Frauen

Frauen

German Women Recall the Third Reich

by
Alison Owings

Rutgers University Press
New Brunswick, New Jersey

Second printing, 1994

Owings, Alison.
   Frauen : German women recall the Third Reich / Alison Owings.
      p.   cm.
   Includes bibliographical references.
ISBN 0-8135-1992-6
   1. World War, 1939–1945—Personal narratives, German.
2. World War, 1939–1945—Women—Germany.   3. Women—
Germany—Interviews.   I. Title.
D811.5.0885   1993
943.086'082—dc20   92-42097
                                                                CIP

British Library Cataloging-in-Publication information available

To the memory of
Kenneth Brown Owings
and
Alice Case Roberts Owings

Contents

Contents

Preface

One cool winter evening in southern Spain, I strolled from my temporary home in an old farmhouse and went to visit my next-door landlady, who had invited me over for a glass of *dos años*—two-year-old Spanish wine. I had gone to Spain for distance, thrift, and quiet (in sum, to write a novel), having quit my job in New York to do so, and by a series of circumstances ended up in a serene and beguiling spot overlooking the Mediterranean. It happened to be in an enclave of elderly Germans. My landlady's name was Señora Marianne Popist, Frau Popist to the very locals.

Like most of the neighbors, Frau Popist was retired and modestly well off. Like theirs, her appearance was conventional, save for her Little Orphan Annie hairdo. Unlike them, however, she was wonderfully and flightily effusive. She squeezed her eyes shut and rhapsodized about such phenomena as blossoming almond trees, and *dos años*. She also peppered me with advice. To raise my arms above my head if I stood nude in front of a man; the stance showed off one's breasts. Not to drink milk from the local goats; they had "not marched here straight from the ministry of health." She never offered, nor did I expect, much self-revelation. That evening, my expectations would prove inadequate and the seed for this book would be sown.

The visit began with customary conviviality in front of her cheerful fireplace fire. We sipped and chatted, presumably about the usual matters—wine, men, and goats. Because Frau Popist spoke less Spanish than even my modicum and only slightly more English, our conversations were in German. Although not my expectation for a Spanish interlude, German was fine by me. I had spent a year at a German university about a decade earlier, and was glad to retrieve my fluency.

At one point in the evening, Frau Popist mentioned a new neighbor, a vacationing American woman we both liked. Her name was Susan Spiegel. Susan herself had spoken a little German with Frau Popist and, knowing Frau Popist came from Hamburg, had also surprised and delighted her with that city's traditional arcane greeting.¹ She explained that her parents had come from Hamburg, too, but had left in the 1930s. She did not even hint at why they had left, but only a fool would not have guessed.

Clearly, Frau Popist was no such fool. In the midst of our affectionate recollection of the meeting, she referred to Susan as "eine Israeli."

Scarcely was the phrase out of her mouth when, without forethought, I was ready. Susan is not "an Israeli," I said.

Well, but I knew what she meant, she said.

Although I certainly did, something inside me compelled contention. She's from Missouri, I said.

Ja, but . . .

She's an American, I said. She may be Jewish, but that . . .

Frau Popist took a deep breath and said—I remember the quote exactly—"Ich kann das Wort nicht aussprechen [I cannot utter that word]."

"Jüdisch? Jüdin? [Jewish? Jew?]"² I remember insisting.

Frau Popist burst like a valve. Ever since she saw those poor people wearing the star and knowing what became of them, she cannot say the word.

It was my turn to take a deep breath.

In the time we had known each other, Frau Popist had talked little about the Third Reich. Once, she described a bicycle trip she had made to a hospital when she was seven months pregnant, to find out if her one child, who was very sick, still lived. As she peddled along, bombing alarms sounded. She scrambled belly-down into a ditch, pulled her bike on top of her, waited until the bombs had dropped and the all-clear was sounded, then peddled onward. Her boy, Joachim, was indeed alive. I had been struck by how casually she had talked of something so dramatic, but my curiosity had not been piqued. I was immersed in my novel.

Also, an exchange with the man she lived with and loved and who had spent part of the war on a U-boat as a meteorologist (as I recall, the work included gauging currents) made me shy from bringing up the Third Reich. In an apogee of naiveté and hopefulness, I asked if he had falsified information. The vehemence of his response (in short, it was *Nein*) and his subsequent contention that Germany did not start the war discouraged my further inquiry toward either of them.

On the evening of the "Israeli" exchange, Frau Popist opened her soul by herself. While the meteorologist snored, she stoked the fire, refilled the

---

1. "Hummel Hummel," says one person. "Mors Mors," replies the other. (*Hummel* was a nickname for men who carried water buckets on a span across their shoulders. *Mors* was slang for posterior. According to the story, someone shouted "Hummel Hummel" to one water carrier, who for whatever reason dropped his pants, showed his rear, and said, "Mors Mors.")
2. *Jüdin* means "female Jew," or that peculiar word, "Jewess."

little ceramic pitchers she used as wine glasses, and told of her belated epiphany about the Third Reich.

As a young woman, she and her friends were active in sports, she said, and kept themselves as far as possible from "Politik" and "Herr Hitler." The distance held for her until a snowy January night in 1942. Married, more than eight months pregnant, and home alone, she happened to look out a window facing the street. Below her she saw "Israeli" laborers shoveling snow. Among them was a woman who had managed to push aside a small pile of apple cores for herself. Frau Popist cupped her hands to show me how small the pile was. Her voice beginning to shake, she described how a Nazi brownshirt, riding by on a bicycle, spotted the pile, kicked it away in a fury, and screamed obscenities at the woman. Not until that moment, said Frau Popist, did she open her eyes and recognize the basic cruelty of her government.

Years later, I had my own epiphany. I realized our evening had been no typical Kaffeeklatsch (or in our case, Weinklatsch). Not only had Frau Popist been talking about a catastrophe of humanity whose combined method and scale was unparalleled in Western memory, and not only had she been talking about it as a witness, she had been talking about it as an insider, as an adult citizen of the Third Reich. She had been part of the reason Susan's parents left Hamburg, part of the reason bombs were falling on the way to the hospital.

My thoughts began dashing both backward and forward. I thought of my nosy, cranky landlady in Freiburg, the Black Forest city whose university I had rapturously attended. After citing my latest infraction, she would tell me you could walk anywhere at night during the Third Reich. You could leave your door *unlocked*, Fräulein Ovinks, things were that safe. With neither the verbal confidence nor the moxie to take on such statements, I had turned away, embarrassed. My interest was not piqued then, either. I was immersed in my studies, Sturm und Drang on paper.

More Freiburg memories returned. On the streetcar I rode to and from class, fares were collected by a man with a steel-hook hand. Downtown, legless men maneuvered themselves along the sidewalks on crude handmade carts. Then I quickly paid my fare to the former and neatly stepped out of the way of the latter. Now I damned my blindered bookishness and embarrassment, as questions erupted. What else would my landlady have to say about the Third Reich? What would the men's wives, or their comrades' widows, have to say? The men themselves, including the walking or rolling wounded, did not interest me. I had heard the satirized line "I was only following orders" so often, I dismissed the lot of German men as murderous, woeful strangers.

Women were not strangers. Nor were they destroyers or warmongers, were they? Women were nurturers and peacemakers, were they not? Those were the messages swirling through the air around me, anyway. At their core seemed to be the assumption that most women were just *better* than most men. I was not sure that was true, or if true, why. But if true, would it not include German women? Of many knotty questions that asserted themselves in the course of this work, that was the first.

Another question was more compelling. Had the voices of the German women of Frau Popist's generation been heard? Granted, the phenomenon of overlooking would-be women witnesses was not without precedent. But the importance of the voices of German "Aryan" women was self-evident, even from the most cursory knowledge of the Holocaust. Whether the women were *better* or not, their voices rife with lessons in valor and introspection, seemed beside the point. They had been there.

There was a fast way to find out if they also had been in print. In 1984, living then in San Francisco, I summoned up my courage and telephoned the person I had learned was the expert in this country on German history, Dr. Gordon A. Craig of Stanford University. I explained my interest, and my inchoate idea to try to fill a gap, if there were a gap to be filled. He cordially bade me come to his office, an hour's drive away. I rented a car sturdier than my own, arrived clammy from nervousness and wrong turns, and was greeted by a dapper man who almost immediately began writing out names of books and contacts, while suggesting possible approaches to delicate questions. Wondering if I were so self-conscious I had missed something, I finally whispered, "You mean, you think it's a good idea?" "An excellent idea!" said he. And he confirmed that, in general, the testimony of few "average" German women had been published, in English or in German. (As of this writing, nearly ten years later, the situation is almost the same.)

The news was challenging, unexpectedly annoying (does nobody listen to "average" women?), and intimidating. As a freelance journalist/writer with the usual standbys of limited time, money, and resources, I had other limitations. Unlike many people who studied the era, I was neither German nor Jewish. And until college, I had not even known, at least knowingly known, anyone Jewish (except for an acquaintanceship with the apparently only Jewish student in high school), nor had I known anyone German. Nor did I know much about the linked disasters of the Third Reich and the Holocaust, or much about World War II.

By the time the idea for this book beckoned (or loomed), my world had widened. I happened to have Jewish friends in the United States and, mostly from Freiburg days, German friends in Germany. I should note that my parents balked mightily at my going to Germany to study. The frivolous circumstances that led to, and from, high school German to German in Freiburg are another story, but the point is, in my parents' opinion, language was one thing, history another. Although my father had not fought in World War II, he had worked for Wright Aircraft for the war effort. My mother had been relatively oblivious to the war, from what I could tell. But like other Americans of that era, my parents knew which side they were on and why, which side they were against and why, and they let their children know, too. Sometimes in conversations about this project, Jewish acquaintances (friends know better) seem mystified if I remark that my parents had been "sort of anti-German" because of the war. Why? They ask. You're not Jewish, are you? For some reason, I get nearly livid. *Why?* Because of what the Germans did to the Jews, I say. And to the Gypsies, and the handicapped, and homosexuals, and dissidents, among others, I add. And because German soldiers killed, wounded, and terrified a lot of American soldiers who *were* fighting Hitler. Germany *was* our enemy, you know. Oh, that's right, is the surprised reply.

At that point, I want to add, you do not have to be Jewish to abhor the Holocaust or the Nazis. And if you are Jewish, you might make room in your sorrow and outrage and memory for this country's Protestant and Catholic farm boys and city kids who may have had other plans than to die fighting Adolf Hitler, but who died fighting Adolf Hitler, or lost their limbs or their minds fighting Adolf Hitler; then you realize there is such a thing as a common enemy.

I was one walking struck nerve. It came, I suppose, from reading about individuals in partial preparation for a "test trip" to Germany I was trying to put together, had to put together. By then I felt compelled to make any contribution I could toward deciphering the ungodly. And I felt swamped by what I knew and what I didn't.

The volume of written material about the Third Reich and the Holocaust seemed beyond even a young speed reader's lifetime. One historian had suggested I read nothing, but go to Germany wide-eyed to get fresher impressions. Fortunately, I rejected that; I would learn I was wide-eyed enough. I needed history and context (the sum of which is in the Introduction). Thanks to a reading list launched by Professor Craig, and his own work, and the suggestions of many others, I was able to dent my ignorance and zero in on my niche. I learned that scholars in the United States and Europe, mostly women, had written much about women in the Third Reich. Their studies, published both before my interest coalesced and in the course of it, were invaluable to me, as was their personal encouragement to a nonacademic newcomer. So I read works by Renate Bridenthal, Elke Fröhlich, Karin Hausen, Claudia Koonz, Jill Stephenson, and fellow nonacademic Gerda Szepansky with interest and gratitude. (It was reassuring, too, to have company in a sometimes hard to explain preoccupation.) I also read accounts about nonmilitary life during the Third Reich. And, of course, I read about the Holocaust.

Sometimes single facts caught me short, underscoring my lack of knowledge. I learned that Germany's Jewish population was less than one percent when the Nazis came to power on January 30, 1933.[3] I learned that most German soldiers were not Nazi Party members. And I gleaned one overall impression. How wide the Third Reich reached, from splintering a friendship to shaking a globe, and how far, how deep, it still reaches. Emotional, economic, and political effects of the era surely will span the century. They certainly have spanned generations.

My readings also underscored that the Third Reich remains unique for what it did when confined to Germany. What other government had a policy of applying such incrementally diverse forms of misery, from petty insults to untempered barbarity, upon one's own unarmed neighbors for being *born* who they were? Also, it was clear that the Third Reich insured its own legacy. There was no question in my mind that Germans who have "heard enough" need not blame continuing cries of outrage or attempts at inquiry on anyone but themselves, or their elders.

That legacy, I saw, showed few signs of diminishing, much less disappearing. What else was the tumult about unifying two Germanies than part of the legacy of the Third Reich? From what legacy came the trappings of the desecration of Jewish cemeteries and memorials in Germany of 1992? What legacy did two thousand attacks that year against "foreigners" by "neo-Nazis" invoke? (Ironically, the Third Reich also gave rise to the huge influx of asylum-seeking "foreigners" into Germany; the liberal asylum law was written in response to a divided Germany, which would not have been divided had there been no Third Reich.) And is the ghastly tale of Bosnia not linked in part to the Third Reich, in terms both of old Nazi allegiances and of echoed inhumanities? That is what legacies do. They live on, because one cannot yet either part with their wondrousness or comprehend their horror.

In the enormous printed legacy of the Third Reich, however, one big gap remained: the voices of half the German population.

I thought about German women a lot. And the more I did, the closer they edged to American women. The idea of common enemy slid toward commonality with the enemy. From appearance alone, German women I knew in Freiburg could have been women I grew up with. The German daughters could have been my friends. Some of them *were* my friends. I myself could be mistaken for a German. Sometimes I was.

In thinking about the young German women who became friends, I recalled how they differed from their stereotype (some were late, some messy) and how almost none had a father who survived the war. Their mothers survived, I remembered. A lot of mothers did. The actuarial fact became ever more amazing. Many German women who lived through the *entire Third Reich* as young adults were still alive, and possibly in better health than their American counterparts. I remembered my earliest hike up into the

---

3. Thanks to Claudia Koonz for first pointing this out to me.

Black Forest: An old German woman was already on her way back down. But even robust grandmothers do not necessarily live another decade. I put the books, and my volume of notes from the books, aside. I had read as much as I could and less than I wanted to—a perfectly familiar state in journalism—and began a race against time.

Using every source and potential interviewee I could conjure—a bank teller's mother, a college friend's housekeeper's mother-in-law, historians' contacts from a professor's wife to a Nazi official—I typed, pre-computer, letter after letter, apologizing for my grammar, went to the mailbox, and waited.

Meanwhile, realizing that the San Francisco Bay area where I lived was fertile Germanic interview territory (a neighbor lent me a copy of the German edition of Albert Speer's autobiography . . . autographed), I conducted trial interviews close to home. For whatever reasons, they felt stiff and unproductive. I decided to save my energy for the Fatherland. But would "real" German women talk, and to a stranger? Truth be told, I sensed they would. For one thing, an intermediary usually was approaching the prospective interviewee on my behalf. And there was the flattery factor. How many times did a foreigner come calling to ask about their lives? Finally, I thought, many old people simply like company.

I had less of a sense what the women might say about their twelve years within the "Thousand Year Reich." No more than anecdotes, prayers, and recipes from the famous domestic triad of "Kinder, Kirche, Küche" [children, church, kitchen]? Or a lot more? What would they say they had known? Had not known? Would they seem honest? But most important, would they talk at all?

Ja, they wrote. They certainly would.

Of some fifty women queried in all (over the years), women from every economic, geographical, social, and political background I could think of, almost all—some with reluctance, most with alacrity—said yes. A message in spidery handwriting began, "Ich bin 1895 geboren. . . . [I was born in 1895]." From younger careerists came typewritten acceptances. Women who said yes included not just the unsung, and sung, resisters. Former members of the Nazi Party said yes. Communists and anti-Communists said yes. Hausfrauen of all political stripes said yes. Anti-Semites said yes. Women who fell in love with men who were "half Jewish" said yes. Women who revealed themselves to be "half Jewish" said yes. Countesses said yes. Farm women said yes. A former antiaircraft gunner said yes. The war widow of a drafted carpenter said yes. The war widow of an SS man said yes. A woman who talked with Hitler said yes. Women who claimed to have known little said yes. Women who claimed to have known much said yes. And a former concentration camp guard said yes.

As I packed my bags for what would be only the first of four trips, I tucked in the naive sisterly shaded hope, tattered though it was by my readings, that the German women would provide a collective sense of reflection and remorse, and perhaps persuade me they had not supported Adolf Hitler after all.

I landed in Hamburg and got to work. Within minutes of the start of the first interview, my hope was history. By the end of the second interview, my expectation of homogeneity had ended, and with it my premise. And by the conclusion of the third interview, I knew I had to rethink my agenda, quickly.

It became to listen to the German women as individual human beings, that is, to regard "the Germans" the opposite of how "the Germans" had regarded "the Jews." I had no other choice. The women were not lining up in the same row. Nor, I noticed, were they taking the high road I so guile-lessly offered them, especially in the form of particularly hopeful (to put the best face on them) questions. Did you suggest your husband desert his regi-ment? Did you think of leaving Germany? The women looked at me as if I were daft and responded accordingly. (Actually, between 1933 and 1941, an estimated thirty-five thousand non-Jewish Germans did leave Germany.)[4] The women were not fulfilling other expectations, either; they said they *had* known about concentration camps.

One expectation that proved inadequate was the women's readiness to talk. Some spoke hesitantly, but most erupted like geysers. It seemed they had been waiting for decades for someone to ask them a question.

In addition to the women I had come specifically to hear, I found will-ing women everywhere. Also, they found me. Having an hour between in-terviews in Berlin one day, I took a walk in the popular Grunewald [the Green Forest] and sat on a bench. Sure enough, two elderly women sat down beside me. I got out a chocolate bar (I seem always to have one on my person in Germany) and offered each woman a square, and, soon, another. As usual, my accent prompted "Where are you from?" and "What brings you to Germany?" With that, we were off. One woman said her late husband had been in the opera and had had lots of Jewish friends and. . . . I took her name and address, but did not follow through. I would never have finished.

Sometimes the ease of the search and its quantitative success were ex-hilarating. Other times, nothing was. When rushing to change schedules or money, or buying more tape cassettes and batteries and more recommended books for background reading, or rewriting more questions, or telephoning, or trying to find an affordable room or restaurant as the dollar plummeted trip by trip, or clumsily lugging my luggage cart down cobblestone streets for want of cab fare, or trying to find the bus, the train, the subway, the street, the building, and finally, in some disarray, the door, I even felt angry.

---

4. David Schoenbaum, *Hitler's Social Revolution* (New York: Doubleday, 1966; paper-back, New York: Norton, 1980), xiii.

Couldn't someone from closer than California (and farther from an ever gaunter savings account) have done this? What an ingrate. I had received two very helpful grants to travel in West Germany, one free ride in East Germany, and was doing what I wanted to (if not precisely *how* I wanted to do it). The anger may just have reflected the emotional accumulation of what the women said. One cannot expect to immerse oneself in the Third Reich and emerge smiling. (Actually, the gallows humor was superb.)

As to the question of why the women talked at all, much less so much, the reason seemed, like many of the women themselves, to be a mixture of disparate parts, including at times whim, anger, shame, pride, self-justification, a sense of being helpful to a stranger or obligated to an intermediary, an urge to bear witness, pent-up memories, loneliness, and, yes, guilt.

Their reasons for talking specifically to me were more evident. I did try to be amiable. Why not? I was grateful to be received, and almost always with hospitality so daunting its description could last pages. Did I have compunctions about accepting it? Sometimes, at first, as during the interview with the former guard. But mostly, no. Why risk offending someone I want to open up to me? (And on my budget?) Furthermore, at the beginning of each interview, there usually was little clue what kind of person sat before me. (And who was I? A goddess of righteousness?) Neither physical appearance nor home decor revealed a woman's personal politics. I did find, though, that the rare untidy German home generally signaled a Hitler opponent.

Because the women knew as little about me and my motives as I did about them and theirs, I told them, truthfully, that my background was in journalism, that I believed they had been overlooked as witnesses and might have something to say. Sometimes their response was like miffed and ruffled feathers plumping in agreement. "My husband," said one still-piqued woman, "never asked me anything."

Why else did the women talk to me? The commonality of being female probably helped. Some matters simply needed no explanation. Also, most women probably felt safer with another woman, especially when an interview went from day to evening to night. And night was when some women got really interesting.

The advantage of female commonality was nothing, though, to the advantage of linguistic commonality. My German is accented, slangy, and error-laced at higher elevations, but it is fluent. I had thought of it as merely a handy (and free) tool, a means of being one-on-one without an interpreter. I was prepared for a smile or two at my mistakes and possibly a hesitantly offered correction, Germans generally being encouraging to anyone trying to learn their language. I was not prepared for awe. As had been the case in Freiburg, people were astonished that an American spoke anything besides English, much less German. Less sophisticated women treated me like a household celebrity, showing me off to relatives and neighbors and, as if I were a talking dog, asking me to speak. Obligingly, I yapped a few words. Such women were indeed flattered by being the subject of a foreigner's attention.

"And she's here to interview *me*," said one woman.

"*Du?*"

As I had guessed, the subject matter seemed irrelevant.

What did seem to matter was that despite being able to speak German, I wasn't one. The distance amid the intimacy helped me to ask and them to answer. A young German woman recently said something that an older woman, a survivor, seconded with fervor. A German never would have asked the purposefully (and not so purposefully) naive questions I did. And the women would not have stood for them. In fact, they might not have spoken to a German at all, especially one the age of their children. German children were known to have asked too much already.

I was an outsider in another way, too. Besides not being one of them, I wasn't one of "them." Only one woman asked if I were Jewish. Others presumably thought I was not. As a result, I am convinced many women said things to me they never would have said to a Jewish interviewer. At times I sensed that if I pretended to empathize with anti-Semitic comments, or made some myself, or expressed regret that I had not been part of a Nazi rally, some women would have been even more revealing than they were. But I could not lie while essentially asking them not to. And they were revealing enough without encouragement. A point I sometimes overlook is that the women trusted me not only with their words; most allowed me to use their names. Only three, as noted in their stories, asked for a pseudonym.

Being an outsider on the inside, I faced my own question of what a proper stance should be. Usually I tried to offer myself as a blank slate, that of a court reporter or oral historian. Occasionally I felt as if I were wearing the façade of an archeologist, carefully noting and evaluating the findings left in the women's sieves of memory, but ready to pounce on a serendipitous shard. Any guise helped when stereotypes crumbled, and complexities, contradictions, and confessions revealed themselves. One woman spoke for hours and hours until, close to midnight, she said she had been a member of the Nazi Party. Hmmm, I said.

At other times, I burned to ask certain questions or make certain comments. The journalist in me cautioned, stay out of it. The rest of me argued, I'm exhausted, horrified, this is my project and I'll say what I want. (Or, I am not following orders.) When that part won, some exchanges became heated and always revealing. Such firestorms were few. Usually we behaved like two ladies, wife of the vanquished, daughter of the victor, sitting together over coffee and talking over what happened, as well as how to stop anything like it from happening again. There were times I dropped the façade, thankfully.

A woman who had hidden a Jewish friend for two years needed no play-acting from me. Other times, the façade fell on its own. A woman for whom I was prepared to have no sympathy made me burst into tears of pity. The tape recorder got the whole commotion—dual snuffling, my search for a tissue, her "Danke," our joint honks.

At emotional encounters of another order, I retreated to near muteness. Within an hour of leaving the home of an active Nazi, I arrived at the home of an anti-Nazi, who erupted in pent-up salvos of outrage and descriptions of horror, delivering almost every word in a buzz of furious yet whispered dialect, while pacing. I gave up trying to track her with the microphone. I gave up asking questions. I was reeling. My pendulum had gone amok. Late that night, the woman's fury spent, she softly put me to bed on her living room couch next to the hammered brass bowl she had made herself, she said, tiptoeing from the room, from an exploded American shell. It gleamed in the moonlight like my own ally. My façade was in shreds.

Disconcerting in a different way were the sweet grandmotherly women. We chatted so cozily, so gemütlich, in the language I was speaking better all the time, learning phrases mostly only old Germans know, like for being excused to go to the bathroom. "I must go where the Kaiser himself must go on foot," I'd gaily announce. I had to remind myself these dears offering me a third piece of kuchen were not necessarily always so dear. My former Freiburg landlady was a case in point. I looked her up, she treated me like a long-lost daughter, acted muddled, and offered nothing of her former sentiments, on tape or off.

Most interviews were with women in what was West Germany. That they spoke of their own free will is self-evident. I also interviewed seven women in what was East Germany, the former German Democratic Republic. It made all the choices and arrangements and did not allow me to find women on my own. My fledgling attempts to do so behind my hosts' backs turned me into a paranoid wreck and I gave up, although not without gaining my first sense of what life in the Third Reich might have been like. In East Germany, I was assigned an escort, who took me to every city and every interview. I was able, however, to insist that each woman and I talk together alone. My escort, a Communist Party member, did sit in on most of the interview with Frau Müller, a Communist heroine, which was fine with me. In all, the women's experiences during the Nazi era overcame most of my misgivings about including them, and did not make me feel it necessary to try to find other women after the East German government collapsed.

Once I had interviewed women in all the categories of experience, background, and viewpoint I could fill, and recognized that I did not have the resources to locate women in a few other categories (such as a woman who admitted she had "reported" someone), I stopped. No woman, I might note, is meant to reflect a certain percentage of other women. Nor are the women collectively meant to represent a statistically accurate picture of Nazi Germany. (For one thing, women who were old during the Third Reich had long since died.)

Back in the United States, between trips and after the final one, I did the other work of the book. I had amassed over one hundred hours of tapes, from roughly thirty-five interviews, not counting many reinterviews, with about fifty women. (As an experiment, I sometimes interviewed women in small groups. The results were lively, but an audio nightmare.)

A major task was figuring how to proceed with the tapes. Had expense not been a factor, I would have sent them all off to be transcribed and translated and awaited perfectly typed pages of German and English texts, along with matching computer disks. A slower method evolved. First, I listened to everything, took notes, and decided who had to be included and who did not, and of those women to be included, what parts of the interview had to be included, and what parts, mostly irrelevant to the Third Reich, did not. Then, in most cases, came the onerous work of transcribing. Some of it was done by friends in Germany who volunteered to take a tape or two. Some tapes I did if the woman spoke clear High German. Most tapes were done by a splendid local troupe, mostly women from Germany or Austria, who were interested enough in the material to work for the modest amounts I could afford. Because I did not want to miss a single word I had gone to such effort to hear, it was they who generally got the more difficult women, those who spoke dialect (I tried to match transcriber and interviewee by region), or who whispered, or chewed food while they talked, or said things I just did not understand.

With each transcript in front of me, I replayed the tape and went through the copy, sometimes finding mistakes, sometimes underlining emphasized words, and sometimes staring in wonder at words I had not known were being said. Then, with the care born of necessity, I translated everything I thought germane. If I saw gaps in the information, I wrote to the woman with questions, or went back again and talked with her. Then I set about writing each woman's chapter. I had considered writing a thematic book, chapters on Women and Anti-Semitism, and so on, but decided not to, in part because one point of this work is to present the women as individuals. I did not want them to get lost in their context.

After writing the chapters, or profiles, I let them simmer, and then rewrote them. During some of the interstices in what had become a nearly decade-long undertaking, I became computerized, applied for more grants, kept in touch with the women, read more, rewrote more, and earned a living from quicker writing.

And between interview trips, I made special efforts to fight grandmotherly seduction. I read more first-person accounts of the Holocaust and saw whatever Holocaust-related films I could. Then, my head filled with written or pictured scenes of a Nazi bayoneting a baby onto a wall, of Jewish family men losing their jobs, of grisly medical experiments, of the fates of dissident students and clergymen, I went back to Germany.

Once I decided to get as close to survivors as I had to the German women. (That some of the women could be considered survivors is another matter.) I interviewed a married couple, both concentration camp survivors, and both Jewish. Hans Hermann Hirschfeld and Inge Korach Hirschfeld had grown up in Berlin and later moved to San Francisco. Their son told me one subject was off-limits. That was Auschwitz. His mother feared his father's nightmares would return. The Hirschfelds were married in 1941, in Berlin, they told me. For the obligatory civil ceremony, Herr Hirschfeld boarded the streetcar at 7 A.M. to pick up his mother and mother-in-law across town so all could get to the marriage office by 8 A.M. Why so early? The marriage office was open to Jews between 8 and 9 A.M. only. The couple recalled the civil functionary (certainly a Nazi Party member) as a person who tried to make things pleasant. He moved some flowers from the large room meant for "Aryan" weddings to the small room meant for Jews.

Later, in a synagogue, the Hirschfelds had a religious wedding, performed by the famous and brave Rabbi Leo Baeck—"more than a Jew," in the groom's words. During the service, they heard a distracting noise of hammering. They learned that while they were being married in one part of the temple, workmen in another part were knocking out the pews. The building was about to become a deportation point to concentration camps.

"Aryan" women had told me a variety of wedding tales. None included hearing the sounds of her own incarceration during her marriage vows.

Even bombing raids, usually the most frightening events "Aryan" women faced, were different for German Jews, who faced the bombs, too. Mrs. Hirschfeld said how awful it was to hear the bombers and want them to harm her own country. She had felt so German.

In a way, I carried the Hirschfelds with me in Germany—in eerily mostly Jew-less Germany. I also carried friends who would not exist had they been born within the reach of the Third Reich. And by the last trips, I carried especially burdensome thoughts and nettlesome questions. How would these "Aryan" women have behaved in my hometown? How would my hometown neighbors, my family, I, have behaved in Germany during the Third Reich? I had faced no test the German women had faced. Sitting in the street in front of the White House and yelling for President Johnson to stop bombing Vietnam, as I had, took less courage than it would have taken a German woman to whisper to a stranger that she doubted Germany would win the war. I thought about past and present anti-Semitism in the lands of the victors. I thought about the term *anti-Semitism* properly meaning anti-Arab as well as anti-Jew. And I thought about the vagaries of human behavior. My old satchel was empty of faint hopes and foolhardy questions, but its new load made it heavy indeed.

At times I felt a great need for a mental break. Only one place in Germany offered it, that is, within the restrictions of my schedule, budget, and relatively demure behavior pattern. It was a German train. Trains not only connected me to cities, they separated me from Frauen. Some days I yearned so much for such separations that the trains became almost hallowed. The blessed Bahnhof shimmered like an isle from a Teutonic myth, beckoning with the promise of the fabled train cars. Oh how they lured Lorelei-like, promising security and succor, summoning me to their cozy little compartments mit pull-out footrests. Oh the legendary dependability. I knew as I sank into spotless upholstery that we would leave the Bahnhof on the button. Soon the window would offer a visual treat, scenes chosen by the German Chamber of Commerce from the nicest travelogues—gardens, inns, vineyards, rivers, castles. Not a swastika or guard tower in sight. No Third Reich to see or think about, that is, think about all the time. From blocks or hours away, I could hardly wait to board.

One afternoon, with special gratitude, I collapsed into an empty train compartment and savored the privacy I guessed would not last long. Sure enough, at different stops several people entered. All were elderly women. (WOULD YOU ALL JUST TAKE A DAY OFF?) We observed the usual customs. A question as to a seat's being free was answered in the affirmative, all lofted the newcomer's luggage to the rack above the seats, thanks were offered, welcomes followed, all resat, laps were smoothed, and that was that. Further conversation was entirely optional. Having silently repeated my new mantra, You-cannot-interview-everyone (it had replaced my old one, Hurry-while-they're-alive), I was minding my own business. More than likely I'd scrabbled in my luggage for the extra roll bagged from the hotel buffet that morning and was looking out the train window, chewing. Because I had hardly spoken, was dressed nonspecifically in terms of country of origin, and yes, may have looked German, the other women probably had no idea I wasn't and took little notice of me. Meanwhile, although apparently strangers to each other, they had started up a conversation. I missed its genesis, but then heard one woman say sharply to her new seatmate, "But I didn't know what went on *in* the camps. Did you?"

I sank back into the seat. Why even try for a mental break in Germany? The Third Reich is not just below the surface or in the backs of people's minds. For the generation that lived it, and for the generations that inherited it—and are doing what they will with its lessons about racism and intolerance—the Third Reich is on the surface and in the front of their minds. The Third Reich *is* the subject.

And from what I could determine in regard to elderly German women who recalled the Third Reich as part of their personal pasts, any generalization breaks down from there.

By having been born who and where and when they were, and by staying, the women in this book lived within the Third Reich throughout its entire twelve-year rule. In most cases the Third Reich corresponded with the women's young adulthood. There are exceptions; the youngest woman was born in 1927, the eldest in 1895. But when Adolf Hitler came to power in 1933, the majority of the women were teenagers or in their early twenties. When the war began in 1939, many had married. By 1945, when the war and the Reich were over, almost all were mothers or widows or both.

The women not only had known the Third Reich from its first cloaked entreaties to its last temporal and spiritual rubble, they *were* the Third Reich. Theirs were the scrubbed faces meant for photographs and posters. Theirs were the hearts and hands and bodies enjoined to beat and bake and beget for the Fatherland. Their minds were discouraged from exertion.

By being born who, where, and when they were, no matter how they and their circumstances differed, the women also happened to have lived at one of the best vantage points for witnessing the Third Reich, the place where the Nazis put their policies to the first cruel tests: the home front. It was at the home front where certain shops were closed, where certain signs appeared, where certain people lost their jobs, where certain slogans were proclaimed, where children got divided from each other, and ridiculed, and beaten up. As home-front battles grew more invidious, with increasing strictures against Jewish Germans (and to a lesser degree against Christian Germans having anything to do with Jewish Germans), witnesses' vantage points became more and more a merger of the personal and the political. Until the war, "Aryan" German men were home-front witnesses too, of course, although they were less likely to be involved with one of Nazism's major focuses, the conquest of children. When the war began, most German men relinquished their home-front witnessing posts. As they left for possible death, remaining Jewish Germans left for almost certain death. These most disparate kinds of departures—soldiers stepping onto trains, civilians shoved onto trucks—took place at the home front, too.

After the war reached full fury, a typical German man still may have witnessed a world narrower than that of a typical German woman. To be sure, women were spared the sights, smells, terror, and danger of front-line battle and the deadly cold of Russia, although accounts of bombing raids and the last weeks of the war seem hardly less terrifying or life threatening. But not even front-line soldiers fought every day, or necessarily saw anyone every day but each other. And when a soldier was not at the front, his world sometimes was safer than a woman's. The story may be apocryphal. A German soldier is home on leave, sirens signal incoming bombs, his wife, as usual, prepares to head for the shelter with the children, and finds her terrified husband cowering in a corner. The front, he says, had not been this close.

For most women, it was.

And bombs were only part of it. The home front in Berlin, not the beaches of Normandy, was where people wore Stars of David. It was in German streets, not in German barracks or battlefields, where Jewish neighbors were pulled from their homes. This is not to overlook either the annihilation camps or the Nazis' assaults on Jewish communities outside Germany, although the argument could be made that the Nazis (that is, the SA brownshirts and the SS blackshirts) tried to keep the majority of drafted German soldiers away from both camps and pogroms. The argument also could be made that the core of the Holocaust began with the core of a policy—Nazis and birth determine who shall prosper and who shall not, who shall live and who shall not—that first was tested on the home front.

At first, the rest of the world may have considered the German women, if they considered them at all, as curiously fanatic, braided but belligerent, and as comical as the man to whom they shot up their right arms over their apron straps. In time, as Adolf Hitler was known less as a buffoon than as a murderer, and as hundreds of thousands of Allied soldiers were mobilized to end his rule, the German women became the wives of the enemy. They were the women who followed the men who followed the orders.

By the time the macabre consequences of those orders were known to the world, German women seem to have been gladly and cursorily dismissed from the world's consciousness as irrelevant to the past, the present, and the future, and certainly to non-Germans. What could their actions and their inactions possibly have to do with us? Theirs certainly was a singular sorority. And they shared the one life-saving privilege that let them into it. They were not Jewish, but were, literally, card-carrying "Aryans," their identification cards free of the big *J* stamped on the IDs of Jewish Germans.

Yet, wasn't that simply fate? What else but fate assured that "Aryan" German women were not singled out for discrimination and then extinction? What else but fate assured that they were not drafted as soldiers, thanks to Hitler's notion of a woman's place? What else but fate assured, too, that mostly on their own and with children in tow, they faced the retaliatory bombs and aggression of their enemies, among other components of war? And what else but fate assured that they faced tests of morality, courage, and intelligence that women beyond the reach of the Reich were spared?

Ingrid Müller-Münch, a postwar journalist who covered a lengthy trial
of women concentration camp guards (including well-known sadists such as
Hermine Ryan-Braunsteiner, once of Queens, New York), raised a particularly vexing point. "In all the years I've been involved with this trial, I cannot
get the thought out of my mind, how would I have behaved at the time,"
especially, she wrote, if she had had the guards' level of intellect.[1]

If fate assured that the German women faced the tests they did, how
well did they face them? As a whole, not well at all, according to Claudia
Koonz's extraordinary work *Mothers in the Fatherland*. She makes the irrefu-
table argument that German women on the whole contributed mightily to
the atrocious success of the Third Reich.[2] By keeping the Nazi flame alive
and/or the home fires burning, German women enabled German men to
set the other conflagrations, those that burned ghettos, barns, countries,
and corpses.

Why did the women behave the way they did? "Fate" is much too easy
a scapegoat. Yet if fate is not culpable, what is? Genetics? Can we believe
that millions and millions of people of often dissimilar roots are born ge-
netically inclined to a behavior pattern ranging from being tidy and punc-
tual, to being gullible and prejudiced, to being hateful and homicidal? And
what about the notion of women's behavior as its own entity? What about
the beatific bequest that supposedly has been oozing since near-eternity
through maternal lineage as the ballyhooed birthright of every female infant? Why did German Womankind not behave like the humane peacemakers, the stouthearted global nurturers that people of both sexes believe
women really are? Goddesses, nest-makers, Überfrauen, Lysistratas in waiting, why did the women not stop the Nazis?

Much of the answer is found not in their common fate but in their
common history. A brief look explains a dreadful lot.

In the first decades of the twentieth century, when most of the women in
these pages were born, Germany itself was an infant democracy, barely two
generations older than they. But neither babe nor democracy came into the
new world unencumbered by the old world. Over the centuries, a host of
traditions and assumptions—some laudable, some odious—had formed in
Europe in general and the Germanic states in particular. And they helped
herald the cauldron of contradictions that was the Third Reich.

Certainly the most respectable political legacy was the idea of a just
state, a "Rechtsstaat," promising equal justice for all. Professor Rudolf von
Thadden of the University of Göttingen related to me what he said was

1. Ingrid Müller-Münch, *Die Frauen von Majdanek* (The women of Majdanek) (Rein-
   beck bei Hamburg: Rowohlt, 1982), 12 (my translation).
2. Claudia Koonz, *Mothers in the Fatherland* (New York: St. Martin's Press, 1987), 5–7.

more than a Rechtsstaat fable among German children. It was legend. The king is kept awake at night by the sound of a mill. He commands the miller to shut it down. The miller refuses. King and miller take the case to a judge. The judge rules in favor of the miller. The king, a law-abiding citizen who adheres to the Rechtsstaat, accepts the ruling. German schoolchildren grow up knowing their country is just.[3]

As students of the Holocaust know, the dual message—our system is fair, our leaders law-abiding—had been as ingrained in German Jews as in Christians. The actions of Herr Dr. Ludwig Bendix, a legal reformer, provide an extreme example of such trust. In 1935, having been released from a concentration camp, Herr Dr. Bendix called the local police to remove an anti-Semitic sticker from the nameplate by his apartment. This astonishingly being done, he then filed a formal complaint about another anti-Semitic sign. Soon afterward the Nazis sent him to Dachau. Two misery-filled years later, he was released. Upon his return home, his son wrote, Herr Dr. Bendix's trust in basic German law still was so intact that "he was preparing a legal brief against the commandant of the Dachau concentration camp!" His children stood guard to intercept the brief until he and his wife were safely out of their country of "Rechtsstaat."[4]

Another concept that remained intact throughout the German political ages was the especially Prussian one of duty [Dienst]. Picture serious men in uniform, lieutenants or letter carriers, following orders. Lothar Brixius, a folklorist scholar and the husband of a woman I interviewed, told a family story that demonstrates the comical vainglory and the exploitable rigor of such an attitude. His great-grandfather, born in 1810, was a government forester who proudly wore his forester uniform while inspecting the trees in his jurisdiction. One day he came across a woman cutting forest grass to feed to her goats. It was a practice he had outlawed. The woman was his wife.

"Halt!" he yelled. Using the formal manner of address, he asked, "What is your name?"

His wife looked at him in stupefaction. "Have you gone mad?" she allegedly replied, not using the formal manner of address. "It's me, your wife."

"That makes no difference," he said. "Ich bin im Dienst [I'm on duty]."

According to the Brixius family legend, he then dutifully wrote out a report noting the time and place of the misdeed and the appropriate fine and handed the paper to his wife. When she pointed out that she had no

---

3. Conversation with Rudolf and Wiebke von Thadden in Göttingen, September 1984.
4. Reinhard Bendix, *From Berlin to Berkeley* (New Brunswick, N.J.: Transaction Books, 1986), 171–172.

money of her own, he reached into his pocket and gave her the proper amount, which she silently handed back to him.

The concept of duty and following orders (within one's beloved and just country) was not limited to "Aryans" either. Many sources confirm the hurt and bewilderment of Jewish Germans at suddenly being treated as if they were not regular upstanding citizens. How can anyone criticize them for not resisting the Nazis more? Apart from the near-futility of fighting a dictatorship from under its boot, had they not grown up, like other Germans, ready to trust the legendary governmental justice and to follow orders? And how could anyone wonder why so many stayed so long? According to countless stories, there was one main reason. Germany was home. They should leave their German language, landscape, and literature, not to mention Fatherland, not to mention work, because of some idiots now in power? Leave everything that was, if flawed, familiar? Jewish Germans rationalized, adjusted, hoped each new insult was the last, and waited for the return of their normal, orderly, German way of life. I thought of a friend who returned crestfallen from a trip to Israel about 1970. There was so much hatred, she said, hatred among Jews. She said that because most Israelis had immigrated from all over the world, they had little in common. And *nobody* liked the German Jews. The German Jews? I repeated, shocked. Why? They were so annoyingly tidy, she said. Sweeping their walks all the time, watering their damn flowers. They were just so *German*.

Another political mind-set that Germans of all backgrounds inherited and the Nazis exploited had a religious overtone. It can be traced to Martin Luther (whose own contributions to anti-Semitism were not minor). In short, it is that some power or authority descends from God to earthly rulers, such as a German emperor—*Kaiser*. When the emperor said "we," people knew he meant himself and Himself. Future leaders (and *Führer* does mean "leader") thus inherited a certain presumption, however subconscious, of a divine edge.

A lay carryover from Germanic ideology to the Nazi one was the notion of the "Romantik," in fact or in fiction. Perhaps to counterbalance their structured morality (or what passed as morality), old Germans, like ancient Greeks, glorified the heroic beings who were sanctioned to act out what workaday mortals could not. The heroic beings' heroic deeds could take many forms, from slaying dragons to writing poetry to serving noble causes—like making Germany Number One again.

Certainly the most repugnant item of ideological dowry the old German states bequeathed to the new German nation was anti-Semitism. Some contend that the increased winds of anti-Semitism blowing through much of Europe during the early twentieth century blew as strongly in France as in Germany, and what Germany got that other countries did not was Adolf Hitler—plus the battalions of soldiers and civil servants trusting their government as just, ready to do their duty by taking orders, and assuming their leader was linked to a higher power. Others contend Germany already was more anti-Semitic than other countries, and trying to increase anti-Semitism there was akin to tossing mushroom spores throughout a damp and expectant forest.

Why either was so remains a matter of excruciating debate, grounded as much on a sociological as a theological chicken-and-egg question. What came first, the ancient Jews' choosing an insular life as a result of being scorned for their beliefs (and their disbeliefs) or being scorned in part for choosing an insular life? Whatever the seed of anti-Semitism, twentieth-century Germans, abetted by a continental array of fellow travelers, unquestionably produced its most acrid fruits.

Although nothing I know of is comparable to that legacy of anti-Semitism, Germany's ideogical dowry contained other forms of antihumanism. One was misogyny. The social strangulation common to most women for millennia throughout most European countries, among others, was especially common to the women of male-ruled German states. "The hopes that women entertained during the period of the Enlightenment faded rapidly in the nineteenth century, and women came under attack as inferior beings who had no right to expect full integration in society," writes Gordon A. Craig. "If the analogy [with Jewish emancipation] cannot be carried futher, it is because Germans who found it possible to conceive of a society without Jews could not comfortably imagine one without women. Even so, the offensiveness of some of the anti-feminist rhetoric was not significantly different from that employed by the anti-Semites."[5] As Professor Craig puts it elsewhere, the situation of German women in the nineteenth century was "truly deplorable."[6]

Besides not being able to vote, most women were not allowed to join political organizations or labor unions, or to help run any aspect of government, or to be on equal legal footing with their husbands, brothers, or sons, Rechtsstaat or no. Furthermore, until the turn of the century, most German girls were denied a good high school education, for few schools existed to teach them, particularly for free. And rich young women in private academies were taught "insipid pablum," in Craig's term.[7] German women could not even enroll in German universities until 1908.

In the earlier, enlightened portion of the nineteenth century, a few lucky and intelligent women had been literary luminaries and/or salon keepers of distinction, the artistic world being less hidebound than other worlds. By century's end, however, Germany had regressed so appallingly

---

5. Gordon A. Craig, *The Germans* (New York: Putnam, 1982), 147.
6. Gordon A. Craig, *Germany 1866–1945* (New York: Oxford University Press, 1978), 207.
7. Ibid., 207–208.

that middle-class and socialist women, among others, started associations to correct the staggering array of blatant inequities. German women novelists of varying viewpoints also brought home to their readers the sense of both the romantic possibilities and the poignant realities facing the female sex.[8] Most German men would not be moved. The famous phrase describing a German woman's life expectations—"Kinder, Kirche, Küche"—summed up reality.

Until the First World War, German women's social and economic bondage continued virtually unchanged. By war's end, the institutions that enforced such bondage had been stretched to a breaking point. By the 1920s, when most of the women in this book were growing up, the young German democracy was changing fast. Added to the shame many Germans felt about losing the war were the victors' demands for payment of what Germans (and others) considered and still consider onerous war debts. The economy ricocheted wildly and ludicrously. People really did need a wheelbarrow instead of a wallet for carrying enough nearly worthless money to buy groceries. With record inflation came record unemployment, and little welfare to ease the misery.

The Weimar Republic, the government in power from the defeat of 1918 to the Nazi takeover, got roundly scapegoated for the troubles. (Of course the traditional scapegoats, the Jews, had "stabbed Germany in the back" as the expression went, never mind how many Jewish soldiers and officers fought in the war, and with honored distinction, for their Fatherland.) Weimar did initiate some monetary reforms, which brought some relief. But the effects of the U.S. stock market crash of 1929 and the subsequent depression sped across the ocean and gouged deeply into a nation still fissured by its war debts. Among women I spoke with who had come of age in the decade or so before the Third Reich, the memory of hard times, theirs or others', crossed all party lines. Images abounded—clothes no longer hung out to dry for fear they would be stolen, a man on a streetcar keeling over from hunger.

When despair was commonplace, the plans of all but the wealthiest families were tempered. For German girls especially, the economic situation meant a lessening of even marginal educational possibilities. Because free public education ended after the equivalent of the fourth grade, many families could not or did not buy the books to keep their sons, much less their daughters, in school. Frau Emmi Heinrich, who came from a learned family, spoke of how appalled she was at the level of illiteracy among the adults of her village, and the level of education of their children. More than one woman spoke of her parents' no longer being able to afford her higher education, rare (but possible) as that was anyway. A more practical, seemly

---

8. Ibid., 209–213.

route was taken: study at a home-economics-cum-finishing school. For other young women, such seemliness (or insipid pablum) was far out of reach. They were exploited as apprentices or were trained, as Germans still train formally for almost every job imaginable, to be saleswomen or clerks. Presumably, when their shifts were over the young women went home to parents or husband. Frau Lotte Elschner of Bochum (whose interview is not included) said in apparent seriousness that there were only two things a woman could do if she left home for any reason other than marriage—she could join a cloister or become an actress.

For many Germans, women or men, any job was preferable to none and any political system was preferable to one in which they hungered. A later argument that Weimar-instigated policies were indeed improving the economy by the early 1930s makes the retrospective pill even more bitter.[9] By the time the policies began working, the Nazi regime was in power and took or got the credit for them. The Nazis also credited themselves with other Weimar achievements. Plans for the famous Autobahn and the "duty year" for young people both started in the Weimar Republic.

Weimar also started, or restarted, enormous opportunities for German women. (This time the Nazis did let Weimar take the credit, or the heat.) For women ready to embrace change and able to afford it, Weimar gave silver linings to economic realities, offering women a blossoming of artistic, political, educational, and work possibilities. As of 1919, women finally could vote, and did so in huge numbers. The women's rights movement, which the First World War had cut short, reemerged, revivified. All in all, Weimar meant a heady time of free expression. German women of ways or means followed their various muses, whether to cabaret nightlife or to law school.

One group of women that took notable advantage of the new freedoms and opportunities, says Claudia Koonz in *Mothers in the Fatherland*, were the Nazis. Using the tolerance of Weimar, they helped build the nascent Nazi Party, then later excoriated Weimar from the Nazi arena in which their voices soon were muted.[10]

Nazi women excepted, only a minority of German women could, or would, plunge into the beckoning brew of Weimar. For others, the era was intimidating and estranging, applicable perhaps to city women, but far from real life on the farm. All in all, children, church, kitchen must have comforted. Freedom frightened, or seemed beside the point.

When Adolf Hitler moved closer to power—a father figure for a gen-

---

9. Lecture by Professor J. J. Lee of the University of Cork, Ireland, at Stanford University, 1986.
10. Koonz, *Mothers in the Fatherland*, 21–49.

eration that had lost its own fathers in World War I[11]—most of the women of this book were young indeed. "Did I vote for him?" said one woman, repeating my question and pulling me up short with her answer. "I wasn't old enough to vote."

How did the Austrian Hitler become the German Führer? In a provocative answer, Professor von Thadden said he sometimes plays a mental game of how the devil could come to power in different countries. In France, he said, a coup d'état might be acceptable, but not in Germany. In the United States, he suggested, the devil might ingratiate himself to voters by taking on a façade of naiveté, or somehow by taking materialism to the extreme. And in 1933 Germany, he said, the devil had to maintain the appearance of governmental legitimacy, of parliamentary procedure, of a Rechtsstaat, no matter what he was plotting behind the scenes.

On January 30, 1933, German President Paul von Hindenburg, beset by senility and political pressure, named Hitler chancellor, legally. The man compared to the devil not only had much of the German government at his command, but German assumptions, from doing one's duty to connecting a Führer to God. It was quite a range.

Hitler used it to move fast. Within a week, the Nazis fired Jewish German civil servants. So much for their Dienst. A temporary exception was made for Jewish men who had fought for Germany at the front in World War I.[12]

Within a month, the Nazis strangled the free press.

Within two months, they established the first concentration camp for the first inmates—political opponents.

They also passed a law taking over powers of legislation from the parliament and handing them to a Nazi cabinet. The law was called, understatedly, the Enabling Act. And it was the end of the Rechtsstaat.

At the start of the third month of power, on April 1, 1933, the Nazis instituted a boycott of Jewish-owned stores.

Shortly after that, all rival political parties and trade unions were banned.

Within half a year, then, while the Fatherland was looking flag-waving terrific on the surface, most of its democratic substructure had been replaced.

Almost from the outset, the Third Reich became a pervasive element

---

11. The observation is Fritz Stern's in "National Socialism as Temptation," a chapter filled with similar insights in his *Dreams and Delusions* (New York: Knopf, 1987), 147–191.
12. Carolin Hilker-Siebenhaar, ed., *Wegweiser durch das jüdische Berlin* (Guide to Jewish Berlin) (Berlin: Nicolai Verlag, 1987), 362.

of Jewish German life, determining work, schooling, home, and future, by restricting and endangering all four. At the same time, much of the "Aryan" Volk began living a life that passed for normal—despite the intrusions, welcomed or not, of the Nazis. The lines of the unemployed and hungry were vanishing. More and more people had work and therefore food. Another hallmark of Weimar, the frequent street fights between Communists and Nazis, ended. The Communists were either locked up or underground. And so, according to innumerable accounts, most people with money in their pockets, food in their bellies, and peace on their sidewalks were more likely to be grateful than not. They were beginning to hold their heads high, proud to be Germans again. And the world seemed to confirm them. Look at the Führer receiving other heads of state.

To "Aryan" German girls and women who had come from a common history short in dignity and equal opportunity, another plus of the Third Reich was the "social" organizations it set up, especially the League of German Girls, the Bund deutscher Mädel (the female version of the Hitler Youth) and the adult women's league, called the Frauenschaft. To hear former members talk, the organizations filled a yearning to have something just for them. Former BdM girls happily recalled handicrafts and singing and the like, and seemed not to recall the political content (much less purpose) of the group and that joining it was close to a command. Frau Gerda Szepansky, author of two books about women in the Third Reich,[13] told me she evaded the BdM as long as she could, with the initially successful ruse that her parents could not afford the uniform. One day she was forced to march in her school's BdM parade anyway, but at the rear with another un-uniformed girl. She said people on the street hissed and catcalled how shameful to march without a uniform. She ran home and cried. Minorities of any kind did not do well in the Third Reich.

The majority of Germans, however, presumably were positive about at least the Reich's early years. They were therefore all the more susceptible to the manipulations of Hitler's infamous master of propaganda, Joseph Goebbels. His ministry exploited the "positive" aspects of the Third Reich so well that there are tales of *some* Jewish Germans caught up in the ardor: Jewish children wanting to buy little swastika flags for their bicycles, Jewish adults approving the order in the streets . . . while waiting for the anti-Semitic aberrations to end.

Goebbels's propagandists also took on the choicest contradictions of Nazi Germany. Surely among the most remarkable was the contention that Germany needed to conquer more living room [Lebensraum] for its suppos-

---

13. *Frauen leisten Widerstand* (Women do resistance) (1983) and *Blitzmädel, Heldenmutter, Kriegerwitwe* (Blitzmädel, hero's mother, war widow) (1986), both published by Fischer in Frankfurt am Main.

edly crowded population, while at the same time the Nazis tried to increase the low German birthrate.[14]

Goebbels himself clearly had a way with words. Reportedly he was an electrifying speaker; some of his most striking images were verbal. The Nazis' slogans were so clever they became part of daily life, said Frau Martha and Herr Dr. Lothar Brixius. For example, listen to the clipped syllables: Feind hört mit. [The enemy is listening.] And listen to the ramification. A child's appearance in a room of adults could be greeted with "Feind hört mit." The message was not only "Do not talk about this in front of a child," but that a child can be an enemy.

As German parents soon learned, their children were encouraged to rat on them for whatever infraction, and they did so, often guilelessly. What did you have for Sunday dinner? asks teacher, who by order or desire probably was a Nazi Party member. If the answer was pork roast and sauerkraut and applesauce, Mutter could be in trouble. That was not the kind of an economical "Eintopf" [casserole-type meal] that the Führer asked all good German Hausfrauen to make.

Finally, one can hardly overstate what effort and effect the Nazi wordsmiths wrought against Jews. In short, *Juden-* and *jüdisch-* became prefixes for anything terrible. The Gentiles' minds gradually became poisoned, commented a Holocaust survivor.[15]

That the poisoning became ingrained was made clear in two incidents some forty years after the Third Reich. Frau Karma Rauhut spoke of visiting a Berlin art gallery in the 1980s with an older woman friend and coming upon a group of paintings involving homosexuals. Her friend snapped, "Judenkunst [Jew art]." Yet she was confused by her own remark, for there was nothing "Jewish" about the paintings. But Frau Rauhut knew what the woman meant. Any art the Nazis disapproved of was called "Jew art." And the Nazis certainly would have disapproved of paintings of homosexuals. Second, a friend of mine related hearing an old woman in Munich cry out, while people were pushing to get on a streetcar, "Nur keine jüdische Hast [No Jewish haste]," then cover her mouth in alarm. She apparently did recognize the source of her words.

As for propaganda relating to women, very early in the Third Reich "Aryan" women were extolled as childbearers and keepers of near-sacred hearths, well away from desks and decisions. Woe to women who wanted to work at Weimar-type jobs, who wanted to be, or remain, legislators, lawyers,

---

14. Jill Stephenson, "'Reichsbund der Kinderreichen': The League of Large Families in the Population Policy of Nazi Germany," *European Studies Review* 9 (1979): 367.

15. Hamburg-born Alice Calder speaking on "Holocaust Survivor Interviews," a cable television production of the Holocaust Oral History Project, San Francisco, 29 April 1991.

or leaders, or independent in action and opinion, or just to have jobs as men did. "Double earners" was a Nazi term of opprobrium. One does not need wonder which half of a double-earning couple was supposed to quit for the good of the greater German economy.

Over the years, especially in the 1940s, when the war did not proceed as Hitler wished, German women were encouraged to extend their hearth-doms after all, even to such sites as bomb factories. Hitler did not believe, however, that women should be drafted for such work any more than for the front lines. (Some contend his sexism cost him battles.)

Amid the contradictions, Nazi Man somehow managed to put "Aryan" Woman on a pedestal, then surround her by attentive armed guards, much like the "protective custody" accorded enemies of the state. A putative majority of German women not only accepted the elevated imprisonment but clambered up the pedestal themselves. It looked safer than feminism. And the elevated attention, the first in their lives for some women, was flattering.

The cynical homage disguised the truth. German women were treated with such misogynistic manipulation, such disregard for any mental acuity (not even Nazi women were allowed in the Nazi "parliament" or at the top of their own organization), it is clear that if women were not childbearers they would not have been accorded even second-class status. They were lucky they had wombs. Nuns, who didn't use theirs, were treated worse.

As the Reich rolled on, democratic institutions like voting, a free press, fair trials, were so long gone that most younger women might not have known what they were missing. Yet they soon knew their pedestal was a little harder to reach. After a full shift making tank parts, standing in line to shop, cooking for and caring for one's children, and dragging them down to the bomb shelter several times a night, the climb back up above the chiseled letters of Motherhood must have been arduous. But the Führer always was there with a last helpful push, and an honorary Mother's Cross for the really procreative.

He was not there in May of 1945, though. Nor were many men. Nor were hardly any Jews. Nor was much of anything in order [in Ordnung]. At what is called Stunde Null [zero hour], the German women were encircled by debris, defeat, hunger, the horrified victors' cries of shame, and films and photographs of what the shame was about. That moment might be their greatest commonality.

The women in this book had so much in common, in fact, that one might ignore their equally important differences, like different ages, different hometowns, different privileges or hardships, different schools, friends, different jobs, lovers, parents, different beliefs, incomes, looks, worries, politics, and different worldviews, or weltanschauungen. Consequently, during the Third Reich German women had different experiences and made different decisions.

Many differences simply reflected their country. When Hitler came to power and so many of the women came of age, Germany was not the homogenous country some seem to think. How could it be after barely sixty years of unification? Divisions ran centuries deep.

Among the deepest was religion. Unlike other major European countries, Germany had two major religions—two often fractious and distrustful major religions—Protestantism and Catholicism, the consequence of the German-based Reformation and the Thirty Years' War that followed. One of many painful ironies relating to the Third Reich is that early Jewish immigrants chose to settle in German states not only because decrees here and there allowed them residency and protection but (supposedly) because of the two Christian religions. A predominantly Protestant village might have a few Catholic families, a Catholic city a few Protestants. All might eye each other warily, but they did coexist. Jewish settlers knew they themselves would not be the only religious minority in town. A tiny minority they were. Berlin, home to about a third of all German Jews, was only four percent Jewish.[16]

The fact that by 1933 Jewish Germans were mostly urban was a consequence of social history, but it also points out another difference among German women. City women likely had Jewish neighbors or friends, or at least acquaintances. Farm or village women likely knew few Jews, and had fewer still as neighbors.

A further difference among Germans as a whole resulted from the large and relatively inflexible social and economic strata, including impoverished apprentices, an aristocracy of stupefying, fairy-tale proportions, and the Volk in between.

The German population was divided by physical appearance, too. The Nazi stereotype of tall robust blonds, a stereotype fostered by Joseph Goebbels, the short brunet with a crippled foot, was skewed. A citizenry that united only in 1871 descended from various tribes and wars and sported various features, heights, and hair colors. "Aryans," of course, did not make up the only genetic hodgepodge in Germany. I heard any number of Jewish German men described as tall, blue-eyed, and blond.

Added to the hodgepodge of looks was that of speech. Then and today, Berliners cannot understand Bavarians and vice versa, unless both can, or will, suppress their dialect and speak High German. Speech differences pointed out emotional differences. A woman from the northern city of Bremen lamented to me that her husband was, after all, a Bavarian. A former Prussian complained that she could not get a straight answer from anyone in the Rhineland. A Rhinelander said she was exasperated with the narrow-mindedness of the Swabians of Stuttgart.

---

16. Hilker-Siebenhaar, ed., *Wegweiser durch das jüdische Berlin*, 361.

Such regional cantankerousness, which Hitler managed to diminish somewhat and replace with nationalism (it was one of his most striking accomplishments), reflected itself in politics. Before the Nazis took full power, voters had their choice of eleven political parties, representing far left, far right, and points in between. Even after the Nazis came to power and there was only one party, basic political differences were notable. Southern Germany, for example, was considered more pro-Nazi than the north. One West German told me an anti-Hitler joke that she said never would have been told in East Prussia.

So, for all their commonalities, the German women varied enormously. It would be reassuring to think they did not, as it is reassuring to think of certain Nazis as "monsters." But there is no getting around biology. All are, or were, individual human beings.

And it is as individuals that German "Aryan" women offer a look at—and indeed, a mirror of—the actions and inactions that accompanied that brief but endless era called the Third Reich. With them comes an admonition that whipped the early wind out of my sails, and kept it out. The late Reinhard Bendix, a Berlin-born survivor and sage (and the son of the man who wanted to write a letter of complaint to his concentration camp commander), said in a seemingly casual way, his brown eyes looking not quite accusatory, "I do hope your book won't make Americans feel smug."

A Note about Language, Translation, and Truth

The women within these pages spoke German with varying degrees of correctness, and so did I. In the first interview trips, my command of German was strained. By the last trip, my vocabulary and accent had improved to the point that I was mistaken for a German. Greater facility with the language did not necessarily improve the interviews; at least one woman was more forthcoming because she felt the need to put her words very basically. The language skills of either party mattered less, however, than one small tape recorder, which I used in every interview. A couple of women were wary about it, but I was able to convince them that I needed it. Therefore, all the women's words, if audible, were retrieved. A few times a woman said something notable when the tape recorder was off. If it was brief, I wrote it down quickly to insure I would not misquote her. If it was not brief, I paraphrased.

The attempt to be completely accurate was tested during the translation. The easiest women to translate were those who spoke High German. They sound quite like themselves in English, I believe. Women who spoke incorrect German, dialect, or both, were more challenging. Rather than try to find equivalent mistakes in English, or jargon, I have opted to point out the women's speech mannerisms to the reader. Now and then I also give a brief example in German of what they said. Beyond often editing out the "umm, let me see, well, you know" and other seemingly extraneous parts of a sentence, I sometimes felt inclined to smooth out a quote. I did not do so, however. With a gadget as miraculous as a tape recorder and with testimony as important (to my mind) as that pertaining to the Third Reich, I felt there was no excuse to be unfaithful to the spoken word. And it is clear these women were not writing essays, but talking.

When faced with a choice of which English words or phrases to use for German ones, I usually erred on the side of a literal translation (especially for a piquant phrase) rather than a literary one. The result may at times "sound" German, but I want the reader to be aware the woman *is* German. To this end, I also included at least one word characteristic of each woman, even something as basic as *ja*, or a typical sentence ending, like *nicht?*

There were other tricky situations, as when certain words had a different feel in German than in English. Like *Mensch*, which means "human being," or the less noble word, "person." I used both, according to context. The most frequently used word that "felt" different was *Jude*—Jew. Having been accustomed to hearing, in English, someone described as "Jewish" rather than a "Jew," not to mention a "Jewess," I tended to use *jüdisch* in my questions. But most of the women, reflecting the prevailing usage of their language and generation, said "Jew" or "Jewess," much more often than "Jewish." Because I was not always able to decide whether *Jude* reflected views about semantics or Semites, I again tried to translate in context.

When uncommon or particularly nettlesome words or phrases faced me, I consulted a native German speaker.

As for often used (mostly German) terms such as "Bund deutscher Mädel," rather than my explaining or translating each one each time it occurs, the terms have been neatly deposited in a glossary, following the main text. (An aside to readers with no knowledge of German: nouns are capitalized.)

Regarding the use of familiar and unfamiliar German words, the fastidious reader may fret that they are not italicized, contrary to common practice. That is because most of this book is "spoken," and I fretted that an italicized word could indicate the speaker was emphasizing a word when she is not. So, only those words she *really* emphasized are italicized.

In terms of the profiles themselves, I tried to insure that none of the women is misquoted in either the overall sense of what she said or a single word. An exception to accuracy is the spelling of a few proper names. Those I was not able to verify are spelled phonetically. At one woman's later request, I changed names of people she mentioned in an unsavory light. And I altered the name of one interviewee who became nervous about signing a release form.

These pages are replete with the fruits of three basic rules I worked out regarding accuracy. If a woman said something that most readers, including myself, would know or assume was untrue (such as Hitler not knowing what was going on in the camps), I left it as it was. If she said something that I had no way of checking because it was private information (what her mother told her fifty years ago) or because I did not have the resources to check it (whether a brother fought in France), I also left it. For various reasons, I did sometimes put in a "she said." But if a woman said something that an average reader might not know and that I could check myself or have checked and if the woman proved to be wrong, intentionally or not, I intervened in the text or a footnote to say so.

The reasons the women do not speak in "pure" unchallenged testimony, either during the interviews or here, are the women themselves and the subject. "Allied" readers are less likely to take the testimony of "Aryan" German women about the Third Reich at face value than they are the testimony of American GIs who fought in Germany. These women simply are suspect. It seemed to me that readers needed a representative. I have tried to keep my presence minimal and unobtrusive, but I am convinced that my absence would have been misleading: no woman was arguing with herself. And the reader has a right to know if a woman was wrestling with a subject on her own or as the result of a question. If I were an anthropologist, historian, or psychoanalyst, the women would have been approached, edited, and/or analyzed differently.[1] But I am not, and they were not.

Finally, I am aware that there must be more experts on different aspects of the Third Reich and the Holocaust than on any other contemporary historical subject, and that I am not an expert on any. Nonetheless, I have tried to the best of my ability to respect the reader by keeping these pages error-free, and accept responsibility for any instance in which I have failed.

---

1. One fascinating example of an analytical approach is "Gender and the Two World Wars," by Annemarie Tröger, a contributor to *Behind the Lines* (New Haven: Yale University Press, 1987).

Frauen

The deep, unadorned, en-un-ci-a-ted voice said, "Perhaps you should expound once again upon the *curvature* of what you wish to know."

The first recorded words of the first interview signaled, among other things, that in the presence of the voice's owner, Frau Margrit Fischer, one had best choose one's own words carefully. In voice, vocabulary, and manner, she did not slouch. In the course of seven years, Frau Fischer and I met four times. And with the exception of a remarkable incident at the end of our third meeting, her demeanor never changed. Yet even as that meeting began, I compliantly clicked the tape recorder off and on several times before getting her all-clear to proceed. One commanded click off came within an eloquent sentence Frau Fischer had not thought through to her satisfaction. Another preceded her request for a recital of planned questions. It was a relief to be able to comply. Frau Fischer was, in a word, imposing.

She and her husband, the historian Fritz Fischer, live in one of Hamburg's finer suburban neighborhoods. Their home, part of a small, discreet development, gives the impression of being well built, well cared for, graceful, proper, and hospitable—somewhat like the Fischers themselves.

Frau Fischer is a tall, handsome woman, her clothing tailored and sensible, her carriage as dignified as her demeanor. She conveyed authority and confidence. Herr Professor Dr. Fischer, soft-spoken, gentlemanly, and natty, is well known not only for his scholarship but for having stirred up an enormous controversy earlier in his career by insisting that Germany shared a great deal of the blame for World War I. The uproar was such that other

Frau Margarete (Margrit) Fischer

Idealism and Chasm

Frauen

German historians ostracized him. Frau Fischer, to her credit, stood by him. As for the origins of World War II and the Third Reich, Herr Dr. Fischer's explanation, historically speaking, was straightforward standard fare. Among his specialties, I gathered, was telling streams of American exchange students his opinion of why what happened did happen. Among his wife's specialties, it was clear, was being the competent hostess of a distinguished professor. Indeed, as he spoke to me of unemployment and the rise of the Nazis, Frau Fischer was in the kitchen preparing refreshments. To be the focal point of American questions herself, however, was a turnabout she took seriously. In time, Herr Dr. Fischer having excused himself, she and I sat alone in the Fischers' living room, sipped tea (her own blend), nibbled little bites of things, and in the most ladylike of ways, plunged. Having just heard her husband's deliberative thoughts, while knowing nothing of her own, I nonetheless looked to Frau Margrit Fischer to set a stunning example for German womankind.

Once satisfied as to curvature, she hit a straight shot to the Third Reich. With posture straight and voice strong, she spoke almost as if reciting an essay. Born in the northern German port of Bremen in 1918, she grew up in a matriarchy headed by her grandmother and her mother, who had divorced her husband, a minister. Margrit had one sibling, a brother. In her teens, she became a rebel, of sorts.

"One must have a certain breaking away," she said. "I *do* believe there is always a group to which one attaches oneself. This experience of the group is perhaps the essential conduit for cutting the cord to one's home. And naturally it is easy to advocate ideals other than those learned at home, perhaps just to protest. I had a wonderful relationship with my mother and my grandmother. That was never tarnished. *But* what is very essential for each young person is the relationship to a teacher."

For sixteen-year-old Margrit Lauth, that teacher was a woman. "She embodied the ideals of National Socialism in such a way that I'd still say, *if* National Socialism really had been how this woman believed it and embodied it, something completely different would have come out of it. She showed us by example what community is, what sacrifice for others is. She never thought of herself. She always lived and worked for others. Exemplary! And that was what she imparted to us as the center of National Socialism. That is what made me so happy. She pulled me into the group, at that time a student union, and personally demonstrated to us in the classroom as well as in the group the best sides, the idealistic sides, of National Socialism. And that convinced me.

"I looked exactly the way Hitler wanted German women to look. Blonde, with braids, and tall and slim and lively. Everything they wanted. But that had nothing to do with conviction. These young people who went in the SS were for the most part exactly as idealistic, especially those who went in the SS early, when it was still voluntary. They were exactly as filled

2

with this belief that there could be a world that was new, better, and more for common goals."

Her candor and sentiments, and the rapid end to my errant expectations, so stunned me, I barely managed a question. It was a most hopeful one at that. When did she begin to have doubts?

"Really first with these Jewish pogroms in 1938." No doubt referring to the November night most Germans call "Kristallnacht"—"crystal night," in English—her answer later seemed remarkable for two reasons. For one, "pogrom" is a word more often used by anti-Nazi groups, including survivors. For another, by "crystal night," the Nazis had perpetuated more than five years of actions against Jews. It was a late, though common, date for doubts to begin.

"I thought to myself," she continued, "how could that really happen? With this idealized view of the future? You have to picture that even though my family was opposed, we nonetheless lived nonpolitically. My parents were divorced, so I had no father, who's mostly the one who embodies a connection to politics. I had a brother, but he had nothing to do with it. He played the cello and because one had to be in the Hitler Youth in some way, he went into the music corps and played cello there. I myself did not join the BdM at all, because I rejected the autocratic form." Frau Fischer went on speaking of her own past, the "pogroms" temporarily eclipsed. After finishing high school, she said, she trained briefly as a kindergarten teacher and went to work in a village. There, BdM leaders came to her and said she was "predestined" to bring the girls of the neighboring villages together for BdM meetings.

"And I said yes, I'll do it gladly. I'll sing with them and take hikes and do handicrafts and make fires and dance and tell them stories. And I got a little bicycle and went to the individual villages. But that belonged to my profession as a kindergarten teacher. It really had no political . . ." she said, trailing off. She continued, briskly, "And if so, it had an idealistic slant. These girls I brought together found it terrific something of this kind was happening in the village. It wasn't like today, where every village has a discothèque and a swimming pool and so on. These were isolated villages. And then naturally there were sometimes nice dance evenings with the Hitler Youth."

Soon, the BdM leaders came calling again. They suggested promotion to "a higher leadership position."

"I said no. I don't really know why. It was not that I didn't want to identify with the thoughts." It was rather, she said, that she was engaged to be married "and did not want to spend my time that way. I was a kindergarten teacher out of passion and really wanted to go further with my profession."

Help in that regard came from a Third Reich organization, the NSV (Nationalsozialistische Volkswohlfahrt [National Socialist People's Welfare

Organization]), which ran the Reich's kindergarten system. It sent her to a two-year course to learn to teach children's health care and gymnastics.

In the meantime, Germany began the Second World War.

"When the war started, I wept so uncontrollably, I'll never forget it." Frau Fischer recalled standing on a balcony in Hanover while below her "young soldiers marched to war. There was no enthusiasm, not a bit. They marched 'stumpf' [gloomily] and in silence into this unhappiness. Perhaps that is what was so tormenting." Thereafter, "I only did my job. One had a profession and one had to work. I also very much wanted to.

"If you want to look back at the political connection," she added, "the first doubts really came with these synagogues, how they smashed them. And the inner resistance began the *moment* the war started. For me, it was all over then. The war freed me far and away from National Socialist thought possession. I already was a pacifist then."

Recollection of the war led Frau Fischer into an extremely heated denunciation of then-President Reagan and the American arms buildup. With enunciated fervor, and rather unpacifistic sentiments, she said she would sacrifice her life and attempt to kill him if doing so could stop another war. She said her antiwar feelings came from her mother, who had "an antipathy against everything warlike. I sucked it in with my mother's milk. Every war is *insanity.*"

Frau Fischer's mother had married in 1916, Frau Fischer in 1941. Like countless others, she thus became the second generation in her family to marry in the middle of a world war.

As a young wife—twenty-three years old—whose training by then was complete and whose husband by then was away as a soldier (her cello-playing brother was in the navy and stationed on a U-boat), "naturally" she continued to work.

Notwithstanding her feelings about the war, it probably advanced her career. Certainly the Nazi regime did. In 1942, the NSV promoted her to a "key position" as head of teacher training for children's health care and gymnastics in all kindergartens in the Hanover and Braunschweig area. Along with the key position came renewed pressure to join the Nazi Party.

"I never joined. On my office door were four names, with *PG* (*Parteigenosse* [party member]) after it. But after Fischer stood *Volksgenosse* [fellow German].[1] They pressured me constantly. As I entered the district leadership, I said, 'Nein, I'm sorry. If you want me, take me, because I'll gladly do my work. But I don't want to be a member of the Party.' "

Frau Fischer said she never gave a reason, other than "not wanting to be bound." But part of her real reason, she said, was that she did not like much of the Nazi hierarchy. "I was against the whole group which sat up

---

1. The term is a Nazi one and would not have been used for a Jewish German.

4

there on high around Hitler. We all had complete reservations. Himmler we all found monstrous. I never wanted to identify with them. Perhaps still with Hitler. He seemed to us still somehow driven by idealism.

"We did not comprehend until '45 what really stood behind it. I had a lot of fights with my husband, who was not a National Socialist. When he came home on leave, it wasn't easy at all. He said, 'I don't see what will come of this.' This eternal question about the concentration camps each of you puts to us is actually irrelevant."

I looked at Frau Fischer in some alarm, in part because I had not brought up the subject, in part because of "irrelevant."

"We knew there were concentration camps," she went on. "But you must picture they were so camouflaged, people who lived in nearby villages hardly knew anything of them. I recently [about 1983] went to East Germany. Our tour guide, an East German woman who didn't identify with the Third Reich at all, said, 'Here you see the prison and there was horrible torture and beheadings and who knew what else, but think, I lived right over there and we didn't know anything about it.' If *she* says that, how should we in Bremen or Hanover know what was going on?"

For the young Frau Fischer, her new key position as teacher of kindergarten teachers enabled her to put similar questions aside. "I really threw my whole life, my whole energy, into [work]. Through the NSV one naturally had huge possibilities." The organization put a youth hostel at her disposal. There she trained the supervisors of some five hundred full-time kindergartens and five hundred part-time "harvest" kindergartens, which operated only during harvests.

She described her schedule in considerable detail. The work involved intensive three-and-a-half-day sessions during which she taught the supervisors courses in children's health care and several related subjects. Then she bicycled to each kindergarten to observe how her information was being applied, critiqued "what was good and what had to be better," rested a little, got back on her bike, and went "on and on, Sundays too, always farther. I didn't do an awful lot of thinking," she concluded.

She added she did not think about herself a lot, either. Nor, she implied, did she think a lot about what some Germans might be doing in the 1940s to other Germans. Asked about rumors, she said, "Ja, one heard rumors. But look, when one was so active, the day-to-day grabbed you like a prisoner. One suppressed it, too. One wanted to hear nothing about it at all."

One could hear something about it by risking listening to verboten foreign radio broadcasts. Asked about that, she did not dismiss the practice as dangerous, which it was, but said, "That was not so easy. All I had was this National Socialist radio." The radio transmitted only Nazi broadcasts. "But when we could, we listened to Switzerland. Naturally, that was forbidden. The broadcaster reported how the world looked from outside. And how the world judged Hitler and our Reich." Frau Fischer said she heard the broadcasts whenever she could, at a cousin's back in Bremen, but the logistics were "very difficult." Apparently, the contents of the broadcasts were "difficult," too. "I didn't believe everything. To us, a lot of it seemed very improbable and also colored. At that time perhaps we also didn't want to believe it all."

Perhaps, I said, it was a matter of protecting oneself.

"One *had* to," she immediately replied. "Otherwise, one could not have gone on living. Somewhere inside, one had to shut oneself off from it. It was more my nature, anyway, to believe more in the good and the best that they always propagandized for the outside world. And I wanted to make it a reality in my own life. I do think that following the example of this very beloved teacher, I applied myself fully to the task that had been put before me. And as far as possible from an idealistic standpoint, I carried it out."

Could one really think of oneself as idealistic while knowing what Hitler was saying (I avoided the word doing) against the Jews?

"It was not that the Jews should be exterminated, but pushed back." She continued, "You must realize, the Jews were not a large percentage of the population. They were actually only in a few cities. There were a lot in Berlin and Frankfurt. Those were the main Jewish centers. And in the cities, they were a very small percentage of the population. In the level of earning, their percentage was much higher. They were incredibly clever. They made up a great proportion of professors. Almost all the critics. Theater people. Journalists. They were the doctors, to a very great extent. They really had all the key positions because of their great ability." (Not all the key positions. In the pre-Nazi years Frau Fischer described, Jews were not welcomed into the higher ranks of two major German institutions: the government and the military. As for professorships, Jews tended to be welcomed mostly into the fields of medicine and law.)

"But, of course, like every people that has been dispersed, whoever had a job pulled in another after him as much as possible. Many great musicians today, too, are Jews, because they're so highly musical."

They pulled not only other Jewish musicians into "their quartet or their orchestra," said Frau Fischer. "In business, too, they naturally always pulled in their own after them. And that irritated everyone.

"Certainly," she added, Jews achieved what they did "because of their own ability. That is clear. But to a great extent, the Jews at least conducted themselves incautiously or awkwardly and did not try to hold back a little." As a result, "the mood against them among everyone definitely was there. There is no doubt about that at all. Overall, where there was commerce, Jews had their hand in it."

Frau Fischer was clearly familiar with some aspects of Jewish history, and agreed that the emphasis on commerce was partially a result of Jews earlier not having been allowed to own (not to mention to farm) land in Germany. "Certainly the Jewish emancipation only began with Napoleon at the beginning of the nineteenth century. Until then, they certainly were limited to extremely specified career slots. For example, everything that had to do with money, no? They weren't allowed to buy land." She added, "And the big department stores were all in the hands of Jews."

Her sources of information seemed an amalgam of historical fact and Third Reich propaganda, the latter having been launched just as she was coming of age. When asked how she knew of acts against Jews, she said she may have learned from movie newsreels or from newspapers, where "it would have been reported with certain pride that the German people de-fended themselves against the 'alien blood' as it was called, and 'parasites,' and however else the Nazis called the Jews. Against this 'economic rule of Jewry.' And now [the Nazis] wanted to send them out of the country. Many emigrated, and could take their money and everything possible with them." It must be interjected that although Frau Fischer recalled some Nazi propa-ganda accurately, she may have been a longtime victim of it, too, as when she spoke of people who could take "everything possible with them." Very early emigrés could take a lot with them *if* they had the means (and pre-science) to do so. Those who had neither, but relied on patience and hope, found their economic situation worsening month by month. And after "Kris-tallnacht" in 1938, most Jewish Germans who tried to emigrate usually had to sell, at extremely reduced value, whatever the Nazis had not already ex-propriated, and could take relatively little with them, if they could get out at all.

"The really bad things that happened to the Jews started in '42," she continued. "Also, the 'final solution,' as it was called, happened first in '43 or '44."

"Really bad things" being a matter of interpretation, but presumably referring to mass murder, Frau Fischer's dates are late even in terms of the "final solution." According to Lucy Davidowicz's *The War Against the Jews,* the first annihilation camps had been built, and completed, in 1941.[2] (Auschwitz began receiving Jews the same year.) Deportations to Poland from some areas began in February 1940.[3] And the "final solution to the Jewish prob-lem" was adopted at the Wannsee Conference in January 1942 and put into

---

2. According to Davidowicz, the first gassings at Auschwitz, the victims "probably 'Communists' and Jews," took place in September 1941. The first death camp at Chelmno, Poland, "intended for the Jews from the ghetto of Lodz . . . began functioning on December 8, 1941, with mobile vans, using engine exhaust gases." Lucy Davidowicz, *The War Against the Jews* (New York: Bantam, 1981), 181.

3. Carolin Hilker-Siebenhaar, ed., *Wegweiser durch das jüdische Berlin* (Guide to Jewish Berlin) (Berlin: Nicolai Verlag, 1987), 366.

high gear shortly thereafter. The genocidal death rates were most intense in the time frame Frau Fischer referred to, however.

She continued, "One believed, through rumor, that whoever was disagreeable, who acted against the government politically, disappeared into concentration camps. But at first there was no torture or the like. That came later." Again, "first" and "later" are matters of debate. People also were sent to camps, said Frau Fischer, if they "made up jokes or expounded publicly" against the Reich. But "one came out again. I had a cousin who was taken to a concentration camp." His crime, which netted him four months of incarceration, was telling a joke involving Hitler. The cousin "had a fresh mouth," she said. "We all made jokes. Who knows how? It only depended on whether one would be denounced. If someone who wanted to do someone else harm overheard him, the person would be denounced. This denouncing always made one shudder. I always opposed it internally."

Her cousin's incarceration was the only example Frau Fischer gave regarding Nazi persecution of someone she knew. And she said she had no personal evidence whatever of the persecution of Jews, because her immediate world had always been "Aryan." "I had no connections to Jews at all. There were very, very few Jews in Bremen. Up to 1863, Jews were not allowed residency to be Bremer. Therefore there weren't terribly many Jews later. In my lifetime, the problem never arose.

"Once, when we went to far Pomerania, we traveled through Berlin, where we stopped for half a day. We went to Kranzler's for ice cream or something. And there I must honestly say I asked my mother, 'What kind of fat women are *they*, all sitting around eating pastries?' And my mother said, 'Those are Jews.' That was really the first and only time in my childhood that a connection or even the consciousness 'Those are Jews' came to me. But it was no problem for me at all. They were no problem at all for people in Bremen."

Frau Fischer later revealed she had meant it literally about having "no connection to Jews at all." Before and during the Third Reich, she said, she never met a single Jewish person. That might have been in part why, for Margrit Fischer personally, the Third Reich was upbeat. "On the whole at that time, I felt thoroughly well in my world and in my daily life and in my human relationships. The political was *very* much on the edge."

Did she consider herself an exception?

"No, I don't think so. On the whole, everyone felt well. During the war, too. No one felt well in the conviction, 'Aren't these terrific times.' But in their daily life, many human beings felt well. One can't feel horrible for years and cry. *Naturally* we cried constantly about our fallen brothers and friends. That's clear. And we were tense about what was going on in the war. But I'd also like to go into the particulars of the time before. It had been basically a productive and *basically* a happy life. The mood, the spirit of the times was certainly *positive*. In the thirties, things went uphill. The order, and there was work. They didn't have these horrible lines of unemployed anymore.

"Many who nowadays always say, 'Yes, we were a hundred percent against it'—all of that one can say very easily afterward. Most human beings tried at the very least, even when they didn't agree one hundred percent with the Third Reich or with National Socialism, to adapt themselves. And there were certainly eighty percent who lived productively and positively throughout the time." She later said, "We also had good years. We had *wonderful* years."

Except for the war, she said. "Nobody wanted the war. We just carried out our duty. This blackout, you can't picture it. I remember how we always longed for the full moon so at least we didn't fall into the holes in our streets. At the time, one really had a relationship to heaven again," she said, laughing.

"Once I had a day trip in Braunschweig with thirty kindergarten teachers and a group of twelve children for a practice demonstration of gymnastics and health care. Then the big alarm came. And I with this group in the cellar and then two bombs went off and all the entrances were sealed shut with rubble, and me completely alone with the responsibility for this group. To talk with these children there below and everything dark, you should picture that sometime." After several hours, she and her group were freed.

She said she was temporarily buried in cellars four times and had to leap from a train during bombing attacks several times. Asked who was cursed in such situations, she said just about everyone. "But you have to picture that, especially in the beginning, Hitler tried to make it clear this war was necessary and we only had to survive it." For relief, she said, she swore loudly. "One was careless sometimes. One said things after which one then said, 'Well, if that goes all right. . . .' One *had* to say things out loud sometimes." The war was "indescribable."

All things considered, it might have been a good idea to get out. Had she considered leaving Germany? Like almost every other woman to whom I put the question before retiring it in embarrassment, she seemed astounded by the idea.

"Nein, nein. I was too nationally minded for that. I wanted to will my strength to the German children."

During the war, Frau Fischer had fallen out of touch with the teacher who had been her National Socialist role model. But after war's end, when Allied forces had done their best to show the German public the atrocities committed in the name of National Socialism, she and the teacher were reunited. She said they wept. "Nothing is more disappointing than throwing one's whole love and one's whole idealism and one's energy into something and having to discover afterward what had been negative and horrendous about it. You cannot imagine there were such human beings, who really believed that now relationships among human beings would change for the better. Naturally during the war, that had died out a lot. But in '45, it all came over us. First, of course, the collapse itself. And then, for the first time, the entire horrendousness.

"Then came all the trials. Everything was disseminated. All accusations were published in detail in the newspapers. And that is when one first became aware of everything that had happened and what they actually wanted. Never again in my life have I been that uncomprehending. That was *bad*. Afterward, one didn't trust so easily. Our whole generation didn't. No ideology in any form. No more running after someone and thinking, '*Those* are the ideals for you!' This idealism we all had, when you get right down to it, was misused scandalously. That it led to war, the complete reverse of what we wrote on our banners, 'For world peace. . . .'"

Frau Fischer did not mention whether she felt the fault of misplaced idealism was in part her own, or if fault were even involved. She and her teacher, who became even closer by being, in her word, "infuriated," remained lifelong friends.

An apparently more fractious postwar reunion took place between Frau and Herr Fischer. For one thing, "he threw at me often enough" her former enthusiasm for Adolf Hitler, although he also knew that "in the last years I distanced myself a lot."

The Fischers' main problem, however, was not about politics per se, but sexual politics. It is generally agreed that from its beginning, the Third Reich treated women in a callous and politically expedient way. Frau Fischer, however, sees things differently. She affirmed that English suffragists had "taken the lead" in women's emancipation early in the twentieth century. Nonetheless, "Women's emancipation in the wide, wide public began fundamentally with National Socialism." Her reasoning included the extensive membership of German girls in the BdM and German women in the Frauenschaft. Both groups "now for the first time" were led by their female peers. "That all really happened in spite of Hitler's wanting the woman to stay with her saucepan. That on the one hand they should return to what was thought feminine, but on the other hand, through this leadership of women by women, emancipation can be spoken of in the larger breadth.

"In addition, during the war, we women here at home replaced all male work. And had to decide, fully self-sufficiently, this way or that way. We had to raise the children. Not I. My first child was born in '45. But women at the time all became self-sufficient because of the war and because of the women's groups.

"Now, when the men came home and tried to reestablish their authoritarian presence, when it didn't lead to divorce, which in many families it often did, at the least it burdened a lot of marriages. Mine was very burdened. Very burdened. We had great difficulties, until we actually . . ." She paused. "Furthermore," she confided darkly, "my husband is Bavarian."

10

In "Bavarian suppositions," she said, "the man is everything and the woman is only the servant." Such an attitude "burdened our marriage *very* much." It might be added that the Fischers now seem a picture of loving and respectful harmony.

"I am still not an emancipated woman," she said. "I have my own opinions, to be sure, and my own areas in which I believe I have the say within the family. But I'm not the one who says *I* must 'realize' myself. Absolutely not. The man must be the one and I was his helper. I worked completely for him and raised my children. And I think I conducted my household quite well. In any case, I was no longer the little dumb girl [das kleine dumme Mädchen] he got to know in 1939. More self-sufficient, more self-assured. I built up a few things organizationally not every woman had done."

Had Herr Dr. Fischer not been proud of her?

"He certainly was, in a certain sense. But he wanted very much to have his say in the house. And he couldn't completely tolerate that in public . . ." After again trailing off, she continued. "As a professor's wife one had to master a certain public. I appeared very independent, with my own opinions, and led my own conversations."

Perhaps things might have been better had she been his sister?

Frau Fischer laughed rather heartily. "Ja, ja. That would have been better."

The aftermath of the war and the Reich also affected the Fischers as their two curious children were growing up. She said explaining the Third Reich to German children, including her own, was "very difficult. Children are always very critical anyway. When they hear about National Socialism at school, there's always the question, 'How could you even have lived? How could you have gone along with it so much that you even lived within it? Why didn't you do anything against it?' Not so much anymore with my children. And my husband can explain wonderfully from a historical perspective how it could have happened and how we managed and lived in this situation. But raising children is not easy in the first place."

Did Frau Fischer think the Third Reich might have been different if women had been in power?

She said she would like to think so. "I believe no women advocated the war." She added that she finds the gruesome acts of the Nazis "completely incomprehensible." She enunciated each syllable for emphasis. "*Un-vor-stell-bar.*"

"What happened in these concentration camps is beyond any power of comprehension, how human beings can do that to other human beings."

Did she not think that women could have done what men did?

"Nein. Nein, I believe not. There are cruel women, no doubt at all. And there are hard women. The concentration camp guards must have had the devil in their bodies." But men, in comparison to women, "certainly are hardened internally," she said. Yet "many men suffered insanely and also a

11

lot went crazy about it and also did something against it. But how could they, in this authoritarian state, do anything at all against it publicly? They disappeared immediately into concentration camps or were imprisoned."

One thing some men did was try to kill Hitler. Frau Fischer remembered well the assassination attempt of July 1944. "Many thought at the time, it's a miracle. It *was* a miracle, no? Three or four near him were killed. And that this table he bent over absorbed the explosion. Is it not"—she changed her voice to imitate Hitler—"the *Vorsehung* [providence] that Herr Hitler affirmed so much?

"*Why* must this people, first of all must *we*, travel this horrible path until the end? If one is religious at *all*, one asks oneself, how could God allow it not to be successful? That we asked ourselves a lot. For what purpose did God still protect this man? When you picture that almost a *third* of the soldiers were killed in the last three-quarters of the year, one simply could go *raving* mad.

"Why didn't it work? If it had, maybe we'd have gone another way and maybe not the way of a democracy. Nobody knows what would have become of us, if there'd been another 'legend,' if we'd have been ultimately unconquerable. Or one says, God allowed it in *order* that we take this horrendous path to the end, in *order* that we completely change ourselves. It's the question that doesn't leave us alone, we who lived through it."

During a primarily social tying-up-loose-ends visit to the Fischer household the following year, Frau Fischer was as straight-backed, in posture and utterance, and as hospitable, as before. The visit included a second invitation to stay for supper. Later, we sat in the living room for an unrecorded postsupper talk. Although the conversation concerned the Third Reich, it was unremarkable, with one exception. Frau Fischer made a passing remark that had to do with "Jewry" and "races." Although I could not remember precisely what she had said, in retrospect it seemed to contradict earlier statements which I had interpreted as more pro- than anti-Semitic. The phantom remark became reason enough to try to see Frau Fischer a third time. The time turned out to be two years later. Although about to leave for a trip out of the country, she graciously squeezed out an hour for a further talk at her home, again over tea. My prepared set of questions turned out to be especially helpful, for Frau Fischer wanted to be even more precise about what was to be asked of her. After I recited all the questions, she elected to answer first, "What was the greatest influence of the Third Reich on your life immediately after the war and now?"

It was, she said with as much passion as she had ever shown, "the indescribable disappointment." Within words, she invoked its still shimmering precedents: "the tangibility of a great deal of idealism and good will and commonly carried sorrow, which mutual assistance required. In the spirit of the time were words like 'community.' It was a band that embraced us all. And that suddenly ripped apart. One's eyes were opened, and saw abysses one had not at all suspected, quite apart from the knowledge of the terrible atrocities the Third Reich carried out, which not only shocked us, but completely demolished us."

It was, she continued, "the worst valley through which I'd ever gone. To build it up again and to fill it up again, with thoughtful and honorable ideas, took years. At first one pulled back completely from thoughts about commonality and common good and concentrated only on one's innermost circle, and tried from that vantage point to build anew with completely new assumptions. That was widely successful. Nonetheless, I'd always say I still sense this break in my life, even today."

After a charged pause that followed what she especially wanted to say came the question I especially wanted to ask, and did so rather raggedly. It was about her "personal differences of opinion about Jews."

The response, understandably, felt cooler in tone and in language than her previous remarks. "I personally never had an aversion to Jews because, as stated, there were very few Jews in Bremen and I'd had no personal relations to Jews at all, neither positive nor negative. The negativity which lay in the air in regard to Jews and which was spread by means of the slogans did not touch me at all. In my profession I had nothing at all to do with it." She characterized the slogans as "downright crude," then added in a lighter voice, "But when one is so bound up with his work and so full of idealism . . ." After trailing off, she resumed, "I actually *wanted* only to see the good. The other I simply shoved aside.

"One must make a distinction," she continued, speaking of her postwar experiences, "between my personal relationship to Jews—after the war, when I met the first—which was very positive. In America and in London we visited a great many immigrant professors, and among them have decidedly good friends. But my opinion about world Jewry and about the role of the Jew in the world has in no way improved since the war. That's connected, of course, to the widest variety of events. For instance, [former German chancellor] Helmut Schmidt's visit to Israel, how [former Prime Minister Menachem] Begin treated him with such hostility. And in regard to Herr [Kurt] Waldheim [the former Austrian president and United Nations Secretary-General], to whom I myself give no good grades, I nonetheless find the way he's treated by world Jewry not to be right." (This portion of the interview took place in 1987 during a public outcry after newly published evidence linked Waldheim to Nazi war crimes.) Frau Fischer also recalled reading in the *Frankfurter Allgemeine* newspaper that a leading Frankfurt rabbi said, "We can't continue as we are or we'll harm ourselves most of all." His reference to "continue as we are," she said, was about what she called "the endless television broadcasts that again and again bring to the screen the concentration camps and the Jewish annihilation and again and again this theme, to the extent that many people have said, '*Again and again* this theme and *can't* there be something else.' "

I asked if she thought German Christians and German Jews were really two different races.

"Ja. That we're two races is completely obvious. But it's no pity that human beings of other races live together. That can be mutually fruitful. One doesn't have to see the one only positively and the other negatively. But I am convinced they're *different*.

"There are things one calls typically Jewish, although of course any generalization is a great danger in which absolutely not everyone can be subsumed. There are neither 'the Germans' nor 'the English.' There are not in that sense 'the Jews.' But there are specific features which are specific as to race." She paused. "Or also specific as to country, which does not necessarily have to do with race."

She brought up, as an example of "race specificity," Jewish authors. "They have a more analytical way of thinking. I'm convinced," she added, "most Jews are more intelligent than we are."

Ja?

"Ja. Most definitely." She added, "Relatively speaking, the percentage of intelligent Jews is higher than among us. There's no doubt at all. But they have a different way of thinking than we do."

It was time to trot out a test case I had developed by then for such occasions. The case was that of a hypothetical Jewish orphan raised since birth in a Protestant family. A family in Bremen, this time. How does the orphan later behave?

"Naturally the environmental influence will cover a lot," Frau Fischer responded. "But in the final analysis, it's exactly the same if you raise a black child somewhere. Another race still remains. And another mentality remains from the other race. Why should one view that as negative?" She had spoken somewhat heatedly, and paused. "It's a very delicate theme you are raising. One could say an extraordinary amount about it. But why do you want to press it? What do you want to hear?"

Whatever there is *to* hear, I thought. My response, however, had to do with the related matter of whether some people really do differ intrinsically from other people, like Germans from Americans, and if so does it have to do with genes. . . . "Of course it has to do with genes and has to do with environment," she interrupted. "I believe anyway that each human being is, crudely speaking, comprised fifty percent by genes and fifty percent by environment."

But is it really fifty-fifty, I asked, and not ten-ninety or ninety-ten? . . .

"Perhaps it's different with each individual," she said. "But I do believe genes play a large role."

There we left it.

Soon thereafter, this third and final interview session (a fourth get-together years later was mostly social) began winding down. As it did, Frau Fischer visibly relaxed. At one point, over the last of the tea, she remembered a happy moment from her youth. It was a huge 1938 Hitler Youth gathering and harvest festival. The event included the blessing of the crops, folk dancing, and singing. She recalled most of all a "Hochstimmung" [exalted mood]. With prompting, she also recollected that she, then twenty years old, wore a dirndl and a wreath on her head and did a folk dance. Through whatever neuron path, the memory prompted another and she said, "Once I shook hands with Hitler."

Nein, I said.

"Ja. I even have a picture of us together. Would you like to see it?" Upon my immediate assent, Frau Fischer, laughing gaily, jumped up and retrieved it from the living room desk a few feet away. She and her mother, she said, had been on vacation in 1935 near Berchtesgaden, Hitler's home in southern Germany, when she learned he was in the immediate area. Wanting to see what he looked like, she left her unenthusiastic mother behind and "marched right up there" to join a group of young women that Hitler was greeting.

Frau Fischer leaned down and handed me the resulting black-and-white photograph. It was riveting. On a hut of sorts a large lightninglike SS symbol had been painted. At the right of the scene stood a smiling Adolf Hitler, wearing a suit rather than the uniform he almost always wore later. At the left were many young girls—all but Margrit Lauth wearing *their* uniforms—smiling up at him. The teenaged Margrit looked very happy, and very pretty. She pointed herself out. "You can tell. My profile's still quite the same." She turned to model. She was right.

And she was right that the photograph was, as she said, "Dokument." I turned it over. There was a stamped imprint bearing the name "H. Hoffmann." Hitler's official photographer. The imprint also stated that reuse without permission was verboten. (Preposterous as it sounds, the long-dead command had enough power to give me a second's pause before having the photograph copied.)

Frau Fischer was saying, "Afterward I went up to him ⌊Hitler⌋ and said, 'Mein Führer, why don't you come to Bremen again soon?' And he said, 'Nein, I don't like to go to Bremen. I don't go over well there.' He had something against Bremen. The people of Bremen were suspicious. They were very circumspect. They didn't shout with jubilation, the way he was used to, the way he liked it.

"He really did make a fascinating impression," she said, now also peering at a man then standing outdoors near Berchtesgaden, now part of a photograph lying in my hand in a nice house on a quiet road newly renamed Anne Frank Street.

"He had eyes that really looked at you and through you. There was a

15

certain charisma. I have to say that from my past impression. Because now when I hear his screaming on the radio, you ask yourself, you grab your head and say 'How could you ever have found that nice or been able to stand it?' But in his expression and relationship to human beings, there was something nonetheless that moved us very much."

As a child, Wilhelmine had a girlfriend who had been born with legs of slightly different lengths, so had trouble walking. "She always liked to walk with me, because she could hang on." While the girl hung on, Wilhelmine happily limped along beside her in imitation—until her mother put a stop to it.

Frau Haferkamp told the anecdote as guilelessly as she did others about her childhood. Her speech had elements of the lowland dialect of northwest Germany, which in short bursts can sound like English (So what? is "Zo vot?"), and it reflected unfamiliarity with proper grammar. But how she talked did not distract from what she just said. A child who helped a lame girl walk and empathized enough to walk the way she did was more likely than other children to become a certain kind of adult: one who helped victims of the Nazis. Frau Haferkamp did. That kind of adult, however, was not usually honored by the Nazi Party, or married to a Party member. Frau Haferkamp was both of those things, too.

Seventy-six years old when we met, Frau Wilhelmine Haferkamp still disported herself beyond convention. Treating physical obstacles no more circumspectly than she had in her childhood, she matter-of-factly referred to an overweight daughter as "die Dicke [the fat one]." And she cheerfully lifted her skirt to jab a needle of insulin into a plumpish thigh. Everyone on her father's side of the family had diabetes, she said.

My first impression of Frau Haferkamp, standing on a corner and energetically waving

Frau Wilhelmine Haferkamp

Motherhood Times Ten, and Food to Spare

down my cab, was of a lively woman in a somewhat dingy town. She lives in a small apartment over a furniture store in Würselen, outside the rather cosmopolitan city of Aachen, in western Germany. My second impression was that she is almost manically generous, and perhaps necessarily so. Her apartment is simply full, partly from gifts, partly from objects produced by her ever moving fingers. Heavily perfumed crocheted flowers suffuse a guest bedroom, itself bursting with flamenco dolls and piles of pillows, bedding, and handicrafts. In her living room a row of crocheted swans with inserts of movable eyes lines part of one wall. Dozens of photographs of children and grandchildren cover part of another. For no apparent reason other than to show the parts of her life not within eyesight, she opened drawers, cabinets, cupboards, closets, to reveal tablecloths, nightgowns, figurines, a broken plate that played "Happy Birthday," a vast display of liquor (which she does not drink), gifts and more gifts, talking about each one. At one point when she leaned closer to say something, I pulled back. "It's my garlic, isn't it?" she asked cheerfully. "I had a bonbon earlier, but it didn't help much." Within no more than an hour of meeting me, she offered not only room and board, but a polyester Christmas tablecloth, a decorative candle, boxed figurines, and two bags of candy. If Frau Wilhelmine Haferkamp were hiding anything physically or materially, it would have been hard to find within her compacted cornucopia. Yet she must have hidden some of her emotions. She was usually an exuberant sort of person, but toward the end of our talks, she looked around her, sighed, and said that things were not going as well as before. "Na, es klappt nicht so wie vorher." Before, she lived with her husband and their ten children. Since then, he has died and so has one child. Five other children have moved to the United States. Frau Haferkamp lives alone.

She was born in 1911 in the city of Oberhausen, part of Germany's industrial area. Her father and his two brothers were train conductors. About 1919, when her family began feeling the devastating financial effects of the First World War, she was sent to Holland to live with relatives who had a restaurant. She recalled the time with pleasure, and showed off her Dutch vocabulary with as much friendly boasting as she did her English one (mostly mild obscenities). She came home from Holland within a year, but, as would be apparent during the war, she did not forget the Dutch people.

While a teenager, she fell in love with a neighborhood boy, Heinrich Haferkamp, who worked in the stone mines and happened to be the brother of the girl she had helped to walk. Wilhelmine's parents strongly opposed the marriage. She was Catholic. He was Protestant. Wilhelmine converted. In 1930, when she was nineteen, they were married in a Protestant church. (Twenty years later she and five of her children converted back, out of anger at the broken promise of a Protestant clergyman to her dying husband to get a nice dress for one of their daughters.)

As might be expected, the families of the newlyweds both voted for the Socialist Party. That is, their fathers did, "for twenty-five years or longer. I know one hundred percent." Frau Haferkamp did not mention how their mothers voted, once they were allowed to. She herself had "no time for politics," she said repeatedly.

"But then all at once it happened. When one had ten children, well, not ten, but a pile of them, one should join the [Nazi] Party; '33 it was, nicht? I already had three children and the fourth on the way. When 'child rich' [kinderreiche] people were in the Party, the children had a great chance to advance. Stake claims and everything. Ja, what else could my husband do? They joined the Party, nicht? There was nothing else we could do. I got thirty marks per child from the Hitler government, came every month, and twenty marks' child aid from the city of Oberhausen. Was fifty marks per child. That was a lot of money. I sometimes got more 'child money' [Kindergeld] than my husband earned." She put it all in separate savings accounts for them, rather than spend it on "expensive sausages," as some mothers did. (After the war, she said, all the savings accounts were nullified.)

Kindergeld was not the least of the family's windfalls, especially when the war came and goods were rationed. "With a lot of children, you also had a lot of ration cards, nicht? And there were cards for cooking, flour cards, all of that."

What did she think when Hitler came to power?

"I didn't know him. I had a lot to do with the children. I always said, I had no time. To think about it, nicht? Ja, I often *complained.* There were meetings there and meetings there and there meetings. Ne, what did one have then? Our 'Dicke,' one of the older children, when she was in school, had to be in the BdM. Otherwise she couldn't go to school. You were not promoted [to the next grade], you had no advantages at all, you didn't have this and didn't have that. You *had* to be in the BdM. I still see ours running with the little shirts and the little blue skirts and the black scarves." Asked what she thought about the organization itself, she said she thought it was like the Girl Scouts, or a gymnastics or singing club. "They got their uniforms, nicht? And marched through the streets. They didn't learn anything harmful." She added that she knew parents who did not want their children to take part in BdM and the Hitler Youth, especially on marches. "Then the Party and the SA were always carping about something. So the children never had any advantages. Ja, the children could not really develop."

Because Herr Haferkamp was a Party member, his children also got more schooling than they would have otherwise. "If you went to high school, the parents had to pay. And if you were in the NSDAP [the Nazi Party], everything was paid." Did she join the Party, too? "Never. My mother wasn't in it, either. To the contrary, a couple times I got a warning."

Frauen

With those words, Frau Haferkamp launched into stories that have become lore in her family.

Most of the stories involved slave laborers, prisoners of war or the human booty of Nazi expansionism, who did hard manual work in Germany, got meager rations, and lived an altogether miserable existence. To help insure their misery, the Nazi regime included them in the category of "enemy" and forbade the German citizenry from having friendly relations with them. Some slave laborers worked on construction projects right outside the Haferkamp home, and especially caught the eye of Frau Haferkamp and her oldest boy. He had the chore of going to the baker's every morning for fresh breakfast rolls.

"I can still see him running with the net bag on his back, with rolls in it, and [past] the ditches in the streets where a new drainage system was being put in. And our boy always had pity. He always threw rolls in the ditches." She said, laughing, "He just went by the row like a farmer sowing his crop." One of her sisters, at the house on a visit, was so distressed to see the freezing prisoners with "icicles in their beards" that she threw them the Christmas cookies she had brought. The gesture brought a rebuke from the Nazis—rather, another rebuke.

By then, Frau Wilhelmine Haferkamp had also committed the crime of "füttern den Feind" [feeding the enemy]. In the Nazis' alliteratively insulting phrase, the "enemy" was further dehumanized by being equated with animals. *Füttern* means "to fodder." In Frau Haferkamp's eyes, however, the "enemy" were merely miserable men. "Now what really happened, was *cold* outside. And every day I cooked a big pot of milk soup for the children, nicht? Nice and hot. Got a lot of milk on the children's ration cards. And then I put a whole cube of butter in it, the pot was full, and a lot of sugar, because sugar nourishes, nicht? And I lived upstairs. My mother-in-law lived downstairs. At the time I was already bombed out. And I looked out the window and pointed to 'the bandolios' [what she called the laborers] that I was putting something in the hallway. They were afraid to get out of the ditches and they wanted to eat it. Then I went to the watchman and I said, 'Listen, you too are married.' I said, 'I have many children.' In the meantime he saw that, because he was at his post until [the prisoners] were done. 'And I cooked a big pot of milk soup.' I say, 'Can I not give it to the poor men? You wouldn't want me to throw it down the toilet.'" In another version, she said she told him to close an eye, that "it hurts me in my soul, I can't sleep the whole night if I have to pour out the soup and the men freeze there.

"He looked at me, he said"—she spat him out in imitation—"'You are an obstinate dame [ein hartnäckiges Weib]. Go ahead and do what you have to, but I have seen *nothing*.' Then I made the soup so hot, put it down in the hallway and with a ladling spoon, not with individual bowls, and then I pointed to it. One by one, they jumped out of the ditches and took the big soup spoon . . ."—Frau Haferkamp delivered a memorable slurping sound—

"until it was empty. One day, my husband got a card from the Party. They would like him to appear in the Party office.

"And they said, 'Listen, your wife is sure doing fine things. How can she fodder our enemies?' 'Ja, well, I can't do anything about it, I'm not always home, I don't see it.' Then when my husband came home, he really yelled at me [hit me with noise], he said, 'You will land me in the *devil's kitchen* if you keep doing that. And I am a Party member.' Had to be, nicht? 'And what do you think will happen when they catch me? They will take me somewhere else.'" The scene was repeated, on the street and off. "They were so *cold*, so cold. They [the Nazis] came a couple times and said to my husband, 'Listen, Herr Haferkamp, if your wife keeps doing that, ne? Then she'll get a warning.'"

She seemed not to have been fazed. "I kept on doing it. Always had something different. Came from the baker, got two big breads, lying there on the table. And there stand the workers." Earlier that day, to her surprise, she overheard some of them speaking Dutch. She quickly spoke a few words to them, to their surprise. Obviously, she was especially eager to give them food, but this time her husband was home. No longer able to work in the mines, he had become a streetcar conductor, a civil service job he likely had, or kept, by being a Party member. That day, "he had a late shift, was just getting dressed." She waited until he left for work, then "made Schmalzbrot [bread smeared with lard] with salt on it and thick pieces of bread and butter, and a paper around them. I went downstairs and wanted to give it to them. My husband was standing right there by the front door. I thought he'd already gone. I was doing it behind his back. Just then I heard the watchman say to my husband, 'Have you posted this man at your door? He won't leave. He said the woman is bringing us bread.'" Frau Haferkamp hurried back upstairs. So did Herr Haferkamp. "My God, my husband came back, 'Where do you want me to end up? Should I go to jail?' But he put up with it. Told him I was [part] Dutch and I had a sister in Holland. . . . I said it made me so sad. He told [the guard or watchman] there's nothing to be done with this woman. Always did it, over and over. *Always.*"

Once, the enemy did something in return. Several of her children were playing near a construction site "canal" when a young daughter, trying to catch up with the older children, fell head-first into a deep hole. "The whole street cried, 'The best-looking Haferkamp child is dead.'" An "enemy" laborer whom Frau Haferkamp had been "foddering" jumped down after the girl and rescued her.

No matter how humanistic and brave Frau Haferkamp was, the people she had spoken thus far of feeding were "Aryans," a safer "enemy" to help than Jews. But by then, were there any Jews in Oberhausen? For the first time since she began her story, her voice became soft. "Ja. There were Jews. There were even a lot of Jews. We even knew a Jew we did not know was a Jew.

21

Eichherz was their name. Bought furniture when we first married. And my husband went to the doctor. Dr. Flöss was his name and was also a Nazi. Had a big buck rank [War ein höher Spiess], but I don't remember what. And my husband laid his jacket over the chair. The [receipt] book fell out of his pocket, that you bought furniture you couldn't pay for all at once. My husband always took the money there until it was paid for. And the doctor saw that. Then he said,"—she yelled in imitation—"'*What?* You as a member of the Party, you buy from a Jew?' And he didn't know at all it was a Jew." She implied that her husband continued the payments.

She also implied that she had defied the quasi-order not to shop at Jewish stores. "You shopped where you liked something. They really made you crazy afterward. 'What?'" she shrieked. "'You shopped at a Jew's store?' How did you know who was a Jew? Now, one knew what one was. What I always thought earlier, it's a difference like Catholic, Protestant. He's a Jew. Nicht?"

In the coming hours, and sessions, Frau Haferkamp brought up many people she claimed not to have known were Jewish. The one whose plight she recalled most passionately was the Haferkamps' "Hausarzt" [family doctor]. "We had a Hausarzt, Dr. Stein. We did not know that was a Jew. [Stein is usually, but not always, a Jewish name.] My God, I was *furious*, was I ever furious, when I once went to Market Street and, because he was a Jew . . . naked, and he had a sign hanging around his neck, 'I am the Jew Dr. Stein.'"

She began to shout. "Stark naked, down the middle of the street they chased him, and behind him with the whip. I *saw* it. Sign on him, on it written, '*Ich bin Jude Dr. Stein.*' And that was our family doctor." He had not done anything at all? "He had not done anything at all. They just found out who was a Jew." She said many people ran after him "to see what was going on. They all ran after him and looked. What they would do to him. Curious. Nein, nobody helped him. They just scared the man and screamed at him, 'Out with the Jews, out with these pigs.'" Asked if he saw her, she said no. "Then I went home and said to my mother, '*Nein*, they chased Dr. Stein naked down the street.' *Naked*, with a sign covering his stomach, sex organs, 'I am a Jew.' That's what the Nazi swine did. Really.

"We had a butcher store, he was a Jew. We *also* didn't know it was Jews. Serfuss was his name. We always got meat there. One day, my mother wanted to buy meat, a whole lot of people are standing there. They would have hit my mother with a club. 'You are buying from Jews, you are buying from Jews.' Wanted to chase her away. My mother bawling, my mother said, 'As long as I've lived here, I buy here.' My mother was *very*, very angry. *Very* angry."

When asked what happened to Dr. Stein, Frau Haferkamp looked distraught. "Ja, they took him away. They took him away. That was terrible." Was it difficult not to be able to help him? "They would have beat us dead. They would have beat us dead. You can believe it." Her mother was so upset about Dr. Stein, she said, she would have screamed "Pfui, pfui, pfui" (a German insult) at his tormentors. Did she? "Nein. My Vati would have told her, 'Nabbed together, hanged together [Mitgefangen, mitgehangen].' Do not get involved. Na, that's how we got through, as a little person."

For a woman supposedly too busy with children and housework to pay attention to the world around her, Frau Haferkamp knew of many more sad fates, including an example of the Nazis' early use of euthanasia.

"In the house where I lived, my brother-in-law's sister also lived and she had a sick child. Looked fifteen, but she was already nineteen. And she was in Essen, near Oberhausen. It was called the Franz Hals [?] House where children who are sort of . . . She got her sickness through a festering in the middle ear. Anni von Thiel. And she came first to the Franz Hals House. And then in the Hitler time, if you inherited something or had something, nicht? I was standing below with my milk jug, the milkman came by at the door, and got milk with Frau von Thiel. And she got a letter from Essen. Anni has been . . . transferred, let us say, to Krefeld, nicht? She had an inflammation of her lungs. And [Frau von Thiel] was bawling. She said, 'My God, look, she's been away a whole week. Couldn't they have told me earlier? I could have gone to visit Anni.' Everything looked like, how upstanding the people all were. And my husband lay in bed. He had night shift at the time, he came home in the mornings. I said, 'Wait, give me the letter and I'll show it to my husband.' And I went to my husband in the bedroom and I say, 'Look, what Trautchen just got. That they [took] Anni to Krefeld. My husband said, 'What?' Looked at it again. 'She's not coming back. They're gassing them all.'

"Because they, och, what do you think? That was that. When they said she was transferred, the child was already dead. And a couple days later she got another letter. When the burial is going to be. I showed that to my husband. My husband looked so . . . 'That was four days ago. She's lain in the earth for four days.' They gassed her, too. Only because she had a disease."

Asked how her husband knew what was happening, she answered, "He could picture it. There was a man who was too lazy to work. But he did not harm anyone, nicht? He always sold postcards, kind of door-to-door. Depending on the time of year, Christmas cards or Easter cards or, whatever, birthday cards. And the man was clean as could be [piekesauber]." He boarded with his sister, said Frau Haferkamp. "When he came home, he washed his hands, then he took a towel, washed himself, and sat down. And one fine day, two police come to the woman's house and said, 'We have a certificate here, eh, that your brother . . .' They had to get his suitcase. They put him in such a home and gassed him, too. The man who would not harm a pig."

She also spoke of a close acquaintance, a Herr Grünewald, whose wife was Jewish. "Suddenly it was learned, mother and children can be sent away. Ja, she was also sent, she never came back. They sent her to the *gas* chamber."

She knew of nonlethal inhumanities, too. One classmate "also had a child every year" and "did not get a penny from Hitler, that is, from Hitler's side, because they all had inherited diseases. You had to be healthy, the children had to be healthy, so that you can propagate your heirs and no sick ones. I got all that child money and she got nothing at all. She often said, 'I can't help it. I have to nourish my children just like you.' I said, 'I can't help it, either.'" Frau Haferkamp was not able to explain why the children were not taken away.

With so many children herself, did Frau Haferkamp get a Mother's Cross? "Oh, ja," with some enthusiasm. "*First* I got the bronze. Then I had two more children and I received the silver one, but had to give the bronze one back. And when I had the ninth child, I got the *gold* one and had to give up the silver one." A son framed the gold cross on a field of velvet. Had she been proud of it? "I was proud of it. Yes indeed, I was proud. Was really proud of it. When I got the gold, also when I got the silver, there was a big celebration in a school, where the mothers were all invited for coffee and cake, nicht?" She had not wanted to go, she said. Why? Precisely because she had so many children to care for. "Then they sent someone who looked after my children and they picked me up in the car."

The question about the Mother's Cross may have been abrupt after her stories of horror. Frau Haferkamp, however, did not break her narrative stride. Nor did she seem to connect the regime that gave birth to those horrors with the one that honored her fertility.

Like many German families during the the first half of the Third Reich, the Haferkamps apparently enjoyed a life apart from the Reich itself. Theirs was centered around family and home. "I was an unbelievable cleaning fanatic [Putzfimmel]." She said her husband once brought home a colleague who said he thought the family had a lot of children (there were seven or eight at the time), but noticed little evidence of them. He wondered if they were not allowed to move. Frau Haferkamp had "a starched table covering here," there, and everywhere. "I made it seem like there were not so many children. Because I was *ambitious*. Ambitious. I didn't want, as I experienced it, that with a lot of children, so poor . . . I was always proud."

She was also lucky. Herr Haferkamp was unusually helpful. "He was very good, very good." He doted on his children—his "Heiligtum [holy riches]," she said. She did not tell him that a man spat on one son for accidentally knocking over a garbage pail. He would have "beat him kaputt." (He did beat up a man who insulted her.) Because she usually had "a big stomach" and had trouble bending, he often gave the younger children their once-a-week baths, two at a time. She exclaimed, What luck they had found a home with a bathroom! If she bathed them, he made supper, like a big pile of potato pancakes. "My children still say it today, Papa always said, 'Now there will be something delicious that will stick to your r-r-r-ribs and you won't need to eat for eight days.'" On Mondays, his day off from work, he told her to take the day off, too, to go enjoy herself in the park, while he cared for the children.

What did such a nice family man, and Party member, think of Jews? "I will honestly say, my husband actually had Jews as friends." With a little laugh, she then pointed out a picture of a grandson whose father, an American, is Jewish. ("Die Dicke" finds the boy so cute "she could gobble him up.") Herr Haferkamp, she said, would not have objected to their daughter marrying a Jewish man but might "at most" have said, "Did it *have* to be a Jew?" Frau Haferkamp also worried about what she considered the anti-Semitism of another American son-in-law, spoke of her grandmother's two Jewish girlfriends, whom she had called Aunt, and concluded, "Well, we did not really think about what a *Jew* is. 'Zo vot?' we always said."

She also mentioned that among the prisoners laying sewer lines in the street, and whom she helped, were Polish Jews. When I questioned this (I doubted they would have made it that far), she asserted, "Ja. They worked there, were all politically persecuted. And I also knew that many Jews were among them."

One thing she did for them, she said, was secretly toss them cigars, a valuable commodity either for enjoyment or trade. Someone occasionally gave some to her husband, who intended that she give them to her father. Her father could buy his own, she figured. So, while her husband slept, she carefully wrapped up each cigar and waited. "*Every* afternoon, in front of my window, people walked by with rifles over their backs. They brought [the prisoners] to work and picked them up from work, nicht?" When the main guard force was gone, she "moved the window a little to the side, then I looked down, then I [tossed] one cigar into the masses. They knew exactly where the window opens and they caught it." Sometimes, she said, she bought cigars and did the same.

Did she ever think she should have done something earlier against the Nazis? As was sometimes the case, she replied to a different question. "We should have left everything the way it was. Why couldn't they have let Jews be Jews?" Angrily, she added, "Did there have to be just *the* Party? They should have let them be, like with the SPD, the way it was with the CDU and the FDP, as I see it."[1] She began to shout. "They should let everyone have his own *Party* and [not kill people]."

When I commented that some people accused the Jews of being at

---

1. The SPD is the Social Democratic Party of Germany, the CDU is the Christian Democratic Union, and the FDP is the Free Democratic Party.

fault themselves, she answered rather sarcastically. "Ja, they've always said so, nicht? If someone wants to sell something expensive or something 'schrappt' [discounted damaged goods], as one says, 'Ja, you aren't a Jew, are you?' One always said. The Jew wants everything, nicht?" Does she agree? "Ne. I personally have *never* . . . Look, I married young. . . ." She went on about her own life until I asked what that had to do with Jews. She took no offense. "Nothing. Only that I had no time for politics."

She brought up the Jewish son of the butcher who married a non-Jewish German girl he met in the store. Both were taken away, he to a "work house." Asked if she meant a concentration camp, she said she did not know. "My mother always said there was no such thing. I mean, the people who did it, they themselves didn't know what they were doing. They howled with the wolves. Whatever the others did, they thought, we have to do, too. Join the Party, hate Jews, and so on, I assume.

"You could not say a lot. Back then in the Nazi time, you were not even allowed to *have* your own opinion, nicht? If it already somehow was known that he or he complained about the Party, nicht? We knew one. He complained. Jeschke. My husband knew the [Jeschke] son from the singing club. They already had an eye on him a long time. He was a thorn in the eye of the Nazis, nicht? They always said to him, Communist, but was not a Communist. The parents were *so* nice. They were such nice people. And one day the word was, they beat up Jeschke. Nobody knew where. Nobody knew how. He's in the hospital." She said their daughter Milli, who worked in the hospital's kitchen, told them. (Frau Haferkamp either was off on a date or a fact, or Milli was extremely young to be working.) The young man's attackers "injured his spine and everything. My husband went there and [Jeschke] said he was attacked on the street. And he said to my husband, 'Hein, can you lend me fifty marks?' We didn't have so much money, that one could . . . My husband said, 'What do you need it for?' Then he said while he's in the hospital he can't get any cigarettes, nothing to read, nothing of that. My husband gave him fifty marks and then he had money, nicht? And then they made difficulties for my husband. That he lent money to this [Communist]. There must have been someone lying in the room, who was paying attention. That was in the newspaper later, too. There were three beds. There must have been one lying there, who paid attention a little to what he said about the Nazis, nicht? And then Milli comes home one evening and she said, 'Papa, you don't have to give Jeschke any more fifty marks.' My husband said, 'Why?' 'Is dead.' Was dead."

Frau Haferkamp learned that one of her relatives had been at least a witness to the beating. "He was in an insane asylum later. He apparently took it so to heart, made reproaches about everything. No one could prove it, but his bad conscience . . . I am no 'church runner,' but I always say, he got his punishment."

The man who reportedly went mad was the son-in-law of Frau Haferkamp's old Uncle Julius, who, like Jeschke, never uttered the words "Heil Hitler!" One morning, he and his wife woke up and drew the blinds. The whole window had been painted black, except for a space in the shape of a swastika.

Frau Haferkamp herself *"never* greeted with 'Heil Hitler,'" she said loudly. "Because that was too stupid. Sometimes I made a joke. If one said, 'Heil Hitler!' I would say, 'Why, is he sick?'" (*Heil* can mean "heal.") She probably did not tell her joke to strangers.

The more Frau Haferkamp spoke, the more her memories resembled her abundant stockpiles. Sometimes she even seemed to be opening drawer after drawer in her mind and holding up the contents for inspection. "One day when my brother came home, he was six years older than I, and said, 'My God, they threw them out like *pigs,* first clubbed them, Communists, too, and when they *could* not walk anymore, they threw them in the wagon and drove them somewhere.' But we knew a good one. Was a Nazi. And he had a high rank and everything and he died. Not that they did something to him. He got an honorary funeral. A wonderful one. We went to see it. A really terrific one from the Nazis with the flag, and then they buried him. His dagger was *on* his grave. But not the real one, you know, one out of stone."

Asked what good he had done, she said the man, whom she identified as a Theo Spickermann, intervened with Rudolf Hess to get permission for a "war wedding" between a soldier in the field and his pregnant fiancée.

More significantly, he also intervened in an abortion case. Under the Nazis, abortions on "Aryan" women were very strictly forbidden. (At the other end of the Nazis' social spectrum, however, the opposite was true; imprisoned Jewish women had compulsory abortions.) In the case Frau Haferkamp related, an acquaintance of hers was "pregnant and did not want the child, had it removed. The woman who did it was an *old* woman, Esser was her name. Then the [pregnant] sister-in-law *also* went there and Frau Esser would not do it. She said, 'I am not making a business out of it. I only took pity on her and helped her.' Then *she* went and reported the woman. And she was put in the clink for half a year or nine months." Learning that, Herr Spickermann "wrote to very high authorities, the woman did it because the [pregnant] woman was very sick and could not have the child and everything and now she [Frau Esser] sits in the clink. They let her off.

"At the time, when you were going to have a child and you didn't want to, the word always was, 'Better ten on the pillow than one on your conscience [Lieber zehn auf dem Kissen wie eins auf dem Gewissen].' When you had a child, you had to have that child, and you were praised, honored, esteemed [gelobt, geehrt, geachtet]." Was that an influence on her? "Ne. I did not want so many children." She said she has told her children that if she went to bed "with the Papa" just after having her period, she would "tremble for four weeks, I hope I get my period, I hope I get my period. I said, 'I was pregnant before I knew it.' That is fact. I did not want so many children." Nor did her husband, she said. "Several times I was already five months pregnant and every month I still hoped I'd get my period. I didn't say anything, until my husband could tell there was life." She laughed. "We lay in bed, nicht? Lay always like in a lap. Then we both turned over, and now we were so that my stomach was on his back. Then he said, 'Stand up. Since when haven't you had your period?' I already had life. Too *cowardly* to say, 'Du, I'm getting something again.'"

Not knowing that birth control had been illegal, I asked if she could have used condoms. "Ja ja, *could, could*. But you didn't get any, nicht? It's not good for the body, not good for the . . ." A condom? "You mean 'die Pariser'? [A "Parisian" was what Germans called condoms.] Ach, my husband could not tolerate them." She did not mention that under the Nazis' anti–birth control for "Aryans" measures, condoms were not easily available, but indicated cost was a factor. "Do you have the money for them?" she asked. "My mother trembled and prayed whenever I got a stomach again. Then my mother said, '*Must* that be?' Today I don't understand why she didn't want me to have so many, since she herself had so many."

As the Haferkamp family expanded, so did the Third Reich, supposedly in part to make room for all the new "Aryan" babies such as hers. This was a lie, of course. Frau Haferkamp's testimony alone makes clear that the Nazis very much encouraged the birth of "Aryan" babies, but, as earlier indicated, they did so because the German birthrate was especially low. German troops did not invade Poland to conquer kindergarten space.

What did she think when the war began? Frau Haferkamp gave no memory of her own. "My husband said, 'My God, my God, we can all poison ourselves. We will lose the war. He said, 'Man, they will kill us.' I got really scared, nicht? But I would be lying if I say it was a bad time. It is not true. Well, for me at the beginning with the ration cards, with doctors and so on, we were not hungry. I was also industrious. I knitted, I sewed. I got some material from this one and some material from that one, I could always make my little ones this, make them that. People came who said, 'Could you make a pair of pants for our boy, make this, make that?' If the collar was worn through, I cut off a piece from here, made a new collar, and put on a piece of white muslin below. Ja, then I always got something for it, nicht?" She said many people also asked her for some of her ration cards. "'Do you have an extra card for milk for me? Do you have a sugar card?' I didn't sell them. I gave them to people."

The "bad time" for the Haferkamps started with the retaliatory bombing raids on Germany. "*Everything* lighted up, everyone wounded, you saw the bombs fly, you saw the bombers, the pilots came, mein Gott." Her description came after I asked if she had witnessed "Kristallnacht," which was years earlier.

It turned out she had. In fact, she, her husband, and their oldest son went to look at the damage. When I commented that "Kristallnacht" was said to have come from the "anger of the people," she replied, "Ja, ja." I added, others believed the Nazis arranged it. "That's also possible," she said, "but I don't believe so." Her logic was this: "They plundered a clothing store, suits for men and so. Then they set the nearby houses on fire, nicht? And ran away with the silk. So [it was] not simply the Party. Was just people who did that."

When I said that some people say the Germans knew a lot, she broke in. "They shut their eyes, nicht?" What does she say to that? "*My* opinion, if they really knew it, and enough knew it, and [if] they would have tried to stop it or do something, they would definitely have been shot. Even just a *dumb* remark, they would have already shot you."

Did she hear any rumors in regard to the Jews? I meant the Holocaust. She did not. "It will happen that Jews will come to power and they will kill us all. You always heard that."

The Haferkamps' more immediate fears, however, came from the sky. "My husband said, 'Out! Out of the beds.' He let me sleep as long as possible, because he knew I needed my rest, nicht? Child on the breast, child in the baby wagon. One who stood up had to dress the other. And then my husband, to the last minute, let me lie there. Then I sometimes stood up, I was *so* turned around, instead of getting dressed, I got undressed, and my husband always said, 'You have to get dressed.' Because I was half in a trance. There were dear people in the bunker, when the noise started, the bombs fell, then the people said, 'Frau Haferkamp isn't here yet, fast, fast.' Then they went to search for me. There I came with a baby wagon, one small baby on top and one child sitting and two in the wagon, I came running. They were already standing there, three of them, took the wagon and into the bunker."

Where was her husband, who figured largely in the beginning of her tale, but by the end was gone? In 1943, he was drafted. Although he was sent not to the front, but to do some kind of office work in Cologne, she said, she was very upset. About the same time, the family was bombed out, and went to live for a while with her mother-in-law, who was "really good, better than my mother. My mother-in-law would also have given the last thing she had. Said ten times, 'I'm already full,' when she was not full. I did the same." She said she sometimes felt weak in the afternoons for lack of food.

When the bombing raids worsened, the Haferkamps were evacuated to a farm near Schwäbish Hall in southwestern Germany. Herr Haferkamp managed to get leave to make sure they were all together and safe. He "did not want one child there and one there and one there" and said he "would not like to scrape my children off the walls later."

Even on a remote farm, Frau Haferkamp found an enemy to help. This time it was a young Russian woman prisoner. "I gave her my little suit, I had

29

shoe ration cards, clothes ration cards. She was the size of my daughter Mia. She went shopping with Mia and Mia told her not to open her mouth. Bought shoes and Mia gave them to the little one. Now a *German* [woman] was also evacuated. She was so terribly jealous and she 'smeared' me. Reported me to the administrator in the village and said I was giving her [the Russian] food. I did always give her food."

Somehow, Frau Haferkamp was not punished. She also fed a French prisoner/farmhand named Louis. He and the Russian were lovers (a relationship that at least three countries must have considered verboten). Louis could not stomach the farm woman's soup—hot water poured over ripped-up old bread and a spoonful of lard. So Frau Haferkamp, as usual making her famous milk soup, began hiding the pot in a place where Louis could help himself, and did. One day she told him he was not getting any more because he never thanked her.

The war ended quietly in the countryside. Frau Haferkamp and all her children were alive, but she not know if her husband was. She had not heard from him in six months. And he did not know she was pregnant again, much less days from delivery.

The first Allies to arrive were French. Louis proved he was grateful for the milk soup, after all; he told the troops what Frau Haferkamp had done. When they departed eight days later, they left the family a load of supplies. "Soap, *everything*. Cookies. We had everything." Next came the Americans, who "were *very* nice to us." But she also said they "slit open the beds and the feathers went flying," and they ransacked the mayor's office and raped the mayor's daughter.

One American officer, whose grandmother was from Berlin, spoke very good German. "He said, 'I think Germans do not love children,' that the Germans were to have marched into France and nailed small children to the church doors. I could not believe it. It is really impossible. I can believe everything, but not that. I always said Germans do love children.'" She still does not believe Germans committed such atrocities against children.

Frau Haferkamp delivered her last child, a daughter named Brigitte. "Gitta was born at four in the morning and that evening at six, my husband was there. On the same day." Herr Haferkamp had not been in a battle, but in a hospital. The old stone dust in his lungs was killing him.

Shortly after the war, the Haferkamps learned that other family members also had helped the "enemy." They included a female cousin who "definitely hid a Jew [a man] for two or two and a half years in her attic" in her home outside Oberhausen. "He even went walking nights, so that he [got] fresh air, could move his legs." Frau Haferkamp said the man wore the clothes of the woman's husband, so that anyone seeing him would think it was he. "At least he came through it, and his other family was killed. His mother, siblings. Kahn was his name." The cousin "was even praised later."

And Frau Haferkamp was, too. One of her sons developed a skin ailment so serious she had to take him to a doctor in another city. The only possible way of going was by train. Because the trains and tracks were still in poor condition from the war, the trip "went piece by piece," interspersed with waits of several hours at various train platforms. "Suddenly a man taps me on the shoulder and spoke such a broken German and said, 'Are you not the Mama with the many children who lived . . .' I said, 'Ja, who are you then?' And now I'm standing in Stuttgart at the station and this man recognized me. And said, 'One of your children fell into the canal?'"

He had been the rescuer.

"Mein Gott, the man bawled. He bawled. He said, 'The good that *you* did.' I was the *only* woman among the German women. . . . They wanted to denounce me, because I did it. That we should let the cockroaches run. I do not want to praise myself. I am happy today to do it. I still do. I do not have too much money. I have no money in storage. I always say, I get new money every month that I haven't done anything for. Nicht?" She laughed.

Frau Marianne Karlsruhen

A Matter of Fate

She met him in July of 1938, while both were vacationing on the German island of Sylt in the North Sea. In years past, she had vacationed with her family—her parents and her three brothers. But because she was older now and living in Berlin, away from home, she was to vacation alone for the first time. Her parents had arranged it all. She was twenty-one years old.

She had gone to Berlin to study, or rather, to sew another stitch in the sampler that comprised a suitable education for an industrialist's daughter. Apart from high school, she had spent a year at a boarding school where "one learned such things which one needs, like cooking, sewing. Also things such as how one must behave. One was guided a little along this whole line."

At the Berlin school, "one could learn various professions there were for women." She said because her father was interested in nutrition, she was studying nutrition. How she might apply the knowledge professionally was not yet a question.

She had wanted, she said, to be a doctor and go to Africa and help people, but her parents did not want her that far from the family. As it was, during her nutrition courses in Berlin, they arranged for her to live with relatives.

And they arranged for her to live at a modest and proper pension on Sylt. But they could not arrange the whole island.

"There I met Peter."

How did it happen?

"Ja. How did it happen?" She laughed a very little. "He later told me he'd noticed the way I walked, the way I moved. That I didn't walk like

other girls, but had a definite swing, which he'd never seen. And my innocent face certainly stirred him, I think. The haircut too. I had sort of a
Gretchen hairdo, the braid twirled around the head, and I believe it all
somehow touched him. As he described it." She laughed again, as if she were
the young woman she was recalling. "Then I noticed wherever I went, I'd
always see him. And he was quite a bit older than I."

The couple had not spoken.

"Then once, I stood in front of a bookstore or something and looked
inside. He was sitting there and looked at me, steadfastly. For the first time
I really saw his face. To me, in that moment, it was a matter of fate. I cannot
say it any other way. That was the beginning of this . . . getting to know
him better. It was, how should I say it? It was also irrevocable."

His glance "was something completely new. It somehow also hurt.
There was something of the melancholy there, too. I couldn't explain his
face at all, but it had to do with compassion. It immediately stirred me. And
when I experience something like that, I can't simply say well, it's done with."

Their contact remained visual until one day on the beach. Marianne
was sitting in her big rattan beach chair. Peter, who was living at the summer
home of a Frau Erichsen in the nearby village of Keitum, walked by with
her. "I saw him with this woman, whom I didn't know, and he motioned
toward me. Then both came over to my beach chair and Frau Erichsen asked
if I'd like to visit her. I said yes, I'd do that gladly, and that was the beginning.
Then I got to know him. We talked. I was always very shy, because I
thought, oh God, he knows so incredibly much and I actually knew very
little and basically nothing at all. He was so grown up, while I was still so
foolish.

"Then we met often. We took walks on the promenade and in the
evenings there were always concerts. I lived in a very simple pension, which
reflected the wishes of my parents, and Peter always rode his bicycle from
Keitum and brought me back to this pension and said, 'Now it's time for you
to go to bed.' And I said, 'What are you going to do?' 'Oh, I'll take a little
look around.' So mostly in the morning hours he went back to Keitum, but
knew me to be protected. That's somehow touching, isn't it?"

She knew his background from the beginning.

"He told me that he's half Jewish." (She used the phrase *ein Halbjude.*)
"He brought to my attention there could be difficulties. But the way I was, I
tossed it to the winds. The difficulties, too. It so angered me, I said, 'You
don't have to worry on my account. That does not affect me at all. Just the
opposite.' It made me fly into a rage there could be difficulties. It didn't matter to me. But it did to my parents."

At summer's end, Marianne returned to Berlin to continue learning
about nutrition. Peter returned to Berlin, too; he worked there as a technical
draftsman. The romance continued. "We met often. Sometimes he took me
sailing, and so."

Frauen

By then, the fall of 1938, Nazi laws for the "purity of German blood," laws forbidding marriage or sex "between Jews and German citizens," had been on the books three years.

Peter Karlsruhen was blond-haired and blue-eyed, had his "Aryan" father's last name, nominally was Christian, and had been living unassailed (as far as Marianne knew) within the Third Reich. His father, from whom he was estranged and from whom his mother was long divorced, was out of the picture. His Jewish mother, to whom he was close, also lived in Berlin. In time, he introduced mother and girlfriend. "We understood one another well. We liked each other very much, from the beginning."

Marianne Jung came from what she called "a Christian home" in the town (she called it a village) of Schalksmühle, part of the industrial Ruhr area. Herr Jung, formerly a widower, had a married daughter, Elsa (whom Marianne referred to as "my sister"), who lived nearby. With his second wife, he had three sons and Marianne. She was, she scarcely needed to say, "very protected."

"I had a decidedly close [innig] relationship to my father. We loved each other very much, I must say. I loved my mother very much too, but my mother was the authority figure, because she had to keep the four children in check. I sat next to my father at the table, for instance, and I always didn't like certain things, which I was supposed to eat up, as my mother expected me to. This is just occurring to me. The moment my mother was doing something, he quickly switched the plates, taking my plate away and putting his empty one in front of me."

Talk at and around the dinner table did not include the business Herr Jung started and developed—an electro-technical firm that occupied an entire factory building. "At home, business was never discussed. It was never mentioned. I only know that in the first, difficult time, as my father became independent, my mother took all deprivations upon herself and stood very bravely at his side. When he sometimes had a bad conscience and said, 'You have to do without so much,' she always made him take heart and told him, 'I'm glad to do it, it doesn't bother me.' She really had presence and stood by him. But later, business was never mentioned. I knew practically nothing at all about what my father did. At school I was asked [by the teacher], as everybody was asked, 'What does your father do?' I still hadn't answered. I was trying to figure what my father actually *is,* and someone loudly called out, 'Manufacturer!' It was a blessing I didn't have to answer. That's the way it was. Earnings were never discussed, how much money or how little we had. I got hardly any allowance at all." It was one German mark a week. If her girlfriends wanted to go have coffee, she could not; she was supposed to show at the end of each week she still had that one mark. "It wasn't meant to be mean. It was simply a way of showing it's not a matter of course to have money, that one also must manage it attentively, that one must save."

Once there was money, however, her mother, who liked fashion and had "excellent taste," splurged on clothes for her daughter. "She'd never deny me anything or say that's too expensive. My father likelier, but not my mother. She'd find something nice for me, and if I liked it too, she'd buy it."

Excellent taste has held. Frau Karlsruhen is a picture of slim, well-heeled, and well-coiffed style. With her beautiful eyes, precise makeup, and understated suit, she was tailored almost to perfection. The only visual snag was her hair, gray near her head and black at the ends, and which she immediately pointed out, saying she had decided to stop dyeing it.

When we met, she was living alone and elegantly in a large, modern condominium in an arbored corner of Wuppertal, also in the Ruhr. Heavy glass doors opened onto a splendid and bright living room appointed with a grand piano, modern paintings, and ancient sculpture. Glossy brochures arranged on a hassock invited her to art openings in other countries. She drew a line at public show, refusing to own a Mercedes. Too ostentatious, she felt. She liked driving her new Volkswagen.

Her manner, unlike her appearance, had a tender and rather melancholy intimacy to it. Seemingly self-conscious and unsure at first meeting, she nonetheless invited close approach. Minutes after I arrived at her front door, she embarked on a discreet getting-to-know-you assessment, one sluiced by the most delicate of ingestions—a split of French champagne poured into ornate Venetian goblets, sculpted canapés. Some qualms must have been quieted, for the conversation soon became intensely personal. She spoke of her nervousness about talking to a stranger about the love and trauma of her life, and into a tape recorder. Later she revealed that her decision to grant an interview was made in defiance of a family member whose objection, on the surface, had to do with not trusting Americans. At the end of two days of talks, she defied the family member on another count, by deciding to use her real name.

Once she decided to talk, talk she did—the first time for more than three hours without a break. She later expressed astonishment at herself and at the hour.

Then she defied convention by leaping across a social barrier that might have taken years, if at all. She suggested we address each other in the familiar *du* form.

No defiances in the modern day, however, compared with those she made in regard to Peter Karlsruhen. Fate may have intended they be together, but the Nazis and her parents had not.

Herr and Frau Jung told her to come home from Berlin immediately, nutrition or no.

"I hadn't written to them about it. They somehow found out about it." She said "my relatives naturally noticed" she was going out with Peter, but she had "no idea" how they found out about his background. She seemed not to want to say point-blank it was her relatives who told her parents about him. Also curious was her explanation of why she had not told her parents herself. "I didn't think it important at all. Not at all.

"But then they knew we saw each other now and then and that it was a friendship. And certainly my father looked further. That's clear. He perhaps could tell what we'd face and understandably wanted to impede it."

She reacted to her parents' command like a good daughter, or, sort of a good daughter. She did go home. "I wasn't mad at my parents, as far as I can remember. I wasn't at all. But in the same way, it was a matter of course the connection with Peter continue.

"We wrote each other a lot. Very, very long letters. It was kind of like an introduction into life, one could say. Through these letters I became familiar with so much. With literature, too. He sometimes wrote poetry and so on and was interested in everything and wrote to me about it all. It meant a lot to me." He did not mail the letters directly to her, but to Elsa, who, along with her husband "took good care of me and also got to know Peter and treasured him." Peter also met Marianne's two eldest brothers, Heinz and Siegfried. The latter, who studied in Berlin, got to know him well. And once, after Marianne had spent a winter ski vacation in Austria with Elsa and a niece, she made a detour to Heidelberg to rendezvous with Peter on her way back home to Schalksmühle.

And it was all secret from her parents?

"Ja." She sighed deeply.

She strongly maintained that Peter's being half Jewish was not her parents' sole or major objection to the relationship. The major objection, she insisted, was her family's religious affiliation. "We didn't belong to a church, but a congregation [Versammlung] of Christians. It was very strict. At the time, there was a great difference whether someone belonged to the church or to this congregation. If someone were a strict Christian, or was devout, that was acceptable, but as soon as it was casual, that was not wished."

Peter was "normal, I mean completely Christian," as she put it. But he was indeed "casual." That his affiliation with Christianity did not extend to his belonging to a church "played a role for my parents, and no small role. That was certainly just as important as the fact that he's half Jewish. Furthermore, my father wanted me to avoid having any male relationships at all. He thought me much too young. I was protected and should remain protected, if possible. That was a very important reason."

Her parents, she said, were not anti-Semitic. Initially, they were not anti-Nazi, either. Although politics, like money and business, was not talked about much in the household, "I do know that my father, who later naturally was the exact opposite, felt positive because Hitler, through the building of the Autobahn and so on, got the jobless off the streets. At the beginning, it all looked positive, or much of it did. I know my father mentioned it and we agreed. But we had no intensive conversations about it."

She said it would have been out of the question for her parents to join the Nazi Party. Asked if her father financially supported the Party, as did other manufacturers—it is inconceivable he did not benefit from the Nazi takeover—she said she did not know, but that if he had, the matter would not have been discussed because money was not discussed.

Before meeting Peter, Marianne had two conflicts herself (that she recalled) with Nazism. One involved the Nazi-ordered boycott of Jewish-owned stores. "I was very, very outraged. Police or whoever [they were SA brownshirts] stood out front and no one was allowed in anymore. I tried to get in because I was so outraged. I knew the owner, I knew these people. We'd always gone there. Naturally, I was pushed back."

The second happened in 1937. She was still in high school, and was a member of the Bund deutscher Mädel. "We were actually all drafted into the BdM. [Almost] everyone in my class was in BdM. At the time, I didn't think about it. I thought, if the others do it and if it's so customary, one goes along, nicht?"

Also customary for someone of her background was to take the rigorous final exam, the Abitur. But she dreaded it, mainly because she had difficulty with mathematics, and kept putting it off. In 1937, her parents insisted she take it. "In my class was a [Jewish] girl I liked very much and she was not allowed to take the Abitur. She had to leave school. Then I was really confronted for the *first* time with this Hitler era. I immediately said, 'I quit [BdM]. I am not going along if such things happen.'" She said others wanted to quit, too. "We were all shocked. Then I was told I'd not be able to take the Abitur. If I really want to quit, then I'm forbidden to take the Abitur. Ja. That's the way it was."

"It" worked. "I then took the Abitur and immediately quit."

The threat was enough, was it?

"What should we do? We were so close to finishing."

She said she did not recall speaking with her parents about the matter. Nor did she know what happened to the Jewish girl, who was "especially gifted and especially beloved by us all."

In 1939, the Nazi government, which tacitly forbade her relationship with Peter, inadvertently fostered it by ordering her to leave home. Like other young Germans, she was to take part in the mandatory "year of duty" program. The duty could entail farm, factory, or domestic drudgery. Elsa saved the day again.

"My sister, who always had a lot to do with the nobility, came up with the idea to put an advertisement in the *Adelsblatt* [*Nobility News*] so I'd get the proper position." The ad "was composed just so. I got mail from the collective nobility and high nobility of Germany. I was cheap labor, nicht? In the advertisement it stated what I could do, special areas of knowledge in

English and what I'd done, my schooling, what I'd done otherwise. Later, I didn't even open the mail, there was so much. Such mountains of mail, I didn't even open it." She laughed.

"This Frau von Rex-Gröning, who had this manor [near the city of Bremen], wrote first. And she wrote in such a nice and friendly way. It was a special delivery letter, afterward dozens of telegrams arrived. I thought, that is certainly meant to be. And I decided immediately. But this deluge of mail, I don't know how long it kept coming." She laughed again. "At this manor, mostly my job was to care for the children, that is, the two youngest." Both needed help with homework, especially mathematics. "So I secretly did mathematics in my room, to be able to help them."

Meanwhile, she and Peter, who had continued to write, using Elsa as postal courier, now wrote to each other directly. They arranged another rendezvous, in Bremen. It must have been exciting, I allowed. "Ja, that it was."

Each rendezvous followed separations lasting months. Although their bond grew closer, it still was secret.

Had she promised her parents she would no longer see him?

"Nein. They hadn't thought of it."

They thought it was over?

"I assume so."

After her "year of duty" at the manor ended, she embarked on her penultimate stitch of education, at a language school in Mannheim. She took a four-month intensive course in advanced English and earned a diploma. Her life seemed so coddled and "normal," apart from her obviously intense involvement with Peter, I wondered if perhaps she did not notice what else was going on in the Third Reich.

"I noticed it very closely," she replied. "I must say, I was completely awake in the time and noticed exactly what was happening. It all interested me. All of it."

By 1941, when Germany declared war on the Soviet Union, among the men Germany had drafted were all three of Marianne's brothers, and Peter. A half-Jew could be ordered not to marry a full "German," but he could be ordered to fight for Germany. The romance continued, by letter and during leaves.

One such leave, and rendezvous, was in Berlin. How was it? This time, her answer had less to do with them than the world around them. "You know, the situation was always getting more critical. It was increasingly more tense. It was becoming ever-clearer what these Nazis wanted. And in Berlin, I came into contact with some people from the resistance, but that was only brief. I almost didn't know it, but only realized it later."

The people belonged to a now well-known resistance group that sent German intelligence to Moscow by a system of radio transmitters. The Nazis discovered the group in 1942, dubbed it the "Rote Kapelle" [Red Or-chestra], and executed most of its leaders. Her contact with some Kapelle members took place at a gathering to which Peter, and by extension she, were invited.

The members she met included the group's two main leaders, Harold Schulze-Boysen and Arvid Harnack, both sons of prominent German fami-lies. Also there was Sven Erichsen, the husband of the woman at whose home Peter stayed in Sylt. "They were all people who had been sought out, and also me. Frau Schulze-Boysen had met me before. [Her] name didn't mean anything to me. She was a highly interesting woman. She knew my point of view, otherwise I'd not have been invited. But this whole thing later blew up. That was pretty terrible, when I heard they were all be-headed. It was horrible.[1] They also had their own radio transmitter. That evening, it was very tense. There also was a speech by a high officer in the air force ministry, a very good-looking man, equal to anyone. And his wife, they were absolutely notable personalities. The whole circle of human be-ings there."

What about Peter's connection to the group?

"Whether he worked with this Rote Kapelle, I don't know. I can't say. I'm completely sure he didn't want to pull me into it. At the time I was rela-tively young, and those people were older than I, and completely differently trained. It was just this one evening when I met some of them. But the or-ganization already existed. There were intimations made, and it was also clear to me that it was a resistance group. I didn't know the name and I didn't know what they did. But there were a load of foreign newspapers there that one no longer ever saw anywhere. And the conversations that took place. I really got scared sometimes. I thought if just *one* person said one word out-side, they'd gambled away their lives."

She and Peter were lucky. Had a spy been in the group when they were there, they, too, could have been named and arrested.

She maintained that despite such connections, Peter did "not really" tell her whatever he knew about what the Nazis were doing or what was being planned against them. Was he trying to protect her or did he not know much himself? "He did not know much himself, not much more than I. How could he have?" From his mother? His mother, she said, was not necessarily any better informed than Peter. What about rumors? They did seep through, she said. About gassing? "Ja. That it happened in the camps and that." She stopped. "I don't know now exactly what I really knew then.

---

1. It was not beheading, but slower. The Nazis killed them with a new method they later used on other resisters, like those who plotted to kill Hitler; victims were hanged by wire suspended from meat hooks and slowly strangulated.

One only suspected terrible things are happening. And one didn't know if [something] were true. It was questioned again and [learned] it's not true at all. But that would have been when terrible things were happening."

She said she and Peter both felt that "a completely unbelievable and unimaginable story was taking place. Everyone we had anything to do with had the same point of view. We often were with Peter's friends and these things often were talked about. But I can't remember any details."

I asked if, when he was stationed in Russia, he had known of the killings of Jews there. She said he did not tell her. "But I am certain he knew of these things. If he had seen them himself, perhaps he'd have talked about them." She added that her brother Siegfried, when stationed in Russia, saw a pogrom, or part of one. Later she wrote me (in script that looks like the tracks of a tiny bird) that she asked him again and he said he saw people being herded into a cellar, "and probably from there into pits. He doesn't know exactly."

Marianne later happened to cross paths with a young German soldier who also knew more about what was going on under German command in the Soviet Union than the German public was being told. In about 1943, she was living and working on a girlfriend's farm in Bavaria, and the soldier, on leave, had been on a hiking trip in the mountains. "It was a completely remarkable meeting, somehow a fateful meeting. He, too, told me about it." His "it" was the shooting to death, by Germans, of prisoners of war.

"After he experienced it, he always volunteered for special commands [Sondereinsätze] to spare others. Fathers of families, for instance. And shortly thereafter, I heard he did not return from one of these things. At the time, it seemed to me he perceived he'd not survive. He even said, 'I won't live long.' And I took him at his word." The soldier wanted to risk his life, she said, not only because he had seen "such horrendous things," but also because he could not prevent them.

On the farm, too, Marianne got an inside glimpse of a potentially deadly act by a German officer against a civilian. It was his own daughter. The young woman, named Marlies, had become friends with Marianne in language school. The small and unprosperous Bavarian farm in effect belonged to Marlies, or was hers to inherit from her divorced father, because nobody but she was interested in it. Marianne had met him and not liked him. "He was sort of a domineering type." But Marlies and he were very close, she said. At the time Marianne met him, he was an army major, and mostly was away in Russia.

"I was there with her a year, I believe, and helped her as well as I could. We did heavy work, including things that farmhands otherwise did. But it was a lovely time." Every morning Marlies took the milk to market. Together the young women did such heavy manual jobs as removing the bark from tree trunks. A Polish farmhand, probably a prisoner of war, did the heaviest tasks. Despite the Nazi law forbidding Germans from having anything but the most cursory relationships with such people, Marlies and he became lovers.

"I mean, he was very handsome and, well . . . But I was astonished, because Marlies never was interested in men and then suddenly said, 'Look at him, how he works,' how he cut down the trees and so. The remark made me reflective." Marianne did not see more of the romance herself, having left as planned to study art history in Munich—the last stitch of her education sampler. But she learned through a mutual friend that Marlies's "life was hanging by a silk thread."

Marlies had become pregnant. By the time she was visibly so, her father again returned from Russia. He learned what had happened and reported his daughter and the farmhand to the Gestapo.

As he must have known, the action could result in the imprisonment and death of not only the farmhand but also his daughter. Somehow, the lover escaped. Then Marlies, learning the Gestapo was coming to arrest her, waited for the night. Very pregnant, and presumably very scared, she sneaked away from the farm, from her father, and from the Gestapo. When her father found her gone, he took an extra step of revenge. He disinherited her. (He later remarried a woman his daughter's age.)

Marlies, in the meantime, eluded the Gestapo, reunited with her lover, and had the baby. At some point, she married the lover, if reluctantly. All lived, but not happily ever after. The farm worker proved "primitive" and "undependable." The last Marianne heard, he was involved "in some smuggling business near the Austrian border."

As for her own life and own verboten romance, Marianne was making the best of both. In Munich, she studied the art the Nazis approved of and hid the literature they banned. "In my room I had all Peter's books, those by forbidden authors which I always kept. Peter gave them to me because, well, naturally he took precautionary measures, that one not find them with him. And it was no problem for me. Other people also brought me their books. People who were afraid in Munich, for instance." Her gesture was not inconsiderable. Discovery of the books could have landed her in jail or a concentration camp.

Her Munich stop did not last long. She was, as the word goes, *dienstverpflichtet*—obligated to take part in the war effort. "I couldn't stay in Munich. There was no justification for studying art history during the war. My father had a factory in Lünen [near the family home in Schalksmühle], and we hoped I could go there. At first it seemed possible, but then the rule was, one wasn't allowed to work in one's parents' factory."

Asked how closely connected her father's firm was with the war, she said she did not know. "I must have known it once, but have forgotten. I also don't know *what* they made. But it's completely possible they manufactured something used for the war." Possible? The opposite is all but impossible. But what was manufactured? At a later point, she said she thought one product was electric switches.

Marianne did get work in Lünen, but at an aluminum works that essentially then was an armaments manufacturer. She worked in the laboratory, doing spectrum analysis. About the same time, Peter, who had been drafted in spite of being half Jewish, was discharged because of being half Jewish. (His case is not unique.) Using his connections with the prosperous and dissident and friendly Erichsen family of Norway, for whom he had worked in Germany in industrial sales, he went to Oslo to work at a construction site under the management of a German-based company Marianne called Nordag. Although Norway was controlled by the Nazis, it was a lot safer for half-Jews than was Germany.

The year was 1942. Peter's life was in some order, but Marianne's increasingly was not. Schalksmühle's Ortsgruppenleiter ("an especially zealous Nazi," she called him) had learned earlier about her relationship with Peter and kept up an active interest. And he, she assumed, informed the Gestapo.

Herr Jung was told to bring his daughter in line, or else. "The pressure on my father and on me kept growing, because they knew I was still in contact with Peter. At the time, they were threatening to expropriate my father's business if it didn't come to an end. That was a very, very difficult time for me, I have to say, because I was causing my father terrible worry and grief and on the other hand I didn't want to leave Peter in the lurch."

How did the Nazis know she was in contact with Peter?

"Ach, they knew everything. They simply knew everything, like later the Gestapo, too, knew everything. Something like that gets talked around."

After working in Lünen during the week, "I came home every weekend. And I knew that these people were pressing my father horribly. He told me all about it and we had long talks about it. My father tried, tried again, to make me cognizant of these dangers. I loved my father very much and therefore it was very difficult for me." It also was difficult, she said, because he and she were similarly strong-willed. After her father kept trying to convince her to break off with Peter, she in turn "always implored he understand me, that I have no choice at all, that I simply must stand by Peter. That he certainly understood. I assume he did. There was so terribly much at risk here, for everyone.

"Furthermore, I was exposed to these great attacks on the armaments company. Sometimes twelve hundred firebombs fell in one night and so on and I never got any quiet, day or night. I was one regular bundle of nerves. At night, when the sirens went off, I didn't even wake up, I was so totally exhausted. Soldiers woke me there and I sometimes literally ran for my life to get to the cellar of this castle near the factory. That was really a very bad time, I can't say it any differently."

Yet in Lünen, she felt politically safe. "Somehow, one always knew which side I stood on. And similarly minded people always find each other. They can somehow tell. All were anti-Hitler. We belonged to no resistance group. It was just a very clear situation. I thought at the time, some solution will be found. It simply cannot continue as it is."

One of the Erichsen men, in Germany at the time, came to her rescue. She asked him on the telephone if he knew of any solution. "I didn't know if I were coming or going. I simply couldn't take it anymore." She said he thought "it was probably best that I get out of everyone's way, out of Germany. It was his opinion I should try to get to Norway, to this Nordag, where Peter was, if that were a possibility."

It was. Peter knew that the head of the aluminum company where she worked was friends with the head of Nordag, where he worked. Peter arranged that Marianne be sent to Oslo to work for Nordag "because of the bombing attacks and so on," she said. "Naturally, they didn't know the other.

"Then I got regular marching orders, like soldiers get, that they needed me there. One cannot do it otherwise. One can't say, 'So, now I'm leaving here and going to Norway.' And I went to Oslo."

She said her parents saw her off with "a very heavy heart. It was a difficult goodbye." The Jungs were concerned not only about their daughter's well-being. None of their sons was home from the fighting. Heinz fought in France and Russia, where he was taken prisoner. (He was released in 1948, "almost starved and very sick.") Siegfried, the one who was friendly with Peter and who saw at least part of a pogrom, was in Russia from 1941 to 1944, and wounded twice, the second time by a shot that exploded his leg. The youngest son, Eberhard, was a teenager when he went to fight. "He took his final exams and then was drafted immediately, completely inexperienced. Taken from the school bench." He was the only Jung child interested in the family business, particularly its technical side. "But Eberhard was missing in action, in Yugoslavia. He never returned. That was very, very bitter for my parents. For all of us. We all loved him especially because he was so especially lovable. He was so nice and looked so nice, was so soft and, . . . And we simply didn't hear any more from him."

Marianne's arrival in Norway was of particular interest not only to Peter. The Gestapo in Norway had been informed, too.

Clearly, she had not been meant for a particular job. An executive with the firm wanted her as his secretary, but she had learned only English stenography, not German. So she was given nine weeks of training at a testing laboratory in Oslo and then sent to a lab at a Nordag construction site in western Norway. Peter remained based in Oslo but occasionally managed inspection trips to where she worked.

At her site she found more kindred spirits. "I learned that a group of anti-Hitler people, Norwegians, all wore something red, a red pullover or a red scarf or whatever, that showed right away they [were anti-Nazi]. And the first thing I did was knit myself a pair of red knee socks and always wore them. I worked in the laboratory with Norwegians. I was the only German and had a very nice, good relationship with them and then became friendly with two German engineers who had my exact sentiments."

Shortly after she began working at the lab and living in the workers' barracks, another crisis literally flared up. "Everything I had up there burned and it really was a lot. The barracks in which I lived burned down. I had nothing. I heard the sirens, left the laboratory, wearing my oldest things, an old pullover and an old pair of pants, and I ran there and this barracks was in bright flames. It was a remarkable feeling, I must say. I looked at it and said, 'My God, one more thing.' Then someone behind me said something and I said, 'Leave me alone.' I was really bold then, you know, and wasn't afraid of anything. Then he walked in front of me and said, 'Tell me, do you really know with whom you're talking?' He had a uniform on, a black uniform. I said, 'I don't know and I'm not interested, either.' And then he said, 'I'm from the Gestapo and am the head of it here.' Then I really . . . I changed inside. I turned around and did not say another word. But this man never wished me ill. Later he somehow also liked me. He certainly knew some things, but didn't do anything to harm me, which he could have. That's what I was afraid of, after I let fly at him."

An investigation into the source of the fire revealed more bad news. "The commission determined the fire broke out in my room. They wanted to hang the whole thing on me, because apparently I'd put an armchair too close to the electric heating or something. Then there was a trial. Well, it was a terrible thing. I'd hardly even got there."

She decided go back home for a while. "I had no more to wear than what I had on my body. I thought, what do I really do now? And naive as I was, I went to the personnel office and said, 'Listen, I'm traveling to Germany. I have to get a few things, there isn't anything way up here, and could you issue me a permit?' And she did. She thought she's somehow protected by the boss or something of the kind. But I had no authorization at all, got the permit, and went to Germany. I stayed there eight weeks, then took a boat back up."

She had told no one at the construction site?

"No, not at all. I only thought, God, it's perfectly self-evident all my things are gone and now I have to see how to get more. I didn't know what I was doing. Also, I didn't have any second thoughts. So, of course one had connections, through my mother and the seamstress whom we had and so on, then I had a few more things again. And, suitcase in hand, returned." She laughed. "Nobody had figured out what I had done. They threw up their hands. '*Ja.* Where were you? Not a single person knew where you were. That has never ever happened, what you did. And stay out of sight of Dr. Zirnriegel.'" He was the boss.

"And the next day, I got the news that I was to go see Dr. Zirnriegel. Now, I knew I was on his good side, from the very beginning. For some reason he liked me, and one could tell, too. So I stood there. He was short, sort of a Napoleon type, and he sat on a kind of platform where he had his desk, sort of raised, and I opened the door and stood there and said 'Good day.' He looked up and acted immediately as if he hadn't seen me and kept writing. I kept standing there, and then suddenly he said, 'Tell me, Fräulein Jung, what did you really *think* you were doing?' "'Well,' I said, 'how do you mean that, Herr Zirnriegel?'"

She imitated his voice of bewildered outrage. "'You *travel* to Germany for eight weeks and then come back? No one knows where you are? What did you really do earlier, before you came to us?' I see it all happening in front of me, which is why I'm describing it so dramatically. I said, 'I studied art history.' 'So. Art history, hm.' He already was soothed. 'Ja, and what do you propose to do now? You have no shelter. . . .' 'Well,' I said. 'I'd like very much not to live in the barracks anymore. I'd much rather live in a hotel'—I'd already gone up to see one—'and I saw such a pretty room. When one lies there in the bed, one can look directly at the mountains.' He thereupon was so perplexed, he looked at me as if he wanted to say, nothing can be done with you. One can do nothing, nicht?" She laughed.

"'Good,' he said. 'You shall have the room.' I got the room in the hotel. It was glorious. It was glorious. Again and again there was something very comforting and good in everyone. I didn't know fear in that sense anyway, but it was not only sad and depressing, nicht?"

Asked if it would have been impossible for Peter to live there too when he was at the site, she said, "Completely. It would have been completely unthinkable." The reason had to do not with convention, but Nazis. "The Gestapo was informed. Ja. We had to avoid letting ourselves be seen together. When he was at the construction site and had something to do there, we somehow managed to meet, but we had to be very careful it wasn't discovered. I mean, somehow one guessed it anyway. Somehow it was in the air. One learned too, how to appraise the dangers."

She also took a few more on. "The Norwegians were not allowed to have any radios, so some brought them to me in my small room and always heard English news broadcasts there. A lot was going on where I lived. I can't say it any differently. Then in the lab we had a Russian whom I always tried to help a little, with bread. He wore, I don't know, but it was falling apart and he made sort of string from the things lying around and sewed his things together. I got him some thread. He was so orderly, you know. He loved me and I loved him. His name was Pjotr. He was an old man. And the Norwegians in general, who always wished me well, supplied me with things, and to that extent it was a completely lovely time. Also, when one is so conscious of danger, one knows how to treasure something."

45

Frauen

In late 1944, she said, the German women working at the construction sites in Norway were evacuated, presumably from the expected Red Army, to return to the "Reich."

"I was among the German women allowed to cross the Swedish border. Of course, I was very happy I could travel home this way, over Sweden. The others were taken away with fast motorboats, the waters around Norway being all mined and that was very dangerous. And I already knew I was expecting a child, from Peter. Ja," she added, noting my expression.

What was her first reaction when she learned she was pregnant?

"That's what I wanted."

Both of you?

"I."

More than he?

"Ja, I wanted it. Because the future was getting ever more uncertain and one didn't know at all if we'd see each other again or what would happen. Things kept getting more critical." She said he wanted a child, too, "but he saw the danger. He also warned me and asked me if I could really cope with it all, and I said yes, I could." She said she knew she was pregnant when she didn't get her period, "and I also was completely certain. I mean, one can tell too, nicht? Some things do change." She had not gone to a doctor. "It was too dangerous."

With Peter remaining for a while in Norway, the pregnant Marianne, supplied with travel necessities by Erichsen friends, left Norway in November 1944, by train for Sweden, Denmark, and Germany. There she faced a reunion with her unknowing parents, a raging war on land and in the air, and a new job order—to work in an air force factory in Augsburg, clearly a bombing target. The job order upset her the most. "I must say, that sort of tore me apart, because I didn't know what I should do now. And there were also constant bombing attacks. Well, it was all an absurdity. I really couldn't have done it."

Peter decided to intervene and, knowingly or unknowingly, to risk his life to save hers. In Norway, he "was allowed a kind of protection" despite being half Jewish. And "he was an important work force in Oslo and one simply didn't hand these human beings over." Now he was to go to Germany, where his protection was nil. His pass did not identify him as half Jewish, she said. But the Gestapo knew he was. So did his employer, Nordag. And so did others.

Peter's plan was to get to Berlin and arrange that Marianne not work where her life was endangered, but be sent to a factory in a town named Egg (pronounced Eck), in Austria. Why Egg? It was where her father's factory had relocated. Who ran it? Her cousin. What did it do? "Made switches, I assume." Her job? It would not matter.

Peter crossed into Germany. "This trip took place because he did not want in any way for me to go to Augsburg. He said, 'I simply have to do that

46

for you, to make it possible for you to get to Egg.' And that's what led to his fate. Otherwise, he probably would have stayed up there, at least at first."

While he set off to fend for her safety, she rather blithely endangered it. On the train trip to her parents, she illegally exchanged Norwegian money for Swedish money, then at a bank in Copenhagen tried to exchange Swedish for Danish. After a suspicious bank teller questioned her, she took her Swedish money and left. She was lucky, but still daring. A hotel clerk changed her Swedish money for Danish.

The reason Marianne wanted Danish money was that, even in war-blasted 1944, the quest for proper clothing still played a role in determining her actions. This time, she wanted to buy a dress to hide her beginning-to-show pregnancy from her parents. She found what she sought. "The dress was lovely, small black and white checks with a small jacket. The jacket hid the stomach a little. And it was trimmed in black velvet. A magical dress. And right for the purpose. I wore it to Schalksmühle."

Her parents welcomed her warmly. "I did *not* tell them I was expecting a child. They would have become insanely concerned. They were always terribly concerned about me anyway."

Their concern lessened considerably when they learned Peter had been successful in Berlin. "He simply bribed the people at the employment office with food we could get from Norway, at the black market in Denmark, and so on." Marianne then went to Egg. She told her cousin and his wife, the Söhnchens, of her pregnancy. Herr Söhnchen told her she need not work at the factory. "I would have, but my cousin thought it wasn't necessary at all." He may have felt he had enough to worry about as it was; according to his widow, Frau Arnhild Söhnchen,[2] he had constant problems from the figurehead factory director, a "one hundred percent" Nazi she also called an "Oberbonzen [top Party hack]" who sent SS men to his office for whatever reason, or held surprise inspections. Employing a cousin with a suspicious pregnancy would not have helped matters.

As for Frau Söhnchen, who in her later years was the epitome of a fairy-tale apple-cheeked grandmother, it seemed a matter of course to help Marianne. She also happened to have much in common with her. She grew up in the same religious assembly (whose minister "didn't preach much against [National Socialism]. He was very careful") and in a home atmosphere where Hitler's early economic successes were considered positively. "We were enthusiastic. There was to be work, and peace." Frau Söhnchen herself spoke with some approval about Hitler ("a friendly man") and Goebbels (he had "wonderful sentence structure"), while also referring to the general rush of enthusiasm about them to be "like a contagious disease." She was influenced toward an anti-Nazi frame of mind, she said, by the reaction of

2. Interviewed July 1987 in Berkeley, California.

her parents and other members of the religious assembly to Jewish persecution. "We had Jewish friends. As a Christian, one always had a good relationship with Jews. We lived with Jews, I played with Jews, our area always had a lot of Jews." She also quoted the Bible as saying, "The Jewish people are equal in my eyes. Who attacks them, attacks me."

By the time Marianne came to Egg, neither of the Söhnchens seemed to have anything good to say about the Nazis. (Herr Söhnchen, said his widow, was dubious long before she was and maintained Hitler never would be sated by any military success. "He'll never fill his throat" was the expression he used.)

When Peter managed to get to Egg, too, to make sure Marianne was all right, the Söhnchens also put him up. He stayed eight days or so, before beginning to make his way back to Norway.

Marianne Karlsruhen resumed the story. "I brought him to the train, and of course he wanted to return to Oslo. In Berlin, he checked in at Nordag. One always had to before one returned to Norway. Then they said, give us your passport. And they took it and held it. They wouldn't give it back to him."

He then went to a part of Berlin where he had lived before, and to the house he had lived. She was not sure why. She guessed he "wanted to know what's happened to him or him and where they were." The couple who owned or managed the house greeted him in a friendly manner. But the man, who was either in the SA or the SS, informed the police that Peter was there. The police told the Gestapo. That night, "he was arrested. Because he was a half-Jew."

He was taken to Oranienburg concentration camp.

Marianne insisted his arrest "had nothing at all to do with me." Could it have had anything to do with any resistance work? She did not know. What about Nordag's connection? "I can't say whether they were conspiring. I don't know. Peter doesn't know either, how it all hung together. He only knew that when he arrived [at his former home in Berlin], these people informed the Gestapo. And he was arrested that night."

She said the people at Nordag did not tell him why they were keeping his passport. "He knew what that meant. In that moment, he probably also knew what was coming. Certainly, he was intelligent enough and knew it. But he did not know the final coup de grace would come from these people. That he certainly didn't know, or he wouldn't have gone there."

She learned of the arrest from Peter's mother. Recalling their earlier meetings, she said the three of them once celebrated Christmas together. "She had a room with a high school teacher, an older man and wife, also Jews. We went there and she introduced us. They had a wonderful library and I admired it. And the man said, 'You may take with you what you like, what you can use. Simply take it.' I said 'No, I could never do that.' And he

48

said, 'We won't be here long.' And the next time we went there, they were gone. They took them away. Then Peter's mother knew it was time. It was only a question of which day. She went underground."

Who knows how a Jewish woman living underground learned that her son had been arrested, and where he had been taken? Or had he got the word to her? And if so, how? Marianne does not know. But somehow the connection was made. And somehow his mother relayed the message to Egg. "And then I heard nothing more."

Marianne stayed put in Egg, eventually taking a room in a house near the Söhnchens, who were "very dear to me." She saw them daily and ate with them at their home. But they were "greatly afraid for me" and "when visitors came from Germany, I had to hide immediately. They were not allowed to see me. It was too dangerous." Everyone was vigilant, she said. "It all could change within a day. No one could predict what was going to happen. Two people were there once. My cousin said they're coming and he really trembled, thinking they were people from the Gestapo who would arrest me the very last minute, nicht? It wasn't unusual that something happened in the last days. It really was tension to the end."

Although "everything was hanging in the balance," as she put it, she said she did not react like the others. "I was the least afraid. The whole time, I knew how bad it was and was uncertain if Peter even was alive. Nonetheless, within myself I had remarkable confidence and sometimes even joyfulness that I myself couldn't even understand. I still can't understand it."

She did keep busy. For one thing, she had to make herself a new wardrobe. Once again hers had been destroyed. This time a truck carrying all her clothes and other possessions was bombed while parked beside an Austrian train station. "For all practical purposes, I had only the clothes on my body. I sewed a skirt by hand from a bathtowel. Someone got me some wool yarn and I knitted a dress. Somehow I got some red material and made a blouse by hand, and a skirt. It was cheap material, but I was naturally very proud and happy." For the baby, she knitted sweaters.

As she sewed and knitted, the war was coming to an end. Suddenly she was more curtailed than before. She said Germans in Austria were not allowed to leave, or to be outside after six in the evening. "Everything was changing radically. The times were upsetting." Concerned that she would start labor at night and not be allowed to get help, she moved to a plain and poor "birthing house" in a nearby village. It was where the local farm wives had their children. Frau Söhnchen visited during the day and planned to help the midwife with the birth.

The baby was late. Marianne still was pregnant when the war ended.

In early June, her labor began. "Arnhild was with me. It began in the morning, I think. She stayed with me until evening, then had to go, and the pains came. But I was confident. I thought, you can do this. It won't be so bad. But the night was bad." As for the midwife, "she kept falling asleep, she was so terribly tired." She laughed. "Ja. Oh, well."

The next morning, Marianne gave birth to a healthy baby boy she named Dorian. "In peace," she said. "I still knew nothing about Peter. I got no news at all."

Shortly after being arrested and sent to Oranienburg, Peter Karlsruhen had been transferred to Sachsenhausen. "He did not talk about it. He did not want to talk about it. But I know a lot was done to him. I never asked him directly. It's been my way. I always waited until one tells me. I never asked him, 'What terrible thing did you encounter or was done to you?' I only know it was terrible. He said that. That he was beaten a lot, and, and that it was a very bad time."

Then the Allies began closing in. Generally, Nazi concentration camp guards reacted in one of two ways to Allied advances. Either they killed the remaining prisoners and fled, or they herded the prisoners along a strenuous march that was scarcely less murderous. Peter Karlsruhen and his debilitated fellow inmates got the second option. "They pushed the prisoners toward the Baltic Sea. Somehow they wanted to drive them into the Baltic, with the SS guarding them. [The prisoners] had no opportunity to shoot or do anything. That was right at the end, you have to realize. And on this march, he collapsed. He himself saw how many fellow prisoners who collapsed were shot. But no one noticed him fall into a large puddle of water."

Shortly thereafter, British troops, presumably in pursuit of the Germans, advanced along the same route. They found Peter.

"He was unconscious. They took him and brought him to their field hospital and took care of him." She said she did not recall how long he was in the hospital, but "it must have been a good long time." She said that in a photograph from the time, "one would scarcely recognize him. Completely emaciated."

The British happened to have saved the life of a man who could help them. Peter Karlsruhen spoke English. When he regained his strength, he began working for them as a translator. But he also had a personal matter to attend to.

After Dorian's birth, Marianne brought him to her room in Egg. Her life was eased by his presence—the only link to her missing lover—and by the graciousness of the innkeepers. "They were so dear. They found a little bed that was completely wrecked and the man nailed it together, set makeshift boards in it. And we took a sack and stuffed it with leaves, dried leaves. That was the mattress. The farm women did it that way, too. And Dorian slept on it very well. It always rustled when he moved."

As for Peter, "I still knew nothing. Nothing at all. Until one evening." Knowing that Arnhild had visited friends nearby, Marianne, pushing the baby carriage, went to the local train station to meet her. "As Arnhild stepped off, she saw me and said, 'Peter is alive. And he's on his way here.'

"I left the baby carriage where it was and threw myself down in the ditch and cried." She laughed at the memory. "It was a kind of collapse, really. That was, well." She paused. "One cannot really describe it. Then I wanted to go home alone. I didn't want anyone to come with me, I was so worked up. And I went to the station every evening because I thought Peter would come on this little train. But he didn't. But, naturally, I was in a completely different world.

"Then one evening, while I sat in my room, Dorian lay in his little bed, he was still awake, and I heard someone below call, 'Does Frau Jung live here?' Of course, my heart stopped. For it was Peter's voice. 'Where is she?' And then he came storming up the steps, and wearing sort of English overalls and, ja, one cannot describe it, this reunion. One really cannot describe it." After a long silence, she began to cry.

Then "Peter looked inside [the bed], and Dorian was such a round and perfect child. Everyone said so. And he looked so understanding, although so small. Peter was naturally enthralled, nicht? He couldn't comprehend it." She laughed a lovely laugh. "It simply was too much. Ja."

How did Peter look when he arrived? I eventually asked.

"Good. Good. He really looked radiant. And he was such a type. I have a completely fantastic remembrance, that he looked dazzling. Then we immediately married, in Egg. Arnhild even made us a beautiful wedding dinner. It was really festive."

Frau Marianne Karlsruhen remembered little of the ceremony itself, other than that it went smoothly. "Questions were asked and answered and there were no difficulties at all." She did remember she wore the dress she had bought in Copenhagen.

With the Reich destroyed, there was no possibility of her parents' coming to the wedding, or of telephoning them. But they knew of the baby, or at least of her pregnancy. From Norway, Marianne had managed to get the news to her sister, who finally told them. The next step was to go to Schalksmühle. The new Karlsruhen family of three had at their disposal the car in which Peter had arrived. "A big Mercedes on which was written in big letters British Military Government. They had let him through all the zones in this car. Naturally, he had all the requisite papers." His bosses knew the reason for the trip. "They were terribly happy about it."

"Then the next morning we set off. The French gave me a certificate of passage without ado, although they held back the other Germans. They didn't let them out of Austria. But I got a certificate right away and could leave." The certificate qualified her as having been persecuted by the Nazis. "It all had suddenly changed. Everything was completely reversed."

Leaving Austria, the family moved from zone to zone with papered ease. "Then at the American sector, we passed all the same people Peter had passed a few days before everything had happened. Now he came back with wife and child. They applauded and said, 'That sure was fast.' I'll never forget it."

The idyll continued in Schalksmühle, where the Jungs received the couple with open arms. Peter then put the covered baby's basket on a table. "He took the cover off and there lay Dorian. And looked as if he'd just been bathed and washed and with these red cheeks and my parents leaned over the basket, and he laughed. My parents were beside themselves. They cried. They couldn't do anything."

Peter became "very, very close" to her parents, she said. "When one later thinks about it, if one had arranged it oneself, one could not have arranged it so wonderfully. To me it seems like a miracle." Peter's mother survived the Reich and the war, too. And "then lived with us and felt very well."

In 1947, the Karlsruhens had a second child, another son. Peter continued to work as an interpreter for the British, then for a sheet-metal-testing company. Her father "always helped him as much as possible," but Peter wanted to prove himself, and did. "They understood each other very, very well." The marriage of Marianne Jung and Peter Karlsruhen continued to his death in 1978.

What about the surveillance on them as lovers, and the events leading to Peter's arrest? They never made any investigations, she said. She knew, she later said, it all started when someone informed on their relationship to the Ortsgruppenleiter in Schalksmühle. She also knew who that someone was. She "would rather not speak about it."

Postscript

Marianne Karlsruhen missed her husband so palpably when we met, nine years after his death, she still was trying to come to terms with her loss. It was clear she also was trying to come to terms with her place in the epoch they lived through. "At the train station, when I saw human beings, Jews with stars, I went up to them, stood with them, and tried to talk with them. Simply to show them I didn't belong to the others, that I was closer to belonging to them. Naturally, today I sometimes think, what if that were to take place today? You have to understand, one grows into these things. First, it happens. One experiences it, but is not entirely clear about it at all. Not until much later was I really alert. And I became very alert after Peter's death. That is a necessity. It somehow changed my life. I sometimes think about this being alert today and also observe other people, what they're doing, how they're doing, whether I can help them, maybe reach out sometime and so on.

"And with the knowledge of all of it from back then, with the alertness and knowledge, I probably should have conducted myself considerably differently. I probably should have done something. Myself. I ask myself today, would I also have done it if it meant pledging my life? For one must include that, if one is really committed.

"I sometimes still make self-reproaches, that I did not intensively research what's really going on here. I believe if one really tried to get behind it, there would have been a possibility . . . But as I said, I probably was too . . . In the meantime, a lot has been generated in me. It wasn't that far along before."

Frau Ursula Meyer-Semlies

National Socialism and Christianity

It was about a year before the Nazis came to power.

"As far as school was concerned, we were forbidden to wear swastikas. That is, one was not supposed to wear any [political] Party symbols. School was supposed to be neutral. And I had a small silver swastika. I always pinned it on a flap of my coat, and when I came into school I turned the flap down somewhat, so it could not always be seen.

"We also were not allowed to go to meetings, to Communists and National Socialists. We weren't supposed to go to the extreme Parties. But we went anyway. We were seventeen, eighteen years old. We wanted to inform ourselves. What's going on, nicht? We often went to such meetings. And then at the end the 'Deutschland' song was always sung, and . . . the 'Horst Wessel Song.' And there, also with the 'Deutschland' song, the Nazis raised their hands high in the greeting. We did too, of course. Enthusiastic, nicht? And sometimes teachers were there, too, but they didn't say anything. Some were already for them." The German government, in its way, was doing what it could to keep National Socialism at bay. State employees, from soldiers to teachers, were forbidden to join the Nazi Party.

In Fräulein Ursula Semlies's history class, National Socialism was discussed vigorously. Once a week, students were allowed to bring in newspapers representing the spectrum of Germany's political groups. "Then it broke loose," she said with the tiny laugh she often used.

"And I was the wildest champion of National Socialism. . . . I tutored after school, because my mother was a teacher's widow and we didn't have much money and there were six of us children. And with my first tutoring money, I bought Hitler's *Mein Kampf.* It was about 1932. I wanted to know what was going on and what he thought and so. If I read it today, I'd read it with completely different eyes.

"Of course, he had something against the Jews, nicht? But he always only said, 'Ja, the Jews have all the money and the stores.' " As she elaborated (the following is compressed from two talks), she sometimes raised her usually quiet, controlled voice to approximate a Nazi official. "It was said, 'The Jews are our unhappiness.' It was always said through propaganda, they are such a small minority and have the most important positions. Especially in every city, in every large place, they had all the stores in their hands. I didn't think anything about it, but at once one became aware of it. And one looked around. Ach ja, the big textile stores, cigar shops. What else was there? School stores, also music supply stores, jewelry stores, were all in the hands of Jews." On the bank of the Memel River were big coffin works, located there to be close to the supplies of logs floated down the river. "The Jews had all that, too," she said.

"And there were Jews among academics, and doctors were Jews. But they really were very beloved, because they were very good." She eventually added musicians, artists, bank directors, and lawyers to the list of Jews in prominent positions. "'You are being ruled only by Jews. Pay attention and see for yourselves whether we're right or not,' ne? And then we saw, 'Well, ja ja, nicht?' And then one said, 'How did that happen?' "

Once, she sort of answered the question herself. She stated that in the Middle Ages Jews "were actually forced into" financial jobs such as tax collectors because Christians were not allowed to engage in such "un-Christian" work. But she expended more attention on the dark ages of the Third Reich. "Hitler said, 'Ja, just look. You all put up with that and they are *strangers.* Those are not really Germans.' And, um, and so, nicht? The people were stirred up. And whoever is young . . . well, not only the young, but also a lot of others, they said, 'Well, it is that way.' We actually thought, completely right, for them not to be the only ones with a say, and if they have all the money.' But that they would be killed, that would never have been the idea."

What about Jews she knew personally?

"Personally, well, we had no friendships with Jews because we were not rich people." She made her little laugh. "My mother a poor teacher's widow, we didn't fit in at all."

Frau Ursula Meyer-Semlies, the eldest of the six children, was born under "the thunder of cannons and the peal of bells," as she liked to put it (and sometimes vice versa), in a quote from her mother. Her birth in September

1914 in the northern East Prussian city of Tilsit coincided with the rout of Russian troops by German troops and with Sunday church services. Nationalism and religion usually, but not always, remained a harmonious duet throughout her life.

Ursula's childhood and youth, which she has written about in two books, call to mind an old woodcut. A family with little means happily sings and plays German folk songs in a snug house while bread bakes and snow falls. Herr Semlies was well known locally as a singing teacher and leader of a children's choir, and for his long red beard. Frau Semlies had been a teacher, too. The family was indeed close, but poor, especially after the First World War. Ursula writes that when she was seven she and her equally skinny brother were sent to live with family friends in the countryside. The two children were so hungry that they ate a dried-up piece of bread they later learned, to their shame, had been meant for the cow. Such stories make up Frau Meyer-Semlies's first book, which goes through 1945, but in which the Third Reich is scarcely mentioned. Was her memory strikingly selective or strikingly apolitical?

Strikingly selective is the answer. Her second book, published after the second of our two meetings, is all about the Third Reich, that is, her Third Reich.

"I still remember exactly how it was the day Hitler came to power," she said. "The [school] class varied. That is, some were very enthusiastic, to whom I also belonged, for we had been raised with such a national consciousness. My mother showed us a book now and then, which areas we had lost from the First World War. The border was [almost literally] at the front door. And we were always very sad things had come to that. Then there was a poem at the time, that the German people were waiting for a Führer, nicht? The poem went, 'O God, send us a Führer who will change our misfortune, by God's word.' And many Germans felt the same way." The poem was written long before Hitler, she said, but she liked it a lot. She thought one "needs a strong man" because Germany was in such chaos. In Tilsit, she said, there were frequent street battles, mostly instigated by Communists.

"Everyone was afraid of the Communists. And all at once the SA, that is, the brownshirts, came. They were the only ones who took them on and didn't put up with everything. Because our government didn't know what to do against them, either." She recalled her enthusiasm when the Nazi brownshirts gathered in town, then took off on a "march and also with music and we ran along on the sidewalk." She laughed her little laugh. "And then Communists came and wanted to break up the march." She spoke with affection about a brother who felt the way she did. He "had a rubber club, wound with wire, and he always kept it under his pillow. He was sixteen years old. And I always said, 'What *is* that thing?' and so on. He said, 'So many Communists live around here. And if they maybe attack me at night, then I have my make-believe gun here on the cupboard,' that was like tear gas or something, 'and my rubber club is under my pillow.' A sixteen-year-old boy," she chuckled. He also went to meetings held in large halls and took part in mock battles "with chair legs and everything. And he found it so exciting." Another chuckle. "The way young people were, nicht?"

Frau Ursula Meyer-Semlies, whose fair skin and bone structure made her look like an Englishwoman, was imparting her memories in her modest and rather dark home in Hamburg, where she lived with her husband, Dr. Andreas Meyer, a retired veterinarian, whom she met in 1941. She kept her maiden name of Semlies, attaching it German-style after his, because there are "so many Meyers." Even though he was elderly and recovering from a heart attack when I met him, he was notably handsome and, in fact, was the rare kind of handsome man who seemed unaware of his looks. By the time I returned to Hamburg the next year, he had died. I knew this; Frau Meyer-Semlies wrote me that his cello stood in the corner all by itself, never to be played by him again.

That first evening, after the three of us rather solemnly had a communal cold German supper, which she had obviously tried to make look festive, she and I retired to another room, where her mood became animated. The reason could have been the subject matter. When the Third Reich took off, she took off with it.

She joined the Bund deutscher Mädel and by 1934 was a "Ringführerin" [literally "ringleader"] for Tilsit. According to a Nazi organizational chart, a Ring contained about six hundred girls.[1] She specialized in the music program. "We sang a lot. Of course, National Socialist songs, too, but also a lot of folk songs." That same year, she took her Abitur exam and was "still very enthusiastic." (She writes in one book that her Abitur theme was based on a passage from *Mein Kampf*.) "Later in '34, I was in 'work duty.' I was still enthusiastic, I know. We graduates had to give lectures in the camp, sometimes about historical things, about the history of East Prussia or whatever, and really not so much about National Socialism. It wasn't like that. We had done that in BdM. Like about the individual [Nazi] leaders." Especially in "work duty" there "was a very nice atmosphere," she said. "We were supposed to get to know each other. Earlier it was the case that the classes cut themselves off from each other a little, nicht? The learned ones among themselves, the craftspeople among themselves, and the simple workers. And here we had girls from all levels of people, from teachers down to factory workers. And I found that good."

By the time her 'work duty' (in her case, farm work) ended, "I was still very enthusiastic about Hitler." Also, she had decided to become a grade school teacher. She applied to a teaching school in Hanover, "the sole wom-

---

1. The chart is reproduced in Erich Blohm, *Hitler-Jugend* (Vlotho/Weser: Verlag für Volkstum und Zeitgeschichtsforschung, 1979), 67.

en's teacher institution" for the whole northern half of Germany. "The others were all for men. Because women should," she laughed, "preferably have a saucepan. They should get married and then give up their profession, nicht? There was great unemployment when Hitler came, and it was often said, 'No double earners.' If the women married, they had to give up their career, so that men get work first."

When she was asked if she agreed with that, her answer was defensive in its circuitousness. "Ach, somehow, we thought, unemployment somehow had to be solved, nicht? Also, 'work duty' was put in effect, so that men got off the street and just had to work, that they not get any dumb ideas. And we all found that good."

One reason she chose to become a grade school teacher was that the training took only four semesters. "We didn't have money for more." Before being accepted into the Hanover school, she had to go there, some thousand kilometers away, to be tested. "And that was an expensive trip." The first part of the test was "in National Socialist weltanschauung. And then maybe four gathered around a table and the theme was named and we had to discuss the theme." One applicant "did not even know" that Joseph Goebbels had written a book called *From the Kaiserhof to the Reichs Chancellory*, but Fräulein Semlies certainly did. "It referred to Hitler. Kaiserhof, that was a restaurant [actually, a hotel with a restaurant] in which they often had meetings. And from there he went to the Reichs Chancellory as the Reichs Chancellor. And she didn't know at all that it was the title of a book. Of course, they noted that, too." Acceptance into the teaching school had to do not only with knowledge, she said, but "also the point of view one had. And furthermore, I came from a family of teachers, that was inherited, it was called 'teaching blood [Lehrerblut].'" Another factor was her family's economic need. Fräulein Semlies met all criteria and was accepted. "One in my class, the daughter of a director, she was not accepted. It was, well, the director has enough money. He can afford another line of study for his daughter." She laughed her little laugh. "And then, when we were already [students] in Hanover, that is where my doubts began.

"A kind of petition was hung up. Everyone who was against religious instruction was supposed to sign . . . that they did not want to teach religion. Many signed it. And my girlfriend, who was also from East Prussia, and I, we both said, 'We're not going along with that. We're hanging a notice next to it, Who *does* want to teach religion? And a lot of people filled it up, too." It might be noted that Frau Meyer-Semlies maintained to me that her interest in teaching religion extended to teaching Jewish religion. When I questioned this (in light of other remarks), she replied that she always included the Old Testament in her curriculum.

About the time of her student days in Hanover, the Nuremberg race laws were passed. Even in retrospect, she did not seem distressed about identification being required by supposed race, but did recognize the value of having "an 'Aryan' grandmother." (She may have been coy in her phrasing. Germans sometimes nervously joked about what if "a Jewish grandmother shows up in my family tree.") She did say, making a point other women did not, that people who made jokes about the race law were those unaffected by it.

After two semesters of study, Ursula Semlies boarded a train to return to Tilsit for Christmas with her family. (Her mother had saved for a ticket.) It was December of 1936. "Suddenly several SS people boarded the train, young ones. And began a conversation and said, 'Ach, wonderful, now we're going home and finally Christmas, the 'Festival of the Family,' and this Christian fuss, no one believes in that anymore.' And I thought, you may not let that go unchallenged. I sent a short prayer to heaven and said, 'Well, for me, Christmas is still always a Christian Christmas.' '*Well* now,' they said, 'you are so young, and only old women and so on believe in the Christian religion.' Then they made fun of me. 'We could discuss it with you.' I said, 'Ja, we can discuss it, but only if you pay as much attention to my point of view as I do to yours.' 'Definitely, ja, ja, we'll do it.' Then we sat there and talked for hours. Then there was another, who had come directly from Schulungsburg Vogelsang [an SS training center]. He said, 'Earlier, I too thought the way you do, but now I've been enlightened about how everything is, and that the Bible's a Jew book,' and so on. And Mary, well, Mary was still pictured as 'Aryan,' nicht? She was still tolerated." Frau Meyer-Semlies allowed herself another little laugh.

"Then I said, 'In political terms, I agree with Hitler. I am really enthusiastic. But in religious terms, I have my own views.' And then these SS people said, 'That *is* precisely the wrong way around. The Führer wants the whole human being, and if there is still *any* region in your heart that does not belong to the Führer, then you are not a convinced National Socialist and then the Führer cannot influence you.' Well, so we talked and then afterward they got off the train and it was well past midnight and they said, 'In ten years, we should talk again and *then* we'll see who was right.'"

Despite such incidents cutting into her enthusiasm for National Socialism, in 1938 or "thereabouts" Ursula Semlies joined the Nazi Party. She spoke as if the decision had been difficult. "I thought to myself, 'Do you join?' 'Do you not join?' Na ja. Because I had been so much for it before, and now should I not be at all anymore? Or what? Well." She paused, then raised her voice. "Na ja, in any case, I joined." And there "wasn't war yet" and the Nazis "were not doing bad things to the Jews," or, she corrected herself, that she knew about. "And much that Hitler did we found good." She named the absence of unemployment and of drunks on the street, the 'work duty' program, the road construction, and "that youth were, again, in order." She added, "A new life had begun, nicht?"

Still, even before the war, "I reproached myself" for joining. Her then-boyfriend, a theology student, reproached her more. "He said, '*What?* You've joined the Party? I don't think that's good.' I always had sort of remnants of affection from before, you see, because at first I had been so enthusiastic about Hitler." She went on to say she thought maybe she should show that she had belonged to the movement. She half laughed. "But I didn't have that good a conscience anymore, either. And I decided I will. I later used it. I thought, as long as I'm in the Party, they won't throw me out as a teacher as fast."

The theology student remained opposed. When the Sudetenland in Czechoslovakia was ceded to Germany in 1938, "he said, 'Well, it looks like war now and what does one get out of it? . . . Then you're just the senior soldier in the grave,' he said. He was completely against National Socialism anyway. When there were collections for 'Winter Help' in the streets and I said, 'Ach, that's such a good thing, collections for poor people, that they get heating material and so on,' he said, '*Everything* they do is terrible because the roots are terrible. Nothing's good. I am not giving a penny.' And when someone came collecting, he waved him away."

Then came "Kristallnacht." She brought it up first in terms of what she would have done. "We said, 'If I were a Jew, I would make sure I got away, but *soon*. One doesn't know what's going to happen next. Many were so *trusting*, the Jews. They stayed and stayed." Downstairs Jewish neighbors named Jaffe (whom she otherwise did not mention) were said to be planning finally to go to Palestine after that night.

Asked what she thought about the event itself, she said, after pausing, "We did not find it good, the ways and means of how they did it, nicht? Of course we thought, 'Jews out' was always the phrase, nicht? 'Jews out, Jews out.' Well, such expressions and refrains were sometimes . . ." She continued in disconnected bursts and pauses. "Anyway, we, but I thought, the methods, well, they should do it another way, but not with force, nicht?" And "most of all, not in such a criminal way."

Another consequence of "Kristallnacht" made much more of an impact on her. By then, she had an entry-level teaching job outside her hometown of Tilsit. Shortly after the events of the night of November 9, she and the fifteen or so other local teachers were called together. Their supervisor "laid a piece of writing in front of us that said Herr vom Rath . . . He was a German diplomat in Paris and he was murdered by a Jew. And because he was murdered by a Jew, we German teachers could no longer take it upon ourselves to teach Christian religion, but we hereby ask to be relieved of doing so.

"And everyone signed. Then it was my turn. And was now one of the youngest, had just started with my teaching career. I read it through once more. I said, 'I'm not signing it.' And he said, 'Whaaaat? Why not?' And so on. I knew exactly what they wanted, nicht? But first I acted like, I said, 'First of all, it's completely illogical. If vom Rath was a Christian, and if a Christian is killed by a Jew, then I'm not supposed to be able to teach Christian religion anymore?

"Furthermore, I *want* to teach Christian religion. Why should I sign that I don't want to? And I'm not signing it.' Anyway, I was the only one. And the others in part were married and I thought, too, someone who's married and possibly will be fired later, for him it's much more difficult. I was completely free. So. Later, I was called alone to the rector, after the others had all gone, and he said to me, 'Ach, you know, that really doesn't have a lot to do with religion. It's really a *political* situation.' I knew that exactly, but I said nothing. Then he said, 'We do *all* want to sign it and why should one person set oneself apart? I would very much like to hand it over, that *all* have agreed to it.' I say, 'But I *cannot* sign it. That's against my conscience and I would prefer to be a 'Putzfrau' [cleaning woman] with a clean conscience than sign it.' "

Another teacher who had been at the meeting told Fräulein Semlies she would not be able to change the course of Germany, that only a few old people went to church, and once they died off, the churches would be done for anyway and Fräulein Semlies would probably lose her job. She still refused. She was ordered to go see the principal and tell him why she would not sign.

"Then I went home on my bike and told my mother. And my mother said, 'You've done well. You won't sign it,' and so on. Na, and then to the principal [Schulrat]. He was not there. His substitute, whom I knew well, he was a nice teacher, and he said, 'Ach, Fräulein Semlies, don't make a big thing out of it. Do sign. Why do you want to cause such unpleasantness?' I say, 'Nein, I cannot.' " He told her he would abide by her decision, but she would have to write out her reasoning.

"And I wrote, 'I hereby state that it is not against my conscience to teach Christian religion. If it were forbidden, then I would not do it.' And then my signature. Well, and *that* made the principal mad at me. I was the only one in the whole area who continued to teach religion, and the people were very enthusiastic that I did it." She said the people also made fun of a male colleague for doing what all the others did.

"The teacher's wife . . . was completely furious that her husband signed it, and said, 'How do you picture it? You want to have your children confirmed, and if you do something like this, then you're against Christianity and I find that terrible.' And he said, 'Ja, little mother, what should I do? When the Nazis came, I was already let go once [for being a Social Democrat]. I was already in a retraining camp a couple of months.' [The phrase *retraining camp* might have been Frau Meyer-Semlies's and not his.] "'And if I don't sign it, they'll fire me. What do you want to do then?' Well, that's how it was."

The story of the rebellion by Fräulein Semlies and a couple of other teachers spread within the regional Nazi organization. Soon, all teachers from the Tilsit area were called together to hear from the Schulrat. She said he seemed possessed by the devil. "He said, 'The *traitors* who have not yet signed, they will see what they have done. When we hoist the swastika flag over the Kremlin, *then* they will see how they have attacked us from behind. And for the last time, I demand of you, Sign!'

"And [an old teacher who had not yet signed] sat next to me. He began to tremble. He whispered, 'I'll sign everything, I'll sign everything.' Well, I thought, the poor man, nicht? For him it's really difficult. But I thought in my heart, 'Now I'll *especially* not sign. I won't let myself be forced into it.'" She later found out another woman teacher and a male teacher refused, too. "He said, 'I also have a family and children, but I'm not signing anyway. I believe the dear Lord will care for me. He will find something I can do.' The woman teacher said, 'I never even considered signing.'" Frau Meyer-Semlies knew of three refusals among three hundred teachers.

The teachers then were called together again, to hear from an Ober-schulrat, who had traveled from the East Prussian capital of Königsberg because of the revolt. She said she was sick and not there, but spoke as if she recalled every word he said: "What is going on with you? What is really going on, to start such an action against teaching religion? That is not what the Führer wants. Some overeager Party member circulated the paper." The Oberschulrat went on to say that Hitler wanted to conquer the Memelland (now part of Lithuania), whose inhabitants were all practicing Christians. "If *they* hear that here in Tilsit everyone's against religion, they won't want to belong to Germany," he said. The petition was to be retracted immediately.

It was. But Fräulein Semlies's intransigence was not forgiven. The Schulrat called her to his office again. He said he knew she had requested an assignment within Tilsit itself because her mother lived there, but unfortunately he could not take someone with her views. He assigned her to a one-room schoolhouse in a rural village, four kilometers from a bus stop.

Before long at her new assignment, Ursula Semlies again established a working pattern of obedience, defiance, and enthusiasm. She spoke about all three in detail and in basically the same tone, as if all really were the same, from her pupils' saying "Heil Hitler!" at the beginning and end of the school day, to their learning the names of the generals, whose pictures she had on the classroom walls, to her instituting various religious Christmas programs at school, rather than the winter solstice ceremonies the Nazis were trying to establish. Her latter actions again brought her to the attention of the Party.

The local Ortsgruppenleiter summoned her to come see him, a trip she complained took a big chunk of time out of her schedule (she adhered to a most precise lesson plan), but which she made. He complained about the religious content of her program. She "decided to slay him with his own weapon" and challenge him. "What do you really want from me? Do you doubt my political reliability? I am a member of the Party." "Ach, I didn't know that." "I said, 'Ja. Now you do.' "

She said that after the incident, "I felt secure again, and did my religious teaching and did what I thought was right, and what I didn't like I left out of the lessons. This and that we were supposed to say, whether racist, and whatever. I left out those things I could not internally square with my conscience, but I said as long as I stay a teacher, I'll join for all the good things. If I had immediately been opposed to it from the beginning, and fired, then perhaps another teacher would have my job, who perhaps would have taught *only* completely in the sense of National Socialism. And therefore I thought, as long as I can stay," she half laughed, "under the protection of being a member of the National Socialists, I can do anything I want. They don't notice it so much. It was a kind of protective shield." Frau Meyer-Semlies otherwise never spoke about how she squared her Christian and her National Socialist beliefs.

Both seemed tested by the war. "I can see us today, sitting around the radio" and learning how the battles were going. The news gave her an "unholy feeling," she said. "We thought the situation is very bad. The same thing will happen to us as in the First World War. The war is already lost. But afterward, with Poland, it went very fast." She and her family were "happy the war was over, that it was over so quickly." As for war with France, she maintained that "Hitler didn't want it. He especially didn't want war with England. He had such crazy ideas regarding England. The English and the Germans . . . are Germanic peoples and they may not fight one another. He should have known that had already been the case in the First World War, nicht?"

She wrote in one book that she wanted Hitler to occupy England and force it to sign a peace treaty, but "he did not do it." She also wrote that Hitler hoped "his friendly gestures" toward England, like "allowing its ships to escape" after Dunkirk, would convince British leaders of his "peaceful intentions."

Dr. Meyer, meantime, was having an unusually peaceful war. He was assigned to care for horses on the far western front, near the Atlantic Ocean. During one long lull, he was even in the Atlantic, bathing as if he were at a health resort. He told her, "Ach, that was so gemütlich." Later, he was sent to the eastern front.

And she was sent to Poland. She stayed there until close to the end of the war. The reason she first went had to do with a trick, or a misunderstanding. One of many men who had impeded her teaching duties suggested she apply to study and work in a new school she thought was near her home. She did apply. But the school was in a "godforsaken" part of occupied Poland. There, too, she eventually made the best of her situation, which included, in effect, trying to reverse the godforsakenness of her surroundings by going to church and singing religious songs with her female charges during unforbidden hours.

One day, in either 1943 or 1944, she said, she ventured beyond her usual world, to the ghetto at Lodz. The reason had to do with her need of a new winter coat. "First, one had to relinquish one's old coat, and then one got a certificate with which to buy a new one." She laughed that the trans-action had to be done in the summer. She heard there were fabric factories that made good coats in the city of Lodz.

"And someone said, 'Do you know about the ghetto? In Lodz there is a ghetto. And one can go through in a streetcar. But it's closed off, because the others, the Jews, are not allowed out [of the ghetto]. But one can travel through.' And I thought, I'll go see it. We traveled through. And were told the Jews have their own administration. And I saw the Jews going around and had the Star of David on their sleeves. I didn't see many, going around, but they looked horribly miserable. I thought, man, they [inaudible] and are not getting enough to eat." The streetcar went farther, "and I don't know." She did not mention the coat anymore.

"Then in the place where we were, in Gostenyn, it was later called Waldrode, there all the Jews had disappeared. . . . In Poland, the Jews were not like they were at home, rich people. They were small craftspeople. And one night they picked them all up and took them away. The houses were empty. I sort of looked in." She said, speaking again almost inaudibly, that she wondered what could be the reason "to take these small craftspeople to a concentration camp. We didn't like it."

Although she spoke of Jews she knew of back in Tilsit as having all been rich, in her second book she described Yiddish-speaking Eastern Jews arriving in town, selling apples and fish. Her book stance is that of a be-mused observer. The Jews gesticulate when they talk and have "secret rites" during their Sabbath. In conclusion she wrote, "Ja, they certainly were strange human beings, these Eastern Jews, but not a single human being in Germany thought about killing them because of it."[2] The words were almost the same ones she had used in connection with rich Jews.

Her description of her stay in Poland, including time at the university in Posen, includes much mention of how nice the Poles were to her and to other Germans. Maybe, she added, they thought if they killed a German they would be killed. But the Poles she met told her they liked working for Germans because Germans paid them on time, whereas Polish estate owners sometimes made them wait two weeks. When she finally left Poland (be-cause the Russians were arriving) one Polish woman begged to go with her, even kissing her hand. "The Poles always kiss so much, nicht?"

---

2. The books are *In den Memelwiesen* (In the Memel pastures) (1983) and *Glockenläuten und Kanonendonner* (Peals of bells and thunder of cannon) (1989), both published by Gollenberg Verlag, the first in Seesen am Harz, the second in Marxen/Auetal.

In Poland, Frau Meyer-Semlies was spared the war, but her family was not. One of her brothers was killed, at nineteen. Her sisters lost boyfriend after boyfriend. She said of one sister, "She had one boyfriend, he was killed. She had another, he too was killed. And so it continued." Her own romantic life, focused on Andreas Meyer, had been interrupted in another way. He was going to visit her after seeing his parents in Hamburg, but the "terrible bombing attacks on Hamburg" happened just then. He went to see to his parents, rather than his girlfriend. He also decided that in such times, there was no reason to marry. Home life, he thought, was like front life. Dr. Meyer, who came from a more cosmopolitan (and, judging from photographs, wealthier) background than she did, may also have been closer to the reality affecting German Jews. After a Jewish friend of his emigrated, he risked visiting the friend's parents.

What about non-Jews emigrating, too? Frau Meyer-Semlies, being an early interviewee, got that retrospectively foolish question, as well as ones about whether she would try to hide a husband or brother rather than let them go to the front. Her answer on all counts was no. "We were Germans and once there was war, one had to stand with his own people." She added, in many different ways, "Should everything now be for nothing? And how many have already fallen in battle? One brother of mine. And four sons of my aunt. She had six sons and four were killed in the war, and another after the war, because he was 'overexerted' from the war. And the last one left, he was also wounded. After a few years he died, too, from his battle wounds. Six sons gone. And one thought, should it all be for nothing?

"Goebbels did say we're sitting in a moving train and no one can get out. And one could not get out. Where did one want to go? Where could one go? . . . Most of Europe was occupied by Hitler. . . . Furthermore I thought, no, one must just hold on." But, she said at another point, "One was just always so torn. I mean, no people wants to lose a war. We thought, if only there could be a cease-fire. I mean, we did not want a *victory*," she said rather sarcastically. "Just a *settlement* somehow, nicht? But it was always said the Americans and English want only unconditional victory. *Unconditional*. Who wants that, ne? One feels so humiliated. And thinks, can one answer it in one's conscience, for his children, for the future, simply to 'throw the rifle into the cornfield'? Nein, we *have* to keep going until the end."

For her that meant shoveling ditches in the snow and rain, against oncoming Russian tanks, while singing. Her overall thought, she said, besides not wanting German soldiers to have died for naught, was, "We *may* not lose the war, we *may* not lose the war. What will happen then?" The victors will "be so furious at us, the Russians and the English and the French and who knows. If only we don't lose the war. On the other hand, we said, 'Ja, but if we win it, what will happen *then*?' That I said, too. 'I'll definitely land in a KZ.' "

65

Frauen

She would land in a concentration camp?

Yes, she said. "I thought, then the real persecution of the Christians will begin." Because, she said, "I didn't agree with what the National Socialists were doing . . . in terms of their racial theories and in terms of their religion and [that] Hitler should be deified. Because I wouldn't have gone along with it."

She said she also knew that "whoever doubted final victory is locked up," so she kept quiet about any such thoughts. She had known a teacher, a woman, who listened to a verboten foreign radio broadcast, was denounced, "immediately taken away," and put in a concentration camp. "And we said, why did she do it? She did know how wild they were about [listening], when it was so tottering, nicht? . . . She *knows* that she'll be picked up. She should have seen it coming."

Frau Meyer-Semlies said she herself never heard a forbidden foreign broadcast, until the 1944 assassination attempt on Hitler. "I said, that's that. Now I'm going to listen to a foreign broadcast." She said one of her brothers during the war was assigned to listen to such broadcasts. He told her, she said, "Ours lie, but the others lie just as much." She laughed. Asked if she could have got information from him, she said, "Ach, we didn't want that at all." Why not? "I didn't want to. I mean, we heard the army reports every day and they were always worse. The front kept getting closer. We noticed it, too."

The German soldiers could do nothing about it, she implied. "The soldier does not ask why, but must obey, nicht?" On the eastern front, she said, German soldiers were so low on supplies that they were told to get their own food, if possible from Russian civilians. One of her brothers was sent on such a mission. She said he went to a terrified Russian family. He tried to put the family at ease by putting his weapon in a corner, then looking pitiful, until they gave him some bread and milk. As he was trying to tell them that he wanted some for his comrades, Russian soldiers were running up to the house, yelling for "Germanski." He thought it was his last hour. But the Russians pointed to a room covered with a curtain, and he hid behind it. When the Russian soldiers were in the house, the family pointed out the window to where he supposedly had gone. He said they saved his life. (In every story Frau Meyer-Semlies recounted, German soldiers and civilians were remarkably popular in occupied countries.)

Meanwhile, Dr. Meyer was taken prisoner by the Russians. Even after four years doing hard labor, he was temperate in his judgment. "My husband said, it was horrible, the Russian imprisonment, but with food, he said, the Russian civilians didn't have a lot to eat either. They didn't get more than we did, he said." She added, "He really didn't say anything bad about the Russians." He had to work hard, was not well fed or clothed, and was treated roughly and strictly, but not cruelly. She thought if he had been tortured, he would have told her.

66

Frau Meyer-Semlies said that the war, from German women's point of view, "was as if a catastrophe broke over us and [we] had to get through it." She said some people were still thinking, "The Führer won't leave us in the lurch," which caused her and others to laugh secretly and say, "Not leave us in the *lurch?* The situation is completely out of his hands." She did not believe talk about a wonder weapon. "I didn't believe any of it anymore. And you couldn't say anything out loud. You just had to see how to save yourself. One didn't think anymore at all. About guilty and not guilty and that. It was like someone's hungry. He had to figure where to get bread from, and this and that. One had to let a lot go by."

But on the question of guilt, Frau Meyer-Semlies also pointed to the countries outside Hitler's reach. If they had taken in the Jews, she said, maybe the National Socialists would not have killed them.

Frau Meyer-Semlies was thirty years old and in Schleswig-Holstein (to which she had been evacuated from Poland) when the war ended. She registered with the British occupiers, stated she had been a member of the Nazi Party, then represented herself at her de-Nazification hearing. Many other refugees were not as honest, she said, laughing, and maintained there had been no Nazi Party in their hometown, or that it had had no members.

After the hearing, she was prohibited from teaching for two years. In some defiance of the rules, she tutored privately. She also spent time trying to get food. The English occupiers "couldn't organize as well. Or maybe didn't want to." She also said they stole cameras and other items. But that happens everywhere, she said. "In every people there are some who do what they're not supposed to."

Frau Liselotte Otting

Retrospective Guilt

In a four-page handwritten letter dealing mostly with health—hers, her family's, her city's, her country's—Frau Liselotte Otting wrote, "How do I see Berlin and Germany? In a bad condition." In 1992, at the age of eighty-four, she was taking a longer view of German history than she had when we met years before. The letter did not refer specifically to increased attacks by right-wing young Germans on foreigners, which that autumn were dominating the covers of German news magazines, which in turn boldly and graphically linked the attacks to the specter of the Third Reich. Her view was all the more chilling for preceding it. "Much," she wrote, "reminds me of the end of the Weimar Republic."

Divisions were becoming deeper, she wrote. Things were going more and more downhill [bergab] for many, especially the young and the old—including her. Sixty years earlier, as the Weimar Republic was ending, her circumstances were just the opposite.

The slim, fair-skinned woman, delicate in feature, gesture, and sometimes in phrase, grew up "a little elite," as she put it. Born in Berlin in 1908, Frau Liselotte Otting was the only child of a cultured daughter of a well-to-do pharmacist and of a "rather high lawyer" in the Prussian finance ministry. His father, a "chief reporter" at a Berlin newspaper, had been a friend of the literati of nineteenth-century

Berlin, including the novelist Theodore Fontane. A portrait of and from Fontane hangs in Frau Otting's exquisitely appointed Berlin apartment. The portrait more or less faces her collection of antique Meissen porcelain and such items as a brocade and beaded bell pull for summoning the servants (it is now on display rather than in use, as it was in her parents' home) and a marquetry table that she has set exquisitely for coffee and conversation. As a last-minute touch, she fetched a doily, to prevent my tape recorder from scratching the delicate wood. A Sanyo on lace was not the only visual juxtaposition in the room. A centuries-old gilded cherub hung from a steam pipe. Glimpses into the kitchen and bathroom revealed a wrestle with form and function. The apartment was in a poorly maintained postwar high-rise in (then) East Berlin.

Frau Liselotte Otting maintained a notably dignified life not only within her East Berlin apartment but, in a way, within her East German government. During our first talk, in May of 1985, she recited at length the organizations, meetings, committees, and trips she had been part of, most purportedly on behalf of women's issues and world peace. She was a member of the Liberal Democratic Party, which she regarded with respect, as if it were a serious contender to the reigning Communists, which it was not. Trying to live a dignified life within a shabby building and trying to work with dignity within a shabby regime were arts of accommodation Frau Otting had acquired much earlier. Her training ground was the Third Reich.

But although she came to terms with the consequences of her life under Communism, she has not done so with her life under Nazism. "There is no reason to have a feeling of guilt," she wrote. "There was no special event. I turned down no one who needed advice or help. I was never in such a situation, to give help. . . . There is another reason for my feeling of guilt. In these dreadful [grauenvollen] years, I was, in human terms, happy in my personal life. While others fought, suffered, died, I was happy. Lived undisturbed, lived in sufficient circumstances, loved and was loved in return. They were the most beautiful years of my life."

Despite an economically privileged youth, which included a large home in Berlin and later in Düsseldorf (where her father worked for a while), as well as private schools and trips abroad, those years were not so "beautiful" to her. She depicted herself as the prototypical poor little rich girl—lonely and courted by suitors more interested in her inheritance and social standing than in her. "The civil servant did not earn so much, so he had to marry a woman with money," she said. "That was also a little bit the case with my father."

Early in her life, she also became aware of the professional injustice meted out to German women. She credited the female doctor/director of a Berlin hospital with saving her father's life after he suffered a severe gunshot wound to his lung in the First World War. The doctor was called in to direct the hospital because men were off at war. But when the war was over, she was fired as "not capable." The incident prompted Frau Otting to study law.

Another hospital anecdote also impressed the teenage girl. The year before her father was wounded, she herself had been hospitalized with appendicitis. While she was recovering, "the Jewish religion teacher visited me. That I still remember. But I know it more from my mother's stories, nicht? It was considered a high honor." Frau Otting told the anecdote each of two times we met. It was only one of a number of references she made to her family's close and extensive circle of Jewish friends. "We were very friendly with the Jews. And at home [in the apartment building] we were the only, at the time, I didn't even know the expression at all, 'Aryan' family, that is, Christian family." The families "socialized together" at each other's homes. Also, one aunt had married a Jewish man. (He converted to Christianity and went to church a lot more than his wife.) "Thank God he died in 1931," said Frau Otting.

Despite the shadows to come, and those of loneliness, the greatest shadow during Liselotte's youth may have been the misery around her. "It was depressing here in Berlin." She mentioned hunger and street fights. "I would say this time lay upon me like a burden." She also said (in another context), "It is indeed bad [schlimm] to be German. I felt that as a child, with the First World War." She also mentioned broken marriages and sudden poverty among people in what she often called "our circles."

By 1925, when her family moved temporarily to Düsseldorf, the widespread economic chaos had motivated her even more to pursue a law career. "The 'means' were gone, through inflation. And one also understood that a woman had the right to [a career]." After finishing a progressive school in Düsseldorf (all the teachers were women "from a very high niveau") she spent another year in a "woman's school," then traveled to England and France for five months each. Part of the French tour, in 1928, involved a stay in the countryside with a group of French people who asked her if it were true the Germans wanted war again. She felt, she said, as if she were "falling from a cloud."

In 1930, when she returned to Berlin to begin studying law, she began falling from other clouds. She recalled bloody battles between right-wing student groups, in particular dueling clubs. She also recalled that the university was a site of arguments between left and right organizations, that professors were noticeably left or right, and that "anti-Semitism made itself known." She recalled the popularity of one Jewish law professor, Martin Wolf. Students crowded a lecture hall to hear the soft-spoken professor, and fell silent as soon as he began to speak. "He was a Jew, but the hall was full. One had to hear him, nicht?"

By 1932, her parents had returned to the Berlin area, to a new and luxurious-sounding apartment in Potsdam, and her father retired from civil service and began his own firm. And "Hitler stepped forth." One step was into her "circle."

"That is where a differentiation began. There were some who found Hitler and his people good." But a greater percentage, including her parents, she said, did not. They once had been on vacation near Berchtesgaden and decided to hear him give a speech. Their verdict was, "Well, one certainly cannot pursue this house painter."

But they could and did talk about him, especially at home in Potsdam. "It began in the circle of acquaintances. And, of course, at birthday and social gatherings one discussed it. Can one accept it or not?" She amended, "That is, less among us young people, relatively seldom, but when parents came together." She continued, "Now begins the great mistake of many in my circles. We never read *Mein Kampf*. We did not find it acceptable. And rejected the fights from the right as well as from the left. I knew none personally, did not come together with Communists. Hardly with Social Democrats." And hardly, she said, with Nazis. But she said that after the Nazis came to power, her father learned that "colleagues of his in Düsseldorf had *long* been members of the National [Socialist] Party of Germany." (Frau Otting repeatedly called it the National Democratic Party.) Her father, however, was out of the Nazis' way professionally. "He had pledged an oath to the emperor. He had pledged an oath to the Weimar time. But *now* he did not need to pledge an oath again to Hitler. For he was self-employed."

Some people in her parents' "circle" liked Hitler so much they joined the Nazi Party. A new social dynamic began to take place. "One continued to invite them. In the early times, one was tolerant. I still remember that at some birthday celebrations, one did sit together at coffee and at dinner." After dinner, "the conversations were in separate rooms. One in *that* direction, and they more over there." Among the guests at her parents' social events were Jewish friends. They "also did not recognize the danger."

As the years passed, her parents continued to invite Nazis to their social gatherings. "We knew, for example, that some [older] single women were particularly bad. They deified Hitler. As if they were mad. Really. But one kept on seeing them. And also some married couples my parents knew, whom we met when there were birthdays or invitations." The reason for the invitations had changed, however. "At first one did not cut off [socializing with Nazis] because one tolerated it and considered it crazy. And afterward one did not cut it off because one was afraid."

Only months into the Nazis' rule, Liselotte got her first sense of its agenda. Returning with a boyfriend from a skiing trip, she found herself in Munich in the middle of the Jewish store boycott. Both were "infuriated," she said, "but we did not . . . We thought, stay out of it. And of course it started, how can I say it? That [you] thanked God you were not a Jew. But one continued to socialize with Jews." Her mother, in fact, left that month for Italy on an art history excursion led by a Jewish professor.

As for her own studies, uproar at the university over the Nazis led to "more and more bloody confrontations," which shut down classes for days. But as for so many other young Germans of the time, Liselotte's life was not all political. Or, as she put it, "Now I must say, of course, in the meantime, I had friendships, had boyfriends, had disappointments. And met my husband on the twenty-ninth of April." He was "thirteen and a half years older than I. He spoke six languages." Asked how they met, Frau Otting paused, then said, "Hardly in a good bourgeois manner."

Her voice took on a lilt. She and some friends, including a girlfriend "who had just married and was not very happy" and the girlfriend's husband and mother, went out that Saturday afternoon to a popular place near Potsdam called Werder. "When the trees are in blossom, one goes there and drinks wine." The group's goal was a "music café" where "one was approached by strangers" to dance. Liselotte was approached, too. "But I never danced. I always said nein. As progressive as I was."

The group stood at the edge of the dance floor while the band played. "When the music ended, a short man came over to me and asked me to dance. And I said very much from above looking down [she did not seem to mean a pun], 'No, thank you, I do not dance.' And a bit away, maybe behind a window, stood a very good-looking gentleman. Alone. And when the music began again, he came and asked me to dance, and I said ja!" She laughed. "After the dance, he asked if he might ask me once again. And I said very snippily to him, I could be very snippy, 'I don't know yet.'" He stepped aside. "And my girlfriend's husband said to me in English, 'He's really very nice.' He apparently had it up to here with three women. 'Why don't you ask him to come with us afterward?'" The group planned to have supper with Liselotte's father in Potsdam. "Thereupon I said to him, 'You're crazy. I can't bring a complete stranger home with us.' In English. The music played again and he asked me again. And we danced. And then he spoke English with me." She laughed again. "He had heard the conversation. Then I said, 'Did you hear everything?' To which he said, 'Ja.' To which I said, 'Well, are you coming with us or not?'" She laughed again. "And he came with us and introduced himself. And worked in the same large company . . . my heart lifted . . . in the same large company where the brother-in-law of this husband who was with us also worked. So, a connection was found.

"Everyone thought later, I had not been completely sober. But I had only drunk one glass. And he came home with us and later he was furious at me, that I had said to my girlfriend, 'Pay attention a little about how he behaves himself.' And he was very nice and very respectable [ordentlich] and we talked and . . ." She wrote me, "From the first day on, we knew that we belonged together. Without exaggeration, nor in glorified hindsight, it was a mutual understanding, mutual esteem, a great love which unfortunately does not happen all that often. Now I was no longer lonesome.

"But," she said, "I noticed something was going on. And there really was. He was still married. And for my mother, that was, when she came back [from Italy], an enormous blow." In brief, which Frau Otting was not on this topic, he had been separated for two years from his wife, a Dane he met while working in Denmark. They had no children. The wife was willing to divorce, for a large sum. The legalities were complicated, too. Liselotte's father balked. She pressed. "I finally have one whom I love, and so on. And he helped us very much as a lawyer. That cost a lot of money and a lot of time and a lot of nerves." And it cost a future woman lawyer.

"In '33 I quit my studies. In part because I did not agree with the situation in the university, and it already was coming out that women had scarcely any chance to become lawyers.[1] The second reason was the financial side. The divorce was expensive." (It came through in 1934.) Herr Otting, her future husband, "did not completely agree that I give up my studies. But I also didn't have the nerves for it, to concentrate. I must say, well, we understood each other wonderfully. Thank God. In every way."

The romance coincided almost exactly with the "Aryan" takeover of the boycotted Jewish stores. Two or three new shopkeepers were "good citizens" in her "circle." (The stores they began running still had the names of the former Jewish owners on the windows.) "You have to remember there was employment again, somewhat more order."

When she added that, in effect, she was glad she did not have to make a decision on the matter, I asked if she ever had thought what would happen if one night there were a knock on her door and . . .

"A house search?" she interrupted.

No. A Jew seeking help.

"I do not know. I must tell you honestly. I do not want to say something untrue. There's no point. From my sense of things today and from my point of view today, [whether I] could look you in the face and say I would have taken her in, that I don't know." She added, "one was happy" not to face such questions.

She did think about them. That is because she grew up in Berlin with a lot of Jews, knew something about the Jewish religion, and "occupied myself with Jewish books." And "of course one had a lot of sympathy. These were human beings whom one knew and valued." But early in the Third

---

1. Her guess, or information, proved right. In 1936, Hitler decreed that women could not become judges or lawyers anymore. Barbara Beuys, *Familienleben in Deutschland* (Family life in Germany) (Reinbek bei Hamburg: Rowohlt, 1984), 479.

Reich, she said, they were not considered in danger, because Hitler was not considered strong. People she knew spoke of his "ruining the economy. That it will come to a dead end. That he can't manage it. We were still full of hope that such a regime won't last."

In 1934, the affianced couple began planning their new home in preparation for their wedding that July, and Adolf Hitler began planning the Roehm Putsch in preparation for his consolidation of power that June. The two events merged.

"Our furniture was being readied by a master carpenter in a carpentry shop in Berlin." He was "a younger man whom I liked a lot" and "who had a 'sympatisch' way about him." The couple had paid the first half of the cost of the furniture when the Roehm Putsch took place. In apparent coincidence to the timing, "my father said, 'Better check on the furniture. I have the feeling his shop is about to go broke.' . . . And we went to the store and he walked up to us in a black SS uniform. We didn't know it before. And told us that he had not slept for three nights, but belonged to a shooting commando in a suburb of Lichterfelde where a cadet place had been. That he told us. He was a hundred percent Nazi and SS man." She continued. "Half was paid. How should we now behave? I never *had* to set foot in the shop again, thank God. But do not ask me how we got out of there."

Pressed on what she had said, she replied, "Nothing at all. What should we say? We spoke about furniture. That it could be delivered. And as quickly as possible ended the conversation." She added, "We were indeed cowardly. Nicht? I mean, he certainly saw the horror in our faces, but we said nothing. What should we say? One was cowardly. And that . . . I was now happy my husband was divorced, that we could marry. I was somehow not suited to resistance."

The Ottings married when she was twenty-six and he thirty-nine. The first year of marriage was, she wrote, "a very nice and carefree time." Frau Otting accompanied her husband on business to Scandinavia and the Balkans. "I learned very, very much from him. First of all, he came from Hamburg. That's not Prussia, nicht? That's a big difference." In their travels, she "gained a wider horizon. But I concerned myself too little with real politics."

At home in Berlin, the Ottings had a loving and "relatively withdrawn" life. He was not interested in her friends, in part because they were much younger than he. And former male friends were especially not welcome. "My husband couldn't stand them." He also traveled without her, sometimes for months. Herr Otting was a salesman and later deputy division director within Europe for "one of biggest firms that distributed medicine." Frau Otting also called it a chemical firm that grew during the Third Reich and resumed business in West Germany after the war, but she refused to name it, or say why. I asked if it had manufactured gas. She said no, and that it was not IG Farben.

While Herr Otting traveled, she stayed home, often sick. "I was in pain a lot for several years." (She had problems involving her abdomen and reproductive organs.) To occupy herself, she saw women friends and read about art history.

When the Ottings were together, they were able to use their frequent separations and her health problems to keep the Nazis out of their private lives. "We always had good excuses." She added, "Well, for me it was somehow not acceptable. Exactly the same as how the Communists had not been acceptable, nicht? I have to add that. Whereby I assumed that Communists were primarily workers and I did not *know* them. Not that I, how can I say it? refused them as human beings. But that was not my milieu. I also hardly knew these sections of Berlin. Not to underrate them, but one did not get together with them a lot. That was the negative, that one did not concern oneself with it."

On some level, Frau Otting also may have been deceiving herself about the impact of the Third Reich on her own "milieu," or may have forgotten it. During our first visit, she said the impact "happened so gradually." Shortly afterward, however, she discovered back issues of her Düsseldorf school yearbook ranging from 1930, just after she had left, to 1934. "With shock [I] ascertained how between '30 and '34 the content of the school in this yearbook had changed completely. It unnerved me so much." The 1930 references were "general, progressive." The 1934 ones were "completely in the direction of National Socialist education. The Abitur themes, the tests, having the 'luck' to go to a National Socialist vacation home, one of the graduates giving up her studies to be active in BdM."

Her husband seemed to have been more alert. "He was the first who really opened my eyes" about the quickening connection between big industry and National Socialism. "He was not a Nazi." She said few of the company's leading people were. In fact, of the many sales representatives in other countries, "most in the Balkan countries were Jews. And now comes something very interesting." It was that "this large company" kept its Jewish sales representatives until 1939, "in spite of National Socialism." She added, "I say that intentionally, to point out the complications of the relationships."

They got more "complicated." Not only were the Ottings "very friendly with a large percentage of these [Jewish] representatives and their families," who often came to Nazi Germany on business (and seem to have been the cornerstone of the Ottings' circumscribed social life), the directors of the unnamed company thought highly of them, too. In fact, when in 1939 the Nazi regime ordered the company to fire them, the company did something else first. It "officially said farewell to them" by holding a formal dinner "at a large restaurant, a very good restaurant, here in Berlin."

Midway through the Third Reich, Liselotte Otting had an operation (by a woman doctor who figured in her life later) that enabled her to become pregnant. The aunt who had been married to the Jewish churchgoer reproached her, asking, "How can one have a child in these times?" But, said Frau Otting, "it was my most fervent wish." (The aunt was killed in a massive bombing attack in Berlin in November 1943.) While Frau Otting was pregnant, German Jews went through "Kristallnacht." She, then living near the fancy Grunewald section of western Berlin, did not witness it, but saw some of the damaged stores later. More Jewish friends in her parents' "circle" finally began emigrating. "And on the same floor next to us lived a Jewish woman by herself. She made sure that her daughter [about fourteen years old] got out. It cost her a lot of money. And we still got together with her."

Frau Otting gave birth to her own daughter in February 1939. "Was the most beautiful time, the first weeks after my daughter was born." That summer, Herr Otting went to a spa for a "cure" for a heart problem, and Frau Otting and the baby went with him. "I had given the Jewish woman the key, to water the plants. And he reproached me. 'How can you do that? They'll hear it downstairs and they'll ask who had the key to the apartment.' Because he understood the significance more, nicht? That was beginning to get dangerous." She called her action "foolhardy, of course. Whom in the house could one trust?" She added, "One did not want somehow to fall directly into the hands of the Gestapo."

Letting a Jewish woman water plants would have been enough?

"That would have been enough. I did not completely grasp it, either. I did not want to believe the danger. You know, I did it, also with the Jewish woman, a little out of opposition. Or we let books by Thomas Mann, Heinrich Mann, Lion Feuchtwanger stay in the bookshelves. And of course, we were never searched by the SS or the SA, but Party members did come to us, about the blackout or something, and there were [the books] openly in the shelves." She added, "To me, that was great literature. And I simply could not comprehend, although I knew the books had been burned, I could not believe that is a crime." She put her relationship with the Jewish neighbor in the same context. "To me, that was a good human being." The women continued a neighborly relationship. It led to another incident the next summer.

By then, the war had begun, as had the first deportations of Jews from Germany. Relationships between Jews and Germans were ever more verboten. From Frau Otting's point of view, however, "I always felt so sovereign. I can do what I want. I sometimes didn't see the danger completely. My daughter . . . was already walking. And we [Frau Otting and her neighbor] were having a conversation and the entrance doors to the apartments were open." Frau Otting's daughter ran into the Jewish woman's apartment and closed the door, which locked it. "Now we had to get a man who could open it. The little one was inside. And she was a Jew. But I didn't think about it." Herr Otting did. He reproached his wife again.

Shortly afterward (probably unrelated to the incident), the neighbor got a notice to move. "One did not speak about it in the house, nicht?" Then "she cleaned out her apartment and gave my daughter a little coffee cup as a present."

Did the women have a regular goodbye?

"Ja," said Frau Otting, softly. "Ja. She rang our bell once more and said goodbye. And I had a servant there, and in front of her, we said goodbye." The woman "did not come in the apartment anymore, but was outside the door."

Did she say why she was moving?

"One knew why. She didn't have to explain."

What did Frau Otting say?

"That I was terrible sorry, and that I hoped she somehow would survive." At another recollection of the meeting, she said, "That was an awful feeling. Nicht? But one could do nothing more about it." Her inhalation is audible on the tape. The woman was "very depressed. But I mean, we did not always assume that all the Jews would be obliterated. Nicht? She then got a room, and had to do forced labor." Leaving Germany was out of the question. "She had no money. She could only get her daughter out. We were there for that. Her daughter . . . was taken by relatives to South America."

Had the woman asked the Ottings for financial help?

"We wouldn't have had it. If we had wanted to. We didn't have it. My husband did not earn that much." The cost was "at least five [to] eight thousand marks," she said. "And later this Jew, she had to wear an armband. I saw her only once at a bus stop. But we didn't talk with each other. We only looked into each other's eyes."

Because of the danger?

"Ja. If I had talked to her, I was at the stop with a lot of people, I would have been arrested. One was not allowed to [speak to Jews publicly]." Frau Otting, who spoke of the woman both times we met, said that at the bus stop the woman "only shook her head. I would have liked most to go up to her, but I couldn't do that either. She had the, uh, the star, nicht? The Jewish star."

Did Frau Otting believe the woman survived?

"She did not survive. She did not survive."

The woman was not the only Holocaust victim Frau Otting knew personally. Another was "an older gentleman," a Jewish banker whose assets the Nazis had taken, and whom her father then employed privately. "Until"—she paused—"the National Socialists came to him and said, 'Listen, that will not do. You cannot do that any longer. Or we have to punish you.' Well. Then he had to let him go. And I believe a short time thereafter, he had no more money, and didn't get out, and they probably picked him up." She again inhaled slowly through her nostrils.

And about 1940, the family learned that their family doctor, "who never hurt a human being" and who was a childhood friend of Frau Otting's Jewish uncle, had been taken to Buchenwald. "After two days, he ran into an electrified fence. We heard that later." The aunt had found out.

Frau Otting also learned about deportations of strangers. "In the street near us was [another] street, a little on the edge. That Jews, always about five in the morning . . . Then were already taken away. They came to these synagogues, were taken away." Everything happened at night, she said. "We never saw anything." But it got talked around? "Ja. Of course."

In 1940 she became pregnant with her second child. "He was not exactly a 'wish child' to me. One was happy that another child was on the way, but one was also afraid. For the air raid attacks did begin in '41." She gave birth to the boy in January of 1941 in a hospital, where she luckily kept her fears to herself. "When I was back home again, someone . . . in one of the nearby houses told me that some other woman in the area also had a son and said, 'Yet more cannon fodder,' and she never even made it home." The woman was arrested in the hospital. Frau Otting, who told this story twice, too, paused after one telling and said, "From then on, one was very quiet."

She might not have said much, but she listened. She learned things from "whisper propaganda" during the two- to three-times-a-night bombing raids. With each warning siren, she would take the children down four flights of stairs, around the corner, and into the air raid shelter. Along the way, "in the street one heard, where a Jewish family lived, 'Did you hear? *They* were picked up in the night,' or '*They* were picked up.'" The "whisper propaganda" was also spread by women standing in line to shop. Information was spoken "carefully, often without any tone," so as not to give away the sentiments of the speaker.

In a letter, Frau Otting described herself during the Third Reich as "not only an observer but a participant, even if only a mosaic stone."

In those same years, Herr Otting continued his business travels. (Because of his age and heart condition, he was not drafted.) He went to Poland and Latvia and did not tell her much, she said. Did she know he was not telling her what he knew? "Nein. Nein," she said. "A great openness really ruled between us. We did talk, within four walls, about problems, also about Jewish problems and the Jewish question, and so on. But he didn't tell me everything. That he could not."

When I suggested he must have known a lot, like about camps, she interrupted. "He did know more, but I now had the little children. . . ." She said that after the war she found a report he had written in a "not pro-Nazi, but careful" way regarding German-occupied territories. From what she read, she learned he knew more about what the Third Reich was doing than he had told her. About concentration camps? That, too. When he was home, he did talk about their foreign Jewish friends (all of whom emigrated, she said) and about the war, which he felt Germany could not win. But he did not talk about extermination. Later, he was not able to talk about anything.

In August of 1943, as the bombing of Berlin intensified, Frau Otting and her children were evacuated from the city. They first went to a young woman, a former employee whom the Ottings had supported "in a private matter" that "was very unpleasant, that her parents did not know about." Later, through a friend whose husband was a "very Nazi" judge, Frau Otting and the children found shelter in a small hotel near Breslau in Silesia and stayed there up to January of 1945. Herr Otting, often in Romania on whatever company business, visited twice. Frau Otting and a few other mothers in her situation spent part of each day working in a vegetable cannery that also was owned by the hotel owners, both Nazi Party members. One day, the wife was "furious" after hearing that in a concentration camp nearby, people "were falling like flies. That the human beings had hardly anything to eat. And that they collapsed in the latrine and so on." The woman also said her husband "was not to know she told us that."

While Frau Otting was in the countryside, her parents were home in Potsdam, one floor below the family of Major General Henning von Tresckow, a conspirator in the June 1944 plot to kill Hitler. (When he learned that Hitler survived, von Tresckow reportedly became afraid the Nazis would be able to torture the names of coconspirators out of him, and committed suicide.) "Frau von Tresckow, when it was out in the open with her husband, came to my parents and telephoned from there, because her telephone was tapped. She was then arrested, too."

And in Romania, so was Herr Otting. Romanians took him and other German civilians prisoner for no apparent reason except that they could. Six weeks later, Frau Otting heard, via a message he sent through Sweden, that he was alive.

Then, one morning before dawn the next January—it was 1945—she and the other residents of the hotel were told they would be evacuated back toward western Germany in three hours. Among the many details of the subsequent harrowing journey that Frau Otting recalled was of being crammed on a farm wagon and seeing, through the snow and ice, that "traveling past us was a sleigh with about eight children and a dead mother. I will never forget it."

After three days, Frau Otting and her children reached the town of Liegnitz, now part of Poland. She left her two suitcases at someone's house for safekeeping, managed to get herself and her children on a train, and arrived in Potsdam that night. She did not get the reception she expected; her father was "furious" she had left her luggage behind. "And sent me back again, to Liegnitz." She went back alone, as ordered.

After the chaos and turmoil that entailed, she managed to reboard a train in Liegnitz only by climbing through a window. On the trip back to

Potsdam, "the only thing talked about was the lost war and what insanity it was. It was said *openly*." The surprise was still in her voice.

The drama of insanity continued. At her father's orders, Frau Otting and her children again left Potsdam, this time for the relative safety of Schleswig-Holstein in northern Germany. There, "we were taken care of so horribly and were treated like refugees, basically spat upon, and 'What do you want here?' and so on. And on the eleventh of March, 1945, I got an attack of agoraphobia [Platzangst], took my children, took my luggage, and went back to Potsdam."

Again, her father was furious, but this time "rightly so." Two days after her arrival in mid-April came the major bombing attack on Potsdam. "It ended at our street. Bombs fell on the street next to us." She said that while she and her family were in one air raid shelter, the ceiling collapsed in the adjoining one and twenty people died. Her father and a servant girl, who had been in the house, came outside and "saw only the mountain of rubble. My father thought we were dead. And then we came out." Her daughter, then six years old, still remembers it, she said. Among the people looking at the dead being carried out was an SS man. "And then he said, 'So? You're not yet all dead?'" She stopped speaking for a moment.

In the following weeks, in Frau Otting's telling, much effort was made to get shelter, and just as much to get family furniture stored or moved. She praised her parents' intrepidity and (as East Germans often did) the behavior of the new Soviet occupiers. She portrayed them as men who tried to be fair, who punished miscreant fellow Soviets, and who shared their bread.

Did the women fear being ra . . .

She broke in, "Nein, nein. They then . . ." and changed the subject. It came up again during our second meeting, which took place in my West Berlin hotel. (As a senior citizen, Frau Otting was allowed some freedom of movement.) Again she praised the behavior of Soviet troops, while again noting the possibility of individual drunken misdeeds by troops who were not always "the elite." I said, to get the record straight, so, she knew of no woman who said . . .

Frau Otting broke in, "I myself was raped." It was as if she had ended my sentence. "I'll tell you openly," she said. But "please turn off the tape recorder." I did.

In January of 1946, Frau Otting learned via another note that her husband was alive, in a Romanian detainment camp. For food, he had "too much to die, too little to live," as the expression went. But he expected to be released that spring. In the meantime, she had found his writings regarding what the Third Reich was doing abroad, and planned to ask him about it.

He was indeed released in the spring, but while he was on a freight train heading to Germany, at the Romanian-Hungarian border, he had a severe stroke. Only when he arrived in Berlin ten days later was he given medical attention. His right side was paralyzed and his speech all but gone. Frau Otting never found out what he had done, or known.

The information locked in her husband's mind may have been the least of Frau Otting's concerns. Her home and her parents' home were destroyed. Her husband's company could not help in any way, and neither could he; at first, he was not even able to sit up. By Christmas, she had got him to walk a couple of steps, but he began to have epileptic attacks. The family lived in a furnished two-room sublet in the Soviet zone. By then, the once-privileged daughter realized she was in charge. "And *now* my conscience began. I had no degree. I had stopped my studies. I had no profession. I was nothing. And now had to support my family. Do not ask me what kinds of reproaches I made, and thought, now you have to be a charwoman."

The first year after the war, "I was completely lethargic, I would say. Not that the war was lost, but what we had done. By degrees, we also had to see the films about concentration camps." Germans were ordered to see them, "but I also wanted to. I wanted to see, I wanted to know." The sights in the films and on the streets of destroyed Berlin, and in her own home, made her "pretty desperate," she said. "I was completely . . . I didn't get my period for three-quarters of a year. I was completely . . . infuriated."

The doctor who had operated on her, making her able to bear children, told her that the Soviets were setting up a new organization meant to help women and children, and asked if she would like a paid job working for it. "I threw my arms around her neck." Frau Otting said she later tried to return to her old neighborhood in West Berlin, but the British occupiers told her that because she had lived in a Soviet sector, she could not. In the meantime, she found she liked her new job and the sense she was doing good. And so she remained in the East.

In our two face-to-face meetings, we had spoken a lot about the East-West chasm, and the travel restrictions, both of which she defended, or seemed to defend, while also admitting that she herself would let the young people travel. (Asked if she agreed with the restrictions, she had said, "I *must* agree.") The day the Berlin Wall came down, I called her. With much excitement in her voice, she said guess where her children were that very hour, then said, "In *West* Berlin!"

Almost two years later, still living in the east, but a citizen of the west, she wrote at length about long and awful physical problems she was having following a fall, of being hospitalized for three months, of now having to pay for nursing help at home, which had been free, and of not being able to afford going to the movies anymore. She sounded rather dismal politically, too. She thought that the good of East Germany, especially in terms of her long interests in women's rights and children's welfare, was being dismissed. And she implied the chasm was still there. "Are we one Germany? Nein."

Frauen

By the next fall, 1992, she wrote that she was still for the unification, but said not everything in the old system was bad, especially for women and children, and that she was not reproaching herself for her conduct "in the Nazi time, or now, either." She added that now, like then, she tried to conduct herself properly.

Sometime after the fall of Nazi Germany and before the fall of the Soviet Union, dozens of older German women began taking an annual sentimental journey "home." Their destination, the spa town of Bad Pyrmont, lies about fifty miles south of Hanover and about five hundred miles west of where they rather would have been—their old homeland of East Prussia. But the Soviets kept it off limits to the yearning exiles.

The women made the pilgrimage to Bad Pyrmont not to relax in the spa's celebrated soothing baths and hot springs but to immerse themselves in the supercharged and recycled air of East Prussian history. They met, ate, and slept in a large East Prussian Federation Society Home a walk away from the Bad Pyrmont baths. And they met, ate, and presumably dreamed East Prussia. Days and evenings were filled with lectures, reminiscences, outrage, and sentimentality. Each of the twenty-five or so bedrooms was dedicated to and decorated with drawings and photographs of a different East Prussian town, which was identified by a small plaque on the bedroom door. A gentle knock on my door came from a woman asking to "visit" her old hometown.

The most memorably terrible event in all these women's lives had to have been leaving East Prussia, or, rather, fleeing it. Apart from the emotional toll, there was no question that the physical circumstances of the leave-takings were dreadful. The early months of 1945 were bitterly cold. And departure dates were geared not to a break in the weather but to stubborn or vindictive or stupid local Nazi officials who often refused to grant people permission to leave until virtually the last minute. Anyone who tried to go earlier

Frau Mathilde Mundt

The History Lesson

might be caught and accused of "defeatism." Defeatism was tantamount to treason. And treason was tantamount to death.

With permission to flee coming so late, three or more generations fled all the more desperately, for hundreds of miles if they made it, by way of rutted roads soon clogged with overloaded carts, wagons, dead horses, and dead people. According to numerous accounts, within days just about everyone was exhausted, cold, and hungry. The well-shod and furred aristocrats, frantically if stylishly fleeing from castle to castle, grateful for their remaining servant and the remaining vintages of the baron, had it better, of course, as they always did. But everyone was fearful. For everyone was fleeing the common enemy that endless Nazi propaganda had warned about: vengeful and "subhuman" soldiers of the Red Army.

As twelve years of Nazi rule drew to a freezing and fiery close, with many Russian soldiers indeed treating the kin of their former occupiers with concomitant mercilessness, many eastern Germans were convinced the blame for their ignoble exodus lay squarely in Moscow.

Among the people who had to flee the farthest were the East Prussians, people sometimes considered more nationalistically German simply because they lived the farthest from "real" Germany. Now, with more than four decades to think, did they still believe the source of their misery and bitter nostalgia was the Russians, rather than, say, other Germans? What would these women have to say about the events that led to their forever painful debacle of departure? The last evening of the retreat I attended featured a tape recording of an East Prussian poet and a reading of an East Prussian tragedy—a woman who committed suicide rather than confide in fellow East Prussians about what Red Army soldiers had done to her. As a finale to the program, we heard a tape recording of bells from an East Prussian church.

While a roomful of eyes was being dried, I was invited to say my piece. Nervous at this first address in German to a large group, and one in anguish, I begged pardon for any grammatical mistakes I would make and said I was interested in hearing what the women recalled from the 1930s to the end of the war. I knew to avoid incendiary nouns, such as "Nazi" and "Jew." About seven women, far fewer than I had anticipated given their friendly behavior throughout the day, followed me to the adjoining library. The reason for the sparse attendance soon became clear. It was the participation of one Frau Mundt.

She was thick of body, reddish-haired and red-faced, with a pugnacious bulldoglike bearing augmented by glasses that rode low on her nose. I had not noticed her until earlier that evening and then had felt sympathy, for she seemed the picture of a rough man, ill-suited to be a female in a country or world that mostly wanted its females feminine. I knew nothing whatever about her. She (rather leading the way), I, and the others seated

84

ourselves at the library's large table. The women talked awhile about the aftermath of World War I. Then Frau Mundt raised her voice.

"Seven million unemployed in Germany, right?"

She was referring to the unemployment statistics when Hitler took power. Another woman responded, "Well, six, no?"[1]

Frau Mundt said perhaps she should give me a history lesson.

No sooner had she spoken those words than some chairs began to scrape and their occupants to leave. Within minutes, the potential interviewees numbered only three, including Frau Mundt. By the time I realized her presence had caused and was causing the others' absence, I knew my plan of interviewing each remaining woman in turn was fading. Although tempted to orchestrate some order, or cut the session short and find a larger sampling of East Prussian women I had traveled a good distance to see, I opted to let Frau Mundt say whatever she wanted. By then I knew that I had happened upon someone whose equal I probably would not meet again, at least in such an unfiltered, unrefined state. The decision proved journalistically correct, but emotionally wrenching. Frau Mathilde Mundt was an out-and-out hater of Jews.

Frau Mundt is, or was, a retired schoolteacher. What she taught, she did not say and I did not care to ask or contemplate. She was born in 1923, not in East Prussia at all, but in northwestern Germany, in the town of Leer, near the Dutch border. She moved to East Prussia during the war, possibly having been evacuated there to escape the bombing. One more background fact: Mathilde Mundt is a pseudonym, the result of my promise to her. If I used her real name, she said with a loud laugh, the Jews would come and get her.

We had gathered in the library about 8:30 in the evening. By about 9:00, Frau Mundt's history lesson began. "In 1919, after the First World War," she was saying, "was this Diktat of Versailles." With one word, her cards were on the table. The correct term is, of course, the Treaty [*Vertrag* in German] of Versailles. Nazis (among others) used *Diktat* instead as a term of loathing to imply its "dictated" imposition.

"Then, in 1922, came this huge inflation," she continued. "Every hour, one had to pay out the money one earned that day. Billions, up to trillions. I still have some of the notes in a box. The mother quickly had to go buy a half-loaf of bread or something. The wash from the clotheslines was stolen. Human beings were so poor. And many were killed, just for someone to get a few marks for food.

"Then, gradually, the controls. But no human being had money. No human being had work. The produce stores went bankrupt. The factories

---

1. Six is closer to official statistics.

went bankrupt. In the big cities, the hunger was so great and then the diseases and who knows what else. The human beings had nothing with which they could defend themselves. We were a Volk doomed to destruction."

When the other remaining women agreed it was a very unhappy time, Frau Mundt shouted over them. "IN BERLIN, IN BERLIN, it was *so* bad, one of my girlfriends, her husband has now died, the man told us so often, there came the Jews."

She gestured to me. "You must know everything, no? They came from the east. And they had such beards, and were greasy, yes?" She ran her hands down her cheeks, as if to demonstrate the look of a greasy face. "They wore a sort of knapsack, and a black hat, and these black beards. To fear. And *slapdash*, completely filthy and greasy [schludrig, ganz dreckig und schmierig] because they did not have even hygienic principles."

An attractive woman, dark-skinned and finely coiffed, cleared her throat. From such a cultured-looking woman, I expected a few well-chosen words of dissent. She said, "It was the eastern Jews, no?"

"The eastern Jews," echoed Frau Mundt, before raising her voice. "And what do you think, a quarter of a year later? They walked around in patent leather shoes, in wonderful suits, and soon they owned a *whole* housing area. They exploited the need of the human beings and bought *everything* for very little money."

"Ja," said the other woman, who later followed Frau Mundt's lead in requesting a pseudonym. She shall be Frau Folgen.

Frau Mundt continued, "And the human beings to whom the houses belonged, or farms or factories, they took their lives, out of despair."

"Good that you explain it," said Frau Folgen.

"This situation was the rule in Vienna, too," said Frau Mundt, rolling even more vigorously with an ally. "And now comes Adolf Hitler. He was in the war, his parents had died, and he was alone, unmarried, a young man."

The other women, including a few who soon left, broke into a free-for-all discussion that Hitler was not so young, that his sister Paula kept house for him, that he was very religious, and that he worked in construction because he did not have any education.

Having recovered somewhat from the first blows of Frau Mundt's club, I broke in to ask if we could step backward and talk about how the eastern Jews bought whole housing areas if the money itself was practically worthless.

Frau Folgen answered, "They all had a little money."

Frau Mundt sighed. "You must understand it this way. In America it's exactly the same. At the banks, at the stock markets, at the diamond exchange, sit the Jews today. Also in Brussels. And the largest diamond exchange in the world is in Jerusalem. They had connections with one another. And it was, ah, Nathan So-and-So wants to buy this entire housing complex and then the mutual friend helped him. And then suddenly they had a whole armful of money and counted . . ."

Did she mean the money came from diamonds?

She spoke as if to a very slow learner. "Nein. Banking connections. You must understand it this way. All these banks had Jews at the top. The top justices in the Justice Department were Jews. If a German went to court with a livestock trader who was a Jew, who had cheated him, then the German lost and the Jew won. That I can actually report to you from one family. Now, Hitler was in Vienna and saw that the Jews moved ahead so fast, without working. Through speculation. And therefore this idea came to him. 'The Jews are our misfortune,' he said. It came from that. One must recognize the roots. Otherwise, one can't report it."

From around the table came a few mumbled assertions that wares sold at Jewish stores had been less expensive. Frau Mundt asserted that Germany's big department stores are "again Jewish." She named several, then said they're "again making German stores kaputt." At that, the other woman disagreed more forcefully, while debating which department stores are and are not Jewish.

"AND NOW TO CONTINUE," blared Frau Mundt, as the others fell silent. "[In] 1930, the failure of the banks. All of a sudden, all credits due. No human being had money. All had to leave hearth and home. Everything taken away. Every day, so and so many human beings had to go to the poverty board." She looked at me. "Do you know what that means? 'I own nothing more.' Now came the unemployed. For seven marks, seven marks a week. Families with two children, ten children and more, seven marks."

Her reference to children caused the others to begin talking excitedly about how large many East Prussian families were. After hearing example after example, Frau Mundt had heard enough. "No money, no work, no bread," she broke in. "As for us, we begged, very horribly, begged. We had nothing. And then came 1931." Her voice lifted, as if describing a heavenly apparition. "At the election, one heard for the first time about the ruling order that made it extremely bad for us. My parents cried a lot. We were defenseless among ourselves, among our neighbors, as a family in Germany. In the Rhineland were the occupying troops, the French, the Belgians. They ran with whips along the sidewalks and the Germans had to get off or be whipped off. Such was the way after the First World War, no?

"Now came 1932. My mother and father took the motorcycle, my mother on the seat in the back, and went and heard Adolf Hitler in a great speech. The next morning they told us what he had for goals, for concepts, how he wanted to be on the side of the unemployed. My mother wept for joy. And my parents prayed dear God would give this man all the votes so that we could get out of need. There was no one else who promised that and who had the concept. And then came '33 and he was elected. . . ."

The others could keep still no longer. They interrupted about Hitler's not having had enough votes to win on his own, that Field Marshal von Hindenburg helped him to power, and about how the election really went, until then Frau Mundt could keep still no longer.

"NOW WE MUST GO FARTHER," she shouted. "He introduced this concept." It was the male and female Hitler Youth organizations. She recited their entire structure. "In 1933," she continued, "I was ten years old and our entire class, with the exception of one girl, decided to be in BdM. Twice a week in the afternoons we got together for activities. There was singing, storytelling, handiwork. We did sports, dancing, folk dancing, and we went to the movies and saw films, at the time cultural films, ja? And I must say, I did not regret that time."

"That is what everyone says," commented Frau Folgen. "But BdM girls did not have the best reputations. . . ."

The free-for-all that ensued was marked by Frau Mundt's strenuous objection to Frau Folgen's remark. It ended when another voice suddenly spoke up. A quiet woman, clad in a tidy dirndl of East Prussian design (she shall be Frau Schmidt), said softly, "My father lost his job as mayor of our village because he would not join the Nazi Party. He said he would obey only God, not Adolf Hitler."

Frau Mundt paid her no mind. "I must say, as the war neared, we were also put into action to help older people, to help on farms, in our free time." (By Nazi law, one must add.) "And things we learned at home were strengthened. When one sat on a train or a bus, if there were old people one stood up. One showed the old people respect. Also, everyone went to church together. That was also the case with us. Nicely, in uniforms, everything clean, nicht? Ja.

"As for my parents, we had a store [it supplied farm machinery] which went very poorly. In '33, when the farms in part were expropriated, there came an order for debt exemption. The farmers who still were extremely weak, that is, financially, no longer had to leave their farms. They received long-term loans and could remain on the soil. That is the truth. And things got better for the farmers, then better for us. And what WE COULD NOT HAVE FORESEEN . . ." Her voice, having again risen, paused in expectation of a great announcement, catching the others' sometimes wandering attention. "In 1935, my father bought his first car."

The others emitted less-than-enthusiastic murmurs.

"Also," said Frau Mundt, "the laws were made so strict, that whoever robbed will be shot. Nobody took anything that belonged to anyone else."

The remark went unchallenged.

"There was someone near us, a Communist," she continued. "Nothing to do with being a Communist, but he hit his wife, hit his children, broke everything in the house. Today it would be said he was sent to a concentration camp because he was a Communist. No. Concentration camps were then called work camps. He was sent to one and had to work, and what he would have been paid, his wife got. She said, 'I don't even want him again.' She got a new kitchen, and raised the children.

"Concentration camps at that time were work camps, for drinkers, and sluggards, and for thieves, and so on. Whoever broke the law more severely went to prison and whoever murdered went to the penitentiary. And when it was proven, then it was the death penalty. Then gradually, in 1938 . . .'"

The misinformation was especially egregious, but the only interruption came from Frau Folgen, about another matter. "Don't forget about taking over areas, like the Rhineland," she said.

Frau Mundt amiably complied. "Ja. We were allowed only one hundred thousand soldiers. They were always traded, however, so there were always one hundred thousand soldiers in uniform. They were trained quickly and sent back home. They also had had no work at all, and therefore were happy that at least they had clothes, provisions, a bed, and something to eat. And also athletics." Before continuing, she reiterated the scene of Germans being whipped off the sidewalks. "Suddenly, our soldiers march in," she said. "They were received with flowers. The others went away, or already were away, and ours marched in. Neither France nor Belgium nor England set up a cry against it. They let it happen. It started in Czechoslovakia. That was the first, no?"

"Don't forget about the Saar," said Frau Folgen. "*That* was before Czechoslovakia."

Mention of the Saar, another disputed French-German area (whose population in 1935 voted to return to German rule), immediately roused Frau Mundt to break into song, Frau Folgen catching up within a second.

Deutsch ist die Saar.
Deutsch immer da.
Und Deutsch ist unser Fluss und Strand
Und ewig Deutsch mein Heimatland.
Mein Heimatland,
Mein Heimatland

[German is the Saar.
German always there.
And German is our river and beach
And my homeland is eternally German.
My homeland,
My homeland.]

Both women remembered every word and every note, including a trill in the third syllable of the second "Heimatland."

Delighted with themselves, they followed their recital with an enthu-

89

siastic recollection of the Nazis' Strength through Joy [Kraft durch Freude] program, which set up extensive and inexpensive trips for low-income Germans. That is, for low-income "Aryans."

"The German workers could now take vacations," said Frau Mundt, turning to me. "Ships were built. This great ship *Wilhelm Gustloff,* which was bringing refugees from East Prussia to the west [and] was sunk by the Russians, was a Strength through Joy ship. A ship went to Montevideo, no? And what do you think, they traveled to Norway, to the fjords, and looked at the beautiful country. They traveled to Madeira and, what was it called, Tenerife, and they also traveled to England. BUT THEY WERE NOT ALLOWED to get closer than fifteen or ten kilometers to the English coast. The English workers, for whom things still were going badly, were not allowed to see how well things were going again for the German workers. That is true."

"Strength through Joy gave trips to the Volk," added Frau Folgen. "To people with many children, to the poor."

"You see," said Frau Mundt, "a worker on the land earned perhaps one hundred or two hundred marks. And he too could take such trips, they were so cheap. It was a completely wonderful privilege."

Their sanctimony did it. Everyone could take the trips? I asked.

"Everyone could take them," said Frau Mundt. "Everyone."

Jews as well?

Frau Mundt developed a hearing problem. "Please?"

Jews. They went too?

"NEIN!" broke in Frau Folgen. "They were rich enough. They didn't need it."

Frau Mundt had recovered her faculties. "They had enough money," she interrupted. "They traveled anyway, in thick fur coats. . . ."

Frau Folgen interrupted next. "The Jews were offered travel," she said. "To sell their stores and leave Germany."

Frau Mundt continued. "The Jews were given a choice. They could sell *everything,* take everything with them, whatever they wanted."

Trying to keep my voice even, I said I had read they did not want to leave because they considered themselves German. That, for instance, they spoke German.

Frau Mundt replied as if to an exceptionally slow student. "Ja. But they were multilingual."

The women moved to the deadlier issue of Jewish Germans who did not take advantage of the Reich's travel opportunities.

"Nothing happened to them for a long time," said Frau Mundt. "It was only eventually in the end, when . . ."

"Afterward, when there was a little conspiring, na?" interrupted Frau Folgen.

"Ja. Ja, ja."

"Well," continued Frau Folgen, "I know that in the house where our office was, was a Dr. Hirsch. He was a physician. He remained completely undisturbed. Afterward, he had to wear the sign. It made me feel bad, that man."

"Ja," said Frau Mundt.

"Ja," echoed Frau Folgen. "But I do not think that he, he somewhere . . ."

"Ach, nonsense," said Frau Mundt.

Frau Schmidt spoke up. "We didn't do anything."

"Nein," said Frau Mundt.

"Merely, we shopped in the stores," said Frau Schmidt. "I can . . ." A tale of shopping, presumably in Jewish stores, did not warrant attention in the opinion of Frau Folgen, who spoke over Frau Schmidt. "This man was a doctor and furthermore owned a large brick-making factory. Rich."

Frau Mundt and Frau Schmidt agreed he must have been. The theme was a winner, and Frau Folgen ran with it. "All of them rich," she said, laughing. "I hardly knew poor Jews."

Frau Mundt held up her hands, her fingers spread wide. "The thick rings here, the diamonds," she said. To make her point more visible, she stood up, and with imaginarily ring-encrusted hands, imitated someone swaggering down the street with a walking stick.

"Gold! Gold!" cried other voices.

Frau Mundt resumed her seat. "They had a lot of gold. Jews were rich. I sometimes looked at them this way." She moved her eyes wider as if confirming the value of what she saw. "Ja," she concluded.

Ten minutes later, the subject had turned from Rich Jew to Honest German.

"Everyone was honest," said Frau Mundt. "Above all, youth was raised to be honest. Clean and honest. And athletic."

"And orderly," said Frau Folgen.

"THIS ORDERLINESS!" shouted Frau Mundt. "At NIGHT we could leave all doors unlocked. No one would come inside. One could let the wash hang on the line. One could leave the car on the street with the key inside. No human being came and stole it or made it kaputt. Nothing."

Was there a lot of obedience?

Frau Mundt missed my edge. "Ja. The children were obedient in the *school*, were obedient to their *parents*. For as long as I went to school, there was singing, but also prayer. It was not forbidden. That's what is said today, but it is not true. One must tell the truth. Not that I was so infatuated by it." She added, "Also, you can't blame us that in that time we felt happy. One can't consider that bad. Parents had work, money, not in superabundance. Then came a law prohibiting 'the effortless ones' from earning money. And that had to do with the Jews."

Effortless ones? I pretended not to know the phrase.

"Haggling business . . ." started Frau Folgen.

"Ja," said Frau Mundt. "Speculation, haggling, and swindling." She leaned forward and asked, with soft-voiced concern, "Do you know what that is?"

As I nodded, Frau Mundt and Frau Folgen broke into a spoken duet of Nazi terminology: "Auf unrechtmässiger Weise [By unlawful means]."

"That was not allowed," continued Frau Mundt. "And through the same means, unemployment was banned. In other words, three thousand marks was the highest that one man, or a family, could earn. No more. Then you'd have to give the work to others. That was a very good law. And so it was a very social matter too."

Frau Folgen looked inspired. "This expression, National Socialism. National, in the highest degree. And Socialism, also."

"Today, that is despised," said Frau Mundt. "I saw the Olympic Games in Los Angeles and how nationalistically you Americans presented yourselves. In 1936, the Olympics were here and Leni Riefenstahl made the first color film in the whole world about them. And we are not now allowed to see it. That is *extremely* sad. There we were, so enthusiastic about our nationalism. Is that not a crime? We were national and social. Social for the human beings who worked and also for those who were helpless and sick, no?"

Launching next upon an extensive discourse about how the Nazis helped tuberculosis patients, an impatient-sounding Frau Folgen finally interrupted her. "I mean," she said, "whoever didn't follow in the tracks was taken hold of harshly."

"Ja," agreed Frau Mundt.

"Certainly. Whoever opposed the regime was consequently . . ."

"I wouldn't say 'regime,'" grumbled Frau Mundt. (*Regime* is a word associated with anti-Nazis.)

"Well, all right. Against the government."

Frau Mundt then managed to change the subject to those she liked better: orderliness, lack of crime, failings of others. "The thieves were the Poles," she said. "They did everything."

Typically for former East Prussians, the other women agreed that Poles are a bad people [ein schlimmes Volk]. A major reason for East Prussians' anti-Polish feeling is that following the Treaty of Versailles, the only land link connecting East Prussia and the rest of Germany was the land mass known as the Polish Corridor, which the Poles controlled. Whenever the Poles decided to shut the borders, the East Prussians were basically stranded, as were their agricultural exports.

Frau Mundt resumed her history lesson. "In 1938, there were negotiations in Munich. We got out of that one. Then came the entry [der Einmarsch] into the Sudetenland in Czechoslovakia, in accordance with the Munich Agreement. The Germans had been so tormented by the Czechs, like by the Poles, the Czechs having been extremely mean and even worse, after the war. They killed half a million Germans. American reporters made films about it, how Germans died along the way, German soldiers. *Horrendous*. I saw it on television once. I *cried* and prayed to God, no? We don't hear about those terrible acts. Anyway, the Sudetenland became part of Germany. Then Czechoslovakia was occupied, and Slovakia. The last piece of Czechoslovakia voluntarily became part of us. Already like a European community." Nobody disputed a fact, or a figure.

"And now it was time for the Poles. Since 1935, they had published a map reaching to the Elbe River, everything with Polish names. [The famous and phony map, meant to convince Germans that Poland planned an invasion, has been acknowledged as the work of Nazis.] And they tormented the Germans so much, forcing a very large number of Germans during a heat wave to make a long march to the other side of Warsaw. Those who couldn't keep going got shot. And they killed sixty thousand Germans. Then Hitler said on the radio one day, I heard it, 'We cannot allow that anymore.' We wanted to avoid war at all costs. But the Poles were so hateful to all the Germans there and those who lived along the border. The Poles also went to Schneider-Mühl, we had a factory there, from which we got the farm machinery. The Poles went to Schneider-Mühl daily and killed the workers who were on their way to work. We always got letters saying 'We lost twenty or twenty-four workers again this week.'"

"In peacetime, please note," said Frau Folgen.

"In peacetime," echoed Frau Mundt. "Now came the war, in '39, in August." (Later comments indicated she meant September, the correct date.) "One saw it couldn't go any farther."

What was her reaction to news that war had started?

"Extremely great alarm. Extremely great alarm. My father said it's terrible, but we must defend ourselves. And we must help the Germans there who suffer so much. That's how we saw it, that we must help. The Germans there are helpless, defenseless, no? Then came the letters from the post office, in the evening, even. Everybody mobilize there and there, whether one had been trained by the navy or to go by foot or in cars or with tanks or horses. They *all* had to go. Within a week, all the men from the village."

Frau Folgen said her husband took part in the Polish campaign. "He said they came at us with *horses*, with horses against our tanks. He said it was such stupidity [Dummheit] to use such means. They were not at all trained. What could they have pictured they would face?"

Frau Mundt was more scornful than ever. "They thought they could use their nonsense army." She stared at me. "Do you know what that is? Horses. Hop hop hop, no? And we were certainly equipped, no?"

I said I had heard that the Poles were defending themselves.

"That's a big lie," said Frau Folgen. "They thought they'd be allowed to do anything, that England and France had turned their backs. They'd never have been so fresh. . . ."

Frau Schmidt worked herself up to an announcement. "The Russian is a different human being. But the Pole is a big scoundrel [ein grosser Lump]."

"Ja," agreed Frau Mundt to the latter. "False. Malicious."

"You see the results now," interjected Frau Folgen. "The Poles got the land that had been Germany's granary. They can't even nourish *themselves*. As for what they can now produce in the way of food, they have to thank the industrious Germans who are still there and to some extent keep things going."

That East Prussia was Germany's granary [die Kornkammer Deutschland] is a common theme among former East Prussians, and the assertion that the Kornkammer fell to ruin because of lazy Poles is a common, if misleading, lament. Most farm workers in the old Kornkammer *were* Poles.[2] Asked if the situation could have to do at all with the Communist system, Frau Mundt answered, "Nein. The Pole is basically lazy."

"Lazy and very drunk," added Frau Folgen.

"The men with vodka," added Frau Mundt. "Day by day, drunk. One speaks of Polish housekeeping. When one comes into a house where there's no order . . . do you know the word *order?*"

I responded that I certainly did.

"Where everything is lying every which way and is dirty and laundry is lying around and so on," she said. "That's Polish housekeeping." (The expression *polnische Wirtschaft* was a Nazi one, too—it also can be translated as "Polish economy" or "Polish goings-on"—and the Nazis used it to depict Poland as a country in chaos.)

When I mentioned that in at least one part of the United States, Polish-American women are known as the best housekeepers and even scrub their ceilings, Frau Folgen commented, "They must have been from *central* Poland." She and the others then plunged into an animated discussion about the filth along the Polish Corridor, until Frau Schmidt, rising to say good night, delivered a gentle parting shot that squelched the topic. "Some Poles are very pious," she said, and walked out of the room.

The hour was approaching eleven. Frau Mundt, obviously not regretting any challenger's departure, resumed her role at the front of the class. "Now, where were we? Thirty-nine. On September third, there came an ultimatum from France and England. If we didn't stop everything in Poland right away and leave, we'd find ourselves at war. You see that as a declaration of war, no?

"Well, we couldn't stop in the middle of the fight. We ended the war in eighteen days. Our people who still lived could return to their houses. The Germans in the cut-off areas returned to Germany. The other area was occupied. That means we did not occupy Poland alone. We marched from this

---

2. Interview with journalist Peter von Zahn, Hamburg, August 1987.

94

side and what one may *not* forget, from the east came . . ." She cued Frau Folgen with her eyes and Frau Folgen responded.

"THE RUSSIANS!" they shouted.

"The Russians had just as much interest in Poland," said Frau Mundt. "They wanted the land. We wanted only that our human beings should suffer no longer. We wanted only the corridor again. Well," she sighed, "then it went farther. We had to go to the west. And there Hitler made a big mistake. We sat at the radio in the evening and there came the signal there'd be a special announcement by the commander of the army.

"Then came the signal, a trumpet sound, which means a halt. My father began to cry and said, 'Now we have lost the war.' What did Hitler do? He let the tanks stay where they were and let the English, who were in retreat, return to England by ship. Had he stopped them, it would have been better. The war would have been over and we would have won it. That was the biggest mistake.

"The week before the war started, in 1939," she added, "we got food ration cards. And up *until the last days* of the war, the system worked *wonderfully.* We never suffered from hunger."

As for the remaining Jewish population, "The Jews got ration cards too, certainly. But there was not so much on them and at times they had well, other things. Not what we had, no? They also had most of what we had on the ration cards. No. They had the same cards. Only they had different times to buy. They were not supposed to be together with Germans. I still know, my uncle had a cheese store in Leer. The Jews were allowed to shop on Friday evenings."

"Because Saturday is their sabbath," said Frau Folgen.

When I worked in my "thought" that their sabbath starts late Friday, Frau Mundt said, "*Before* the sabbath. Before their sabbath they were allowed to buy everything."[3]

So, why could they not shop with Germans? I asked, then corrected myself. With other Germans?

Frau Mundt sighed. "Ja. That I cannot tell you. Why not with Germans?"

No one spoke. It seemed, so far, the only question for which there was no answer.

After a long pause, Frau Folgen switched the subject to the more comfortable one of countries that turned away ships filled with German Jewish

---

3. Jewish ration cards, stamped with a *J,* were indeed very restrictive as to what might be bought and when. Picking them up at a distribution center was not without risk, either. Would-be recipients could find themselves being rounded up for transport to a concentration camp. Some Jews therefore went underground and out of the dangerous tracking system and had to figure other means of finding food.

refugees. That led to Hitler's idea for another Jewish homeland. Frau Mundt summed it up. "Hitler wanted the Jews to emigrate to Madagascar."

In 1940, the Nazis did promote solving "the Jewish problem" by making the African island a Jewish colony—under the reign of Heinrich Himmler.

Said Frau Folgen, "About killing there was absolutely . . ."

Frau Mundt interrupted more quickly than usual. "*Neiiiiiin*. He did not want to kill them." She looked at me. "Have you ever heard that?" When I answered, firmly, no, she continued, in regard to the Madagascar plan, "It is a *wonderfully* beautiful island, magnificent climate, and also a good soil, no? And the Jews perhaps would have been ready. But England and France prevented it. And in this context, at that time I always had a little package from my mother when I went to school. Sometimes bacon in it, sometimes eggs, sometimes wurst, and bread and also vegetables. For a Jewish family. The family Gans. Today, they have on, what's the biggest street? Fifth Avenue. They have a large jewelry store there. You could ask there.[4] I rode my bicycle nine miles to school in the morning. And my mother always packed the bag full and I had to deliver it to the family. Then I rang the bell. And I was not the only one. A lot of people went there."

Frau Folgen asked, "Were they nice people?"

"Ja. And once she opened the door in her bathrobe and there was nothing but such bags and little packages. They were supported, but privately, no?"

Why did Frau Mundt's mother do it? Were they friends?

"No, not at all," said Frau Mundt.

Frau Folgen stepped in to help. "From pity, no? From neighborly love. From Christian neighborly love."

In the spring of 1945, Frau Mundt managed to leave East Prussia (she did not describe how) and return to her home village and her parents to wait out the end of the war with her family. Her mind was burdened, she said, not only by the "goalless" bombings of German cities but by the "tragic number of German traitors.

"Then the war came to an end. German soldiers came to our village and wanted to defend it. We said, 'Young men, let it be. Find safety for yourselves. Look there above you and see the tanks coming.' I saw the tanks from the roof, with a telescope. And they came and [she shouted louder than ever] THEY SHOT AT EVERYTHING, THEY SHOT WHERE NO ONE WAS STANDING. They shot the house kaputt, they . . ."

---

4. Much later, I did, quite cursorily. The New York telephone operator had no listing for Gans or Ganz jewelry on Fifth Avenue.

Who? Who?

"The Americans." she said. "And the English and the Canadians. Click, click, click, click, everything through the houses, at every angle. Then the tanks stood still. My mother and I were home, in an earth bunker my father built. And father was with the others, with my brother, with my sister, with our prisoners of war, in another bunker outside the village. Then I said to mother, 'We must get out and see what they're doing,' and I went out and pshhhhhhh, one shot at me. Hands up, no? I said, 'Yes, that is good, but I have nothing, I do not shoot, I do not do anything. My mother,' I said, 'I must get the Mama, no? Yes, everything in order.' I knew more English then than I do today. But when I saw how they behaved, I did not speak another word of English. I'm not speaking with you if you behave that way.

"The first came up to me with a typewriter. I said, 'Hey, hello, what is that supposed to be?' I said, 'I thought you wanted to liberate us from Hitler, not from typewriters.' He told me to hide it in the hay, but instead I hid it between two beehives. No one came in. The bees went bzzzz, no? They were afraid. In the evening one of them came and wanted to get the typewriter for his comrade. I said, 'Comrade is already away with typewriter, other comrade.' I still have it today.

"Anyway, they *stole, robbed, raped women*. It was indescribable. The English, the Canadians, and the Americans. Indescribable."

Frau Folgen, having waited her turn, said, "I was in Mecklenburg [in northern Germany] then. They didn't do anything to us. The Russians, who came afterward, then we got it. And the commander, he was a Jew, a German-hater. But I must say that nonetheless he put the brakes on his people."

Bluntly, I asked them if they knew about the gassings.

Frau Mundt responded evenly. "It is said today human beings were burned. Human beings are burned today. They're put into an urn and become a very small grave. It's the same in America."

Neither Frau Folgen nor I said a word.

"And regarding that time," Frau Mundt continued, "you have to think of it this way. In our village, diphtheria broke out. There was no serum. There was no doctor who could help. The same was the case in the concentration camps. The human beings there also had diseases. Diphtheria, typhus . . ."

"And were weakened, too," said Frau Folgen.

"And were weakened, no? And there were bombing raids. Many camps were bombed and people there were killed. Then the bodies were burned."

"Ja," said Frau Folgen. "Where should they bury them all?"

I asked Frau Mundt if she meant there was no gassing.

"I do not want to strike that out. I do not want to strike that out. But how one suddenly can say, 'You gassed six million Jews.' Where does the six million number come from? They guessed. But there weren't six million in Europe. Barely two million. And of them, there's still a long line alive today whom we did not kill, no? I killed none."

A silence followed.

Frau Mundt broke it by adding that Simon Wiesenthal, the Nazi hunter, was scheduled to speak at her local high school and that she had signed up to ask a question: where did he get the figure of six million? Frau Folgen was agape at her notion.

Frau Mundt also said there was "one thing I want to learn before I die." That is, what happened at the concentration camp in Dachau. She said "it is said" there were no gas chambers built there, but she planned to go to Dachau herself to "find out from the local people" if there were gas chambers in the camp.[5]

Thinking Frau Mundt perhaps had been affected after all by the widely disseminated reports, photographs, and films about the atrocities of the camps, I asked what her reaction was after the war, when she realized what had happened.

"We cried for at least fourteen days. At least fourteen days of crying. Day by day crying."

Because . . . I prompted.

"Because we lost the war."

---

5. A gas chamber was installed in Dachau (and may be seen today), but according to guide material at the site, it was never used. Prisoners were sent to other camps to be gassed, however. And 31,591 prisoners died at Dachau from other causes.

There was one time in her life, and one time only, when Verena Groth liked to stand out in a crowd simply for being who she was. It was when she was young. Her sense of stardom was in being the daughter of a respected doctor.

She also had her own round of childhood celebrity. Between the ages of three and ten, she broke her right arm six times. "I found myself quite interesting. Everyone asked, '*How* many times did you break your arm?' and at the doctor's each immediately fumbled around it."

After the last break, a specialist advised her father to let it stay in a cast for six months. That agreed, when the last cast finally came off, "my father and the specialist stood there and looked at the X-ray and found it so great how it was healed, except the arm was crooked, and still is. You can't tell, and it's never bothered me. Then the specialist said to my father, 'Ach, you know what? The arm is crooked, that's dumb, we'll break it once more and set it straight.' Then my father said, "A half dozen times is enough, for both my wife and me. If she doesn't get a husband because of a bent arm, it's best she stay single.' I was ten. I know it like it was today." She let out one great laugh.

Verena Groth is a tall, hearty, big-footed woman, a steady smoker with a smoker's voice, laugh, and cough. She met me at the train station, about an hour from Munich, and led me to her little Ford, which seemed too small even for her alone. Soon she was conducting a quick and enthusiastic tour of the nearby lake and hills. By profession Frau Groth is a landscape architect, with the botanical politics of an ecologist. (She has retired since we met.) Holding firm both to ecological standards and to scrupulously honest

Frau Verena Groth

An "Exotic" Past

accounting procedures (she recited with outrage attempts to make her compromise on both) has cost her business, she said. She appeared to be generous, and of modest means.

En route to her home, before we talked seriously about anything, she revealed her heartiness in humor, and her mastery of rollicking, obscure, and untranslatable German slang. She recounted with gusto a time she lived in Liechtenstein. When "her majesty" entered the bank, she said, all other business stopped. Her majesty did, however, touch her subjects' hands. Frau Groth said she told her boss at the flower nursery that she supposed she should never wash her touched hand again. Living in Liechtenstein was "like living in an operetta," she laughed.

Later, I learned that just behind the funny stories huddled the sad ones. What happened to her doctor father. Why she had gone to Liechtenstein. And why she stopped liking to stand out in a crowd.

When we reached her home, a small rented house where she lives alone—having been divorced long ago, her two daughters having been on their own long since—almost all I could see was the exuberant garden. Masses of overflowing pots, blossoms, and arbors cascaded every which way. Amid the visual frenzy was a small lily pond she built, with a goose decoy. The inside of her home had something of the celebration of natural disorder about it, too, but the outside reflected her best. And she obviously loved being there, inhaling her flowers and her smoke. A chain-smoking plant lover was not the oddest of juxtapositions. And it was not the only one in her life.

Frau Groth's political point of view held no juxtapositions at all, or none that was evident. The German past sparked in her a lifelong suspicion about nationalism, and she paid abiding attention to whatever manifestations of it she saw occurring in Germany, or elsewhere. When we met, German newspapers were full of reports about many Americans' orgy of enthusiasm for Lt. Col. Oliver North, a figure in the then-raging Iran/contra scandal. Frau Groth, in her kitchen fixing lunch before sitting down to talk into a tape recorder, was flabbergasted both by him and by the reaction to him. The way "der Olly," as she called him, had hooked onto a sense of patriotism that seemed to have caught so many people's emotions rather than their minds reminded her of no less than the Third Reich. (She, incidentally, was not alone in comparing the North hysteria to the Hitler hysteria.) By the summer of 1992, her alarm again was focused back on her own country. She sent me a copy of an essay against the outbreak of racist antiforeign violence there, and added in a letter, "I often am ashamed to be German."

When we talked, years before the appearance of the young neo-Nazis of the 1990s, it was the old Nazis from the 1930s and 1940s who concerned her. She maintained that they still were hooked by the Third Reich, and she thought she knew why. "Before the war, many had no big careers or were nothing special themselves. Then they had careers as being true Party members. And in 1945, the career was over and they were only average citizens. Now they cling to this time. It was their golden age. They simply do not admit that they erred, or more carefully put, that they were seduced." Or, as she put it in the kitchen, before the Third Reich they were nothing and after the Third Reich they were nothing, but during the Third Reich they thought they were a big deal. A later metaphor popped with pique. "And now one scratches their lacquer [Und jetzt kratzt man denen am Lack] like Mr. Waldheim's lacquer was scratched and they feel solidarity with him.[1] They've LEARNED NOTHING in forty years. They remain as stupid as they were."

It was obvious that the emotional impact of the Third Reich hit her strongly. "Today I have a distinctly disturbed relationship to the concept of Fatherland, for example. In my youth, it was so overdone [überstrapaziert] I have no more connection to it. My father, who was very German national, never grasped it. I said, I try to raise my children first of all as good human beings, maybe as good Europeans, but certainly not as 'good Germans.' My brother's Canadian, one uncle is Brazilian, the other is an American, a cousin of mine was born in Italy, my mother came from Russia, I have relatives in Russia and Poland, we are German, we have relatives in England, too, how should I explain to my children, 'Deutschland, Deutschland über alles'? It's idiotic. I can't say only the Germans are good human beings. That is somehow unworthy of being believed. But some cling to that. I really regret it when some say that Germans have no real historical consciousness. It's absolutely tied up with the fact one really had a disturbed feeling of nationality. You can't just sweep it under the rug. The masses unfortunately are that way. They say, 'We don't want to hear any more about it.' That's something that always horrifies me.

"Naturally, no one [alone] carries the guilt. You bear no guilt[2] for what happened in Vietnam. But one cannot also say we don't know anything," she continued. "It did happen and somehow one must come to terms with it."

Frau Groth then brought up the famous "historians' fight" that was also raging. It concerned whether the Third Reich and Holocaust were unique, as most historians argued, or should be seen in a wider context of other reigns of terror, as the maligned minority said. In seeming conflict with her other liberal views, she sided with the minority. "In the span of history, it really does not play a large role, when one thinks of the Crusades. The knights going into the Holy Land did not always behave themselves so

1. Former Austrian president Kurt Waldheim denied published reports about his involvement in the deportation of Jews.
2. To the vexation of the English-speaking world, the German word for "guilt," *Schuld*, also may be translated as "fault," "cause," "blame," "offense," "sin," *and* "debt" or "obligation."

nobly. They also murdered and plundered, to free Jerusalem from the infidels. Cruelties have always occurred." In a hundred years, she said, the Third Reich will start being considered in the way the Thirty Years' War is now. "But we are living in the time when it's all so *current,* and what really always horrifies me is this anti-Semitism that still exists. It is so indestructible [unausrottbar] in most people, one is continually horrified.

"One notices it, for instance, in completely ludicrous comments. It just happened to me again. I did a garden for a builder. He's an art dealer who came from one of these Baltic Sea states belonging to Russia. He showed me his paintings, and acquaintances for whom I'd also done a garden collect paintings. I called them up and said, 'Do call Herr Levkowitz, he has beautiful paintings for sale.' They are pretty well-to-do, and then they spoke to him. He speaks good German with a very heavy eastern accent. Then [the wife of the collectors] said to me she would like to be in touch with him but hadn't [met him] yet, and 'Tell me, Frau Groth. Is that a Jew?' It was said so disapprovingly. 'Is that a Jew?' I was so shocked. And I said, 'Why, just because he comes from the east?' I could not get to the point because I was so shocked, that it allegedly still plays a role. People don't think much of it, but *that* is exactly what's so shattering. That it's still inside.

"I was at my hairdresser's a few years ago and there in some magazine was an article about Auschwitz. She came over to me, and I knew her father was a pretty active Party member here in the Third Reich, and she said, 'This is soiling one's own nest. Now they're writing yet again that six million died in Auschwitz or the concentration camps, and one doesn't even know if it was six million.' And in rage, I screamed at her and said, 'It's all the same if it's three million, four million, or thirty million, or just three. Each one is too many.' Then she was quiet. But what horrified me so much was this foregone assumption that I had the same opinion."

Frau Groth lit another cigarette and soon was talking about recently seeing, in Berlin, a policeman with a machine gun patrolling a Jewish kindergarten, other police escorting a leader of a Jewish cultural group. "They all still live as if they're locked up," she said. "I find it so awful, as if it's to be expected, that precisely those . . ." She stopped. "I am somewhat affected by it. As it so happens, I am a half-Jew."

And that is why she did not want to stand out in a crowd again, simply for being who she is.

Verena Goldmann Groth, born in 1922, grew up knowing nothing of her Jewish background. She knew no Jewish children, either. She considered herself just a typical German schoolgirl, living happily in Stuttgart with her brother and her parents. The marriage "was not very happy" (for reasons she did not give), but it was intact. Her mother was a Mennonite. Her "very German national" father (a "super German," she also called him) was Jewish.

She said she read an article about Jews having an "unlucky love" to

Germany, of being 150 percent Germans. That he was. "My father's family had lived in Germany for five hundred years. My father was a doctor, highly decorated in the First World War, and could not picture that something would happen to him." Her mother, she said, "opened her mouth more than my father. She always saw things more realistically" than he did.

At one time, Herr Dr. Rolf Goldmann must have been considered a leading Stuttgart citizen. He was the medical director of the dental clinic at a Stuttgart city hospital and worked in the clinic as a dental surgeon, specializing in mouth and jaw diseases. He seems to have been a good father, too, protective and instructive—not aware of the coming world, but doubly aware of the one around him. His daughter has only "very, very vague" childhood memories of the famous unemployment of the 1920s. "I mean, things were good for me. But as a child, you don't pay attention. It was all taken for granted. We did not live ostentatiously, but I noticed my father was unbelievably clever as a teacher. He was still medical director, so it was before 1933, maybe '32 or '31. And the word from school was, you could take an airplane trip over Stuttgart for ten or fifteen marks, I believe. It was naturally more than today, but still not a lot. And I went home and said, 'Vati, give me ten marks, so I can go on a flight over Stuttgart.' And then he said to me, 'Is everyone in your class going to fly?' 'Noooo,' I said, 'of course not.' 'Well, why not?' 'Their parents don't have the money.' That was already clear to me. Then he said, 'Then you don't fly *either*. You must not think that because your father is medical director, you can do everything.' He was very, I won't say despotic, but when he said no, he meant no. Pleading or begging didn't help. Thereupon I probably made a downright forlorn-looking face and he said, 'But when you graduate from high school, I'll give you a present of a flight over the Alps.' At the time, that was the greatest thing imaginable. And then came the war. And nothing. To the horror of my brother, I've still never flown."[3]

Another reason Herr Dr. Goldmann must have felt safe in his world was that in terms of religion, he was not Jewish. The last two generations of his family had converted to Christianity. He himself was a Protestant. His brother had converted again, to Catholicism.

And little Verena considered herself a Christian too, just like her parents. But when she was ten years old and visiting her father's mother, she learned more.

"My grandmother, that is, the Jewish grandmother, sat at her sewing table in her house in Cannstatt [a part of Stuttgart] and said to me, 'You know what? Let's go to the cemetery sometime, to the grave of your great-

---

3. In 1988, she boarded a plane for the first time, to visit her brother and his family in Vancouver. She was entranced, she wrote, not by flying, but by Vancouver, where people from so many cultural ancestries got along so well.

grandparents." I said, 'Ja, when are we going and why haven't we been there before?' That was the end of '32, shortly before Hitler came to power. She said, 'They're buried in the Jewish cemetery.' And completely astonished, I said, 'Why are they buried in a Jewish cemetery?' And she said, 'They were Jews, and we are Jews too, as Hitler wants to see it, and your father cannot bring himself to tell you. But at some point someone must tell you, for Hitler will come to power and things will be quite bad for us.'

"I realized much later that even when I was a child, if something weighed upon me or if I needed to cope with something, I went into the garden. I went into my grandparents' garden. I can still see myself standing at the fence and looking into the schoolyard of a girls' school. It was recess and these untroubled girls romped about. And I stood there at the fence with my ten years and thought, 'Now your childhood is over.'

"I felt it with such crystal clarity. Now it sounds so boastful [geschwollen], but I simply knew everything will be different. Some kind of era is over. Now come bad times."

In terms of her father being the medical director of a public hospital clinic, bad times came very soon. "It was in April 1933. As a civil servant, he was tossed out immediately."

The Goldmanns moved into a smaller apartment. "We had had a very 'noble' apartment, and afterward it was not so noble, but it wasn't so bad either. And there we remained."

The reason for remaining was simple. Herr Dr. Goldmann could not picture leaving. In Stuttgart, he started a private practice as a dentist and also performed dental and jaw surgery, which was the core of his profession and what he most loved doing. "He built up a practice, which he had to 1939. Then the 'offer' was made that he could continue, for Jewish patients only. He said, 'I don't do that.' He'd rather stop completely. That is when I first saw my father cry. I was an apprentice in the garden, a hospital garden. He called me up and said, 'Come to the office, they've taken away my certificate.' His practice was maybe ten minutes away by foot, and I dropped everything and went there. And there at his desk sat my father, sobbing like a child. He was so very attached to his profession. It was terrible for him. He was always so tall and stately, very heroic, so 'Praised be, what makes one hard [Gelobt sei, was hart macht],' and to see him like that. . . ."

His daughter drew on her cigarette.

"Gelobt sei, was hart macht"? When asked later where the phrase came from, Frau Groth said she had no idea. Her response may exemplify, if ironically, the subconscious power of Nazi propaganda. The phrase was a Nazi slogan used to describe "Aryans." Actually, the Nazis misused it, after appropriating it from a work by Friedrich Nietzsche.[4]

---

4. It is from "Der Wanderer" in *Also sprach Zarathustra*. Thanks to Linda Wheeler.

She continued, speaking of her father, "I remember exactly, I wanted to comfort him and said, 'It will all end sometime. It will not stay like this forever.' He was so despondent. He always thought it will never change." His reactions, she said, were part of his "unlucky love for Germany." People like her father "thought that without Germany, they could not live."

Herr Dr. Goldmann had lost his spirit, his work, and his home to the Nazis, but they did not have claim to his body. "Because he was married to an 'Aryan,' nothing happened, he was not sent to Auschwitz." Nor were his parents. His father died in 1933. His mother "had to wear a star. My father didn't because of the 'Aryan' marriage. That made all the difference.[5] If my mother had divorced him, he'd have been in a concentration camp immediately. At the time, many divorced.

"My mother would never have divorced, even in what was an unhappy marriage and especially not after she knew it would be his downfall. Especially not then. I mean, many men sent their wives to England. I know of several who said, we'll divorce pro forma and later I'll come get you. And many, along with their wives, broke down. They went with the Jewish part, they could not bear the strains, and they killed themselves."

She said her mother faced no direct pressure to divorce. "Naturally, my mother could have got a divorce with the stroke of a pen. One put it quite directly to the 'Aryan' half. If you want to, then you can. It is a grounds for divorce." As for her parents' basic relationship, "that didn't change. It was the way it was. I did say I'll stay with you in good days and bad, and these are the bad days and one just stays together. That was really just a matter of course for her." She said that her mother's brother had married a Jewish woman, and they stayed married, too. "That was a decidedly happy marriage. And there was *never* a debate about it."

Frau Groth noted that many "Aryans" yielded to the pressure (or opportunity) not only to divorce, but to shed Jewish colleagues. "Granted, it is very easy to judge it later. My father suffered a lot because many of his colleagues and fellow club members cut him, wanted nothing more to do with him, and threw him out of their organizations. To his dying day, he never had the strength to cope with it. And when 'the ghost vanished [the Third Reich ended]' and they said he could rejoin, he said, 'Thank you, I don't wish to anymore.'

"But you know, I sometimes reconsidered it afterward and talked about it with my father when he complained they didn't want anything more to do with him. I said, 'Vati, think about it. If I'm honest, I don't know for certain if under the same conditions I'd not have acted the same way. If it's a matter of existence or one's profession or one's family, not everyone is born to be a

5. Another reason neither he nor Verena had to wear the star was probably because they were not "registered" as practicing Jews.

martyr. I'm not so sure whether I, too, wouldn't have been cowardly because of fear."

During the Third Reich, while the adults in her family adjusted to their fates, Verena Goldmann continued to go to her school, a large public girls' school. "I was just half, nicht?" The other girls' treatment of her did not change after the Nazi takeover, she said. "There were no problems with my classmates." They knew she had a Jewish father? "Ja." The name was a clue. "There's a bunch of 'Aryan' Goldmanns, but still."

But still, too, she was alone in her category. "I was really the single exotic one among seven hundred girls. And that was certainly burdensome." She said she had not felt "exotic" earlier. "Before '33, it really wasn't there. I also went with the other schoolgirls to their homes. The parents, too, were always completely normal to me. I really never had the feeling, now I'll be treated badly or the parents would say, you can't bring her home anymore. Those were the things that later made me think many people did not feel so well 'under their skins' or found the hatred against the Jews not so optimal. If they had been two hundred percent Nazis, they would have forbidden their children to have any private contact with me.

"There's no bad memory that [the children] placed themselves apart from me. I was just there and I was lucky. It could have gone another way. But, one always stood apart. The others ran around in their uniforms because they were in BdM, this girls' organization. And I as the only one of seven hundred girls . . . not to be part of it, when you're twelve, thirteen years old, that was very hard."

Did she herself want to join?

"Probably."

Was she herself part of what she called "a mass psychosis?"

"Ja, certainly. At the very least, in order not to have to stand apart. My father did not want to leave Germany, and therefore, out of necessity, one more or less adjusted oneself. That simply came from the alternative. Either adjust somewhat to live through it, or leave."

She took part in the requisite Nazi marches. "For the first of May and so, the school was sent and you simply went along. To place yourself apart would have been superhuman." And she knew more and more how it felt to be "placed apart."

One day, one of her teachers "had something to say about the Jews and he didn't want me there. 'It's really better that you go now.' So I went, bawling of course. Those are always situations when one feels like a pariah. All thirty-five stayed there and I should leave. I mean, on the one hand, I later thought maybe he really only wanted to protect me. He had to take this theme through the history lesson and didn't want to hurt my feelings and therefore threw me out. So, which was better?"

At the age of fourteen she decided to quit school, as was allowed, and become a gardener, a highly unusual career choice for a girl then. She remembered her father's response clearly. "Shortly before my father died, I was in Stuttgart again and I told him, 'For your time you were unbelievably modern. When I said I wanted to be a gardener, you said, ach, I'll speak with the head nurse in the hospital,' it was a Catholic hospital with nuns, and 'You'll go to the nursery there three weeks during your summer vacation and see if you really like it.' And I did and enjoyed it, but at the time I was always the daughter of Doktor Goldmann and something completely special and I thought it always will be so."

She said she also told her father he was modern in not pointing out that she would never get rich by gardening. "He looked right at me and said, 'That seems to me a very secondary consideration. I thought, perhaps you must have a profession you'll be doing when you're old, and then it's much more important you enjoy it rather than earn a lot of money and don't like it.'"

During the Third Reich, she continued to enjoy learning her trade. Indeed, it must have been a refuge. A later difficulty, however, in being a half-Jewish would-be gardener, was getting apprenticeship papers. Without an official apprenticeship, she could not be certified. No certification, no good job. Finally, a bureaucrat relented. (After the war, he numbered among those who sought out people like her to request "a 'Persilschein' [an 'Ivory Snow certificate'] that they had no 'brown spots' on their vests. One should certify they always treated us humanely and correctly so they wouldn't be classified as Nazis. I was supposed to certify what a noble human being he was." She signed the form, she said. He had helped.)

Once Herr Dr. Goldmann himself was unable to do the work he loved, he too eventually "mucked around," as she put it, as a gardener. His situation was not as felicitous as hers. "Some gardener he'd known before took him on. But they were not very Christian. They did not treat him very nobly, either. They let him know it a lot. There was no more Herr Doktor So and So."

Although her immediate personal world was kinder, the Third Reich made her suffer a sociological rite of passage unique to the era. "It was so terrible for me in my youth. After I met someone, at some point I had to tell him or her, 'Listen, I'm half Aryan.' And then never know what the reaction is going to be. Astonishingly, they all reacted completely normally and said, 'So? You're a nice girl and all the rest doesn't interest us.' Those are friends with whom I'm still friendly today. If I say to them, 'You have no idea what that meant to me then,' they start up and say, 'You're imagining things, that was so self-evident.' Then I say, 'For all of you it was astonishingly self-evident. For me at the time it was not self-evident.' This angst from the Third Reich that someone could reject me because of this dumb origin [dieser blöden Abstammung] has stuck in me since I was a child."

Frauen

While her father and she tended their separate gardens, Germany started the Second World War. Evidence of that war lies within the pages of her photograph album, itself an almost unbearably poignant document of her teenage years. One snapshot is of a very young woman, looking as German as can be, with a nice-looking young man. They are Verena and her boyfriend.

Did he believe in the war?

"Ach, he was a theology student. He did not believe in the war. He was fairly . . ." She stopped and restarted. "He was killed in January 1945."

In another snapshot, he and she are sitting on a log. She is wearing a dirndl. "That was in the mountains once. A dirndl will never be unfashionable." He is wearing casual clothes and their backpack. Both are smiling, somewhat shyly. On the back of the snapshot she wrote, "Zwei Glückliche [two happy ones] on a trip to Wendelstein in August 1940."

We faced a snapshot of another young man, a friend of a friend, bound for Poland. Did *he* believe in the war?

"He had a kind of intuition he was not going to make it home. I still remember when I took him to the train station, he was so distressed and so strange. And within two weeks he was dead. So, somehow he could tell. He definitely knew it."

She turned a page to a small paper pennant with a swastika on it, and was baffled. It seemed to have come from some German automobile club. "I mean, afterward they had swastikas everywhere, instead of the eagle." She kept pondering, remembering she did not have access to a car, but her girlfriend did. The light bulb went on. "ACH! We drove veterans somewhere to take a walk, who had no cars. That was it." Aha, I said, for the Fatherland. "For the Fatherland," she repeated. And for the effort, a tiny souvenir.

Frau Groth once had written remembrances, too, from the era. "In 1981 I found a box in my cellar, which I hadn't cleaned up for an eternity, and it was filled with nothing but letters which I'd written to my then boyfriend at the front and he'd written me." This was the theology student killed in January 1945. "I took this box, sat down, and spent a whole afternoon reading the letters through once more. At the end I burned them, because I thought, it's my private matter, and my love life of thirty, forty years ago is not my daughters' business. Then I thought, were *we* ever trying to kid each other. I wrote for example—all the letters were sent back after he was killed—'There was another bombing attack tonight. Quite a few houses are kaputt,' as if it were the most natural thing in the world. And he wrote, 'I have to stop writing now, the Russians are attacking,' also as if someone were just walking by. In other words, each was trying not to cause the other to get more upset." Also, she said, "at the time, everything was so everyday one did not see it as that dramatic anymore."

During the war, she mostly "marched around," as she put it, in different nurseries, managing at one point to work in relative racial freedom in Liech-

108

tenstein, the rest of the time in Germany. "I enjoy practical work, but after five or six years of war, I had the feeling my soul was drying out. So I learned poems by heart, and while I watered violets I recited poems that today I find completely stupid." A famous one she recited, by Friedrich Hölderlin, which she finds worse than stupid, was about loving to be among the ranks of soldiers who die for "the Fatherland."

She was watering violets, her father was swallowing his pride, but what was happening to her grandmother, Frau Goldmann senior? The family had managed to move her to a remote village (well east of Stuttgart) to help protect her from the bombings. There, to Verena's wonder, her grandmother maintained the look of a "lady" under the most primitive conditions. I asked what happened when she wore her star outside. "She didn't go out much anymore. She mostly stayed home. And in the village, she didn't wear the star much. There they weren't so . . . it was also so far removed, and it was such a singularly Swabian village. I always had the feeling it was a completely different race. At one time, they were certainly Sicilians or Gypsies, who settled there. It is a completely different branch of people—short, wiry, black-haired. They also had a somewhat different dialect, and nothing but brightly painted houses, which was very noticeable. They clung to the mountain like an Italian farm village. And [the villagers] really were quite tolerant."

She said she believes that unlike "half-educated people or intellectuals who consider every step and every sentence and every gesture, what cause it might have or not," country people with "an education of the heart" were not "so fanatic at that time. They sensed much earlier what was false."

She said the Nazis sent an official to the village to shape it up, but he was essentially ignored.

The villagers may have made Frau Goldmann senior's life easier, but her son may have saved it. Frau Groth thinks her father "used some kinds of tricks" to keep his mother from deportation. She does not know what they were, only that they worked. (Frau Goldmann senior died in 1950.) Frau Groth said she herself did not know at the time what exact fate awaited her.

She did know something of what the Nazis and their supporters were doing at the home front, for she witnessed the "everyday occurrence" of anti-Semitic comments. And she knew she could not "dare say anything [against the Nazis] out loud in the streetcar." She also knew not to speak her opinion to anyone she did not trust, or to do anything verboten. She knew of encouraged denunciations by one person of another, the denounc-ers—children and adults—often convinced they were doing the correct thing. "There was a system to it. It was remarkable how National Socialism psychologically got the Volk perfectly in its hand. It was indeed demonic, devilish, because *no one* trusted the other."

Could she herself have done something against the Nazis?

"I?" She paused. "Absolutely not. Absolutely not. I wouldn't have known what I could have done. I personally didn't even learn how to do resistance. It was from this time I really learned one must stand up in opposition and then one must resist and then one must open one's mouth. But that's in a *democracy*. And a democracy with all its shortcomings, and our stupid government ['with all its empty bottles sitting there,' she later said], is still the best possible formulation for a state. I can write a letter to the editor."

In Frau Groth's opinion, it was precisely the lack of trust the Nazis promoted among the citizenry that led to a lack of knowledge about the fate of Nazism's victims. "For a long time, one did not know much of exactly what was going on. You hardly trusted talking to anyone else, like in all totalitarian states, and the Third Reich in particular. One didn't trust the neighbor across the way, like if you listened to foreign broadcasts, the Gestapo came and took you away."

Like most of the other German women interviewed, she said she knew of the existence of concentration camps, but not what went on in them. "That so many died and what happened with gassings and so on, one did not know for a long time. Certainly not until the end of the war. That they weren't handled with velvet gloves, that was pretty clear. But *how* bad it was, *how* one beat them or shot them in a row and under which *in*humane circumstances they vegetated there, and the stories of the gassings, and that one tore out their gold teeth, nothing but such horrors, that I, too, first knew after the war."

She really learned of the gassings only after the war?

"I first learned about them after the war."

What else had she known, and when, and how?

"Ach, that I don't know. But it certainly was toward the end of the war. Perhaps '44. Somebody did say once, 'They're making soap out of Jews.' That I remember exactly. Somewhere the remark was made. Where, who, and when, I don't know. I mean it would indeed be spoken in a kind of smoldering-under-the-surface way, in secret. Or, 'Lampshades are made from human skin' or something like that. But it was so far beyond the ability of comprehension, closer to cannibalism sort of, that one simply did not want to *believe* it. With the concentration camps, too. I mean, no one can say to me he didn't know about them. The concept of concentration camps definitely was known quite early on. When suddenly people were picked up and they weren't there anymore, they're not in prison either and no one knows where they are, I mean that wasn't just Jews, that was also Socialists or Communists or up-to-then honorable citizens or ministers, and suddenly they're *gone*. But the details of what happened, I mean, perhaps at the beginning one pictured they're in a camp and it's similar to a large prison, only that they're not locked in cells, but are free to move around. But that they starved or, or these cruelties, one did not know about them. That is true. Because those who got out, if they got out, naturally shut up. They were afraid they'd go back in."

She said, regarding her father, "I do not believe he knew anything. And if he had known, he wouldn't have told us, in order not to endanger us."

Frau Groth spoke with particular anger about how the Nazis affected Germany's young people. "Their good feelings, their enthusiasm, their idealism, was absolutely misused. They were stirred up [and] sent them off to war and the wool was pulled over their eyes that they'd be dying for greater Germany. Everything for Germany, everything for the Fatherland. That's why I have a disturbed relationship to the concept of Fatherland and the concept of nation. I think, I've heard that song before. Yet I was always happy when I was allowed to be a part of it. I had the feeling, sometime it will be over and then I'll be fully integrated. I always thought it's only a period of time. The shock came afterward, when the whole extent of the danger became clear to me. If Hitler had been in power two more years, I probably would have landed in Auschwitz too. That is reality. He'd have done away with the rest, too. I thought, it was just a hair's breadth away. Concentration camp. Dachau. Auschwitz.[6] But what idiotic conclusions one came to! My father, under all circumstances, wanted to stay in Germany. The Third Reich fostered such special, dumb exceptions. If they absolutely wanted to save someone of Jewish origin, one could initiate an 'Aryanization' proceeding."

The Goldmanns did.

"In the fall of 1944, my father said, now we'll try it with 'Aryanization.' And my grandmama, we always called her Madame Etiquette, was very distinguished. She lived in a village without regular toilets and went through the village with a black dress and white collars and gloves and the children always bowed or curtsied. She was a person of respect. And then she signed a statement that her children might not be descended from the Jewish Berthold Goldmann, but she'd had a relationship with a manufacturer from the Black Forest. That was flat-out *perjury*. But in order to help us, she signed it. Then we were ordered to Tübingen."

In Tübingen was an institute where people of questionable origin were "scientifically" tested to determine their race.

The group that set off for it consisted of "my father, my brother, and me, my aunt—that is, my father's sister—and my [male] cousin. My cousin and my brother look awfully Germanic, blond and tall. My father also was

---

6. Her fear is well justified. Reinhard Heydrich, the administrator of the concentration camps, proposed casting many half-Jewish "Mischlingen" into the lot with "full" Jews to be deported and murdered. Wolfgang Benz, "Eine Besprechung mit anschliessendem Frühstück," *Süddeutsche Zeitung*, January 18/19, 1992.

very stately." As she had said earlier, her aunt was happily married to a Christian. He insisted on going to Tübingen, too. "My uncle, the 'Aryan' uncle, said to his wife, 'I'm not leaving you alone. I'm going with you.' This 'Aryan' uncle," added Frau Groth, "looked incredibly Jewish."

"We went up there, indeed to a castle in Tübingen, and the professor walked over purposefully to this uncle and said, 'Good day, Herr Dr. Goldmann.' And my uncle said, 'You have erred, Herr Professor. I'm the 'Aryan' part of the family.'

"And you could not *laugh*," said Frau Groth, her husky voice filled with the humor and outrage of the story. "We just about exploded [geplatzt]. The scientists got very red faces. I'll show you a picture of my father. He looked more like Kaiser *Wilhelm*. Anyway, their whole theory was overturned within a quarter of a minute.

"They stumbled around and then measured us—nose, ears, head, and made anthropological studies. But then, thank God, the war was over." She laughed and laughed. "Thank God, the Americans were faster."

The end of the Third Reich meant to Frau Verena Groth personally that she could stop being half this and half that and resume being what she longed to be: one whole person.

"When the war was over, I thought, thank God, the ghost has vanished. I was twenty-three. And I went to the university from 1946 to 1948. I had no inhibitions at all. I talked about it with all my fellow students, because I thought, now everything's done with and thank God no one is looking crooked at you."

Like others in her situation, she was eligible for various forms of restitution. "As a student after the war, I could have tried. The nice expression was 'Persecuted by the Nazi Regime.' They got privileges. Otherwise you had to finance your studies yourself. My fellow students with whom I talked about it a lot said, 'Are you crazy? Go there and at least you will get a tuition waiver.' Already then, I said no. Not to be exotic again. Now I finally belong to the great masses and I do not want to dig up privileges from a time that's behind me. I'd rather give up my studies than go there and say now it's my turn, pay for me."

Although personally at ease in those years, she was upset about the Allies' system of justice toward former Nazis. "They prosecuted the little ones and let the big ones run. Once again, they held high and worthy office. Doctors who perpetuated euthanasia were not forbidden from resuming their careers. But some small bureaucrat, they throw him *out*. I really don't understand it. But it's a little like with North. He violated laws and marched away like an American hero. One asks oneself, is that really happening? What a courageous human being who disregards all the laws in order to serve the nation. He gave the Nicaraguans money, but to fight the bad old enemy, the Communists. And it was similar here. He did everything to fight the bad old enemy, the Jews, or the Gypsies, or whomever. Suddenly law has no more meaning."

Yet in her own life, she was happy not to be singled out as either enemy or victim. Her sense of ease lasted less than two decades.

"In the sixties, during a parliamentary election, the National Democratic Party, a successor to the NSDAP, got ten percent of the votes in Germany. I really almost flipped out. Our friends continually calmed me and said, 'You're imagining things.' I always said I will not survive a new edition of the Third Reich. I'd rather drown myself in the lake. I told my father, 'I'm taking my rucksack and going over the mountain and not even looking back when I reach Austria. I will leave this country behind like a nightmare.'

"I actually thought, until 1933 I lived a very peaceful and trouble-free childhood, and then from 1945 to the beginning of the sixties were the times I lived unafraid. But otherwise, I always had anxieties just beneath the surface. That comes from the time I still don't like to speak about." She is, she said, "hypersensitive."

"I know precisely who knows of my origin and who does not. I mull it over for years before I say something. That is part of me. My friends have said I must go to a psychiatrist, that I have a trauma. I tell them, 'I have reached the age of sixty-five with this trauma, and I'll keep it until I die.'"

I asked if she had felt an urge to tell the hairdresser who questioned the death toll of the Holocaust that her father was Jewish. "I have never been able to say it. Not to this day. Only very few people know it." What about her other neighbors? Like the friendly man who stopped by during our talk to give her some drafting supplies he thought she could use? "Not a single person here knows it," she said, lighting another cigarette.

She continued, "You know, when one has another relationship to the Jewish religion and culture, it's probably less of a burden, but when one has none at all. . . . My grandparents were already baptized, I grew up in an absolutely Christian home, and suddenly one is put in a caste to which one has no relation at all. That sticks to you for the rest of your life. Somehow idiotically. I couldn't even speak about it with my daughters. You would not believe how many running starts I took until I could speak to my daughters. Always thinking, 'Now you have to talk about it.' Then my throat seemed to close and once again I could not.

"It was the same with my son-in-law, when I found out he was in a club [a student club that once was nationalistic]. I had sleepless nights and I thought, the exact same thing is going to happen to [her daughter] that happened to me." (Frau Groth presumably meant what she feared would happen to her.) "He will suddenly drop her and say 'you with the funny origins.' I told her, 'You have to talk about it with him and if you don't, I'll have to.' 'Ach,' she said, 'that doesn't matter at all.' Then I said, 'For you it doesn't matter, but for me it does. I won't be able to have any contact with him if I have these inhibitions that he'll look at me crooked.' Fortunately, he reacted in a 'stinking normal [stinknormal]' way and said, 'What about it?' So, often I'm imagining the fears."

She said she noticed later that her daughters listen to information about the Third Reich "as if it's a story that no longer has anything to do with them. And the Nuremberg [race] laws, I've not yet been able to bring myself to tell them about that. Ja, you two are also still a quarter not 'Aryan.' It's not *reality* to them. And then I always think, well, these details of the Third Reich, why should I rub their noses in it, if no one cares about it anymore and it doesn't bother anyone? And then they're spared these whole schisms and burdens which, which, which, I had. And that was really the reason."

Apparently, Frau Groth was not alone in her wish to keep her "exotic" status quiet. She spoke of an evening with her former husband. "By complete coincidence, we got to know three couples of whom one half was 'Aryan.' We were often invited out together, but you would not believe that anyone ever began to talk about it? I always thought, no one has the confidence to speak about it. Each knows it about the other, but each has the feeling, not to want to be something exotic again.

"It's so terribly difficult for me. A few years ago I was in Stuttgart and met up with some old girlfriends from school and they said, 'You're crazy. Why do you always consider it a *burden*? Consider what the Jewish intelligentsia created in Germany, why are there no more Nobel Prize winners here.' First, a great part of this whole generation was killed. A whole generation of young men was indeed practically erased, and all the intelligent Jews were either gassed or emigrated, and they get their Nobel Prizes as Americans. 'And you must be proud of your cultural inheritance of Judaism.' When I hear or see Leonard Bernstein or hear Horowitz or all these super artists, I find it ravishing and terrific, but I simply don't get it, that internally I myself should be proud I now also belong to this caste. There is such a chasm between us, I cannot overcome it."

Nor can she overcome the anxiety that her neighbors learn she is half Jewish. That is why her town has not been named, nor has she. "Verena Groth" is our concoction.

Her anxiety about being who she was, where she was, and what was going on politically was never far from the surface when we talked, on a summer day in 1987. But on balance, she was "glad to be here." She liked "a lot of Germans, but a lot of Germans I can't stomach. I find their point of view horrible. But I find that has nothing to do with nationality. There are jerks everywhere and pleasant people everywhere. I get wild with this lumping everyone together."

She added that she did not like to hear of "*the* Jews" any more than she does "*the* Germans and *the* Americans. It still annoys me. I think the Third Reich somehow damaged the German people. Now the hate is starting toward the Turks." She said, "Whether I say 'Jews out' or 'Turks out,' it's still this elite claim, that we are somewhat better than the others." She also was upset about the treatment of Germany's "asylum seekers." The phrase was rather new then.

Despite her prescient concerns, Frau Groth was hopeful about Germany's future. She thought young Germans were more tolerant. "I always think things will be better when our generation, the old generation, is dead. The younger ones will do it better. I hope so, anyway."

Five years later, in the reunited Germany of 1992, the world beyond Germany knew well the term *asylum seekers*, both for their numbers and for the neo-Nazi attacks against them and other "foreigners," like the German Turks she had been concerned about. The world also knew of the attacks against the physical remnants of the memories of German Jews, and knew the symbol defacing those remnants was a swastika. Frau Verena Groth was no longer using the word *hope*. Her letter, dated September of 1992, had more to do with worry.

"I have feared this development for decades. The 'trauma' that friends laughed at me about. I would emigrate, if I were not too old." Sometimes one thought calms her, she wrote. In an emergency, if it gets really bad, she could find a little place with her brother, in Canada.

Frau Maria von Lingen

A Cosmopolitan View of the World

Were it not for war and madness, the twentieth century might have been just another agreeable hundred years in the von Lingen lineage. Asked to describe her "Elternhaus" [a word that means a parental home, but implies the circumstances of childhood], former Countess Maria-Carla von Lingen summoned the fourteenth century. Within seconds, epochs and branches of diverse von Lingens, from Sweden's Queen Christina granting some von Lingens an island, to one grandfather's tobacco export business in Baltimore, were swirling through the air. Despite years as "really powerful families," most branches have died off. Just like in Thomas Mann's *Buddenbrooks*, she said.

As precisely as she named her relatives and would name her well-connected friends ("My dearest friend is a Countess Schenk von Stauffenberg," she wrote me in her first letter), so would she name her aversions, some of which she capped with sniffs of disapproval. One sniff accompanied her lamentation about the existence of supermarkets. One punctuated the news that the tasteless Poles, having turned her former castle into an agricultural school, had painted the decorative white plasterwork in *colors*. Another sniff was accorded that "little philistine," Adolf Hitler. Not to mention the terrible shade of brown the Nazis chose for their uniforms.

The sniffs issued from the patrician nose of a woman whose reddish-brown pageboy and curvaceous figure (and satin-and-lace bedroom) called to mind a retired Hollywood star. Frau von Lingen, however, also rides a motorbike. And at a local inn, she drinks schnapps like one of the girls; neat and down the hatch, in one gulp. She long has had her common touches. A mutual friend said that decades earlier, whenever he was out of what she wanted at his produce stand and he offered to walk to the field to pick it fresh, she walked with him to help.

After a relatively peripatetic life, Frau von Lingen put down her own roots in the pretty south German town of Überlingen, a hometown of her youth, but she rued her return. The accursed weather of whatever season, especially the bedeviling Föhn wind that wreaks havoc with her delicate constitution, is not to her liking. So she travels a lot—to more soothing climates, to spas, to relatives and old friends. This was gleaned not only from our meetings but from years of her singular correspondence, a mix of exhaustion and enthusiasm, nobility and Nazis, German and English, legend and politics, religion and race, complaints and worries, and touchingly personal inquiries and greetings, mostly typed on filmy airmail paper. Her fountain pen then underlined words of emphasis and circled the margins with afterthoughts. In person and by mail, she had so much to say it seemed she might explode. The wonder is that she has not.

Frau von Lingen did not strike me as the kind of person well equipped to slough off traumas, and hers have been abundant. Her home, a modern, modest, comfortable walk-up apartment, sums up the least of them: a complete reversal of fortune. Fine prints on the living room walls provide the only apparent clue to an opulent past. Photograph albums provide more. Late one night she flipped through the pages almost perfunctorily, to scene after scene of the old castle in the eastern German province of Silesia. A standing suit of armor in the huge entrance hall, sumptuous salons, a long table festively decorated for Christmas—for the staff. Snapshots in another album show Frau von Lingen as the young bride of the castle's count. Sunning herself on the castle grounds. Striking casual poses with nobility in mufti. Uncle/Count Ebert at his hunting cabin. The "head forester" and "under forester." How elegant, I said. Frau von Lingen replied that she lived there only a month of peacetime. Her finger went back to the faces and pointed out who was killed in the war.

She spoke flatly, as she usually did in our two days of talks. At first her tone seemed attributable to her being world-weary, low, or a former countess. But there were times her voice became swollen and unsteady, she repeatedly clicked the lid of her porcelain-and-brass cigarette box open and shut, and the flatness seemed to have been only a façade.

Her life did begin auspiciously, as did her parents'. Herr von Lingen, who married his cultured cousin, also a von Lingen, studied music, took voice lessons, composed, and "lived from his means." The couple had a grand home in Überlingen overlooking Lake Constance. Frau von Lingen senior oversaw the household staff, the gardens, and the canning, and gave birth to two presentable children, Maria and her brother. But in the inflation crises of the 1920s, "We lost the whole fortune, everything." Through a friend, Herr von Lingen got a job in the Berlin branch of SKF, a large Swedish-based manufacturer of ball bearings. The Überlingen home was vacated, the furnishings stored. While Herr von Lingen was "finding his footing" in Berlin, his wife and son went to her hometown of Bremen, while Maria, about nine years old (she evaded saying when she was born, but one might guess about 1917), was sent to boarding school. Asked what the mood at home was, she answered, "We had no home."

By about 1930, Herr von Lingen had found his footing and brought his wife to a suitable home in Berlin. "A city girl at heart," she began living a pleasantly bourgeois life, joining "the best women's club in Berlin" while the children remained in school in Bremen. At the time, Maria faced a limited future, even in liberated Weimar Germany. Like her social peers who were expected to spend their lives presiding over a husband's estate, she took courses in home economics (in a school in a castle). She wanted to become more than an upper-class Hausfrau, however. She wanted to become a doctor. "But studying medicine takes a long time and my father couldn't pay for it. It was out of the question to expect it of him." So she returned to Berlin and attended secretarial school. If she combined that training with her interest in foreign languages, she might find work as a multilingual secretary, then a prestigious job for a woman.

Her plan was interrupted by the von Lingen family demon, the emotional instability of Frau von Lingen senior. Beginning in the First World War, after learning her husband was severely wounded, and every few years thereafter, she got an attack of depression that developed into a "Raptus" [fit of madness]. Once, she slit her wrists. In early 1932, SKF announced it was moving its offices from Berlin to the city of Schweinfurt, about a hundred miles east of Frankfurt, to be closer to its factories. Herr von Lingen had to relocate or lose his job. Schweinfurt, needless to say, is and was no Berlin. A Raptus soon began. Nonetheless, the whole family relocated and reunited in Schweinfurt, and hoped the senior Frau von Lingen's Raptus would go away. "The first day my father returned to work at SKF, my brother went to school, I was at home alone with her, and she poisoned herself. She put muriatic acid in her tea."

In long and torturous detail, Maria von Lingen recited the minutes, days, and months that followed. The details included coming home from shopping on the day her mother had exploratory surgery and seeing her father, "always very calm, always very strict," lying across his desk and weeping so hard he was shaking. "When I saw him like that, my world fell apart." He had learned his wife's esophagus had fused and that she would not live. But she did, for a total of four months of self-reproach and agony. "*That* was the trauma of my life. *Nothing,* not the flight from Silesia, the death of both my husbands, the war with its range of horrors and the bombs and all that, nothing traumatized me *so much* as the death of my mother."

The Third Reich arrived the next year, apparently little noticed in the von Lingen household. Maria left for England to improve her English and her health, and to flee not Nazis but memories. After her mother's death, "I got all possible nerve problems," including an ulcer and colitis and the temporary abatement of her menstrual period. Doctors advised her to go, but her leavetaking left her shattered father alone. "Another daughter perhaps would have stayed with her father, would have said after all you've been through, I'm not leaving you alone. But I could not hold on anymore." While she was in England, they corresponded, but not about Germany's new regime. "He never bothered with politics and never joined the Party either." She said he was one of only two Germans at SKF who refused. He claimed to be "too independent." She said he had not voted for Hitler, nor had she, being too young anyway. Yet he liked some of National Socialism's consequences. "He was satisfied that order reigned again, that people had work, that the economy was going forward, and that Germany again enjoyed a certain respect."

But on a boat returning her to England from a visit to Holland, she overheard people "complaining about the Nazis and these impossible politics and about Hitler. I thought, what *is* it with these people? What are they talking about? Everything's 'in Ordnung' at home." Being furious was one thing, curious another. She was still in England in 1934, going to art museums and making friends, when London newspaper headlines screamed about the putsch against Hitler's old ally SA chief Ernst Roehm. "I looked at it all and thought, who *is* this person Roehm?"

At another juncture in our talks, Frau von Lingen indicated that at some point she was quite aware of what was going on in Germany. "In Schweinfurt, I had a Jewish friend, Ruth Dreifuss, and her father was a livestock trader and very rich. They arrested him. The Gestapo. And took him away. Then I went to Ruth and her mother and they were completely frightened and cried terribly. Everything was horrible and so on. I said, 'I'll visit you again,.' 'Ja, but be careful and it's so dangerous and we don't know what to do.' One day Papi came to me and said, 'Listen, this won't do. The Party has brought to my attention that you have a Jewish girlfriend here and visit her. If you keep doing that, you risk my job. I'm terribly sorry, but I cannot do anything about it. Please don't go there anymore.' So I didn't, because I did not want to harm my father." She said she later learned through mutual friends that Herr Dreifuss was set free and the family emigrated to the United States.

While Maria von Lingen was in London (whether before or after her Dreifuss affair was not clear), her father remarried. Betty was thirty years his junior and came from a carpenter's family. Maria refused to attend the wedding. She spoke at length about her objections to the marriage (it lasted until Herr von Lingen's death), about her father's pleas, and about Betty's attempts to educate herself. "She had entered another niveau afterward, that's for sure." When Maria had to return to Germany to earn a living, she scorned Schweinfurt and the newlyweds and went to her mother's hometown of Bremen. After "a lot of effort," she got a job at an English import-export firm, then, through an aristocratic connection, got a better job at an ear, nose, and throat clinic in the Rhineland spa town of Bad Ems. The head doctor, needing someone to help with English- and French-speaking patients, was "an anti-Nazi of the first order" who spoke of "the beginning of the end being played out."

By then, she herself had seen Hitler and Goebbels "a couple of times." She was not impressed, she said. "I always had the impression these are small people who somehow have made themselves big by means of power. Because people who really are something do not go screaming around like they did." She warmed to her theme. "When one is really a personality and has a certain cultural niveau, one does not find it necessary to thunder around hitting everything. Only parvenus do that." Furthermore, she said, most of the Nazi "parvenus" were Austrians, and not only Austrians, but lapsed Catholics who had become atheists. "They are the worst because they continually have a bad conscience and cannot get rid of it."

Frau von Lingen herself is a most unlapsed Roman Catholic. On a walking tour of the medieval center of Überlingen, she provided a biography of every side-altar saint in her church. And she broached no criticism of the Catholic church in regard to the Third Reich. "Vatican diplomacy is the best in the world. They did *that* that they could, and they could do no more. If they had been provocative, there would have been murder and fighting to the death." As for the famous/infamous Concordat, she disputed the general historical perception that it was the Roman Catholic church's pact with the devil. "They adhered to it, the Nazis. They arrested a few preachers and so and locked them up, but did no more than that." She was simply wrong, and in a later letter mentioned reading that three thousand priests in Austria and Germany were taken to concentration camps. In the same letter, she wrote that if there had been no Concordat, the Vatican would have been occupied and the Pope deported. The Vatican's representative became Pope Pius XII, "the greatest Pope I have ever known" (and whose birthday, she said, is the same as hers).

Her recollection of hearing one lapsed Catholic, Nazi Propaganda Minister Joseph Goebbels, speak at a hall in Breslau, was that "he screamed all over the place. He spoke fabulously. He had been in a Jesuit school in Bad Godesberg where he learned rhetoric. The Jesuits are really the best in rhetoric. And because of the way he spoke, when one left, one was almost convinced he was right. Afterward one thought about it back and forth and said no, no. The Volk, of course, ran along. They always run along. If someone appears and makes a loud hue and cry you can be certain the Volk will come running along, even if they don't know why. But if one has a certain educational niveau or cultural niveau or intelligence niveau, one asks oneself *why*, what did he really *say*, what does it all *mean*. Hitler gave me the impression of a little philistine. You could only laugh."

What about supposed sexual pulls of the thundering Nazis? Did women think the SA and SA men in their uniforms were sexy?

"Nein! Nein! It is true that men in uniform somehow always look more impressive than when they come along in a civilian suit. So that women naturally somehow always look at those in uniform. Always. Whether they're in the Luftwaffe uniform or the navy, which was even more chic. Whoever was in uniform was naturally very chic to look at, no? And the SS, who had to be a certain height and blond and blue-eyed and had to look so and so, naturally were very good-looking men. One cannot say otherwise. Naturally women looked at them. But I never socialized in such circles where one concerned oneself with such things."

Frau von Lingen did, to a certain extent, concern herself with "Kristallnacht." She brought up on her own that she had witnessed it. "I was working at Opel AG in Rüsselsheim in the technical division, as a secretary, and lived in Wiesbaden. I had a nice room with a very nice family and always took the train in the morning to Rüsselsheim and back again in the evening. That evening, I wrote a letter and wanted to go mail it. And I saw an enormous crowd on the streets, and the most elegant street of Wiesbaden. It's a long, wide street with very elegant shops. They were almost all Jewish-owned. The synagogues were burning. And the SA was everywhere and a crowd of human beings and cries and wailing and they were pushed together. I saw it! An SA man grabbed my arm and told me, 'Fräulein, get away. There's nothing here for you.' And I ran home with my letter and never mailed it. I was completely in shock, completely in shock. The next day one heard, ja, it was the anger of the Volk that caused the synagogues to burn. The anger of the Volk unloaded itself on the Jews. But it was not the anger of the Volk. It was the SA that did it all. I saw all the SA men on the streets, how they pushed the Jews together and how they threw stones through the panes of glass, and destroyed the stores, tore everything out and threw it in the street. Went up in the homes, threw all the furniture out the windows, and took the Jews away. It was horrible. One thought, 'For God's sake, what is going on? What kind of government *is that* we have? It's *impossible!* One cannot do that in a civilized country!' But what should you then do? After all, I was in the technical division of Opel AG. They produced only military goods. We were all under oath not to talk and so on. Tanks and such things were produced. It was all what you call 'secret.' Naturally, I was shocked. But when one is very young and not interested in politics, then of course one somehow didn't bother all that much about these things. But I thought, what they do is impossible. For my part one could tell the people, well, you must leave Germany. You can take so and so much with you and the rest you must leave here, and please leave for America or England, somewhere. But not in this manner. For that is absolutely barbaric. And of course I already was very opposed to this whole. . . . Well, the Party was not popular with a lot of people, anyway."

Nor was "Kristallnacht," according to many reports. But although it was a major catalyst in making hesitant German Jews finally try to leave Germany, it may have prompted some "Aryans" to try to make the most out of staying. In the spring of 1939, for example, Maria von Lingen accepted an invitation to an outing at an acquaintance's estate. There she met Count Ortwin von Pfeil und Klein-Ellguth, better known as Count Ortwin Pfeil-Minutoli, from a connection to the aristocracy of Naples. Frau von Lingen called him "a Swedish aristocrat who paid no attention to the Party." Count Ortwin also was a German reserve officer and once a year was called up for a few weeks of duty. The rest of the time he spent at his family castle near the Silesian village of Friedersdorf. Within months, Maria and Ortwin became engaged. They planned to marry in October.

The aristocrat may have dismissed politics, but politics did not dismiss the aristocrat. On August 15, two weeks before Germany declared war, he got a draft notice. Maria was at her grandparents' in Bremen, preparing what sounded like an elaborate wedding. "Then I got a telegram. 'I have been drafted. Please come immediately.'" She did. The "war wedding" was "only a civil wedding, in the castle. Then he had to go to his troops." She insisted she and he have a religious wedding, too. "I told him I want to get married in a church and I can't wait until the damn war is over." The couple remarried during a three-day leave.

Count Ortwin fought in Poland, France, and the Soviet Union. But he was not away as much as most soldiers. Because his estate included forest and farmland whose output was deemed important for the war effort and "the nourishment of the Volk," he got not only military leaves, but month-long "economy leaves" to oversee his holdings. As for the war itself, "*He* was *convinced* we would win the war. My grandfather in Bremen told me [she imitated his accent], 'My dear, I would not go to Silesia to marry.' 'Why not?' I said. He said, 'What that guy [Hitler] has put his foot into will cost us head and home. I would not go east.' That was the grandfather who knew so much about overseas and exactly what was being said abroad. Here one knew nothing. The whole press was censored. When the war broke out, it was a prison offense to listen to foreign broadcasts. Of course one did it secretly. I always listened to the BBC, which one could receive very well." Her former boss at the Bad Ems clinic also advised her not to go to Silesia. He said Germany was embarking upon "a catastrophe." "I said, 'How can that be? All we do is win.'" She added, "Rational people knew it could never go well. And with such people as the Nazis. I was interrogated three times by the Gestapo."

Frau von Lingen imparted this rather startling information the same way she would impart other startling dispatches. Her delivery was flat, her timing that of an actress. Although she was not inclined toward hand gestures, her apparent agitation, along with her delivery, did give theatrical force to much that she said. Regarding the Gestapo interrogation, the first incident involved her English friend Jane [a pseudonym], who was married to a Munich lawyer. "Munich was always being bombed, and furthermore they had nothing to eat," so Jane and her daughter spent summers at the castle. "And Jane always listened to the BBC and didn't turn the radio dial back to a German station. Then the staff came down in the morning and turned on the radio because they wanted to hear some music or something and the bells of Big Ben clanged and I was denounced. I was in Italy at the time. My own staff, *some* of them, that is, the housekeeper, the nanny, and a kitchen maid went to the Ortsgruppenleiter and said foreign broadcasts are heard in the castle. I wasn't even there. But I had to return immediately, because my husband had been killed in battle."

This was her first specific mention of his death. (She subsequently wrote that he was killed in Caucasia in September 1942.) Asked if she was afraid something might happen to him, she said, "No. Not at all. Never! Never thought something could happen to my husband. I miscalculated completely." After stumbling a while, she said, "I could not grasp that at all. Months later, I received my husband's suitcase. For a year I had it put in a guest room and never touched it at all. I couldn't. So," she continued, turning a page of the castle album, "there's the entrance, from the street side."

As for the Gestapo incident, on her way back home from Italy, she stopped in Munich, to which Jane had returned. "She gave me a few black things so that I not turn up in Silesia in light colors, and I took the night train back. About fourteen days after I'd returned and we had had the funeral service and everything for my husband, I was called up by the Kreisleitung [local Nazi group, or "circle"]. Said a Mr. Greisler, 'Frau Gräfin [literally, Mrs. Countess], Herr Kreisleiter [literally, Mr. Circle-Leader] would like to speak with you.' I said, 'It's eight in the morning.' 'Ja, he'll be there in a half hour.' Well, I was not at all ready." She quickly drank a cup of coffee, pulled herself together, and "then came this Kreisleiter who was *very* polite, I must say that. Excused himself a hundred times. That he was frightfully sorry to come into a house of mourning, but he had to do it. That a report about me had been delivered regarding listening to foreign broadcasts.

"At that point I said, 'I want to tell you something. I was not even here. I was in Italy. Here's my pass, here's my travel permit and my reentry permit.' 'Ja, you're responsible for what happens in your house.' Naturally, this was Jane. That was clear. And I said, 'I can only tell you I know nothing and that I was not here at all during the time in question.' And he said, 'I want to tell you something. For one thing, you are in deep mourning for your husband, who fell on the field of honor. And furthermore I'd advise you to give this to your attorney. This was placed on my desk and as a Party official, I cannot simply sweep it off. Otherwise I would.' So I gave it to our family lawyer and he handled it. How he did, I don't know."

Jane later got her in trouble again. "Erika [a housemaid] came to me and said, 'Countess, the police are here, but in civilian clothes and from Breslau.' I said, 'What? In civilian clothes and from Breslau? What kind of car?' 'A black Mercedes.' I thought, '*So.* That's the Gestapo.' It *was* the Gestapo, too. A short man came in wearing sort of puttees and a completely unbelievable appearance and introduced himself, Herr So und So, secret police. 'We would like to question you in a matter regarding spying.' I said, 'Ja, please.' The other one, who had a typewriter, wrote down each word I said, and the other took the testimony. He said, 'You have a friend who is an Englishwoman.' I said, 'She's not English. She is, but she's also German. She married a German. She has an English and a German passport.' 'Ja, she is suspected of spying and what do you know about her, what can you tell us, and her husband is the officer in charge of a camp of English prisoners.'

"I considered each word precisely and said, 'I have no idea what you're speaking about. She never said anything to me.' I never was told about some letter being secretly smuggled to England. Anyway, to make it short, he questioned me for one and a half hours. I told myself either you're getting out of this or they are taking you with them. And if they take you with them, it's good night. Then they squeeze out what one has not even done, no? Under duress and certain methods of handling they had. At the end he said, 'I must tell you that your testimony is in accord with what our colleagues in Munich have got, and the matter is closed.' Then they left. And then came the horrible story with the assassination attempt on Hitler on the twentieth of July 1944, and I had a friend"—she pointed to his framed photograph—"who was an adjutant in Air Fleet One."

The ensuing point was that the man, a Colonel Hans Bader, whom she met in a military hospital after he had had a nervous breakdown following the death of his wife in a bombing raid, looked very much like Count Claus Stauffenberg, the man who tried to assassinate Hitler. Also, both had the same kind of honorary badge, which was worn at the throat. "Then [the Gestapo] came and claimed Count von Stauffenberg entered and left my house. I said, 'You're very mistaken. That was not Count Stauffenberg. That was Colonel Bader who looks similar and has the same badge." She added that if they did not believe her to go ask Colonel Bader's general. They left.

Still to contend with was her major Nazi nemesis, the local Ortsgruppenleiter with whom she had "one fight after the other." But he had met his match in the widow. "One day he came and said he would like to use the *worthy* premises of the castle for official Party marriages and christenings." "*Worthy*" got a particularly gusty sniff. "I said, 'Listen. I'm afraid I cannot do that. You must contact the executor, my late husband's cousin. Count Carl-Friedrich von Pfeil und Klein-Ellguth at his estate of Wildschütz.'"

She won that one. But their skirmishes were not over. "As the Russians kept getting closer, whoever was relatively able-bodied was sent to East Prussia to dig antitank ditches. Then the Ortsgruppenleiter said to me one day, 'Countess, you will also be sent to dig ditches.' I said, 'So. I have a child under six.'" (This was her first mention of his existence.) "The law states," she continued, "a mother with a child under six years old cannot be sent to dig ditches.' 'You can hand the child over to farmers.' I said, 'We'll see about that.' And I thought to myself, a warning's been offered here."

She hurried to a nearby town where there was an air force clinic whose head doctor and head nurse she knew. "I said, 'Dear people, you must help. The Party's out to get me.'" After she explained the situation, they called the leaders of an institute of aviation medicine that had been relocated in a nearby castle after being bombed out of Berlin. "They hired me *immediately*. And I got a pass as a Luftwaffe helper. The Party couldn't touch me." Her job was to translate Italian and English books about aviation medicine and altitude sicknesses. "Naturally, they just did it pro forma. It probably wasn't very important, because what they wanted to know, they knew anyway." The Ortsgruppenleiter was furious.

"He came another day and said, 'I'm going to draft your horse. He'll have other purposes.' I said, 'I want to tell you something. First of all, the horse is very old. Second, I need it to get to my job.'" The institute was about three miles away. "He told me, 'You could walk there and back.' I said, 'Listen. That I will *not* do. I refuse.' You can see what kind of people they were. He was a farmer from the village. And before the Nazis, he was jailed for sodomy. They made such people Ortsgruppenleiter. To name one example." Sniff. "Then he said to me, *word for word*, 'You'll be walking completely different routes if the Russians come.'"

The statement was defeatist, and treasonous. And "Mrs. Countess" pounced. "I said, 'So. Perhaps I have not heard right. Should I now repeat what you've just said to me? Or would you prefer I keep my mouth closed?' He did not ask me about my horse anymore. I kept it."

What the Ortsgruppenleiter had said, however, was what Frau von Lingen had long thought. "The Russians kept coming closer and closer. Of course one saw the war was lost. One knew for certain, since Stalingrad. After it fell, I had a mover come and I had huge crates and baskets, great travel baskets like one earlier used, and trunks. . . . And my dishes and my books and my silver and my linens and everything possible that belonged to *me* . . ." She trailed into the list of princes with castles and Stauffenberg relations she wrote to, asking to store things with them. Her father wrote she was crazy. To send her things west, where all the train stations were being bombed, rather than leave them safely in Silesia where there were no bombs at all?

He was not alone in his delusion about the safety of Silesia. In 1943 the German government designated her castle a storage place for Berlin art treasures. "I had to have all the salons emptied, all our things put in one salon, and the rest at the disposal of the conservator of Berlin. He stored things from the state library, from galleries, from museums and private collections and then had it all sealed shut. I grabbed my head and thought, 'What kind of a government do we have? They send their things to Silesia? And I send my things to Austria and Bavaria. It was not to *fathom*. My husband's family was so *stubborn*. I'd told them I could send away more. 'Nein. You'll send nothing. That's all defeatism and you've always had something against Silesia in the first place. We'll remain here, no question about it.' That's how they talked."

She said the only way she could send away what she did was by lying that she was fulfilling her husband's will, sending to various people the things he had left them. She could not have told the truth? "Um *Gottes* Willen [for God's sake] that would have been defeatism. If you had just said a syllable about thinking the Russians could come eventually, that would have been it. We'd have been shot on the spot."

When the Russian Army was about twenty-five miles away, Frau von Lingen had to reckon with another force—the refugees fleeing the Russians. Her castle was on a major east-west refugee route. The designation as an art repository meant she did not have to take in refugees (no people, just paintings), but she opened the doors anyway, she said. "I already was housing the German military. Then Breslau was evacuated and the great stream of refugees from Upper Silesia came. All the streets were stopped up with treks, people with handcarts, people with bicycles, with baby carriages, people on foot. It was completely ghastly. And it was twenty-five [Celsius] below freezing. It was insane. There were people whose children had died in their arms. The old people died, and one had laid them in the street ditches. The minister came and said, 'For God's sake, where shall we bury the people?' The earth was frozen hard as stone.

"I had straw thrown everywhere for the refugees so they could *sleep* somewhere or lie down. Then came the treks with very proper people, Count Garnier-Turava and others. I had to put them up in the guest rooms. The next day they complained like crazy everything possible had been stolen from their carts. Ja, I couldn't do anything about it. Chaos already had begun, no? And I packed and packed and packed. Suitcases and suitcases and still more suitcases and crates and trunks. And I thought, maybe somehow my military pass will work. Every day I went to the train station. But you could not get on a single train. People hung from the running boards, from the roofs, between the cars, on the buffers. Then their hands froze and they fell to the ground. It was completely *impossible* to get on these trains. It was ghastly. I told myself, you can't do that. You won't make it, and certainly Jürgen [her son] won't. Then I thought, what do you do? What do you do? I could not flee on a trek or I'd be shot. I could only flee when the Ortsgruppenleiter gave the order. And he waited until the last moment."

She was basically alone. "They had drafted my entire staff into the munitions factories. At the end I had only Erika. The butler was drafted, and killed. All the housemaids were drafted into military concerns and factories." But Frau von Lingen had prepared herself for a confrontation with the Russians. "I had a Walthers police pistol and diligently practiced skeet shooting with our forester. I was completely decided they're not going to get me alive, me nor my son. First I'll shoot him and then myself. That was firm."

A wounded, recovering German officer she had put up came to her rescue. "He said to me, 'Countess, I have to go to the military hospital in Görlitz tomorrow. I will get the horses ready, you get the wagon ready, and make sure you and your child get away from here. We'll also take everything you've packed and see to it you get to the Görlitz station and use your military travel pass there.' And then . . .'"—she paused to light a cigarette—"the next day we set off." Her travel outfit included riding pants, boots, a fur coat, and two pistols. "Görlitz was not that far, about twenty-eight miles away, but it took us the whole day to get there. The main roads were completely clogged with refugee treks. You could not go forward or backward. So, with these horses and the wagon we circumvented it all and got to Görlitz. First we went to the train station, and with my military pass handed over all my things. All I had was Jürgen and two rucksacks and two fur coats and two suitcases and some things to eat. I'd had food prepared to last a week for the two of us." The officer brought her and Jürgen to his aunt's home in Görlitz for the night. Frau von Lingen hoped to leave the next day for Schweinfurt by way of Dresden. But that night, Dresden was destroyed.

"I could not get to Berlin. I could not get to Dresden. And I could not get back where I'd come from. So I thought, first of all, I have to leave the aunt. In such circumstances, you just can't sit on your duff, and with a small child." The officer having left as planned for the hospital, Frau von Lingen availed herself of other male help. "I went to the Four Seasons. That was the hotel where my husband and I always stayed when in Görlitz. In the hotel was a division of the Waffen-SS. I had myself announced to the general. I said I'm so and so and come from such and such, and I no longer know what I'm supposed to do. Then I was taken to a major and he said, 'First of all, you and your child must get off the streets. I'll clear a room of one of the men. They'll have to share another room.' They helped incredibly. At the time, the Waffen-SS did nothing other than help women and children get away."

Asked, disingenuously, why they did so much for her, she answered, "Probably because of my name." A brisk sniff. "If I had been Frau Müller or Schulz or Schmidt, they probably would have said, 'Dear woman, go to the station and wait for the next train.' It made a difference if you had a name, that's obvious. And then they looked at me and so on, no? In any event, they gave me the room. Then they sent me all over the place and to a liaison officer of the air force, Officer Ungewitter."

My shell of suspended surrealism shattered and I burst out laughing, as did she. *Ungewitter* means "bad weather." "I will never forget that name my whole life," she said. "Anyway, the first thing he gave me was a bar of soap, because no one could get soap anymore, but of course the Wehrmacht had everything. Then he said, 'Now listen, Countess. Tomorrow a convoy of the Luftwaffe is going to Prague.' I said, "Ja, dear officer, what am I to do in Prague?" Officer Ungewitter listed alternative routes that were no longer options, including one that led to a refugee camp. She had just seen junior officers forcibly stuffing women and children into trains heading there. He convinced her it made more sense to try getting to Germany from Prague than "to get anywhere from this damned Görlitz." She decided, "Schön. I'll come along."

Thus, in February 1945, Countess Maria-Carla von Pfeil-Minutoli and four-year-old Jürgen von Pfeil-Minutoli took off in a German air force convoy of twelve trucks toward Prague. "The major had fixed up one of the trucks as a salon. The junior officers sat up front in the cabs. And *everybody* drank. All we did was drink, all day long. When I was in the hotel [in Görlitz] where the SS were, in the major's office, all anyone did was drink cognac and whiskey and schnapps and constantly smoke cigarettes, because one knew it's now *over*." She snapped the lid of her cigarette box. "Either we come out alive, or it's over." She said when the drink and smoke in the major's "salon" made her start getting sick to her stomach, she asked if she might sit up front with "your people in the cab," and that he replied, "If that will make you more comfortable, go right ahead." In her account, both addressed each other formally.

The next day, the group reached Prague's airport. Complaining that that was hardly Prague, she got a ride to the city in an army kitchen truck, and along the way met yet another helpful officer, who helped find her a hotel room. The hotel's Czech owners refused to give her sheets and towels. "They already were looking at you as if we know it's all over soon and we'll get you." She sympathized. "We occupied Czechoslovakia, made it a protectorate. We really played tricks on them. Anyway, this good man went and brought me bed linens and hand towels and everything possible. He also got me food and so on. I spent my days running from one German organization to the next to see how I could get out of Prague. Then I told myself, something's about to go bad here soon, and then it's over. They will finish off the Germans. The Poles and the Czechs were much worse than the Russians, because they had a different kind of hate."

Her efforts paid off. Through her military pass she got admittance to a special military personnel train heading west. "There was a very nice air force officer on board. And they all concerned themselves with Jürgen, put him on their laps and gave him food. He got candy and whatever and I didn't have to concern myself with the child at all. But scarcely had we arrived in Nuremberg, around midnight, when there was a massive bombing attack by the Royal Air Force. First we had to go down to the station's bunker with all our luggage and everything. After the attack, we went to a hotel across the street. It's very large and chic. The window panes were all kaputt. The door-man let us in. And just as we *were*, with everything, we threw ourselves on the bed, the child between us, and spent the night. Or a few hours. The next morning we got on the train to Fürth. If I had not had the man, I would not have been able to get on at all. It was *horrendous* what was going on at the station. Masses of people, all shoving to get in these trains going west. And there was such a mess after the bombing attack. You cannot imagine the number of refugees and everything. It was completely *horrible*."

After her new officer said goodbye at his stop, she had to transfer once more and ended up in a compartment "of nothing but Hungarian soldiers who had fought on our side in German uniform. They were such terrible people. It *stank* in the compartment."

And it rained bombs outside. "Of course, the train stopped and the people had to run outside and throw themselves on the embankment. We did that two or three times. And I had enough. I took Jürgen, my rucksacks, my suitcases, and all my things and walked to the road. I said to myself, 'If one of these bombers sees me, then please, send me to paradise. It's all the same to me.' You know, in such extreme cases, it doesn't matter.

"So I stood in the middle of the road and the *first* truck that came by was from SKF, Schweinfurt. I just stood there and the man, furious, looked out and said, 'Man! Look at the likes of that. And a child!' And [she imitated his dialect], 'Dear woman, where did you come from?' I said, 'I came from Silesia and I am the daughter of Herr von Lingen.' 'My *God*.' And he got down and loaded everything and drove us to our front door."

Betty answered the ring. She and everyone else who came running looked at Maria as if she were a ghost, she said. They had heard on the radio the Russian army had captured her town, and they assumed they would never see her again.

Schweinfurt turned out to be no refuge either. "It was terrible. One bombing attack after the next. One was constantly in the cellar. You took your things down there, jewelry and papers and the essentials, always up and down and up and down, and between bombing attacks raced to town to try to buy some food and so on."

One Saturday morning in April, she went to do some grocery shop-ping and heard "a remarkable hissing sound, a crazy whistling sound. Some-one grabbed me by the arm and said, 'For God's sake! Come inside now! That's artillery.'" The Americans had arrived.

She said they requested that Schweinfurt declare itself an "open city" to avoid both bombers and artillery, but "this idiot of a Kreisleiter said 'Nein!' and the mayor said, 'The city shall be defended!' although nothing was left." The artillery fire alone, she said, lasted five straight days. "All one did was sit in the cellar. At night the English, by day the Americans, the artillery in between, and the German flak to the rear. At the end, I didn't even go to the cellar anymore. Just sat upstairs. It was all the same to me, much to the great horror of my father who complained terribly and said, 'You have a duty to your son to stay alive and go to the cellar.' I said to myself, 'If this house gets a direct hit, the cellar's gone and everything's gone. We're all gone.'"

Although Herr von Lingen knew the war was lost (she said he remarked he was experiencing complete defeat for the second time), he had been doing more than sitting out bombing raids. He had been commuting by train to a town where SKF relocated. When bombing attacks on the trains stepped up, he commuted by bicycle. "That was twenty miles! And he was already over sixty!" He complained he was never getting all his work done. "He was iron. *Iron.* I'd never have done it."

The war ended in a burst of silence. "One knew," she said. "Jetzt ist Schluss [Now it's over]." Perhaps because of the concentrated noise of the Third Reich—the shouted speeches and rallies, then bombs and guns— what Frau von Lingen said she remembered more than anything about the arrival of the American troops was how quietly they walked. "These boots came to here," she said, pointing to her lower leg, "and were laced. They were like cats. Our boots made a horrible noise. German soldiers clattered. The Americans had rubber soles. They walked so softly you heard nothing."

The Americans in Schweinfurt requisitioned a tower of the von Lingens' home—the tallest point of the city. In the tower, they set up a radar station. She said when soldiers wanted someone's house, they usually told the inhabitants to get out within a day, but the von Lingens were told they could stay. Two "very young" American soldiers manned the makeshift lookout, working and sleeping in shifts. "They were very nice and we understood each other well. I spoke good English and they gave us a lot of things for the children. Chocolate and cookies and so on. Then one day, one of them came with a copy of *Stars and Stripes* [the U.S. military newspaper] and was beside himself. His face was chalk-white and he said [she quoted him in English], 'Look at this. Look at this.' And that was . . . The Americans had discovered and entered the concentration camps. And saw what had gone on. They were so completely beside themselves with horror, that, well, the whole mood was ruined, no? They became very circumspect. That it was grisly and how could such a thing be possible and whether we had known anything about it. We said as for known, one heard something and guessed, and so. There had been rumors. But one never knew anything definitely. It was also too dangerous. One could not ask, for if one had, one would have been on the spot immediately. And to whom should one have . . . Well, I already knew it. I knew such [places] existed, where they first did euthanasia.

They did away with it later, because the people began to rebel. Then they built the camps. One knew of Dachau and Oranienburg. And one knew that in Poland were camps where, well"—she paused—"eh, there were extermination camps. But *how* it all was and who . . . And that the Jews were deported, that one had seen. They were simply picked up and taken away." But, as it turned out, she was referring to what she had witnessed on "Kristallnacht."

The young Americans were not satisfied with her answer. She recalled their outrage probably more accurately than their exact words. "They said, 'We simply don't *understand* this. How is it possible in a country where the people are exactly like us? How it is possible that such things happened?'"

What did she say?

"Ja, what, what should we say? Of course we were horrified. And said, that"—she stumbled—"that those were things one heard about and were whispered but had never experienced because that simply was too dangerous. If you asked, you'd simply be taken away." Clapping her cigarette box on each syllable, she said, "You could *not open your mouth* and say a word. Or you were lost."

The Americans were beyond explanations. "They were really beside themselves with horror. Because they did not comprehend it. They were from some American," she added in English, "God knows where, Middle West or somewhere. Never heard of such a thing in all their lives." Switching back to German, "And then were confronted by such atrocities." She added, in English, "Of course it made me feel awful. It made us all feel awful. But what could you say? We were Germans. And this happened in our . . . not in our country because all those extermination camps were in Poland."

As midnight approached in Frau von Lingen's Überlingen living room, she seemed increasingly energized, brought out the photograph albums— there's the coachman with the minister's children—and whether by design or not, told a remarkable tale. It started by my asking what her first husband thought of the Third Reich. She said she would like to have known, too, but they never talked about it because he was not interested. Asked if she knew what he thought of the pogroms against the Jews, she foundered awhile, and hit a memory involving his being in Lublin, Poland, and seeing the SS shoot a Polish count and throw his wife into the street. He became "sick and frantically worried" when he thought of the same thing happening to her.

"And the second [husband] saw the shooting of Jews. He was the commander of an airport in the Ukraine or wherever it happened. Where this insane number of Jews were shot. There wasn't a camp, but they simply, simply killed them all. And he took photographs. Then he went to headquarters and complained about the disgusting behavior. That it was an impossible situation. That it was unheard of for his soldiers to see such a thing.

And everything that was going on. Anyway, he was taken before a military judge. The only reason they let him go free, I have the papers somewhere, is that he always was an irreproachable officer and all his people counted on him."

What happened to the photographs?

"I burned them."

The reasons seemed to have to do with panic. She said that she came upon the photographs when cleaning out her husband's desk after his death, but that he had shown them to her before. The man, Karl Hübschle, had been a professor in civilian life. They married after the war, and in 1950 he died of a heart attack. It was brought on, she thought, from heart disease he contracted in a POW camp in France, a camp in which, she said, two-thirds of the prisoners died of hunger and typhus. (French POW camps had reputations as filthy hellholes.) When he died, "there was a terrible brouhaha" involving his four children from a previous marriage. He had left no will.

"If someone found such photographs on me, or, or, or if I were to die and had these photographs somewhere, one would think I'd had something to do with such things." So, no one else can see what she saw, and still sees. "It was horrible. The people had to take off all their clothes and had to stand by the graves, which they themselves first had to shovel out. And then after a shot in the back of the neck, they were thrown in. And when one layer was full, the next came. And then wherever there was any movement, they shot at it. Ja, those are things no normal human being can cope with." She added, "Of these SS, young people, many went crazy [durchgedreht]. Many went crazy. They could not cope."[1]

Asked if her late husband had shown the photographs to a wider circle, she said no. "For him it was settled and that was that." She returned to pointing out photographs she had kept, another girlfriend who spent the summer at the castle. Trying to get her back, I said it must have been terrible for him to have seen what he did. "Ja! He complained vigorously about the contemptible goings-on and that one could not demand such a thing from his people and they should be sent somewhere else and so on. Here's Constanze when she was very young and . . ." Whether his sentiments or hers came from another layer of self-protection is unknown, but she had twice quoted her husband as having been upset not about what he had seen, but about its effect on his men. Perhaps that was all he could tell the judge.

Frau von Lingen's personal postwar responses to the Holocaust do not fit into a neat category. She has never been to a concentration camp, although

---

1. There is mention in Helmuth von Moltke's memoirs, *Letters to Freya* (see interview with Freya von Moltke), of a wartime psychiatric institution for disturbed SS men.

Dachau is relatively near. "Why should I look at that? For what reason?" Yet she bought a television set just to watch the series "Holocaust,"[2] even though she does not like television "because it made me nervous." She also sent away for the extensive background material the German government provided to accompany the series. She said the overall effect was "deeply moving [erschütternd], of course."

"I want to tell you something," she said soon thereafter. "One always heard things. Through foreign broadcasts and through rumors, which emanated from circles of people who were close to the German resistance and somehow were informed. One heard there was annihilation. There were euthanasia camps. For people who were 'worthless.'" She asked, "What could you do? What could you prove?" Asked if she considered, even in a fantasy, being in a resistance group, she said resistance was in the hands of "all possible groups schooled in that" and made up solely of men.

Seemingly as a substitute, she recited with relish old anti-Nazi nicknames and slogans. Joseph Goebbels, whom she called a "half-devil," was known as "'der nachgedunkelte Schrumpfgerman [the darkened, shrunken Teuton].' Consider the expression! The people were fresh. They were often shameless. They wrote on the Odeonsplatz in Munich in front of the hall of martyrs for National Socialism, 'Besser ein König von Gottes Gnaden als ein verkrachten Maler aus Berchtesgaden.'" [In unrhymed translation, "Better a king by God's grace than a failed painter from Berchtesgaden."]

Frau von Lingen certainly was well aware how the Nazis could reach into a family that was not the Nazi ideal. Her mother's brother, who worked in the 1930s for a German steamship company in Spain, "came back with severe depressions. He once tried to commit suicide. The attempt had to be reported to the state health office. And he had a forced sterilization. Forced sterilization! The man got a shock for the rest of his life.[3] He was a very handsome man. And the word was, something's not right in your family. One had to go back to find what the matter was, because families with inherited diseases were disinherited. That was the [Nazi estate] law." She said her family tree also was checked because of her mother's history, but her mother's problem was determined not to have been inherited. "It must have been a mutation which came about by the marriage and the children. Many women get such conditions."

---

2. The U.S. series, involving family drama interspersed with documentary footage, was broadcast in Germany on four successive nights in 1979, to enormous attention. Thanks to Kathryn Kerns of the Hoover Library.
3. For more on the widespread use of compulsory sterilization (made law within a year of Hitler's takeover) see the essay by Gisela Bock in *When Biology Became Destiny*, edited by Renate Bridenthal, Atina Grossmann, and Marion Kaplan (New York: Monthly Review Press, New Feminist Library, 1984), 271–296.

Frauen

Frau von Lingen had found ghosts in Count Ortwin's family, too. She learned his father had not been killed in a hunting accident, as she had been told, but had shot himself, as had a female cousin. She started observing her "peculiar" brother-in-law. A linguist and businessman, he was drafted, and sent to northern Norway, where he got "polar frenzy" from the darkness. "He began to get these attacks and scream against the Führer, against the Reich, against the damn war and against everything. They immediately sent him to a military psychiatric institution." The poor man was demoted, sent again to fight, taken prisoner by the French, and later released. He never recovered emotionally.

Had the Nazis known of the Count's family mental problems, which she diagnosed as schizophrenia, she was sure they would have dispossessed them. Had she herself known, she was sure she would not have become, as she labeled a charming and youthful photo of herself, Maria-Carla Countess Pfeil-Minutoli.

I asked Frau von Lingen how she evaluated herself.

"You mean in relation to the Jewish question?"

Yes.

"Well, from the beginning I found that impossible, no? One learned later the people were deported and never came back from these camps." Was she evading on purpose? Or had her train of thought simply gone off track? "One had the feeling," she was saying, "revenge will follow in the same footsteps, no? After all, we did lose the war and paid penance. And how! We lost a third of our land, we had all the refugees, we had so and so many dead, we had our bombed cities."

She said one of her father's best friends was a Jewish municipal lawyer who after the war helped validate him as a non-Nazi. She said her parents had "nothing against Jews." She continued, "Berlin was completely ruled by Jews before the Nazis came." Did she mean she thought Jews should have been more "reserved [zurückhaltend]"? "They don't do that. They aren't reserved. They seize hold of everything. First of all, they had the big banks in their hands, then all the finance institutions. There were a lot of Jewish moneylenders in the country. Then there were a whole lot of Jewish livestock traders, and they really fleeced the farmers. So, they weren't always, eh . . ." again she stumbled until hitting it. "They had their own idiosyncrasies."

Another series of stumbles resulted in: "It is just a *foreign people* [ein fremdes Volk] which *lives among other people*. But they never completely belong. They're always somehow foreign. Because even if they no longer believe in their Jehovah and their religion and carry out their Jewish rituals, they're *racially* all bound together. This Jewish blood always makes its way through. Always. Even if it takes two generations, or three. It's exactly the same if you married a Negro." She spoke of a German woman she knew who

134

got pregnant by an apparently white American and had a black baby, later to learn the man was part black. "It's the same with Jews. If you have Jewish blood *once* in the family," she said, tapping her cigarette box lid with each syllable, "it will *come through again and again*. This race maintains itself through all generations. It is just another *race*. It's a Mediterranean race."

It was time again for my hypothetical orphan. If a Jewish baby grows up in a Catholic family, I asked, how will it behave?

"They have certain idiosyncrasies. Even if they're raised differently. It's a character trait or way of being. They are just *different*. They're different from us." She paused. "They think differently and feel differently and are different. Maybe it's because of their long two-thousand-year history [sic], when they were thrown out of Jerusalem and threw themselves to the four winds. They've always lived more or less as *guests* within another people. They never had their own home. And stayed together nonetheless, no? They have not assimilated." (In a much later letter, she referred to a book about the Arab-Israeli conflict, and added in English, "One feels sorry for the latter, they seem to get no real home in this world.")

How precisely might the Jewish orphan behave as an adult?

"Some kind of disunity will appear, no? A divided being. It's always the same. For example, if a northern European married a Spaniard or an Italian. The children of both are always divided. Those are completely contrary races. In other words, there are two souls in one breast."

Is that not the same with every child?

"No. It depends on the parents, where they're from." She turned to Gypsies, "persecuted just like the Jews. Gypsy blood is Gypsy blood." And "Jewish blood" remains Jewish blood. I asked Frau von Lingen how she thought anti-Semitism could be avoided. She answered with uncharacteristic softness. "Yes, anti-Semitism. Well. It hardly exists in Germany anymore." That was spoken in 1985.

Then, one could see no evidence of anti-Semitism, or of the Third Reich, in Überlingen. But what one could see resulted in part from the efforts by one concerned citizen, Maria von Lingen. She mentioned, during my visit, that she corresponded with a professor at the Yad Vashem Holocaust Memorial Institute in Jerusalem. She sends him German newspaper clippings "about Jewish events." She also wrote him about a love affair in Überlingen between a Jewish survivor and the anti-Semitic widow of the town's former Nazi leader. (The widow accused Frau von Lingen of being a spy for Israel.) Why had Frau von Lingen contacted Yad Vashem in the first place? Because she learned there had been a concentration camp in Überlingen.

The mayor did not want to have anything to do with putting up a memorial. She, among others, was "furious [stinkwütend]" about his attitude. She wrote to Yad Vashem to find out about the camp, learned most of the victims had been Italian prisoners, went with a local group into Überlingen's woods to see the camp's remains, and later helped arrange a service at the site and the installation of a memorial marker.

Why not forget about it, as the Überlingen mayor wanted? "Because I find that an injustice! The people labored here and died here, died of hunger and deprivation and mishandling, and then one should not . . ." She interrupted herself. "Every other concentration camp has a memorial. Why couldn't they have one in Überlingen? Because they want to hush up [vertuscheln] there was something here? That made me angry."

In the autumn of 1992, she was angry again.

Among the racist acts of violence that were scarring Germany's majority, its minorities, and its overall reputation, was one in Überlingen. On October 23, some "vandals," as the *New York Times* described them, defaced the memorial with swastikas. Fifty gravestones at the adjacent cemetery were wrecked.

Frau von Lingen had been among the many Germans disgruntled about the large numbers of immigrants to Germany after the country's unification. But, at least to her, the subsequent violence against them, and against Holocaust-related sites, was a separate matter of condemnation. In a letter, she described the Überlingen attack (in English) as "scandalous destruction." She later continued (in German), "It's getting worse and worse here. Not a day goes by in which a home for asylum seekers is not attacked or a Jewish cemetery destroyed or a concentration camp memorial ruined. It's the neo-Nazis, and the government does absolutely nothing against them but talk and talk."

It is fitting that Frau von Lingen, both during the Third Reich and in later response to it, would condemn various German governments and help plan a memorial that condemned the most heinous era of German behavior. To her mind, she was not really German herself.

"I was *never* very nationalistically minded. *Never!* And I always thought more like a European than a German. Because France interested me as much and Italy interested me as much and also England. I always thought in each people there are weak and strong sides. In each people is a pro and a con. My mother-in-law always reproached me, 'You've traveled too much. You've seen too much of other people.' I was always more tuned in to the cosmopolitan. I don't know why."

In many ways, Irene Grünwald had a perfect childhood. She was the eldest of three girls born to farmers in East Prussia. Her father was the community mayor. She lived surrounded by the embrace of her family, a profusion of East Prussian traditions she felt part of, and the beautiful and fertile fields that gave the "granary of Germany" its reputation.

The Grünwald farm was small, about ninety acres. It was part of an Ort [locality] of about seven hundred people. Four localities made up the Kirchdorf [church village] of Tolnicken. Farther away were the cities of East Prussia, and much, much farther away was the rest of Germany. Irene's world not only was close, but closed, the result of East Prussia, a fat chunk of land embracing a corner of the Baltic Sea, having been cut off from the rest of Germany after the First World War. Then, as noted earlier, it was made part of Poland after the Second World War. Many observers see both remappings as the consequence of ultimately failed German military aggression. Others either do not, or cannot.

When Frau Burchert and I met, in interviews years apart, she lived with her husband in a neat, modern house outside a rural village near the northern German city of Kiel. Not far away was the (then) East German border. She even gestured out an east-facing window, as if watchful for an invasion. (With the collapse of the Soviet empire, however, it

Frau
Irene
Burchert

Learning
How
Communism
Works

was Frau Burchert who went east. She visited her beloved farm and homeland, became terribly upset about what she saw, she wrote me, and returned four more times.)

It was clear from our first meeting that although she was not then allowed to go back to East Prussia, she had carried as much of East Prussia to the west as she could. Reminders of East Prussia lined her walls and covered her body. She had gone to weaving school as a teenager, and now was wearing a snug dirndl in an East Prussian pattern she had woven herself. She seemed altogether precise and composed. Her face was scrubbed, her hair tidy, her brown eyes wide and soulful. Her form was petite, her movements and voice delicate. She also seemed aware that she was projecting (to my eyes) an image of a small proud creature who has suffered. She often punctuated her remarks with "emmm . . ." and pauses that were like the dabbing of lips with a napkin. And unlike many Germans who end sentences with variations of "no?" she more frequently ended hers with a soft "ja?" Her hands would have seemed in perfect repose on her lap or reaching for a skein of wool. But what she reached for during our meetings were brochures, books, articles, photographs. All pertained to the subject that has occupied her much of her adult life: the deceitful, murderous, twentieth-century political system visited upon Germany, among other countries, the system that gained idealistic supporters through conniving and treachery and left millions of innocents dead in its wake. To further her point, Frau Burchert introduced a photograph. A man and a woman, looking dull-faced, stand behind a table. On it are the remains of their child, whom they had partially eaten.

The family, she said, were Russians, driven to cannibalism by Joseph Stalin. To Frau Burchert, he was the devil of the twentieth century. Hell was Communism. And hell's foot soldiers were the Soviets.

Little she said about the troika, especially Stalin, was a matter of debate. But that, bluntly speaking, was another story. What about the stated topic of our interviews? The regime that took over her East Prussian world when she was ten years old and in which she lived for the next twelve years? What about the Third Reich? Politely, pleasantly, she accepted a variety of questions about it, mostly answered briefly, and then returned to the indignities and atrocities of Stalin, Communism, and Soviet soldiers. Many indignities and atrocities she had read about. Others she had experienced herself.

In January 1945, when Irene Grünwald was twenty-one years old, Soviet soldiers invaded Tolnicken. Within a week, she and her sisters were on their way to a Soviet labor camp in Siberia.

Irene Grünwald was brought up a Roman Catholic, a minority religion in East Prussia, although not in her region. She spoke often of her faith, and how it tempered baser instincts. When she spoke of her one child, a son, it often had to do with what she had taught him about conscience and morality.

As a young woman herself, taking in the variety of lessons her world offered her, she may also have been learning a maxim seemingly endemic to the region. It was to blame your political dilemmas on others. In the 1920s, the others were Poles. Whenever they shut down access from East Prussia through the Polish Corridor to the rest of Germany, the goods trapped in East Prussia included those of the Grünwald farm.

"The Pole did not allow any transportation into the Reich," said Frau Burchert. "And my parents could not get rid of the grain or the livestock if the traders came. They [the traders] didn't want to pay a lot, because they could scarcely sell it to anyone else."

"The Pole"? Like the equally fungible and featureless "the Russian" (which both she and Herr Burchert referred to), the term is thought by some Germans to be simplistic and insulting, and an indication of "conservative" politics.

"And then my mother, emmm, also took butter to the market in [the nearby city of] Allenstein. She took me with her. That was before '33, ja? She said, 'I'll do it. I don't like to at all,' she said, 'but I have to buy things. I have to buy you clothes.' Or material. She sewed everything herself. The day before, butter was made. And then the people from the city came to taste. 'Ach, the butter is rancid.' My mother said that was the worst thing she had to do. But she said, we had too much milk. We had too much butter. We cannot eat it up ourselves."

Frau Burchert said her husband, a year older than she, was "closer to what was going on before '33. There were riots with the Communists, who wanted to expand." No such riots took place in her village, she said, pointing to a framed map of East Prussia. "In the bigger places [there] was more unrest. So that the population really said, now we can elect Hitler. Maybe he'll bring order." Asked if politics was talked about in her family, she replied, "It certainly was." Her parents did not vote for the National Socialists, she said. They cast their votes for the losing Catholic party, Zentrum.

Among the Nazis' first acts of power were to end freedom of the press, to order a boycott of Jewish stores, to kick Jews out of civil service positions, to set up concentration camps for political opponents, to burn books, and to negotiate a treaty with Poland that opened up the corridor between East Prussia and the rest of Germany.

"After '33, things were better on the farms. Somehow there was an agreement with Poland. The Pole allowed transportation through the corridor. My parents could sell the products they grew."

Another consequence of the Nazi government was that mayors had to be Nazis. There may have been exceptions, but the practice was to dismiss any mayor who refused Party membership. Mayor Grünwald remained in the job. Did he think Hitler would be good for Germany? "He would bring about order, nicht?" She added, "We didn't know him."

Herr Grünwald did know something of a wider world than East Prussia. He had fought in Russia in the First World War, was captured, put in a prisoner-of-war camp near Lake Baikal (north of Mongolia), escaped, and slogged back to Germany on his own, meeting both White and Red Russian contingents along the way. Frau Burchert said he boarded a train during part of the trip back and Russian civilians protected him from passport inspectors by hiding him under the seats. (The point of the anecdote seemed to be that ordinary Russians liked Germans.) By the time he returned to East Prussia in 1920, he spoke some Russian, and became friendly with the village outcasts, a family of White Russians. In one of the countless paradoxes of European history, one of his best friends in the village was his mirror image—a Russian World War I veteran who had been in a German POW camp. Herr Grünwald's experiences in the Soviet Union taught him, said his daughter, that if Communism ever got to Germany, Germany would be lost.

In the first half of the Third Reich, life went well for the Grünwalds. The Grünwald girls grew up healthy and secure. And for diversion they had the activities of the Bund deutscher Mädel. "That somehow came from school automatically." There is no doubt the BdM group filled a social gap, especially as "rival" organizations were banned. "We were glad to be able to go somewhere. We did sports, we did handicrafts. Who didn't join?" She claimed the BdM was not political, and bolstered her assertion by saying she recently met a woman who agreed.

Frau Burchert did recall a tiny "political" intrusion in her life. "When I went to take a [home economics] test, we were warned there could be trick questions. Then the question came up, 'What comes after the Third Reich?' Somebody answered, 'The fourth!' That was wrong. One wanted to hear, the Third Reich is the One Thousand Year Reich, ja? The same answer came up a lot. But the question was not put to me."

It is difficult to gauge the Nazis' overall impact on the relatively isolated farming village of Tolnicken. Something in their message drew early enthusiasts, but only a few, said Frau Burchert. "They were mostly, let us say, those who were nothing before. There they could rise quickly or, how can I put it? Emmm, types of people who liked to make a lot of noise. Earlier they were with the Communists, ja? Such types, I had the feeling, joined the SA [brownshirts]." She continued, "There are human beings who have no conscience. And they can *be* somebody. Whoever was the freshest, who had the most courage, was the ringleader. And those were not always the most educated. That's how I want to put it." She recalled one young farm boy "who could not get anywhere" in the village who left and supposedly joined the SA.

The Ort officialdom seems to have adjusted to and become part of

Nazi rule without strain, even in religious matters. Although a basic Nazi Party line was to mock organized religion, keep it as impotent as possible, and deal with any dissident anti-Nazi clergy about the same as with any dissident, the Nazis knew to stop short of closing churches. And many German churchgoers kept going to church, Nazis or not. In fact, some Nazi officials kept going to church. Frau Burchert said her village Ortsgruppenleiter went to ten o'clock church mass in full uniform and straight from there to the eleven o'clock Nazi meeting. "That's the way it was."

She volunteered another gentle glimpse of local Nazis in action. "I finished school in 1938. One experience from my school years. I came from a Catholic region. The crucifix [in the classroom hung] in the middle. And Hindenburg hung on one side and Adolf Hitler on one side. Then the principal came one day and said, 'Take the cross off the wall. We are well away from *that* time.' And [he] lay it on the cupboard. When the principal had gone, our teacher took the cross from the cupboard and said, 'Hindenburg certainly would have nothing against my hanging it up again. And I believe Adolf Hitler has nothing against it, either' and hung the cross up again. So the cross remained throughout my years at school."

She said she was told when she left home to attend weaving school in another town not to ask about attending church, but she decided to anyway. "I went to the leader. I asked first if I may go. She said, 'It is not looked upon kindly.' Then I said, 'I am Catholic and I am obligated to go to church on Sunday and I also like to go. But if you do not allow me to,'—I was seventeen or eighteen—'there will be no obligation.' She said, 'You may go.' Afterward, others went too. Protestants as well. It was allowed. Someone just had to have the courage to ask."

What about courageous responses to anti-Semitism? Frau Burchert said she had known of no anti-Semitism personally. As if to illustrate its dearth in her family, she said her mother and grandmother shopped in a store in Allenstein "and it did not bother them at all that the owner was a Jew. Not at all."

What about envy toward Jews? "No, we didn't know it. I was raised as a Christian, by a very religious teacher. [And was in] a Christian home, where envy was suppressed."

Frau Burchert offered no comments relative to any negative influence by the Nazis on her village, region, or country during the first half of the Third Reich. (She did confirm, when asked, that villagers were careful not to express their political opinions openly.) Then, shortly before September 1939, Mayor Grünwald was called away to attend a conference. Frau Burchert said she does not know what he learned, but assumes it had to do with war preparations, for he returned with food ration cards to be distributed within the community. "And after that, he didn't speak anymore. That was before the invasion of Poland. Then the day the war began, my father got sick. He knew it [war] from before. Not physically, but emotionally." She repeated, "He did not say another word. When the war began, my father was a different person." He and his wife (who was "very interested in everything, about everything new, also about history") took to meeting with friends behind closed doors. All Irene knew was that "those were very earnest discussions." Before the war, "when there was a conversation with someone, we children always were there. But no longer afterward."

The war had another impact on her father. "He wanted to give up the mayoralty. But he was not allowed to." She said he was told he could give it up after the war. He remained "a changed man. 'That did not have to be,' he said." She saw the changes "in his face. It was as if he had turned to stone. He was totally against the war. 'That did not have to be.'"

One might think that the events leading to her father's distress, such as the printing up of ration cards before any fighting took place, would have prompted Irene Burchert then or later to believe Germany started the war. She did not.

"I remember something else. Before '39, before the war with Poland started. I didn't see it, but it was talked about at home. That Polish airplanes crossed into the country. Then leaflets were found. 'Betet noch ein Vaterunser. Morgen seid Ihr unser.' [In unrhymed English: 'Say the Lord's prayer. Tomorrow you belong to us.'] That Poland planned to take East Prussia."

The leaflets are famous. They are famous for being fakes. The general belief of historians is that the Nazi government printed them as part of a plan to trick German citizens into thinking Poland was about to invade Germany. After Frau Burchert went on at some length about Poland's government and intentions, I asked if the leaflets were not German. She seemed to have heard the suggestion before. "Perhaps different sides picture it that way."

She then brought up another well-publicized prewar action, a group of "Polish soldiers" sneaking into Germany just before the war and looting German homes. Again, most historians agree the men were not Poles but Germans in Polish uniforms, and that this incident, too, was staged to prompt German civilians to support retaliation. The following remarkable passage concerns Frau Burchert's rebuttal of that version, via an acquaintance. "She was from Silesia, from *that* area. She said, 'Such a lie. The Poles came in the night and looted.' Her husband went, too. They kept watch during the night. She said, 'Our men chased them away with clubs.' Those were not German soldiers. Those were Poles. And came over the border and looted houses everywhere. She died several years ago. Such a lie to say it was German soldiers. Although Hitler . . . What I learned after Hitler, that we . . . Anyway, I did not know and I believe my parents did not either. They didn't know about concentration camps. That . . . what one heard happened."

What was remarkable, although not unique among the women, was the transition from one unrelated subject to the Holocaust. And like other women who had done so, Frau Burchert then quickly stepped back. She repeated her father's opposition to the war.

We eventually returned to the looting. If Poles really did it, was that a reason for Germany to start a war?

"Ja. Poland provoked."

She cited a book by a Polish writer who also claimed the provocation was intended to goad Hitler to war. Pressed on the issue of justification, she answered, "It's still no reason to start a war. But as I've always tried to tell our son, when a small human being who has no conscience gets power, he uses that power without constraints. Hitler had no conscience."

She then returned, as she had before and would again, to the safer territory of pre-Nazi German history, the eras of the emperor and the Hohenzollern rulers. Later, she brought up the allegedly Polish-made leaflets again. She cited a letter to a Kiel newspaper from a woman who said she had lived near the Polish border and must bear witness that "the Pole wreaked a lot of havoc with the Germans," chasing them out of their homes and farms, and that she also found the leaflets.

Not sharing Frau Burchert's line of reasoning that the leaflets thus were authentic, I asked if she were one hundred percent convinced they were Polish-made.

"That I cannot prove. I never saw one. Only that my parents knew it."

For what *reason* would Poland have dropped them?

"Poland wanted East Prussia. Since after the First World War."

Yet if that were true, was it not unlikely that Poland would publicize its intentions? And to the very people most likely angered by them?

"Ja, I understand you. Well, you could see it that way. That's why it is a little odd to me. If I planned to conquer another country, I wouldn't throw around such leaflets first." She then amended herself, saying the leaflets "came less from the government" than "single hotheads." Polish hotheads.

Frau Burchert, as may have been evident, simply was not forthcoming about the first eleven and a half years of the Third Reich. Then the chronology got to the point when Soviet troops were moving toward Tolnicken. And Irene Burchert became a different witness.

"The orders came to get ready to flee. January 20, 1945. The Ortsgruppenleiter gave the order. Then we packed the cart on a sled, and then the order came not to leave. The route we should take would be named later. The whole community together. The order did not come. Sunday was the twentieth. The next day, Monday, my father sent me to the Ortsgruppenleiter. We just went in. He had already fled, with both farmers from the neighboring village. Without telling us. And on the radio it still was being said the Russian would be held at the border. But in reality, Danzig [Gdansk] was already broken through and for all practical purposes we were cut off, ja? In the village, there were three men on leave, two of whom were soldiers on the eastern front who had not gone back. Afterward, they lay on the side of the street, shot. [As deserters, presumably.] They'd wanted to go home, too. That was Monday. Monday evening, an uncle of my father's came from Allenstein. He'd been a teacher in West Prussia and had retired to Allenstein. And brought two nieces who'd lived with him and went to school there. He was fifteen years older than my father, my grandfather's brother. And that evening he sat with my father and looked at the map. 'Let's *go.*' We had already packed, were loaded up. 'Let's go,' he said. And the adults decided to leave early the next morning. That was Tuesday. Soldiers, German Army, were still stationed in the village. At two in the morning, my mother and my father went to the village and the army was still there. They said, 'Good, if they're still there in the morning, we can go.' When we went to the village at six in the morning, we lived outside it, the German Army was gone. And then everyone came out on the street. 'What? You want to go and leave us here alone?' So we went back home. I was so happy, because I didn't want to leave. There were livestock. The stalls had been full of livestock. We had released them. The cows, the pigs. We'd given them all fodder. And we tied up the livestock again and, ja. But on Tuesday, the Russian was there." She had barely paused.

She later mentioned that she and her sisters had had a chance to escape "the Russian." Shortly before the invasion, a German officer stationed in the village urged her father to send the girls away with an army unit heading west. There was not enough room for the whole family, but the girls were in the most danger. Frau Grünwald told Irene the decision was hers. Irene decided not to leave her parents.

When the Soviet troops arrived, they did not come by way of the regular roads, as expected, but by old military roads. Why? According to Herr Grünwald, they were using their old maps from the First World War.

Frau Burchert's testimony about the Red Army's advance is sometimes jumbled, but vivid, and detailed. "Now we could see, we lived a little farther away, they first got the livestock. The horses, the cattle, the pigs. The livestock was herded together and the people had to get it to Russia. They had a horrible fate, those who had to drive the cattle. And then they came in the houses. They came from the Ort with a wagon and we could watch it. They came in the houses and looted. They opened the cupboards, they ripped the doors open, they ripped the beds apart. First they were in the luggage from the family [a family seeking refuge in the Grünwalds' home]. They found a clock. We were all standing against the wall. They wanted to shoot us all. This uncle of my father's could speak Polish. And he talked to them. That was an old man. He was over seventy. They then didn't do it, didn't shoot us. [Why her father did not try intervening in Russian is not clear.] Then they took my father with them and we were sure they would shoot him, because the mayors were all shot first. But they didn't shoot him right then. They took him to the neighbors, a White Russian family. And they'd had a hard time with their neighbors and my father always helped them. And then this White Russian said, 'What? You want to shoot him? He's always helped us. Let him go.' And really, they let my father go. He was not shot. Then the officers from the village came and he had to take so and so many people to work in the village. It was only women, the men were gone."

The work included cooking for Soviet troops. The Soviets chose Herr Grünwald's old friend, the Russian who had been a German POW, to oversee both the cooking and the provisions—a lot of provisions. Frau Burchert said the Soviets filled a room with food they took from the farms. Sides of ham were piled so high they reached the ceiling. The Soviets also collected the German staple of Schmalz [lard]. "They drove from farm to farm, got the Schmalz pots, all the cooking equipment, and we had to fill pails with it. That Schmalz then went to Russia. And then I saw they also took our Schmalz pot. 'Ach,' I say, 'now you've found our last Schmalz pot.' And then this [Russian cook] said, 'Take it with you again this evening.' So, there was that too, ja? We didn't have anything to eat. Everything had been taken from us. That was Schmalz from home butchering. We asked whether we could take the brown part. They didn't use it. That they allowed. Then my mother rendered it again and then we had fat, ja?"

Without pause, Frau Burchert recalled in minute detail (repeated with hardly a changed word during the second interview) being told to cook breakfast for the Soviet officers the next morning. Her father had her go to one house to ask a certain German-speaking Russian officer when to show up.

"He told me I had to be there at seven to make breakfast. And I say, 'But we have no more clocks. I cannot guarantee I'll be here at seven. We don't know the time anymore. Everything has been taken from us.' He turned around. There was a kind of display case and there stood a whole row of alarm clocks. 'Ach,' I say, 'there is our alarm clock.' And he took it and gave it to me and said the following. 'Hide it. Do not put it *on* your cupboard, but *in* your cupboard. And what you still have, hide. Otherwise everything will be taken.' That's what a Russian officer said to me in accent-free German."

She thinks the officer was Alexander Solzhenitsyn. She said it is known he was among the troops in Allenstein and was arrested not far from her village. "And he held himself apart from the other officers. The others did not think well of him. And Solzhenitsyn began to write back to Russia what they were doing here, that someday it would be avenged, that they were doing great injustice here. That's why he was arrested."

Was the man of dark hair and average height Solzhenitsyn? He did not answer letters of inquiry. A woman who once knew him well considered the above information and more of what Frau Burchert said and concluded that she thought not.[1]

Another task assigned Irene Grünwald was one she described as "horrible. We had to go to the village to bury the dead. Simply in the ground. One woman was brought in and the rats had already started chewing her face. That was so . . . There was no coffin, nothing. There was only a bed-sheet. And in the earth. A whole family was shot. Seven. The girls had clung to the parents. I wasn't there."

Other dead included a young local man, Albert. Deemed unfit to fight because of a heart problem, he had spent the war years at home, going from farm to farm to help the farm women with light tasks. Frau Burchert said that shortly after the Russians arrived, Albert's mother was at the Grünwalds', heard screams she knew were his, rushed toward the sounds, and found Albert dead. He had been shot in the back of the neck. Frau Burchert said the Russians, observing him go from one farm to another, had concluded he was a spy. They were heard to call him that as they shot him.

Frau Burchert delivered her testimony about the Soviet invasion of Tolnicken in such detail that the one subject she left out nearly screams its omission. The subject is rape. Individual rapes and gang rapes by Soviet soldiers of German women were so pervasive, it would have been an exception if any Grünwald female escaped. In fact, a documentary film calculates that at the end of the war at least two million German women were raped, the majority by Red Army soldiers.[2] Finally, without saying so directly, Frau Burchert indicated she was no exception. When the subject was neared, she whispered, "There are things I still do not talk about . . . ," then dropped into inaudibility. In her 1992 letter, she brought up the subject herself, saying she was asked to write a report about her experiences for an East Prussian museum. "I determined that I would not speak about the worst thing that could happen to a woman, rape. Not in conversation with you, either. I must repress a lot in order, to some extent, to be able to live."

One morning several days after the invasion, Russian soldiers roamed the streets of Tolnicken and grabbed people. Among them were Irene, her sisters, cousins, and Herr Grünwald. They did not grab Frau Grünwald. Why they chose whom they did is anyone's guess. Frau Burchert did not suggest her family members were taken for political reasons, but her father was the mayor and a Party member, and she and her sisters were in the BdM. And she "thought" her mother had not joined the Frauenschaft.

---

1. Thanks to Agnes Peterson for trying to help me reach him, and to Olga Carlisle for her insight.
2. It also reports considerable raping by soldiers of every other Allied force, except the British. *Befreier und Befreite* (translated as *Liberators take liberties*), directed by Helke Sander, 1992.

Before the exodus began, prisoners were interrogated. Because the village outcasts vouched for Herr Grünwald's character, Russian soldiers apparently held him in some regard. Frau Burchert said that after they questioned him they cut short questioning her, saying they could use the same information for "the daughters of Anton Grünwald." Then, in one of the more convoluted ironies of the Third Reich, the other local Russian, the former POW-turned-cook, sneaked the Grünwalds departure presents. He brought them a long woolen shawl and a spoon, and told them they would need both wherever they ended up.

Frau Burchert said she knew the destination was Siberia. Her father, who had his own experience in the matter, had told her so.

Some two thousand prisoners, mostly women and girls, and their guards, took off toward the east. Frau Burchert said that for a while she could see her family's farm. The group traveled by foot and in freight trains. An area south of Moscow would be the halfway point. The destination was indeed Siberia, a camp called Chelyabinsk, about 2,600 miles from Tolnicken. According to a book that former East Prussian inmates (not including Frau Burchert) wrote of their experiences,[3] the journey lasted three weeks. She indicated it took twice that.

However long it lasted, fear, cold, hunger, and death were part of it. Frau Burchert spoke about the overall experience episodically. At an early stop, she and her sisters volunteered to do the laundry because the payoff was "a bread" apiece. As they returned with their breads, the male prisoners were being led away. Among them was her father. She was not able to speak with him, but was able to give him her bread. That was the last time she saw him.

She did know, from him, that as the eldest she was now in charge of her sisters. She was to make sure she and they did everything they could to avoid attention.

That was only one of many concerns. The places where the prisoners were to sleep were filthy and crammed. Among the worst, as she described it, was in the East Prussian city of Insterburg. About fifty women were put in a cell meant for one or two people, and were given a single pail for a toilet. Days were wretched in other ways. Somehow Irene's thumb got painfully infected, and when she tried to protect it from a guard by pulling back, he hit her and threatened to shoot her. Other prisoners then put her among them to keep her out of sight. The same guard, observing her sister but not knowing the relationship, expressed concern that her shoes were so thin.

Provisions were meager and sometimes so bad that people eating them

---

3. *Verschleppt* (Deported) has as its subtitle "Women and Girls Deported from East Prussia to Siberia." It was published by the East Prussian exile organization, the Landsmannschaft Ostpreussen, in Hamburg about 1981. (No date is given.)

got sick and increasingly weak. Eventually some people could not go any farther. She said they were shot.

The farm-fed Grünwald girls started out healthy. But a younger sister became so sick and weak that Irene and the third sister all but carried her along. The sick sister wrapped herself ever tighter in the Russian's shawl. Irene believed it saved her life.

The change from walking to riding in freight cars was scarcely better. Frau Burchert said she noticed attempts were made to separate family and friends, so she and her sisters tried always to be on the same car, along with dozens and dozens of other women stuffed inside. Once a car was loaded, it was closed. There were no windows, and no toilet facilities. At one stop, the women were given some cabbage soup. They all got diarrhea. She said if the train stopped, women who had tin cans held them out between the slats to plead for water, the first Russian word Frau Burchert learned. She herself had managed to retrieve a small pail of her family's, but it did not fit between the slats.

Many prisoners died along the way, among them "a woman who fought death so long." As Frau Burchert spoke of the woman, her face changed. She seemed to be back with her.

After any woman died, the prisoners waited until the next stop and knocked on the train door. When a guard appeared, the women would say, in the guards' own fractured German phrase, "Frau kaputt." The guard then would take the body away. After one such knock, a guard opened the door, asked "Frau kaputt?" they answered, "Frau kaputt," he picked the woman up, saw a little movement in the body, yelled "Nix kaputt," and threw her back in.

During stops, one prisoner from each train car was allowed to retrieve food rations for herself and the other women in her car. One woman came back "chalk-white," said Frau Burchert. The woman had managed to peek into the car behind the engine, the car that carried the coal. On top of a pile of coal were naked bodies. It was apparent they were being used for fuel, too.

Did Frau Burchert, in relating such grotesque scenes, think about train cars filled with victims of Nazis? The similarities were so stark—a long, fearful, and sometimes deadly journey in crammed, dark airlessness to an unknown destination. And what of the perverted practical disposal of the human beings who did not survive the trip or the fate that followed it? Starved bodies fueling a train, cremated bodies making annihilation camp cabbages grow. Did she consider any such similarities? Furthermore, did she connect Russian treatment of German civilians with German treatment of Russian civilians? Did she connect the planned German invasion of the Soviet Union to her own unplanned journey in the same direction? She did not say so yet.

When the surviving prisoners finally reached Chelyabinsk, it was spring-time in Germany, but still winter in Siberia. There was snow on the ground. It was melting, however. Winter really was near an end. So was the Third Reich. Hitler killed himself.

A Russian guard told her, "Hitler kaputt."

Her reaction?

"There was no reaction. Nothing at all mattered to us. We were no Hitler fans, even if I was in the Bund deutscher Mädel. We had no rights, were treated like cattle. . . ."

Frau Burchert said the book about Chelyabinsk paints a better picture than existed, because most essays were written by women who worked in the camp's kitchen. "Those who had to work in the tile factory had it bad. I worked in the tile factory. I was so miserable, I couldn't move anymore." She said none of the mechanized parts of the tile-making operation was oiled, so she had to push and shove the various components into position. "That was terribly difficult. And I didn't have a fever. I couldn't be written up as sick. I had sciatica, ja? In the back. My right leg is also thinner. If it had been shorter, I would have been an invalid. But it was only thinner, ja?" She said "a nice Volga German doctor" in the camp prescribed lighter work for her. "I got lighter work. Loading tiles. Sometimes all day long."

Many conditions at Chelyabinsk, as Frau Burchert described them, also seemed similar to those at Nazi-run concentration camps. Homesickness, hard, hard work, followed by long evening roll calls in the cold, exhaustion, and almost above all else, hunger. As in concentration camps, the two unreliable links to life were labor and food. There was little to eat in Chelyabinsk, as Frau Burchert described the rations, and what there was, was often bad. The aforementioned book about the camp described one soup as consisting of a horse head boiled in water. As in the memories of Holocaust survivors, Frau Burchert recalled some meals in detail. There was, for example, salted herring that made everyone sick. She later got permission to rinse it. But she said few people died of hunger. "You were always hungry, but there was a little too much to starve to death."

Prisoners died of other causes, mostly disease. The conditions at the camp contributed to many cases of dysentery, which, if untreated, can lead to death. Frau Burchert said two thousand people arrived with her at Chelyabinsk. By the end of the first year, only eight hundred were alive.

"Every night a wagon was driven by with bodies in it, naked. A little bit of straw over them. And my sister and some [other prisoners] went and dug a large, deep hole. The next day, the corpses were in it with a little straw over them. And we had to dig a new hole." One of the dead who did not die of disease was a young woman named Monika. She went insane. She suddenly began yelling, "The trains are coming! We are definitely going home!" ran into a fence, and was shot.

Frauen

Had Frau Burchert read of cartloads of Nazi victims, not even covered with straw, thrown into other holes, dug by people who themselves would soon lie in them? Had she seen photographs of people who, insane or sane, had run into electrified fences? She did not mention them yet.

On one crucial point, similarities with concentration camps ended. Prisoners were not beaten, she said. (Nor did they die as a result of medical experiments, commando squads, or gas.)

They could be punished, however, for infractions such as lying during their formal interrogation about their background. Knowing this and fearing a discrepancy could get them in trouble, the Grünwalds rehearsed. "We learned it by heart. How many cows my parents had, how many sheep, how many pigs and horses, et cetera. Pity whoever gave a wrong answer. Then we'd be locked up in a sort of hole in the ground.

"And then I was asked, 'How many foreign workers did you have?' ["Foreign worker" was a common German euphemism for prisoner of war.] I said, 'One Frenchman.' Then this Russian officer screamed at me, 'You're lying! You could not work the land with only *one* Frenchman.' 'Indeed we could,' say I. 'We could. We three girls and this Frenchman harvested the fields.' He did not say another word. I probably had been too fresh." She had not meant to be, she said. "I talked to him exactly as he talked to me. I answered back exactly as loud and only told the truth. We did always work together in the fields during harvest."

Her retort cost her. "I had the 'Red 6' on my card and my sisters didn't. And I was sent to the prisoner-of-war camp." The "Red 6" indicated a politically suspect person. Irene Grünwald did not then know she had a "Red 6," nor what other consequence it would entail.

But the prisoner-of-war camp was a boon. "It really was better for us, because we didn't have to do the hardest work." She volunteered for kitchen duty and got it. She implied her labors were appreciated. She "cooked honestly," as she had been taught at home and in home economics school. "For instance, not to add cold water to soup. It wouldn't taste good." Kitchen duty did not last long. When her health improved, she was assigned night shift in the tile factory, with "nothing to eat all night long."

In speaking of her time at the camp, she seemed to find the emotional deprivations as trying and as unfair as the physical ones. To a degree, the emotional aftermath also mirrored that of Holocaust survivors, in that she said she did not talk about the experience for years, but "repressed" it. Religious holidays were especially hard. "The first Christmas we were there, we were not allowed to sing church songs. We were not even allowed to sing Christmas songs. We were hauled outside to clear the tracks, just as a trick, ja? It was almost midnight and we had to shovel snow from the train tracks. And someone began to sing 'Silent Night.' A Russian guard was there, too. He must have known it was our Christmas Eve, ja? Then no one shoveled any more snow and we all bawled, ja? And, and some began to pray. And then he went back with us to the camp. The stretches [of track] were practically clean. We'd already cleaned them that day. That was only a trick."

She also resented having to sing the Communist anthem, "The Internationale," and being forced to sing songs about Communist folk heroes such as Rosa Luxemburg or, she said with a touch of disdain, being "brothers together for freedom." When she and others burst into their own folk songs, the guards quieted them with "Nix, nix, nix."

What kept her going both on the trek to Chelyabinsk and in the camp itself, she said, were two things. One was hope. "We hoped to return home. Whoever had no hope, died." The other thing was faith. The prisoners got Sundays off and spent the time doing "a lot of praying" secretly. "Now, one did sometimes ask oneself, 'Dear God, why us? Why must we be in this hell?'"

Unlike other hells, Chelyabinsk had a most unusual angel: the wife of the camp commandant. Irene briefly was assigned to her as a housekeeper. With the Russian words she had picked up and with sign language, they were able to introduce themselves and communicate. Not only was the wife "good" to her, so was the husband. ("The Russian as a human being is a pleasant human being," she said at one point, when "the Russian" was not the subject.) The relationship with the commandant's wife lasted longer than the arrangement. After Irene was reassigned to more arduous work, the wife sometimes sent for her and gave her food. And once after Irene finished a shift unloading coal cars, there stood the commandant's wife with a plate of potato pancakes.

Frau Burchert said she and other prisoner women also were helped by a Polish Jewish Communist man who was in charge of one part of the camp. He warned them not to steal food from the fields that day, for there would be an inspection. He "did not hate" Germans, added Frau Burchert. Her remark can be considered a variation of the phenomenon of the "house Jew"—the former Jewish neighbor or colleague with whom the "Aryan" had a good relationship and, more importantly, supposedly bore the "Aryan" no ill will. This was the first "camp Jew" I had heard of performing the role.

Despite kindnesses from unexpected grantors of it, Frau Burchert's life at Chelyabinsk unquestionably was dismal. An especially low point came after she requested a transfer to a collective farm where one sister was assigned. The person in charge of transfers looked up her papers, discovered the "Red 6," and said she could not go. Irene did not know what else the stigma signified, but she eventually found out. Her sisters were released without her. She had no idea when, if ever, she would be freed.

She was finally released in 1949.

It is a given that Irene Grünwald Burchert suffered a long and traumatic ordeal. Yet throughout her telling of it, certain nagging questions remained both unanswered and unasked. Did the ordeal so traumatize her that she saw only it and not the trauma her countrymen inflicted on others? Or did

151

she one day recognize the comparisons? And did she connect her trauma to other events that cruelly but logically led to it? I broached the subject by asking if she had seen or heard of German concentration camps.

"Ja," she answered. "And I also saw the films. I know how it looked. Only I didn't know it then. That was unjust, what happened to the human beings. That was unjust. And the two hundred people to a barracks. . . ."

What barracks? Her barracks. Similar questions led to similar answers. It seemed that in her mind, the sources of her four years of misery all lay outside Germany. They lay in the Allied countries of the First World War, in Poland, and most of all in the Soviet Union. "My husband and I both got to know Communism, and we are afraid of it." She buttressed her answers with her lapful and tableful of source notes. There was the American journalist who had been at the Nuremberg war trials and wondered how a people could sink so low, until he began studying the Soviet Union, where people got twenty-five years' forced labor "for nothing." Then she found a German edition of a book by an Englishman about Stalin's policies leading to widespread hunger. Admittedly both bored and annoyed by the unremitting deflections from the Third Reich, I said I knew about people starving under Stalin.

Frau Burchert looked genuinely surprised. "You do?"

It is fairly common knowledge, I replied.

She seemed to lose a degree of steam, but continued on a course by then predictable. "Because here, only the cruelties of the Germans are discussed, over and over. But that was only twelve years of German history." The familiarity of the only-twelve-years argument made it (to me) no less repugnant, and I asked about its significance.

"Twelve years in the whole span of German history. We could go back to the beginning of recorded time. When we only think of those twelve years, we get no correct picture of Germans. There will be . . ." She switched subjects and proffered more photographs. "Here are concentration camps in Poland after the First World War, filled with Germans."

Frau Burchert then asked me to locate in the United States a certain book said to contain a chart showing which countries in the last five hundred or so years had been at war the most (whether in offense, defense, or both did not seem to matter). It was her understanding Germanic territories did not encompass the number-one spot. Later, I located a copy of the book and sent her a photocopy of the chart she wanted to see. Germany did not lead the pack.[4]

Frau Burchert did make connections from one historical event to another. But they leapfrogged backward over the Third Reich entirely and

---

4. Although I forget the book's title and who supposedly fought the most wars, it is my recollection the finger of accusation pointed at Portugal and the Netherlands.

landed on earlier years. "You cannot write about this time [separately]. You must start at least with the First World War." She often repeated the theme. "If the German people had not been treated like serfs after the First World War, Hitler never would have been able to get a foothold."

But what was going on when she was old enough to observe it got short shrift. What about Hitler taking back the Rhineland and the Sudeten part of Czechoslovakia? Answer: Both belonged to Germany. What about the German-Soviet pact? Stalin had Hitler "in his pocket" and Hitler did not know he was being used. Soon she was back to the First World War and reading from a book about Polish and Czech diplomats trying to deport Germans.

She had read so much about the entire period of time, I said, might she be able to recommend a book about the behavior of German troops toward the Russian civilian population?

There was one, but she had not read it. A pause. (What would she say? That in retrospect the miserable Verschleppte such as herself should not have been entirely surprised by Russian hostility?) The pause ended. "The Russian people," she answered, "regarded the German soldiers as liberators."

Liberators?

"That I know from my husband. Whoever plundered—I'm speaking of the army [Wehrmacht]—was punished." She began looking for a paper about it.

Finally, she did have a book to suggest regarding conditions in the Soviet Union. *The First Circle of Hell*, by Solzhenitsyn. She acknowledged, while continuing to go through her papers, "it is not about the German Wehrmacht." The object of her current search was a document showing how, contrary to the treatment of German prisoners in Russia, "Russian prisoners in Germany were treated better."

I'm not talking about prisoners of war. . . .

"Yes, but it hangs together. The war saved Communism in Russia, ja? Stalin was through, his cruelties almost at an end. Now, because of the invasion by the Germans, he could call for a war of the Motherland."

Had she read about what German SS commandos in Russia did?

She said softly, "Nein, nein. Nein."

Perhaps it is a part of it. Because there was so much revenge vis-à-vis the Germans. . . .

"Perhaps one can say that. One can see it that way, too." She paused. "And nonetheless there are other Russians who saw it differently. 'What we are doing is crueler.'"

After a while, I tried again. In Siberia, did she ever think how it came to this? That it was not as if Russian men woke up one day and said, Let's go rape German women.

"Nein, but Russia had armed itself for war. And if our soldiers had not marched in, they would have invaded us."

Frauen

More than four decades after the war ended, did she ever think, if only she had done something different?

"Nein, nein. After all, we never persecuted."

The conscience of Irene Grünwald Burchert is clear. "You know, at the time I also saw things a bit from the religious side. We're Catholic, ja? And we prayed to our Lord Jesus, we are voluntarily prepared to atone for the sins of other human beings. Perhaps God accepts my word. That's how I interpreted it. I myself am not knowingly guilty, but I prayed this prayer. With my heart. Not only with my voice."

What had she learned during the whole time?

"'Learned' is hard to say. Does one learn from injustice? Yes, one should learn from injustice. Learned. Me personally. Emmm. I learned how Communism works, how they treat their own people. Emmm. I cannot say anything else."

"When the girls went to be shot, I asked the Polish Maria, who was going too, 'Where will you be this evening?' They all had their packages of belongings with them. 'Look up at Ursa Major this evening. I'll be there.' 'What?' I stood still, right at the gate where I asked that."

Eight young Polish women prisoners of Ravensbrück Concentration Camp, including the one named Maria, had been ordered to come to the camp's administration office that evening. They were told to bring their packets of possessions with them. Soon thereafter, Frau Lotte Müller and her fellow prisoners learned the fate of the eight young women not by looking into the stars, but into the office. "There lay eight packets on the table. We knew what had happened. They'd shot them all."

Ravensbrück was the Nazis' concentration camp especially for women. Lotte Müller arrived there when she was forty-one years old. The charge against her was "preparation for high treason," and her papers carried the notation *Rückkehr unerwünschst* [Return not wanted]. The phrase basically meant a death sentence.

In Ravensbrück, death could come by many means. It could come not only by shooting but by hunger, or exposure, or disease, especially tuberculosis and typhus, or by the effects of gruesome medical experiments, or by trying to escape. An estimated fifty thousand women—Catholics, Jews, Protestants, Gypsies, nuns, Communists, women from twenty-three different countries—died in the hellhole of Ravensbrück, located about fifty miles north of Berlin. Babies died there, too. Born to

Frau Charlotte (Lotte) Müller

Solidarity and Survival

newly arrived, newly pregnant women, the babies usually lived only briefly, often dying of "natural" causes such as freezing or starvation, their mothers too cold and malnourished to offer warmth and milk.

Other deaths only started in Ravensbrück. Frau Müller remembered a wagonload of women prisoners who had been reduced to raving, blithering skeletons being sent to another camp to be finished off by gassing. Children, too—imprisoned orphans tenderly cared for by imprisoned adoptive "mothers"—were sent away to be gassed.

Frau Müller also remembered other women so far gone in weakness and sickness that they lay nearly motionless upon bedding straw, their excrement caked to them. The straw was removed and replaced as if the women were animals. Many women began their incarceration with relatively sound bodies and minds. They then faced, among other deprivations, not only poor to decreasing rations, but, because of overcrowding, sometimes not even a utensil or plate for eating what food there was. The camp was meant for six thousand prisoners. At one point it held at least thirty-six thousand.

The majority of prisoners did not have warm clothes, or a warm blanket, or sometimes, because of overcrowding, any blanket at all. (The camp's storerooms were jammed with an abundance of pilfered goods. But they were meant for guards, not prisoners.) In addition, those prisoners who could work, worked very, very hard. Indoors, bloodied bare feet pushed the treadles of looms. Outdoors, backbreaking work of all kinds was the norm in all kinds of weather.

Then there were the SS guards and commanders, of both sexes. By mistreating their prisoners, said Frau Müller, they were "better respected" by their peers. With such an impetus, each seemed to outdo the other in ordering or effecting whimsically heinous barbarities and day-to-day cruelties. Lotte Müller spent 1,095 days and nights in Ravensbrück. She survived because of one major reason. She had a profession valuable enough to the camp's SS administrators that they wanted to keep her alive, if barely. She was a plumber.

She was, in fact, the head of a five-woman plumbing "battalion." (Actually, only three of the women worked. The two others were so sick and weak she sneaked them into the group as a cover to save their lives.) Frau Müller's status did not prevent her, too, from being beaten and otherwise punished. But it did give her more freedom of movement than other prisoners had, thus enabling her to witness more than other prisoners might have. What she saw was a lifetime's worth of inhumanity on the part of her overseers and a lifetime's worth of humanity on the part of many—by no means all—of her fellow prisoners.

Her eyes may have been open, but her mind had been set long before, in her hometown of Berlin. The Nazi court that sent her to Ravensbrück did so to put her in "protective custody," a phrase as cynical then as now. She was to be "reeducated," a term less cynical than ludicrous. "Na, how can they reeducate me? That I'd like to know." Nazi reeducation did not work for Lotte Müller. It never would have.

Lotte's beliefs were formed when she was a schoolgirl. From all evidence, she never deviated an iota from them. Her teacher, in terms of the first person she really listened to, was her father. He was a plumber in the metal-workers' union (the German word for plumber, *Klempner,* also means "metal worker") and a member of the Social Democratic Party. Herr Müller had received his political convictions from his father, also an active member of the Social Democratic movement.

In the early years of this century, the Müller family—Lotte's father, mother, sister, and she—lived a Berlin working family life fused to their political beliefs. The Müllers lived in a Social Democratic–built workers' apartment and bought their food in a Social Democratic co-op. The children went to a Social Democratic kindergarten. "Everywhere there were Social Democrats my father was *there,*" added Frau Müller, going low on the last word. Her voice, bass from smoking, also was characterized by an unwavering Berlin accent (*y* for *g* making *Gott* sound like *Yott*), a good deal of slang, much of it crude, and poor grammar. Lotte Müller was not fancy. (It is doubtful anyone ever called her by her full first name, Charlotte.)

"Naturally, my father heard about politics from my grandfather. And as a manual laborer [Handwerker], of course he doesn't join the party where the employers are. He goes where the employees are. So my father was in the Social Democratic Party and in the union and was an official. Then he got no jobs because of his political work. Already then, around 1900, he was on the blacklist. So he became an independent worker.

"I was influenced by him. And I was interested in his trade, even as a child. After school I went to his workshop. First I had to do my homework and he oversaw it or talked with me. Then he told me about nature, as I had to hold the long pipes when he sweated them or whatever. He discussed it with me, in a way for children still. I remember exactly and can repeat the sayings he told me. And it was there I learned from him to hate the police and to be there for the workers.

"I was still in school and I wrote my essays that way, so the teacher wrote underneath, 'Where did you get *that?*' 'Ja, my father told me,' this and that. 'I don't find it quite right.' I had to write 'Mein Vaterland, mein Vaterland.' Ja, if our Fatherland were for the poor, it would have been a good Fatherland. But that it was not. For workers, there wasn't such a Fatherland. In the First World War, everyone got into the war for the capitalists. And that's how I wrote my essays."

She said one teacher took her aside to confide he thought she was right in her thinking. Another teacher thrashed her. "I defended myself, too," she added. "Father said to that, 'You get something to eat here and therefore must go to school. I have to defend myself, too, against the capitalists.'

"Once he took me with him, to the capitalists. He was invited early Sunday by a director to his beautiful home and took me with him. Naturally I couldn't go up with him, but had to wait below." She said she was about ten, the same age as the director's daughter (the "chic Mädchen," she called her), who came down and played with her until a governess snatched the other girl away. "I was dressed in clean clothes," said still-smarting Frau Müller, "but maybe hers were cleaner or prettier. That can be." The lesson in class differences took. "One already started to think then, nicht?"

When she was only sixteen, her father died. But by then, Herr Müller had taught her enough about politics to risk her life and enough about plumbing to save it.

After his death, she continued her plumbing apprenticeship by going to a trade school, despite the taunts of neighborhood children and despite the more conventional wishes of her mother. "My mother said I should be a 'chic Madame.' That she never accomplished." Frau Müller nearly choked on her laugh. "I just remained the way I *was*."

Whichever way she was, she also needed to earn money. During the financial roller coaster of the 1920s, besides trying to get what plumbing work she could, Frau Müller learned to play the violin and taught beginning classes at a conservatory. "In the needy time, I earned countless money under the table." During one period of unemployment, she saw a sign to take a test as a children's swimming instructor. She took it, passed, and in 1928 got a job as a "Schwimmeisterin" at a public pool. There, she became acquainted with a social ranking one step higher than that of "worker." It was "employee."

She extended her approval. "They're workers too," she said. "They're not better and are just as exploited as workers, nicht? That is clear."

The same year, Lotte Müller joined the Communist Party.

If she was a fraction as enthusiastic then about being a Party member as she was in her much later years, she must have made quite an impression. Since the war's end, and possibly to her death, she made her home in East Berlin. (Attempts to reach her in the years after our meeting were unsuccessful; she may not have lived to see her dream repudiated.) High in an old apartment building, in a crowded, cozy living room overlooking a noisy intersection of traffic and playground, Lotte Müller reigned like the respected old fighter she was. Her frizzy white hair parted in the middle and tied back with brightly colored yarn, thick glasses extending her eyes like light bulbs, she in turn scoffed at a doctor's report on her cancer, pounded a small completed portion of a handicraft rug on her lap, gestured for hours with an unlighted cigarette, snapped at a female companion, refused (or ignored) almost any interruption to her often bewilderingly meandering tales, and remained impassioned and unswerving in her admiration for communism. Nearly any mention of it, in fact, prompted her to burst into a workers' song or verse. Conversely, she showed an equally impassioned loathing for communism's antithesis. "I would *not* want to live in a capitalist country, because then I would have to put up with capitalism again."

And as bad in her book as capitalism was Nazism. It immediately changed her life, by banning labor unions and opposition political parties, especially Communists and Social Democrats, and the organizations—in which Lotte Müller had spent many years—connected with them. "Everything was dissolved and no one asked any more questions."

The Nazis' intrusion into her life included the swimming pool where she still worked. She was, by then, thirty-two years old. Her boss had assigned her to the cash register and the accounting division. "He could put me anywhere and didn't want to lose me. Then I was supposed to work in the administrative office." But an SS man was put in overall charge of managing the pool. "Sometimes they were really dumb pigs [Manchmal ganz dumme Schweine waren das]. They were stupider than the ones the police allowed in. I walked in, said, 'A good day to you.' I did not say 'Heil Hitler!' So! Therefore I was fired, because of communistic . . . well, they called everything communist."

Her world was not so one-sided that she did not know Hitler supporters. "Ja. I knew some. They did it because they were afraid and they wanted work, because there was a lot of unemployment. Many of us workers gave in. It happened."

She also saw Adolf Hitler herself, she said. She was on her way to visit her mother. "In front of the palace there's a view of the Wilhelmsplatz and it was *full* of dames." (Frau Müller used the word *Weiber*, which straddles the linguistic border between being common and being disrespectful.) She lowered her husky smoke-choked voice even lower and mimicked what the Weiber were screaming. "We want to see our Führer. We want to see our Führer."

"I got off [the streetcar] and peeked at this big deal with the Weiber. They were completely in love with him. It's a mentality like with soccer, the whole stadium goes crazy. And here were these dopey German Weiber. Whether they had no man of their own, I don't know. There's always an excess of women. And they stood down there, 'We want to see our Führer.' A *scream* I tell you, like at a soccer field. When the soccer people down there don't 'play toward their snout' or whatever. Anyway, making a lot of noise. That was the mentality back then."

Frau Müller said she assumed the crowd was made up of the bourgeoisie [Bürgerlichen] and "not real workers. Because I cannot imagine a worker from Siemens who works all day, eight hours and more, taking up a position at the Wilhelmsplatz and saying, 'We want to see our Führer.'"

Afterward she went on her way, as unimpressed then as later. In her recollection of the incident, she did not even allude to what Hitler looked like.

"Hitler said he'd rule for a thousand years. And the apes believed it. But there weren't many," she added. "And do you know how I know exactly what was going on with the Führer? My brother-in-law is a trained riding instructor. And his brother was, too, and their father worked for the czar, to care for his horses. They were in Russia a long time. My brother-in-law's brother took care of [President Paul von] Hindenburg's horses. Well. Now Hindenburg goes and Hitler comes to the same house with the horses and could not stand horses." Frau Müller paused for effect. "And everyone in the house all knew Hitler personally."

Their opinion was, she said, "He was not completely *normal.* When there was some dispute, he threw himself to the ground—my brother-in-law saw it—and he bit the carpet."

After savoring her remark, Frau Müller added, "He didn't drink schnapps, only seltzer. But he got into such a rage when something went wrong. And that was what the capitalists needed, to make the working class kaputt. . . ."

In the autumn of 1933, several months after losing her job at the swimming pool, Lotte Müller got a new position. She began doing illegal work for the Communist Party. "When one does illegal work, one must have a certain aura," she said. "First, one must hate the capitalists. One must know where one belongs. Second, to feel correct within this hate and do one's illegal work. With the friendliest face, do something else."

She started working in Germany, but soon had to leave. "The Party told me, 'You have to get away. Someone in Cologne "went high" and named your name.' We already knew it. The Party was well organized. And I crossed over the border, through Essen, to Holland. I was there to 1936 and was arrested because we had no identity cards and was shoved over to Belgium. It was better in Belgium. There I got an identity card, but no work permit. Now we had to live from the solidarity of the Belgian workers, nicht? [The Party] wanted to use me in Germany, but then it came out they were looking for me there."

She continued talking, accompanied by a persistent cuckoo clock calling the hour over the din of the traffic and the playground, saying that working illegally in Holland and Belgium "for our Party" involved working among colleagues she called the "emigrants." The overall job description was doing "illegal work against Hitler in Germany. We had the sections of the Rhineland and the Pfalz. The French had the areas farther below, Lothringen and whatever, and the Norwegians had everything up here. Everything was divided by illegal work." Part of what she did, she said, was help Belgian, Norwegian, and Dutch Communists get to Spain to fight in its civil war.

"They all went through my lists. The workers have doors from one country into another."

In Holland, "friendly workers" provided food and a place to sleep. "But we never had a cent. For three years I never had a penny in my pocket." She then found a coin worth twenty-five cents and splurged. "I went in a store and wanted to buy something nice. I bought two washcloths, for six cents, so that I had something left over. Then I went back to the house and showed the people and they said, 'We could have sewn washcloths ourselves.' I said, 'No, that's not the point. The point is, I went in a *store* and *bought* something.'

"Anyway, in the emigration, we collected money for our illegal fight. First to care for ourselves, more or less so that we could sleep, and then we wrote articles for the newspaper. I wrote several, for the Dutch papers, too.

"We collected money for our illegal newspaper, *The Red Flag* [*Die Rote Fahne*]. Very thin paper and it was printed in Antwerp. Sometimes there was no money to pay the printer." So she went to "Belgian people with names," including a professor who contributed a lot. "We didn't buy ourselves any shoes with it. We gave the money to our elders, our Party secretary."

Frau Müller seemed particularly pleased with two actions. She said Communist "cells" in a pharmaceutical factory, mostly young Belgians, stole sheets of the printed medical instructions that were to be inserted in bottles of medicine. Other party members printed the Communist manifesto on the reverse side, and Belgian packers inserted the two-sided data in every thousand or so medicine bottles to be shipped to Germany.

Belgian workers made similar efforts with a weekly German newspaper that was sent to Belgium. They removed the inner pages and substituted their own. "Inside, all the pages were full of things against Hitler. They switched all the packets at the train station and people came to the kiosk and bought our newspaper. Is that not right? There were such idealistic things. And before they realized it was another newspaper, all the newspapers in the kiosk were sold. That is illegal work. And the workers always feel correct in such a situation, because it had to do with 'hindering' the war.

"If we get a war, a new war, and we are not for war," she added, "the whole world will be socialistic. Socialism is coming to our world."

While Frau Müller was fulfilling her missions in the Low Countries, the Gestapo was trying to find her through her sister, whom they tailed. "They didn't know where I was. When my mother and my sister moved to East Prussia to live with relatives, when they went to the forest to pick blueberries, there was even a man there, dressed as a woman, who looked to see if I'd appear. They did that. They went with my sister every morning as she rode her bicycle to work at Siemens. Someone on a bicycle always rode behind her. They wanted me at all costs, nicht? And didn't get me." She said they did not mistreat her sister. "They didn't mistreat me either, because they didn't get me. If they had got me, they would have mistreated me. I know

Party members they mistreated horribly." She also knew friends who were mistreated to the point of death, or killed outright.

"Our Jewish girls in Brussels. I was with them in the emigration. They ended up in the gas chambers. Even their children were taken from them. One was shot to death because of antimilitary work." But first the woman was "versaut." [The nondictionary word means acting like a pig to someone. In this case, it includes rape.] "She was pretty as a picture," added her old friend. "And the SS all had their way with her until she almost died."

Throughout her years of illegal work against Hitler, Frau Müller maintained her love not only for Communism, but for Germany. "I had a Party assignment to leave the country. Without it I wouldn't have left. I maintained discipline. One must. And there's nothing more beautiful than to live in such circles. Do you understand? You feel what I'm saying. Not to be misused by anyone. And we all had good comrades in this circle, if we also starved or whatever. Such enthusiasm! We were attached to our Heimat. I was free. I could have married in Holland or in Belgium. I had admirers. You can imagine that when one is young, one has admirers. But I wouldn't marry a foreigner. I said, I *stay* German and I don't care how it goes. Then, such bastards . . . I did see that one married an Italian woman, the other an Indonesian woman and so on. The marriages are so *different.* Only with a German man can I talk and work together with him. Either have joy or go under. I remain German and that's *that.*" ("Basta!" she said.)

Frau Müller never married. "But I lived with a man. And because we couldn't get a house, we built ourselves a little cottage. He was a carpenter and I helped and we had a pretty house. Below a room and a kitchen and above the sleeping area." They had no children, "out of a sense of responsibility. Then what would happen if I'd had a child? It would have been in the Hitler Youth or the Hitler girls. There was nothing to be done about it. I knew that from the girls around me."

In the spring of 1940, Lotte Müller's life as a free spirit in an unfree world ended. "The Germans came to Belgium. Hitler would have conquered the whole world if that had been possible. He probably would have come to America. He would have packed England in a sack. He packed France in a sack."

On the morning of October 27, the Gestapo arrested Frau Müller. Her specific arresting agent was a Berliner. She said she told him, "I didn't know how I was getting back to Germany. It cost too much money to travel there. It's good you've come so I can get back for free."

She was tried in the Moabit section of Berlin on an old charge involving her connection with a Communist workers' group. "There was *no* betrayal among us in the emigration. No one! The Gestapo never knew who our boss was. I knew it. Because I was the only one who went to his home. Had there been a betrayal, I as a Party member would have been suspected first, nicht? That is a heavy duty." She laughed, mockingly.

162

She was sentenced to a year and a quarter in prison, which she served. On the day of her release, in April 1942, instead of gaining freedom, she and other women prisoners were handcuffed in the prison hallway and put on a train to Ravensbrück.

She already knew about the camp. "We were all afraid. No one wasn't. But there are human beings who don't show their fear. I'm one of them. When there was something difficult, I always thought of a way out and somehow found it, nicht? And later I had second thoughts about it and my heart slid away from me. Or when I worked illegally, I did my assignment and had to be in control afterward to make sure everything was in order. Then I got scared about what could have happened."

But Ravensbrück seemed even more dangerous. "We did not know, you see, when you went to sleep at night if you'd wake the next morning. They could have had something else planned to keep us reined in. They could pull us all out of bed and make us stand naked at the block [for outdoor roll call] in winter, which they often did. The SS got sudden ideas and carried them out."

The considerable remains of where they carried them out have been turned into a memorial and museum, but the site alone makes an oppressive impact. For example, on display outside the camp gate is a mammoth concrete roller, taller than a person, at least twelve feet wide, and designed to be pulled by a truck to grade streets. Frau Müller said forty to fifty Jewish women pulled it, overseen by a guard and her dog.

To hear her talk, it seemed there was nothing in Ravensbrück she had not known about, heard about, or seen herself.

She had an especially vivid and personal memory of one woman guard's cruelty. Frau Müller's plumbing battalion was called to the rightfully feared "Strafblock" [punishment area] to make some repairs in the adjoining washroom. As they finished, they heard an enormous commotion behind the Strafblock door and the voice of a female SS guard screeching and vilely cursing. When the noise did not let up and the waiting became unbearable, Frau Müller and her crew opened the door. The SS guard, a Frau Lehmann, in a towering rage and with an inhuman look on her face, was thrashing the women prisoners with a club, hitting randomly everyone she could reach and then pounding a group that had sought refuge behind overturned furniture. "The SS Weiber could really beat a prisoner. She was beating the girls, the table knocked over, the chairs kaputt and everything every which way and didn't let anyone get out. She stood there in the doorway, hitting all around her with a club. And we looked at her and didn't say a word and she turned and said, 'Ach, you all want to leave, don't you? I also have to give my child something to drink. It's time.'" The guard then hung up her club and escorted the horrified plumbing battalion out the door as if nothing had happened.

163

"She had to nurse her child," continued Frau Müller. "When she was gone I told the girls, 'She must have sour milk in her breasts, this Weib.' That is a *woman*." Frau Müller fell silent. "Such a thing happened. They are *beasts*, is what they are. It is simply unbelievable that human beings can be that way. What do you as a woman say to that?"

Frau Müller had her own answer. "They wanted to move up, to get more money. Or they had a boyfriend in the SS who was in the shooting commando. They had 'yearnings for validity [Geltungsbedürfnisse—a very ornate word for Frau Müller].' Were as stupid as all get out," she added, back to her usual way of talking.

"Picture this. An Austrian girl comes and enters Block One across the way. A second Austrian girl who was with us leaves, and says, 'Servus! [It is Austrian dialect for "Hello!"]' She [a guard] starts to scream at her and pound her. 'No French is to be spoken here,' and so on. Just picture that! Beat her for saying 'Servus!' From behind I bellowed, because we all stood together with our plates in our hands because there was no more room at the table to eat, I yelled, '*Servus* is Latin.' She turned around, because she wanted to get me. I just stood there and kept eating. And the other girls protected me. Situations could flare up so quickly in the camp. She also had a dog, a black German shepherd."

All the guards, said Frau Müller, carried a club for hitting people, and for variety, a riding whip. She said she herself was beaten especially severely and for no apparent reason. The head female SS guard had ordered her to find another guard to accompany her to repair a water faucet in the head guard's apartment. After she asked a room of guards for one to come with her, one came outside and thrashed her. "I kept screaming, 'I have to do this assignment for Frau Aufseherin [Mrs. Guard],' again and again. And she beat me. But I did not feel a thing. I can stand beatings, nicht? You can imagine what kind of skin I have. Kept screaming again and again. She [the head guard] must have seen it."

Acts of humanity by guards did exist, she said, but were punished by the camp commandant. "We had two female guards who were prisoners with us in the concentration camp. They delivered letters to the families of the prisoners or gave prisoners bread or whatever. Anyway, somehow they had contact with our prisoners and did something against the camp order. Then the guards came 'inside.'"

Asked if the average guards (those with no such humane gestures) had something against women from a particular country, she immediately responded "Ja!" and then said, "Most of all, Jews. Jews and Poles." And if a woman were both Jewish and Polish? "That was worse yet. Even worse is a Polish Communist. They didn't even get to the camp. They shot them earlier.

"Ja, a thing happened with Polish girls," she continued, and told a story that seems almost unbelievable in the annals of Ravensbrück. "Two pretty

Polish girls fell in love with two SS men and the other way around of course, too. The two SS with the Polish girls. There are pretty Polish girls. It's well known. And we knew what was going on, we already knew. One day the two girls were gone. How they got out nobody knows for sure, even today. Whether they were in SS uniforms or what." She went on, "The two SS people picked them up, had an airplane ready, and off they went, to Switzerland." There, she said, they married.

Frau Müller's companion, interjecting perhaps because of my look of disbelief, said, "Well, they're all human beings. I can understand it."

The Polish girls did not leave empty-handed, added Frau Müller. They took with them a list of names of other Polish women in Ravensbrück who were "death candidates." The women were in a special block, where they were considered "Nacht und Nebel" [night and fog] prisoners. The reference —a cynical appropriation from Goethe—is to Hitler's decree to have persons who endangered Germany disappear without a trace, into the night and fog.

According to Frau Müller, the newly escaped Polish brides of SS men found their way to the Pope and gave him the list. At his instigation, a charity began sending goods to the women on the Nacht und Nebel list. "Then the packages started coming. Everyone went crazy, as you can imagine." Earlier, she said, the guards helped themselves to any packages sent to the prisoners. "They stole. Cigarettes, chocolate. And the small amount remaining they [the prisoners] got. Now it gets interesting, I can tell you." The cuckoo clock struck again, as if in agreement. "A package sent by the Pope. From: Pope."

The hard-to-follow tale that ensued, with mumbled phrases that passed into inaudibility, had to do with the guards, facing punishment if they tampered with packages closed with a papal seal, finally letting prisoners open their own packages and standing over them while they did so. In a camp where hunger was a daily fact of life (prisoner rations included two pieces of bread a day, sometimes-rotten turnip soup, and one spoonful of marmalade a week), the edible and untampered riches that came "From: Pope" were dazzling. So was the recognition of what the guards had been taking. "They didn't hold their traps, our girls," said Frau Müller. "That's how we all knew."

If camp policy had been followed, the escape-elopement that led to the packages might have resulted in terrible punishments of the other prisoners. Indeed, the threat of what would happen to one's peers was one of many inducements not to try an escape. But Ravensbrück's administration did nothing this time.

Unquestionably, the behavior of the two smitten SS guards was an exception. According to Frau Müller's recollections, there was notably little demonstrable humanity by SS guards of either sex, or by the camp's administrators. The prisoners therefore learned to help each other, however risky the help might be.

Frauen

Tales of how they did so, or tried to, or were punished for trying to, are contained in a book she wrote of her experiences, *Die Klempnerkolonne in Ravensbrück/Erinnerungen des Häftlings Nr. 10787* (The Plumbing Battalion of Ravensbrück/Memories of Prisoner Number 10787).[1] Published in East Germany, the book was translated into Russian and sold almost two hundred thousand copies, she said. Although the number sounds high, the reception must have been enthusiastic, for the book is not only a first-person account of the camp, but a hymn to the Soviet Union. One chapter involves Communist prisoners gazing with great enthusiasm at a smuggled picture of Stalin in uniform. Other chapters describe the brave actions—and brave they were—of the women in the Red Army Block, others the unbelievable punishment they withstood. And throughout the book are constant references to the brave Red Army that is going to liberate them. If readers knew no more, they would assume the Red Army alone fought Hitler. Incidentally, Frau Müller's only story of SS humanity (the "elopement" with the two Polish women) does not appear in the book.

For all the objections one might have to the narrowness of Lotte Müller's (or her publisher's) viewpoint, there is no question that her sense of survival in Ravensbrück was linked to what she called her solidarity with other Communist political prisoners. As at other concentration camps, prisoners were separated by and identified by categories of country and background and/or transgression, whether Polish, homosexual, Jewish, Jehovah's Witness, Belgian, criminal, German, and so on. On their striped concentration camp uniforms, prisoners wore one or more colored triangles and letters encapsulating who they were and what they had done. A green triangle meant a criminal. A black triangle meant signified the wearer as "antisocial." Whatever the infraction on the outside, inside Ravensbrück green- and black-triangle women were considered the kind who would rat on someone to gain a favor from a guard. "We knew exactly who they were. Most were Germans. They were the shit dogs. We had to suffer them, I can tell you that." Nonetheless, Frau Müller said she and her colleagues tried to make contact with green- and black-triangle women. One never knew from whom one might need help.

Red-triangle women always signified help, as least to Lotte Müller. Red was for political prisoners. "On the left sleeve of the blouse and the jacket there was the red triangle and my number. I had to identify myself. Three steps away from the body of the guard, not look at her, look down, and say, 'Protective custody prisoner. Müller, Charlotte.' And then the number. 10787." The red triangle let prisoner number 10787 find potential allies and let them find her. But rivalry also existed among the reds. "There were a load

---

1. Berlin (East): Dietz Verlag, 1981.

of Socialists in the camp who said, 'I'll never be a Communist.' I can even name names. And I just laughed, nicht? What did they want? After all, the Social Democrats fell apart with Hitler. They said, 'Let him just run everything into the ground economically, which he'll do, and then the Social Democrats will take charge.'"

Communist women not only were smarter on the outside, she implied, but on the inside they were more unified than any other group. "We practiced such solidarity. Everywhere it was necessary, whatever I encountered, I always did something to distract attention or did something in order to pull the prisoners out of their misery, nicht?" To her, solidarity also meant strength. "The strongest women were the political ones. They knew the reason they were inside and were convinced Hitler would not last, that another government would come and that would be the government we wanted."

As for religion building strength, Frau Müller's opinion was equally unequivocal. "Ne, *ach*. Do you think the dear God,[2] I must say what I think, ja? and you must not think poorly of me that I don't believe in the dear God because I know Darwin and so on, that everything is in evolution. Whoever believes *should* believe." She did not finish her original point, but made her other one, that faith was no help. "Nein. Never. Because it was *too* terrible. They became *mute*. They became passive. More passive."

Every religion had the same effect, she said. "Protestant, completely. Catholic, too." As for Jewish prisoners, "they weren't all religious, the Jewish women. You know? They were also already democratically progressive, so to speak. As for them and the dear God, no. . . . With so many terrible things and so many days in the camp, they lost their beliefs. So, 365 days in a year and each time wake up and go to sleep and so on, nicht? That ground a human being down. Ground them down. The dear God cannot help. That has nothing anymore to do with the Bible."

If a prisoner were able to maintain her faith, she had best maintain it privately. Practicing religion openly was forbidden. "You went to the bunker for that, or got another punishment." The bunker was a hellhole within a hellhole, a clammy underground cell with neither bed nor toilet nor light. But many women defied such threats. "The Poles held their own mass among themselves, Sunday mornings. They had sort of a rhythm going, almost like they were in a church. They posted someone outside in case one of the SS came into view. She'd pass the alarm, nicht? And then they'd talk about something else. Ja, belief was important for the Poles. One should allow

---

2. Many Germans, including atheists such as Frau Müller, use the phrase "the good Lord" (or more precisely, "the dear God" [der liebe Gott]) as a matter of course, eschewing just plain *Gott*.

people to do that, if they're believers, nicht?"

Despite the potential punishment and her own sentiments toward religion, Frau Müller once reached out to a group of newly imprisoned nuns. She had been on assignment in the washroom where the nuns had been stripped and had made to leave their clothes (to be stored) and possessions (to be thrown out). After the nuns were led off (to be insulted by the SS and defiled by the camp doctor), Frau Müller, seeing no one around, grabbed rosaries, a crucifix, and a prayer book from the throwaway pile. That evening, she sneaked into the "arrival block," evading the block elder, whom she did not trust, and quickly asked the nuns who their "senior person" was.

"When the young woman appeared, I say, 'Come with me to the washroom.' Said *du* to her right away. I say, 'Can you keep your mouth shut? If you promise by your faith not to say where you got what you're about to get. Just say they forgot to take it away.' I had about nine rosaries and a breviary, a white thing, a small one. I said, 'I've made it unholy because I'm not a believer, but you need it for praying and you're against Hitler. And because you're for praying and against Hitler, I've stolen this crucifix for you.' Then she wanted to kiss my hand and who knows what, she was carrying on so with me. So, the front of solidarity was closed and I did what I was supposed to, according to Thälmann.'" German Communist leader Ernst Thälmann seemed a close second, in Frau Müller's affections, to her father.

The sense of solidarity, sometimes conveyed by such acts as making eye contact with doomed prisoners, helped Frau Müller withstand not only the miserable and frightful conditions in which she and the other prisoners lived, but the ghastly sights she saw. She wrote of one prisoner, a Gypsy, who escaped for about a day. The description of her condition when the SS-manhunt brought her back, beaten bloody, holding her spilled intestines to her body in her last hours of life, is almost unreadable.

Frau Müller spoke about another wretched memory, a four-o'clock-in-the-morning deportation. "I had to get up and see what's going on. They loaded all the Jewish women. Took them all to Bergen-Belsen." The women had been incarcerated in Ravensbrück's "crazy house," or what she later referred to as a "nerve clinic." "There they were in a narrow little room, so. Gassed with a hundred human beings in Bergen-Belsen. All their things came back. 'Klamotten [rags],' as one says. Ja. No one survived." Frau Müller paused a long while before she spoke again.

When she did, her mind had moved from the gassing of Ravensbrück's adults to the gassing of its children. "No single human being can picture it, that one must say goodbye to children whom one liked very much." Some children were not gassed, and also managed to survive the other avenues of death at the camp. "Some live today, that we know." One man, orphaned from his own mother, invited his surviving Ravensbrück "mothers" to take her place at his wedding.

168

There was no redeeming aspect to a tale from one winter at the camp. Thousands of Hungarian women and children had been shoved into an unheated tent set up to relieve the overcrowding. The freezing prisoners had almost no clothing or food. They died, and died, and died.

Frau Müller was called in to solve a monumental plumbing problem. "The whole camp was stopped up. The main pipes behind the camp that led to the lake, where all the dreck went into the lake. They pumped the water, and the clogging was in one drain after the other. That much they'd figured out. If there's no water in the last drain, the stoppage is behind it. Three days or longer, *none* of us could use the toilets. We went outside for that. I hacked out a hole with a rod so that ours could, like it is with farmers, nicht? At many blocks it looked like a small church cemetery. Everywhere little hills, with pieces of paper, like a gravestone. You can imagine when the SS walked by, the girls had to sit there because they had to go and the SS men saw them doing it. All *shame* was gone.

"So, there was this tent. The toilets were built above it, where the drain entered. They had five toilets and everything flowed into another drain. It was stopped up. They pumped there, and pumped and pumped. It was crazy. The pipes weren't wide. And there stood the Gypsies who had the job to deal with the clogging. They couldn't manage, though, so the men from the next camp pumped and pumped and pumped. Day and night."

Finally, after days of pumping, "we stood there and I said, 'It's gurgling. Water's coming from below. Something is coming loose.' I stood above with the Gypsies and we opened the drain. More water was coming, gurgling great. Suddenly our drain was full. I said, 'The clogging is here.' I yelled to the men and they all came over. Then the water flowed away and there lay everything that didn't go with it.

"A man reached down and told us, 'It's a pig down there, a little pig.' Because it was light-colored. What do they pull out? A boy. A newborn baby boy. From someone in the tent of the Hungarian Jews, nicht? I don't mean to say they were bad, but it was all Hungarian Jewish women inside, and among them probably was a pregnant mother who gave birth to the child and said, 'I'm going to die anyway, and what's to become of the child? I'll throw him in there.'"

In her book, Frau Müller discribed the incident much less roughly (and much more literarily) than she talked about it. "Which tragedy happened there," she wrote, "unnoticed by anyone? Was the boy born dead? Did he die shortly after birth, or did the mother, to spare him an agonizing death from hunger, kill him herself?"[3] Frau Müller said no one could find out who the mother was.

---

3. Müller, *Die Klempnerkolonne*, 184.

Frauen

Having witnessed all that she had, and knowing what she did, Frau Müller must have had horrible nightmares, I suggested.

"Not at all," she said firmly. "Never. I have such strong nerves, you know. I shake it off. But my heart bleeds."

On April 28, 1945, the Nazis ordered everyone in Ravensbrück to evacuate. The order came three years to the day after Lotte Müller had arrived.

Guards and prisoners then left on a forced march out of the camp, the guards still in charge. Along the way, their cruelties continued. So did the prisoners' attempts to help each other. The latter tried to relieve the oldest and most exhausted women from their task of pulling the cartloads of the guards' plundered goods. Finally, the prisoners spotted a jeep of Americans and later, officers of the beloved Red Army.

"We yelled afterward, 'We're free! We're free!' Everyone came out of their houses. And the SS crawled away. They stuck their weapons in the beds, hid them, and headed west."

Frau Müller was convinced that is where they and their like-minded colleagues remained. She spoke of one Ravensbrück doctor, "a Schweinehund," who gave deadly injections. She called them by their sardonic name of "Himmelfahrtsspritzen [injections to travel to heaven]." He and similar doctors "adapted themselves" to West Germany, she said. One set up a pediatrics practice. "*That* happened. And people go with their child and don't know that they gave death injections in a concentration camp."

Frau Müller's companion spoke up for Germans less informed than Frau Müller about what went on in concentration camps. "Not everyone knew what was going on," she said. "I lived on the other side of the Oder [River—by Poland] and knew nothing at all, until I went to Buchenwald. It was if I'd just awakened."

As a free woman, Frau Müller immediately made her way back to her beloved Berlin. It was partitioned, but there was no question which partition she belonged in. She got a job with "the People's Solidarity Central Committee."

She did go to West Germany for one special occasion. The English authorities asked her to be a witness in the trial of former Ravensbrück guards. "They picked me up one morning. I said at least they have to let me tell my mother." That was done, apparently in Mülleresque style. "I said, 'I have to go to Hamburg for a trial.' Four of us flew there. Arrived by airplane." In Hamburg, she saw her former nemesis, the "Schweinehund" head guard. Her name, she said, was Frau Binz.

"I had to testify what really happened. To make up nothing and to add nothing. The judge asked questions and 'Have you anything to say to that.' And I said what I'd seen." The women guards sat in the room during the proceedings. "Afterward they were all sentenced to death. And hanged."

Frau Müller immediately added, "You can get a copy of the trial [transcripts] from the English. But they want a lot of money."

In the decades that followed, Frau Müller worked on the executive committee for the "People's Solidarity," and as a civil servant, in particular for the police. Could she have been connected to the infamous East German Stasi secret police? I do not know.

As far as I could determine, as long as she lived, she never looked back. She and the Russians, she said, want above all that "the heavens stay clear. Is that not a beautiful life, to fight for something like that? I've done that my whole life and I'm satisfied it has been so. I have *nothing* to ask of life," she said, as if aware she was concluding a soliloquy. "I enjoyed my life, although the personal was pushed to the rear, nicht? But I can be comforted and say I had a successful life as a simple woman. And not everyone can say that."

Frau Ellen Frey

"We Did Love Our Führer, Really!"

That she was uncomfortable was more evident in play-back than in person. Represented only by her voice, neatly cassetted and smoothly circling the tape hubs, she seemed snarled in unfinished phrases and incomplete thoughts, in contradictions amid justifications. Within seconds, her words were both defiant and abashed. Her revelations came mid-sentence.

There was no real reason for surprise. She never claimed to have thought her way through the Third Reich to a conclusion. To the contrary. She cannot talk with her children about it, she said. They do not understand. On the other side of the spectrum were her friends. And they, she implied, spoke the unspeakable. In fact, the afternoon she and I sat down in the living room of her largish house outside Munich, Frau Ellen Frey may have been trying for the first time to come to terms with the two worlds represented by her children and her friends: that of accusers and that of defendants. When the interview began, I knew nothing of that. I did know her a little. Years earlier, we had been neighbors in southern Spain, where she owned a second home. There she seemed a brisk, confident sort, with hobbies—ceramics then. She had given me a small plaque showing the ruins of the local castle. She later turned from ceramics to golf.

When we got together in the 1980s to talk, her second husband, whom she married in 1951, had recently died. He was dim in my memory, a seemingly quiet man, at least in comparison to her more forceful personality. She did not display much grief over his death, I thought. Maybe she still considered him alive, for at times she referred to him in the present tense. Mention of her first husband, however, seemed to touch her more deeply.

She and I began talking chattily, catching up over the requisite coffee and cake. Like almost all the women I had met and would meet, she dazzled me with hospitality. This time, however, the coffee was poor, which was unusual for any of the women, and the cakes were store-bought. Frau Frey may have run households, but she was no Hausfrau. She projected more the energetic committeewoman or businesswoman. "I can organize very well," she said. She also described how, within a day of war's end, she organized her family's well-being, sending off her "Kindermädchen" [live-in baby sitter] to get quantities of potatoes and carrots. And she described how shortly after that she organized the remains of her parents' bed linen factory in Stuttgart—obtaining cloth from various sources, hiring seamstresses, getting the business going again.

She spoke High German, but with a toothsome Swabian-Bavarian overlay. For *ein Bisschen* [a little bit] she said *ein Bissel*. Routinely she punctuated sentences and phrases with the all-purpose regionalism *gel?* She spoke and acted, it seemed to me, as if she were relatively at ease. Her movements had always been quick, I thought. Only in retrospect, and upon hearing her voice in those stopped-short sentences, did I realize she might well have refused to talk to a stranger.

Soon after the tape recorder began rolling, she did chuckle, while reciting Nazi propaganda. "It was sort of a slogan of the Nazis. 'The German woman doesn't smoke.' 'The German woman brings children into the world.'" She laughed, as if it were ludicrous to her. "Like that, gel?"

"Hitler understood how to fascinate women," she continued. "I was born in 1915 and I was *very* patriotic. I still remember that before the whole thing with Hitler happened, I'd said to a girlfriend, 'In our generation there is *nothing* going on with heroes and nothing going on that one can really stand up for.' And then came Hitler. And he did it right for us young people. He said 'Volk und Vaterland' and 'We must bring our people together' and what all he had for slogans, that somehow had *value* for young people, to fight for something, let's say. Just for Volk and Fatherland and what is really German again. I still remember I had a friend, a neighborhood kid, and he was a half-Jew and I often discussed things with him. He always said, 'I'm a pacifist,' and so on and then I always said, 'Ach, Viktor, you have to be for Volk and Fatherland,' although he was a half-Jew, gel? That wasn't clear to me at all. Later he went to America like *many* girlfriends who were in school with me. *All, all,* emigrated. I know personally no Jews who stayed here. They all went to Switzerland first and then to America. And now they come back and visit."

About the same years they were leaving, she was spending more of her time with the Bund deutscher Mädel, eventually becoming a youth leader. "I had a small group, about twenty-five girls, and we always had group evenings and [I] told them stories and the girls adored me and somehow that was appealing to one as a young girl." She pointed out she did not have to "fill out a paper or donate something or make a report, nothing at all. It was just nice. One *played* and I really could give the young girls something, because I talked to them a lot. About everything possible, gel? And we pored over problems. It was absolutely nice. And naturally one sang songs for Volk and Fatherland and had the opinion it was worthwhile to live for that, and so on."

Did she know then that Jews were not allowed to be in the BdM?

"Ja," she said. "One already knew. That was really *clear*. As a young girl, you didn't think about it. No, no Jews there, one basically thought, but that it somehow was *against* them . . . In my school, in my class, they did all leave."

Did any of her Jewish girlfriends want to join the BdM? The question was not facetious; there are accounts of young Jewish Germans who got caught up early in the pro-German mood and did want to join the Hitler Youth.

Her voice became soft. "Not these Jews, no. They knew that wouldn't work." She paused. "They did know that. And at the time there was after all, the propaganda. I remember it. I was just recently talking about it with my son. 'The Jews,' our parents always told us, 'the Jews are *everywhere*. They're in the *theater*, at the highest positions. They're sitting everywhere and have us in the palm of their hand.' That's what our parents told us. And that was the opinion. They're everywhere and sort of push us Germans aside and take the best jobs. I mean, the Jews are intelligent and all and naturally did a lot and. . . . Ja, one thought, perhaps it's very good if they leave, so we get a turn. We Germans. That was the opinion of us young girls then, gel?"

I asked if it were true there was a big difference between the Jews one knew personally and the Jews one heard about.

"Ja, that's exactly right. Everyone had his 'house Jew [Hausjude]' as one put it then, gel? And everyone had a good friend who was a Jew or a half-Jew. It was obvious he's a Jew and he is not now loved in our area." She added, again softly, "One really didn't think about it much."

What about Viktor?

"He said, 'It is *insane* what Hitler is doing and I'm a pacifist and we must all be brothers' and so on. During the war, I still wrote to him, that I was so much for Germany and remained for Germany. In that style, really. To that point when this Roehm thing began, when Hitler did this Roehm Putsch. From there on in, one listened a little closer and was mistrustful."

Her chronology, it must be noted, is way off. Hitler's purge of his old "brownshirt" friends in the SA, including the murder of one of his former close friends, SA leader Ernst Roehm, took place in 1934—five years before the war began.

She continued, "A girlfriend I'd had since I was six, whose father was a doctor, when the Roehm thing happened he said, 'I am *through* with Hitler,

if he kills his friends in such a manner.' It was a big disappointment for us.
And I must say that *was* possible, which is doubted very much today."

The "that" which was possible, was, she said, that "one simply left the
Party" without reprisal. She is partly right, but the situation varied greatly
with the person and the year.

Asked if the man would have made the same declaration in a Munich
beer hall, she said he would have, then added, both buttressing and negating
her point, "I had an uncle, a banker. And this Uncle Willi constantly said in
every bar, 'These idiots! What they are doing!' Then I said," she whispered,
"'Man, be quiet, or you're going to a concentration camp if you're not' and
so on and we laughed about it and already knew, well, some things. But we
did not know anything for sure."

She added she was asked to take over a bigger group in the BdM but
did not want to. It would have involved a lot of "writing stuff" [Schreibkram]
and bureaucracy and would not have been as gemütlich. So she just quit.
And "*nothing* happened."

An only child, she seems to have been of one political mind with both
her parents. "I really grew up in a circle that was for National Socialism. My
father was a Freemason and at first not in the [Nazi] Party. And we had a
linen factory and the 'Arbeiterinnen [women workers]' often were in the
Party. They got so fresh my father said, 'Soon I won't have any say. They
keep threatening me with the Party. I must join.' He did join, just so that he
had a voice in his own business. And after a while a notice came. He was
being thrown out of the Party because he's a Freemason. Lodge brothers and
all, that wouldn't do."[1]

As for the politics of her mother, she "thought the same as my father.
In general, it's always been the case. They all vote *exactly* the same as their
husbands. My daughter, too, who grew up completely differently. We always voted CSU or so [it's similar to U.S. Republicans] and she votes SPD
[similar to U.S. Democrats] because her husband votes SPD. They always,
always, adjust themselves to the men. I never heard that the men adjust
themselves to the women."

What does Frau Frey think would have been different during the Third

---

1. To Hitler and his supporters, Freemasons were a suspicious and treasonous group
who helped Germany lose the First World War, and who accepted Communists
and Jews as members. Hitler wrote of his distrust and dislike of Freemasons in
Mein Kampf. When he came to power, he essentially banned them. Or as *Brockhaus
Enzyklopädie,* 17th ed. (Wiesbaden: F. A. Brockhaus, 1968), 6:574, put it (my
translation), "Under National Socialism, as of 1933 all Lodges had to dissolve;
many Lodge members subsequently were persecuted and arrested; all Lodge
property, archives, and libraries were confiscated." Thanks to Linda Wheeler for
the research.

Reich if women had been in power? Her response is remarkable, but not because of what she said about women. What is striking is that like other German women, she took a rather neutral question and turned the answer to the Holocaust.

"I believe women also can be very bad. If they'd been in the concentration camps, I can imagine. What is interesting, what I still cannot comprehend today and what nobody can take away from me is that we knew *nothing* about the concentration camps, that specifically Jews were tortured there. We did know, well, that a concentration camp was something completely unpleasant. And we were afraid that if our *own* people and acquaintances said something, they'd go to a concentration camp. So it wasn't just Jews who were inside, but also those who politically did not do like the government wanted them to, as Hitler wanted, nicht? Who'd become dangerous to them. Because of that."

It was striking, too, and also not unique, for a woman to retreat from the Holocaust to the subject of her own situation or fear.

Frau Frey, however, then brought up "this 'Kristallnacht.' How they destroyed these stores. *Then* my parents did say, 'These SA people, there are such *commoners* [Proleten] among them and when they have power they commit such nonsense. Such *stupidity*,' we always said. 'How can they make the stores of the Jews kaputt? How can they do that?' But"—she paused—"we never thought that it somehow was directed from above to below. We always said Hitler is just [Recht].

"The feeling was, ja, last night they lit the *synagogues* on fire and smashed the Jews' windows. One was *really* outraged and said, 'That is *un*-believable. How could they?' one said at the time. 'And if they want the Jews out, why don't they do it in a nicer way [auf feinere Weise]?' That's what *we* always said. In a normal manner. But they were such boors, such rowdies."

Frau Frey was in Stuttgart at the time, but did not witness "Kristallnacht" herself. "One didn't go there." She did, however, see the resultant damage. "I saw the shops with their windows 'in,' and so, and I also saw these Jews running around. They had to wear the Star of David and we said, 'Man, the poor fellows, it's unbelievable that something like that . . .' But you know, one had so many problems oneself. I don't know either. That toward one's closest fellow humans . . ." She trailed off again, omitting the verb that would have completed her thought, and said instead, "I don't know why."

She had trailed off on her history, too, recalling two very visual but anachronistic scenes of Jewish persecution as one. "These Jews running around" in the days after "Kristallnacht" would not have been wearing Stars of David; the decree ordering Jews to wear them was issued in 1941.

I asked her about a much earlier event, the boycott of Jewish-owned stores. Had she ever gone in a store bearing a sign that said "Don't buy from Jews"? She took some time before answering. "At the time, we hardly bought anything."

After adding that she would not have "become involved with it, either," she said, "I am a human being to whom it doesn't matter, while my mother-in-law was a 150 percent Nazi, gel? I still remember how my first husband, in her eyes, did not go punctually enough to his job in the SA. He was an SA man. Nazi. Ja, my first husband was an SA man."

The connection was probably that it was SA men who enforced the boycott of the Jewish stores.

Why did he join the SA?

"Ach, Gott. He was in the student movement, where there were *many* SA men or SS men. You know, that was simply sort of pro-Germany. And one was in the Party, but was a civil servant. My husband was a government advisor. That was really completely obvious [to be a member of the Nazi Party]. Most of them were in the SA or the SS." She added, "Naturally, many whom one asks today don't say so. Unfortunately."

What did her husband do as a Nazi brownshirt? We talked later, when the tape recorder happened to be off. She really did not know, she said. She really did not know what he did in Germany, or in France, or in Russia, except to be a regular soldier. And she did not take me up on an offer to find out.

She and he met when she was seventeen. He was twenty-three and just out of college. The year would have been 1932. She thought everything between them was "completely wonderful. I was completely enthusiastic about it. And he said, 'Nothing will come of us. You are a girl to marry, and I am nothing and have nothing, and I don't know if I'll get anything soon.' That was actually the time they went past our house. I recall it very well. [Men carried] placards and had written on them, 'We want work and bread. We are hungry,' and demonstrated. That was before Hitler, before he became chancellor of the Reich. And naturally that all changed with one blow. My husband immediately got a job, too, and everyone suddenly got work and bread and therefore people naturally were pro-Hitler." It was obvious that her husband (whom she finally married in 1938) had been for Hitler from the beginning. Had she been, too?

"And me *too*, ja. Gel? Also, I didn't hear anything bad about him. I still remember, there was this putsch against Hitler, when he was supposed to be killed [in July 1944] and I'd already been evacuated with the children to the countryside. It came across the radio there's been an assassination attempt on Hitler's life. And I thought, just myself alone, 'Man, it's a shame that," she whispered, "the attempt failed, because we in the Heimat had long noticed it's not going well and the man has become crazy and he should stop and why does he not *stop* with this war and keep going and keep going. And then my husband wrote from the battlefield, 'Is that not unbelievable, that they want to stab him in the back. That our Führer fights and we fight for our Fatherland and *they* stab us in the back.' Ja? Suddenly things were seen much differently from the Heimat than from the soldiers in the field."

Frauen

She said she never would have let her husband know her feelings. "It was his *ideal* to fight there for his Fatherland and for his family and, and, and, if the soldiers didn't know what they were fighting for anymore, if *they* had panicked. . . . One thought, one could not tell them at all how we thought."

Her husband's response to the assassination attempt, she claimed, had nothing to do with fear of censorship. "Our letters were never read. Never." Does she still have them? No, she said. A short while ago, she went through them and put most in the trash.

His last letter arrived shortly after their third child was born, in February 1945. "In his last letter, his *last* letter, he wrote me that 'I would gladly give my life that things go well for you in the Heimat.' He knew about Heide, and chose the name Heide, too, but he never saw her."

She said of their marriage, she didn't know "whether it would have remained so ideal. One does change. But when I was married, I was really in love and that was the man for me. At night, how one slept in the marriage bed, when I'd wake up, I often thought, that cannot go well. It cannot be true that one is so happy or that one wants somebody like him. He *was* that way, so tender with me, so nice and dear and darling."

Frau Frey said she also went through her second husband's photographs from the war. "I sat there and looked at them and threw most of them away." She did not describe them as depicting anything but the dismal life of soldiers on the Russian front. As she went through them, "I thought, man, you poor fellows, who had to experience that. It certainly was terrible there in Russia in the dreck and in the war and with the gnats and in the cold. It's simply terrible, a war like that. And I thought, too, how *little* one asked them, the soldiers who came back. First of all, I believe, they didn't want to talk about it, since the experience in part was so awful. Not once did I say, 'Now, do show me your pictures, tell me about it.' Not once."

She also said men did want to talk about it, at least with other men. "The *men* always start it up about the war. Always. They talk and talk about the war. Much earlier even, I thought that war for men is perhaps what giving birth is for women, or something. It's a completely incredible experience for them. Also the experience of comradeship in war. My [second] husband said he'd never want to have missed it. That he'd learned a lot. Whenever I was impatient, he'd say, 'I learned in the war to wait.'"

She said her father and uncle, who were in the First World War, "spoke of nothing but the war" when they were together. "And we women always said, 'Ach, we can't listen to any more, now they're starting up again.'" The tradition continued, her second husband talking with fellow soldiers about the Second World War, while around them the women sounded complaints and told the men to be happy the war was over. "I thought about that as I got rid of the pictures. It really is unbelievable how little . . . that is, after all, one's partner . . . that one didn't say, 'Tell me, was it awful and how was it?' Nothing! Nothing! Nothing!"

Did the men ever ask the women, how was it for you?

"Nein nein, nein nein. That was never the case. I told my present husband some things, but it really didn't interest him. Perhaps my first husband would have been different. I always thought that when he comes back, I must tell him everything possible. He would have listened."

She pointed out a small painting he had done of himself as a soldier and sent to her. Until Herr Frey died, she said, she kept it out of sight so he would not get jealous.

The "everything possible" she planned to talk about may have had some gaps. When he was home on leave, "I must honestly say, one spoke little about politics. Actually, not at all. You know, in the war, when things with the Jews probably also were going on, we had so many problems ourselves. To keep our heads above water, that one had enough to eat, or got everything the children needed. One really had so many problems and . . . My son always says, 'I know exactly how it was. You didn't *want* to see it.' That's not *true*. I really didn't see it. He says, 'In your subconscious you didn't want to.' But I say *no*, 'I really didn't see it.' I only saw once, when I was taking the streetcar to town and only Jews boarded it. Only Jews, carrying rucksacks and wearing stars. They were sort of poorer ones and sort of average. . . . Well, the Jews were not poor. Anyway, average people. I stared at them, really. Suddenly I felt, what is *that?* I thought, where do they have to go now, to the train station or where? *That* one probably suppressed through one's own . . . I already sensed, that couldn't be, it's terrible, and where are they going? Again and again I kept telling some people that I saw a few Jews, I said, and how they . . ."

Their reaction? I broke in.

She responded in another whisper. "They said, 'Ja, ja, I saw it too, that's terrible, where do they have to go? It must be awful in the concentration camps and they're treated terribly, the poor Jews, why didn't they leave in good time?' And so on, one said. And especially these poorer ones who didn't have the connections to leave, gel? The richer ones figured it out very quickly and they . . . I already said, in my class there were seven or eight Jewish girls and they *all* left. I mean, they were all Jews who had houses in a nice neighborhood. Probably the parents quickly organized everything and had connections."

What about the seven or eight Jewish girls? Had she been friends with . . .

"Ach Gott," she interrupted. "I mean, I was never really close friends with them. I was invited to children's gatherings and so on." But that was before the Third Reich. "When I was eighteen or so, they weren't there anymore."

If her dates are correct, that means the families left early indeed—in 1933.

She recalled happily attending the Jewish girls' birthday parties. "That was *nice*. They had nice birthday parties, *gel?* And there one didn't think at all. . . . One did know, that's a Jewish girl [eine Jüdin], but exactly that she's a Pole or something in particular. . . ."

But one did know they were Jews?

"Ja ja, one always knew that. That was essentially clear. And *I* personally must say that overall, I had a bad opinion of the Jewish boys [die Judenbuben]. It's quite peculiar. As young girls, about fifteen years old, we often played table tennis with them, these Levis and whatever their names were, and then one said, 'Yech, they're somehow so . . .'" She paused for the word. "Unpleasant. They weren't at all sort of upright fellows or so. That was simply a different . . . They were . . . Somehow one had to protect oneself from them. *My* feeling as a young girl. I don't know. I mean, nobody stirred me up against them or so. Huh. Strange, *gel?* One thought, well, they're not so completely hate-free either. *So!*" she said, in a rather challenging manner. "Somehow that one not come too close, in an unpleasant way. And a girlfriend of mine, too. *Yech.* They are . . . 'Careful of them.' I don't know."

Frau Frey swiftly and seriously dismissed my conjecture that maybe because the boys were verboten in her world, she really was attracted to them.

"Nein. It wasn't that. It wasn't that. I don't know, either. In any case, we had an aversion to these Judenbengel. What we always called them. 'Judenjungen' [Jewish youths], *gel?*"

It may have been linguistic circumstance, but whenever Frau Frey referred to the girls, she used nonpejorative words, such as *Mädchen* or *Jüdinnen*, literally, "Jewesses." But the words she used for Jewish boys in her school—*Judenbuben, Judenjungen,* and *Judenbengel*—ranged from questionable to insulting. The Nazis frequently used *Juden* as the beginning of an anti-Semitic word, such as *Judenfeind* ["Jew enemy"]. The stigma has not gone. Still, *Judenbuben,* for example, *may* be translated fairly as "Jewish boys." (The alternative translation is "Jew boys," which would make her sound worse in English than she does in German.) But there is nothing ambivalent about *Judenbengel. Bengel* means something like "teenage rascal" and can be affectionate by itself. When preceded by *Juden,* however, it is not an affectionate word. And as we know, she did not like the people she was talking about.

"They were *fresh,* the boys. *Fresh.* Not the girls. Strange, the girls all had our sympathy. The girls were dear and nice and darling, and we really liked them a lot, all of them."

There was an echo. "Dear and nice and darling" were precisely the words she had used to describe her first husband.

It is doubtful whether her second husband, Herr Frey, ever dissuaded her in any of her negative sentiments about Jews. Out of the blue, she said of him, "My husband was an SS man. My present one. Who died." But, as in her

Frau Ellen Frey

mention of her first husband, the SA man, she had virtually nothing more to say on the matter. It later seemed the reason she revealed her husbands' backgrounds was not as a prelude to talking about what she knew, feared, or suspected of their involvement in the Third Reich, but to make the point that these two men and their colleagues, the men of the SS and the SA, really were nice.

Then what about Adolf Hitler, the person who in a sense had brought them all together? Considering what he had brought to bear on and in Germany, had she been disappointed or angry about him? I listened to hear "Ja."

"Nein. Nein. That's the funny thing. Nein. *Not one* of my children understands it. They always say, you lost your husband, and I loved my husband very much, my first one. We had a terrific marriage." She again lowered her voice to a whisper. "I was not disappointed. It is *such* a peculiar phenomenon. I don't comprehend it myself. I should be *mad* at this person. [In February 1944, bombs also totally destroyed her family's "beautiful large house and the factory building," she said.] And nonetheless I am, if I am *honest*, in my inner being, not against this Hitler. That certainly is very peculiar. I do not understand it. Don't get it, don't get it at all. I must say, I've never been to Dachau. I should go sometime. I always say, nein, I don't want to see it and so on. And because I hear from good friends, from earlier, who say everything in Dachau is. . . . Well, one must not say what they all say."

What do they say?

"Well. That a lot was tidied up [zurechtgemacht]. I mean, definitely a lot happened. I have not seen Dachau and actually I cannot speak about it with any person of your generation, because they all say that is the worst thing there is [das ist das Schlimmste überhaupt]. Or just now, my son said," she continued, interrupting herself, "or my son-in-law, and I cannot speak about the topic of Jews at all. With this generation. They find it such a terrible . . . And it *is* terrible. I myself find it all terrible, what was done. And I cannot say . . . I don't know what it is, this phenomenon." She paused, noticeably struggling. "Maybe it's if someone brings so many ideals to a young person for which one had waited, that maybe it cannot all be taken away. I don't know." She paused again. "Because as a young person one would like to live for something, to be there for something. And I'm a little susceptible to enthusiasm."

She said even when her own daughter pointed out what she lost and what she experienced, she still defends Hitler.

"I say, *ja,* I also find it awful and it was an error and the man went crazy, but I say that, *too.* Everything. But what he gave us young girls back then somehow must still be there, that one cannot condemn it all. Or. I don't know. And my husband who just died felt the same. He felt exactly the same. We differed on many things, but in that point we were, without saying anything about it. . . . Whenever we saw something from the time, we were glad. Somehow that was a lovely time for us. Not in a bad way, but in the idealistic good way.

"For example, when we heard Hitler speak or something like that. One sees him on television sometimes. Then we'd laugh and say, 'Hey, look at Adolf.' *So!*" she said, the same way as before. She laughed and laughed again. "So! Or we'd say, 'Man, now they're showing pictures again, which we've never seen, so *distorted*.' Or we'd say, when one examines it now, 'Ach, did he ever spin a wicked lie.' One does sometimes say that."

What especially upset her was a reaction to the widely watched U.S.-produced television series "Holocaust." While visiting Madrid with German friends, she met some friendly Spanish schoolchildren. Soon a guessing game began: where were the grown-ups from? When the children gave up, Frau Frey cheerfully told them, "Somos allemanas [We are Germans]." The children shrank back, she said, and fearfully whispered, "Holocaust, Holocaust."

The widow of an SA and an SS man, the woman who still agonized over her feeling for Hitler, was outraged.

She did not like the "Holocaust" series either. "It's just so much bias [Tendenz], done on purpose. Maybe rightfully so, that such a thing never happens again. I mean, it must not happen again. But that it had such an effect on children, 'Those are the Germans. . . .'"

More upsetting were encounters within her own family about the Holocaust itself. The most volatile time she described was what she called a "conversation" with her son-in-law, a teacher, while she was visiting him and her daughter.

"A book was lying on the table at their place and I leafed through it a little. Then I said to my son-in-law, at the time I didn't know him so well, gel? He is completely in the current generation. I said, 'What's written in there is manure. It is all greatly biased.' Did he ever get *mad* at me! And we got into such a conversation he'd have thrown something in my direction, from anger. My daughter stood up and defended me. That was the only time that he and I . . . Since then we *never* touch this topic again. Never again. Now we understand each other perfectly, because we do not talk at all about this topic. We cannot talk about it. It's impossible, gel? There is such a chasm in Germany, you cannot even picture it."

We returned to the friends on her side of the chasm. What else do they say?

"Well, I don't know whether one can say it. They say that much was arranged at Dachau that does not reflect the truth and that not so many had been gassed, I mean. And they say the numbers aren't right. That's what *they* claim, gel? That they aren't right at all and that much was reconstructed. But my feeling is, even if it's only three who were gassed or so, it's completely out of the realm of discussion. Impossible. Because one does not begrudge any human being . . . that somehow one has no right at all. I mean, for me that is completely different from this other time that I experienced with Hitler, or, what do I know. I don't know." Her last words were almost inaudible.

I kept pressing her on the odious debate about whether the slaughter of the Jews was as extensive as most people believe.

"I'm not an expert," she said. "I just keep hearing over and over that they say it's not true at all. Certainly there are many . . . I ask myself. . . . Just a little while ago a woman friend asked me, 'Do you know *one* 'Jüdin' who was gassed? We know all of them and they all are still *there.*'"

Frau Frey continued without pause, stumbling. "But there are probably, maybe, those from, the other ones, or . . . I don't know. I mean, it's perfectly obvious that's the way it is. And that is clear to me today. I don't know. I don't *know*. Because my first husband and my second husband, our friends too. . . . I mean, *really* terrific people, gel? Really nice human beings who have also done things for other people and not only for themselves and who were capable and everything . . ." She whispered again. "I don't know either."

Asked if she knew whether these really nice human beings ever had changed their minds about the topic, Frau Frey said this. "The people with whom you speak today, *all* these former SA or SS men [say], 'Let's drop this topic.' You know, something went kaputt for them, for the men more than for the women, I believe. I don't know. The men believed in it more than the women, about the idea of . . . They don't want to talk about it much." (Except, it seemed, with the women or when the women did not want to hear about it.) "They also say the time had much good about it, that afterward it degenerated so much, there's no way we could know that everything was . . ." She paused. "Of *most* of the SA and SS men whom I know, all whom I know, nobody knew it. That something so bad. . . . They thought, it's an idealistic thing, or whatever. [Hitler] really understood how to seize the younger generation. Somehow, he really understood, but that it . . ." After several more disjointed phrases, she almost completed this sentence. "What is funneled into you in your youth, maybe, 'We love our Führer . . .' So! We did love our Führer, really! It was true. And when that's inside you as a young person, it doesn't leave so quickly. Or so. Nonsense, gel?

"When I see him today, it's always a wonder it was possible not to see through this human being. Something struggles against it internally. It can't be possible that everything was all lies and all false, because"—she paused again—"we definitely did not want to harm anyone. No foreigner and no Jew or . . . One didn't think about Jews so much anymore. But. Odd. I mean, some of us from home were opposed [to the Nazis]. There certainly were many. Certainly. But, oddly, we just didn't belong to that."

Frau Frey said she did read Hitler's *Mein Kampf*. And she read Hans Grimm's *Volk ohne Raum* (People without space), which she incorrectly attributed to the Nazi ideologue and anti-Semite qua non Alfred Rosenberg.

"We read it and said, 'Man, there are so many people in Germany and we're in such a narrow space, they can give something up for us, no?' That [Hitler] somehow manages to get room," she suddenly laughed, "but in a proper manner, one had thought. One thought nothing bad, gel? Somehow one didn't think so far, that it would bring war and what went with it. We weren't as educated politically as they are today."

Frau Frey talked on, about such matters as in the early weeks after the war, often sitting in her garden and looking toward the road to see if her husband were returning from the front. She said (in a later letter) that "worn-down and tired" soldiers came back that way, some pushing "a baby carriage in which they had their possessions."

I took command of a pause and asked how she thought one could hinder anti-Semitism. She jumped in before the question was quite finished. "There is no more anti-Semitism. It does not *exist* in your generation. But the Jews finally must be at the same level with us and not always. . . . They always want not to forget, but sometime they have to. I mean, it's terrible. Everything. But we will never be able to change it and at some point they must integrate, so one simply can just speak with them, like with a minority, like with the Turks here or . . . Well, they're not like them. They are not guest workers. But simply like it's normal. But they're always so convinced 'I am a Jew and I have a right to that and that.' With that they make more enemies again, unfortunately. My opinion, gel? But like I say, your generation thinks much differently. And whatever our generation does, it's always afraid to do something wrong, so that one *somehow* thinks, they're still Nazis or so. And that definitely is not the case, in no way at all in our government. But the fear is there. My present husband always says it will end only when our generation dies. But I don't know. It's a big problem. I also have the feeling the Jews don't want to forget. They want an eye for an eye and . . . And it's obvious. If someone had murdered my father, I would say exactly the same thing. Probably. I don't know."

Frau Ursula Kretzschmar

Before, During, and After the Firebombing

When Frau Ursula Kretzschmar goes berry picking with her grandchildren for pleasure, she remembers something similar she did for survival when she was a child. "I went with my mother to glean potatoes. You know, when the potatoes have been harvested, then afterward into the fields once more with a hoe, and gather them. Or glean corn. When the field is fallow, glean a bundle, then put [it] on the handcart . . . and then take it to the mill . . . and like that the whole summer through."

Despite such efforts at economy, at one point her mother and she were so poor that the state stepped in. Mother and daughter were evicted from their home in the town of Teuchern (about twenty-five miles southwest of Leipzig) and taken to Dresden "by force, really force. Our furniture loaded onto a furniture truck, and to Dresden whether we wanted to or not. And when we arrived, the furniture [was] put in storage and we first went to a homeless shelter, my mother and I." Yet Frau Kretzschmar did not call her childhood poor, *arm* in German. She called it *ärmlich*, a word that implies something less harsh, or more discreet. Other words in her vocabulary also circumvented reality. Instead of *schwanger* [the usual word for "pregnant"], she used the more delicate and rather antiquated phrase *in anderen Umständen* [in different circumstances]. But her vocabulary may have had less to do with age than with geography. The old ways of talking are typical of the language of East Germany.

Frauen

Once taken to Dresden by force, she stayed by choice. And she became active in East Germany's Communist Party, the Socialist Unity Party. This was not something she mentioned. But the Communist guide assigned to me had written it in his notes, and I peeked. Even if I had not, other aspects of Frau Kretzschmar's vocabulary would have made her position clear. Still, politics were not, of course, the main reason to hear her memories. The main reason was Dresden. She had been there through the night of February 13, 1945. She had witnessed the firebombing.

She also had witnessed considerably more than that.

Long before becoming an enthusiastic supporter of Communists, she had been an enthusiastic supporter of Nazis. The "fault," in a way, was her intelligence. Born in 1923, growing up as an "ärmlich" child, Ursula could have expected nothing more from the Weimar Republic but the most cursory primary school education. But, as she modestly described what happened, "because of my [school] achievements, it happened very seldom, I went to the Bürger [middle-class or bourgeois] school after fourth grade. I received a [tuition-] free position because I was"—she lowered her voice—"because I was very good and because my mother could not raise the tuition money. That was essentially a special privilege." It also meant "I automatically landed with the Jungmädels."

The Jungmädels (for "Aryan" girls ten to fourteen years old) was the junior division of the Bund deutscher Mädel. "At that age, naturally, one did not yet grasp it. I was, in fact, very proud. That I admit. Ja, then the brown jacket." The rest of her uniform consisted of a white blouse and a dark blue skirt. Because of her intelligence and her mother's poverty, she got the uniform gratis, too.

The Jungmädels did not reflect a political direction either of her parents would have chosen. Ursula's father, who was from Dresden himself and who had died when she was very young, had been "an artist and actor and everything in one, a little all thrown together." He would, for instance, paint a bouquet of roses in front of an audience, then throw the roses to them. His family was more or less aligned with the Social Democrats and "were somewhat well to do," even though his death left his widow and daughter virtually penniless. Ursula's mother had come from a family of Communists who were not well off at all, but she joined the Social Democrats, to the annoyance of her brother. "Then there was a little . . . not that there would have been a real quarrel, you know, not that [they] would have thrashed it out in public. But my mother always wanted, as it was called, to be better." A Socialist was a social step up from a Communist.

In postwar East Germany, the difference was beside the point. Frau Kretzschmar, when we met, lived in an apartment in a Communist "workers' association" building she helped build. She had put in six hundred hours of

186

manual labor, she said, and now paid thirty-nine marks (about twenty dollars) a month rent. Her living room was a nice, friendly size, if somewhat close in smell and feel. Mustard-colored drapes lined the windows. A large, old-fashioned tile oven seemed to be the sole source of heat. Decoration tended toward items that could be used by children, like a red yarn octopus, and—not atypical for East German travelers—a toy samovar.

Frau Kretzschmar, clad in a blue cowboy shirt, was a mostly friendly woman who had been a Dresden city guide for more than thirty years. She loved the job, she said, thought of it as a "paid hobby," and strongly resented West German tourists thinking she needed it to supplement her pension. If she had anything positive to say about anyone or anything from the west, she did not say it to me. Nor did she accept (or maybe understand) my contention that many people who had been pro-Nazi might still live in her new country. She said East Germans who went to the west (she did not say how) now wrote pleading letters to come back. "I am naturally of the opinion they should not be accepted. If they betrayed the GDR [East Germany], they should stay away." She was unquestionably more objective when talking about the political system she had chosen in her youth.

Even in a homeless shelter, the young Ursula's intelligence again was noticed. "So then I had to go to school, and because of my foundations of learning, that I wasn't exactly the dumbest, here, too, I again received a 'free place.' It was a 'parallel class' for 'higher expectations.' And after a while, we got a small place to live." It was in a narrow house in an alley behind the old marketplace, reached by climbing high, narrow wooden steps. "Then my mother got work sewing in a tailor shop and after a while, a couple of years, we got a bigger home, at least a little bigger. And as the war kept going and then the 'total war,' naturally the company where my mother worked made bombs instead of sewing. And later I noticed, my mother was often sick and so on . . . a lot of times did not go to work. When I was more mature, she told me that she did it on purpose, ne? So, a little sabotage, ne? That she was fighting privately. Well, I mean, to do the work wrong or something . . . She didn't risk doing that."

Although Ursula was concerned about her mother's health and did not know the claims of sickness were a means of hindering the war effort, she did recognize that her mother did not share her own enthusiasm about the war, or the Nazis' earlier actions, like building the Autobahn. "Through the construction [the Nazis] got rid of unemployment all at once. And there was such enthusiasm, ja? But I still remember that sometimes there were discussions. 'When the Autobahn is finished, tanks will roll on it.' They already knew that, in circles my family was in." Her mother told her that things do "not look so rosy." Ursula paid little mind. She purposefully went to Nazi parades in which she made the "Heil Hitler!" salute with great pride.

"That I admit. But my mother always got out of the way, and when I was with her, she always pulled me into a side alley." Did she have any idea how many other citizens of Dresden were enthusiastic? The majority, she said. "In Dresden, certainly. Dresden is, or was, definitely a civil service city [Beamtenstadt]."

One time Ursula and her mother especially clashed. It was shortly after the death of German President Paul von Hindenburg in August 1934. Never mind that the Nazis had manipulated the old man shamelessly to gain power. They knew to make the funeral mammoth and the memorials widespread. One memorial was in Ursula's own little town. "There was a stairwell leading to the church in Teuchern, I can still see myself today. I sometimes asked myself how one was so 'pasted together,' and how we went to this mourning procession and I had a kind of mourning crape on my brown vest and you can imagine how proud I was. When I came home and told my mother about it, she said, 'You should *stop* it, I cannot *listen* to any more,' and so on."

Ursula "graduated" from the Jungmädels to the Bund deutscher Mädel. "Then fighting songs were sung. We did sing 'Today Germany belongs to us, tomorrow the whole world.' And my mother often complained. I was not allowed to sing that at home." Her mother also got upset "when I sometimes came home full of enthusiasm, or had turned on the radio that was called the 'Goebbels Snout.'"

The official name for the small black radio that could broadcast only the Nazi station, and from which often emanated the voice of Propaganda Minister Joseph Goebbels, was the Volksempfänger [People's Receiver]. But Goebbelsschnauze [Goebbels Snout] was not an uncommon nickname for it.

In 1939 and 1940, the broadcasts were full of self-praise for the early military conquests, and Ursula reacted as planned. "Mutti, look! Victory, victory, victory!" But "Mutti" then "always turned it off. Had I heard enough and so on, that it will end horribly. That she said, ja? But naturally not that I understood.

"In later years, when I was mature, I sometimes talked about it, said, 'You made a mistake with me.' I said, 'Why didn't you sit me down and exactly say this and this? Or why didn't you forbid me directly? You did let me go.' And then she told me, 'It would not have been possible at all to state I forbid you.' They would have taken *me* away from my mother if she had forbidden it. That's how it was, ja. Would have said the child is gifted, ja? She just did it on the basis of 'I cannot listen to anymore, it gives me a headache,' and so on."

Ursula was loyal to her mother's memory. "My father was already dead and my mother was afraid that as her *daughter*, well, she probably did not necessarily have the courage, like maybe in other families, where there was a father and he was against the Nazis. In any case, she didn't do it, or perhaps she couldn't do it, because probably in that sense her education was not high enough to see it coming. *Nein,* I don't want to say that she did not see it. But a *fear* inside stopped her from speaking." Her mother had another reason not to risk talking about her aversion to National Socialism. Her brother Reinhold, the Communist, had been arrested.

It happened "about 1939 or 1940" in the family's hometown of Teuchern. "And naturally that was terrible for my mother and naturally she became even more afraid. You can imagine." As far as Frau Kretzschmar knows, he was not arrested for having been a Communist, but for trying to get information from a radio source beyond the "Goebbels Snout."

"He apparently was caught listening to . . . one then called it enemy radio. There was such a thing with directional equipment and so on. And then they suddenly stormed in, in the door, and saw that the dial pointed to a different station. And then they just took him away. And then [he] was in a concentration camp for many years, to the end. In Buchenwald. He survived. But at the end, he was not completely okay in his head, because of what he had been through." She did not know if he had been betrayed. "I only know that it was really very bad." She sighed.

Early in the Third Reich, during the anti-Jewish boycott, she and her mother themselves got a sense of the consequences of noncompliance. The two were walking down a shopping street. "In one store window there was a white suit on sale. Displayed there. Was very, very cheap. I don't remember how much anymore, but anyway, my mother said, 'We will get that. I will alter it a little and you will have a chic white suit.' But 'Don't buy from Jews' and so on was painted on the windows. Then my mother and I went in together, without being stopped. And when we came out, we were spat upon.

"But my mother had the courage to do it. Said, 'I have to go where it's cheap.'" As a result, "I had the chicest white suit." In a letter, Frau Kretzschmar wrote me that the people who spat at them and insulted them were "SA people in brown uniforms" or, as she described them, "Nazi-Faschisten." The incident still did not seem to change her youthful enthusiasm.

It was hardly the only complication within the family. While her uncle Reinhold was in Buchenwald, her cousin Walter (her mother's sister's oldest son) was fighting for Germany in the Soviet Union. His mind may have broken before Reinhold's. "He was in the army at the time and he was already a sergeant. In any case, this Walter, he went crazy. I did not experience it, my mother just told me about it." The "it" began while Walter was home on leave and sitting down with relatives to eat. "Then suddenly during the meal, he began to telephone, and to fantasize, and he said some stuff, that made everyone stare. . . . He . . . but in a foggy state, ja?" She wrote that he had held his hand to his ear as if he were listening and talking on the telephone. "It had gone to his head, what he experienced with the soldiers. And from that, they realized not everything was in Ordnung the way it had been made to seem." Walter spoke "about shootings and everything. But really in his subconscious, as my mother told me." He did not seem to know what he was doing or saying. She added, "Then he was taken to an insane asylum and then suddenly died.

"Whether my cousin was killed, I cannot say with certainty," she wrote in answer to the question I had been unable to ask earlier. "I only know that the Fascists had homes where one did not let incurable people live long. There was no doubt that my cousin was sick."

Frau Ursula Kretzschmar's one act of youthful rebellion was not against National Socialism, but against her mother. Apparently as a kind of homage to her father, she took acting lessons, secretly. When her mother later found out, she was, for whatever reasons, furious. But Ursula, as later with her "paid hobby," loved to entertain. There was not much theater left in Dresden once the war began, so her teacher and his students went to military hospitals (formerly schools) in the area and performed for wounded soldiers. Rather than the Hollywood-type hoopla shows American GIs received, wounded Germans got recitals of heroic poems about keeping up the fighting spirit. "Everything" had to be "auf Nazistisch," she said.

They were delivered, though, by girls such as Ursula, who would have been about sixteen. Among the wounded recipients of rhyme one day was a certain soldier Kretzschmar, who happened to be from Dresden. His wounds were relatively minor; two fingers had been sliced off at an angle. When he recovered, "naturally he went back in the field again."

In the summer of 1943, four years after meeting, the couple married. The wedding took place during Herr Kretzschmar's home leave from the Soviet Union. The couple then moved into his parents' "gigantic home" in Dresden. In civilian life, "my husband was with the railroad [Reichsbahn]. At the time, he was an inspector and my father-in-law was a railroad official. So, my father-in-law was in the Party. Official is certainly something, ja? And then, when my husband came home on leave, there was a huge scene one *night*. My father-in-law believed one hundred percent what Hitler said." Maybe two hundred percent, she added. "Everything was 'right.' And one night my husband kicked up such an uproar, that he said, 'Father, you have no *idea* at all what's going on out there, ja, you can't even *talk* with me about it.' He was really mad, my husband, and also insulted him and insulted Hitler. Then my father-in-law said, 'If you do not stop this at *once*,' this to his own son, and then it began to dawn on me, I began to think about things myself, [about] what was happening, and then my father-in-law said, 'If you don't stop, I'll bring in the Gestapo.' That he said to his *own* son."

Where was the mother-in-law? There, too. "She wanted to smooth things over." What did she say? "Well, of course she was infuriated. 'What! You should be ashamed of yourself, your own boy!' And without saying goodbye, my husband left [the room.]" He had said, "You all have no *idea*,

190

when [it's] victory, victory, victory. All the while out there in the trenches, you don't know at all what's going on, how the soldiers are croaking [verrecken] and how they're shot [if they] open their mouths."

"My husband wanted to desert. But his mother pleaded with him. She said, 'Son, that will come *out* and they will *find* you.'" He wanted to hide with relatives in another town, but his mother prevailed. When his leave was over, he returned to the front.

His outburst did not have to do with concentration camps (which Frau Kretzschmar said she had thought were "reeducation camps") or the shootings of civilians. It had to do solely with "soldiers among themselves, what they were going through."

The following January Frau Kretzschmar gave birth to a daughter, Sabine.

One year and one month later, the Allies staged the ferocious firebombing of Dresden.

"We were *all* convinced, in all of Dresden, everyone was convinced, that there would be no attack *here*. First, there was the rumor that a sister of Hitler's was living [nearby]. That was said." Another rumor she said she remembered only vaguely was that "Americans had invested a lot of money in these big factories. That was said a lot, and everyone believed it." Another reason for assurance was that houses in a nearby village had been bombed in the fall of 1944, but the attack had been considered an error.

Dresden was no error, at least logistically. The question is still being asked about whether the Allied attack on the beautiful "art city," housing so many civilians, so near the end of the war, was justified. (It is a question Frau Kretzschmar herself never brought up.) The reasons Dresden was bombed are clear. It was a communications center, thus a military target. And, of course, it was part of the Third Reich. And the Third Reich had bombed one Ally, England, first.

Yet Dresden's local leaders and citizenry were so convinced the Allies would not bomb them that in the whole city, said Frau Kretzschmar, there was not a single public bombing shelter. "Only the cellars of houses. In that sense, no preparations. There were air raid drills, they were done. But other than that, *nobody* thought. . . . Just because the civil servant presumptuousness [Beamtendünkel] and so on was so strong in Dresden. In that sense, there was nothing. And when the attack came, in an instant, the sirens didn't work. There were no sirens to hear at all."

On the evening of February 13, 1944, Frau Kretzschmar, who was pregnant again, was home with her in-laws and Sabine. From the "Goebbels Snout" came an announcement that groups of bombers were nearing Hanover and Sachsen. "One did not take that seriously, either. It had often been the case that they then turned off, and so." This time, however, "the moment it was ten o'clock, suddenly *everything* was bright, nicht? The sky was bright and, I mean, if it weren't so ghastly, that the end was there, one could say it was a pretty piece of theater, these Christmas trees [flare bombs], nicht? And everything bright as day. And now one noticed that it would be serious. The din already had begun." She said it would be impossible to re-create what it sounded like. "Sort of a muffled rolling."

"When the din began, we were in the cellar. One already heard the detonations, nicht? Cracking. Quickly into the cellar. There couldn't have been a lot of panic, because there weren't many of us in the house." Another family, by then just a mother and child, lived in another part of the house and used the cellar, too. In the cellar, as always, were the families' already packed suitcases, a spare baby carriage, and a couple of old armchairs Frau Kretzschmar had taken down. "The cellar was not built like a bunker or anything, ja? It was a normal cellar, which had been altered for use as an air raid shelter." The ceiling and walls had not been reinforced, but the windows had been refitted on the inside with heavy iron shutters, "iron windows," she called them, on hinges.

During that first attack, there might not have been panic, but there were no longer delusions about safety, either; the house was located fairly close to the main railroad station. Frau Kretzschmar heard "crashes and bangs." The cellar itself sustained little damage. "We just heard it. Then after everything had quieted down a little, my father-in-law peeped around a little [upstairs and outside] and said, 'Everything is quiet. But it's burning, it's burning.' He said nothing in our house was on fire, but a lot of windowpanes were broken. In the living area everything was all thrown together, whatever had not been fastened down. Tables and chairs were all every which way."

Everyone went upstairs about three-quarters of an hour after the attack. "Then we began to clean up, the most basic things. So, the home looked . . . everything thrown around, but nothing had burned. Just dirty, and the broken glass panes." The first thing they did was lay a few blankets on Sabine, the cold February night now being inside as well as outside. "Then we began nailing up the windows with cardboard, and *then* suddenly we heard another humming and these sounds of engines. And now naturally the fear was even greater, that's clear. Immediately down again in the cellar." Frau Kretzschmar said that once again, the planes came too fast for warning sirens to react. "When we were going down the cellar steps, it was already roaring. It roared continuously. I sat down, put my child on my lap, and in front of the child another pillow. Suddenly, it was like a sixth sense, instinctively, I heard from far away, zzzzzzhhhhhhhhh, as if really a bomb were coming toward us. That is what it sounded like to me. Instinctively, I threw the child to the floor, that is, the pillow, the child on top of it, and me over it. And [the bomb] already roared. And *how!*

"After the noise was over, we slowly shook off the dirt." She then saw that her instinct had saved her life and her daughter's. The force of the bomb had lifted an entire iron shutter up out of its hinges and thrown it across the room.

"If I had been sitting up, it would have hit me on the head. But instead it went over me and skidded down the other wall vertically. That was an experience," she concluded.

"Afterward, after the second attack, we just stayed there, until dawn. And then we came upstairs and saw the 'present.' *Everything* was demolished." That included the house itself, and almost everything in it. "My mother-in-law and my father-in-law, they had both immediately become hysterical and howled and, ja, for me, I must say in that moment, my mother was more important." Leaving her hysterical in-laws behind, Frau Kretzschmar took her screaming daughter in her arms and left on foot for her mother's house.

"I went with my child along the railroad tracks. On the other side, where we lived, everything was burning. And there came, one heard screams and goings on and so forth and some human beings came through wrapped in blankets and said, 'You cannot cross over, everything is burning, you can't get through.' And the streets were all so narrow. Some got through and called to me, 'Don't go there, don't go there, you won't get through and there are dead . . . there are a lot of dead.'"

Nobody knows how many. People died not only from bombs, of course—which flattened an estimated sixteen hundred acres of central Dresden—but from the fireball that followed. Estimates of fatalities have varied from tens of thousands to hundreds of thousands. An authoritative statistic, from an East German publisher, is that thirty-five thousand people were killed.[1] (Frau Kretzschmar said that the bodies of ninety thousand people, most pulled from the rubble around the old market area, were piled up and burned.)

Surrounded by pandemonium, fires, and the thickening smoke, Frau Kretzschmar made her way past some of the dead. She spoke as if she were still in shock. "Then I went up, and my hair was all plastered together, and then I went along the tracks and . . . toward the west, where my mother lived, and she came to me on the tracks. She had the same thought, that there was no other way to get through. She saw me. I didn't see her. My mother found me through the screaming of the child."

After the relief of the astounding reunion, the question became where to go. Fire had destroyed Frau Kretzschmar's mother's home, too. They decided to return to the in-laws' cellar. Along the way, the women passed more and more dead. They were "everywhere. I can recall I [saw] sort of a tangle and I said to my mother, 'Look here at this, what an odd kind of tree trunk.' My mother said, 'That's not a . . . Look, those are clasped-together human

---

1. Walter Weidauer, *Inferno Dresden* (Berlin [East]: Dietz Verlag, 1983), 205. Many thanks to Agnes Peterson.

beings, carbonized.'" Frau Kretzschmar looked closer. Her mother was right. The form was made from "a few human beings, together, who probably in their need. . . . And then one saw rib cages, and then one saw several eyes and hands. I saw it."

When asked her first thought, she said, "That was clear. That was the fault of Hitler. The Third Reich was at fault, or it wouldn't have happened."

She and her mother made their way back to the cellar. "But my in-laws were not there anymore. And we took the baby carriage and then together we carried it up. And then we went in the wrong direction. Then out toward the southern part of the city and when it was morning, as it was then light, then we saw many, many human beings and the word was that on Mommsen Street there's a central place for the injured." They decided to try to go there, but through the worsening smoke, destruction, and chaos around them, kept getting turned around. "And I was 'in other circumstances' and now it was so, through the smoke I could not see anymore. I said, 'I see nothing at all.' I could see nothing, only completely blurred. Then [when] the eleven o'clock attack came, we had more luck." During the attack of the morning of the fourteenth of February, although they were outdoors, they "sort of half and half found some shelter, but nothing much happened." That is, nothing much happened where they were.

After the attack, they continued wandering around and getting lost, but then had another piece of luck. They happened to see an evacuation bus. In addition to dealing with the dead and wounded and the fires, civil authorities had been spending part of their efforts trying to get buses from other cities to come in and get the survivors out, because conditions were not only dangerous, but cold. "And on the afternoon of February fourteenth, I was loaded into a bus with the child. Then my mother went crazy. She howled like mad and said, 'I cannot leave my daughter alone, don't you see, she cannot see and then the small child, in these 'other circumstances.' . . . Basically, only smaller children with mothers were to be taken away, and not the older ones. But my mother, she was so, so was half-hysterical and screamed so much, that they let her on the bus. It was true, I could not *see* anything."

The bus was going to a village named Kummersdorf, about seventy-five miles north of Dresden. "We arrived there that evening, in this village. We were immediately all put together in an inn." The local population met the refugees to help. "The children here and there. And then with my child, just imagine, the whole day long we had had nothing to eat, that is we had a little zwieback or so. And it hadn't been possible to change her. It was cold. I decided to let it be instead." When she finally did go to clean her up, "The feces were coming up out of the collar. Ja. And then in the dance hall, we [laid down] straw and so on and we were all. . . . It was like a bed in heaven. We were there, and now quiet, and had lived through it. We were all very thankful."

194

In Ursula Kretzschmar's family, the only person who felt the same about the Third Reich at the end as at the beginning, and who remained basically unchanged in spirit, was her mother. She never did like the Nazis. And once they were gone, her major concern remained, as it had been before and during their reign, her daughter's (and now granddaughter's) welfare. She went to farmers near the evacuation village and volunteered to work for free in exchange for a place for them to stay and for food. The offer was accepted. The threesome moved into a living space, reached by a ladder, at the top of a barn. The arrangement worked well, but her mother was exploited, said Frau Kretzschmar. Apparently, the farm family also exploited the city people who, as throughout Germany, came to trade possessions for food. The farmers had so much, they "lacked only a carpet in the cow stall," said Frau Kretzschmar, reciting the familiar slogan.

In fact, they had so much that her mother was encouraged to take over "when the beggars came." She proved adept, too, trading food from her own stock for something in return. She got her son-in-law, not yet back from the Eastern front, a pocket watch.

Meanwhile, shortly after Frau Kretzschmar was more or less settled, she made her way back to the ruins of her in-laws' house. They were not there. She then did what people were doing all over Germany. She wrote on a wall that she was alive, and where she was living.

Within the month, they came and found her. They brought the news that she and her mother and the baby had been fortunate indeed to get out of Dresden as early as they did. They said that everyone who remained in the city lived in a panicked frame of mind that lasted for weeks.

Frau Kretzschmar soon learned that her in-laws, especially her father-in-law, were less deeply affected by the psychological stress of the future—fear of another attack, than they were about the past—reports of what the Nazis had done. "He died in the year '45 from *grief*, from inside, because he had been so mistaken. He also said, 'That scoundrel [Lump] Hitler. How could he?' And so on and so forth. He did not think it right, what happened then. Na? He died at the end of the year '45. One saw . . . from day to day he shrank more and more, internally. He did not overcome it. He simply slowly withered." She paused.

His wife died a short time later. Frau Kretzschmar wrote me that "they could not overcome the loss of their home, and that they suddenly stood before a nothing. They had no courage to start all over." When we met, she did not mention their destroyed house as a factor, but solely their destroyed faith.

Had she ever felt personally guilty?

"Individually, no. To the contrary, everyone said, 'We must, we must.' 'Must' became the excuse. We couldn't do anything else. We must."

And her almost-dissident husband? He survived the war, was taken prisoner by the Soviets, and released in 1946. He once told her, she said, that during the war "many" German soldiers went over to the Soviet side. Even after captivity, his view of the Soviet system remained positive. She said he reported that prisoners "were not handled with velvet gloves," but that was to be expected, and that prisoners were not hit or tortured. Somewhere along the way, however, his experiences must have affected him. She did not go into details, but referred briefly to his being a changed man when he returned. Her implication was that when he returned to Germany he drank heavily and slept around frequently. Frau Kretzschmar and her husband were divorced not long after he came back.

By then, she had already suffered another kind of loss. In August of 1945 she gave birth to a son, but "I could not carry him through." That November, he died.

For a while after the war, Frau Kretzschmar's focus, like her mother's, was apolitical. In May, while she was playing in the courtyard with Sabine, some Soviet soldiers rode up on horseback. Frau Kretzschmar said that because German propaganda portrayed Russians as men with a "knife clenched in their teeth" who "would butcher everything," she was terrified. She called out to her mother, just as one soldier took Sabine and placed her on his horse.

"What went through me in *that* moment, I cannot describe. Now he had the child, stroked its sweater, gave the child something, and gave it back to me." She said he had seen the fear in her eyes, and told her, "Nix gut, nix gut." After they left, she climbed up into their home. The soldiers came back, and climbed up, too. The one who had picked up Sabine put a bag on the table and said, "'Everything for child, everything for child [Alles für Kind, alles für Kind].' And in it was half a pig's head."

Frau Kretzschmar explained (which took some doing) this was a welcome present. She said that from the head she made jellied meat [Sülze] that lasted a month. After she happily accepted the present, another Russian soldier, who knew German better than his colleague, told her about him. He said he "'also had a wife like you, and child. And SS took child, at the wall. Brains out.' That's what was said." Frau Kretzschmar took a deep breath. "You know, when you think what he could have done to my child in revenge. . . . Would have been completely possible, ne? To the contrary, they left again, hugged the child, and said, 'Alles gut, wird alles gut [Everything will be fine].' Now the tears come, when I think about it." She paused. "So, I did not experience anything bad with the Russians."

The only incident she mentioned knowing that concerned any Russian soldiers doing anything "bad" was to shoot a Hitler Youth fanatic who was shooting at them.

She knew of no other instances of "mishandling"?

She said *nein* five times.

The town of Marburg, about an hour's train ride north of Frankfurt, is celebrated for its lovely setting, its centuries-old university and library and other cultural jewels, and for being the workplace of the famous chroniclers of German fairy tales, the Brothers Grimm. As fearful children and frowning parents around the world know, most of the tales are filled not only with obstacles but with cruelty and violence, and typically end only after a plucky male hero saves and gets the female and/or the kingdom—the Reich, in German.

For some Germans in the 1920s, another fairy tale about another Reich was just beginning. And one local Marburg girl who must have looked perfect for a role as a Teutonic fairy tale princess was Martha Fenner. She was tall, blonde, and, given her striking looks in her seventies and eighties, exceptionally pretty. And she, too, numbered among the German youth pulled to the seemingly heroic Nazi movement.

For her and her classmates, the lure came early, about 1928. She was about seventeen. "We went to an office here called the 'donation ring.' It was a precursor to the Party. You could donate something, money or whatever. It was already very National Socialistic. We were *full* of enthusiasm and marched right over. I did it just once, went there and donated three marks or something so they could do something good with it."

Had her gesture met with enthusiasm or apathy at home, her course might have been

Frau Martha Brixius

The Ambivalence of Avoidance

different. But, upon hearing of the donation, "my mother, who was very political and very alert, enlightened me. She talked about what kinds of dangers were coming, how horrible she found the whole thing. She'd already surmised there could be a war. My mother was very keen of ear and eye." And as for Martha's inchoate enthusiasm for National Socialism, "that was the end of it." The larger tale, however, had just begun.

Among the families it would affect was the small united matriarchy headed by Frau Klara Fenner, a First World War widow with two children, Martha and Justus. Frau Brixius mentioned, many years after we first met, that her father had been a lawyer who was assigned during the war to rule on desertion cases. She said he began empathizing so much with the scared young soldiers who had run from battle that he was unable to sentence them to jail and refused to continue in his job. As punishment, he was sent to the front as a soldier himself. There, he was killed in battle.

The family he left behind knew well the potential price of opposing the government.

Thanks in part to both her parents, Frau Martha Brixius has the clear conscience not to have been a Nazi. But at the outset of our interviews, she said she was not the "active anti-Nazi" described to me by the American man who put us in touch. Meeting my first and rather eager question directly, she said an active anti-Nazi would imply someone who had hidden a Jew or done something along those lines. And, she said, she had not.

Barely disguising my disappointment, I asked on. Eventually Frau Brixius proved to be, although less brave than advertised, more intriguing. It is easy to judge heroes or criminals or even fellow travelers by their responses to the Third Reich, but it is not easy to judge a person who represents what might be called a universal dilemma of degree—a person who opposed the Third Reich more with heart and brain than with life and limb, a person who chose not to go along rather than to go against, a person who was, in sum, a passive anti-Nazi.

Frau Brixius still lives in Marburg, in a bright, attractive home she designed herself. She shares it with her second husband, Lothar Brixius, a folklore scholar. He is a thoughtful man of droll humor. It was evident from the start the Brixiuses live a comfortable, and readerly, life. Their home exudes careful taste and much evidence of her family's prosperous past, including such treasures as a lovely oval oil painting of her lovely mother and the remainder of her father's antique beer stein collection. (Frau Brixius said most of it was destroyed in the weeks after the war, when American occupation soldiers tossed the steins out the window and onto the sidewalk, apparently after drinking from them.) Herr Dr. Brixius's collection of prints of old Marburg lines one room. Thousands of books are here and there, neatly, in bookcases. The wooden floors gleam, the tea is choice, the bedsheets are of ironed linen (Frau Brixius had invited me to stay before we met), and the herbs are homegrown, in Dr. Brixius's organic garden.

It also was evident from the start that the couple's life is cultured old-world conservative every way but politically. The reason seems largely to be the Third Reich. The passive anti-Nazi turned into an active antimilitarist and antinationalist. But being active in the 1980s helped no more than being passive in the 1930s and '40s, said Frau Brixius. Freedom to protest changed nothing. She listed all she had done, to no apparent avail, she said, against nuclear weapons. And being horrified by the Germany of the early 1990s, and reading about it constantly, helped nothing either.

Yet the lessons of the Third Reich permeate the way the Brixiuses see the world. During a first and extensive discussion, they mentioned, for instance, being wary of the Greens' movement. They did not like its celebratory view of "Made in Germany" products. The emphasis seemed nationalistic. And as the Berlin Wall came down, the Brixiuses were aghast at other Germans driving to East Germany, buying carloads of cheap state-supported goods, and gleefully showing them off back home. "We're ashamed," she wrote me. Herr Dr. Brixius, who had retired after careers in teaching and radio programming and an avocation in peaceful protest, said at one point he has given up and just works in his garden.

But Frau Brixius continued to fulminate. Her letters to me usually included a neatly clipped and underlined newspaper article about something that she deplored, from the United States' bombing of Iraq, to West Germany's politics toward East Germany, to the neo-Nazi hate crimes. It sometimes seemed to me that she had never relaxed since the Third Reich ended, or began.

The Nazis' boycott of Jewish-owned stores in April of 1933 may have been Martha Fenner's first confrontation of conscience. Her mother led her through it.

"She always went into Jewish stores, even when the SA stood out front to see who entered. Once I went in with her. SA men in uniform stood outside. My mother really gave me courage.

"This Jewish merchant was someone from whom one could buy sewing needles and cloth and wool and scissors and so on. It was so terrible—such a very large store and completely empty. The owner came over to us. He was so *thankful* that someone *came*. My mother really had nothing to buy, but wanted to show him, I'm still coming. So she bought two small spools of thread. And in his zeal and happiness that someone was there, this man, Herr Blumenfeld, said, 'Shall I have them sent to your home?' But it was sad, naturally, he said it."

Frau Fenner, declining the offer, put the thread in her purse and left with Martha. There were no consequences from the Nazis at the door. "We probably were very lucky. More could have happened. Nothing really did. They just half looked at us and could have recognized us, but didn't write down our names. One stood at each side of the door. It was so dumb. They'd been ordered there, probably hadn't thought about it a lot."

Soon after similar shopping excursions, "the stores were closed. The problem was taken care of." Frau Fenner then followed a personal dictum of not buying from Nazis.

"My mother loved chocolate and went to a fine small shop where the best chocolate was. And one noted very early on in conversation, they were Nazis. So we never went there again. In a certain sense it wasn't that simple, since she liked this chocolate so much, but she didn't go again. Those are such *small* things one could do. It's really only that one relinquished something, but one did nothing active. Not that."

Thinking of "nothing active," I asked what happened to the family that owned the dry goods store. Speaking very slowly, Frau Brixius said, "They left, but I believe they got out in time. To the U.S. I did not hear they were killed." She said specific fates generally were learned after the war, when a survivor wrote to old friends. "It was talked around who still lived and who did not. But it took years until one knew."

In the meantime, she herself saw some of what was happening in her hometown. "Once, to my horror, I saw, who can that be? A lawyer suddenly having to do road work, to dig out the tracks for the streetcars. I could see him. He'd dug a deep hole in which he stood. He'd hacked it out. Suddenly I recognized him as a fine gentleman I'd seen on the street."

The Nazis also went after one of Martha's friends, "an *unbelievably* beloved gymnastics teacher. She had so many students. She was also very musical and always played beautiful piano accompaniment to the exercises, especially beautiful. And she put a little box on the piano and one threw one's money in for the gymnastics course. She never checked to see if everyone paid. There were so many, she couldn't. She was so beloved. Then suddenly came word she's half Jewish and can't give classes anymore. From one day to the next.

"There was another gym teacher here who worked at the school and was a Nazi. She had made it known. And my friend, who was married to a lawyer, moved to Berlin and hid, so to speak. You can do that easier in a big city. Two small daughters. They lived in a rented apartment in the middle of Berlin and I visited her there a lot. She gave classes to me and another friend, in her room. Her husband later was punished for marrying a half-Jew. He was put in the Waffen-SS, on what one called a 'commando trip to heaven,' with which one figured you didn't return. But he did." Safely.

I asked if he might be one of the Waffen-SS soldiers buried in the cemetery in Bitburg. She said yes.

Back in Marburg, the prevailing mood was pro-Hitler. Frau Brixius said she would gauge her own neighborhood as 90 percent for and 10 percent against. "You could not say anything on the street. There was something called the German look [der deutsche Blick]." She demonstrated it by looking behind her and to each side before talking. Another street routine, she said, was to develop a wait-and-see attitude with people whose politics you did not know. "If they liked Hitler, you could tell very fast. For instance, I met one on the street, from my old school class. I noted *immediately* she'd become a Nazi, and since then we didn't speak." She said the classmate would not have greeted her with "Heil Hitler!" although it was compulsory. More likely, she said, the woman "had spoken enthusiastically about the war, 'Now we have another great victory,' and so on.

"Most apparent was who was for [the Nazis]. They said it loudly and acted the same way. You could tell by their uniforms or insignia. The opponents, naturally, were much softer and quieter and more hidden. It's hard to say how many opponents there were. The supporters certainly were in the majority." In tallying supporters, she included the "ones who simply went along with it and didn't get outraged by it."

One time, the pull of the Nazi phenomenon came close to nabbing her again, too. She happened to be in Hanover on a day Hitler was there for a rally. And she happened to be standing where the Nazi motorcade drove by. From an open car, Hitler waved to the wildly cheering crowd. "I noticed, although I was opposed, how such a mass of people screamed so enthusiastically and raised their hands and threw flowers, that I was in danger of being pulled along. It is very dangerous to stand in such a throng of people. Somehow it's fascinating. The throng's so enthusiastic, it can infect you. And you think, could you be wrong and all the others be right? One does become uncertain."

She recalled a related pull. "I am very much against the military. But when I hear military music, somehow I get goose bumps." She paused. "And I must make it clear to myself I don't want anything to do with that. It is a danger."

She also spoke (as noted in the Introduction) of the dangerous pull of words during the Third Reich, that is, the diabolically and alliteratively clever nouns and phrases that emanated from Joseph Goebbels's propaganda ministry. One example was the slangy double-*k Kohlenklau*. It meant a "coal snatcher," but implied a person who squandered precious fuel. "If someone merely came into the heated room of a house, the rest of the house was cold, and left the door open, someone would say, 'Kohlenklau, close the door.'"

Were such words and slogans repeated on the street?

"Oh, always, always. Everyone knew them. They were used a lot." Her husband added, "You heard it once, then you knew it. Goebbels was really a master in such things. And in the face of this clever psychological work, a normal human being could hardly defend himself, hardly preserve himself."

Frauen

Neither the lure of the crowd nor the cleverness of the phrase swayed Frau Fenner, however. She continued thwarting the Nazis in her own way, by trying to ignore their directives. One directive was to buy a Nazi flag. The encircled black swastika on a field of red—the bigger the flag the better—was required decor for many German homes, especially those facing a street on which Nazis paraded.

"It eventually got very difficult. People were always coming and saying why haven't you hung out a flag, for Hitler's birthday and so on," said Frau Brixius. "You almost went to jail. It was very dangerous if you didn't do it. One person after the other came, rang the doorbell, and said you haven't hung out your flag yet. Finally, my mother bought a real tiny one. You were supposed to hang it on a pole. She simply hung it over the balcony like a little rug you put by the bed."

The degree of maternal heroism may seem negligible in comparison to that shown by others. But for the daughter who lived through the time and the fears with her, the admiration never wavered. "My mother was a brave anti-Nazi. I really got my attitude from her. It's not something I earned on my own, but I thank my mother for it. She was incredibly courageous and not always very careful, so we really were afraid for her.

"She was consistently against the Nazis. She was supposed to attend evening meetings of Nazi groups. She always said, ach, she couldn't, she couldn't walk that far. It was a bit away from town and it was too dark in the evening and she'd be afraid. Nothing but such excuses. Then a terrible neighbor came over, an Ortsgruppenleiter, and he told my mother, 'If you're afraid, I'll take you there and bring you back home.' My mother told me, 'For God's sake, I'm more afraid of him than I am of the dark.'"

Frau Brixius laughed high and delightedly at the memory. "She never went once."

One evening, the ever-hopeful Ortsgruppenleiter's attempts to get Frau Fenner to attend a meeting put both women in danger. "This horrid man came into the house to persuade her to go with him and we had our radio dial set to the enemy station. My mother literally trembled that he'd look over and notice where the dial was set. But he didn't, and nothing happened."

If the consequences of going into Jewish stores, of dallying about flying a Nazi flag, and of resisting attendance at Nazi meetings were not precisely known (although still feared), there was no mystery about what happened to people caught listening to verboten foreign radio broadcasts. One person who was caught listening was Martha Brixius's religion teacher. Unbeknownst to Frau Brixius, the teacher was Jewish and had converted to Christianity. (My initial confusion as to which way the conversion went prompted Frau Brixius to explain, "Jewish race. Christian belief.") The teacher, "a *highly* intelligent woman," not only taught religion at the high school, but also lectured at Giessen University about Christianity. "She probably hardly thought of herself as a Jew. For many, it was a surprise to return to the consciousness, 'I am a Jew.' She lived, I later learned, with a non-Jewish girlfriend in an apartment. The apartment being relatively large, I never saw it, they rented rooms to two or three women students. These students heard that the two ladies listened to foreign radio broadcasts and told their professor [Herr Pfannenstiel]. This professor was a super-Nazi. And he made sure that the two, the Jew and the non-Jew, were sent to a prison nearby. The one who was not Jewish died there. She couldn't take the punishment.

"[Later], to my great surprise, I suddenly saw my old teacher again, on the street. I went to her, spoke her name, and wanted to ask how she was, and she said . . ."—Frau Brixius lowered her voice to a whisper—"'Get away fast, get away fast.' Then I learned she had only a short time, a day or two, to get some papers before being taken to a concentration camp." She paused. "To Theresienstadt." A longer pause. "I found it so decent of her, that she didn't want to put me in danger. Nothing worse could happen to her, but she didn't want something to happen to anyone else. Ja, if someone had seen us together, I probably would have gone with her to the camp."

"Probably" is debatable, but the danger certainly was there. And so was the other danger. Still, Frau Fenner continued to tune in to the enemy. "Always, even during the war, she listened to foreign broadcasts, which was strictly forbidden. And she was always afraid someone could hear at the wall of the house that we were listening. My mother and I were completely unschooled technically and racked our brains trying to figure if someone could install a device on the house to hear from outside that inside we heard foreign broadcasts. We never knew if it were a danger or not. But nothing happened." And through the broadcasts, "we learned that a lot they had told us here wasn't true."

Frau Fenner also may have expressed her anti-Nazi feelings in other ways. "Certainly if an SS man had sat next to her on the bus or the trolley, she'd have stood up and walked away. *That* I am sure of." Frau Brixius said she worried that her mother spoke her mind more freely than was prudent. But, again, nothing ever happened. They continued living at the crossroads of bravery, timidity, luck, and fear.

Frau Brixius had a vantage point other than that of Marburg. She had Berlin. Although she often returned to Marburg to visit, she moved to Berlin in the late spring of 1933 and lived there for five years. She had gone to pursue her career as a librarian. I had assumed it was what she wanted, but much later she indicated that she had lowered her sights to being a librarian, rather than raised them.

As for Berlin itself, true to its reputation, it was "unbelievably stimulating and lively," Nazis or no. Martha, then about twenty-three, got a job in a branch of the central Berlin library. Among her first sights was one especially distressing to a young librarian. It was the Nazis' book burning.

"I suddenly heard that books were being burned. And I went there with some acquaintances to see it, if it were really true. I saw that gigantic fire." Volume after volume by Marxist and Jewish and other disapproved authors, such as Thomas Mann (who had a Jewish wife), were destroyed. "They kept throwing in the books with great enthusiasm. Most were enthusiastic. Those who found it horrible, naturally didn't go."

The Nazis' heavy-handed clamp on German culture prompted one of her cousins, a young woman sculpture student, to flee Germany. Asked if she herself considered doing so, Frau Brixius said, "No. If I must be honest, no. I did not have that much courage, nor that much independence."

Nor did she leave her Berlin library job, even though her boss, predictably, was a Nazi Party member. "I would not say he was a great supporter of Hitler, but someone who was most proud of the Nordic race." He was a disciple, she said, of a then-famous professor, Hermann Wirth, who had immersed himself in old Nordic traditions, studying everything from runic script to ancient Germanic Christmas customs.

And he was smitten with his new employee. "It was ludicrous. Everything I said was terrific and wonderful only because I was blonde. We always took books home with us, which we had to read and discuss so we could advise the readers about them. Because we couldn't read every book, it was divided, and we all sat together once a week and told the others, this kind of book is for simple people and that's a fantastic book, very complicated in style and should be recommended only to exacting readers, and so on. And when I said what I'd read and thought, his reaction was, 'Fabulous, that is really the natural and healthy sensibility.'

"And in the library, we wore white smocks. It's always so dusty when one works with books. A smock is very practical. And because I had only a furnished room in Berlin, I sent my wash home to my mother. She was fed up with these white smocks she had to keep washing and sending back. So she made a brightly striped smock which looked cleaner longer. One day, I appeared wearing it and the reaction was, '*That* is again the correct sensibility. Not this *sterile* one, but *again* the healthy *color*.' So, it was again right.

"Whenever we wanted the afternoon off for whatever reason, I was the one to go and ask. Mostly the answer was yes. Only because of my blonde hair. But one day it came to an end."

That day was years later, in 1938. She no longer was a single librarian, but a married woman (married to her first husband, a Herr Koch) with a baby girl, named Annette.

"I was taking a walk in Berlin with my daughter, she in her baby carriage, and I met this library director. He said, 'Ach, may I peek in?' and surely thought there would be this completely wonderful blue-eyed blonde child inside. At the beginning my daughter had very black hair and looked like she was from the Caucasus steppes or something. All he said was, 'Oh!'"

She laughed. "Horrified! 'Oh!' Since then he never spoke with me again." She laughed again. "That was the end of his enthusiasm. He probably thought I'd married some foreigner and not a racially pure German or whatever."

Incidentally, Lothar Brixius, whom she married long after the war, was having difficulties with racial stereotypes himself. The Brixiuses now make an unusually arresting couple as they walk along holding hands, but alone in the 1930s, he could not walk along the sidewalk with the ease she could. "I was treated as if I were a Jew. I was short, had a curved nose, I had dark hair, curls, and, what do I know? Anyhow, I got it too, even though I'm not." During his undergraduate days at Marburg, he said, he was walking up the steps to a classroom building when uniformed SA men blocked the door. They yelled at him, "Out! Jews out!" To escape such treatment, he fled—to the German army. He was sent to France and Russia, and was wounded five times.

The day the war began, said Frau Brixius, she fled for home. "I was going shopping for something or another that morning and read, in huge posters everywhere, war has been declared. I was insanely terrified and thought it's all going to happen at once with the bombs, which took a good deal longer. I took my child and the most important things and came here to Marburg, where my mother lived, because I thought it can't be as bad in a small town as a big city, which also was right."

Frau Fenner turned out to be as prescient as ever. "I sat with my mother and on the radio heard big speeches about cannons instead of butter. My mother immediately said, 'It's all over for us. It won't go well. It's the worst thing that can happen.' She saw immediately we'd lose the war and what kinds of losses there'd be for all sides. She pictured it right away."

Family concern about the war immediately turned to the draft, and her brother Justus. "My brother had to be a soldier, against my mother's wishes. He had no choice. But he didn't have to fight, because he was the only son of a father who died in battle [in the First World War]. The last male of the family didn't have to go to the front. To the contrary, he could even go to college. He studied medicine during the war. But he had some difficulties."

She said a junior officer complained in the barracks that Justus had not laid out his underwear in an orderly enough way. Justus replied that that was beside the point with a war going on, and added, "You're nothing to me but a little piece of shit." The remark consituted a criminal offense. Justus was summoned before a military tribunal. His panicked family then "mobilized everyone possible" to help and found a "very nice lawyer. He *was* in the Party. But he was not a Nazi. There's that, too. And he helped my brother." Justus was released.

Spared both jail and the front line, Justus nonetheless was sent to France and Russia. At one point, he was made an officer himself.

Frauen

Back at the Marburg home front, a matriarchy of four had evolved: Frau Fenner, the future Frau Brixius, and two children, Annette and Justus (named after his uncle), born in 1944. Life was made up partly of drudgery and partly of terror.

The drudgery included milk buying, which Frau Brixius said took at least two hours every day—forty-five minutes for the round-trip walk to get it, the rest of the time waiting for it. "When the man who sold the milk finally came, some fifty women were standing there with their little milk cans. This milkman was such a sadist, he really enjoyed it. He saw how we all stood, greedily waiting for the milk, and he moved very slowly, making us all more nervous and waiting even longer. Then he made jokes. Finally, we got our little bit of milk. It was completely light blue, not white, it was so thin." Sometimes she took Annette or the baby with her. By the end of the war, Annette no longer went to school; it was shut down, partly because of the bombing raids. (The effect of the bombs on Annette showed itself decades later, when mother and daughter and others were on a walk in the mountains. A stunt pilot suddenly flew so low—probably to impress a girl-friend—that everyone ducked. But Annette disappeared. "We found her crouched in a ditch. She'd hidden herself, in terror. A war child.")

An advantage of living away from major targets, as the family did, was that fewer bombs were dropped. A disadvantage was that there were fewer bomb shelters. Everyone was frightened wherever they sought shelter, said Frau Brixius. "We could only go to our cellar. That could have been a lot worse if you're trapped there by rubble. In the last year, my son was just born and I didn't go to the cellar at all because I didn't want to wake him. We hoped for luck. I didn't want to make the child nervous. During the day, we often went into the woods. I took the baby carriage and a bicycle, too, because in between I had to go back to the house to get food or clean dia-pers for the baby. We couldn't take everything with us at once. And some-times I quickly warmed the milk or made soup. We could hang the can of milk on the handlebars of the bicycle, so I'd take that in the woods."

The war also came to Marburg in the person of prisoners.

"A French prisoner of war was assigned to the local coal store and hauled coal in a sack to the customers. Although we didn't have much, we could give him an apple or something. Not in the light of day, of course. But what is a terrible memory, we lived on a street where you could see everything. And every morning around four o'clock, I heard steps, steps, steps. It was Russian prisoners from a nearby camp going to work. They were brought here to our little train station. Every morning at four I woke and got up and saw these sad figures going by, some without shoes. In the *winter*. There was ice and snow. And *completely* starving and completely in rags. But I couldn't give them anything. There were always guards, German soldiers. It wasn't possible."

Frau Brixius felt that such memories, unlike those the soldiers had, led to much estrangement between German men and women. "At home, one experiences very grave things, upsetting things, unusual things. And the other [person] lives in Russia or France or somewhere in captivity and experiences things with which the woman could not empathize. Then suddenly he comes back. For everybody, that certainly was very difficult, and for many, it simply was impossible to be together again. The woman had learned how to forge ahead and help in emergencies and protect her children and earn money and get food or even steal it, if she couldn't find anything else to eat. She could no longer be the true devoted wife who only did what the man wants."

Frau Brixius thought the war affected her first marriage, too. "Less my independence, maybe, than the completely different experiences. I kept evolving more to the *anti*–National Socialist side. And my husband, oddly enough, did not. I know he didn't take part in the worst aspects of the war. He saw no action. He wasn't in any battle. He always had plenty to eat. He was always somewhat"—she paused—"to the rear."

She continued, haltingly. "Perhaps it sounds perverse, but I sometimes wished . . . that he [would] experience something completely horrible. I did wish that on him. So that he really understood it, that it [would] really make an impression on his innermost being and not remain on the surface.

"Oh, he brought back nice things," she added, rather scornfully. "First of all, something to eat and also clothes. I do believe he bought it all. I mean, as an officer, he got paid and could buy things. Nonetheless, it wasn't very nice. We were momentarily happy for something to eat, that's obvious. Or if I had something for the children to wear. But I always felt terrible we had invaded the countries and also took something away from them."

When her husband was home on leave, however, their political differences were not that great, she said. "He was no Nazi. It was a sense of duty. 'Everyone's doing it, and so do I.'"

The couple's main differences were not political, but personal. Yet the political were great enough to involve the personal. "I wasn't a member of anything except in 1944, at the end, when I wanted to divorce my husband. He did not want a divorce. I was very scared he'd do something to me politically. And there I'd stand with really nothing to prove I'd done anything for the Third Reich. I thought, what in God's name *can* I do to show proof of something? So I went into the lowest-level organization there was. . . . It was some do-good undertaking." The organization, she later confirmed, was the Nationalsozialistische Volkswohlfahrt (NSV) [National Socialist People's Welfare Organization]. (It was the same organization that furthered Frau Fischer's career.) About the process of joining, Frau Brixius said, "It all went so fast, I don't know now if I even paid something, but I had some receipt in my hand."

Whatever else her act proved, it also proved pointless. "He didn't try to do anything to me politically. I didn't need it. But I wasn't sure, and I was worried about my children. My fear of him wasn't that I thought he's such a big Nazi, but that he's so furious at me for wanting to leave, he might do whatever he wanted, in order to harm me."

Toward war's end, the divorce still pending, she made a gesture in the opposite direction. "Three or four weeks before the war was over, he was here on leave. And I knew, *clearly*, like anyone who could think, observe a little, it was ending. That we'd lost the war or would soon lose it. And I said to him, 'Stay here. Hide yourself here. Don't go back.' I'd have hidden him."

The offer was significant. The crime of desertion or hiding a deserter was treasonous.

"He said, 'I can*not* do that' and went away on a *bicycle*. No more trains were running, there was chaos everywhere, and he left on a bicycle just so he could get [to his unit]. Then he was taken prisoner. I didn't know where he was. He could have stayed here, but that sense of duty said 'No, I may not. Keep going.'"

What did he think of her suggestion? That it was sweet of a woman?

She laughed. "I don't think he found it so sweet, but completely impossible. 'A woman does not know a man's duty.'"

While her husband departed from his doorstep to his duty, German soldiers, looking "thin and gaunt," arrived from their duty to his doorstep. "They rang the doorbell and said, 'Take us, we need a hideout.' My mother said, 'No, I cannot.' Certainly, some of them were very frightened people who'd gone through terrible things and really hadn't wanted to. It was a hard decision to say no. But. For political reasons, one had to hold firm, to show one was against the war and against the soldiers, even if you felt sorry for the individuals.

"And a cousin of mine came, the black sheep in the family. He was an SS man. A completely dear human being, a completely faithful relative still. Who certainly never did anything bad, but was enthusiastic about this war. He had some gold medal, and was an SS officer. He came to us as he was fleeing. As a human being we liked him very much—helpful and loving and attentive and faithful and we let him stay here *one* night. Then my mother said, 'As hard as it is, you have to move on. We can't keep you here.' He had to go."

A "completely dear human being"? Without an investigation, neither of us would know how "completely dear" her cousin was.

The war ended.

"We sat there in the cellar of our house. For the first time, there were no more bombs and planes, but artillery. The shooting sounded very close. Then it suddenly stopped. And one heard that the Americans were marching in. Then we heard them. They weren't loud like our Germans, who had hobnailed shoes. The Americans, I think, had rubber soles. But when hundreds marched at once, one heard it. We'd have liked most to run up to them with flowers or something, but we were too scared and didn't do it. You weren't sure of the situation or if you might get shot."

Asked her first impression of the American soldiers, she sighed. "They looked very healthy. Well nourished and healthy and red-cheeked. Well dressed, the uniforms still in one piece and new. From our point of view, they looked fantastic. Ach, to us they looked like gods.

"We were crazy with happiness when the Americans came," she said. "Certainly not everyone was happy. We were, although afterward there was a big disappointment about how they treated us and absolutely did not want to know if one had been for or against. What the Americans did here was quite a disappointment that hit our family pretty hard. *Many, many* Nazis got away with no problem at all, but *us* they threw out of our house."

She said that between 1945 and 1957, she and her children and her mother had to move twenty-one times.

The American troops threw not only her family out of the house, but also their possessions, she said. In addition to the antique beer steins, the family china, among other things, landed smashed on the sidewalk, too.

You *were* the enemy, I said.

"Ja. They broke everything, and threw it all outside. Later, we found only piles of rubbish. There wasn't much left."

But to Frau Brixius, there were two distinct "they"s among the American troops: the fighters and the occupiers. "Those who came in the first few days were fighting troops and they had seen something of the war. But those who came later, from the USA, hadn't seen anything at all. And many of these very young soldiers wanted to experience something, like repeat a little of the war, nicht? Have some adventure. One could understand it, but when you're part of it, it's not so nice. An old man was walking down the street. They kicked him and threw him over a garden fence. And such things.

"We had original watercolors and so forth on the walls, which weren't framed, and they wrote all over them. In the cellar we had bottles of apple juice. When we wanted to get some later, after the Americans had left, they'd drunk it all up and filled the bottles with urine. Or, in our cooking pots was toilet paper, used toilet paper. And such, such dumb things."

She said, after a while, that although she agreed their actions were understandable, "it seemed as if the local commander might have taken a little more trouble to differentiate. To disappoint old non-Nazis was hard."

Disappointed or not, she applied for and got a job as a secretary with the American forces. There she met "a very nice Jewish officer" who tried to intervene with his commander to let her family back into its house, but without success. The commander could well have his doubts; back on the streets of Marburg there was nary a Nazi. "It was extremely embarrassing. No one was part of it anymore. It happened very quickly. They suddenly were dressed differently, all uniforms were gone, no insignia at all, and they'd all been 'forced.' . . . The turnabout happened so fast, it was a joke. I never saw anything like it."

After several months of semihomelessness, the family was allowed back into its cellar, thanks to the intervention of "a very nice American" who was newly responsible for the house. He also later, secretly, allowed them to sleep in the attic, and finally to use the bathroom, rather than a pail.

Frau Brixius did not say whether the Americans' behavior was influenced in any way by whatever they knew or were learning about the newly freed concentration camp prisoners, or if they had asked her what she knew about the Holocaust.

But I certainly asked her what she knew. The subject came up in our first interview session and in several more over the years, years in which the Brixiuses offered friendship as well as hospitality. In fact, the friendship was one reason I felt obliged to press her more than I did other women. We were on a *du* basis, which she had extended; I could hardly let a *du* off the hook. Another reason for pressing her was that she seemed to have spent a good deal of effort in soul-searching and thinking about the Third Reich and her own place within it. Another reason was that I simply trusted her as at least trying to tell the truth.

That trust was confirmed when we experienced a bit of the aftermath of the Holocaust together. The Brixiuses had taken me to their vacation home, a two-hundred-fifty-year-old house in Herr Brixius's native village in the Eifel mountains. (At the puffy-cake kind of bakery run by a relative, he whispered, "Not a single ingredient has been ripped from nature.") One day, in typical German custom, we all, along with his cousin and wife, took a long walk in the nearby forest. Along the way, the cousin, a seemingly affable man, deliberately fell in step with Frau Brixius and me. He wanted to tell me about something that happened to him as a soldier in the Second World War, he said. It raised a question he thought an American could answer.

At the end of the war, in southern Germany, he began, American troops captured his unit. The American commander ordered the German soldiers to exhume an enormous pit of bodies, and lay the bodies side by side. (The Americans presumably wanted to count the bodies, try to identify them, and reinter them.) While we continued to walk, the man continued to talk. Of standing thigh-deep within the pile of corpses. Of pulling at one body and the skin coming off. That was the trouble with moving them, he said. You'd pull on an arm and all you'd have in your hands was the skin. And boy, did it smell. When you went inside to sleep, you had to leave your clothes outside.

Throughout, he volunteered not a word about who the victims might have been, nor how they might have died. Nor did he mention the inhumanity that had led to this pit of horror, nor what it was like for him emotionally to undertake such a grisly task. Granted, I had no idea of his subconscious. But on the surface, he did not seem to be hiding anything. He seemed simply not to feel it. Then he got to his point. His friends laughed him off and didn't believe him when he told them about it, the skin slipping right off the arms like that. Could I find out which American troops had been in charge at the pit, to help him prove it was true?

Frau Brixius and I had the same response. Horrified as we were by his story, we were equally horrified by how coldly he told it. I suggested, coldly in response, he write the Pentagon.

The incident reestablished my trust in Frau Brixius (Martha to me by then), and of course made pressing her about the Holocaust more difficult. But press I did. Still, nothing she said changed over the years; it just became more pointed.

The first time the subject approached, I opened a wide gate by asking her response when she meets someone who claims not to have known "what was going on." She answered that anyone who read a newspaper could tell what was going on. I quoted a village woman as saying she had had neither the time, the money, nor the inclination to read a newspaper.

"One must grant her that," she said. "That can be right. Moreover, I believe it varies. I'd believe it of many, because there was much I myself didn't know. I *never suspected* there were so many concentration camps. I'd have thought two or three. And I only learned particulars about a concentration camp by pure accident.

"During the Third Reich, we lived in a two-family house that belonged to my mother. We lived in one half and the director of the humanities high school lived in the other half. He was a good anti-Nazi and had a lot of anti-Nazi friends who visited him. One day, a friend who'd been released from a concentration camp came to him and said a few things. Not a lot, but we heard about them too. Otherwise I'd have heard *nothing* about all the cruelties and the horrid games they played. For instance, when there was bread, the SS took the pieces, sort of big scraps, and threw them in the air and the hungry prisoners had to catch them. A completely humiliating, degrading thing. I heard about things like that." She said the neighbor also said his friend must have been shackled a long time, for he stood and slept as if he were still tied up.

The neighbor did put himself in what she called "a certain danger" to let his old friend stay with him and had to be careful whom he told about him, lest he endanger them both. (The Nazis forbade ex-prisoners to talk about camp experiences.) Yet in Frau Brixius's eyes, the neighbor was not altogether a good person. "A very cultivated man who ate and lived with great seriousness," as she described him, he missed the prewar good life. So when he was drafted and stationed "at some transportation place in France," he availed himself of whatever luxuries were to be had. "I really got angry about him. He sent an enormous number of things here from France. Vast quantities of tobacco and canned meat and everything, and a beautiful Jewish lamp. We did not find that nice. They had so much, they asked us to store things in our cellar."

She said she did not believe he stole the items, but took advantage of a terrible situation. "Maybe one could buy the crates of things from poor Jews, I don't know. But I couldn't have bought a Jewish lamp if it had cost five cents. Because one could think of its history, no? He was no enemy of Jews [Judengegner], and maybe one could say things were safe with him and he cared for them and and knew their history. One *could* say."

She could not. But had she not known him, she maintained, she would not have known any details of the camps. "Therefore I can believe many people who knew little or nothing."

Herr Brixius, sitting with us just then, related an incident confirming his wife's statement. He said that during the war, he and some fellow soldiers tried to find out about the closing of a road in Weimar—near Buchenwald concentration camp. They had not even got to the barricade, he said, when armed SS guards peremptorily turned them away. If uniformed German soldiers could not find out what was going on, he asked, how could the German public?

One possible way was by rumor, or so-called whisper propaganda. I asked Frau Brixius about it. She said it "was not all that frequent. It certainly existed. But it certainly went right by a lot of people. One didn't even *risk* saying something of the kind. You'd be scared telling it to someone you didn't know well, for what he'd do with the news, if he'd report you and say, 'She's a defeatist, she's hindering our victory.'"

Such "defeatism" could, and did, lead to concentration camps.

Frau Brixius said her family's source of information remained mostly the forbidden radio broadcasts. I asked if they included reports of gassing. She whispered, "That I cannot tell you exactly. I don't know. I don't know."

I asked when she knew what.

"I did not see the transports," she said. "And learned the details definitely after the capitulation."

By "details" she meant gassing?

"Ja. One certainly had *heard* that. One thought everything possible, but whether it really was true was almost too terrible to believe. Only afterward, when one saw *pictures*, did one really believe it."

I tried to pin her down on when she heard which rumors. She said she had to disappoint me, that she simply did not know.

Then what were the specifics she did hear?

"That the Jews were being deported. First, we saw they had to work, lawyers and so on our streets, having to dig out the tracks for the trolleys." She added softly, "And didn't ride on them themselves. There they worked, very hard work which they weren't used to and which took away their strength. And one knew after they'd done that awhile, they were taken away. To a camp. One could not *imagine* more."

Yes, but rumors, I insisted . . .

"Perhaps it is unbelievable to you, but I did not hear much before the end of the war. It was more like a gloomy feeling [of] who knows what horrible things are happening to the people? But I did not hear particulars."

Particulars?

"Well, I did not know where the concentration camps were, how many concentration camps there were, what one was doing with them. And *gassing* certainly went on a long time before I knew about it." She whispered. "Even heard about it."

She also said she was unsure when she learned something, whether she learned something she knows now during the war, or after it.

What had she done with whatever she had known during the war?

She said her sole recourse was to tell her friends, and agonize together. "Things had gone so far, you could not undertake anything without being killed. It was already too late. We all woke up too late. It didn't help either, if you yourself were done away with." She said that because German women were responsible for elderly parents and children, they were the least independent and therefore least likely to risk their lives. "The man in the Third Reich thought, 'I can risk everything. My children are cared for.' The woman *did* concern herself with the children. But women could not count on a man to concern himself with the children."

"Furthermore," she said, "you needed a lot of courage. And it is my opinion not everyone is a hero. I believe one cannot expect every human being to be so courageous. That is asking too much."

Frau Margarete (Gretl) Sasowski

From the Emperor to a Mud Hole

When Gretl was a little girl, she watched the emperor eat lunch. "I saw him in Breslau twice. He always came to the crown prince's estate to hunt. And in Breslau he always stopped in the home for blind children. That was associated with our boarding school. He always had lunch there (sauerkraut with this smoked meat) and always got tipsy. Then he stayed with the children through coffee. He ordered this Silesian streussel cake everyone liked to eat." She laughed. Her whole boarding school, "more than ninety girls" and their nuns, showed up at the home for blind children to see him. What impression did he make? "He was nice. He waved to us." He "really made a good impression." The emperor, Kaiser Wilhelm II, wore his cuirassier (dragoon) uniform, she said. She laughed again. "Those were such wonderful times. There's nothing going on today."

She was born in 1895. In her opinion, life went downhill from about 1910 on.

The year we talked, she was ninety years old, scratchy-voiced and largely toothless, but bright-eyed and mentally sharp. That is, she acted as if she thought she were sharp. She often spoke in a wildly disjointed manner. She also might fairly be described as spiteful, stubborn, suspicious, and uninterested in modern notions of personal hygiene, to the dismay of her son's family, with whom she lived. Their home was a converted schoolhouse in an isolated village near Belgium. The name of the village is Hohn, which in German can mean "scorn." She may as well have named it herself.

Gretl was the elder of two girls born into a

well-to-do family in the town of Leobschütz in Germany's far eastern territory of Upper Silesia, an area considered, at least by Frau Sasowski, part of
Prussia. The wealth came from her mother, whose grandfather had owned
"three estates." In the line of inheritance, "we two girls each had 100,000
marks in gold. We could have lived like 'God in France.' Sometimes my father said, 'I don't have to worry about my children. They have enough.'"

Gretl's grandfather made a hobby of photography, which her father (a
son-in-law in the equation) "really built up, very big" into a business. In a
striking posed photograph from the business and the "wonderful times,"
Gretl, age about six, is sitting, smiling, and wearing an enormous hat of
ostrich plumes.

One reason the photography store boomed was that Leobshütz was
the headquarters of a squadron of Hussars. "That was a real gold mine, because a lot of military kept coming back. Our father sometimes sweated
through three shirts [a day] from running back and forth, the way he
worked." For help, he had apprentices and assistants, but not her. "I was not
interested at all." She added, "Such a business brings a lot of bother. Many
wanted to be a lot better looking than they really were and that simply did
not work." She laughed the way she often did during our sessions—a high,
distinct "ha ha ha" as dry as her speaking voice.

The family lived in a large and "wunderschön" house taken care of by
a housekeeper. Gretl's mother sewed the family's clothes, and painted. Because of the house's size, seven rooms on each floor, part was rented out to
a married couple, a Herr and Frau Kassel, who were Jewish.

Gretl's wonderful times began ending when her mother came down
with pneumonia. Gretl said she rarely left her side then, and said of her now,
"I would dig her up with my hands if I could." She added, "Now all the graves
lie there, demolished. The Poles make everything kaputt." Frau Sasowski's
feelings against Poles—only one of many peoples she berated over the next
hours and days—stemmed in part from Leobschütz becoming part of Poland after the Second World War. She said she did not know its new name,
but bitingly guessed "Leobschützski." (It is Glubczyce.) She never commented on the roots of her own married name. "Our area was the best farmland of Germany. Now nothing but thistles as high as a man grow there.
They should work. They're too lazy." My standard suggestion that the land's
condition might have to do with the Communist system brought her response, "I've heard that, too. But it was always the case."

Gretl's mother died at the age of thirty-one. "I have so much behind
me. I would not want to repeat my life. It was so wonderful, the first nine
years when my mother was alive. If you don't have a mother, there's nothing.
My father, he was very good, but my sister was sickly. And all the love that
burst from him belonged to my sister. I always felt like an orphan. I hung in
the air." A great-aunt stepped in to fill a maternal role, but after a few years
Gretl was sent away to the boarding school in Breslau. "It was a school for

home economics and German and everything that went with it. It was very nice."

Gretl was well aware that beyond her privileged world was poverty. In Leobschütz, "in the winter, we cooked for the poor. They could come get a meal every day. And at the big grammar school there was a big kitchen and they cooked there. The Fatherland Women's Club, it was called." (Frau Kassel, the Jewish renter, ran it.) "A lot was done for the poor." She said her father administered the distribution of free bread and coal, and she helped him write up the lists of recipients.

At the time, the only men Gretl seemed to want in her life were her father, grandfather, and the Kaiser. Asked if he were very loved, she said, "Ja, *ooch*," in a Silesian-Rhineland amalgam that means "ach." Frau Sasowski, for all the highbrow aspects of her early years, spoke downright lowbrow in her later years, both in accent and vocabulary. Asked about boyfriends, she said, "Ooch, those we never had. We never bothered about men. My aunt once said I always made such dark looks, if your face grows that way, you won't get a man. I said I don't need a man. I wasn't interested. I would not have married, either."

In the spring of 1914, her male world narrowed. Within a month, both her father and grandfather died.

Then came an event that brightened her life: the beginning of the First World War. "There was such enthusiasm! Everyone wanted to be part of it. My brother-in-law, too. He went all the way to Breslau just to be drafted." Why were people so enthusiastic? "I don't know. I can't even describe it. At the time we had such a love of the Fatherland. It was in the schools.

"You cannot picture at all how we felt as children," she said at another point. "We would have let ourselves be torn to pieces for Germany. That was how it was in school. When I was five years old, the first school year, I had to recite a poem I still know today. 'The Kaiser is a dear, dear man. He lives in Berlin. And if it weren't so far from here, I'd go now to see him.'" She added that as much as she loved Germany, she hated the French.

During the war, Gretl's personal world unraveled more. "My aunt died and my sister had a relationship [with the man who had enlisted in Breslau] and I sat there all alone."

At another aunt's birthday party, she met Karl Sasowski, a school-teacher from Berlin. Throughout much of the war, he was stationed in Constantinople (Istanbul), she said. They began corresponding. What did she like about him? "Most of all, he was anständig." The word, which may be translated as "decent," "reliable," and/or "proper" and which she used often in other circumstances, implies someone you can count on. "That was the most important thing to me. And also, very nice."

The Sasowskis married in 1921. By then, both had witnessed slices of the postwar political and economic upheaval that would help bring National Socialism to power. Frau Sasowski recalled seeing defeated soldiers getting off the train in Leobschütz, and gangs (of Communists, she said) roughing them up and ripping off their shoulder insignia. When Karl Sasowski returned briefly to Berlin because his father had died, he encountered a condition close to anarchy. "There was nobody who would dig his [father's] grave. And my husband had to go to the registry office to report it and a bullet went through his coat. There were such street battles in Berlin."

The 1920s were a bad time to be a beginning teacher. Frau Sasowski's long lamentations about her husband's early career problems were confusing, but came down to his having a hard time finding any teaching job, much less a good one. He once was assigned to a Polish-speaking village in Silesia, although he spoke no Polish himself, and had eighty-five children to teach. But even that was a job of the past. She could not help much, either. Massive inflation and Germany's defeat ended her glory years. "I was able to save only six thousand marks. Nothing more. It was just from the sale of the house. Everything else was lost in the war. We had the money in Anatolian Railroad stocks. My grandfather invested it and it was all nullified." Her summation of the reversed circumstances included no hint of self-pity.

The family must have been close to homeless. She spoke of their living several years in an abbey and receiving a very small subsistence. "Those were the worst times we had. I was pregnant with the second child and couldn't eat margarine. And we could not buy butter and I always had to have dry bread and then twice a week I made a little potato soup without anything else. There was nothing more." The second child, Bernhard, was born more than two months premature and weighed three pounds. "You could not even look at him." (She happily recalled that her first child, Käthe, looked "like a peeled hard-boiled egg" at birth.) "I thought, he won't grow old." How did she keep him alive? "He drank enough for six." She said she could not nurse him much, but a doctor helped her get ingredients for a fortified milk.

In 1928 Herr Sasowski was offered the job of schoolteacher in Hohn. She said that because they were Catholic they had to be assigned to a Catholic village. The job paid poorly, 335 marks a month, but it included housing—space in the schoolhouse over the classroom. Her husband told her he would accept "just so we have something to eat." Traveling from far eastern Germany to far western Germany, what they came to, from her description, was an impoverished mud hole. The population numbered three hundred. It was clear, she said, the job was open because no one else wanted it. "I never wanted to come here. I'm still not warmed up to it. I'm a Silesian. The anger I feel toward the Poles I cannot describe. That beautiful land."

Hohn's acreage could not compare. "It yielded so little. It was all stones." The poverty of Hohn's farmland determined the poverty of its farmers. She said the people had so little that one small boy ran around in his father's old undershirt, to which his mother had sewn on opened socks as sleeves. "The people here were so poor. The dirt in the streets, all over your shoes. I always complained they sent my husband to such a manure hole.

You cannot picture the poor. They first got rich through Hitler. He put a lot into the farm economy. When we got here, there was a single horse and only oxen in the pastures. Ooch."

As for the Sasowskis' own accommodations, they were crude, with nothing "modern" like hot running water or central heating, or, presumably, indoor plumbing. And the cellar was full of water. But the little girl of the ostrich plume hat became as industrious as she was fertile. She would have a total of five children, three boys and two girls, took care of them, did virtually all the housework (by hand), and worked a large garden. "I never bought a vegetable." Her husband's salary stretched just far enough for other food. "How we saved. We turned over every penny. But we never had any debts. Never." Still, "we couldn't make great leaps, a trip or so on. We never took a vacation once." She envied her childless sister, whose husband was also a teacher. "They traveled a lot on vacation. But I had to raise the children. I didn't get any of it."

Frau Sasowski did not better her life in Hohn by making friends. "Ooch, those were such dumb people. At first, I didn't understand them at all. They had other words for things. I only said, 'Ja, ja.' My husband said, 'You're always saying ja, ja.' I say, 'What should I say? I don't understand them.' 'Then say nothing.'" So she had no women friends? "Nein, nein. With them you couldn't. They were under one's own niveau. What should one have a conversation about, anyway?" And "I didn't have any time" and "I didn't want to get mixed up with the village chatter [Dorfklatsch]. That was bad enough for my husband. In the winter, when they had free time, [farmers] came in the evening to talk. And when *he* was there, *he* complained about *him* and when the other was there, *he* complained about *him*. Sometimes it was a scream. My husband said, 'Just keep your mouth closed.' Herr Sasowski extended himself well beyond listening. She described at length his intervention on behalf of children whose infected injuries were worsening. In one case, he took a little girl to get an emergency eye operation and paid for it with the Sasowski family savings. "There was *no house* where he hadn't helped. But thanks we did not get."

While Hohn was living its dramas, the National Socialists were preparing theirs. In the 1930 election, almost everyone in Hohn, she said, voted "black"—for the Catholic centrist party. But four chose the National Socialists. And one voted Communist. She said that when the votes came in, people wondered who voted for the Nazis, and finally figured it was the village fanatic (a woman who would reappear in Frau Sasowski's life), her brother, and their parents. "We never did find out [at first] who voted Communist. The little Bergrath girl came to us and said it's definitely Herr Haselmann. But it turned out there was old Frau Rommel, who wasn't right in the head, who was Catholic and she put a mark by the *K*, thinking it meant Katholisch, when it really meant Kommunist."

By 1933, such misunderstandings were beside the point. Hohn may have looked like the last place on earth anyone could find or want to. But National Socialism found it. Indeed, Hohners may have felt it was the first government that bothered with them. And, thanks to Frau Sasowski's re-membrances, Hohn also demonstrates the dilemmas the Third Reich posed to ordinary people who might not be Nazi enthusiasts. Living under National Socialism in a city or town was one thing, in a village another.

One issue was Party membership. Civil servants, including teachers, were supposed to join the Nazi Party or lose their jobs, but for years Herr Sasowski hesitated. Then the Nazi district leader came by to give him a list of Nazi sayings to be recited each morning before classes began. Instead, "my husband always said a prayer." Herr Sasowski also was told not to teach religion. "My husband always did. I said, if someone reports you, you'll go to a KZ. Ja, that would have happened. But we had a leader here who was friendly and dear. All it would have taken was for a child to say, 'We always pray in school' or something like that. No one said anything. And my husband kept doing it. He said, 'You see, the good Lord blesses me.'" She laughed.

"One had to keep one's mouth shut. Whoever said anything against [the Party] had had it. Worries kept me awake many nights. My husband was that way [to say something against it]."

Herr Sasowski apparently was just as worried about his wife. "My husband always said, 'Keep your mouth closed and be quiet. Let them do what they want. We can't change anything anyway.'" She repeated the above, with slightly different words, at least two other times. Once she quoted her husband as telling her, "One day you'll be gone." Another time she implied she spoke her mind anyway. "I let it be. I couldn't defend myself. They did what they wanted with us."

Despite whatever hesitation their parents expressed, Käthe and Bernhard enthusiastically joined the Hitler Youth. So did "all the young people," said Frau Sasowski. "They all went in the Hitler Youth. And the farmers were organized again. You know, [Hitler] understood how to organize. Perfectly. No one could compare. As for the rest, he wasn't bad. In my opinion he had something entirely different in mind. He himself wasn't so bad. . . . There had indeed been unemployment. There was nothing. And everything kaputt."

Around 1936, Herr Sasowski faced another test. Adolf Hitler was coming to town. That is, he was going to be in a parade in the larger town of Gmünd. Not only was the Hohn Fire Department going in its firetruck, it was selling seats on the truck to the citizenry. "There were some free seats and someone came to my husband and asked if he'd like to ride along. He said no, he couldn't, because of school. He could have if he wanted. Was happy he had an excuse. For this occasion, he could easily have shut the school." His son, in effect, shielded him. "Our Bernhard was so for Hitler. And he said, 'Oh Mutti, let us go, let us go.' And I went along." The Hohn group took up a position on a bridge over a culvert. "Hitler went by us very slowly. I could have taken off his cap. He wasn't afraid." What kind of impression did he make? "You know, I wasn't very interested. But he was a good-looking [hübscher] man. One can say that." When he went by, she said, people "all screamed 'Heil Hitler!' It was like they were crazy, I can tell you." She insisted she did not yell along. "I had to make sure we kept our balance, there on that thing. Then we went and had some coffee."

Also in 1936, Herr Sasowski got a summons to justify why he was not in the Party. She said he asked her, "What should I do? I'm against Hitler." One afternoon around three, the doorbell rang. Standing there were two teachers Herr Sasowski knew from neighboring villages. "They got the same piece of paper. They said, 'What should we do? What should we do?' Then the youngest said, 'I'll say it's too expensive for me. Three marks a month is too *expensive* for me. I'll write that and send it in. Then we'll hear and decide what we do.' He did it and two days later I went with my husband to Münstereifel [the nearby shopping town] to the bank." The young teacher happened to be there, too. "He said, 'Karl, just join the old shit Party. I've already got my transfer.' They sent the poor fellow out of the village to a thing where he had to, God knows what else, fetch water. They gave him that kind of terrible job. That was thanks for his saying it was too expensive." She laughed her kind of laugh. "Then the other [teacher] came to my husband and said, 'What should we do?' 'Ja,' my husband said, 'there's nothing else we can do or they'll do the same to us. But I'll add I want a free hand with my pupils.' He sent that in and had to join the Party. And the Party book was validated to 1933. They did things like that. As if he'd been a member since '33.'"

Back in Upper Silesia, her sister's husband, also a teacher and war veteran (he had lost an eye when his plane was shot down), was having Party problems of his own in his attempt to be promoted to headmaster. He had joined the Party as ordered and had hung a picture of Hitler in the classroom as ordered, but he had also put up a crucifix. And he was childless. "They even asked him why he had no children. My sister went to two gynecologists. And they chalked that one up. If he had no children, then he didn't need to be the headmaster and such stuff. It was terrible." She said because "he had such an uproar with the Party, he volunteered to join the fighting. Finally to get some quiet away from the endless back and forth." He was "emotionally kaputt." (He was assigned as an airplane courier between Germany and the Crimea, and barely survived his second war.)

Herr Sasowski also learned that joining the Nazi Party did not get the Nazi Party out of his life. He was hounded about not subscribing to the local Nazi Party newspaper, the *Westdeutsche Beobachter*, until he finally gave in. "Then we took it and paid for it, but always threw it away. We never read it."

Frau Sasowski did not read much of anything, it seemed. She literally had no time. "Up at 5:30 every morning, also before the war. And maybe around 2:00 to bed." She said that during the day she cooked, did the laundry, tended the children and the vegetable garden, and in the evenings "I had to knit and mend and patch" and iron and prepare the food for the next day. A woman came some Saturdays to help clean, but Herr Sasowski objected to how she dusted and had his wife resume that, too. "In the household itself, he didn't help, although he knew how to. He could peel potatoes with his right and left hand. But he said that's why he married, so he didn't have to do that anymore." She added, "He always said, 'If I die and came back to earth again, I don't want to marry anyone but you.' Then I said, 'I've had enough. I'll never marry again.' That he believed."

His evenings were indeed spent reading. "And then he said, 'Here's a good book, you should read it.' Ja, I read maybe six pages, then he'd say, 'You know what? You could peel a couple of apples for me.' I had to get up, had to peel the apples for him. Sit back down, and there was something else. I said, 'You know, two, three pages, what do I get out of it? I'd rather go in the kitchen and do my work.'" She called her husband "good, but odd" and "an egoist," yet said she had a "love marriage." For her birthday, "I would get a present, but it was always something useful. A new cooking pot. Or a coal shuttle." When I laughed about the latter, she became defensive and said people did not have the expectations they do today.

Frau Sasowski may have been exhaustively busy as Hausfrau and Mutter (she once mentioned she was never alone one minute), but the Party approached her, too. As the wife of a civil servant, she was enjoined to join the Frauenschaft. "I tried to avoid it. They came to me and said, 'Oh please.' I played dumb. I said no, I have four children to take care of and I can't. And then my husband said we [*sic*] have to be in the Frauenschaft. Otherwise something else will happen." She joined. A group of local women came on Thursdays for two hours and met in an empty classroom, which Frau Sasowski pointed out she had to heat herself. The women mostly knitted socks for poor people, or brought their mending. They liked to come. "They always heard something new, nicht?" Once she attended a Frauenschaft meeting in another village. In front of every cup at the table was a picture of Hitler. "It was such a nice photograph. He looked so handsome in it." She put it up in her home.

After the Thursday afternoons went on awhile, Herr Sasowski suggested she make the get-togethers more festive, with a little singing, perhaps bake a little something. "I did that and then I got a reprimand. I should have asked for permission." A half-century later, Frau Sasowski was still mightily annoyed. It turned out that the women had enjoyed the festive afternoon so much they made the mistake of talking about it, and the news got passed to the local Frauenschaft leader by the Hohn fanatic, the woman who voted for Hitler in 1930. (The same woman also yelled at the Sasowskis for saying "Good morning" instead of "Heil Hitler" as they left for mass.) And she wanted to be the Frauenschaft leader of Hohn. The mayor told her no, the group needed someone who at least could write [well] and get things done. Frau Sasowski might have been named as a possibility. Not long thereafter, Frau Sasowski got a visit from a Frauenschaft official bearing an anonymous letter. It said the Sasowskis were not really Hitler supporters and the Hohn branch of the Frauenschaft needed a leader who was. The leader asked Frau Sasowski if she recognized the handwriting. "'OOCH!' I said. 'It's from her, I know it.'"[1]

Hohn was relatively isolated from what was happening to Jewish Germans, because, according to Frau Sasowski, it had none. But Münstereifel did. The Sasowskis happened to be there the night of November 9, 1938. "Suddenly a car came up to the gate where one enters, there was a great cry and these SA sprang out, all SA people. And suddenly, there was a Jewish store, I don't remember its name, and we saw the bullets fly through the window and my husband said, 'Come, come, we don't want to be in that.' That was the beginning of that. . . . They burned the synagogues. At home in Leobschütz they burned it. It was such a beautiful big thing. A fabulous, beautiful temple. Big. Ten towers and everything." She was never inside, but her sister "was in a church choir that sang at a wedding there. And she told us how it was. The men all sat there with top hats." Frau Sasowski laughed. Asked her reaction to "Kristallnacht," she paused. "We were outraged. I mean, that freedom was always here. Confession of faith."

She then happily recalled a scene from her childhood. In preparation for a Jewish festival, Frau Kassel made round cut-out cookies and gave her the scraps of dough from the outsides as a treat. It was Frau Sasowski's almost only positive recollection of anything or anyone Jewish. To the list of people she berated—Poles, Communists, French, Hohners—must be added Jews.

The first and lasting bad impression was made by Herr Kassel, a lawyer. "I couldn't stand him. He was such a black one and had such a long face and the eyes, you know, such real crafty eyes. It's how I always pictured the devil. Only the horns were lacking. But he was very nice to me, I can't say otherwise. His wife, too. But he made us angry." She claimed he abused her father by not paying for things he should have, while paying rock-bottom rent. "I can tell you, how he played tricks on us, the fellow. My grandfather said, 'I'll pay the whole rent, the whole time, just throw the fellow out.' And

1. Frau Sasowski said people in Hohn later saw the woman run after American troops and shout, "If you find Hitler, I want you to break every little bone in his body." The woman was alive when I visited Hohn but told a Sasowski family member she did not have time to talk. Something about problems with her roof.

he [Herr Kassel] said, 'I have such a good landlord, I'll never move out of the house.'"

When asked why she thought Hitler had such anger toward Jews, Frau Sasowski answered, "I'll tell you something. The Jews are at fault themselves, that it happened. At home [in Leobschütz] we had a population of fourteen thousand and of them three hundred were Jews. And they were nothing but business people, big capitalists, and lawyers. All such things where you didn't have to work. We had three fabric factories. That was three Jews, all brothers." She described one laborious factory job involving shawl making. Workers had to "tie threads in a knot, at least five times and on both sides. And for that they got twenty-five pennies." She said an acquaintance's pay for sewing open stitchwork on a large tablecloth and twelve napkins was only fifteen marks. "I'd rather lie in bed than work for them.

"At home there was a lot of anger toward them. They cheated people." When asked if she had had only bad experiences with Jews, she said no, then spoke of going with her husband in Leobshütz to a men's clothier, "the Jew Boehm." (Asked if her husband really said, "I'll go to the Jew Boehm," she replied, "That was the only large store.") The Christian Sasowski had only his father's old tattered winter coat, but little money for a new one. The couple had saved thirty marks between them. "Then he said, 'I'll go ask Jew Boehm if he has a rejected coat.' And he went there and asked if he had something he'd put aside, he can't afford more, and so and so is the situation." Herr Boehm suggested Herr Sasowski try on a particularly handsome coat. Herr Sasowski protested. Herr Boehm insisted. "He [sold] him the coat. I tell you it was a beautiful coat. He wore it at least ten years, and he only took thirty marks for it."

After her husband earned extra money by giving lessons at the military unit, he returned to Herr Boehm's store to buy other items. Of Herr Boehm's thirty-mark gesture, she said, "He did it to get customers. But he was a proper one." Not proper at all was "the Jew Bitomski," who sold "terrible" shoes. The store went broke, but then the Jews helped him get back up and he opened the store again under his wife's name. The Jews help each other, always. But in our class for two, three years, we had one Jewish girl [Jüdin]. She was irreproachable, that girl. The brother even was killed in the First World War. He even got the Iron Cross. That was the Jew Goldmann."

She talked of "the Jew Hachs," a livestock trader. When he and his wife became old, they sold their house and moved into a home for the elderly and lived there throughout and after the Third Reich. "They didn't do anything to them."

How is that possible?

"Everything is possible," she said, laughing. "But I know it. You can count on it, what I say is true."

She also said, "In Münstereifel, a lot of Jews were killed. The one friend of my daughter's, Müller, she was in the Hitler Youth at first, in the BdM.

And then they found out her mother was of Jewish descent and she had to get out [of the BdM] and she was so upset, because she liked it so much. Ja, and those two [mother and daughter Müller], I didn't see it, but they loaded them into cars and took them away. And the mother, Frau Müller, and the daughter jumped out of the cars. And then they were in a cloister and worked in the kitchen and saved their lives."

She described the "cars" as "the open cars they used for transporting the people, to be gassed or whatever. That I don't know. We didn't know about that at all at first. This gassing business [Vergaserei]. We always heard, you'll go to a KZ, but we thought they'd be prisoners."

Before the deportations, the Nazis isolated Jews by making them politically poison, as Frau Sasowski inadvertently described. In Münstereifel one day, she and her husband happened to meet "'the Jew Nathan.' And we were still talking with him and everything and later Karl said, 'I'm going to catch shit if they photographed us.'" She laughed her laugh. "But it didn't happen."

She also named, as did many women, German Jews who escaped early. And she said that if Jews had noticed that Hitler was so "crazy on the subject," they could have "stepped aside" and gone to England or America, as many in Münstereifel did. The Müllers could have got away, she said. She indicated she wished they had. Frau Müller was so "fresh." At some point after the war, this "Judenfrau" returned to Münstereifel, and one day went to the butcher shop to buy a roast. When it was her turn, "*that* she didn't like that and nein, she didn't like that piece, and she took a quarter of an hour until she found the roast she wanted. If he had to do that with all his customers, where would that get us? I'd have been very quiet if I'd been a Jew and would have fled the whole theater, mein Gott. You see, that's a Jew."

Maybe Frau Müller wanted to prove something to the butcher?

Frau Sasowski laughed and said again, Jews are "fresh."

Asked what would she have done in respect to the Jews if she had been in power instead of Hitler, Frau Sasowski, like other women, reacted first by scoffing at the notion of such power. Then, like other women, she spoke minimally about what she might have done, before changing the subject to herself. "Most of all, I'd have left the people alone so they could do what they wanted. That was terrible. We didn't have a will of our own. We didn't even vote anymore. A couple of times my husband said he was sick." Pressed on the question, she said, "I'd never have got the power, so I can't even consider it." She laughed. "I'm much too dumb for that. You know, I'm too good-natured. I'd rather give than take."

When the Second World War began, Frau Sasowski apparently was much less enthusiastic than she had been about its predecessor. "I wonder why Hitler started it," she said. "We weren't ready at all." What might the emperor, Kaiser Wilhelm, have said to Hitler? "He would have been amazed.

Hitler was only a corporal. He didn't know a thing about winning a war. And he didn't let our people do what they wanted to. They told him for a long time to end it. But he never did."

At the start of the war, Bernhard Sasowski was wildly prowar. His father almost certainly was not, and his estrangement from the Nazis seemed ever-growing. He had become a "black sheep" among the teaching community, Frau Sasowski said. Interfamily differences had been played out, too. Bernhard was supposed to go to a "training school run by the National Socialists" after high school. Herr Sasowski adamantly refused to let him. But Bernhard immediately signed up to fight. Asked if there had been family discussions about it, she said, "There was no reason to. They would have taken him. In the end, they took them all."

When the war expanded to the Soviet Union, "two young people" came to the Sasowskis' home to tell their teacher the news. She said he replied, "'We are finished, Mother. We have lost the war.' That's what he said. And this young man who had told him then said, 'You say that as a teacher! You'll have to go to a concentration camp.'" Herr Sasowski's highly dangerous comment, if true, apparently went no farther. But his sentiments had become well enough known to prompt an act of Nazi revenge. At about the age of forty-five, Herr Sasowski was drafted. The person behind the action was the local Ortsgruppenleiter, a teacher himself.

When the draft notice came, Frau Sasowski was pregnant with her fifth child, her son Heinz. She was furious at the Nazis on behalf of her husband. "They only did it because he didn't dance to the Party's tune." Some of her anger she released at her "handsome" photograph of Hitler. "When my husband was drafted, I took it and tore it up and burned it." She said that the older woman who sometimes helped clean asked, "Oh, where is your pretty picture of Hitler? That was always so nice." (It is my recollection, although it is not on the tapes, that Frau Sasowski said she told the woman what she had done, told her husband she had told her so, and that he reprimanded her for her indiscretion.)

Herr Sasowski left as ordered for the front, but not to fight. He was assigned to help build a wall on the French border. "He got so cold, he became sick. They drafted the people and had no shelter for them. They lay on benches and in horse stalls." While he was away, Heinz was born. The number-five "Aryan" child brought with him the Nazi honor of fecundity. Frau Sasowski received a bronze Mother's Cross. Evidently not bothered by being rewarded by the same group that punitively drafted her husband, she kept the medal. In fact, she got it out and showed it to me.

She soon would have crosses to bear. While her youngest son was still a baby, her oldest son was wounded in battle. A grenade ripped Bernhard's hand apart. Frau Sasowski said the doctor wanted to amputate it, but a specialist tied it together so well "with silver threads," Bernhard later "could screw the finest screws again." She recalled walking with him while he was home on leave, he wearing gloves to protect that hand especially, and being confronted by a lieutenant who angrily demanded, "Why is a corporal wearing gloves?" Later, Bernhard was sent to the Russian front. Despite his hand injury, along with whatever else he might have experienced, he continued to be zealously prowar. "He said, 'I can tell you this. When Hitler has only two men left, one of them is Bernhard.' He was *so* enthusiastic. Then he said, 'I'm going to Russia to fight for Silesia.'"

Why was Bernhard so enthusiastic about Hitler? His mother said softly, "That I don't know." She said his biggest goal was to get to England. (Ridiculously, I thought she meant as a tourist. Nein, she clarified. As a soldier.)

In Russia, where fighting life apparently was not enough for him, Bernhard volunteered for a special commando. A team of nine soldiers was trained, she said, "to smoke out Russian bunkers" with some kind of long poles. "Ja. And then we got the news, 'Missing in action.'" She stopped for a rare and long pause.

"He had sent back a picture frame. While this commando was there they made a shed out of branches. And each time they left, the Russians made it kaputt. Then they captured three Russians and told them, 'We'll leave you here if you make sure they don't make everything kaputt. And we'll also share our food with you.' That went so beautifully, he said, 'We were like brothers.' And the one with a razor blade cut a picture frame out of oak. So beautiful, I tell you." He gave it to Bernhard as a thank-you present, she said. She still has that, too.

The war also came home to the Sasowskis in other ways. Käthe, having enjoyed BdM so much she became a leader, was in Czechoslovakia caring for German children sent there to escape the bombs. "She liked it a lot." Then Herr Sasowski was sent home, sickly from the deprivations he had gone through. He died in 1947, a direct result of them, she felt.

While he was back, bombs began falling on and near Hohn. Frau Sasowski described the attacks as "constant." Adding to her and her husband's concern was that their young son Peter got so excited when enemy bombers flew over the village, he ran outside to watch them. "That was terrible. He always wanted to go see them and Karl was afraid something would happen, and always ran after him."

Frau Sasowski claimed that once when she was ice skating with her children during the war, an English fighter plane shot a child. She also claimed that the English dropped poisonous candy and explosive dolls and pen holders, all to attract and harm German children. She said the daughter of a woman she knew lost three fingers opening one pen holder. No attempts of mine to question even the logic of the purported actions swayed her. (No attempt to find corroboration was successful, either.)

The Sasowskis had another problem on the ground. The German military requisitioned the schoolhouse and all but two of the family's rooms, for housing soldiers. It was Frau Sasowski, of course, who had to share her kitchen with them and organize her family around them. She spoke repeatedly about the imposition and inconvenience of the soldiers' presence. But she did feel safe. "Nobody would have done anything to us or attacked us or anything. There was really order."

Yet her clearest memory about that time, she said, was "hunger. Hunger everywhere. I had to sacrifice myself for the children. There wasn't enough bread to go around. We usually needed two loaves of bread a day." The farmers did not help, she said. She said she used to buy two to three liters of milk a day and two pounds of butter a week from them. But the farmers had found more desperate and/or appreciative customers—city people. "My husband had double pleurisy and the doctor prescribed for him, on the rations card, a quarter-liter of milk a day. Then it was, 'It's not worth it, to measure a quarter-liter.' That's how it was."

The bombings also made it more difficult to get to food stores. "We could only go buy meat at five in the morning, to five-thirty or six, in Münstereifel." The situation worsened. To get more fat than the little bit on the rations, the whole family went to the forest and picked beechnuts. "It was a tedious thing" and cold, for the nuts had fallen off the trees. "For fifty pounds one got a certificate and could buy a pound of margarine. Peter always complained. He didn't like it. But Brigitte could pick with both hands. And then at home my husband had to look through them all. If there was a hole, it wouldn't be accepted." She added that people who go to a store these days and see the varieties of margarine and butter have no idea how it was. "You know what I think? Today's youth should spend at least *one* day the way we did, so they know how it was. They don't know at all. The dumb brats [Fratzen] were born after the war and everything went uphill right away."

In the midst of the bombs and the other miseries came the news that an attempt had been made to assassinate Hitler.

"Many were sorry. We would have been out of it faster. But he was so protected, there was nothing to do. And the poor fellows were all hanged." She said of Hitler, "He was a fool. He just did what the others wanted. In leading the war, he was a washout. He was, after all, only a corporal."

She added, he "plunged the whole Volk into unhappiness."

From her perspective, toward the end of the war everything was getting worse at the same time. As elsewhere throughout Germany, city people streamed into Hohn to trade household items for food. In their wake came the Nazis, knocking again at the Sasowskis' door.

"If we had not been so proper and had opened our mouths, half the village would have been in a KZ. Someone from the Geheimpolizei [Gestapo] rang the bell one evening. He asked me if my husband's there. He would like to speak with him. And I let him into the living room and from the kitchen I heard them talking and talking. I thought good Lord, I have no more quiet. There's going to be something else. My husband was supposed to function as an informer. And was supposed to let the Geheimpolizei know when a woman from Cologne is here and sells everything. She even brought a bathtub. She was there two or three times a week. My husband was supposed to tell them that, so they could catch her. And he said, 'I won't do that. I must live with these people.' They wanted to know everything. And then he left, but they nabbed the woman anyway."

Then the Sasowskis learned that their daughter Käthe was reassigned back to Germany, to train in beaming searchlights on Allied planes. Soon she commanded three batteries. She lived through two carpet bombings of the city of Wesel in the Ruhr area, but "in one night, she lost sixty girls."

Frau Sasowski said no Volk but the Germans could have made it through the war. She mentioned an Englishwoman who said she had been bombed twice. Frau Sasowski told her she had no idea of what a "bomb war" was, that such an attitude was "laughable," that (in England) "they shot up one city kaputt, but otherwise nothing was kaputt."

What about London?

"London wasn't much." Wasn't "much"? German bombs killed an estimated 65,000 British civilians, many in London.[2] "They should have thrown more on it," added Frau Sasowski.

Asked why, she said, "Because they ruined us. Shooting children who are ice skating. That's no war. And then with the dolls and stuff. A German would never have done that. So malicious."

What about disguising gas ovens as showers?

"We couldn't do anything about it, nicht?"

After an unsteady silence, I added that the first bombs fell on England, not Germany.

"I don't know," she said.

Asked if she had "something against the English personally," she said, "No, not at all. I just was furious about the Poles." She got just as furious, it seemed, about the last group on her list. That was the SS.

For during the final months of the war, while retreating from the plunder of western Europe, the SS too sought shelter, or rather took it, at the schoolhouse. "The SS was terrible. I was afraid of them. They didn't even ask and went in the cellar and took coal, which you could only get on ration cards. But we couldn't say anything." And they stole the Sasowskis' food, including their meat ration for the week. Frau Sasowski even complained to the SS boss. He said sarcastically, "I cannot look in everyone's mouth to try to find a fiber of meat." Maybe he ate it all himself, she thought. Once the

---

2. R. Ernest and Trevor N. Dupuy, *The Encyclopedia of Military History* (New York: Harper and Row, 1970), 1198. Thanks to Linda Wheeler for ferreting. Allied bombs killed an estimated 600,000 Germans, mostly civilians.

SS brought a whole goose from somewhere, had her cook it, and did not give the Sasowskis a morsel. "And they had everything. Chocolate in almost every variety. Cookies and candies in huge jars. They had everything. I saw it." And they had the effrontery to steal some of the Sasowskis' potatoes and have her roast them. They did provide their own margarine, she said. They did not take it from the stash the Sasowskis traded for fifty pounds of beechnuts.

Then more German infantry troops arrived, and were put up in the classroom, too. They were "from the last undertaking in the Ardennes. But they were proper, the troops. That was no SS." Frau Sasowski said the troops, presumably exhausted, were about fifteen years old, and very hungry. The SS was not moved toward generosity. "I mean, when they have everything, they should give the boys something. Nein, these Grosskotz- kerle [big vomit guys], they lived high on the hog. Wine and *everything.* They could have everything, all from France.

"Once I made some potato soup and Karl said to me, 'Do give the rest to the boys, they don't have anything either.' I tell you, how they licked up that little bit of soup. And as I was just coming back upstairs with the empty pot, this fellow from the SS came by and said"—she raised her voice— "'What are *you* doing there?' I say, 'I gave the poor fellows a little bit of soup.' '*They* have enough.' I say, 'Ja, water with three leaves of cabbage in it. That's a meal.' That's what I told him. Then Karl bawled me out. He said I would put my foot in it yet."

For Gretl Sasowski, the last weeks of the war were almost intolerable. "I sometimes said it would be better to be dead. One had no joy of living at all anymore. Everyone in the school, this pack of soldiers, and ooch." And constant bombing attacks. Once the family stayed in the cellar two weeks straight. She said they had had no electricity since November of 1944, and no candles, either, but the "military gave us their stumps and my husband remelted them."

Then came word that Hitler was dead. "We said, it's good he's gone. I often thought either he'll kill himself or take poison. It made me mad when he talked so much about war and peace. Why didn't he go to the front and fight? Wilhelm and the others were on the front." When I suggested maybe Hitler was not very brave, she said, "He was an Austrian, not a German. Hitler. Ha! Such a crazy people, taking an Austrian as their leader."

At the end, the Americans found Hohn, too. She said, laughing, "I'll be quiet about what they did to us. They stole from us like no one else. They took all our valuables." Those included, she said, the family radio and her husband's stamp collection. The Americans also made Herr Sasowski provisionally the mayor. Because he spoke French, as did one American, that was the language they communicated in. She also said the Americans were afraid of the Germans. "You should have seen the tanks they had. There were two in our garden. They were everywhere. No one walked in front of one. They weren't like ours [troops]. Ours went right up front, they went on top of them. That's love of Fatherland, you see."

How does the Holocaust fit into such love? Simply to jog her memory, I showed Frau Sasowski photographs from a book called *Frauen unter Hakenkreuz* (Women under the swastika).[3] After scenes of smiling youth groups, we got to ones of naked Jewish women on the rim of a mass grave. Asked if they were publicized after the war, she said, "No, I never saw them. I also don't think that's true."

She does not believe these pictures are authentic?

"I don't believe it's all true. It's propaganda." She made a little laugh.

By whom?

"I cannot judge. I don't know. I didn't hear it, either." She repeated that she and others had thought the Nazis punished people by putting them in concentration camps, but not by killing them. Asked her reaction when she learned what had happened, she answered, "Of course we judged it. The Jews, too, do have a right to live, nicht?"

After a long pause, she said, "But you can be assured the *Russians* weren't any better." She was speaking of the Russian soldiers' rapes of German women. And she said she knew of an American soldier who raped a girl.

Asked how she feels as a German, knowing this is what the German people did, that they built concentration camps, she said, "The terrible thing was, one could do nothing oneself. We were completely powerless under Hitler. One could not utter a free thought, for God's sake."

Yet does she feel less proud to be a German?

"Ooch, I'm a Prussian."

---

3. Munich: Deutscher Taschenbuch Verlag, 1985.

Frau Barbara Amschel, Frau Anna Lieb, Frau Anna Maier

Rural Perspectives

German farm women have an uneven reputation in Germany, at least among nonfarmers. Because Nazi propagandists treated the farmer like an "ideological darling,"[1] tilling the true German soil or butchering the plump German pig, far from evil urban— that is, Jewish—influences, and because this flattering attention did not fall entirely on deaf ears, German farmers are thought to have been in general pro-Nazi. Many were. But according to one historian, "The frequency of Party membership among farmers chronically lagged behind the frequency of farmers in the working population."[2]

To the German population at large, the political affiliation of farm women was less compelling than the women's behavior, especially at the end of and just after the Third Reich. By circumstance and default, they became power players in a practice that came to be known as *hamstern*.[3] It derived from four facts. Farm families had food. City families, mostly women and children by then, did not. Farm families did not have a lot of citified possessions. City families did.

City women then packed up some belongings, somehow made their way to the countryside, and tried to trade a treasure for food. The transaction was almost always all-

---

1. David Schoenbaum, *Hitler's Social Revolution* (New York: Norton, 1980), 153.
2. Ibid, 156.
3. *Hamstern* otherwise means "to hoard."

female. Most farmers, if they were not huge landowners, were at the front, or in POW camps like other German men. Even if they were in grain fields rather than in battlefields, they usually left hamstern to the women. The farm women responded to their new role, say many city women, by taking cruel advantage of it. Farm families were said to have accumulated so many luxuries that, according to a new expression (used by Frau Kretzschmar, among others), "they lacked only a carpet in the cow stall."

In the tiny Franconian farm village of Kemmern, on a bright spring day that happened to fall within a week of the fortieth anniversary of the end of the Second World War, two old felt-slippered friends, Frau Barbara Amschel and Frau Anna Lieb, both born in 1908, talked about these matters, and more. They spoke separately, in unison, and sometimes as in a roundelay, with one picking up the last words of the other and adding a few of her own. They clearly knew each other's stories and opinions well. And even without my comprehending all they were saying (and vice versa, as the transcript shows—apart from occasional efforts to speak High German, they mostly spoke in a dialect so dense that at times the only words I understood were my own), it also was clear they agreed with each other. Later, when a younger neighbor joined the twosome, unanimity seemed to break down.

Kemmern, which lies about 6 miles from the thousand-year-old city of Bamberg, itself about 150 miles north of Munich, has handsome half-timbered barns and clean-swept streets. Except for modern road signs, the village looks centuries old.

The Amschels' upstairs living-dining room was scrubbed clean. Most of the furniture, including a big table in the center of the room, looked new, and relatively inexpensive. Frau Amschel was accompanied by her daughter-in-law, Maria, an intermediary in arranging the discussion, who obviously had taken on the responsibility of making sure things went smoothly. Early on, she intervened often with her elders, trying to cajole High German out of them, or explain, in dialect, my questions. The housekeeper to another woman who attended, she knew enough of the world in which High German was used at home that she seemed to want her people to do well. Although the older women each turned out to have a relative in the United States, they had not ventured far from Kemmern themselves and seemed happily unworldly. Frau Barbara Amschel (hereafter referred to as Frau Amschel) essentially laughed off her daughter-in-law's pleadings. She could only speak frankly—"the way the snout grows," she said, laughing.

Asked about her childhood, she said she was one of eight children—five "Buben" [boys] and three "Madla" [girls].

"*Mädchen*," remonstrated Frau Maria Amschel.

Frau Amschel said she grew up on a small farm meant to nourish the family. Kemmern must have been a place of meager means, although none of the women mentioned the words *poor* or *poverty*; farmers tried to earn extra money by selling and transporting wood for such concerns as a coffin-maker. Her family "just did a little farming, a little pig raising." Was anyone interested in politics? No, no time for it. She added, as if apropos of politics, that her father had died in France during the First World War. "I still know that."

When Frau Lieb arrived, Frau Maria Amschel introduced her rather formally as the widow of the blacksmith, and said she was from "over there." ("Over there" meant a nearby village.) Frau Lieb smiled a little (she seemed to be hiding the absence of teeth) and sat down at the far end of the table. She was thin, with watery eyes, and spoke softly, usually deferring when anyone was louder, which was often. Frau Amschel seemed the sturdier of the pair, with a deep voice that sounded nearly like a man's. Both women dressed alike, from their thick felt slippers to their "Kittels" [smocklike neck-to-knee aprons]. They gave the appearance of having momentarily left their kitchen or barn chores, planning to return to them forthwith.

When Frau Amschel told Frau Lieb we had been speaking about the First World War (instead of *erst* for "first," she said *urscht*), Frau Lieb responded in even stronger dialect, "What do *you* know about that? That's when we started school, no?" In higher German the second sentence would have been, "Dann sind wir gleich in die Schule gekommen, nicht?" Frau Lieb's version was, "Da simma lei in d'Schul kumma, ne?" She later said that when she went to school, she "had nothing, no exercise book [Heft] . . . nothing."

Frau Maria Amschel, looking rather pained, asked Frau Lieb to please speak somewhat "nach der Schrift [as in writing, or High German]." Frau Lieb also laughed her off. "Ja, I can't speak so fine 'nach der Schrift.'"

She said she was the oldest of three children, including two little boys [zwa Büble]. Her father was, it seemed, a kind of painter, and her parents also did "a little farming. A cow and goats. And in the stall, rabbits and just, whatever. What went with it." Any political interests in her family? She said her father did go to the inn.

Frau Amschel, like Frau Lieb, did not marry a farmer. Herr Amschel worked for more than forty years for the public waterworks. His daughter-in-law, Frau Maria Amschel, in bringing up what happened to him, made the first mention of the Third Reich. "Then the Party came. And whoever was not in the Party, he lost his job. That's how it was." Her mother-in-law confirmed that Herr Amschel had joined. "He didn't want to, but he *had* to, because he would have lost his job, ne?" Asked if the decision had been talked about at home, she said, "Certainly [freilich] it was talked about. Ja, he went in the Party, had to go in." And he told her, "Keep your mouth shut, or you will land in the slammer [Kittchen]."

The other women joined in, seconding her, and laughing. Frau Lieb said her husband also told her that if she said anything, she would land "in the hole." She worked in, "And one had to raise his hand. 'Heil Hitler,' ne?"

She added, "That was force [Zwang]." She added, among the few words intelligible over the din of agreement, "Obviously, there were people who perhaps would have betrayed you."

Frau Amschel picked up the thought. "Others took in everything and then 'hung it on the big bell' [made it public], ne? What one had said and how one said it."

"Fanatics," said Frau Lieb.

The women spoke, in fragments, of a woman whose husband had died, who had five or six children she was working to support, and who faced arrest and imprisonment for having said something against Hitler. The gist of the tale was that witnesses would not confirm the woman had made the comment and the authorities therefore did not take her away, although they told her they would have, despite her being the sole support of her children. Frau Maria Amschel commented, "It was really bad. In the village it was bad, too, not only in the city."

Frau Lieb and her husband, who apparently were not Nazis, had landlords who were. The wife kept trying to recruit her. "She was always coming by. 'Frau Anna, you can come to us in the Frauenschaft.' Say I, 'I have enough Frauenschaft, if I have my family and my housekeeping, I don't need any other Frauenschaft.' And then she often grew bitter, ne?" She added, "I always said it's pointless, 'You're wasting your breath on me.' And I had my mother, because the brothers were all gone, ne? And the farming, we had to work on that, too, ne? And the fields. Everything. No one else was there."

"Everything" was no overstatement. The women later revealed, in an offhand way underscoring that it was a matter of course, that they cut those fields by hand, with scythes.

Frau Lieb's oldest boy was in the Hitler Youth, she said, until he was beaten up by the Youth "Führer" on the Sportplatz. The boy "had just come from work. He also had to take care of the children at the farm, so he ate his bread over there. [The Youth Führer] *punished* him because he ate his bread. Came home, he was bawling. 'Mother, I am *never* going there again.'" Frau Maria Amschel remembered that her brothers, five and six years old, were punished for not attending some function. "They had to run maybe ten kilometers. They herded them, just herded them in front. Was just Party fanatics."

The Amschels encountered at least one strong-minded person on the other side, a woman named Eva. "She once reproached me, 'Your husband is in the Party.' I said, 'He had to.' 'Well, my Hans,' she always said, 'he's not going. If we have to stay home,' she said, 'we have our fields, ne? We don't need any Party.' Then I said, 'That's something *you* can say easily enough, because you have your farming. But we have *nothing*,' I said, ne?" Hans, the women said, was not fired after all, for not joining the Party.

Frau Lieb spoke up softly. "The people were afraid."

The others agreed, more loudly, that everyone was afraid of the Party and of informers. As Frau Amschel put it, "There were always some on the prowl, if you 'scalded your mouth [said something dangerous].'" She added, "Nobody had the confidence to say anything." Frau Lieb annexed her colloquial affirmation, "Na, na." (Because her pronunciation was more toward "naw" or "no," it sounded like a negative. But she meant "Ja, ja.")

At this point, the women had expressed nothing but negative sentiments about the Nazi Party. Even giving them the benefit of the doubt, that they had felt the same way during the Third Reich, their village surely was not an anti-Nazi bastion. Or was it?

It was not. Frau Amschel said her friends mostly felt the way she did, but named a local man who went along, as did other "small workers." Asked what percent of people in the village were for the Party, Frau Lieb said, "Well, there certainly were some." Frau Amschel said, "The workers, mostly, ne?" They all agreed it was not the farmers.

"Where you could nourish yourself from your own farm," said Frau Lieb, "where you didn't need work from the state and anybody at all, like that."

Frau Amschel said it was obvious that Party membership was growing. Added Frau Lieb, "Well, whoever just needed work, ne?" Added Frau Amschel, "Of course, he joined the Party. And when he was in the Party, he also got work." It seemed as simple as that.

Frau Maria Amschel estimated that sixty to seventy percent of Kemmern, which itself had many more "workers" than farmers, was for the Party. The statement was debated, but no consensus was reached. Asked if the Nazi Party brought improvement to Kemmern itself, the women fell silent for the first time. Frau Amschel Junior finally said it solved unemployment. Frau Lieb agreed. None of the women offered another answer.

They divulged, eventually, that although they were frightened of going against the Party, they and their friends did so a little. Someone brought up that a "Frau Mitzke always listened to black [forbidden foreign broadcasts]," and the two old friends said they did, too. "Then we heard something," said Frau Amschel. "Whatever was going on," said Frau Lieb. "It was curiosity," said Frau Amschel. They tittered a little.

Not many people in Kemmern had radios that could get the foreign stations. Frau Lieb said "a good acquaintance, Strelker, he had one." She continued, "He bought it in *installments*, ne?" Her emphasis may have been to make a point about the importance of the broadcasts. Because farm people at the time mostly bought a major item like a radio by cash in full, or not at all, Herr Strelker's taking the unfamiliar route of buying a radio in installments was an indication of how badly he wanted it.[4]

"One didn't turn it on so loud, ne?" Frau Amschel asked rhetorically.

---

4. Thanks to transcriber Nina Helgren for the insight.

"That the neighbors heard it. It was very quiet. Each person was afraid."

"Ach, that was a difficult time," said Frau Lieb softly. "That was a difficult time."

The women may have been better informed and politically more astute than their unworldliness might make them seem. When asked if they had known there would be a war, Frau Amschel replied, "That we already knew, ne?" She said they saw the preparations for war. What kinds? "That they were in the club, ne? The Hitler club, that was all preparations, ne?" She meant Hitler Youth was thought of as preparation for a war? They all agreed, at once. When I said that many Germans believed it was only a club . . .

Frau Lieb, in a rare moment, interrupted. "They were always there on the Sportplatz. They had to exercise and jump. . . ."

"March and sing," put in Frau Amschel.

Frau Lieb made a noise of aversion.

Frau Amschel junior said that when her brother was thirteen, "my father once told him, 'Adam, pay attention, that you learn how to mow. I'll have to go to war.' And it actually happened."

The women recalled a neighbor woman who liked Adolf Hitler so much that she referred to him as "our magnificent Führer." Frau Amschel said, "We laughed about it," adding, "and you had to keep your mouth closed. If you said anything, *she* would have reported everything. We didn't trust saying anything. You wouldn't believe it. She would have had you taken away. Definitely true." A local man "pleaded to *her* on bended knee to let him go. They got a little excited, because . . . Complained about Hitler and everything, ne?" It seemed the woman knew that the man and some of his friends had "complained" about Hitler. The fear the women expressed on their behalf was underscored by Frau Lieb. "They would have gone to Dachau, if they had reported it."

They said they all had known about Dachau through newspapers and "black radio."

Frau Amschel added, "There were more camps, ne?"

"Freilich," said Frau Lieb. She said, "If you didn't raise your hand, ne? You always thought, they're going to report you."

Frau Amschel recalled that a man in Kemmern who had been knocked on the head and "could not talk right" was given special permission not to have to say "Heil Hitler!"

Asked how they felt when they said "Heil Hitler!" Frau Lieb replied, half-laughing, "Very mocking." Her friend echoed, "It was mockery, ne? A *must. Forced.*" She added that she still remembers being with her friend Christel near a pedestrian bridge (she tried quite a while to remember its name until her daughter-in-law said it did not matter) that both had to cross to go to a factory. On it, they encountered a man crossing the other way. He said

"Heil Hitler!" She did, too. But of Christel, she said, dropping her voice, "She never raised her hand. We always said, 'Christel, they'll take you away yet.' 'Should take me with them right now,' she always said. 'I won't put up my hand.'" Frau Amschel continued, "We said, 'One day they will grab you by your jacket and pull you with them.'" She added, laughing, "We all laughed about it, saying we'll all land in the slammer." But they did not. Luck, someone said. "Ja, ja," breathed Frau Lieb. A woman who had refused to say "Heil Hitler!" had become a local legend.

No Jews had lived in Kemmern, said the women, but a good many, especially shopkeepers, lived in Bamberg. (In an interview not included, a Bamberg shopkeeper, whose shop was on a street she said used to be Adolf Hitler Strasse, described the "many" Jewish shopkeepers she and her husband had known in Bamberg as being "nice, wonderful, pleasant business partners." She mentioned that some had visited from America after the war.)[5]

"Where Hertie [department store] is now, that's where Tietz's was," said Frau Amschel, speaking of downtown Bamberg. Tietz's was a Jewish-owned store where the Kemmern women used to buy their dress material. They knew the inventory well. So did the local Nazi fanatics, who sometimes stopped any local woman on the street and challenged her to state where she bought the material for the dress on her back. "They even reported it, that the material was bought at Tietz's. It was that bad. Because it was a Jew, ne? Where Hertie is now."

At this point in the roundelay, Frau Anna Maier, clad in store-bought beige knit, arrived. She was notably younger than Frau Amschel and Lieb, and bustling. Her arrival seemed to change the mood. The reason (if correct) revealed itself slowly. At the outset, she acted more outwardly confident, as well as more worldly, than the others. She turned out to be the only one of the three who watched television, and the only one who commented on watching the war film footage recently rebroadcast in connection with the anniversary of the war's end. When introductions and greetings were over, and Frau Maier was settled at the table, I brought her up to date on the conversation thus far, including the matter of whether to go in Jewish stores. She said she did not know so much about that, being born in 1923.

Frau Amschel Junior then pointed out that in 1939, she would have been sixteen. A hint of challenge was in the air.

Frau Maier responded she may have been sixteen, "but look, I didn't really know so much about the Jews. I first became conscious of it when I saw the stars, ne? Jewish stars. That's when I really grasped what was going

---

5. Interview with Frau Anna Pretti, Bamberg, September 1984.

on. We didn't know about the other camps at all, only Dachau, ne? We didn't know about the others at all."

"Auschwitz," said Frau Amschel.

"Auschwitz I cannot really remember. I was really astonished that so many existed."

The others made sounds of agreement. "And such a large cemetery," said Frau Lieb.

Frau Maria Amschel asked Frau Maier about Tietz's. "Did you go in and buy something?" she asked.

"Of course we went in."

"Weren't you afraid that you'd be reported?"

"Was not afraid." She then changed the subject. She said her father had worked in the state "food office" and had been asked to join the Party, but said, "I'm not joining. You can stand on your heads. I'm still not joining." His stance did have consequences. "They threw him out, ne? Had to join the war." She said when he got his draft notice at home, he knew it was a result of his refusal to join the Party. He was sent to the front to be what he considered cannon fodder.

She returned to the Stars of David she had seen, and said she had seen them in Bamberg. "Well, and earlier, so that I tell no lie, Bercher, a livestock trader, he always came by. Then my mother was always so afraid. And my father always said, 'Don't be afraid, he'll do nothing to you.' 'Ja, he wants money and he repossesses, and so.' She was always a little afraid."

Frau Maria Amschel commented, "Ja, who traded with the Jews was afraid a little. My husband, he . . ."

Frau Maier interrupted. "I remember we once transported potatoes for a Jewish family. I was fourteen or fifteen and I got such a nice dress from the Jews. Oh, I was so happy. I didn't know there was hate against the Jews and so on. And I wore the dress a long time. We were four children at home. We didn't have a lot, ne?" She made another sympathetic reference to a Jew, in the middle of a tale about other matters. "He was a Jew and he didn't get any more contracts. He had to let his people go." She also brought up that "we didn't hear any more from Bercher, the livestock trader."

None of the women did.

When the war began, life for the women of Kemmern, and presumably for most women related to small farmers, became considerably more difficult. Their families' agricultural holdings were too small to qualify as "essential" for the nourishment of the Volk and thus exempt the farmer from military duty, and were too small to receive free labor from the government, whether a German teenager or a prisoner of war. So the women essentially were left to do everything. That meant not only "women's work," like cooking, sewing, laundry, caring for children, and maintaining a garden, it also meant "men's work," taking care of animals, planting, and harvesting. The primitive nature of that work first became clear when the women mentioned that Frau Lieb's husband got deferments from fighting. Frau Amschel said, "The only blacksmith in the village, ne?"

"The farmers had to have the cows shod, ne? And the scythes whetted," said his widow, Frau Lieb.

"And the tools adjusted," added Frau Amschel.

Frau Maier commented it was "so nice, the way it used to be. Today it's all gone, the smith whetting the scythes . . ." The women went down a kind of memory lane together, being especially nostalgic about the old frog pond. Frau Lieb recalled that her husband always said when the frogs croak at night, it will rain in the morning.

But it must have been a physical and emotional strain to have been a Kemmern woman then. "Everything by hand," said Frau Amschel. Frau Lieb recalled that "one was *so* happy" when postwar farmers with binders or mowing machines helped out even a little. But during the war, not only was such help nonexistent, women out scything fields were particularly vulnerable to bombs. Amid one racket of memories about the bombs, a voice (it sounded like Frau Amschel) spoke about running for shelter, and finally crouching next to a cow.

Adding considerably to the strain of war, the women indicated, was that the government kept tabs on virtually all the work they did (not to mention other aspects of their lives). Everything their fields or animals produced, no matter how small the enterprise, had to be accounted for. Frau Amschel put it this way: "How many hens do you have? You have to deliver this many eggs. How many cows do you have? Then you have to deliver this much milk. If you had four cows and you only delivered milk from three, they would have noticed. Stop. Something is missing. Then they came after you. One already had to watch out." The government did pay for the products, if not a lot.

The women then began to talk, all at once, about a common response to the system: cheating. Not much happened in the daylight hours, during which people simply hid their private stashes—items as small as an egg or as large as a cow. Night was the time for action. Frau Lieb, who married in 1933 and by 1942 had five children to feed, told of sneaking off to the mill at night to have small amounts of flour ground, which she then hid. Laughing a little, she said she awoke about three in the morning to dig up potatoes secretly.

"Everything secretly," said Frau Amschel. "*Everything* secretly." The women talked about making butter secretly, and leaving the butter in the churns where no one might look. They also talked about that most secret of secret practices, "black" butchering. How else to kill the fatted pig that had not been registered? In the commotion of the women's remarks about the

239

practice (they probably worked together), Frau Lieb remembered how she hung cloth in the windows to keep out the light, and how everyone had to be finished at a certain hour, before the first hint of daylight.

Toward the end of the war, the women of Kemmern had another distraction. Hamstern had begun. "A *lot* of women came," said one voice in the tumult that broke out when the subject was introduced. Frau Amschel said, "They just asked for food, and they had dishes, and dolls, clothing, children's things, ne? Whether you didn't need some, ne? A few eggs, they always said. Or a little flour." The others, who had been agreeing with the inventory, added that many women brought Christmas tree ornaments. A factory nearby had made them.

What did the women of Kemmern say to the city women?

Frau Amschel said, "Well, if you had anything, or needed anything, ne?"

What were their feelings about them?

Frau Lieb said, "We felt bad for them."

"Ja, they really made us feel sorry for them," said Frau Amschel. "One often gave them something to eat, ne? When they came. With the Huckelkörb [back basket] that they always had."

What kind of people were these city women? "*Always* nice" and "friendly" were heard in the outpouring of response. Frau Maier said the city women "always asked if you would take something, should trade something, ne? Usually you didn't really need it and took it, also when you didn't urgently need it. We knew how much hunger hurts."

"That's why they gave away their things," added Frau Lieb.

"Freilich," said Frau Amschel.

"They didn't want to beg directly, they gave something for it."

"We felt sorry for them, the people," said Frau Amschel. "Going peddling, they made us feel sorry."

Asked what the city women might trade, for instance, for three eggs, Frau Lieb and Frau Amschel listed "a couple of plates, a couple of cups. Coffee cups. If you had children, something was always getting broken. Toys. They all had clothing."

"They even had bed linens," said Frau Lieb. "When they were in need, what they had extra. That's what they talked about, what they could do without, they said."

What happened when the Kemmern women did not need anything?

Frau Maier said, "Then they left again, without hesitation. When you said you didn't need anything today, they left again."

"They didn't complain, didn't do anything. Honestly," said Frau Lieb. She and Frau Amschel spoke of giving them at least some food when they had cooked something, or a piece of bread.

And if a woman wanted to trade a sheet for some soup and they did not need any sheets? Frau Lieb and Frau Amschel said in almost complete unison that they did not take anything for soup, or a piece of bread, or a couple of eggs. Frau Lieb added, "I mean, nobody wants to beg, ne? Actually beg. They took something with them for it, because maybe they thought it wasn't begging, ne?"

"They were *fine* women, ne?" said Frau Amschel.

"Agreed," said Frau Lieb.

"They weren't obtrusive," said Frau Maier. "They were never obtrusive. If you didn't take anything, then they went to the next house."

All in all, this was not the response I expected. When I tried to explain the general reputation of German farm women among "hamstering" German city women, Frau Lieb and Frau Amschel both thought I was saying something else and began talking even more sympathetically about the city women.

They also spoke about their own fear of being caught "hamstering." Caught? Such trading was not forbidden, as they confirmed. But, as Frau Maier tried to explain, the situation had to do with ration points and with how many goods people could have. The farm women did not want the authorities to know what had been traded. "One did it only when one urgently needed something." If Frau Maier's implication were correct, the reputation of German farm women as greedy ogres may be off. No doubt some or many women did take advantage of the situation, did furnish their homes with everything short of the carpet in the cow stall (especially after the Third Reich ended). But if the women of Kemmern are representative, and accurately portrayed, many simply were being careful. They could not trade much more than what they had told the authorities they had. They were trading out of their private stashes. Asked if they felt they were "using" the city women, they all said, more or less, they did not.

Frau Maier said she herself had an arrangement with one city woman, whose husband worked at a department store in Bamberg. The woman came to Kemmern and got milk or potatoes from the Maiers. "Was so thankful." In return, she took the Maiers' clothing ration cards to town, and through her husband's connection stretched them further than they would otherwise go.

The woman figured in another story, too. The biggest Allied bombing attacks on Bamberg were reported in April of 1945, but the one Frau Maier remembered happened on February 22. As bombers approached the city, somebody saw the woman of the ration cards standing in the street and acting rather strange. Everyone else was running to the shelters, said Frau Maier, but not that woman. Just before the bombs fell, "the woman looked around, three, four times. Looked around and waved." Whoever saw her said "she looked around as if she could tell she was not coming back," as if, in fact, she were waving goodbye. When the bombs fell, "she was in the air raid shelter [with her ten-year-old daughter]. At home, her house remained standing. And in the air raid shelter, she and her child were killed."

Frau Maier added that the woman had the clothing ration cards with her when she died. "Of course, we got them again." The reputation of German farm families for pragmatism was not diminished by the Maiers.

The farm women did not dispute that the countryside was a much safer place from bombs than cities. But their countryside happened to be en route to bombing targets. So when Bamberg, Schweinfurt, Würzberg, and Nuremberg were bombed, people in and around Kemmern knew it. "We heard every hit," said Frau Amschel. Frau Lieb said everyone watched the night bombing of Nuremberg.

The Kemmern countryside also happened to have its own targets—train tracks. The women related many, many close calls. Frau Amschel recalled taking a handcart to town with her friend Gretl to pick up a harrow, and on the way back home encountering dive bombers [Tiefflieger] that came so low she could see the pilots' faces. "Three times we lay in the ditches, had to lie under the handcart." She did not mention her own fright, but emphasized repeatedly how scared her mother was when she and Gretl were not back on time. Frau Lieb recalled bicycling to town when bombers hit some railway tracks close to the street where she was riding. She threw her bicycle in the ditch and lay beside it until the attack was over. It was March, 8, 1945, she said. "Won't ever forget it."

The bombs seemed to have been particularly frightening to the very old and the very young. Frau Maier remembered her two-year-old son, Franz, running around and around the big tile oven in the middle of the house crying "The Bumm-bumm is coming." Frau Lieb's youngest child, also two years old, hung on her skirts and cried the same. Frau Lieb whispered that her grandmother was so scared she rarely left their storage cellar, but stayed there with the "little one," who slept in the wooden baking trough.

Kemmern itself never was bombed, but it was invaded. During the last months of the war, strangers came from all directions. They included not only city women, but German soldiers retreating from the west and German refugees fleeing from the east. As clearly as the women remembered the arrival of the city women, so did they recall the refugees, carrying all they could on their bodies, being part of "treks, everything loaded up, horses, handcarts." The Kemmern villagers put them up, six or seven to a room. Frau Lieb recalled "old Kupske with his nag and all his things on it" being there a long time. The women also remembered one refugee named "Martie, who hung himself out of despair" because he had to give his horse away.

How long did they stay? A few days, or . . .

"Some are still here," said Frau Maier.

The villagers had long decided to stay put, too. Frau Maier said nobody knew where else to go. "Whether it's the Russian or whoever, it's the same. We're staying, ne?" She said one German soldier told her mother, "Mütterlein, enjoy the war. The peace is horrible." The women around the Amschels' table laughed a little, for the first time in a long while.

In all the turmoil at the end of the war, did the women ever think why it happened? Or who was at fault?

"We already thought, the war is senseless," said Frau Maier. "What was it for?"

Frau Lieb spoke up. "Hitler wanted to conquer the whole world. The *whole* world. He always kept up the war, ne?"

Frau Maier, fifteen years younger, disagreed. "I believe it wasn't Hitler alone. He didn't know a tenth of it at all, I believe, what the others all did. I don't believe that he knew everything, the brutality, how one saw the bodies in the camps, ne? I also said to myself, ja, that can't be true, that's impossible, that Hitler was in charge of that, something so, so brutal. One saw the people, only the bones were showing. I honestly cried from anger. *So* bad. Who has to answer for it, I said, to do that, ne? That was horrible. I didn't *ever* know that, that there was something like that. I myself was completely astonished. It was like I was hit on the head."

The entire time she spoke, no one interrupted. Because most of the women's interruptions had been signs of agreement of one form or another, the silence seemed to signal disagreement with Frau Maier's core contention—that Hitler was less than fully culpable or aware of what was happening in the camps. I asked Frau Maier if she had trusted him.

"What does trust mean? I myself, honestly said, [was] not able to keep up with it, because I was still a child, gel? I had no idea what it all meant. We would have liked a radio, because in school we had to write essays about Hitler's speeches and stuff like that. We could have got one, because we were 'child rich,' but Mama always said, I have enough radio, I don't need another."

The other women laughed.

Frau Maier continued, "We had to write essays in school, when someone talked about the Führer. We had to go along. What else could we do? We were forced to, we had to write essays."

"A difficult time" murmured someone. The intent of the remark may have been to stop Frau Maier from going on about Hitler. If so, it did not work. She spoke about the Hitler Youth groups, of having "no time for it. We couldn't join, we had to go in the fields, take care of the children. And we had no money to buy the 'rags,' that stuff, gel?" She said her father said if the children all went to Hitler Jugend and the Bund deutscher Mädel, "who is going to be doing the work at home?"

Frau Amschel spoke lightly of one boy in a "brown shirt and open tie" being proud to be in the organization.

Frau Maier then compared the Hitler regime to East Germany's and returned to the issue of German youth under Hitler, especially her brothers, born in 1923 and 1924. "Those were fifteen-, sixteen-year-old boys, what could they do? They had to go, too, gel?" After circling into contemporary politics, she returned to her earlier theme. "Hitler could not have known at all, I believe," about concentration camps, about "what they did with the people."

Still, there had been virtually no interruptions.

Frau Lieb finally spoke. "Well," she said, "we don't want to get all riled up. It's all over, ne? It's all over."

Frau Maier did not take the out. She immediately said, in the same tone of outrage, "But honestly, the poor human beings made me feel sorry, how they threw them, in a pile, into the pits."

Only then did the others join in, and agree with her.

The afternoon closed on easier agreements. The women all said they wanted no more war. When asked how to avoid one, they said they could do nothing but pray.

Frau Maier then spoke happily, and at length, about doing laundry for American soldiers at the end of the war. She liked the friendly GI who said, "Annie, you my friend," she liked learning how to iron "the extra folds" in the soldiers' shirts, she liked how the soldiers always paid her something, and maybe brought chocolate for her children, and, once, coffee for her. She liked doing the work with her sisters. And she especially liked being with the American soldiers at Christmas—less than a year after the U.S. Armed Forces bombed her country.

"They were there on Christmas Eve when I decorated the Christmas tree. They sang so nicely with us. 'Stille Nacht [Silent Night],' in English. It was really joyful, ne?"

As we said our goodbyes, Frau Amschel shyly asked if it might be possible to hear some of the tape. Besides never having been interviewed before, the women obviously never had heard their voices before. Glad to oblige, I partially rewound the cassette and hit the play button. The Frau Amschels, Frau Lieb, and Frau Maier began giggling, then began pointing to each other when they recognized each other's voices, Frau Lieb covering her mouth with her knobby farm-worked hands as she laughed. Soon the women all were guffawing so hard they all but fell off their chairs.

There was no question which side Freya von Moltke had been on during the Third Reich. Kreisau, her former home, is part of the vocabulary of anti-Nazi resistance.

A rural village, Kreisau lay in what then was the eastern German province of Silesia and now is part of Poland. For generations Kreisau's most prominent residents surely had been the von Moltkes, who lived in the nearby Palace Moltke and oversaw their thousand acres of farm and forest. During the Third Reich, however, the estate took on a role well beyond agriculture and forestry. Within its walls some twenty-five outraged souls worked on the highly treasonous task of planning, on paper, a new government for a defeated Germany. The treason lay in acting on the belief that Germany would be defeated. The group never named itself. But when the Nazis discovered it, they did. Skilled as they were at alliterative wordplay, they came up with "Kreisauer Kreis" [Kreisau Circle].

At the time, the name Kreisau was nothing in comparison to the name von Moltke. To Germans it was the equivalent of the names Washington, Grant, and Eisenhower—not the presidents, but the generals. Field Marshal Helmuth von Moltke was the military hero of nineteenth-century Prussia. His closest descendant and titled namesake was his great-grandnephew, Count Helmuth James von Moltke.

The woman who was to be his wife was Freya Deichmann, just "a regular burgher's daughter," as she put it. The description was humble to the point of inaccuracy. She came

Mrs. Freya von Moltke

A Modest Woman of the Resistance

from one of Cologne's leading families, her parents' marriage representing a merger of bankers and financiers. Before the Deichmanns lost most of their money in the depression of the early 1930s, they had had grand homes and other accoutrements of wealth, such as a carriage with liveried footmen.[1]

Like the Deichmanns, the von Moltkes had become cash poor, too. In the fall of 1929, the Kreisau estate was in such critical financial shape that Herr von Moltke senior summoned home Helmuth, his eldest son, to save it. The twenty-two-year-old law student did go home, and from Kreisau kept up a correspondence with Freya, an eighteen-year-old university student. The couple had met that summer in Austria at "a wonderful vacation place where an Austrian woman brought her friends together. They were all anti-Nazi and they remained so, too." The hostess, she said, had "Jewish roots." (She did not say the woman and her husband were Eugenie and Hermann Schwarzwald, social activists involved with many of the artists and intellectuals of the German-speaking world.)[2]

The correspondence to and from Kreisau lasted two years, which "felt like ten." He had other romances "for sure. For me, none," she added with a laugh. The couple did not seem destined to marry. "He saw life very skeptically. He always said, 'I will not marry and I do not want children.' And I said, 'Who's talking about marriage? Not I.' But he kept saying it over and over. I said, 'Stop that. I don't need to start a marriage at the age of twenty.'" Her plans, she said, were to study law, too, and to see the world.

Then, in 1931, she received "the remarkable letter [der merkwurdige Brief] that said now he has to marry me. His mother was going back to South Africa and he had to marry to take care of his younger brothers and sister."[3] Freya von Moltke agreed the proposal was not very flattering "but nonetheless very nice. And he said 'So.' And I said 'So. I want to, too.'" She laughed. "And that was that." They married that year.

"In every way living with him was foremost, so naturally I went to Silesia. My relatives were surprised I'd go that far east, but they understood it was what I wanted. So I went to the strange other world, which is how western Germany considered eastern Germany. For me, it was the most important thing in my life. There is nothing at all about me of the liberated woman, but I have always lived an extraordinarily liberated life. I had the luck to come into a family where the men were not autocratic and totalitarian, which they are in most German households. The women had the

---

1. From "Der Ordinäre," a profile about Mrs. von Moltke's brother Hans Deichmann, *The New Yorker*, June 4, 1990, 50, 55.
2. Ibid, 54.
3. Frau Dorothy von Moltke, a South African of Scottish background, was going to pay a long visit to her parents.

same rights. That held true for my mother-in-law and for my sister-in-law and for me."

By all accounts, the marriage was glorious. "Some marriages are made in heaven. Nothing much is thought about them. They go fabulously. I certainly had such a marriage. It was never very comfortable or easy, for our life was demanding. There was no money, there was nothing there, we had to work, we were poor. But these always were second-rung things. What we had would not be called a comfortable life today. But there was such beauty. The countryside, the energetic family, the interesting activities, the other lovable people there. All that made me happy.

"You won't often find such happiness with many women. That is the remarkable thing about our existence. When one has such a wonderful thing, it doesn't last. It was a gigantic gift. Then there was nothing. That was not so pleasant." By "nothing" she meant her husband's death. The Nazis murdered him in January 1945.

Forty years to the month later, seemingly coincidental to the date, three generations of von Moltke family and friends gathered in Freya von Moltke's old clapboard house in eastern Vermont. It overlooked a placid New England landscape of snow-covered fields and split-rail fences. She moved to the United States to be with a friend, not to turn her back on Germany. But once in this country, she stayed.

The view outside seemed all the more still when contrasted to the gentle end-of-Christmas-season hubbub inside. Freya von Moltke's beloved sister-in-law, Asta von Moltke Henssel, visiting with her husband from Berlin, said the Vermont home—not the pinnacle of German household order—reminded her pleasantly of life in Kreisau. There always was "viel los" [a lot going on].

The "viel los" was most evident from the house's large first-floor keeping room, which contained a Christmas tree hung German-style with apples and cookies, a huge round table where ten people would eat that evening, and a variety of comfortable places to sit among remains of Christmas wrappings. A granddaughter and her friend sat in stuffed armchairs, reading. A baby grandson toddled in and out. From another room came the sound of a recorder. A clock chimed, family members came and went from local outings, the telephone rang off and on. Freya von Moltke took it all in stride.

Her appearance was pleasantly striking. A tall, blue-eyed, dark-skinned woman, with a profile that remained handsome, she was slim to the point that relatives urge her to eat more. Her manner was unaffected and straightforward. We sat on an antique sofa, in front of us a tray of herb tea and her homemade Christmas stollen. Even before she began talking of her life as a young woman, it was obvious from her surroundings and her behavior she does not live in the past. But she draws from it.

247

"I still live from the resistance we carried out. It is completely alive to me. Not so much the horrible Nazism, but the effort we made. The high point of my life was with my husband *and* the time we stood against the Nazis."

He was, she said, "an extremely unusual man." How often does she think about him? Her answer, two minutes into the interview, was, "There is no day in which I do not think about my husband." I had assumed, while nervously boarding ever smaller planes to get to her home, that I would find a woman of bravery and dignity, and I did. I was not prepared to find a woman in love.

Helmuth von Moltke's death was presaged on January 30, 1933, the day Hitler was named chancellor. "We had a Social Democratic district magistrate to lunch, whom my husband knew well, and he said, 'Ach, now the Nazis have come to power. That is much better. One lets them take over. And they will mismanage themselves like any other ruling party.'

"Then my husband said, 'You're *insane!* [Du bist *wahnsinnig!*] You have no idea what kind of horrendous catastrophe, what kind of a day this is. You cannot see it.' And that he told the man on the 30th of January.

"My husband was an exception. That is why he remained so meaningful to me in my life. I completely trusted his leadership. To be sure, I had a great influence on him. He listened to me, he questioned me. And sometimes he had such high-flown ideas, I would say, 'Don't be so crazy.' It's not as if I were subordinate to him. It's hard to describe, but I mean, that is a good marriage."

As newlyweds, the von Moltkes lived in Berlin, he working as a junior lawyer, she studying law. Later, she quit her studies and then resumed them, getting her degree "quickly and poorly" at the "very nice Humboldt University in Berlin." She added that she has used the credential only when writing a reference letter for someone.

Earlier in the month that the Social Democrat had come to lunch, Freya von Moltke herself had a glimpse of what was coming to Germany. She had gone to the theater in Berlin with a friend to see a film premiere but, having arrived late, had to wait in the darkened vestibule for a light to be turned on before being led in. "A man stood next to me, directly next to me, and I saw his eyes [only]. It was already dark. They were terrible, dreadfully unquiet eyes. I thought, 'Who *is* this next to me? What kind of eyes are those?' And then the light went on and it was Hitler."

He and his entourage sat down directly next to her. She looked at them, she said, "like wild animals." By the end of that month, the "wild animals" were in power.

She said she and her husband soon became more and more upset about "the treatment of the Jews and those whom Hitler considered inferior. They were human beings like us, and the treatment contradicted what we thought civilization stood for. We found it a treason against humanity, as humanity had been taught to us. And we had personal ties to Jewish human beings. Many Germans did not. For them everything they heard was"—she paused—"theory. For us, it was our own skin. Those were our friends. Then it's very simple to be in opposition."

Yet virulent anti-Semitism, she said, was not the norm. "In the majority of the German population, crass anti-Semitism was not liked. There were anti-Semites. But they were against the crassness. Many women were against it. But naturally, they were afraid. What should we do against it? That's it, you see? What should we do against it?"

The question may have seemed increasingly unanswerable. She referred to one of the Nazis' earliest measures, passed in March 1933. It was called the Enabling Act [Ermächtigungsgesetz]. "It authorized the Nazis to take away basic rights. You could be imprisoned without seeing a judge. That took care of freedom of rights. And my husband said to me, 'That is the end of the constitutional state.'" The constitutional state [Rechtsstaat] was to Germans what the Bill of Rights is to Americans.

"Then came these terrible murders, in 1934, of the SA, and the intrigues. [She is referring to the Roehm Putsch.] It was so obvious everything was completely lawless. The people no longer had the rights they'd grown up with. The Nazis said what was legal and what was not. And the people didn't notice."

Obviously, Helmuth von Moltke did more than notice. "From the very beginning, he wanted to do things against the Nazis," she said. "To help." Among his earliest responses to the Nazis was to help the couple's own Jewish friends emigrate. "My husband said to them constantly, 'Out! Out! Holland is not far enough away,' he said. 'The Nazis will do whatever they want. Far away! Out! And I'll help you,' to those we knew. He helped many get out. To England, America."

Claims of lack of patriotism made later against the von Moltkes were valid, she said. "Our complete being was not at all nationalistic, but had a lot more to do with principles. We *never* did anything for nationalistic reasons. That was thrown at us like, 'These people, they're no patriots.' No. We were not."

But who were they? The American historian and diplomat George Kennan called Helmuth von Moltke "the greatest person, morally, and the largest and most enlightened in his concepts" he met on "either side of the battlelines in the Second World War."[4] It is no overstatement to say that von

---

4. George F. Kennan, *Memoirs 1925–1950* (Boston: Little, Brown, 1967), 121–122. Cited in Helmuth James von Moltke, *Letters to Freya 1939–1945* (New York: Knopf, 1990), 4.

Moltke applied those concepts to do everything in his power to save the lives of any victims of Nazism he could, from Jewish German friends to foreign prisoners of war. Considering the reputation of her husband, it is understandable that Freya von Moltke's story is less that of her own life than of theirs. But it would be an oversight not to think of her as her own person, both then and now. In the 1980s alone, as international history began rearranging itself, over and over she faced the public's interest with intelligent grace. She rejected any claim on the Kreisau manor in Poland, in part not to dispute Poland's new borders. And at a later address by survivors of the Munich student resistance group, the White Rose (she heads the American branch of the White Rose Foundation), at a Jewish organization, it was she who stood up to make the point that in comparison to the horrors that National Socialism perpetuated, resisters were small minorities. "All we can do is be modest," she said.[5] In a way, that is what she always was: a modest woman.

It was one thing during the Third Reich for the von Moltkes to recognize injustice and to act upon it within legal limits. But then what? And where? From her conversation and his published letters, it is clear the couple's emotional home was Kreisau. He had practiced law in the area, she said, but once the Nazis were in power found it difficult to work the way he wanted. Silesia was too small-town in nature and his name too well known to insure privacy. So he went to Berlin, five hours away, to work where, as she put it, "what one did was not so visible." Yet in Berlin and Kreisau, as the years and edicts passed, he felt torn. Mrs. von Moltke said he tried to fight the Nazis however he could, for example, interceding on behalf of Jewish businessmen whose firms the Nazis had expropriated, but he felt crushed by the overall atmosphere and his own pessimism.

In part "to get some air," she said, he often went to England, where he had contacts, and, of course, his British roots from his mother's side. He also used the time to get an English law degree. He did more than that. He engaged in acts of treason that Mrs. von Moltke did not mention. In the summer of 1939, he was one of several Germans who gained access to British leaders, including Prime Minister Neville Chamberlain and Lord of the Admiralty Winston Churchill, to warn them of Hitler's planned attack on Poland. And he tried to inform the English and through his connections to American journalists, Americans, what else the Nazis were up to.

Back in Germany, anticipating that war was inevitable, he sought work that would absolve him from orders to fight for Hitler, and also give him power behind the scenes. He found it in the foreign branch of German intelligence (a center of opposition to the Nazis) as a legal advisor to the

---

5. Address to Hillel Foundation, Berkeley, California, March 4, 1992.

German Armed Forces' High Command. Once the war began, part of von Moltke's strategy was to convince the Nazis that maintaining the norm of international law even during a war would help the Third Reich more than hinder it.[6] His posthumous book, *Letters to Freya*, contains his accounts of the agonizing difficulties, his failures, his growing despair about situations he learned about and could scarcely alter, and his eked-out successes (such as getting rescinded an order that war prisoners be shackled).

At one point, she said, he had heard that Nazis in Holland, Brussels, and France were "obliterating" their prisoners. "He worked very, very hard against the shooting of hostages, that people not simply kill innocent people. He even spoke to the SS in the countries and said, 'That serves no purpose. It only provokes the population. It's fully counterproductive.' Helmuth always worked from the standpoint not that what you do is horrendous, but that it does not gain anything for you."

She said he found it remarkable that he had such success with the SS. Such success was not remarkable to her. "The Nazis honored the great heroes of German wars," like "this General von Moltke. That was a great name to the Nazis. My husband carried the most direct inheritance of that name. It impressed them. Therefore, he could undertake things another could not. In fact, that's what they told me when they counted him with the other resistance people who had to be put to death. Himmler explicitly let it be said to me, through my brother-in-law who'd tried to save him, 'Now we can take no more consideration because of the name.' That means they *did* take consideration. [Helmuth] knew that too. He said, 'I am better off.' "

Part of his response to the Nazis was to make "the greatest effort" finding out what they were doing. She referred to one of his longest letters about how difficult it was to learn what was going on without secure telephones, mail, or messengers (if caught they could be tortured), and about how the Nazis tried to mask the truth from the German public.[7] Through his contacts in Munich, he found out about anti-Nazi leaflets being written and distributed in 1942 and 1943 by the White Rose. Mrs. von Moltke said, as if in passing, at the previously-mentioned White Rose survivors' gathering, that he managed to get copies of the leaflets and take them to Sweden, and from there get them smuggled to England. There they were reprinted by the hundreds of thousands and dropped by plane over Germany.

And through his diligence and contacts, he found out where German Jews were really being deported. As a group of letters from 1941 indicates,

6. Barbara Beuys, *Vergesst uns Nicht/Menschen im Widerstand 1933–1945* (Do not forget us/People in the resistance 1933–1945) (Reinbek bei Hamburg: Rowohlt, 1987), 415.

7. The 1943 letter, printed in *Letters to Freya* but not meant for her, was partially memorized by a nervous contact and recited to its recipient in England.

he then seemingly used every bit of energy and prestige he commanded to try to change the policy. Following his efforts at a November 1941 ministerial meeting, he actually succeeded, but only for a few days.[8]

He also wrote to her, she said, of a German officer "who's come back from Russia, through Poland, who tells things so horrible, one can scarcely believe them. But they are said to be." She said the man was describing Auschwitz. Her brother Hans also told her of the horrors of Auschwitz, after he was sent there to recruit Italian laborers. "So," she said, "it wasn't impossible to know it."

Most of her husband's efforts were carried out from his work base in Berlin, while she stayed in Kreisau, taking on more and more the running of the agricultural estate. His letters, which often singe with frustration and sorrow, also refer to that work, to his concern she is doing too much, and to "lovely" reunions in Berlin or Kreisau. "He always pushed a great deal of responsibility at me and always saw me as his *partner*. There is this gigantic correspondence, because we were apart a lot. Daily letters back and forth. I have them all, still.[9] The letters my husband wrote me were the dangerous ones, but he mailed them in public boxes and they could be checked only in Kreisau. We knew and completely trusted the mailman and the woman at the post office. One naturally could have said, 'We must open the letters of von Moltke,' but that never happened. And everything got more chaotic. So fabulous the Nazis were not. And I wrote only completely uninteresting things. About cows and children, visitors, harvests, and so on." She said, though, her husband claimed to "live" from her letters, once writing her, "No letter yesterday, but thank God, two today."

Her role in running Kreisau, with its work force of sixty people, was as intermediary between her husband and the farm manager. She said her husband "always said, laughing, but meaning it earnestly, 'You must learn everything, because I won't live long.' He really said, 'There will be a revolution and they will hang me from this tree.' I said, 'Don't *say* such horrible things.' But in the very deepest part of my being, I always felt it was true. And I thought, 'For God's sake, not yet.'"

Helmuth and Freya von Moltke had ample opportunity to emigrate. In 1934 and 1937, for example, they visited some of his relatives in South Africa (his grandfather was a well-known liberal judge), but never hesitated to return to Germany. "Perhaps I underestimated the dangers. But my husband did not want to stay away, because he was the eldest and ran the farm. Also, he became increasingly willing to stand against the Nazis."

He also became willing to have children. In the first years of marriage,

---

8. Von Moltke, *Letters to Freya*, 15. Also, von Moltke's department was not invited to attend the subsequent meeting that resulted in the "final solution."
9. They became, of course, the basis for *Letters to Freya*.

he continued not to want any "because he found *life* so hard and the dangers so great. But I didn't give up." She changed his mind, she said, by convincing him that life also means to be accepting. They had two boys, Caspar and Konrad, born in 1937 and 1941.

The Kreisau Circle was conceived in 1940. To its members, it was a spiritual counterpoint to the war. "At the very beginning of the war, Helmuth said Germany would not win. His deepest despair came when France was conquered and it seemed the Nazis would go to England. Those months were frightful for him. And in those frightful months, he decided on the gathering. He thought, if I don't do something now that sustains my hope, I won't be able to stand it."

In a sense, the Kreisau Circle was no more than an intellectual study group. Disparate thinkers united in an attempt to plan a future Germany that would be fair and peaceful. Although the group was criticized then (and after the war) for taking an ivory tower approach to slaughter, an ivory tower was no sanctuary within the Third Reich. To prepare for a Nazi defeat was almost as forbidden as trying to bring one about. The participants in the Kreisau Circle knew they were committing treason and knew the likely punishment was death.

The first glimmer of the Circle was contained in a 1940 letter from Helmuth von Moltke, in Berlin, to his wife. She said he wrote that he had just met two people and "we understand each other extraordinarily." The two, a married couple, lived in a little house in Berlin, and they would all be seeing each other often, he wrote. The couple was Peter and Marion Yorck von Wartenburg. The two men had more in common than politics. Peter Yorck also was a count and a descendant of a famous German general.

Freya von Moltke vividly remembered her first visit to the Yorcks' home with her husband, even recalling the meal was wonderfully cooked beef prepared by the Yorcks' housekeeper. Marion Yorck, for her part, recalled young Freya as delightfully energetic and enthusiastic. There was not a lot of open physical affection between the von Moltkes, she recalled, and surmised that may have had to do with his being half British.[10]

"So it began with a friendship," said Freya von Moltke. "Then they started trying to find others. Helmuth got the Social Democrats he'd known. . . ." She said the group's general frame of mind was to go ahead "as if sometime there will be an end," even though in 1940 such optimism did not seem possible. The group's pervading sense was that the Nazis would dominate all of Europe. Her husband "considered that a greater catastrophe than if it had been the Communists. I must say that, too. He always thought the Communists' fight was a legitimate revolution, while the Nazis' was a counterrevolution, a *miserable* counterrevolution that had nothing real to

---

10. Conversation, May 1985, Berlin.

offer humanity. Only exaggerated nationalism, narcissism, that slew everything Europe stood for.

"There was a long period in which my husband doubted how anyone could do anything in opposition. The Nazis had an overwhelming might, not only materially, but a might over the German people. There was no question most Germans were Nazis. Or were fellow travelers [Mitläufer]. They didn't want to see, or couldn't see, what was really happening. The despising of human beings, which lay in the Nazi system, which treated people like herds and lied to them and manipulated them, made it possible that, paired with material gains, Germans really had the feeling it was a terrific regime. And when something was not terrific, they had the feeling we can't change it, we shall rather look away. And opposite them, my husband, pessimistic and really despairing and still not wanting to leave, because he thought, I must do something against it. To be there when it's all over. Fear that it goes farther. I'm not leaving. I do not have to leave." She said his concentration was so intense, it seemed at first he would never be able to do something with it, but that "he went from strength to strength."

For its participants, the Kreisau Circle must have been a tonic. The first and smaller meetings were held, circumspectly, in the Yorck home in Berlin. "It was not at all noticeable that in the evening a few people gathered and spoke. The larger meetings were in Kreisau." A great effort was made, she said, to include a diverse group of thinkers. "People who opposed the regime and had different points of view were much more ready to try to defeat their own prejudices, because they wanted to serve the same goal." She said the group included no Communists but did include Socialists and capitalists, and, reflecting two other major groups, Protestants and Catholics.

"There's this remarkable split from the Counter-Reformation between Catholics and Protestants. One had to bring them together. Then they confronted the state of affairs. Slowly, matters got closer together and there were those who'd lead discussions and then it all played out in larger circles." Discussions, she said, moved systematically from topic to topic. "About building up the state, about schools, rural economy, about economy in general, about foreign policy." In *Letters to Freya*, one gets a sense of the arduous care with which participants were approached, chosen, and encouraged to work together, and the care with which each draft of each position paper was studied. The intense and futile gesture that comprised the work of the Kreisau Circle could have been Germany's new constitution.

She said the participants not only gave the group no name, "the word *resistance* did not come up either. They merely were a group of people who planned for the future." As for the Nazis' label of Kreisauer Kreis, she called it "a very appropriate name, really. It's an excellent name."

The group's first meeting in Kreisau took place in May 1942, during Whitsuntide. A dozen people attended. The guests slept in the castle (a large, solid, un-fairy-talelike castle) that had been abandoned for year-round family use because it was too expensive to heat. During working sessions in a spacious but smaller house on the property, participants were guided by caution and carried by conviction.

"We were *lifted* during this time like never before. I can't even describe it. We all had such a feeling we are doing what we have to do, that one cannot do otherwise at all. And what will happen will happen. In that sense we were completely devout [gläubig]. Whether one believed that Mary personally is lifted to heaven, that's not it. But we all basically had a devout attitude. And naturally my husband did it because he said his Christian faith demanded it."

Other Nazi opponents did not share the Kreisau group's enthusiasm for its work. "A lot of people came and said, 'We have to kill Hitler and it's all the same what you think besides that. [Your plan] is much too theoretical. It won't work.'"

Mrs. von Moltke said she believed there was room for theory as well as assassination. Although she and her husband worked on the former, he had certainly considered the latter. She said that early in the war he had sent a message to Claus von Stauffenberg, who eventually tried to assassinate Hitler. In the message he asked, as she put it, "if he wanted to engage in practical work against Hitler." She said Stauffenberg sent back the reply: first we have to win the war, and then free ourselves of the brown plague.

That approach, she said, "obviously was completely wrong. But my husband also spoke with several people about whether or not it was possible to do away with Hitler."

The above contradicts a common belief that Helmuth von Moltke opposed the assassination because of his religious beliefs. The contradiction, however, must be tempered. Mrs. von Moltke stated that although her husband "was not so much against murdering Hitler," he did have what she called "scruples" about it. (She said she, on the other hand, had "no scruples.") She added, "It is not at all that he found it fully 'impossible.' But he always pondered *how* one could do it, *whether* one could do it. And he came to the firm conviction, Stauffenberg and his friends could not pull it off successfully.

"Helmuth said, 'You don't have anyone who can do it right. And it won't help, anyway. Everything's too far gone, and so horrendous. You can't change anything. We have to leave it to the Allies whether you want to or not.' He said, 'We are dilettantes. It won't succeed for us.'" She said he also worried that an unsuccessful attempt would cost the lives of people needed to govern postwar Germany.

Another consideration in regard to killing Hitler was that his death alone might not be enough. "They thought, besides Hitler, without question they still had to kill Goebbels, Himmler, and Goering. Otherwise they would never be free of the government. And Stauffenberg kept waiting again and again for the chance where he'd at least get Himmler, too. And that was impossible.

"The question remains, one asks oneself in hindsight, whether it would not be better for the Germans to try something anyway. That's what the Stauffenbergs [Claus and his brother Berthold] thought. They decided it had to be attempted no matter how it came out. If it weren't tried it would be even worse, for the honor of Germany." The question of "honor," she said, posed a double bind for the officers involved. "They had to come to terms with the oaths they'd sworn, whether they could break them, nothing but such difficult questions. Germans *are* that way. They pose such questions endlessly."

For Helmuth von Moltke, the choice was easier. Oppose the Nazis by subterfuge while on duty, and prepare for their defeat while off duty. The work of the Kreisau Circle continued. Although never utilized after the war, the Kreisau documents eventually were printed. Before meeting with Freya von Moltke, I read them and found them in a way both impressive and somehow naive. But two points snagged me. One concerned the election to a would-be parliamentary body. Qualifications included being twenty-seven years old and male.

"Yes, that also shocked me," she said. "Somebody brought it to my attention and I said it's not true. I didn't believe it, because I know my husband didn't think that way."

She blamed the error, as she clearly considered it to be, on the haste with which the documents were pulled together for public consumption. And she said she recently reread a letter in which her husband wrote about the would-be office of president. He used the word *der Vorsitzende*, with the masculine article, then excused himself and said he meant *der* or *die*, the feminine article. "He is not that way," she said.

My second snagging point concerned religion. Much emphasis was placed on Christianity "as the basis for the moral and spiritual renewal of our people." The "two Christian churches" would have a major role in "shaping public life." The question begged to be asked: what about Judaism?

Mrs. von Moltke replied that the emphasis on the Catholic and Protestant churches had to do with the chasm between them. It was not meant to exclude Jews or any other minority, such as Jehovah's Witnesses, whom the Nazis also singled out for persecution. "Tolerance," she said, "was most important of all.

"In the last fifty years before the Nazis, the Jewish religion did not play a large role," she added. "We didn't know any Jews at all who were of 'Mosesian' belief. We didn't see at all it was a religious matter, not like the role the Jewish religion plays today. We weren't anti-Semitic, but we considered the Jews basically as if they were us."

Also, she said, the documents were not in their final form. "We were ready to change a lot." She also added that she herself only later realized what a "Jewish community of faith" was. "I said, 'Look, that is a *religion*.' I'd never seen it that way."

If the Kreisau group was ignorant about Judaism, it was not so about politics. In the village of Kreisau itself, the von Moltkes treated old acquaintances with new caution. "Naturally, they more or less were Nazis. Some were in the Party, some were not. But they did go along. And they didn't understand why we didn't, why we were opposed."

They knew?

"It was completely open we weren't Nazis. They didn't know we were actively against them, but they knew we didn't go along."

The big clue was the ordained Nazi greeting. "We always said 'Good morning!' first, not 'Heil Hitler!' The bad ones *then* said 'Heil Hitler!' But if they said 'Heil Hitler!' first and *then* we said 'Good morning!' it was a great affront. We didn't do that all the time. Sometimes we too said 'Heil Hitler!' It was not worth risking a lot only because one didn't say it."

Prudence on the street was echoed at lunch breaks during the Kreisau Circle meetings. "My husband said we were never to include anything political in a prayer." He was especially uneasy about a young servant known to be very nationalistic. "She was a good, true girl. And after July 20th [the day of the assassination attempt on Hitler] she went and denounced us."

Mrs. von Moltke said the girl testified that "at those people's there were always visitors and it certainly didn't have to do with correct things. And then she, her mother, and her family said, 'If our soldiers have to die because these people are against the Nazis, we have to denounce them quickly.' It is certainly understandable people thought that. If one could have removed the Nazis earlier, fewer soldiers would have died. They died because the Nazis started the war. But they couldn't think that far. It was all horribly complicated."

But she said, the members of the Kreisau Circle were not fearful. "We lived with the feeling what we did was right. That was much stronger. It's really true. We weren't afraid."

For any German who opposed the Nazis, doing what one thought was right often was tempered by the consideration of doing what one hoped was safe. Freya von Moltke faced her own personal dilemmas of degree not only along the streets of Kreisau, but a short walk away. There, forced laborers from a nearby "work camp" (the lowest rung of concentration camp) shored up a riverbank. She said the first workers on the project had been part of the German labor service. Later, working under heavy guard, came Russian war prisoners, then Jewish prisoners.

"We always saw them and we couldn't do anything for them. We couldn't give them anything. Never. You couldn't even pass them bread." Yet sister-in-law Asta von Moltke Henssel, who at her brother's urging had left the wartime dangers of Berlin to live in Kreisau, later told me the two women did sometimes "accidentally" drop bread or other food while walking by.

Frauen

Freya von Moltke said the efforts she and her husband already were making against the Nazis made them especially circumspect. But her admiration is unequaled for anti-Nazis who were not. "There were people . . . *all* were killed. There was the well-known Paul Schneider, a pastor. He always screamed in the concentration camp, from his cell, 'It's all criminal and horrendous,' and then they stopped up his mouth. Then they finally killed him. Screamed until he was dead. There are fabulous people." She said they "saved the German soul."

Such people, she said, are now discounted. "The resistance movement is not beloved today in Germany, among the Volk. People say, 'You didn't accomplish anything. You're no better than us.' "[11]

Freya von Moltke also judged the actions of her two brothers and herself, all of whom, she said, had been influenced by their open-minded and progressive mother more than by their Kaiser-yearning conservative father. She said her older brother, Carl, fled to Holland, then to Switzerland, to escape the Nazis and "falsified passports and helped as much as he could, but little." The Germans sent her other brother, Hans, to Italy, as a representative of the German government's chemical division.

"He sabotaged *enormously* and risked a lot. He was *shameless*. He was a young man, but nonetheless a leading businessman. And he always attended the meetings in Rome where the military situations were talked about, in the late part of the war. The German army people reported such and such a bridge had been bombed but now was repaired. He left, and outside stood his Italian friend, and he told him the bridge had been repaired. The next day, it was kaputt.[12]

"So, *he* risked something. But nothing happened to him. My brothers really hated the Nazis, and they reacted differently. Perhaps I would have been an anti-Nazi too, but I can't picture myself without my husband. I don't think I'd have had the courage. Don't make my role too big."

She made it even smaller. "I say that no one who survived in Germany is guiltless. Such a person does not exist. Such people do not exist. People who lived through the Nazi time and who still live, who did not lose their lives because they were opposed, all had to make compromises at whatever point. And among them, I also count myself."

---

11. The situation seems ever-changing, at least among younger Germans. She made the comment in 1985. In 1992, at the Hillel Foundation in Berkeley, Franz Josef Müller, head of the White Rose Foundation, said his organization could not keep up with requests to visit schools in western Germany to talk about resistance to the Nazis, but indicated that eastern Germans scorned the deeds of what they called "anti-Fascists" and had no interest in them.

12. For a fuller look at Hans Deichmann's resistance work, see "Der Ordinäre," 47–77.

Helmuth von Moltke, who wanted to live to see a new Germany, made compromises, too, but not enough to save his own life. In the autumn of 1943 he learned through a contact in the Luftwaffe that a Gestapo spy posing as an anti-Nazi recently had attended a Berlin anti-Nazi "salon," and that the Gestapo was about to arrest everyone the spy had seen and named. (The spy, supposedly a doctor, was the guest of a regular member, Elisabeth von Thadden, whom he had tricked, and named, and who was executed as a result.)[13] It has been written that von Moltke himself frequently attended the salon, although not that evening, but Mrs. von Moltke stated (in a letter in English) that he "did not attend the salon." She went on, "Helmuth always feared that people would *just talk* and endanger themselves for nothing. That is precisely what happened to that group."

Learning of the anticipated Gestapo roundup, von Moltke managed to warn his friend and colleague Otto Kiep, who warned the others. Despite the warnings, in January 1944 the participants were arrested.[14] So was von Moltke. In her letter, years after our meeting, Mrs. von Moltke named the fateful link to his arrest. "Helmuth was arrested because Kiep, under pressure, gave away Helmuth's name."

Shortly after the arrest, she got an oddly circuitous phone call from a friend. "It took a long time before I understood. He called up one morning in Kreisau and said, 'Helmuth is traveling.' I said, 'Oh? Where did he go?' Something like that. 'Yes, one doesn't know when he'll get back.' *Then* it began to dawn on me, he had been arrested." Technically, he had not been arrested, but been given "protective custody." But he was locked up.

Leaving the children in the care of her sister-in-law, Mrs. von Moltke immediately left for Berlin. On the trip, she figured out an approach to gain visiting rights. "At the prison, I said the firm was important to the war effort ["firms" producing food were indeed considered "important to the war effort"], that without his decision I couldn't do anything and I had to speak with him. And they let me."

A few days later, a large bombing attack near the prison prompted the Nazis to move their prisoners to another prison an hour's ride away. It was next to Ravensbrück women's concentration camp. Mrs. von Moltke said the prison had been a police school with barracks. She then made her way there, and got permission for monthly visits. The visits were long and almost private. "The barracks I entered contained an office and a narrow room, and in the corner a bench and table and an SS man, but less than that, an SA

---

13. For more on the calamitous downfall of the group, see Irmgard von der Lühe, *Eine Frau im Widerstand, Elisabeth von Thadden und das Dritte Reich* (A woman in the resistance, Elisabeth von Thadden and the Third Reich) (Freiburg im Breisgau: Herderbucherei, 1980). My thanks to her nephew, Dr. Rudolf von Thadden, for the gift of it and his insights.
14. Among those executed as a result of being named was Kiep.

man. My husband and I sat behind him. We were with each other for two hours. And my husband brought a pan with him and said, 'My wife has to travel soon, could you make some tea for her?' And he made me tea, and there we sat, and talked."

That her husband had what she called "a privileged position" was made even clearer on another visit. When she arrived, they were designated a private room for their visit. But caution defined the walk to it. "As we went up the stairs, my husband made a sign to me to start talking and be heard by the man in the corner. We talked of children and the farm, things we also talked about very happily. But never about political matters. He gave me a few warnings for people, not to return to Germany or they'd immediately be arrested. Such things naturally were said, too." She said she delivered the warnings to a man who had safe passage through Germany and Switzerland.

Asked her mood during the visits, she said, "Oh, I was happy that I saw him. My mood was good." His mood was good, too, she said. Between visits, as always, they wrote. His letters got through fine, if "a little censored. Then the people said his letters were too long, he shouldn't write so much. But they didn't censor my letters. And they were always insanely interested in what I wrote. Remarkable, how interested they were. Naturally, I again wrote mostly about the farm. They read it all. They were always very friendly to me, these men."

The men belonged to a diabolically powerful group, the SD (Sicherheitsdienst), the intelligence branch of the SS. Their "friendly" interest in the von Moltkes once took a bizarre twist.

Arriving one day for a scheduled visit, Mrs. von Moltke was greeted at the door by an agent who had obviously been reading her last letters. "Oh, Countess von Moltke!" he said. "I am *so* sorry you're having such trouble with your geese."

She repeated the incident to her husband. "I told Helmuth, 'These are really very friendly people,' and he said, 'Apart from the fact that they tear your fingernails out.'"

That he himself was not tortured was an unusual luxury. In fact, he had a relatively comfortable stay at the Ravensbrück site. The von Moltkes even had hopes he would be released that autumn. One positive sign was that his office in Foreign Intelligence had begun sending him paperwork to complete. "When he was in jail, I did not think it would turn out badly." But an event that summer insured it would.

One of the many grotesque ironies of the Nazi era is that Helmuth von Moltke is known today primarily for his one major act against the Nazis that led to nothing—forming the Kreisau Circle—and that his fate was determined not by the many actions he did undertake against them, but by the one he disavowed—the 1944 attempted assassination of Adolf Hitler.

As the situation inside and outside Germany worsened and the war grew, so too grew an increasing passion among certain people in Germany to get rid of Hitler. But an inverse proportion was at work. The more people wanted to kill Hitler, the less chance Hitler gave them. Paranoid (and with reason, considering earlier failed attempts to kill him), he was rarely seen in public; in private ever fewer people had access to him. As Freya von Moltke pointed out, the very nature of a dictatorship makes it "extraordinarily difficult" to get rid of a dictator.

By the summer of 1944, Hitler was visible in person only to a small and trusted inner circle. The circle included Lt. Col. Claus von Stauffenberg. On July 20, 1944, while Helmuth von Moltke was a prisoner of the Nazis, von Stauffenberg arrived at a meeting of Hitler's inner circle, placed his briefcase containing a time bomb under the section of the table where Hitler was sitting, and left the room on a pretext. It might be noted to anyone unfamiliar with the story that von Stauffenberg, because of his battle injuries, was missing one eye, one hand, and two fingers of his other hand, and presumably could not have managed a quick draw of a gun. Presumably, too, he did not want to be a martyr. To sum up the familiar sequence of what happened next, the bomb went off, but merely injured Hitler. His wrath, however, was unrestrained.

Among the first of nearly two hundred people put to death was von Stauffenberg himself. A major participant sentenced to death soon thereafter was Peter Yorck, not only von Stauffenberg's cousin but Helmuth von Moltke's close friend and fellow Kreisau Circle founder. Yorck's execution, like that of many others, was gruesome. His widow, Marion, like her lifetime friend Freya, never remarried.

The assassination attempt also was fatal to Helmuth von Moltke. Although he claimed not to have known of the conspiracy itself, a claim his widow vigorously seconded, he certainly knew the conspirators.

She learned of the attempt from a newspaper while in Kreisau, and realized she had been quite close to it. During the preceding months, some of the men involved had visited her. "They were very nice, but did not tell me about what they were doing. It would have been too dangerous, for them and for me. One didn't know if I'd be picked up or if it came out, you know? When too many know, it's always a very dangerous matter."

She visited her husband at Ravensbrück in early August. "They didn't yet know he was so well acquainted with these people, that he was a friend of those involved." But he was afraid the link would be discovered and he would not be able to write her what was going on. So he worked out a code.

"Forty acres must be harvested without delay," she said, meant "it's hopeless." "Twenty acres must be harvested" meant "I have a chance, but it bodes poorly." Finally, "If I write nothing about acres, they haven't found out anything."

During the trials of the assassination conspirators, Helmuth von Moltke's friendships were discovered. (She did not know what effect the young servant's testimony had.) The Nazis "naturally were furious, when they realized they'd had him sitting there." She said she did not know how his name was brought out. "He definitely was not denounced. But if one is being tried under terrible conditions, one says some things."

In Kreisau, she got a letter that said twenty acres must be harvested.

On September 29, her husband was transferred to a prison in Berlin to be tried before the infamous People's Court. The letters stopped coming. "After a month of not hearing anything, I went to Ravensbrück and took a few things with me. A suit, undershirts. And they immediately gave me all his clothes, all the things he had there." She was told it was good she had come, that "he's just gone to Berlin and needs a suit." She then went to the designated prison in Berlin, was told "der Lange" [the tall one—he was 6'6"] was not there. Because another bombing attack had destroyed all the cells, he had been transferred to Berlin's Tegel Prison. "And not only was he there, but so was our friend Poelchau, the prison pastor."

The name Harald Poelchau lights up the face of anyone who knew him. Active in the resistance, and indeed a member of the Kreisau Circle, he became not only an intermediary between prisoners and their families but a spiritual helpmeet to the prisoners condemned to die for their opposition to the Nazis. It was to him they spoke their last words.

"I shouldn't have called him, but I did and said, 'Helmuth is there.' He said, 'Come early tomorrow, in my visitors' time.' Then I went there early in the morning and got an appointment, and I saw Helmuth at the gate. He was in a striped concentration camp suit." She said she later got permission from the People's Court to visit. "I saw him a few times. Always very brief, with the prison director in the same room. But it was nonetheless *meeting*."

Sometimes she and the wife of another prisoner sat outside the prison door, waiting to visit, and talking. The other couple maintained one had to think positively, that the men would survive. Her husband did not agree. "Helmuth always said, 'We have to leave it open. It can go this way or that, but one can't just say that in any event we'll survive. We can't know that.' And that's the way we lived."

"There could have been something that saved him. Some were saved. We thought maybe the Allies would still come. Maybe the Russians would come quickly. A bomb could have fallen in the prison and he could escape. That one I never believed. He was *gigantic*. [Not in girth, but height.] He'd never have been able to hide. One would have known immediately it was he."

With his status in Tegel clearly more precarious than in Ravensbrück, Mrs. von Moltke's visits to her husband no longer were low-key get-togethers meant to bide time until his release, but urgent missions connected with working out his trial defense, and saving his and others' lives. "I always left the children with Asta and then went to Berlin and tried this and that and brought food and had visiting permission and tried to report to the others what their line of defense might be. Then I had to go to the other prisons where the others were, with whom he was later sentenced, and tried to smuggle in information."

He wanted her to do that?

"Someone *had* to do it," she replied. "And I got inside. We also had women who brought sandwiches and there were papers in them. . . . All that belongs to the world of prisons," she said, laughing.

But Freya von Moltke did not need to rely on communication by sandwich, for she had her own smuggler. "At the prison, the good Poelchau always took my letters inside, daily letters that were carried in and taken out. Up to the end. Four months long, Poelchau did that."

One day her husband gave her an especially difficult mission. He thought that if he could talk privately with Heinrich Himmler's second in command, Gestapo chief Heinrich Müller, he could convince him he had had nothing to do with the assassination plot. She was to go to the Gestapo headquarters in Berlin, housed in a large and intimidating building, meet Müller, and persuade him to meet with her husband.

"That was a fright. I went up there, inside this 'palace.' There was an anteroom where I waited and then was led to Herr Müller. I said, 'It's not at all true, what is being said about my husband. You must speak with him.' I acted, of course, as if I knew nothing. Obviously. I don't know if he believed me or if he *wanted* to believe me." In any event, Müller's reply was, "I'll do it gladly."

But he also wanted to tell her something else. "He said that 'your husband did insane things and later I'll tell you all about it and then you will *understand* us.' That is how he spoke to me. I was beside myself, and I said, 'This I will say to you, General Müller. I will raise my children to *respect* their father.' That's what I told him. Then he said"—she imitated him—"'*That* you may do, *that* you may do.' It all *impressed* him. Ach, and thereby I saved my soul."

Müller, she said, was typical of members of the Nazi hierarchy who criticized her husband but praised her. "And that was always monstrous to me."

Her encounter was not yet over. "Müller was so polite, he ran after me in the hall and then said, 'When everything is all over . . . ' That means when my husband is *dead*. 'Then do come back to us. We're not at all like you think. Come back to us.'

"Imagine that! They offered money, maintenance, to many wives because they actually respected them for having the courage to be against them. They wanted to win over the wives and above all to make the children Nazis. They're a remarkable people, aren't they? They had the concept of an elite, a Nazi elite. We were people whom they gladly would have won over. Precisely because we were the way we were. That was the Nazis for you. *Completely* different from the Communists. Because the Communists hated the old classes, no? And we were of the old classes and the Nazis found that wonderful. I wasn't, I was a regular burgher's daughter. But the von Moltke family naturally got different consideration."

The meeting between Helmuth von Moltke and Heinrich Müller took place at Gestapo headquarters. "It didn't help. Müller did not understand him. My husband is difficult to understand. He's completely atypical. He was a man unto himself alone."

The ordeal of trying to save her husband wiped out most of her optimism. "It was horrendous, when I think about it again. There was nothing that worked, nothing that bore fruit, nothing came of anything. I always had the feeling it's not working, it's not working, it's going badly."

In addition, another major problem literally came to the Kreisau doorstep. As 1944 drew to a close, the Russian Army rolled westward, preceded by a massive early warning system—enormous numbers of panicked and fleeing German civilians.

In anticipation of the Russians, the Nazi government had evacuated pregnant women, among them Helmuth von Moltke's pregnant sister, Asta, to military hospitals in western Germany. She left Kreisau after Freya von Moltke had temporarily returned from Berlin, just as the refugees began arriving. "One had to be there. There was a terrible commotion. One could not always be going to Berlin."

Another ghastly irony was upon her. The advancing Russian Army, which caused the panicked stampede she felt she had to face in Kreisau, was the same force that determined her husband's final fate in Berlin. "The Justice Minister had to sign any death sentences before they could be carried out," she said, her voice ever calm. "We heard he [the minister] would be away from Berlin for four weeks. But then the Russians moved through the west with such might, the Nazis got scared." They called the Justice Minister back "and he signed *ten* death sentences. The one for my husband was among them. It was so . . . surprising."

There was no way of knowing when the verdict would be carried out. "I thought to myself, I cannot go to Berlin again. I simply must leave to the future whatever happens. There were people going to Berlin who would tell him I could not be with him, that I couldn't come until something settled down. It was simply too dangerous to leave the children there alone. We were agreed about it. He wrote back, yes, it's completely right, you must keep watch and see how things progress."

Eventually, she did feel able to leave her children safely in Kreisau, and went to Berlin. When she got there, she hid in the home of Pastor Poelchau, hiding to protect him, not her. He continued to smuggle letters back and forth between the couple, now in their thirteenth year of marriage.

One afternoon in January 1945, "Poelchau, the dear pastor, came home and I sat there and I wrote him a letter for the next day, you see. He came to the house in the afternoon around three, and had presided at a funeral for, oh, I don't know for whom. He also had friends outside and had done this funeral for someone. And I said, 'How did it go?' Completely friendly, about the funeral. And then he told me.

"I hadn't noticed anything, so to speak. By then he was already dead." Freya von Moltke's voice dropped until it was almost inaudible. "Three o'clock he came to the house. 'At two o'clock Helmuth lost his life.' "

Amid the tangle of aftermath was a thought.

"He himself wasn't even so *proud* of what he had done. I don't know if it ever will be recognized what we did, and that we did it. He didn't even know whether it would be acknowledged later, how it would be judged. He had no notion at all. He died despised and not knowing if what he did had any effect."

He knew one major effort did not. According to remarkable U.S. Office of Strategic Services documents released by the CIA in 1990 (and the basis of an article in the October 1992 edition of the *Vierteljahrshefte für Zeitgeschichte* [Quarterly historical journal] of the Historical Institute in Munich), von Moltke had a U.S. code name, "Herman." He offered the OSS a secret "Herman Plan," to coordinate resistance efforts inside Germany with Allied troops. The OSS gathered lengthy written responses from experts (some highly suspicious about "Herman's" motives), then turned him down.

After her husband's murder, Freya von Moltke returned to Kreisau, and her two young sons. "The small one understood nothing at all and the bigger one understood everything. It was one of the worst hours of my life, when I had to tell him that his father was dead.

"But then came an extraordinary comfort. Two days later, in the morning, he came into my room and found me in bed and I was crying. And he said, 'You're crying? Why are you crying?' And I said, 'Well, now.' And he said, '*Still* because of Pa?' That comforted me so *extraordinarily*, that a child could not comprehend it after all. *Still* because of his father? I said to myself, thank God, he does not understand what happened." She laughed. "I still see him before me.

"Women who lost their husbands in the horrendous war and even here, in this country, experienced far worse than I. For them it was horrible, the men simply going off to war and then never coming back. Many lost husbands who hated Hitler and they nonetheless were killed. That is *bitter*. But for me, everything was worthwhile. I thought, he has fulfilled his life. And he did. Definitely.

"When you talk with me for a long while," she said, "you understand that one lives a whole lifetime from such an experience. When he was killed, I had two delightful children, two dear sons. I thought, so. That is enough for a whole life."

Frau Erna Tietz

The Schisms of a "Flakwaffenhelferin"

"Not only do I trust men now much, much less, but my esteem toward men has been absolutely destroyed. Absolutely." Did she ever marry? "Nein." Perhaps for that reason? "Nein. Perhaps I may explain it to you this way." She said that when she was a young person and always for justice, it was common for girls and boys to play together. "And I was always furious then that *only* the boys decided. . . . Even with the smallest games, they always had the say." The children all had been "playful, there was no hate, but it was just 'We boys have the say. We boys are the stronger ones and we will prove it.' That rankled me and then I said, 'So. That is not fair.' "

When Erna Tietz grew up, she shot down airplanes.

The first time we talked, Frau Tietz and I were riding a loud-braking train south to her home in Marburg from Bad Pyrmont, the site of a gathering of former East Prussians such as herself. She was born in the city of Preussisch Eylau in 1921. Her one sibling, a sister named Annemarie, was born a year later. Frau Tietz said their childhood was secure at first. Their father worked for the "regional construction office," which oversaw road-building programs, but then, like many men during the upheavals of the 1920s, he lost his job. She remembered his having stomach trouble and always being "gehandikapt." To live more cheaply, the Tietzes moved to the countryside, and eventually built a small cottage. In the country, Herr Tietz got whatever work he could and his wife got work in a dairy outlet "where milk, butter, and cheese and all [was sold] right from the central [farms], nicht? She almost directed it for more then ten years. And therefore things were good for us. We lacked for nothing, nicht? We grew up very well. Strong and healthy." Her daughter laughed. "Mother was a *thoroughly* dear woman who was always there for the family."

She also was the center of an incident Frau Tietz remembered clearly and repeated twice. The year was 1943. By then, Erna had spent years in the Bund deutscher Mädel, a group she recalled with "enthusiasm," especially for its "cohesion." She liked that "the simple child of a worker sat next to the daughter of the mayor." Erna also had spent several years in a "sport training curriculum" before joining the German army. At the time of the incident, she was in uniform, and home on leave.

"My mother said to me, she said, 'Erna,' said she, 'I have to go to Ullenberg.' And Ullenberg was a clothing store that belonged to a Jew. My mother always shopped there. My mother was a thoroughly brave woman." When I expressed surprise that a Jewish shop was still in business, Frau Tietz insisted that Ullenberg's was, although it had "Don't Buy From Jews" placards on the windows. She said there were no SA men at the door, but there were some in town, and they knew everyone.

"And you can imagine, everyone who nonetheless bought from Jews, we were then already so, eh, somewhat spied on, nicht? But I said, 'Mutti,' I can still hear myself today as I was then, 'Mutti, I cannot go inside with you.' You know, this schism. I am now in the army and then I should go in a Jewish store as a young person? And then Mutti said, 'Why not then? Come along.' Then I said, 'Mutti, I can't.' There, can you picture this being torn back and forth of a young person? I would *like* to. I have nothing against the human beings, but I *may* not. Well, I still see this schism in me, I see the store in front of me, and then my mother did go inside, and bought . . . Jawohl, my mother was very courageous. Perhaps I got my courage from her. And I stood there outside, but had a very, very, very bad feeling. I cannot describe the feeling, eh, menschlich [from a human point of view]. I knew that menschlich it was not the right way. But from the point of view of the Party, if they had seen me in uniform. . . . For the first time I knew that the humane stood to the rear of the Party-political. And I can never forgive myself.

"If someone is persecuted today, if he proved himself a human being and had committed no criminal act, I would bring him into my home. I would help him. Whoever does not learn that is poorer for it. And many have not yet learned that, and that is what depresses me and also perplexes me."

While her mother was inside, Erna stayed outside and looked in, hearing nothing, but following the hand motions of her mother and the proprietor throughout the transaction. "I waited until my mother came out and then she said, 'Well then, shall we go?' My mother did not discuss things very long, but she said, 'Ernachen, I want to tell you something. Jews are also human beings.' And what my mother told me, that always got to me. I was someone not very easy to convince and had a thick head, a thoroughly, thoroughly, immensely thick head. But I have learned. Therefore I say today, Negro, Jew, it's the same to me. If he behaves toward me like a human being, if he didn't, eh, I should say, somehow didn't do anything inhuman, like for example, rob a bank or hit someone or shoot or whatever, and if I have to share my last piece of bread with him and share my last money with him, that's how I see it today."

More accurately, that is partly how she sees it.

At the East Prussian gathering, Frau Tietz had not stood out, that I observed. But in the intimacy of a European train compartment, she seemed to be opening up by the second, even though we had barely met. Plainly dressed, with no makeup, she gave rather the appearance of a mature camp counselor who will keep the girls singing on the hike even after the rain starts. Once the tape recorder began rolling, she gave her date of birth and headed straight to the war. "Germany was fighting on many fronts at the time, nicht?" Sometimes, over the sounds of the wheels, only phrases came through: about wear and tear on the soldiers, about a lack of reserves in the Heimat, and about "getting the enemy airplanes in the cross hairs."

Around 1937, when Erna Tietz was a teenager, she saw Adolf Hitler in a procession in Königsberg. She was with her BdM group. What did Hitler look like? A "normal human being." He went by quickly, past a "wide, enormous mass of people." What happened when he went by? "Jubilation. Jubilation. And I cheered with jubilation, too, nicht?"

She said (another time we met) that she now thinks of Hitler as "a devil in a human form." But then, "I would have said he is a human being who promised to help us in a difficult situation, in a crisis situation. And we at the time blindly, I would like to say with complete honesty, trusted . . . And *this* trust was *so horribly* and dreadfully disappointed."

During the war, did she consider him a leader?

"Nein, nein. I must contradict you." She said she thought whoever was in charge of any branch of the armed forces "needed first of all a thoroughly solid education. He had to have gone to college and not be just a little corporal." She got worried, she said, as soon as former Corporal Hitler took over the army himself. "Why are generals there who have studied a long time, who knew about the whole story exactly? And then along comes someone like that, who was politically very engaging and showed that he could accomplish something, but I doubted it would go well. That was already my opinion." She was right on target. German generals would have agreed with her then, as historians do now.[1] Frau Tietz said at another point the reason she had "an unholy feeling" the war would not go well was because Germany "assaulted" and "marched" into too many fronts, and had neither enough soldiers nor weaponry to win. (And Hitler remained intractable on the subject of drafting women for any military role.)

Assuming her perception about the lack of soldiers was made then, it not only was correct but was precisely the reason the German armed forces began employing tens of thousands of women such as Erna in military jobs. The women freed the men to fight.[2]

In 1943, when she was about twenty-two, Erna Tietz learned how to operate the searchlights that sought out Allied planes in the night skies. Following her training, she was sent to Berlin and assigned to a searchlight mission [Scheinwerfereinsatz]. The searchlights could reach up to nine thousand meters, she said. But when die Englander und die Amerikaner flew at ten thousand meters to avoid them, "our searchlights were too small."

So, in 1944, she was retrained, as a Flakwaffenhelferin. In a direct translation of the German euphemism, she was a female "flak weapons helper." In more straightforward English, she was an antiaircraft gunner. Rather than aim a searchlight at Allied airplanes, she aimed a gun. She called it "a big gun," an "eight-eight." What was it? The first expert I asked knew right away. Ed Green of the Presidio Army Museum in San Francisco called the German eighty-eight-caliber antiaircraft gun "a hundred times better than anything we had." The famous, accurate, powerful, long-barreled gun was so big, he said, it required a team of at least three people to operate it: someone to focus, someone to load the shells, someone to fire. ("We each had a function," said Frau Tietz.) Mr. Green called it a "good tank-killing gun," too, and said it could hit a person from fifteen hundred yards.[3] But its main purpose was to hit airplanes. And that is what Frau Tietz and two batteries of women under her command used it for.

---

1. For a fascinating and lucidly written summary of how Hitler conducted the war, see the last chapter of Gordon A. Craig's *Germany 1866–1945*, called "Hitler's War." (New York: Oxford University Press, 1980), 714–764.
2. Ursula von Gersdorff, *Frauen im Kriegsdienst 1914–1945* (Women in war duty 1914–1945) (Stuttgart: Deutsche Verlags-Anstalt, 1969). See also Jutta Rüdiger, *Zur Problematik von Soldatinnen* (On the ambiguity regarding female soldiers) (Lindhorst: Askania, 1987), about the role of the Flakwaffenhelferinnen. Thanks to Agnes Peterson.
3. Telephone interview, June 22, 1992.

Frauen

If she had been trained a fraction as carefully as she was evaluated, she must have done her duty well.

Rendsburg, March 5, 1944

Evaluation

Flakwaffenhelferin Erna Tietz

a. *Mental and physical predispositions:* spiritual [or intellectual], capable, interested, good memory, catches on easily
   Physical: tall, well-grown, athletic, sturdy, open, cheerful look, hardy [literally, capable of resistance]
b. *Individual Characteristics:* brisk, industrious, willing, dependable

Record: very good
Punishments: none

A year later, she received more training and another report:

Leipzig, April 2, 1945

Evaluation

Special training   8.8 cm Flak 37

Mental and physical predispositions—Mentally good, capable, physically strong, athletically proportioned

Adolf Hitler would kill himself within four weeks and the war would end within five, but the Wehrmacht took time to note that Flakwaffenhelferin Erna Tietz not only was mentally sound, but athletically proportioned.

Frankly, it was Erna Tietz's mental state that interested me. She did mention, as the train stopped and started, that her assignment to shoot down Allied airplanes had bothered her. Why? Because she did not like that the Nazis were hiding from the German public the fact that women were being used to shoot down planes. Frau Tietz's identification "only says ZBV [zur besonderen Verwendung (for special use)]. That means they did not admit that I was with the eight-eight and schooled in how to use it." ZBV could mean a lot of things, she said. "Maybe I could have been active in news gathering for the Wehrmacht, or in the secretarial pool, or distribution of clothing, or so. One wanted to avoid that the public learn that women were assigned to weapons. That one wanted to veil. You see, I am entirely honest. I also have the courage to tell you everything. I have always been courageous."

She also said the ZBV designation did give the women "a small cloak of protection" from any Allied soldiers who may have read the women's identification. "They could have questioned me so long, and maybe also under pressure, until I was ready to declare which 'purpose.' But they did not ask."

Frau Tietz's primary assignment as a Flakwaffenhelferin was at an installation of eighty-eights near Frankfurt am Main.

Did she know if she hit any planes?

She said nein three times, then added, "Well, I did not know, because several guns were in position everywhere around us and I don't know if *our* gun, that *we* had in position, shot down a plane. One could, one knew. . . . That I still don't know today. And thank God, I also was *only* there a short time, because the capitulation was in May and I was not there that long, that is, not a whole year and maybe. . . . But must have been about half a year on assignment, nicht?" (The first evaluation shows she was a Flakwaffenhelferin more than a year, although not necessarily on assignment.)

Her flak colleagues in Frankfurt were all young women about her age, some as young as eighteen. Asked about their mood, she said, "Partly this way, part that way. I came from East Prussia where there was scarcely any fighting or airplanes. The mood among the girls was basically good, but in part also not good if they [came] from Hamburg, from Frankfurt or also from bigger . . . Cologne, the whole Ruhr, where there was a lot of industry. When, for example, these bombing attacks kept getting stronger, then they said, 'What is all this for?' They saw this misery. We did not." She acknowledged that such candor meant her colleagues trusted her. "For we could not pass it on, nicht? They would definitely have been punished, nicht? But"— she paused—"today it would be entirely the same to me, whoever was in need, whether a Negro, an Indian, a white, or a black, I have already said, *I* see first of all a human being. Nationality or skin color are exactly the same to me, whoever meets me as a human being and needs my help, but without weapons, never again take a weapon in my hand. Never again. I mean, I'm not asked anymore, purely because of age alone. I would also *hesitate* today, even if only a pistol, and so on, nicht? [I would] help any human being who is in need. But nothing more than that."

During the war, however, her view (which she repeated several times) was different. "Our soldiers are at the front and are supposed to protect us, the people, and the land. And we were ordered to contribute a very little bit. But today, never again. No more 'Einsatz' [assignment]. I would reject it on principle." She added that she now very much opposes women being soldiers. "I would say, in secretarial assignments, information desk, ja, but *not* the way we were. And this concealment under ZBV, not to have the courage. . . . These were young girls in a very dangerous situation. And if the Americans, English, French, or the Russian come and then surprise these girls *at* their weapons, we definitely would have been [treated] just like the soldiers, and rightly so, for we also shot."

She had implied at one point that she considered the Second World War to have been defensive (from the German point of view), but pinning her down on the matter proved difficult. She reiterated her opposition to any war, repeated that the German soldiers were "defending us, helping us, wanting to protect us," spoke of archives in various "states" having different documents claiming different things, then said, "The Second World War was in my mind a war of defense. That is how I see it." Questioned closely, she backtracked. "But no longer as, I want to say, as convinced as I was then. I waver [schwanke]. I now waver somewhat." She should. On this military matter, she is completely wrong.

She continued, after a while, "I don't believe anymore, I must honestly say. I only now believe what I myself see, what I myself hear, what I myself can read. I don't believe any more politicians today. I don't believe any of them, no high general and so on. I have become almost an unbeliever, in that I think the political parquet has lost its polish. Many tripped on this political parquet."

Does she trust men less than she did?

"Absolutely. Absolutely." The word she used was *restlos*, which she trilled for emphasis. Rrrrrestlos.

It was men who ordered Erna Tietz and other Helferinnen to Frankfurt am Main and men who, in the face of advancing American troops, ordered the young women to stay put. "When the Americans came and our barracks already were beginning to shake, our battery officer said, well, the battery command ordered that the 'helpers' must stay where they've been assigned. That meant to wait until the Americans are *there*, nicht? And maybe oppose them afterward with a couple guns, eh, still a couple of lines. But then *our* battery leader said, 'I am taking over responsibility. *My* battery packs it in immediately and then we try to take over another position. We are setting ourselves apart from this battery order,' nicht? So the 'helpers' will not be delivered to the Americans. And then later we were underway, no longer during the day, all of us leaders [Führerinnen], we each got a troop of girls in our command and . . . we then had to steer a course and then always brought our 'helpers' to this goal."

Of her own rank, she explained, "I was a Führerin at the time and that means in the range of a lieutenant. I never admitted it, though. I had an incredible amount of fear this rank would become known, nicht?" She said the rebellious battery officer led two large batteries of troops comprised of "*nothing* but girls in my age range" away from Frankfurt and the American front and toward Leipzig . . . and the Russian front. She said she and the other Flakwaffenhelferinnen prayed that the Americans would get to them first.

The young women and their commander, traveling only under cover of darkness, arrived in Leipzig around April 1945, she said. (Her certified last segment of training was dated early April.) There they encountered retreating German soldiers from the east who "always called us 'children.' [The term is meant paternally.] They didn't say 'girls,' nicht? Or 'helpers.'" One

272

soldier said that no one from the east should even try to get home, but that anyone from the west was free to hide on the weapons under his tarpaulin and make a run from the Russians for the west with his unit. The condition was, if Frau Tietz and the other Führerinnen said they could. "And then I thought, *my* God, you have the responsibility. You now have a troop of girls in your command, and then I also saw, what is more important . . . One did not know anymore at all *where* the enemy is anyway, how much longer will the war go on. Then on my responsibility, I let the girls who came from the west get up, simply covered them with the tarp. They left, and then I still had a small group." They all ran off during the night. Of those who left under the tarp, Frau Tietz said, "maybe I even saved some." She said the incident taught her "that I also had the courage my mother did."

Shortly after arriving in Leipzig, rather than taking over another flak installation as they had expected to, they were met by an army paymaster. "One more time we received a little sum and a small piece of soap, I remember as if it were today, in the hand. And then it was, we could now go wherever we wanted to."

But they had no idea where. They were between American and Russian troops, wearing German uniforms, carrying German identification, and, to hear her tell it, seething at German commanders. "Madness, what they did with us. Madness. Nobody in the leadership of the armed forces really knew what was going on, who was coming from the east, who was coming from the west, who is where. Everything afterward was fully chaotic, nicht?"

The Russians got to them first. Unbeknownst to Frau Tietz, her sister and parents were enduring unchecked Russian wrath back in East Prussia, but she herself, the only person in the family active in the war, "had the best luck" with her Russian captors. She was able to convince them she had been assigned to her Einsatz because of a lack of soldiers and had only been assigned within Germany, rather than in the east. "That was decisive for me. Otherwise I wouldn't be here today. Otherwise I would long have been in the ground." Thanks to a fellow "helper" who had connections, Frau Tietz "landed in good hands and came through the three years of the whole Russian time very well," by working on a farm.

Not until she was on the Russian-controlled POW farm, said Frau Tietz, did she learn about the consequences of not following orders. Among her fellow prisoners were German women who had been imprisoned for listening to forbidden radio broadcasts. (It seems the Russians took over the farm and detained the Germans already there, along with the new prisoners.) She said that some of her friends had listened to the verboten broadcasts, but she had not known the act was punishable by arrest. And she herself had not listened to them, but had *watched* people listening.

"I just looked in and noticed what was going on. I never heard the broadcasts once. Just peeked in and only waved and then saw how they all listened in front of the set. Shhhhhh, nicht?" She described the people as being in a multifamily house, their heads "under the pillow and they sat together and then people outside in front of the door standing guard, looking out the window and so on. Woe if someone moves on the stairs. Turn it off. Turn it off. Turn it off. And only then look outside, who's there, everything is okay, someone else comes, let in, everything locked up again, nicht? And then there they sat at the radio. I still see many groups sitting with their ears on the set, so that the tone was not too loud." The set was put as far as possible from the corridor in apartments, she said, and in "lightly built" homes "one sought out a room where one had the opportunity to listen fairly undisturbed and without a stranger being able to."

After the broadcasts, the listeners repeated what was said. "And then, naturally, it started. In any event, everything was discussed. Can that be? Do you all believe that? The 'Ami [American]' said that, the Frenchman that, the Englishman that, and so on. We do not believe it, we *cannot* believe it, we may simply not believe it. And Goebbels told us this, the Wehrmacht told us this and this, and now the Englishman [said] exactly the opposite. Ja, what now should we believe? They doubted.

"I must say with complete honesty, we, the younger ones, did not see it as so severe, that someone who heard a foreign broadcast, that he would be taken away. And at the time, as young people we said, well, they just want to hear once what the 'Ami' and the Englishman and the Frenchman says, but they lie. . . . [With] the older people, who had *more* experience, the broadcasts threw them into doubt, made them think, also discussed it, said there *must* be something true in it. But then again and again this counterpropaganda, this entirely clever subverting propaganda from Goebbels. Invalidating everything."

The reason she never listened to the broadcasts, she said, was that they were "uninteresting." Plus, "I just believed thoroughly in what our government said. Not only Goebbels alone, but our army reports. And that's how it was."

In such broadcasts, something about the concentration camps may have come up. Was that discussed in the group? "Ja, that, too . . . And they then, ja, they were thrown into doubts, because we ourselves did not *know* a lot. And that came from a foreign country and then we said, 'That's only counterpropaganda.' Do you understand correctly? We never somehow saw a KZ camp." She also said that she and her friends did not know the initials stood for concentration camp. "We always said a concert camp [Konzertlager]. Well, that's a jolly camp for, eh, for a place to vacation."

Then she learned that her local shoe repair man had been released from a camp himself. "And then I asked, 'Shoemaker Menz, what is that really, a KZ?' And he said, 'Ja, I have been there, but I'm not allowed to speak about it.' Never learned anything from him. I thought, well, if he doesn't want to, or may not speak about it, or whatever, I, I didn't consider it important. Never brought up the theme again. And the others, they, ach, 'concert camp,' nicht?" She seemed to have known the term was a joke (she would have been only twelve when the first camps were built and barely a teenager when *KZ* was becoming part of the Third Reich vocabulary), but she insisted she did not know what a camp really was. "We only knew, that is a place somewhere, or a house."

She did not know that *K* stood for *Konzentration?*

"Nein, nein. Only always [said] KZ, but concentration camp, that we didn't know. And we then later made 'Konzertlager' out of it. We were . . . Who knows, what they said against Hitler or Goering or whomever. They disappeared. Gone."

What she does not understand, she said, is why leading politicians outside Germany who could affect world history with great ease ("shake it out of their sleeves") and who, she said, knew what Hitler wanted to do, did not stop him. She quickly added, "I mean, I do not somehow now want to shift the blame somehow in *that* direction. That is what I as [a] small lay person cannot comprehend. And what I also do not comprehend is, if our officers could peek behind the scenes and knew that in part everything already was lost," why none of them had the courage to act. "And there may have been one possibility, no matter how harsh it sounds from the mouth of a woman. [She presumably meant killing Hitler.] But I mean, they did see *which* situation we would face if it kept going. They knew a lot more than we little citizens did."

In a related context, she said, "I am for an entirely clear ja, for an entirely hard no. I am not for this seesawing, when the other doesn't know how I feel. And I also have the courage always to stand behind this clear yes, behind this hard no." Frau Tietz wended her way to the more personal. "That is which perhaps brought me, eh, I would like to say, not to marry." She said her father knew her to a T. "He always said, 'Mädchen, if you don't change, you will never marry.'" She is not, "I would like to say, 'eine Emanze,' that is, a woman who always has to be right, or as one says here in Germany, a 'Mannweib,' more man than woman. I am not that." Another reason she did not marry, she said, was that the war destroyed something within her.

But what came through over and over in Frau Tietz's testimony is that she lost her trust of men. Decades of work after the war in a utility company did not improve her trust. "Today it's still, if the woman accomplishes more, only then will the men recognize her. But if the woman accomplishes the same as a man, then nothing."

In the cozy, if loud, train compartment, a day after hearing at Bad Pyrmont the worst anti-Semite I could have conjured, Frau Tietz seemed downright noble. Having had nobody else to talk to, I told her what Frau Mundt had said. If I expected someone to reflect my reactions, I was wrong. Frau Tietz responded with somber consideration. When I said Frau Mundt doubted there was gassing, Frau Tietz said, "Nein, I do not see it that way."

But she quoted a supposed expert who had just addressed the East Prussians on the question. "He said that this number cannot be found anywhere, in no archive. Therefore I am very skeptical. Please, try to understand that I say if I myself had counted, I would believe it."

Soon she said, in reference to a concentration camp, there "is a feeling of guilt that burdens many Germans very much."

I told her she was the first person I heard refer to it.

"It distresses me very much. Eh, well, now and then there are sort of excerpts, there are films which in part lay buried somewhere or maybe the conquering powers [Siegermächte] here and there . . . And in a roundabout way these films came to Germany. They are always shown here. It is horrifying."

One certainly horrified her. She and her sister were eating supper one evening while the television was on. "We were not paying attention at all to what was being broadcast and then came a report about the, I don't know, about which KZ. Auschwitz or, or where, I don't know anymore. So, I can't say exactly. It was horrifying. My sister and I, we took our plates to the kitchen as *quickly* as we could. The last bite, that did not go down. It shook us so much, insane, we *never* did . . . well, in this whole Nazi time, never knew what happened there. We didn't know anything at all. Nobody would accept that from us. I can understand that. But in absolute honesty, whether you accept it from me or not, how many of my generation say, 'Erna,' that is my first name, 'if we had known *that*, we would have thought entirely differently.' Already then. It was so horrifying. I could not have swallowed another drop, could not have [eaten] another bite. We took our plates out, but then we said, 'We do have the courage now and we must be able to look at this misery, this thoroughly horrible misery, to the end. And we . . . But it was horrible. So I saw, also with my sister, nicht? But she had a completely different mentality, maternal, nicht? I am a little more the motor for us both, cranking up the engine a little.

"But we both sat there. It was horrifying. Afterward, we turned off the television. Afterward, we could not have [listened] to any music or anything, there could have been the most beautiful broadcast. Nothing more. It was horrible. So my sister then said, 'Erna, I will read something.' And I also like to read a lot. Then I said, 'Ja, Annemarie, me too.' I was, we, we do not need to talk a lot about anything. We understand each other so, we turned it off and that meant for us, well, for us for the first time it was brought home to us, that we first had to try to work through, and then away, each in her room, door shut. I did read, but I always saw the pictures in front of me. For I had only taken something [to read] to skim through. I did not want to 'react away' through this reading and escape these pictures, and I was afraid that I could not sleep, and that these pictures would follow me. But it was good that we got to see it." She said the scenes shook her. "Because we had not known about it, and if we had known, I believe, some of it would not have happened. And that is a powerful feeling of guilt."

On the day after the broadcast, she said, "We were on the phone constantly" telling friends and acquaintances what they had seen and that they, too, had to see it. Whenever anything like it came on, "Then we said, 'Now there's a broadcast, turn it on right away.' I do that. They should see it."

The broadcast that shook her so much was in the early 1980s, she said. Asked if she had seen similar films before, she said nein six times. She said she also thinks there are many Germans like her who have not seen such films. I asked her what in the film affected her so much. "Like for instance, it began, how the SS and SA went into the stores and there where Jews were. So now especially in reference to the Jews, where they, where they now picked up the Jews, set the synagogues on fire, and made them kaputt and so on. Then the Jews were brought together and then were . . . and then the old were sorted and the young were sorted and often pulled from each other, children and so on, but sometimes also whole families brought to trucks and one saw it all in the film. *Or* in a larger city, brought to a train . . . and then somewhere later into a KZ. That we all saw for the first time. Horrifying. And then afterward again, then sort of a . . . the train was shown, then it was that they were going to be deloused, but that meant . . ."

The tape ran out.

By the time I changed it, Frau Tietz was talking about something else. I did not ask her to speak more about the grisly end of the Holocaust film, because to me the end was self-evident, whereas almost everything short of the end was not. I asked about the family that ran the Ullenberg store. "They later, they later took them away, too. I was only there on leave, nicht?"

She said the incident at the store "fell into the forgotten, nicht? But only in this moment, there I was, a young human being [Menschenkind], nicht? And this being pulled back and forth. There stands politics and the politics of the Party and there stands the human being opposite the Party politics. To which side do I decide to go? Today I would know the way, definitely." She said she knew that her mother tried not to show her disappointment in her, but Erna felt it. "And *that* still makes me sorry today, now after I experienced everything and then afterward came these," she stumbled, "seeing the KZ, about *suffering* human beings. And these hollowed-out eyes which I believe will follow me until I'm no longer here. And they no longer had the strength to cry. One noticed, well, somehow an alleviation must still come, maybe through tears." But, she said, few could cry and so "one had *only* this terrible expression of these eyes. It follows me endlessly. And something like it would *not* repeat itself in Germany. We would all go to the barricades. But all.

"I will also tell you honestly, Germans adhere to this feeling of guilt. Many, the majority. I mean, [there are] very few, very obstinate, who have learned nothing, or did not want to learn anything, or only can see what's on their small horizon."

She also said, "Today, if I were to encounter a Jew . . . That is, I have not spoken to one in a long time. Have no opportunity." But if she did, "I would speak to him exactly the same way, regard him first of all as a human being."

Was Erna Tietz, in sum, a very young woman full of enthusiasm for her country's new regime who had proudly done her duty by shooting down Allied planes and who later learned her lesson about the regime? I thought so. For no particular reason, when I decided to stop in Marburg the next year to interview someone else, I wrote Frau Tietz that I was coming, and when. To my surprise, she met the train. To my further surprise, she had booked me a room at a nearby hotel, to which she essentially marched me. She allotted me time to wash up, then packed me into her car (it was indeed easier to follow than demur), drove me to her home, introduced me to her sister, and prepared a nice supper. At some point, I realized with great chagrin that I was very short of cash for expenses the next day. She immediately lent me some. All in all, Frau Tietz could not have been personally kinder. We spent that evening and the next together. The first began with an amiable filling in of loose ends. The last ended, in my recollection, with my screaming at her. Yet on the cassette, my voice merely sounds tense. The screams must have been internal.

The buildup was gradual. At one point, Frau Tietz was not even there, but away for a short while. Her sister, Frau Annemarie Zettler, who was indeed in manner and voice much softer than her sister, spoke some about her past, including horror stories from the Soviet invasion of their East Prussian town—apparently indiscriminate killings, the disappearance of the sisters' father, the deportation of their mother, and the gang-raping of German women, whose cries throughout one night made Frau Zettler think she would go mad. The Soviets also commonly bit their rape victims bloody, she said. She herself, nearly nine months pregnant, was not raped.

"*We* asked ourselves," said Frau Tietz, who returned about then, "how did it happen, that such human beings turned into such beasts? We discuss this a lot. Sometimes we do say, why should we simply burden ourselves? But we have said, one must indeed understand the Russians *exactly* as well, too. We did go into their country and we did also murder human beings and killed and shot. It was war, that's how it was, there had to be defense, but that they then later had their revenge . . ." Asked if they had read about what German soldiers did in Russian villages, as opposed to battlefields, both said they had not.

The subject led Frau Tietz to fret about all the "asylum seekers" coming to Germany, bringing disquiet, that Germany cannot take them all, that after such people have helped Germany build itself up, one should offer them the opportunity to go home and pay them enough so they can build a house there. "But they must also have an understanding for our country. We simply cannot take any more." The sentiment (spoken in 1985, years before the refugees and asylum seekers reached much higher numbers) seemed to diverge from her earlier expressed welcoming of all strangers. She then sort of dipped back into that stance, by enormous praise of Jesse Owens, the American star of the 1936 Berlin Olympics. Frau Tietz was unaware of Hitler's snub of the black Owens (Hitler refused suggestions he meet him),[4] but was very aware of Owens's popularity in Germany. She described him glowingly as wonderfully loved and admired, how in addition to his track accomplishments, "in terms of humanity he was very much in Ordnung." Owens, however, was just one person, and was not seeking asylum.

We moved closer to the subject of race. "I cannot imagine breeding a Nordic race, a master race, so to speak, who then will control everything later," said Frau Tietz. She reaffirmed how skin color is all the same to her, and said Germans are not really a master race. "But, again and again, [the German] through his straightforwardness, through his honesty, through his thrift, through . . . I would say that one can depend on him, through his industriousness, [was] always really pictured as the 'model boy' to the whole world." She spoke about how quickly Germany rebuilt itself after being "knocked to the ground." She went on to say that she believes other countries greatly envy what Germans have accomplished. She did single out as an exception the Japanese, and invoked the German expression that they are "the Prussians of Asia."

Somehow, her avowal of open arms to all had slipped some, what with her dismay about asylum seekers and her bringing up German behavior when the subject was about a master race, which she otherwise claimed to disavow. Still, my antennae were not activated. But they were soon after asking, basically just to fill in a blank, whether there had been a "crystal night" in their hometown.

There was, said Frau Tietz. "We had a synagogue and as . . ."

"Burned, the synagogue," said Frau Zettler.

"Nein, did not burn, they only knocked out the windows, nicht?" said Frau Tietz. "That was all. And at the time, because we were also young, we also did not think about it at all. We only always thought, because this propaganda against the Jews and that was also in connection with this 'Kristallnacht,' that was very, very severe and many thought what was written in the newspapers about Jews, was true. And we only [had] a little idea of 'Kristallnacht.' And we as young human beings had no understanding why they were hit. We had our churches, they had their belief."

---

4. For a fuller story, see Duff Hart-Davis's *Hitler's Games: The 1936 Olympics* (New York: Harper & Row, 1986), 176 and 177.

Something about "only" the synagogue windows being knocked out was troubling. But then, after Frau Zettler called the local Jews she had known, including the Ullenbergs, "entirely magnificent human beings," Frau Tietz agreed, before referring to her parents shopping at the "Jew Prokofza" fabric store. She knew that Herr Prokofza Senior had been decorated in the First World War, and "we could not understand why they took them away."

The subject narrowed toward her feelings about Jews after I asked her what she thought would have happened if Germany had won the Second World War. She answered with remarkable hesitation, as if feeling disloyal, that "I believe it would not have been good for Europe." Pressed on the subject, she amended, for "all Europeans." How about for minorities? Her answer had to do with Huguenots who arrived in East Prussia in the seventeenth century.

What about other minorities, such as Jews?

She paused, taking the absurd question seriously. "With Jews." She sighed. "Ja, well." Another pause. From what she saw after the war, "I believe the [conquerors] somehow would have tried to get out them out of other countries, somehow." Also in answer to this "very difficult question," she said she believes that Jews would "not have been accepted as a minority."

And during the Third Reich, she began to say, Jews really always were portrayed as if only they . . . Her sister completed the sentence, "handeln." There is no perfect English equivalent, but "deal," trading this for that, comes closest. "Trading in animals. And stores and so on," Frau Tietz continued. "And that they have an entirely special *talent*, eh, to close a good deal, but that they can gain a great profit from it and then, that is, then afterward also took advantage of many. In that direction. The Jews were known for that. We already knew that. That is, when dealing with Jews, pay close attention. He always works happily for his own pocket. He always makes sure that he will get a big profit and take advantage of the others, also if it's not fair and he takes from them, I would like to say, more money than it really should be."

Within one minute, Frau Tietz seemed to have changed from the guilt-laden woman I thought I had known to someone else. So much for invocations of black skin, red skin, and lessons learned, not to mention the Ullenbergs. Almost beside the point, this was the last evening of a nonstop three-and-a-half-week research trip from Hamburg to Berlin to Munich and many stops in between, my mental state was not cheery, and I succumbed to the dual temptations of exhaustion and anger. Do Christian Germans never take an unfair profit?

"Also. They do it too," said Frau Zettler.

"Eh, ja, they do. Of course, of course," said Frau Tietz. "But here it was reinforced, and one did then see afterward, like when, like for example now farms became impoverished and then, eh, then the Jews came and they did have, through all of their international banking things, already at that time, they did always have the opportunity to work with a lot of money and then it was always, eh, 'the Jew plunged us into our misery.'"

But she later read how that had been falsely portrayed, did she not?

She paused before answering. "Well, falsely portrayed. In which direction? Now I do not understand you. That the Jews did not take advantage, but did respectable business or how?" Interrupting my sputtery response, she soon said, "We always heard over and over, whether it was a horse trade or so on, it was always, be careful about the Jews. He deals this way. He always tries to cheat, always tries to get in his pocket what he set out to. Whether it was right or not right."

Frau Zettler then declared that she could not recall any Jews in the countryside where she had lived ever really *working*. "Our farmers worked, but I cannot recall at all if Jews did, being always active, let us say. A farmer does have to work with his *hands*, earlier in part, but that the Jew . . ."

"For the most part, they were the 'Händler,'" said Frau Tietz.

That was not work?

"Ja, of course that is work," said Frau Tietz. "Ja."

"If it had to do with obtaining a piece of property or so," said Frau Zettler, to which Frau Tietz added a fast "Ja."

Did one then know that for centuries the Jews were not allowed to own land? This was not completely accurate on my part, but close. It gave Frau Tietz pause again. "Nein, one did not then . . . one did not then speak about it at all."

Did she know it? "Ja, of course we know it, we know that, too." Her voice became faster. "And nein, I mean, then we did not know that. Today, yes."

Frau Zettler and I wandered off (or retreated) thematically, talking about manual labor, Israel, and Jewish exclusion from certain guilds and professions. Frau Tietz was silent, until she said she had to contradict the assertion that handeln had been one of few options for Jews. Speaking faster and faster, she said, "I must say with complete honesty, I see that from the human side. There are other minorities, there are other human beings, who, who really are *also* without a home and I mean, the Jews had that especially. Maybe in their unhappiness they are . . . at fault themselves. I mean, in world history it's the case, too, *Poland* was 'off the map' and the Poles always had a 'nationality consciousness' that they always said, Poland is not lost. And *why* did the Jews not say at the time, Israel is not lost, so we'll fight, or in any case, we will try somehow to find a homeland?"

After a time, I said maybe German Jews were not so set on fighting for a homeland because they considered themselves Germans. The sisters, both of whom had been talking at once, fell silent.

After a spate of needless (and premature) crowing on my part, and a few other diversions, Frau Tietz was back, and as if nothing had changed. She said what "makes me think the most is that the majority of Jews have achieved no other work, or very little, than just handeln and banking." And that it was not just Nazi propaganda, but that as a child her relatives warned her about doing business with Jews. "We should be careful because they always wanted to take advantage. . . ."

"Tried," put in Frau Zettler.

"Always tried. That is the mentality of the . . ."

"Well," said Frau Zettler, "business people are always that way, whether they are Jews or other people . . ."

"But the Jew was especially known for it. And that was before the Nazi time, nicht? That I remember as a child."

What about people they knew well, like in the Ullenbergs' store and the fabric store? Did one say, watch out for them?

"Nein," said Frau Tietz. "Well, the Jews we got to know, Ullenberg, where we shopped, and Prokofza and so on, then we *never*, my father never, my mother *never* said anything like that."

When they quoted what they heard about Jews it was negative, I said (tensely), but when they spoke of Jews they knew it was all positive.

"Ja!" said Frau Tietz.

"Ja, so the cliché is not true . . ." began Frau Zettler.

"Ja, ja, exactly," said Frau Tietz. She spoke of "many human beings" not fitting into a cliché, but "they're all put together, *the* Germans, *the* French, *the* English, *the* Russians, *the* Negro." She added, when she, being sometimes "very impulsive," says "*the* youth," her sister always says, "Careful." But when the subject of Jews returned, it was about how their Händler tactics are so skillful a person does not know what is going on until it is time to pay. I suggested that the reference is different with a Christian Händler. Frau Tietz disagreed, and spoke very fast. "One did not say the Christian, but one [called] him by his name, when one did business with him himself. And one also had the *proof* that he took advantage of me and that came out then. And then later, one never said the Christian, but *then* I said, him or him with the name."

She understood the difference?

"Ja, I do understand. Here one said in general *the* Jews, nicht? And one did not say the Christians, nicht? Here one said just the human being, or one said the Jew so and so, nicht?"

So, to her it was always "the Jew," but the Christian always had a name? Frau Tietz paused. "Ja."

It makes her despair, she added, that some people have learned nothing.

Frau Zettler said it is most important to reconsider things, and "we have learned that."

Frau Tietz agreed.

The same evening, she also said in regard to anti-Semitic propaganda, "We did not let ourselves be influenced by it. Ach, definitely not."

Frau Zettler added, "We also didn't do anything against them."

Frau Tietz said that if a Jew came to their home "and there was the fear of death in his face, we definitely would have hidden him. And my mother [would have] definitely." Like if it had been Frau Ullenberg, she said. Frau Zettler commented, regarding the Ullenberg store boycott, "It was talked about all over, no one should go in, no one should buy there, and then people became uncertain and then always said, 'My God, if I go in there now . . .'" "I'll lose my job, nicht?" ended Frau Tietz.

The sisters eventually spoke again about their mother, who took in and hid a terrified German soldier who had deserted. They believed, and were probably right, that she would have been shot for harboring him. "Our best role model is our mother," said Frau Tietz. "And father, too, of course, but more mother. And that's how we are *too*, and humane. And I have said, if today someone comes with a yellow, with a red, or black skin and shows himself to be a human being and is in need . . ."

Could either sister think of one incident in the Third Reich when she asked herself whether "it" was completely right?

After a long pause, Frau Tietz said, "Well, I cannot."

Frau Zettler did. It was the firing of a doctor who was married to a Jewish woman. She said she herself sometimes cannot understand how much they did not know. "We sometimes said, we simply cannot comprehend that. Where was our common sense? That we also never heard or saw something at all, that we didn't know anything."

Frau Tietz agreed, "They simply do not *believe* us."

About a month later, she wrote to thank me for the repayment of the loan, and added that her sister and she thought so happily about the hours we spent together. Half a year later, after acknowledging my Christmas greetings, she wrote that they still often think about our last evening together. "Not only the 'Punsch' loosened our tongues," she wrote, "but it was also the feeling to be able to discuss so much openly and honestly."

Frau Anna Rigl

On Megalomaniacs and Little People

"You have a genuine child of Munich in front of you," said Frau Anna Rigl with half-jesting pride, and a very rare laugh. "Child of Munich" (*Münchner Kindl* in the Bavarian dialect she used) is a symbol of the city, and also a well-known brand of beer. "There aren't very many left," she continued. "They're all from outside. The foreigners we have . . . I don't want to say foreigners.[1] Basically immigrants, from cities and from villages, from the countryside. Many came for work. There was great unemployment, and here there was more opportunity to find work. And then when Hitler came, they built the Autobahn. They got paid fifty cents an hour and the people were happy they had earned a little something. Hitler just built the Autobahn to get rid of the unemployed, and then the arms buildup got going."

Frau Anna Rigl's own buildup was startling. Within two minutes, she had brought up not only Hitler and the familiar saw about his solving the great unemployment problem by building the Autobahn, she had gone beyond the saw in two unusual ways. She implied the building of the Autobahn was

---

1. This interview was conducted in 1985, well before the large migration from eastern Europe.

a precursor to the militarization of Germany, which it was. And she proved herself someone for whom earning a living meant more than political theory. Many women mentioned the unemployment/Autobahn connection. Only Frau Rigl mentioned the pay.

Her lifelong perception of herself, and her view of the world, clearly has been that of "Arbeiter" [worker]. Asked to describe her parents, she replied they were "just workers."

Her father was a bricklayer. He and Anna's mother also were live-in caretakers of "a gentlemen's house, a good house" in Schwabing, a section of Munich. They had four children. Anna was born in 1916.

She stayed put in her city. Apart from fleeing the bombs of war for the peace of a farm near Augsburg in 1943, Anna Rigl has lived in Munich all her life. (Her mother, who wanted nothing to do with country life, bombs or no, stayed in Munich throughout the war.) For more than half a century, Frau Rigl lived in the same street-facing ground-floor apartment in a handsome, solid building near the Isar Gate, just a walk from downtown.

In the building, Frau Rigl had a reputation of being the person to leave the key with, the person who stows packages and waters the houseplants of whoever is away. I assumed she was at least the concierge. She simply was *there*, rooted in her home, her neighborhood, and her city.

And one October afternoon, I saw from a block away, there indeed she was, leaning out her front window, smiling, talking with two women on the sidewalk. They were wearing the region's ubiquitous felt hats with feathers in them and carrying the ubiquitous net shopping bags. They must have paused for a nice Bavarian chat on the way to the grocery store. By the time Frau Rigl closed the window and opened the door, her demeanor had changed entirely. It was obvious she preferred talking with friends about life now to talking with a near-stranger about life then. Nonetheless, she led the way to her scrubbed living room.

It was furnished in the postwar style not unusual in German households where everything old may have been bombed, abandoned, burned, stolen, or traded. Ornament was garish or humble—a huge orange glass vase on a cupboard, a plastic flower arrangement on the coffee table. Frau Rigl herself was more in tune with the plain, no-nonsense furniture than with the knickknacks. She looked sturdy and thick, a sweater and wool skirt for warmth, no makeup, although her curls may have been set professionally. She sat in an upholstered chair next to a small coal oven from which emanated a flush of heat. With a gesture as easy and accurate as that of a basketball player, she occasionally tossed a piece of coal into the oven's open mouth. She never missed. And, unique among the women, she never offered or mentioned any refreshment. (She did accept my present of wine.) Instead, she started by asking agitatedly what was expected of her, listened to a few words of explanation, then brusquely interrupted. "How it all happened, or with that Hitler? I was still young then."

Frauen

In time, her hesitancy, agitation, even the absence of the hospitality ritual, explained themselves. To Frau Anna Rigl, this was in no way a sociable occasion. To her, the Third Reich did not bring forth memories about idealism on behalf of National Socialism, or about the outrage of opposition, or about the ambivalence of blindered and stumbling fellow travelers. To her, the era meant something much narrower and yet encompassing: its intrusion into her own family.

Possibly adding to her discomfort with the subject was the language she needed to convey it. Her native Bavarian dialect would not work with a North German, much less a North American. So she strained to talk in High German (while I strained to understand her, and be understood). Although the conversation was not easy and led to piquant misunderstandings, language was less an impediment than her aversion to the subject.

One exception was her early childhood, which she sketched as uneventful—with one retrospective exception. She had gone to school with Eva Braun.

"Her sister went to school with me, too," she added. "Eva was one or two years older, and was in the same school we went to. I knew her well."

Well! Not everyone knew Eva Braun before she became Adolf Hitler's girlfriend. She has been described as "the daughter of lower-middle-class Bavarian parents, who at first strenuously opposed her illicit relation with Hitler."[2] What might Anna Rigl know about her, or him, or them, that had eluded historians? I asked if Eva Braun had been noticeable in any way.

"No, no. They were well brought up."

Prodded, she said the Braun sisters were "nette Mädchen [nice girls]." Prodded further, she said she knew at the time of the Braun-Hitler relationship. (Historians and other Germans contend the public did not know of it until after the war.) "She was always more in public because she went to Berchtesgaden, into that bunker thing. One knew it. Maybe not everybody, but in any case I knew it."

And that was that. It was clear from the start that there was no point trying to prod Anna Rigl any more than Anna Rigl let herself be prodded. Besides, she had much to say about the Third Reich that would prove considerably more interesting than what she did not have to say about Eva Braun.

Anna was still a child when Hitler was becoming a public figure in her hometown. She recalled that the Nazis named Munich the city of something or other, racked her brain trying to recall what, but initially only came up with Munich's present public relations label, the "City with Heart." *That*

---

2. William L. Shirer, *The Rise and Fall of the Third Reich* (New York: Fawcett Crest, 1950), 1442.

was not it, we agreed. The next day she cheerfully related that what the Nazis called Munich was the "City of the Movement [Stadt der Bewegung]." It had come to her in the middle of the night.

As a child, she might not have been aware of what was going on in the "City of the Movement," but her parents likely were. Asked about their politics, her first response was, "We were not for Hitler." She said she did not know how they voted before 1933, that "children were not so interested then." Nor, she said, were women. "They didn't bother with politics. At that time they all had a batch of children, three, four, and still more. The woman had enough to do and no time for politics. I wasn't interested, either. Politics wasn't like it is today. Now people all get foolish. And if you don't vote the result's the same, because they all pull our legs."

Prompted to give more reaction of her parents to Hitler before he became chancellor, she said, "Of course people saw that if Hitler came to power, it would lead to war. Everyone said so. That is, most people said so. When he takes the wheel, there'll be war. We weren't keen on Hitler, because we knew what kind of misery he'd bring. I can't have a good impression about a person who only lies to us that we're going to get it so good.

"And the arms buildup did get going, of the air force and everything. And everything did change because of this arming, and then people got work again, no? We had a lot of people who were for Hitler. We had some in the house. Listen, if you didn't greet them with 'Heil Hitler!' that was bad." How bad? "We'd get out of the way or we looked away or something, because I never liked to say it. You had to be alert right away, so they wouldn't have you hanged."

She said the Nazi supporters she knew "were mostly not workers, but more the middle class, let's say. Employees and low-rung civil servants, like that." She began speaking more willingly. "Those with good positions, those who worked in offices, were for Hitler already, because they had a good job and didn't have to leave to go to war. In part they were 'essential' [a military classification]. So the dumb one had to go fight the war."

Asked about the enthusiasm of Hitler supporters for the war, she answered, "They were very enthusiastic at the beginning, of course, while we did nothing but conquer, marching into Poland and into France and England. That was completely different from say, '43, '44, when one already noticed we weren't winning, that we'd lose the war." Once it was lost, her Nazi neighbors got lost, too—"made dust of themselves," as she put it. Others "turned themselves around. They became small again, you know? They saw we lost the war, that they had to be different and can't be so enthusiastic anymore. Because many people lost relatives. Their husband, their brother. And until the end, the word was, 'We'll conquer.' They really played us for fools. 'We'll conquer.' Huh!" Frau Rigl sort of laughed.

The loss of the war was a long time off when she suffered her first personal loss. In 1933, her father died. Then the remaining family (two children already were on their own) lost its home. The owners of the building needed a caretaker who could manage the heating system's large boilers. So, in 1934, Anna, a brother, and their mother moved to the apartment that is Frau Rigl's present home. My question of whether she owned it, or the whole building—which seemed entirely possible, given the combinations of hard work, thrift, and longevity—made her burst with incredulity. "ME? Nein, I'm no homeowner. If I were THAT! Nein, a renter since '34." Nor is she the concierge. "I just do a few things on my own" out of "good-naturedness." But she must get something off her rent? "*That* would be good," she laughed. The idea seemed beyond her.

After her father's death, her mother got a "very small" pension and supplemented it with part-time cleaning jobs. Anna, then a teenager, took a course in sales clerking, found a job at a high-grade grocery store, and gave her mother her earnings. Anna enjoyed the work a lot. "Actually I wanted a store myself, but didn't have the money for one."

She also enjoyed going out. One memorable evening she wore a mask and fancy dress to a Fasching [Mardi Gras] dance. There she met Ludwig Rigl. He was a construction worker who liked to dance, was five years older than she, and a man with whom she "had a son while very young." Later, when a few numbers came together, indicating the son was born in 1936, it became clear what she had meant. Anna and Ludwig married in 1938.

The mid-1930s to very early 1940s were a time of relative prosperity for many Germans. They had jobs and food. And if they nurtured Nazi contacts, they had even better jobs and more food. Asked if that period of time helped her, however, Frau Rigl's response showed she was not thinking in economic terms. "Nein, it didn't help us. Nein, nein. For one thing, my husband had to join the military."

She referred to 1939, the year the war began, as "eine schlechte Zeit [a wretched time]." What did she mean? Again, she was referring to the personal. "Above all, it was the blackout measures. Then there were the bombing attacks. You had to stay home after dusk, everything darkened. And as for food, there was nothing. There were ration cards. It was a bad time, as the war really got going. A terrible time. Then every day, when there were air raid alarms, you had to go down in the cellar. No sooner were the children in bed [the Rigls had a daughter, born two years after their son] than you had to get them out again, get them dressed again, and into the cellar again with the suitcase as the bombs fell. After waiting for the all-clear, we went upstairs again, and if we had bad luck we were upstairs for maybe an hour and then we had to go below again. Often one had to go down a couple of times a night." She said sometimes the stay in the bomb shelter, which was cold in winter, lasted an hour or longer. People "grumbled" about the attacks, said Frau Rigl.

About whom did they grumble?

"Of course, one grumbled about the English and about the 'Amis.'"

Presumably one did not "grumble" about one's own government?

"But we bombed too, no?"

Despite the shortcomings of the bomb shelter, it did keep her family safe. Not everyone in the neighborhood was so lucky. "Near us, in one house, there were 128 dead. Near us on Isartorplatz, where there'd been a direct hit. There were a lot of dead. Ja, ja, a lot of dead."

Her point of view was unmistakable—Big Them against Little Us. Politicians pulling one's leg instigated the war, the "dumb one" who did not have a cushy Nazi desk job fought it, and warring governments brought it down on frazzled women with sleeping children and on houses of neighbors. How would such a point of view continue in terms of the as-yet unmentioned Jewish population? It was my experience by then that the subject generally required a tiptoe approach, lest a direct hit kill the answer. I commented that there must have been a lot going on in Munich early on. Parades and . . .

"Ja, ja," she interrupted. "At the Königsplatz, downtown, on Brienner Street. There was the house where, what was the name of that Hitler house, where he always went when the parade was over? Dear God, what was the name of that house?" Although frustrated that she had forgotten, she continued, and came to my intended subject on her own. "Then it got going and 1938 was, after all, 'Kristallnacht' where they smashed everything, everything. Made everything kaputt. The big department stores, everything, kaputt. Ach Gott, ach Gott, that's when it got going, 1938. That's when it began with the Jews. We all grumbled, you know? We all grumbled, although actually, the Jews for the most part . . ." She interrupted herself. "I was in Schwabing working in a store, where most of our customers were Jews. [The store itself apparently was not Jewish-owned.] But those who had money, they had all left earlier for America or wherever. They already sensed what was coming, no? They were already there and now they're sitting pretty there in America and rule us."

Thus we began. Frau Rigl insisted, repeatedly, she was correct. As to the source of her information, "Well, it's generally heard. You can also see it with the Jews again here. Where there's a store or something bigger, Jews are involved. I myself don't care for Jews much." (The phrase she used was, "I don't have anything extra for" them.) "And it was in the Bible. The Jew will be persecuted as long as there is a Jew,[3] and that's true. He can go wherever he wants, no one likes him. Look down there at Israel, how they fight, everything with the Jews."

---

3. Young's Analytical Concordance to the Bible has no such quotation, or anything similar. I thank the Reverend William M. Perdue for checking.

She said she did not know how such a situation came about, but "Jews are another people and that's the truth." She paused. "Ja, and look now in the offices and so. In America, too. Most people sitting in them are Jews."

She again insisted, repeatedly, this also was true. "It is so. I know it. Doch doch, doch doch. [*Doch* is an intensified *ja.*] One reads newspapers and one hears a lot and, doch doch." The newspaper she cited was the *Süddeutsche*, a well-regarded Munich daily.

And in regard to the Holocaust, Frau Rigl was among those who voiced an opinion heard before. "I don't believe they killed that many Jews," she said.

My assertion that the statistics came from the German government failed to impress her. "Ja, but nonetheless. There were so many Polish Jews who came. We have a lot of Jews again today. Jews here have good jobs. For example, look, we have Jews on television, we have Jews on the radio." Asked if they are any good, she answered, "Ach ja, you can't tell any difference. Someone can't hang out a sign, he's a Jew or he's a Christian. He just does the broadcast. Just like us, no? There's no difference."

Frau Rigl had only begun to baffle. What about her personal experience with Jews?

"Well, personally there's less to say. I got to know nice Jews through the store, but they are real Händler. Dealers is what they are, making a ten-penny piece out of a five. Ja, downright dealers they are. And he gets results, the Jew."

"He can also shit on people," she later said. "The Jew says, 'That is gold.' It's not gold, you see. That's sort of how he does it."

Asked if she had personal experience in that particular regard, Frau Rigl said, "Nein. But I know it." She then added, "It's the same with us. The same with Christians. There are nice Christians and nice Jews."

On the whole, Frau Rigl did not think much of Jewish women. "I know a few Jewish women. I mean they're typical Jews, not politically, I don't mean to say that at all. But I've often said, that's a typical Jewish woman, always in the right. She knows everything better, wants her own way, one must do it *so*, and that is *so*. She always has the last word. That's a typical Jewish woman, I always say.

"Back then we had Jewish ladies [Judendamen]. I mean we had real rich ladies as customers, no? *Clean* Jews, whose homes were clean and everything. They had maids, no? But for their staff it was this way. The ladies ate and invited people over and the staff got nothing. Not once did they get something substantial to eat." Frau Rigl said she knew one of the maids. "She got a small sausage. And if you threw them out the door they came in the other," she added.

"I have the experience from working in the store. Ja, and there were real clean Jews and then there were real dirty ones, too. That's the case for any group. It's the same for us, no?"

290

Her words that followed those, and follow these, must be prefaced with an explanation. Frau Rigl began speaking in an especially convoluted and confusing manner, more like a stream of consciousness than not. Although editing would make the following "story" clearer, she spoke with such striking and blunt anguish, it has been left verbatim.

"Naturally there were Jewish stores here, too. They had a sort of dry goods store and they were dealers. You could always bargain with them. That you can do only with Jews. He's a real businessman, the Jew. They gassed him, took him away. He was gassed, ja. Had *four* children. And they were nice people. If, let's say, the apple cost thirty cents, and if you said thirty cents is too expensive for me, he'd give it to you for fifteen cents. You see, one could bargain with them. Right nearby he had a store. They gassed him. They took him away."

In the course of telling the above, Frau Rigl's manner had changed. Because she generally was brusque in her delivery, any change in voice or manner indicated much more than it might with a highly expressive person. When she spoke of the Jewish shop owner, a drop in her voice and a change in her face magnified what looked like grief. When asked how she knew what happened to him (he lived, she said, on Zweibrücken Street, which is several blocks away from her home), she made several false starts of a sentence before finding one she could end.

"Well, the store was closed and then it got spoken around that he was taken to Dachau. Or wherever he was taken. I don't know where he went. I think the whole family was taken away. They closed the store and took them away in the middle of the night and one never saw them again. Mostly they did it at night. They took them right out of bed and took them away. And they had to leave everything behind." Her voice lowered again, and slowed. "It was a fright [ein Schreck]. That was a horrible time."

Then she said, "But there are so many Jews again today. They are not doing badly, the Jews. As long as they live, I believe, they'll be supported. Because we lost the war, we were guilty of everything, and therefore we have to pay. What I want is justice. That things go well for us too. Look at me, for example. I'm a war widow. You can believe we were badly off after the war. We didn't get anything. We had no golden time, like we do today. Having to sell everything, one thing after the other, to have something to live on." Of her status as a war widow, she also said, "When you're alone, behind you there's nothing, in front of you nothing."

For whatever reason, it was difficult, but not impossible, to bring her back to the Jewish storekeeper and his family, whom she never named. She said no, she does not think about them, but added, "Only when one is in a conversation, I say ja, they're not there anymore, but farther away. Ach Gott, one has one's own problems, no?"

It was the shopkeeper himself she seemed to remember the most. "He was a right nice man [ein recht netter Mann]."

Frauen

What were the children like? "They were simply, ja, small children, growing up." Well behaved? "Ja, ja." Especially remarkable? "Nein, nein."

"Ja, they treated the Jews badly. That was true. They had to wear the Jewish star and then they had to stay home even during the day, they were so afraid. Ja, it went bitterly for them, the Jews. We felt sorry for them, you know? Because they couldn't help it that they were Jews."

If Hitler's seizure of power presaged Frau Rigl's sense of powerlessness, her own and others', his war confirmed it.

And its memory, to her, remained in the realm of the personal. Many women, asked to recall their impression of the war's first days, when German troops marched into Poland, answered in terms of politics or the military. Not Frau Rigl.

"My impression? I was scared every day. My husband was part of the invasion."

One of the first men drafted, Ludwig Rigl immediately was sent to the infantry's front line. He was "not at all" enthusiastic. "Nor was any man we knew. They all grumbled and still do." The grumbling then was in private. "One talked among one's friends. I didn't go to some tavern and make a big announcement, for I didn't know who sat next to me. That was dangerous."

In 1940, when Germany conquered its old enemy, France, many Germans felt proud and vindicated. Frau Rigl's reaction, as she recalled it, was that "with France, things were not yet so bad. The French campaign wasn't tragic. It had all just started."

Still, "proud" she was not. "I was never proud about the war. I really wasn't, because . . ." She stopped and intensified her indignation. "I'd like to know who was. If my husband had had bad luck, he would already have been killed. He was in France, and faced England on the coast. They were shipped over to Calais. I can't be proud if I have to be afraid every day what kind of a notice I'm going to get. One never knew from day to day what was coming. Every day a death thing, a death notice, could come. No woman was proud of the war. All we did was grumble.

"We really had a bad time. You couldn't buy anything. You had to mend every day, repair socks and darn everything together, because we didn't get anything. There were ration tickets, a few, for fat and all. Ach Gott, ach Gott.

"And destruction everywhere, you know? Cities, everything, wrecked. One talked about the Americans and the English, who covered us with bombs. One grumbled angrily about that. And during the very last days the American still bombed, even knowing we're played out and we're about to capitulate. That was sure a misery. Ja, one certainly grumbled about the Americans. They didn't have to do that."

One reason the Allies entered the war, she said, was that "the Jews stirred things up. Because many had gone to America. But by then it was too late. Everything was too late."

She continued, "We all said we wouldn't win. The soldiers had more of an insight into that than we did, they saw, after all. But no one could say anything, the soldiers either. They just had to fight. Because if I don't shoot him, he shoots me. They were simply enemies, in that sense. That's what war is."

Her husband, she added, was wounded "a few times." He was decorated a few times, too. "My husband had all the medals. Wounded in battle, Iron Cross I, Iron Cross II. All such medals there were, he had." Throughout the war, he and she kept in touch by mail. He wrote often, she said. He got leave, too, "but not often." Once a full year went by without his getting home.

It would seem that at such times friendships among women would get closer. But Frau Rigl said, "I really had no one. I'll tell you something. Where could one have gone? There was nothing going on. Nothing." How about visiting each other at home? Out of the question. "Everyone had to make sure to be in one's own home by evening. We didn't know when there'd be an air raid alarm. You couldn't leave. You weren't safe a single minute. You took your little bit of money and went quickly to buy something and then you're home again." There was a little bit of socializing, she said, but "real sitting down together didn't exist anymore." Had she been lonely? "You're not lonely with children."

Frau Rigl also had the social benefits of a paying job. In 1942, she went back to work in the grocery store where she had worked before. Her mother managed the household.

For many German women, changes on the home front during the war caused strains within the marriage. Sometimes such strains became evident when the husband came home on leave. Not with the Rigls. "Nein, nein, nein. It was very nice when he came back. We were always on a honeymoon. A couple of times we took a vacation, one time to Vienna, for fourteen days, once to Freiburg. One time he got sick with dysentery in Allenstein in Poland [at the time, it was East Prussia] and I traveled up there. When I arrived, he was gone, having been transferred to Zwickau back in the Reich and we didn't even see each other." She laughed. "Oh, that was a disappointment."

In 1941, Herr Rigl was on active duty about twenty-five miles from Moscow. "He wrote we're here, and now we're there. And in 1941 was the great freeze in Russia. You can imagine what the men went through. Good Lord, so many had frozen feet, frozen hands. Here, we knitted. Everyone knitted. We knitted socks, we knitted gloves. And one sent it all there and then they often didn't even get anything. The ones at the rear took it. Those who were not at the front, they got it. Na, it's the same everywhere.

"He took part in the whole return march, to 1945. Then came the retreat, when we were beaten farther and farther back as the Russians advanced more and more, into Prussia."

In January of 1945, he was wounded again. For a time, he was in Denmark, and was supposed to get home leave from there. Instead, he was ordered back to Russia immediately.

"And then he was missing in action," she said, and paused. "In February 1945." She paused again. "Two months before the end. And after taking part in everything."

On a nearby table stood his framed picture. He looked young and fine. She never found out what happened to him. "At first, I waited and waited. But then I gave up hope, because one knew how it had gone there."

Their son was then ten, their daughter eight. Frau Rigl referred to the children by slang, rather than by name. The boy was "der Bub," the girl "das Dirndl." (There is no English equivalent.) Both children understood "that he was no more, that we were alone." She said she "registered him with the Red Cross as missing and waited, and waited, and waited. And children, mein Gott, if children have their lives and their food, it doesn't bother them so much."

Almost three decades passed until she heard anything.

"In 1973, the Red Cross wrote me the great probability was that he died in action. They all died in action. There weren't many left."

Nonetheless, in 1985 Frau Rigl made one more try to find out what happened to her husband. She went to a reunion of his unit, the Seventh Infantry Division.

Her brother accompanied her to the gathering, which was held in Munich. His fate had been luckier. Stationed elsewhere, he had been severely injured and taken prisoner, but "he got out." The reunion, which she said was the division's first, marked the fortieth anniversary of the end of the war. It also marked the fortieth anniversary of Frau Rigl's widowhood.

"There weren't many there, you know? Back then, they were young men. Now they're just grandpas. I went because I thought, maybe I'd learn something from . . . That someone would be there who'd known him. But nothing. One of them said we were there and there, and he must have been there, too. But he didn't know him. You see, at the end they were all simply mixed together because there were always fewer of them. They mixed different divisions together."

Despite her disappointment, Frau Rigl stayed and listened to the speeches. "Former generals spoke. They talked wonderfully. That was very nice. But they described it exactly." It was "difficult, hard [schwer, hart]" leaving without the answer she had tried to find, she said. "That was no easy path. It was a hard path. But I went, because one thought maybe. But there was nothing to be done."

Not knowing specifically how her husband died, she blamed his death

294

on the whole fighting world. "The Frenchman bears a share of it. Everyone, the American, the Englishman. All took part in the war. The Russian, the Pole, all fought the war. At the end, the Japanese too. They were all guilty. Not Hitler alone. Otherwise they couldn't have joined in right away, if they hadn't armed. The Russian always arms."

She modified her words by saying she did not mean guilty exactly, but having participated in guilt. "If they had only stopped, but who stops? We should have stopped, because we certainly saw we were losing the war at the end, '44, '45. That it went downhill for us. They should have capitulated. But Hitler didn't do that. He fought to the last man. They share the guilt all together."

When pressed, however, she gave Hitler his due for starting the war. "Ja, of course he was guilty. He invaded Poland. He invaded Austria in '38. He invaded France. Hitler had megalomania. He wanted to conquer the whole world."

To Frau Rigl, Hitler's war did not stand alone. "There were wars before the war and there will be wars after Hitler and there will always be wars. You can't blame Hitler alone, because there had been wars before him." She said she does not know why. "I didn't need one. You wouldn't have wanted one either. But they just keep coming, no? Because human beings keep coming who like them, who have megalomania."

Asked to comment on one woman's assertion (it was Frau Mundt's) that Germany did not start the war, Frau Rigl bluntly replied, "She most probably did real well. That was simply a Nazi, a real Nazi. Ja, that's how they talked." Hearing that the woman was a retired teacher, Frau Rigl interrupted with a pronouncement. "That was just a Nazi incarnate." The phrase is more graphic in German: "eine eingefleischte Nazi."

"They were the ones Hitler hypnotized. Nicht? But whoever opens his eyes a little and thought a little saw where it was all leading." Frau Rigl got increasingly agitated. "Ja, and she must have seen that they destroyed everything here in the Reich, the cities and everything. Ja, when one is so stupid, I don't know. She must be really stupid."

The way Hitler conquered Germany, she said, was "with his speeches. After all, he 'screamed' everywhere." She continued, "That was a brutal person. When he spoke, so dictatorially and so egotistically that there's no one else . . ." She trailed off.

Asked if she had heard the speeches herself, she seemed perturbed. "Of course one heard them. They were on the radio. I never went to hear them. Are you asking if I went to the Königsplatz and listened to his trash [Schmarrn]? If you're already against him, you don't go there. We didn't go to any of it. Speeches, meetings, we didn't have any interest in it."

I would have gone out of curiosity, I said.

She looked astonished. "You would have gone? Can you imagine how he blubbered? You heard him on the radio, on the first of May, when there were rallies. Oh my, oh my, there was always something going on."

Asked if he had talked "good," she replied with disdain, "All he talked about was about good. That Germany would have it good, and my God, the Thousand Year Reich, no? He wanted the whole world."

So does everyone else, she said, embarking on a then-current theme of Russian and "Ami" megalomania and joint fears about the other's nuclear bombs. "Who has to atone for it? The little people, no? The small man. Do you know what my husband always said? For the big man, war is sport. The biggest sport. And it's true. They all have megalomania. Now they even want to go into space and take weapons and build a station there. Ja, they should give something to the poor people. The 'Ami' has so many poor people, we have so many poor people, too. Look in New York, what's going on with the Negroes. No work and nothing."

The Catholic church should ante up big, too, she said. Frau Rigl, herself a Catholic, expressed little interest in the Third Reich controversy surrounding the future Pope Pius XII for negotiating the Concordat with Hitler. "I don't know whether he interfered as much as the present one. He travels everywhere. He should stay home in his Vatican and shouldn't just give the poor people his blessing, but should give them something. He should sell something pretty. The richest man in the world should, after all, give something to them below him."

Frau Rigl said she went to church during the Third Reich, but heard nothing from her priest against the Nazis. "He wasn't allowed to say anything either. Because they took several priests away and killed them, those who said anything. Every human being saw the injustice."

Big Them against Little Us was proceeding, in its way, true to form. Yet, what if a Little Us had been a Big Them? What if a person like Anna Rigl had been in power? Putting such a notion to any of the women almost always was too much, or too absurd, for them to consider. Many were used to feeling powerless outside their front doors. And Frau Rigl had felt lowly for decades.

Nonetheless, she had opinions about what she would have done if she had been in power. I asked her about the Nazis' 1935 Nuremberg laws "to Protect German Blood and German Honor." Among other provisions, they stipulated that marriages "between Jews and German citizens [or 'Aryans'] are forbidden." She answered with a very German expression indicating she did not care. "It was all sausage to me." She added, "It was the same to me who married whom. Although I believe most of them married among themselves, Jews to Jews, not Jews and Christians. It was not so frequent that a Christian married a Jew. A Jewish woman married a Jewish man.[4] What hap-

---

4. Not always. According to German government statistics pertaining to 1932 (the last sociologically "normal" year), of 3,182 Jewish men who married, 875 (27

pened often among Jews was that they married their relatives and then there were children who weren't normal. Jewish children very often were not normal. I knew some who weren't. Because again and again, most married each other, Jews and again Jews. It was called inbreeding." Still, "Ach, I wouldn't have forbidden it. It was all the same to me who got married. Love knows no borders, the expression goes."

It was time for another "if." The year is 1933. Hitler says the Jews have too much. He tells Frau Rigl to decide what to do about it. What would she have done? "For the Jews?" she asked. "Ja, what should I do for the Jews? We didn't have anything ourselves." Once our misunderstanding was straightened out, the answers changed. Would she have taken anything away from them?

"Nein."

Or removed them from government jobs?

"Well, one said, ja, there sit the Jews. One said that. They're everywhere in the big companies and in the big department stores. The Jews had it all, but that was all the same to us."

Did she think it right to take something away from them?

"Nein, that was not right, not just. You know, maybe somehow they could have curtailed it. But not take everything and 'Away with you.' We were already angry they were so radical with the Jews. They might have, let's say, taken a little more. Because the Jews really did have a lot of money."

She also said, "Everyone said they had pity for them. Because it wasn't the Jews' fault, and those who were there were Jews who didn't have much themselves. The Jews were to pity. Ja, the Jews were really poor."

A minute later she said, "Jews were indeed rich."

There was no apparent contradiction to Frau Rigl.

What she would have done to very rich Christians? How about taxing them more? The notion seemed new to her, and she seemed to like it. "They could have done that, of course. Well, they also paid taxes. . . ." She added, "One said there are also Christian Jews. Who are keen on money."

On her own, Frau Rigl brought up another "if." What if Hitler were back in power. "We wouldn't have the trouble with the youth. He'd restore order better, Hitler. The punks and the rowdies, the young who don't want to work. Hitler would be right, people say. Our government is much too lax. He'd get them all somewhere and they'd all have to work. Look, you can't even go out after dark anymore. You have to stay home because you're

---

percent) married non-Jews. Of 2,810 Jewish women who married, 503 (18 percent) married non-Jews. *1934 Statistisches Jahrbuch für das Deutsche Reich*, Volume 2, Bewegung der Bevölkerung, section 9, Religionszugehörigkeit der Eheschliessungen, page 32. Statistics also show that in 1933 intermarriage increased: 35 percent of Jewish men and 20 percent of Jewish women married non-Jews. Thanks to Agnes Peterson and Linda Wheeler.

afraid someone will take your pocketbook or knock you down. People say it wouldn't be this way with Hitler. Anyway, that was the only good, so to speak, with Hitler."

In the flattest sense, Frau Rigl's life was like that of the majority of German women her age, it later occurred to me. Her country, with or without her encouragement, was taken over by a dictator for whom, or against whom, she actually was too young to vote. Her country, with or without her encouragement, issued harsh strictures against her Jewish neighbors. Her country, with or without her encouragement, went to war and drafted her husband to fight it. He did, and he died.

And throughout the whole period, if she is telling the truth, she scrabbled through, neither liking nor trusting the people who thrust the epoch upon her, and seeing herself as a pawn of those she considered, rightly or wrongly, to be the mighty. That meant, in addition to enemy bomber pilots, Nazis and Jews. Having them all occupy the same position was not typical of the other women I met.

And as her voice and manner indicated, the two people who most touched her heart also were an unlikely pair: her soldier husband and the Jewish merchant. Perhaps reflecting her own self-image, both men were pawns of others' wills, and both died because of their impotence. Presumably making the deaths even more difficult for her was never knowing how, where, or when they happened.

When, later, I asked if she had seen films of the liberation of the concentration camps, she said only "Na ja." [*Na ja* is an untranslatable German time-filler.] Finally, she said, "I too saw a couple. After the war." After several similarly truncated replies to promptings about her reaction to the Holocaust, she let loose, with words as pure and sincere, and as depressing, as anything any of the women said. Frau Anna Rigl's reaction to the Holocaust was this.

"It was bad and didn't have to happen. If they didn't like the Jews, they should just lock them up, but not gas them, kill them. They didn't have to kill them. I also don't know how that would have gone further, with the Jews. I don't know. They didn't have to punish them. They were also human beings, no? Hitler could have taken their possessions away from them, no? Possessions and jewelry, that they all had. But for heaven's sake not push them out, into the camps, and kill them. They didn't have to do that."

At first glance and last, Frau Emmi Heinrich was the kind of woman whose lap almost any lost child would seek. She has sparkling blue eyes and a curly kind of laugh, is rather short and rather stout (a festively laden coffee table helped explain the latter), and, when we met, was dressed in a cheerful blue-and-white skirt and white blouse. And she was the product of a happy home.

A happy, well-to-do home. "I come from a bourgeois family. My father came from a very old farm family and my mother from, if you will, a learned family. My mother's forefathers were overwhelmingly theologians, doctors, lawyers. In the course of time, there have been many pastors in Mecklenburg [a part of Germany north of Berlin], all of whom came from my mother's family. And my father was very German National. He always regretted there was no more emperor." She began to chuckle. "And always gauged everything in terms of the Kaiser. To his old age, we always laughed, he still was so taken by this earlier time that he never would have said 'emperor.' Only spoke of 'His Majesty,' even to my children." She was still chuckling and, as she was wont to do when especially merry, squeezed her plump arms to her sides as if they were a bellows, pumping herself with air. When she and her siblings were very young, she continued, their father always made them learn patriotic songs and verses, such as "My Prussia stands so proud and great, therefore I love it without restraint." She said that she and one of her brothers assumed he meant a high wooden tower that supported electricity lines and that they liked to climb. It was the only thing they knew that stood "so proud and great." Not

Frau Emmi Heinrich

Dissident Clergy and Dissident Actions

until their mother questioned their request to go to "our Prussia" did they learn their father had meant something else entirely. Finishing the story, Frau Emmi Heinrich all but burst with merriment.

Her other memories often contained images, but few brought even a smile, much less a laugh.

If it is true that people develop altruistic personalities in part because of a strongly moral parental figure,[1] it was Emmi's mother who must have been that person to her. She had no political opinions, said her daughter, "none at all. My mother was a deeply devout woman. My mother measured everything in terms of Christianity. And therefore during the war she really helped many whom one was not supposed to help, according to Nazi theology, out of her Christianity, because that was her 'neighbor.'" (She used the word *Nächster* [nearest], presumably referring to Jesus' commandment "Thou shalt love thy neighbor as thyself.") She continued, "And one must help a 'neighbor' who's in need. So for her it was all the same if it had to do with a Jew, a Frenchman, or a Russian war prisoner."

Emmi was the eldest of the six children—three girls, three boys. (All but one child reached adulthood; her eldest brother died of infantile paralysis when he was eight.) She was born in 1914 in the city of Parchim in Mecklenburg and essentially grew up in an oasis of cultural and creature comforts amid an impoverished and largely illiterate rural population. Do not blame those people for National Socialism, she implied. "You must not forget one thing. At home in the countryside, I believe scarcely anyone had a radio. My parents first had electricity installed in '23. Until then, there was nothing at all. And then, in Mecklenburg, the *miserable* education. Everyone in *one* classroom. All pupils. [In keeping with her family's status, however, Emmi presumably attended a private girls' school.] And *after* '45, there were always flyers, today there's sugar, today there's butter, and everyone could go and get some. And when this slip of paper arrived, there were not a few in the village who said, 'Let him read it. He can read without stuttering.' Books were read very seldom in the village simply because people's education was not up to it. There wasn't any interest in literature and poetry and so on, nicht? At the time, it was the exception to go to high school. We had very poor soil. The farmers were not among the richest farmers. Anyway, that was very difficult."

Do not blame her, either, for National Socialism, she more than implied; in 1933, she was only eighteen. "We were allowed to vote at the age

---

1. For an intriguing exploration of the subject, see Samuel P. Oliner and Pearl M. Oliner, *The Altruistic Personality: Rescuers of Jews in Nazi Europe* (New York: The Free Press, 1988).

of twenty-one. And by then I wasn't asked to anymore. So when one always says our generation is at fault for the arrival of Fascism. . . . [It is] they who were older." Furthermore, Germany's political leaders "were always changing. Ach du lieber Gott! One did not take anyone seriously. Then it was Hindenburg, then him, then him. So when Hitler came, each person thought, well, not each, that's probably going to end just as fast."

Asked if she had known any Jews in those pre-Nazi years, she answered she had two Jewish classmates. "You know, for us the Jew meant nothing more than another religion. When I think about it, we were really all predominantly Protestant. And we had these two Jewish girls in school and one Catholic. She was stranger to us than the Jews, simply because we were more strongly oriented toward Luther and his Reformation. That the Jews accepted the whole Old Testament just like we did and did not see God's son in Jesus Christ, but a prophet, actually seemed to us more believable than our belief. Therefore, we embraced them. We knew what separated us from the Catholics." She laughed her laugh. "And I never really came to terms with . . . Hitler's whole race thing. Because I knew [Jews], some of whom had German wives. They not only had German wives, they had German grandmothers. Or were baptized and whatever. So I always said, this is no *race* in and of itself. And they look just like *us*. How is that a race?"

Years before she concerned herself with such issues, she was concerned about her own future. "When I finished school, it was the time of the great unemployment. And many professions were closed to women. One said no woman was allowed to be hired whenever a man had a substantial family to feed. I would have liked terribly much to be a librarian or a bookseller or something like that." The injustice of the system still rankled. It was "unbelievable," she said. "First one went to school and then everything was cut off. My father did not find it bad at all. He said, learn properly how to run a household, for you'll get married someday and can always use it. So."

The story was familiar in that generation of Germany's well-educated (and hence well-off) young women. Now that times are tougher, forget about the career you worked toward during the liberal Weimar Republic, and get a "woman's job." Through "family contacts" with the owners of a large estate, Emmi became a cooking apprentice.

"Now I experienced something. Earlier we had our beautiful farm home [Hof]. My grandfather a lawyer, mayor of the city of Parchim. Let us say, we really always belonged to the elevated citizenry. And now I was a cooking apprentice and things went exactly the other way around. *Now* I experienced humankind being treated as the last piece of filth. And *there* is where my social conscience somehow revealed itself. We were told, 'We do not wish you to have contact with the workers.' And we thought, 'Why not? What kind of human beings are they?' And we sought them out and determined they were much more honest in their way than our gentlemen of the estate, who hid everything behind a smile." She said that criticizing someone one day and acting friendly days later "was really foreign to a worker."

She and the other apprentices of good homes ate with the estate family. "And in the evenings when we were finished work, [we] were allowed to spend a half hour socializing with them." Her voice had somewhat of a practiced edge to it.

"Then I had an experience that angered me terribly. I set a table for the evening meal. And the youngest son of the estate owner had a visitor from the city." Through an open door from the dining room into the corridor, she overheard the two talking. "Then I heard the owner's son say to the visitor, 'Listen. If you need a girl, go to the harvesters' barracks. If you can't argue your way out of it [that he made the girl pregnant], it will cost you seventeen marks a month. But don't mess with my wife's cooking apprentice. That will cost you a lot.'"

According to the law at the time, she said, child support was based on the mother's class. A mother with education had a right to raise her child a certain way and could demand more from the father. "So the fun cost fifty marks. But there were Polish girls in the harvesters' barracks. And *that* infuriated me. I always thought whoever had a proper education and wore a proper suit had a proper character." She said she told the cook, who had warned her earlier about the family. The cook said, "'Now you're finally wising up to what kind of people they are.' And so it went. One suddenly opens one's ears. Many have said to me, 'You really don't come from a worker family. How, then, did you become a social worker and really help those who really could not help themselves often because of their inadequate educations, because they were imprisoned,' and on and on? And I said, 'Because I experienced that.'"

If Frau Emmi Heinrich's vocabulary and view of the world seem out of the ordinary, it is because the place she made her home after the war was East Berlin.

When we met, she was living in an old apartment building whose hallways had the usual East Berlin look of a maintenance workers' strike. But her apartment itself was intact and attractive, with tall ceilings, a big tile heating oven, and pieces of old family furniture a little too large for the space. Frau Heinrich was, it seemed, a minor star among East Germans. A few sentences sounded like part of an often-delivered talk, and may have been. And if she spoke in terms of assessing her life, that stemmed in part from having been diagnosed a year earlier with inoperable cancer of the spine. She was being treated with radiation, she said, then changed the subject.

She did say cancer and age made her decide to go through the many papers she had relating to the Third Reich and to donate them to a receptive organization. One paper was a verboten flyer printed with the words of Martin Niemoeller, the noted pastor who helped found the anti-Nazi Protestant denomination called the Confessional Church. Martin Niemoeller had been her pastor. Yet during the Third Reich, he was only one of many people who opened the eyes of Frau Emmi Heinrich.

Just about as the Weimar Republic was ending, so was her two-year cooking apprenticeship, a kind of indentured servitude typical of the times. "The training, as one so nicely said then, was tit for tat. I did not need to pay for anything, but I got paid nothing. But I was allowed to get up at five in the morning and sometimes we were not finished by ten in the evening. In the summer there was baking and in the winter there was butchering."

And in the meantime there were Nazis. "They unleashed a *huge* enthusiasm among young boys and girls. In workers' circles and where industry was strong, that is, in big cities, there was already a Communist Party. In part, there was a somewhat left-leaning Social Democratic Party, let's say counterinfluences, which were minimal at home [in Mecklenburg]. The [Hitler Youth] boys found it terrific to go into the countryside on Sundays and put up their tents and get together."

Emmi's lot and future seemed considerably less exuberant. Her apprenticeship over, she took a final exam, passed, got the requisite certificate and a job with a local minister and his wife as a "Haustochter" [house daughter]—a job like being a maid, a cook, and an au pair. She worked ten- to twelve-hour days, received room and board, and only "seven marks a month spending money." She paused, still outraged. She did get one break a week. Every Saturday morning, she accompanied the minister's wife to town to do the marketing. (Emmi did have to return early, to cook the midday meal.) The trip included a stop at a "nice" confectionery store for coffee and cake, where Frau Minister also picked up her sweets for the week. "One day we went there and an SA man stood in front of the door and warned us [not to go in], it was a Jewish store. And as we went farther down the street, it was everywhere. *Everywhere* people were standing and warning one couldn't go in anymore. That was the first Jewish boycott."

Frau Heinrich said she found it "unbelievable," but she and the minister's wife did not go in the store. "It somehow had to do with fear." The next Saturday the store was closed.

"A few days later, SA people in brown uniforms went through the village and searched houses. The homes of the estate's workers. The word was that some of them leaned in favor of the Social Democrats." She said the brownshirts presumably were looking for Social Democratic literature or similar things. "And you know, a young person has a very strong feeling of justice. I found that unbelievable, too, that they simply went in the houses and rummaged around simply because they had on brown uniforms. And the others stood in front and no one was allowed to go in."

A month later, in April of 1933, the Nazis tied their noose tighter around the printed word and people who wrote or read it, by consigning works of newly verboten authors to the flames. "My grandfather was very democratically oriented. And Grandfather said to me, 'Child, go to the bookcase.'" She acted him out, pointing to the same handsome oak bookcase in her apartment. "*Behind* the first row stood a second row. He said, 'You may take the books out sometime. Read them. And you make a judgment whether or not that is worthwhile German literature, what they've burned. There is Thomas Mann, there is Heinrich Mann, above all [Heinrich] Heine.'" The latter they read most of all. "And he said, 'And we live in a state which burns these people.'" She said he retired early rather than let the Nazis dismiss him. She did not mention that if his verboten books had been discovered, he might have lost more than his job.

By February of 1934, Emmi had had enough of being a "house daughter" with seven marks a month spending money. She moved to Berlin to study nursing (one of the few approved professions for women) at an evangelical-affiliated hospital in the city's Grunewald section. Her eyes opened wider.

She and other nursing students were members of what she called "the evangelical deacons' organization," which involved Bible discussions with an assigned minister. She did not like his "German Christian" (pro-Nazi) line of thinking. "And not far away, in the village church in Dahlem, was Niemoeller. I still remember saying to the other nurses one day, 'You know what? We're going to Niemoeller.' And we went to Niemoeller, we wore our outfits, and wanted to talk with him, and told him [our concerns]." They discussed his version of certain biblical lessons vis-à-vis the preachings of the Third Reich. "So, next Bible hour, we showed up snappily [at the Bible lesson of the other minister] and said we'd thought about that. And why is that not so? And isn't that so? And he got nothing but trouble from us." She laughed. "I knew Niemoeller already had been set upon and we went back there again and I said we sometimes were worried about him. And at that he said . . . He always stooped slightly, even then. I can still see him in front of me, how he stood there and said, 'Nurse Emmi, I must say as Luther did, Here I stand. I cannot do otherwise. God help me.' Can *never* forget it. And that was two years before his arrest."

Frau Heinrich said she "belonged to his circle and wrote letters to those who belonged to [it]." Yet she said the members of the Confessional Church knew each other only by face, not name. She said the flyer she had had contained Niemoeller's reference to the first commandment, "Thou shall have no other God but me," and his admonition that the Nazis were trying to make a God out of Hitler. (In 1937, Niemoeller was arrested, imprisoned, set free, rearrested, and sent to concentration camps. Allied troops liberated him from Dachau in 1945.)

At almost the same time she sought out Niemoeller, Frau Heinrich got what may have been her first personal lesson about crossing the creed of the Third Reich. "I had a head nurse whose nephew was a personal advisor to

Hitler. The lad's name was Kurt Gerdisch.[2] I never met him, but our head nurse was no little bit proud of this nephew. Ja. And over coffee I am to have said something in a casual way, well, that my father didn't think much of this upstart [Hitler]. She took me to her room and said I would be advised to be careful about my utterances. That she, for example, was the aunt of Kurt Gerdisch and he was the personal advisor to Hitler. That's when I first noticed one had to be somewhat careful. And then came this 30th of June, '34, the Roehm revolts, where Hitler had a group of his supporters killed, who somehow didn't want things completely the way he'd planned.

"It was a Saturday. I had had night duty that night. We had a doctor, whose name was Dr. Heineke. I heard he committed suicide, but much later. And *he* also was the doctor for Hitler's bodyguards." (The bodyguard regiment, called the Leibstandarte-SS Adolf Hitler, did more than protect Hitler. It was like a small army of terrorists, and was active in the Roehm Putsch.) "That summer evening," she continued, the doctor "was summoned to western Berlin, to the bodyguards. At approximately five in the morning, the man came back, pale as a corpse, shook himself and said, 'Please, a very strong cup of coffee.' I put it down next to him and then he said just one sentence. 'Do you know how terrible it is to have to confirm the deaths of *over* one hundred human beings?'" She paused. "I didn't say anything. He didn't say anything. And afterward he just said"—she spoke rapidly in imitation—"'Tell me, what did I say?' It had simply poured out.

"And the next day I went to Dahlem to hear Niemoeller and *everywhere* there are SS on the streets. *Every*where. You could not walk a hundred meters without it being the same. 'Please move on, do not form a group. Please move on, do not form a group. [The expression was *Keine Haufen bilden* (Do not build a pile.)] Somehow, one got an eerie feeling. Although at first we didn't know what had happened." She continued on her way, stopping at her girlfriend's, a former classmate who happened to live next door to the Leibstandarte headquarters. The friend said that "in the evening, SS people came and said we should close our windows and not look outside. And throughout the night, we heard shooting over and over, and now and again a scream." The friend "just sat there trembling and not knowing what was going on. That was the thirtieth of June. And from *then* on, I could not sympathize with them at all. To me, it was so horrible one lived in a state which simply could kill people. And my own father was a *member* of the NSDAP."

She said he belonged to the Stahlhelm [Steel Helmets], a nationalistic organization consisting mostly of First World War veterans who wanted a

---

2. The spelling of his name, and others to come, is a guess. Frau Heinrich never responded to my later inquiry about (among other matters) the names of people she mentioned.

return to the German monarchy. Its leader was Franz Seldte, who in her words "transferred" the Stahlhelm members over to the Party. "And my father did not have *that* amount of courage to say, I want to get out of it." According to another source, at the end of 1933, Hitler incorporated the Stahlhelm into the SA to cut opposition. The move was not popular among members of either organization.[3]

Her father, she said, decided to stay in the Party for his children's welfare. "But he always warned my brothers about overeagerness, that they should not go along with things, but study more instead. Then, afterward, the owner of an estate in the neighborhood also was shot to death, in the course of this whole situation. Then my father always said, 'If only one *single* person was shot without a judicial sentence, that is murder.' "

The following year, 1935, another public event, the enactment of the Nuremberg race laws, touched Emmi's private life. One person who fell under its provisions was her new best friend, Anneliese Tack, from the well-known Tack shoe manufacturing family. They had met in nursing school. Anneliese was the daughter of a Jewish father who had died in the First World War and an "Aryan" mother. Although the mother had remarried an "Aryan," the Jew who had died for his "Fatherland" now endangered his daughter's life by having been who he was. Anneliese emigrated. Frau Heinrich recalled another half-Jewish girlfriend who did, too.

But her most detailed memory concerned a young doctor named Max Arnold Mairovski (as she pronounced it—the spelling is a guess). "His father was professor of dermatology in Cologne [University]. And he [Max] was at our hospital and wanted to specialize in neurosurgery. Then the Nuremberg laws came down. His family fell *completely* under its terms. Father came from a Jewish family. Mother came from a Jewish family. Whether baptized or not played no role. He had a sister who earlier had joined a cloister in Italy and later was arrested when the Nazis combed through it, and died in a German concentration camp. And the family, Professor Mairovski, his wife, both his sons, his family, then left Germany in 1937." The family's immediate destination was England.

Before departing, Max Arnold Mairovski wrote a formal farewell letter to Emmi Heinrich. When I expressed interest in it, she retrieved it within seconds and read it out loud with the care she might have given a poem by Heine. Max Arnold Mairovski's German prose was achingly beautiful.

Writing to "Most esteemed Nurse Emmi" on August 4, 1936, he thanked her "from my heart for the great helpfulness you rendered me at a time in which the majority turned away." He wrote of his recognition that "after the foundations of life that I considered the sole worthwhile ones for

---

3. Louis L. Snyder, *Encyclopedia of the Third Reich* (New York: McGraw-Hill, 1976; New York: Paragon House, 1980), 331.

me ultimately were destroyed . . . in my closest family I am needed more today than I ever have been." His life now would be "without dividends" but "built upon waiting for the moment when the Fatherland again will need all those who are prepared to be true to it . . . in spite of everything. Pythagoras once was asked how one should behave toward an ungrateful Fatherland. And he answered, as toward your own mother."

The Mairovski family went from England to Tennessee. Frau Heinrich said she heard through a mutual friend that a young neurosurgeon in Nashville was named Mairovski.

"And you know," she said, "the fate of these human beings contributed to the fact that I never would have been able to marry a man who was connected to this system. It just wasn't in the cards anymore." Asked if she had not been so opposed earlier, she said, "Nein, nein. I did find it impossible, what the SS [sic] did with the house searches and the Jewish boycott. *But*," she said, pausing, "at that time, I would have married someone I liked and even had been a [Nazi Party] member. If he had been able to explain it to me. Ja."

The someone she did marry she met in 1938 on an estate in Mecklenburg, where he was working. Herr Heinrich, far from being a Nazi, had been in the "Young Socialists" and "made no concessions" to National Socialism. She said she often asked him what he had done and was doing in that regard, but he would not say. "He didn't want to burden me, nor the people he knew well and who felt the same way he did." He was going to tell her later, she said.

The same year she met a good man, she also met a "very, very good" woman who hired her as a nurse. So, a year after the Nazis caused Frau Heinrich to lose two people close to her—Max Mairovski fled Germany and Pastor Niemoeller was arrested—she replaced them, in effect, with an anti-Nazi husband and an anti-Nazi employer.

Frau Dr. Briefert was the wife of a man who had been married to Frau Heinrich's aunt. Frau Heinrich found even that much of a "familiar connection" to be reassuring at a time when, she said, government-paid nurses had to be National Socialists. Nurse Emmi asked Frau Doktor if she might work with her in her private practice; she consented. "And so it remained." (The women stayed close until the doctor's death in 1984.)

"I began with her in 1938 and in '39 the war broke out. And then later patients came and told us horrible things. One [a civilian man] came and said, 'Could you please write me up as sick a couple of days? I cannot bear to hear it anymore.' Well, we said, '*What* can you not stand to hear anymore?' And he said he works near Plötzensee [prison] and always hears a little bell tinkle. And whenever he hears the little bell tinkle, someone else is beheaded. And he *cannot* stand to hear that anymore. Could we write him up as sick a couple of days? And that's the *first* time I heard about that."

She said she did not know how he learned that the tinkling of the bell at the prison meant a beheading, but he was sure "there were not a few" who were beheaded. Frau Heinrich, at first incredulous about the man's claim, asked one patient (a woman later honored for her resistance work) to help her verify it. The woman said she and her husband were close to Plötzensee's Pastor Harald Poelchau[4] and would ask him to receive "Nurse Emmi," so she could tell him about it. "I was at Pastor Poelchau's and told him and he only nodded his head and said, 'Unfortunately, it is true.'"

Frau Heinrich paused a good while before she spoke again.

"A lot of Jews were still living here in Berlin. And Frau Dr. Briefert earlier had had many Jewish patients. That happened simply because they lived [in the neighborhood]." The doctor's office was on the Chausseestrasse in central Berlin, east of where the Berlin Wall was. Frau Heinrich went on to say that the Jews had to put Stars of David on their doors "so when the SS rounded them up, they had it terribly easy. And the Jews at the time were not allowed to seek out a normal medical practice, only go to one of their own. And were not allowed to walk on certain streets here and not allowed to travel on the streetcars at certain times and they weren't allowed to sit anyway, had to stand, and got other ration cards. Well, it was pretty awful. And they were not allowed to go to movies and they were not allowed to go to the theater and afterward they were not allowed to have pets, no parrot and no dog. It was all verboten. And now we had Jewish patients. We were not allowed to write prescriptions for any." But, she said, she and Frau Dr. Briefert had their own medicine, stashed in a wall-long cabinet of drawers. "We called it doctor samples. The pharmaceutical firms came and offered their newest developments and medications and pills, so Frau Doktor could order them. We had medicine for the heart, for circulation, gall bladder, things for the liver and kidneys. And now we began to give out these medications to former Jewish patients and to take them there. We always had a signal." She demonstrated, rapping on her chair arm: two knocks, a pause, three more knocks. "And then they knew it was us. They were completely scared and we only passed it in to them. We also falsified prescriptions. Frau Doktor said to me, 'So, now I'll write this prescription out for you. Or for whom can we write it?'" The woman patient who approached Pastor Poelchau helped in the scheme, too. She "got many a prescription for things she never had and she also delivered them." But when she left, she sometimes got "a bad feeling" that someone on the stairs had seen her and might report her.

Frau Heinrich had her own moments of extreme panic. Herr Heinrich was off at war in the navy artillery, and she lived alone in two rooms con-

---

4. For more about the remarkable Pastor Poelchau, see the interview with Freya von Moltke.

nected to the medical offices. Sometimes the bell rang at night. She felt "as wretched as a dog, because one did not know if it was someone who had observed you. Sometimes it was someone who didn't know that Frau Doktor didn't live there and who desperately needed a doctor."

One day a woman Frau Dr. Briefert and Nurse Emmi knew entered the medical practice and made a brief statement. "Frau Doktor, I hid a Jew." Frau Dr. Briefert answered, "Ja?" in a way that in Frau Heinrich's telling meant "Yes, so?"

The woman continued. "He died. What can I do with the corpse?"

The death, due to illness (Frau Heinrich indicated that Frau Dr. Briefert had supplied the man with medicine) occurred in an apartment building about five houses away. "Now everyone was endangered. Do you know what they did? During a bombing raid, they carried him out and set him somewhere on the stairs. There were always bombing attacks." The other inhabitants, upon returning from the shelter, were to assume that the stranger had sought shelter in the building during the bombing and died.

"That's when I first knew how dangerous it was to hide people. Until then, one thought, ach Gott, that's just . . . One always called those who had gone under 'U-boats,' nicht? And one sometimes thought, ach Gott, perhaps it's not so bad at all. And then I noticed how bad it could be. And they could not say he died. They really would have been taken away that morning, to a concentration camp or whatever."

Some elements of day-to-day life under the Nazis did remain normal, said Frau Heinrich, but not in smaller places. A case in point was "the greeting" of "Heil Hitler!"

"Here in Berlin, you could still get in and out with a 'Good day' and so on. *But* in Parchim, it was noticed if you didn't greet. I remember at home my sister had to get something done at the blacksmith. And came into the smithy and said 'Heil Hitler!' and the smith asked her in Plattdeutsch [dialect] if she'd cracked up."

Her sister had said it only for protection?

"Ja, ja. She didn't know his opinions and it was such a matter of course in school, and she'd been in the 'work duty' program." She added, "You didn't need to raise your arm, but that was just the greeting. It simply belonged to daily routine not to stand out. And one did not want to stand out."

In Parchim, even innocent comments stood out. The following is a perfect example of how German civilians were kept in line. "We had a [woman] shopkeeper who had a combined store, half bookstore, half stationery store. And when the war with the Soviet Union broke out, the winter was ghastly cold. The soldiers were not at all prepared and therefore did not have proper clothing. And someone came in the store and [spoke of] well, our soldiers. And she [the shopkeeper] said, she was always thinking about the poor soldiers. And some Hitler supporter heard that and immediately denounced this woman at the regional headquarters. As a result, she was ordered to go to the regional headquarters. And every day for *four* weeks she had to show up at the headquarters and say the sentence, 'Not our *poor* soldiers. Our *brave* soldiers. Heil Hitler!' " Frau Heinrich laughed.

She also gave an example of how German soldiers were kept in line. The example involved her husband. Herr Heinrich, having returned to the front from leave, was asked, apparently amid a trusted group, what he thought about the war. She said he replied that it would be revealed that the Soviet system had its positive sides and was not just as the Nazis tried to picture it. A man in the group denounced him that night. "My husband was taken in a special boat to Germany and appeared before a military judge. For 'disruption of the state and the people,' three years of prison. He got off well, for the times. Had it been two years later, after Stalingrad, things would probably have gone much worse."

Learning of his sentence, Herr Heinrich again tried to hide the truth from his wife, who was about to give birth to their first child. "He had *only* written, 'If you don't hear from me for a long time, don't worry. I'm probably going to special training, where I'm not allowed to write.' And I was such a fool, I believed it." She said shortly after their daughter's birth, she happened to see a professor she and her husband both knew. "He said, 'Where is your husband now?' And I said, 'Ja, he's on a special teaching program and I can't reach him.' And he looked at me so peculiarly. I thought, 'Why is he looking at me so strange?' " Herr Heinrich was not in prison long. "After a good three-quarters of a year, Hitler issued a decree that everyone under a certain [level of sentencing] was going to the front. And the remainder of the sentence to be served would be decided *after* the war."

Later, while Herr Heinrich was back at the front, another decree came out that nurses who were not pregnant or did not have many children also were to be sent to military hospitals at the front. "In January 1943, I knew I had to go to the examination, during which I said, 'I believe I am pregnant.' Whereupon the doctor screamed at me, 'One either *is* pregnant or one is not. One knows which.' I said I didn't get my period and my husband had been home on leave and I assumed I was." She was.

She stayed in Berlin, continuing to work for Frau Dr. Briefert and their patients and against the Nazis. "It really was not political resistance. It really only came from purely humanistic reasons. There were humanistic reasons that separated someone from the system and there were humanistic reasons that we helped them, but no political motive as such."

In the midst of the war, Frau Heinrich met yet another anti-Nazi personage, the artist Käthe Kollwitz. She was married to a doctor with whom Frau Dr. Briefert had a working relationship. The meeting occurred when Nurse Emmi went to Dr. Kurt Kollwitz's office to pick up a patient's file. Frau Heinrich said she knew Käthe Kollwitz was verboten as an artist but did not know much about her, except that she had sculpted a memorial to the dead of the First World War and that the dead included her son.

"It was a cold January day and her husband wasn't there and I had to wait. And then Käthe Kollwitz asked me, 'Do you also have relatives at the front? I answered, 'Ja. My husband. My brothers. My father.' " She said only, very sweetly, 'You poor child.' And I asked her if she also had relatives [there]. I said I knew about her son Peter from the First World War. And she had a grandchild who was named in honor of the fallen Peter. And he, too, was killed. In the Polish campaign. And she told me [regarding her son's death], never in her life has she come to terms with that. Maybe never. Because she persuaded him to volunteer for the fighting. And fourteen days later he was no longer alive. And she said she got such terrible fits of depression and isolated herself so much, it almost cost her marriage."

Over time, Frau Emmi Heinrich got her own reckoning from the front. "My other two brothers died in 1943, in the war. And my husband, imprisoned for political reasons, then was sent to the Eastern Front for reinforcements, and was missing in action. We did not hear from him for a long time. The last news was in March 1945. And after that, nothing more."

The only male in the family to survive was her Kaiser-loving Steel Helmet father.

Toward the end of the war, Frau Heinrich left Berlin (no doubt as part of the evacuation of women and children from the city) and returned to Mecklenburg. She was there when Soviet troops came through. Unlike women from other eastern parts of Germany, not to mention Berlin, Frau Heinrich did not bring up a word about the Soviet soldiers raping or looting or killing. Instead, she spoke of a Soviet officer asking her to use her medical skills to help prevent a typhoid epidemic that threatened nearby villages. She agreed. She said her in-laws turned up from the west and asked her to come live with them so the family could stay together. They also offered to help care for the children so she would be free to work. "Ja, should I just leave my villages in the lurch?" She whispered, "I couldn't do that. I couldn't do that. I was needed." She said she decided that where she was, was where she could "fulfill her duty."

Frau Emmi Heinrich remained in East Germany. In 1948 she was asked to be a social worker in the new mother-and-child division of the country's health ministry. Having known in her nursing days of young unmarried women's attempts to commit suicide because of being pregnant (the Nazis forbade "Aryan" women to get abortions), she grabbed the chance to equalize the treatment of legitimate and illegitimate children. (She said that under old German law and throughout the Nazi era, if a woman had an illegitimate child before marriage and gave it away for adoption, she had to tell her future husband, but he did not have to tell his wife if he had fathered a child.) "I said *that* is a thing for which you can commit yourself and make propaganda for and can break this monopoly of only a certain class being able to send its children to higher education, as I experienced it. Why not the talented child of a worker?"

She remained a believer in the new system all her life, it seemed. She even was active in East Germany's very subordinate opposition party. But, in her new antireligious country, did she keep her Christian faith? "Ja. I profess my Christian faith now as before. For me, everything I do stems from the basis of my belief." She said she also had spoken about Christianity with Dietrich Bonhoeffer, another prominent Protestant anti-Nazi theologian. (He died in a concentration camp days before the end of the war.) "He told me, 'To be a Christian really means nothing else than to be there for others.' And from when I was small, I always had to be there for others. I had siblings who were nine and ten years younger. As the oldest, one always had to be there for the littler ones. Well, when one comes from such a big family and then the farm, there were always duties. It began with feeding chicks and hens, but somehow one always had to be useful. And so it was my whole way of being, that consequently led toward becoming a nurse and then later still, becoming a social worker. Always out of this need to want to be there for others where help is needed and to be able to help as long as one is asked."

Anna Fest's childhood memories, as she described them, were about nothing remarkable—just commonplace tragedy, followed by economic survival. Born in 1920 in a central German village of approximately four hundred people, most of them farmers, manual laborers, and their families, she was two years old when her father was killed in a train accident. As a result of his death, her mother received a small annuity to help support herself, Anna, and Anna's baby sister, Erika. She also resumed her earlier trade as a seamstress.

Of the 1933 election that brought Hitler to power, then-thirteen-year-old Anna Kupfer later recalled there was only one no vote in her village. Everyone knew of the vote, she said, if not who cast it. She said the election itself did not make a big impression on her, but she does remember that after the Nazis came to power the family's annuity increased.

Her mother "obviously" joined the Frauenschaft, and because of her "good school education"[1] took over its local treasury.

At home, Anna found no "unrestrained enthusiasm" for the Nazis. If her mother said Goebbels should not talk so big, someone else would say be quiet, then someone else would say, "These two hundred percent Nazis will make us all kaputt." Anna's uncle, a member of the leftish Social Democratic Party, did not like the Nazis at all. Talk about them ricocheted around the house.

Frau
Anna
Fest

A Job in Its Own Category

---

1. Basic "Schulbildung," roughly equal to completing ninth grade.

Frauen

In the mid-1930s Frau Kupfer decided to move her family of three to a larger town where she could earn more money. She was specifically a "white seamstress" [Weiss-Näherin], which meant she went to private homes to sew private garments of fine white linen. The work, said her daughter, entailed "attaching lace and doing the embroidery on elegant underclothes for ladies."

The town in which she chose to employ her fine hand more fruitfully was Sonnenfeld, in north-central Germany. There, Anna joined the Bund deutscher Mädel. "I found it very nice. We sang folk songs, there was a gymnastics group. And still today, with the best attempts I cannot remember any direct political instruction. I've tried so hard to remember something like that. There was *nothing*. We liked it so well anyway."

From the Kupfers' point of view, the Nazis' best accomplishments were jobs and the family's increased pension. Frau Fest said she cannot understand why other Germans deny their early enthusiasm. "Why don't they admit it?" she whispered. "So many were enthusiastic. We all were more or less enthusiastic." She continued, "We were young people. We were spoken to. It's not so difficult to produce patriotic feelings in a young person and fill him with enthusiasm. Why shouldn't one admit it later?"

Throughout the coming years of the Third Reich and the war, her mother and Erika lived a relatively unremarkable existence. Anna, however, spent the latter part of the period as a concentration camp guard.

Frau Fest now lives with her husband, Otto, a former postal worker, in the pin-tidy village of Wackersdorf, some ten miles from Sonnenfeld. Their children, a daughter and two sons, have long been on their own. (At Frau Fest's request, family and place names and some details have been fictionalized.) The Fests own a prototypically German house, which at first glance is nearly overwhelmed by the front-yard flower garden. Inside, the furnishings are prototypically German, too, of the postwar style. Cleanliness and modesty reign, along with touches bespeaking house pride—on a polished table a large vase of different colored roses from the garden, a breakfront holding the crystal. Judging from what could be gleaned of the neighborhood, it seemed the Fests were a blue-collar family on a white-collar street, and felt it. Toward a down-the-street neighbor, a retired psychologist named Frau Dr. Diener, the Fests behaved with noticeable deference.

Frau Dr. Diener, who had put us in touch, knew virtually nothing about Frau Fest except that she was boisterously friendly to everybody, was a nurse's aide, and had been a guard. That, to my surprise, was neighborhood knowledge. But why had she said yes to Frau Dr. Diener's inquiry about talking to a stranger? Was she used to discussing her past? Did she have a clear conscience, justified or not? A muddled memory? An urge to confess?

314

Later, it dawned on me she simply may have been trying to please Frau Dr. Diener.

Frau Fest probably saw me coming up the walk. She probably wondered why it was taking me so long to knock. The emotion of standing for the first time at the door of a former concentration camp guard is difficult to describe. Finally, I raised my hand.

The woman who opened the door was stout and graying and wore a white uniform on which was pinned a Red Cross service medal. Frau Anna Fest and I shook hands and introduced ourselves. The interview was to take place between her stints of caring for a bedridden old woman.

Frau Fest's face showed signs of prettiness and was devoid of makeup. It also carried a troubled expression, at odds with her local reputation. The reason was clear. Contrary to one of my guesses, she was not at all used to talking about her past. This was the first time, she said, that she would be talking freely about it to anyone outside her immediate family.

We sat down in her living room, and struggled through several minutes of laden and leaden chat. It must have been clear to us both how uneasy we both were. Finally, Frau Fest suggested we have "a small glass of wine [ein Gläschen Wein]." All right, I said. The moment was transforming. She hopped up, apparently relieved to do something she was used to doing— serving refreshments to company; I relaxed when she relaxed, and, thanks in part to a fine local vintage, we were off.

Frau Fest tripped through the village years, the move to Sonnenfeld, and arrived at Germany's declaration of war. At the time, she was nineteen years old.

She got the news at work, the Behringwerke pharmaceutical company, which was involved indirectly with the military. From the loudspeaker came a command for employees to gather in the factory's inner yard for an announcement from the director.

"He said that as of a certain time there's war, our troops had marched into Poland, and so on. I know there was no enthusiasm. Many women cried. They simply knew, okay, now the men would be going away. Perhaps there *were* some who said yes, it has to be, and there may have been some who were a little more interested in politics, who could have seen what was coming. But we ourselves really weren't interested in that."

In addition to her job in a factory laboratory, involving typhus immunization research, Frau Fest immediately was made part of the war effort. Under the aegis of the Red Cross, with which she had been affiliated since 1936, she was sent to the local train station to help care for soldiers when the troop transports stopped. There, some women dispensed coffee, soup, and the like, while she was posted to an adjoining medical unit, somewhat stunned, it seems.

Frauen

"When I think back about it, I must honestly say that when the war began we were a little bit surprised and taken unawares [überrascht und überrumpelt]. One simply was in the middle of it. One didn't come to any *consciousness* to think differently."

Frau Fest's fiancé, Otto, was sent to the western front. Many other men from both their families were drafted.

"It's quite clear one will be fearful. That will happen to every mother. That will happen to every woman. And when everyone kept being told to be brave, and the first news of the fatalities came . . ." She trailed off. "You know, at some point you don't want to be brave anymore. You want to be able to cry. Then you're extremely sad inside, but can't risk showing anything. It's terrible. Of my father's family, six brothers were called up and four were killed. One *never* comes out of the blackness that follows."

Doing double duty at the home front prompted Frau Fest to complain to her mother that she was exhausted and wanted to have Sundays free. Her mother, she said, responded that Otto was at the front, so Anna would not be going anywhere on Sundays anyway. And if everyone gave up, no one would do anything. So Anna reactivated "the perhaps stupid sense of duty" and the maxims "be brave" and "don't cry" and kept going.

In 1940, after more than a year of active duty, Otto Fest got his first home leave. He and Anna used it to get married. The couple received from the state the standard wedding present for "Aryan" betrothals, a copy of *Mein Kampf*. Giggling, Frau Fest said she still has it and still means to take the time to read it, but has not. As for the newlyweds, Frau Fest herself joined the Frauenschaft and Herr Fest returned to the front.

"The war probably had completely different consequences for women than men," she said. Women were "forced to be self-sufficient and really had to struggle, and the men were away." Her own plunge into self-sufficiency led her to be one of many German women whose marriage became a post-war battleground. Like other women, she saw the nuptial phenomenon as going beyond her individual situation. "As far as the men were concerned, we'd basically become too self-sufficient. We'd become what one strives for today. Emancipated. And I was always sort of the type anyway who wasn't so easily ordered about and did defend my personality a bit. When my husband came back from the war, that was downright difficult."

While he was away on one front, another front came to her. During a bombing raid, her laboratory was hit. She was not injured in the attack itself, but while helping clean up the damage, badly injured her hand. It became temporarily paralyzed. She could no longer hold a test tube. Behringwerke assigned her the less skilled job of packing serum.

She said that a new publication by a local history study group reported that Behringwerke elsewhere conducted medical experiments on humans. "None of us here, of course, knew about it." According to the publication, Behringwerke (which in 1929 became a division of IG Farben) conducted

medical experiments on prisoners in Buchenwald. From such tests as inject-
ing prisoners with high amounts of serums or the pathogenic agents themselves, especially typhus, more than six hundred prisoners died.[2] Frau Fest
said if you now ask Behringwerke, one of Germany's postwar success stories,
about its past, you are "up against a wall. There's silence. There's nothing."

In the fall of 1944, the Nazis called for Germany to attain "totaler
Kriegseinsatz" [mobilization for total war]. Frau Fest said each company was
ordered to release a certain percentage of its employees for the mobilization.
She, whose stiffened hand relegated her to "the ones they could use the
least," was among those released. She said Behringwerke sent her to the local
employment office, which in turn sent her to the employment office in the
town of Allendorf.

There she was assigned her total mobilization job. She was told, she
said, that she had been "drafted to watch over foreign work forces." She said
her impression was that she would oversee their work in a factory and be
helpful in whatever way she could be. She was, she added, "so dumb."

"Then with ten or twelve other women who'd also been taken from
work, we were sent to what we'd been told was instruction at a manufacturing plant. We were sent, however, to Ravensbrück."

There, the women would receive two weeks of "instruction," and some
searing memories. Survivors of Ravensbrück concentration camp for women
(see interview with Frau Lotte Müller) considered it hell. Anna Fest, then
twenty-four years old, said her group of young women was unaware of the
destination and had "incredible fun" on the train ride there. "We were being
foolish, like young things sort of are, no?" Then they asked a male passenger,
a civilian from the area, where they should get off. "He said, 'Well, don't you
know where you're going?' and he told us, and it was, of course, an insane
shock."

Yet, she said, even when she saw the sign, Ravensbrück Concentration
Camp, she misunderstood. "I thought it was a manufacturing plant. And we
thought we'd be trained to learn the manufacturing procedures and then
instruct the foreign workers. There was absolutely no talk of that. . . ." She
stopped. "We arrived at the holding room, sort of at the camp gate, and we
saw how they were being brought in and out and guards stood there and
already we saw a kick and sometimes a box on the ear too, and we began to
grumble. One of the guards said, 'Go ahead, you can grumble. I don't have
anything against it. But if you want to be on the inside too, that's your business. I'd advise you to keep your mouths shut.'

"It was such a shock to me. Even today it practically makes me crazy.

---

2. *Braukessel & Presslufthammer, Abriss einer Industriegeschichte* (Brewery vat & jackhammer,
   Summary of an industrial history) (Marburg: Geschichtswerkstatt Marburg,
   1985), 28.

When I think about it, I could burst out weeping in front of you. Something so *'fürchterlich'* [horrendous]. They were human beings and should be treated like human beings."

The second year we met, she related a similar incident that "incredibly horrified" her. She had been eating with her group at a table overlooking the gate area when a group of prisoners arrived from Poland. Ravensbrück's male SS guards "received" them. One guard "got among them and began beating a woman. I jumped up. A guard who sat next to me pushed me back down and she said, 'Obviously, you are tired of living. Stay seated if you can and look away. You have no idea how many of your kind who have rebelled are already prisoners themselves.' Of course, I didn't say another thing."

Frau Fest and the other young guards-in-training were kept in a closely regulated group, she said, and told "to trouble ourselves with as little as possible. We weren't allowed in the camp itself, but had to stay at the outside gate. And then [we] were trained how to observe the people you had to guard, to make sure no one got away, and so on."

Frau Fest also indicated she knew the worst of what went on inside, even if she did not see it. Having been to Ravensbrück myself, I said I was told that "the ashes" were dumped into the nearby lake. Frau Fest responded that she and another woman had taken out a paddleboat on the lake one afternoon, that she must have noticed something, chided herself how could she have, and concluded if they did it, they must have dumped the ashes at night. Neither of us had mentioned where "the ashes" came from.

During the two-week training period, Frau Fest and her young colleagues were inducted into the SS. Then they were issued SS uniforms. When the two weeks were up, the group was given temporary leave. "I was *so* happy when I came back home. Then my mother saw I wore an SS uniform. She said, 'Child, that is my death.' It was true. She got so insanely upset and was a little unstable in terms of nerves. She got stomach cancer during that time. She always swallowed all upsetting things."

Frau Fest soon learned she was not to be assigned to Ravensbrück after all, but to one of fourteen "work camps" specializing in munitions, near Allendorf. The camps were under the jurisdiction of Buchenwald.[3]

About half the "work camps" had paid employees. The other camps, including hers, would fit the world's basic sense of concentration camp. Frau Fest described her camp (and the third year we met drew a map to help explain the layout) as a large camouflaged complex with separate, isolated areas, among which numbered an underground munitions factory with its own security system. The factory itself was reached by going through one

---

3. Bernd Klewitz, *Die Arbeitssklaven der Dynamit Nobel* (The work slaves of Nobel Dynamite) (Schalksmühle: Engelbrecht Verlag, 1986), 9, 119.

gate into an "enormously large" area and then through "a massive fence." Her area inside the factory was further cordoned off.

The prisoner barracks were farther away in the forest, as were the guard barracks. Although most prisoners were women, some men, who, she said, did the heavier work, also were there, as were male SS guards who patrolled the camp's outer perimeter. She said the whole camp was so disguised that Allied pilots could not spot it.

Herr Fest, who in the late 1950s walked around the camp as it was being converted into a housing and factory site, described the smokestacks as reaching higher than the trees. When there was a bombing raid, he said, they were retracted and the smoke was diverted into underground ducts and released throughout the forest. He also said all buildings, at most a story high, were covered with earth planted with camouflaging shrubs and bushes.

Frau Fest said her relative good fortune at being sent to Allendorf, rather than having to stay at Ravensbrück, was compounded by the kind of women she was to guard. From her first mention of them and every time thereafter, her voice and her face reflected awe. The women were Hungarian Jews.

"I had the luck to get a small detachment of [about ten] women who were very intelligent. I was alone with them. And outside the central camp area, we essentially could do what we wanted, no one looking over us."

She said her job spanned what was considered "a completely normal working day." She got up about 5 A.M. and usually was back in her barracks by 6 P.M.

Every day was about the same. "In the morning, I had to be at the gate. They came out and then I had to receive them, so to speak. To sign that so many women went with me to the plant." (Her prisoners' work shift started at eight, she said.) "The same thing happened in the evening, when we returned." She said she never was allowed in the inner camp where the women slept and ate. During work hours, she said, she stayed in the factory with her group. "I looked to see what they were doing individually and talked with them. They all spoke German. Only intelligent women could be used for this work. I sometimes asked questions, how are you doing that and so forth, and," she whispered, "sometimes I was able to help them a little. Although that really was not allowed."

She said the prisoners had a fifteen-minute breakfast break and at most a half-hour lunch break. In the evening, she took them to the gate of their barracks and returned to hers, to which she was "basically confined." Some evenings she took a walk with other guards, and, infrequently, went to the nearby village for a movie. But usually she stayed in her bunk, writing or reading. It was less trouble, she said.

"If we wanted to go out, we had to have a certificate of passage and if we wanted to go home, a certificate of leave. If I could get the time, I'd go home to Sonnenfeld. And because I was one of the few who lived there, I did some shopping for the camp. I remember, for example, buying things for Christmas, all possible kinds of baking ingredients and setting some of it aside for my mother and mother-in-law so they could bake for Christmas, too. And I bought pencils and so on for myself, and then the prisoners baked and made Christmas tree ornaments."

The irony went beyond Jewish concentration camp inmates making Christmas ornaments: one common German Christmas symbol the prisoners probably made is a six-pointed star.

As for the factory work in Allendorf, neither Frau Fest nor the prisoners apparently knew exactly what they were making, or so it seemed at our first meeting. "They were separate pieces of some 'special program' which later were sent somewhere else where it was all assembled. It was all kept so *secret*. The whole complex was kept so secret. Even people who lived in the area didn't know where it was." She later said the work involved "experiments with gunpowder, making a new weapon, I don't know."

Her walk with the prisoners to and from the plant took twenty minutes to half an hour and wound through the woods. Frau Fest spoke as if she treasured it. "As long as we were within sight of the camp," she laughed slightly, "we were very good, marching in a straight line. Later the whole thing got a bit looser and then one could have conversations and that was quite nice, when you were there alone. If there'd been two or three guards, you don't know what the next person would do, if you'd be denounced because you spoke with the prisoners, or if you got involved with private things."

Could she really be denounced just for speaking with them?

"Well, not for *speaking*, but if you discussed private things or what I sometimes did, when I was home and my mother baked a cake or so and said, 'Come, take some with you,' then I'd arrive in the morning carrying my pocketbook with the cake for me. And when we were out of sight, I'd divide it to give each of them a piece. Or I'd bring a few pairs of socks with me or once a sweater, which naturally I *never* was allowed to do. I'd have been punished immediately if that had come out."

What she was supposed to be doing was making sure "none of them somehow, well, fled or so." If someone did try to escape, she was supposed to "report it immediately." She insisted she did not have a weapon.

"*Nein*. Nein, nein, nein, nein. Nein, for God's sakes, that would have been the *last* thing." Frau Fest added that she was terrified of guns. Nor, she replied to further questioning, did she have a dog or a stick. Nothing.

She said she doubted any woman would have attempted escape, anyway. "They all knew, probably with certainty, they were not going back to Hungary. Hungary, well, Hungary was occupied, no?"

What about just escaping from the camp?

"That would have been senseless. Those who were halfway intelligent knew they as women couldn't get through alone. They couldn't hope that somehow they would get help from Germans. And when things were even halfway tolerable in the camp, one knew one had the best opportunity to survive.

"It's very possible," she added, "that the women, the group I knew, collectively highly intelligent women, also maybe had a more political and worldly view than I did. I didn't *have* any such thing then. Where would I have got it from? I'd only learned what was fair and unfair, but *no* more than that."

Her assessment that she was handicapped by her background came up again in regard to anti-Nazi Germans. "As a simple person one didn't have the overview. Like when I speak with Frau Dr. Diener, she had an entirely different overview about the whole thing. Her circle of acquaintances was more, let's say, in part influential people. And they might say this and this is going to happen. We didn't *have* any of that."

Frau Fest also implied that her own modest background made her feel worse for having to guard women she felt were her superiors in terms of education and social class. She sighed deeply. The situation was "very, very difficult" for her, she said. "Let's say we have, as I did, a group of people. And it included a woman doctor. And it included women theologians. And it included women scientists and women who were accustomed to managing a large home, and wives of professors and so on, who told us what they had at home and *how* they used to live. I could speak with them because I was alone with them. That was very depressing for us, that now you somehow are supposed to supervise the women. That was an extreme degradation.

"You didn't even think how it all evolved. You just tried to make the best you could of the day. I always thought, you can't make things unnecessarily bad for the women. They have it bad enough. Then they cried and kept hoping some kind of mail would come and no mail *came*. And when you as a woman are alone and don't know where the other family members are and when new women came and were asked right away, have you seen her or him and have you any idea, that oppressed you very much, without question. I was always very happy when I could go home and talk about it all to my mother and cry myself out. It was quite a burden on my nerves."

Frau Fest said if she had had to work inside the camp itself or with another guard who might have reported her transgressions, she could not have made it. In fact, she got the assignment she did, she said, because the camp commander saw how distressed she was "about everything." She said it was he who sometimes gave her a break by sending her to the city to buy supplies.

Asked about changes among the prisoners, Frau Fest answered in terms not of physical but of mental health.

"Evening after evening, when one had to return to the barracks, together with so countless many other human beings and doesn't know what's happened to family members who were home and so, and they often cried and said whatever would happen to their children and everything, it's obvious there would be changes. And some things enormously burdened *us* along with them, because one simply was so helpless. One couldn't do anything at all. What could you do? My husband was a career soldier, and one thought then we'd win the war; if I'd complained and had been punished, things would have been impossible for my husband. He'd have been discharged and, furthermore, not honorably." Concern about her husband's military career also was a big reason, she said, she had kept her mouth shut in Ravensbrück.

According to a book published later about Allendorf, the Hungarian Jewish women had more than obvious reasons for being so troubled about the fates of family members. The women had come from Auschwitz.

They had been loaded onto locked cattle cars in Hungary, endured the trip to Auschwitz, and endured months in Auschwitz, including having physical examinations in which soldiers checked their vaginas for valuables. They also endured an inspection by the infamous Dr. Josef Mengele.[4] One thousand "selected" healthy women then were loaded and locked back into cattle cars for the trip to Allendorf. When the women arrived three days later, all were still alive. It was August 1944.

Anna Fest arrived the next month. As she told it, living conditions at the camp were tolerable, but the guards' treatment of the prisoners varied widely. She first said, in effect, that the majority of the guards were all right, but that there were exceptions, then spoke less favorably of the group as a whole. Asked how the guards saw their work, she said for most it was just work. Frowning, she added it bothered her for a long time that authorities had not sought out more "suitable" people with "character." Many guards were "uncomfortable people who had not worked well" in their previous jobs. "In part they simply were very primitive, and that was what was bad.

"And when you flatter yourself you're someone special, and I then say, 'Listen, you can't do that, that's not right, to deal with the people that way, and most of them are far more intelligent than you all are,' I got 'Aren't you conceited,' and so it went." Frau Fest said that if "someone risked walking alongside someone else" for a few steps, rather than single file, a guard would scream at her to get back in line. "I found that such complete nonsense."

In her recollection of conversations among fellow guards, Frau Fest used the familiar *du* form, later confirming that "We all used *du* among our-

4. Ibid., 212.

selves." She said the prisoners used the formal respectful *Sie* form to the guards and addressed them as "Mrs. Guard" [Frau Aufseherin]. "I found that very funny. I didn't use *du* with them. I couldn't. I said *Sie.* "But a lot of guards "said *du*, from above looking down."

What about the guards' nonverbal behavior? Frau Fest's answers were circumspect. She said one woman always carried a stick, and although she said she never saw her hit anyone, "I would have thought it provoking." She also claimed there was no "real mishandling" other than a kick or punch, which she said she never saw, but heard about later. The lack of "real mis-handling," she said, "all had to do more or less with the boss, a very nice older man who was in charge of the whole thing. I had the feeling it was not exactly pleasant for him, that he was sent to this job and tried to make the best of it. He always preached, 'Treat the people like human beings.' But he could not be everywhere."

What about the food? Frau Fest said it was neither great nor bad, that there were many one-dish [Eintopf] meals, as well as bread, cheese, and wurst, and sometimes margarine. She said prisoners were not starved.

What about medical care? She described the camp infirmary in almost pleasant terms, saying she knew it "quite well, because they took care of us, too." She said it was run by two women prisoners who were doctors, assisted by two prisoner nurses.

Were medical experiments done on prisoners? "Nein nein, nein nein. Not in the smaller work camps. These experiments no doubt were done in the larger camps. Mauthausen. Ravensbrück. And all of them. Not to forget Buchenwald. I had no insight, no idea, what specifically went on [at bigger camps]. There was so *much* people didn't know at all."

Allendorf, she later said, was "nicht das Schlimmste [not the worst]." Other camps "must have been horrible." But how bad was Allendorf? A lot worse than how she first described it.

The second year we met, she said a group of young people had been re-searching Allendorf and reported that punishment of the prisoners included beatings and withdrawal of food. The third year we met, she herself revealed more. "One time I saw someone had been beaten. I spoke to her and asked, 'What have you done?' She said she'd tripped and fallen. Naturally, I didn't believe her. That's absolutely clear. She couldn't have said anything else. She probably was afraid."

Someone not to fear, according to Frau Fest, was the earlier mentioned camp commander "with whom I got along well, and who was very humane." She continued, "[He] always tried hard to make sure the people had enough to eat and everything and also that those who wanted to read got books sometimes. And sometimes I went to Sonnenfeld and got colored pencils so they could draw. But those are all only such very tiny things that don't weigh very much, in comparison to the rest of it, I mean."

The memories seemed to activate and anger her, and to prompt her to say what she had not talked about specifically before. It was that the prisoners' major job was the extremely arduous and dangerous one of putting explosives in bombs—grenades, she called them. "The prisoners had to do the hardest work and never where one wanted to be. For a time I went with them, for maybe two or three weeks, to where the grenades were filled. In [only that time] I got red hair, my skin and everything was completely orange colored. Sure, in the first moments it was unpleasant, and then they got used to the smell. But one didn't consider at all that the prisoners worked there week after week and maybe for years." (Years they did not; the camp existed less than a year.) "They all had red hair, their hands were red, everything was red, all their underwear was red. They couldn't get it out even by boiling it in water. It was everywhere. The ponds where the runoff water came out, everything was completely red."

She agreed it must have been in the prisoners' lungs, too.

Did it scare them?

"Probably. Not one said anything. And it probably was quite dangerous to work there. They all had to take off their shoes. You couldn't go in with nailed shoes, only with wooden shoes. That was also a sign only clear in hindsight, that there were explosives."

In Frau Fest's explanation of the prisoners' work, they faced rows of empty grenades, which they had placed on wagons, then filled the grenades with dusty orange-red liquid that came from a hose hanging above the rows. (According to other reports, the shells weighed thirty-five pounds each, and each prisoner had to handle hundreds of them a day.)[5] When the grenades were filled, the women pushed the wagons farther on.

This then, after three years, was her story of what the prisoners did in the factory. Had I misunderstood they had done something else, or "only that?" "Only that," she repeated. Minutes later, she spoke of working "for a good while" with prisoners in the camp laundry. It seemed she, and they, were moved about as needed.

Had Frau Fest herself not brought up the explosives work, it would have been time to ask her about it. The study group she mentioned earlier subsequently published a book about the Allendorf camp, *Die Arbeitssklaven der Dynamit Nobel* (The work slaves of Nobel Dynamite). The title refers to one of the factory's corporate owners, Dynamit-Aktien Gesellschaft, or DAG, formerly Alfred Nobel and Company. As *The Work Slaves* made clear, DAG was the leading German manufacturer of explosives at the time, and the Allendorf munitions factory/"work camps" were of major importance to the Nazi regime. The book, which began as a school research project, in-

---

5. Ibid., 225.

cluded the results of extensive reports about the Allendorf camps as well as testimonies from former prisoners.

At first reading, the book painted a much different and worse composite picture than the one described by Frau Fest. It gave example after example of inadequate food, of "crass and primitive" medical care, and—not unlike Frau Fest's own testimony—terrible and dangerous working conditions. (It said that the explosives the women were filling into the grenades included TNT.)

The Work Slaves was especially censorious toward the nearly fifty female guards at the camp where Frau Fest worked. It detailed acts of meanness, viciousness, and deadly trickery. It also singled out ten or so guards, not including Frau Fest, who were especially cruel and/or who had joined the SS voluntarily. There was nothing to do with the new information but take it to her. Before doing so, I reexamined the book's overall evidence from her situation and time frame, and compared the specifics of what it said to what she had said.

Tentative findings determined that both the book and she could be right, up to a point. Frau Fest arrived in Allendorf only a month after the camp opened and was there only three or so months before being transferred to another camp. The book did state that in the first months at Allendorf, prisoners found the amount of food "sufficient," and it quoted one report that the meals in the first two months were "rather substantial." The prisoners then were reduced to a starvation diet.

It is likely that in Allendorf, as at other camps, all situations deteriorated rapidly in 1945, and that some or many of the horrors the book alluded to occurred after she left. (When American troops arrived in late March 1945, "it probably was high time," she said.) It also was possible that because Frau Fest was not allowed inside the prisoners' barracks and therefore did not see their sleeping, eating, and toilet areas, she missed a lot.

As to the specifics, from what I could determine, in almost every case she and *The Work Slaves* were in basic accord. For example, regarding the "humane" camp commandant, the book said former Allendorf prisoners did ascribe to the man referred to, SS-Hauptscharführer Arthur Wuttke, "a certain humanity." Asked about deaths at Allendorf, Frau Fest said she knew of none. The assertion strained credulity, but *The Work Slaves* all but seconded her. Quoting documents provided by the Red Cross, it said "with few exceptions, all the Hungarian women survived the slave work in Allendorf."

It must be noted that I already knew, from the first interview with Frau Fest, what a postwar Allied court had decided in her case, and the decision influenced my sense of her. Still, even the journalistic act of looking for consistencies and inconsistencies made me feel painfully like someone who wails "it can't be true" when charges of war crimes are made against a relative. Perhaps that is why I felt especially obliged to press Frau Fest about what

The Work Slaves said. I did not want to say what text informed my questions, however. I wanted her to open up, not close down. So I used the book's data, but not its existence. Although she may have known or assumed where the information came from, she never asked.

At our final formal interview I began, as always, with the easier questions. She proved to be on target with the book about the prisoners' ages (the average was twenty-six) and off on how many prisoners there were. She guessed "at least three hundred," far short of the one thousand women *The Work Slaves* reports.

The book singled out three female guards as being particularly inhumane. The worst was Käte H., the head female guard [Oberaufseherin]. (Inexplicably, the authorial outrage that permeated the book stopped short of providing the guards' last names.) Käte H., who had free rein inside the prisoners' living areas, reportedly woke one woman by punching her in the ear, and beat sick prisoners to force them to work.

"Käte Hoern," immediately confirmed Frau Fest. She said she herself did not know the accusations against her until after the war, but that Käte H., who looked "very good" physically, had a "looking down from above" attitude. "She already was a little conceited and let us know we were only such small things, that we had to obey what she said."

Frau Fest and I went over point by point by point. By the time we were done, and I rechecked her testimony with the book, I had found one instance of specific contradiction. *The Work Slaves* quoted a woman who described "four or six" women guards, and two older SS men, as being "accompanied by bloodhounds as they brought us through the forest." Frau Fest insisted, repeatedly, that no guard in Allendorf had a dog. "None at all."

But two larger general contradictions remained. One involved the infirmary and the treatment of the sick. The book said there was no doctor until December, whereas Frau Fest had spoken of prisoner doctors providing care. (It is possible the prisoners were not licensed doctors.)

The second contradiction involved the guards' treatment of the prisoners. For whatever reason, Frau Fest's criticism was quite careful and more individual than not. *The Work Slaves* is more sweepingly condemnatory. In one passage, it said numerous testimonies from prisoners "substantiate the official proceedings that with few exceptions, the SS women guards were considered brutal women who intensified the fascist rule of the KZ."

None of the exceptions was named.

Early in 1945, Anna Fest was transferred to another munitions "work camp." It was Sömmerda, near the Thüringen Forest in eastern Germany.

There she had no group to herself, but was collectively in charge of guarding about two hundred prisoners, also Hungarian Jewish women. The only thing better about Sömmerda, she said, was that the work was cleaner. Prisoners in the camp's factory dealt only with rifle ammunition, "and that was considerably more pleasant."

More pleasant?

"Ja. In quotation marks."

For the guards, however, Sömmerda posed a "somewhat more difficult" situation. Taking the prisoners back and forth to the factory meant marching them not through the woods, but through the local town of Thüringen. "We were there with a great many of them, and the people cursed us a lot."

The Germans cursed the guards?

"Ja, ja. And kept trying over and over to slip something to the people, bread or sausage or whatever. It was a good idea to look the other way and simply allow it. Otherwise one could have been attacked by the Germans. It did happen."

She said guards who refused to allow local citizens to pass food to the prisoners but threatened them with jail instead had it "really hard" later and were afraid to walk alone in the town after dark. She said the anger of the local Germans against the guards as a group was so great that the latter were not allowed to visit Thüringen in uniform during their breaks.

People on the street—old people, women, and children—had shouted, "You're worse than worse [Ihr seid ja schlimmer als schlimm]." It was obvious, she said, the prisoners were hungry. "Why shouldn't we give them something? Of course, from my point of view, we didn't think we'd lose the war."

That was not her only delusion still holding strong in the early months of 1945.

How old was she as a teenager, I asked, when it dawned on her the Nazi regime was not necessarily as "good" as she thought?

With notable embarrassment, she answered that it was well after her teens. It happened while she was at Sömmerda, the *third* concentration camp she had been in. Furthermore, she did not open her own eyes. A Waffen-SS officer did. She said that because she was the only woman guard in Sömmerda who could play chess, and because she was terribly homesick, the officer, a former mathematics professor in Austria, often played chess with her. He and she also both played with the camp commander.

Once, when the commander was out of the room, the officer erupted about her naiveté. "I don't know what you're expecting," she quoted him as saying. "Have you *really* taken it into your head we're going to win the war?" He went on and on, she said, "with that and that and everything" and ended with, "*Think* about it. Put two and two together."

A later version of the story placed the camp commander in the room, grinning. "They obviously knew each other so well, and they probably knew everything. It was just us dummies [wir Doofen] who didn't know the war was as good as lost."

The Waffen-SS officer "made me open my eyes about so many different things. That was the first time I had doubts."

The *first time?* Had she thought what went on back in Allendorf just was part of it?

Was part of it, she repeated. "It was simply war and our men at the front needed munitions. And if they didn't have any, they couldn't shoot and the others could. For us, that was simply a matter of course, as strange as it now sounds. But in Allendorf, I didn't have a minute's doubt."

What about the prisoners' misery? That was part of it, too?

"Ja, that it was not for us to judge and that we couldn't do anything about it." What really convinced her, she said, was the often-repeated rationale that the prisoners "had not been picked up by the Germans, but the Hungarian government essentially had sold the prisoners to Germany, and each month Germany paid the Hungarian government a certain sum for each prisoner." She added that at the time young people such as herself did not have the information, the overview, "perhaps not the interest either" to know what really was going on.

It turned out that what really was going on in Frau Fest's life at the time was more, and different, than she had said. Not until midway through the final interview did she tell the tale, and only because of an innocent question. When I had asked earlier why she had been transferred, she said that individual guards commonly were transferred from one camp to another, as she had been, according to various needs. Now I asked if there were a specific reason in her case. She became immediately and obviously uncomfortable. Her answer was short. "Ja. That I know."

A pause turned to a wait. Finally, may I ask?

"You may ask." There was another pause. "I have told my husband and my children, too."

Mystified, I waited and waited. Then came the answer.

"I met a very, very nice young woman there, in Allendorf, who was from Berlin. We were together a lot. She came home with me, too, because she couldn't get back to Berlin. When I had free time, we always arranged to be together. And to Frau Hoern, that stank. She didn't like it, she couldn't stand it, and then she went and reported that we were both lesbian."

The report went to Allendorf's commanding camp, Buchenwald.

"Then I went to our boss, Herr Wuttke, and said this and this is the situation and Käte Hoern said that and that, and what can I do against it?"

He told her there was only one thing to do. Go to Buchenwald herself, with the travel permit he would provide, and ask to see the disciplinary procedure against her.

"I did, and they wrote me a rather scornful letter. They said the only way to break this thing is that Frau Oschlivsky or whatever—in addition, she had a Polish-sounding name—stays in Allendorf and Frau Fest goes to

Sömmerda. 'Then the thing is broken once and for all and we'll keep an eye on Frau Fest.' "

"I have to tell you truthfully, when this complaint came," she said, "I had no idea what it was. I knew neither the expression nor the relationship. I never knew there was such a thing, a relationship of woman to woman."

You knew of man to man. . . .

"Nein. Not that, either. Nothing."

You really were a village girl, I said.

"I really was. A 'klein Doofi mit Plüschohren' [a little dummy with plush ears]. I asked Herr Wuttke, 'What does that actually mean?' He said, 'Child, you don't really know?' I said no I didn't and please explain. So he did."

SS-Hauptscharführer Wuttke not only explained homosexuality to Frau Fest, he took it upon himself to tell her the incident was her own fault. She should not have distanced herself from the men at Allendorf.

"I said, 'Herr Wuttke, let me tell you something. I am, after all, married. And my husband is a soldier at the front. So what should this mean? I should take up with your primitive male guards or some other man, just to avoid anyone claiming anything else about me? You cannot demand that of me.' And he said, 'They're keeping an eye on you, and when you're there [in Sömmerda], the same thing can happen again. Do try to develop at least friendships with some man or another.' "

He then gave her a letter to present to the commander at Sömmerda, whom he knew, to "take care of you a little."

"And that's the reason," she concluded, "they invited me to play chess. So that no such thing happened to me again."

Frau Fest read one of my thoughts. "It's something," she said, "someone with a normal understanding cannot comprehend."

The Sömmerda assignment proved to be short. And for Frau Fest, it ended with substantially more trauma than it began. In the early spring of 1945, not long after her arrival, an order came from Nazi headquarters for everyone to pack up, evacuate, and head east, on foot.

As guards and prisoners alike began packing their bundles, the chess-playing Waffen-SS officer took Frau Fest aside. "He said to me, 'Are you really so dumb? What are you thinking of? Make sure you get home. Go to your aunt's and get some civilian clothes and go home from there. Jump on some train, or walk the whole way as far as I'm concerned. Are you crazy, to march along with this group?' And I said, 'Well, my husband is, after all, an active soldier and if it comes out later and he loses his . . . ' and he said, 'He's going to lose his position anyway and won't be an active soldier for long. When the war is over, we won't have any more active soldiers.' I didn't believe him."

She sighed, "I always believed [the government]. Everything was in Ordnung, and, I don't know."

Not even the marches with the prisoners through Thüringen had changed her mind?

"Not at all. I always said, 'How can people say such things?' We have to believe and have to hold on. What do we have otherwise? We have nothing at all if we don't hold on."

So Anna Fest, who once described herself as "not so easily ordered about," set off, as ordered, with the others.

Their first stop was another camp, where two hundred or so more prisoners and guards, including men, joined them. Along the way, her officer friend (who visited her after the war) and the Sömmerda commander both took off. The trek, which was to end near Pilsen, Czechoslovakia, one hundred miles away, continued to the east, and the Soviet Army. Frau Fest had described the experience in the first interview with tones of horror. One great difficulty was that the collapsing Reich provided almost no food. "It was terrible. We received neither enough for ourselves nor the prisoners." She said, "You were happy if you got a piece of bread."

In Czechoslovakia, where she said she felt more like a prisoner than a guard, people threw stones and spat at the Germans. She said the prisoners got between them and told the Czechs, "Don't do that, they've been good to us." She insisted this was true, and also said that when local citizens cooked up a vat of potatoes for the prisoners, the latter would sneak one to her and other women guards.

The march was "decisively worse" than the camps, she said. Her voice lowered, and became very emotional. "It was the worst thing one can imagine. I mean, the people fell from weakness along the way. They simply remained *lying* in ditches by the side of the road. They couldn't move any farther. Each one just . . . I don't know if you can imagine it if you haven't experienced it. Each person just groping forward and, and, having only the basic feeling always just to set one foot in front of the other, to stay with the group and not remain back . . . not to stay back alone, lying somewhere in a ditch. Then, in between came the, the bombing attacks. We once went a little way in a train and then were unloaded, then it was, 'Quick, quick, out,' and then get to the open field and lie flat. Then came the bombing attack. Then machine guns shooting into [the group], then you were happy when you didn't get something yourself. The one next to you just lies there and . . . And when you experience that, how the wounded lie there and no human being can really help them and no one even has the *will* to help the other, but each just . . . protects his own skin and tries to get away in one piece. That is something so *horrible*, that one cannot normally even imagine it. And what, for one as a woman . . . what is especially awful, there next to you lies someone who's been shot. He lies there, and limbs torn off and so on and so forth and you have to *see* that and you get sick to your stomach and vomit and on the other side someone is screaming for help, you have to *help* him. And then the whistle is blown and that means everyone reassemble again and get back in line again and the human beings lie there and you cannot help them. And you have to get back in line and they're screaming and then you're back in the line and then the *next* bombing attacks come and bombs start falling on the defenseless human beings. Those are experiences one never forgets. Those are such incisive [einschneidene] experiences, one is never finished with them."

Nor was she that day we talked. The following afternoon, Frau Fest, who said she had had to take a sleeping pill the night before, went into more detail. To be true to the emotion of her recollection, at the expense of instant clarity, her words are left virtually as spoken.

"Along the way, I had to experience several shootings and also was rebuked by certain people and then got massive warnings. I basically was told, just endure, for we take no regard of you at all and if you put yourself on the same level with them, compare yourself with them, then you can march with them. And I myself didn't comprehend, when it was old, sick people. As far as I was concerned, one could have let them lie by the roadside. There were villages all over and there definitely were people who perhaps might have come and taken them in and could have helped them. One didn't have to wander around, not to mention that we crept around half starved to death. You know, the whole time was so terrible, the people who simply could not continue, who were so weakened they fell down. Then, there were some there who weren't even part of us, but so many came together there, men among them too, all streaming somehow, ridiculously, toward the east. And among them were some who had pistols and who just kept pulling the trigger. It was so *terrible*."

Who "kept pulling the trigger"?

"The men. Some of them. I still remember it. We'd always positioned ourselves together, and shut our eyes, so as not to sweeten it by looking on. And when afterward the shot went off, one automatically looked away and absolutely couldn't watch. It was *bad* to such a degree I don't know if you can understand it. It was so horrendous. For one, as a woman, to have to go along with it. And it wasn't one thing alone, but several—hunger, bombing raids, *and* then that."

She turned out to have been referring in particular to one man, who was among the "countless" numbers of people who "attached themselves to us" as the trek began to resemble "a worm that moved itself along." The man was an officer, she said, the only one still among them, the others having "all more or less discharged themselves." The officer's actions finally prompted one of her own. She said she approached him during a rest stop.

"I went up to the head of the line and he stood there in the middle of a few people. The prisoners were sitting along the sides. They all heard it. I did it without regard to myself. I said this is unheard of, that it makes no

331

sense and he must see that everyone is so powerless and he certainly should spare them, if there was room for that in his conscience. And then he said I should leave my dizzy feelings alone, that it was totally ridiculous. They were all the scum of society and one more or less didn't matter and it didn't matter to him either, that he also had a bullet for me. And so on, in that style. So I said, 'Then just go right ahead and try it. I've had it up to here, anyway. That for me, too, one more or less doesn't matter. I see only what injustice is being done and I would have thought you at least would have had enough morality and not have rotted away to such an extent to do a thing like this.'

"And I said, 'And finally, when all is said and done, you are an officer and you swore your officer's oath and I don't know if you also swore at the same time to shoot defenseless people to death.' Then I said, 'They *are* defenseless people.' And I said, 'Since they are also weakened, and you say they are the dregs of society, how can you make the judgment that they are dregs?' I said, 'For instance, I happen to know that among our women there are many who in terms of intelligence when compared with you, leave you far behind. And can you, regarding these poor, shriveled souls, say these are the dregs. One perhaps could sooner say you are the dregs.'

"The others said afterward, 'Menschenskind! [Holy Jesus! approaches an English equivalent.] Have you gone completely crazy? You have such courage to say that!' I said once I was in it, I simply had to. I could *not* keep my mouth closed. And I must say, somehow it did help a little. For two days, it was really quiet. I heard nothing more. You couldn't see what was going on, either. I stayed way to the back because I thought he shouldn't see me. Get out of his sight to stay out of danger. And the women, our prisoners, always said, 'Frau Fest, come and stand among us so he won't see you at all.'"

On the third day, a bombing attack insured the officer's cease-fire. "He was killed. I don't think anyone crooked a finger to save him. I don't think I was the only one who could not accept what he did. There were very many. Just, I was the only one who had the courage to say something."

She said his victims on the march numbered "five, six, definitely. Otherwise I wouldn't have become so insanely upset. Perhaps I'd also have made him speak to me if it were two, but would have thought, well, perhaps he behaved this way because he panicked or something. But somehow I couldn't take it anymore. It had dammed up in me and no other move was possible."

When the man died, Frau Fest felt "first of all, relief. Second, as I said to some of my colleagues, 'Nothing remains unpunished.'"

About the time of the man's death, the march was nearing its end. But its goal remained undefined. "Today, when I think back, I realize there was no goal at all. One simply set off, practically up against the Russians. I found the whole thing so insane. Simply march off without sense, without goal, just toward the east. There was nobody left who might have said we do this or this. Afterward, it almost was like a deliverance. We crossed Russian battle lines. The Russians came with their tanks, circled us, and quasi rolled over us, then brought out the prisoners who were in the barns, then 'You can go,' and they scattered in all directions."

For lack of an alternative, the guards eventually scattered, too. Frau Fest said she wandered through Russian lines in her SS uniform virtually unstopped. (She no longer had her jacket and cap, the parts of the uniform with SS insignia, but wore only the uniform's gray pullover and skirt.) Finally, she came to the conclusion it was time to turn back.

After hooking up with about seven other women in her general situation, they began heading west, mostly through forests, staying on the alert for Russian troops and hiding when any came near. Then, "idiotically," they entered a Russian-occupied town. It was Karlsbad, in northwestern Czechoslovakia. They were arrested immediately and held for several days. But they were given food, she pointed out. Every once in a while some were taken aside for questioning, by "Russian women in uniform." Then "one fine day," a Russian officer told them they should leave. Frau Fest said the women stared uncomprehendingly at him until he said, "Go home! Go home!"

That was easier said than managed. Even getting out of town was difficult, Karlsbad being filled with refugees, and with Russians and Czechs, still shooting. Nonetheless, she and two other women did manage to leave together. They ran into a German army unit whose soldiers shared some clothes with them. Then, going farther, the women eventually stumbled upon most unexpected help: an outpost of American GIs.

Frau Fest said the women approached them very hesitantly, as the men waved and one called to them, "Come here." They did.

"One asked where we came from, and one of them spoke very good German, and we poured out our hearts a little, and one said, 'My *God*, look at you,' we understood him a little, 'how starved you look.'" The GIs gave the women all the food they had, which amounted to some cookies. "Just a few," said Frau Fest, adding, as if in past deference, "but they were very good. And it probably was just as well we had only that. Otherwise we'd have eaten too much."

The GIs began taking on the role of protectors. They also decided to hide their "guests" from their commanding officer.

"The one said, 'Stay here. We'll put up a tent later and you all can sleep in it. You don't have to be afraid of anything. No one will do anything to you.' Because we were still afraid." The soldier told the women to stay in the tent and keep quiet when the evening rations were delivered. He said there would be more than enough food, that after the food deliverers had left, the men would cook a common meal and give the women a lot to eat. Frau Fest, laughing a little, said when the rations arrived, the women in the tent were as quiet as tiny mice.

The Americans were as good as their word. One soldier, who was supposed to return home the next week, even offered to mail a letter from Frau Fest to Otto, by then an American prisoner of war in the United States.

The next morning, the GIs gave their guests more food and set them on their way. Frau Fest said the women had told the GIs they had been guards, but that seemed to make no difference. The GIs apparently were not bothered by another fact, either. The war was still going on.

Because of the danger of being caught by less friendly enemy soldiers, the women again traveled mostly through forests, at night. Frau Fest said that during the march east, she had tried to suppress even the thought of home. "Nobody knew if he or she ever would get home again or how to get home again. You couldn't let yourself consider such thoughts, because they were unendurable. You just went from one moment to the next."

She did make it home, to a mother who scarcely recognized her. Anna Fest said she weighed about seventy pounds.

In the meantime, the war finally ended.

"I came back here free, and then registered myself. I had to do that to get food ration coupons." She said she registered at the German employment office, where she was advised also to register with the American Counter Intelligence Corps (CIC). "I had the best of intentions and nothing to hide. Why shouldn I register? Then I went to the CIC and registered there too." She said the process including giving "all the particulars" about what she had done and where. Six weeks later she was arrested.

Members of the American occupation forces came by in a car to her home, told her to pack a few things, and be ready in half an hour. "Then it started. Such a feeling of helplessness, when three or four heavily armed military police stand in front of you. You just panic. I cried terribly. My mother was completely beside herself and said, 'You can't do this. She registered just as she was supposed to.' Then she said, 'If only you'd gone somewhere else and had hidden.' But I consider that *senseless*, because I did not feel guilty."

Frau Fest said she never was told why she was under arrest and received nothing in writing. "That was the way it went with everyone, with no reason given." Her tone was a verbal shrug. "With no judicial examinations at all, we arrived and met various acquaintances. 'Why are you here?' 'Mein Gott, because I was in the Frauenschaft,' or the men said, 'I was in the SA. . . .'"

Frau Fest, of course, was in the SS.

Although she said that was reason enough to be picked up eventually, she thought she came to the Allies' attention earlier because she was denounced. "There was a very, very bad lot of Germans who denounced one another in order to get whatever advantage. That actually depressed me even more than being arrested." She was certain her denouncer was a former fellow guard in Allendorf, a "primitive," emotionally unstable poor lost soul, as she portrayed her, who had lived for a while with her and her mother, who had "gone to so much trouble" for her. Frau Fest said the woman was told when arrested that she would get off earlier if she named names. She named Anna Fest.

In the weeks following her arrest, Frau Fest was moved to several different installations before being taken to an internment camp in Ludwigsburg to stand trial. In the meantime, she was interrogated. She spoke of "very, very bad experiences."

"Both officers who took our testimony were former German Jews. They must have seen some terrible aggression, I'd certainly maintain that. But the terrible thing was, the German men had to watch. That was a horrible, horrible experience."

Pressed to explain, Frau Fest, obviously upset, tried to change the subject. I tried to change it back. She admitted at first only to being manhandled, and said the subject was too difficult for her. Was she talking about the two officers? She said yes, and took a deep breath. "I still know the names today. The one was Schmidt, the other Rosenstein. The one was arrested, for whatever reason, and the other somehow was killed in an accident. Neither of them is alive. An American later told me that, when it came up in the hearings. And then we were taken in trucks. . . ."

I interrupted again. Was she raped?

"Nein. Nein, not that. Really, not that. Only, well, physical abuse and hitting and so on." With another deep breath, she moved away, saying there was more, but she could not talk about it.

A year later, in fits and starts, and a fast and shaking voice, she continued. She said she was taken to a small hut. Inside were the two officers and a couple of German shepherd dogs. One officer screamed questions and accusations at her. If she did not answer "as he wished, he kicked me in the back and the other hit me" with his fist. The dogs insured she did not get away.

Apparently the most volatile point had to do with whether she had been armed. "They kept saying we must have been armed, have had pistols or so. But we had no weapons, none of us."

The "primitive" poor lost soul had testified just before her, however, and had broken down during questioning and claimed (to be left in peace, in Frau Fest's view) that she did have a weapon.

"I had no pistol. I couldn't say, just so they'd maybe leave me in peace, yes, we had pistols. The same thing would happen to the next person to testify."

It did anyway, she said, and other women also broke down and added their false confessions to the first one.

What she referred to as "the bad part," however, was that during the proceedings, the door of the hut was left open so that German men standing outside, waiting to be questioned, had to see and hear it all. "That must have been terrible for them. When I went outside, several of them stood there with tears running down their cheeks. What could they have done? They could do nothing."

She said that toward the end of the interrogations, a German woman in charge of the area where the women prisoners stayed made and hung a large sign reading Caution! Contagious Diseases. "We weren't interrogated any longer after that. The Americans, this is nothing against you personally, at that time had an insane fear about contagious diseases."

Contagious or not, she and the others were taken to another camp for six more weeks. Her mother, learning her whereabouts from some prisoners who had been released, went to see her but was not allowed any contact. Frau Fest was moved again, for several weeks, to Dachau.

There she and others faced former prisoners who had been assembled to single out their former tormentors. Although maintaining her innocence, she described the experience as frightening. "We were interrogated on the stage, which was all lit up. We had to walk back and forth with stage lights on us. And down in the darkness sat the people who looked at us."

Later, the accusers went down a hall "where there was a door with a flap on it, and they looked through to see if somehow they recognized us, if any of us had done anything. Many were hauled out. What happened to them individually, I don't know."

Frau Fest said she was not hauled out.

Most of her fellow prisoners in Dachau, she said, had been either guards or members of the Frauenschaft. But one prisoner was in a classification all her own.

"Frau Koch also was there with us. I got to know her."

Ilse Koch, wife of the commandant of Buchenwald, became notorious for the ghastly hobby she reportedly had, of collecting lampshades made from Jewish skin. Frau Fest said Koch, as a prisoner, was led wherever she went, and kept apart by others' initiatives as well as her own.

"Now and then I talked with her, but she was very, very closed. She said nothing at all. She admitted everything they demanded of her."

It was believed Koch also admitted more than what she had done, said Frau Fest, in order to be rid of her interrogators. But "what was true was bad enough for my way of thinking. I saw her earlier in the camp in Ludwigsburg. She was on the same hall as us but in a separate room, and she didn't have to show up in the morning with the rest of us to be counted. When she went along the hallway, I always had a feeling. . . . How can I describe my first impression? As though a beast of prey were skulking. She never walked in the middle of the hallway. She was always against the wall, and if anyone else walked down the hall, she jumped back quickly to her room. Furthermore, she was a little 'unheimlich' [sinister]. One knew who she was."

Frau Fest said the opinion of the other prisoners toward Ilse Koch was about the same as hers. "One had no contact with her other than 'Good day' and 'How are you?' and 'Don't you want to join us sometime when we have readings?' And we had a choir too, where we sang. She didn't want any of that at all. She closed herself up, over and over. We'd met her halfway and thought we could bring her out of her isolation a little. But that wasn't possible."

I finally managed to choke out a question. *Why try?*

"Well, somehow she was ultimately, in the long run, also a woman. . . . And she made you feel bad when she always slunk around and never was with others. We thought it's terrible enough for us to be locked up and when a person is completely isolated, it's really terrible. Actually, well, from what one heard about her, there was also a little . . ." Frau Fest finally came up with the word she wanted. It was "disdain. She could not be a good person," she added. "But there were many who weren't good, and one must sort of accept them as they were, in a sense. In another sense, they made one feel bad, so one thought one really should try a little to make life easier."

Among the other prisoners in Ludwigsburg was Käte Hoern, whose life Frau Fest did not try to make a little easier. The Oberaufseherin was sentenced to seven years' labor.[6]

Soon after the stay in Dachau, Frau Fest had a nervous breakdown. She did not discuss it (with me). When she recovered, she was sent back to the camp at Ludwigsburg to await trial.

The long delay between her arrest and the trial itself, she said matter-of-factly, had to do with the Allies' difficulty setting up a judicial administration and with the prosecutors' needing to familiarize themselves with the various organizations and job categories of the Third Reich. Furthermore, she said, as an SS member she was in Group 1, the most suspect of all, and was not to be processed until defendants in less suspicious groups were out of the way.

For her own case, she decided to act as her own lawyer. "I told myself, no one else can say better than I myself how things really were. And at the time one remembered it very well." She prepared by consulting almost daily for a quarter of a year with an American judge assigned to her group. He "went over everything with me, about what was what. We worked together very, very well. And he was the one who heard my case. I had the feeling he was, well, he must have been prejudiced, but he wasn't as filled with hatred as others were. I could tell him things I couldn't have said elsewhere."

In the meantime, Herr Fest, back home and free (and proud of the American slang he had picked up as a POW), also was busy working on his wife's defense. He sought out former prisoners to testify on her behalf. Many still were in and around Allendorf, in part to recuperate, in part to act as witnesses for the prosecutors. The Fests both said the women he reached

---

6. Ibid., 222.

told him they would like to help but "their organization" (unnamed) forbade them to testify *for* someone, only against. He did get former fellow guards to sign a deposition that his wife had acted humanely, but as she said with a sigh, "that was just the workers" and the paper "naturally didn't have the same weight [as] if it had come from a prisoner."

Herr Fest also had obtained and shown to the appropriate Allied forces a crucial certificate issued by Behringwerke. It stated Anna Fest had been "Dienstverpflichtet [called to duty]" to Allendorf. In other words, she had not volunteered. Frau Fest called the document "unbelievably important" because "the Americans had thought we'd all gone of our own free will." She added she "really can't quite comprehend" why anyone would volunteer for such a job, but that some must have or such a document would not have been needed.

Because of the document, Frau Fest's case was one of the first of her Group 1 to be tried. She did not get former prisoners to testify in her defense, but did get a former boss. Her Behringwerke supervisor traveled to Ludwigsdorf and corroborated that she was sent involuntarily to Allendorf, and was "a decent human being [ein anständiger Mensch]."

In 1947, before learning the outcome of her trial, Frau Fest was sent to a camp in Darmstadt. (The transfer seemed to have to do with a geographic or jurisdictional question among the occupational forces.) There, after a rehearing, for which she again acted as her own defense lawyer, she was acquitted.

She said the authorities at the hearing "excused themselves and said the entire thing basically was automatic." Afterward, she and her husband, who was allowed to be with her, "were led through the streets by two American soldiers with fixed bayonets." She laughed. "We even smiled about it among ourselves. They said we're only doing it because those were the orders."

She was not free for long. That summer, she was put back in Darmstadt for another stay for what she said were unspecified reasons. She remembered the circumstances of her final release, and homecoming, vividly and emotionally. Without warning or hope, events "happened quite fast. I was called to the office for my personal papers to be looked at. And the person there said to figure on being set free in two or three days." Two days later, she was told to come by the office again. "One seldom thought about something good. I thought they'd retract what they said." She was told instead to pack and that she would be released the next day, August 28, 1947. She remembered the date in part because it was her sister's birthday. "I stood there as if rooted to the spot and said absolutely nothing at all. I have no idea how I got back to the barracks. I only know once I was inside, I threw myself on the bed and wept horribly and the others couldn't figure what the matter was until the next woman came and said we're going home." Frau Fest had been a prisoner for more than two years.

The next day, she and other women entered a free and strange civilian world. "They even brought us to the railroad and furthermore not in the big trucks, but in a perfectly normal *car*. And they bought us tickets and we were seated in the train and nobody was there to guard us and nobody locked us in. We essentially could do and let happen whatever we wanted, but we were *afraid*. We didn't even know how to move around freely on the train and maybe walk down the aisle. We didn't dare do that. We sat there just so, a couple bawling miserably."

When they reached the closest station to their homes, about nine o'clock that evening, the women got off the train, but had no idea what to do next. Frau Fest's voice dropped to a whisper, as she continued. "I thought, 'Is there no one here to tell you where you should go and what do you do now and how do you even start? How do you get home?' " One of the group suggested they try to find a bus. To Frau Fest's surprise, "there really *was* a bus and we asked if we could ride, but we had no money. Then the bus driver said, 'Where did the likes of *this* come from? Where'd they let you out of?' We said we'd come from the holding camp in Darmstadt and we'd like very much to go home."

He let them on. "As the bus went along its way, the people all turned to look at us, at our appearance. From our point of view, they were so well dressed and they found it natural just to sit there on the bus. We couldn't even fathom that."

Frau Fest reached her home in Sonnenfeld late that night, and rang the bell. "My husband peered from the window above and I said," she whispered again, "'Otto, it's *me*.' He shut the window and one heard a terrible noise on the stairs and then at first he, naturally, hugged me and then asked 'How did you ever get here?' and 'What's going on? But first come upstairs,' and he carried me up. I was a feather, not so fat like I am today. In the meantime my mother-in-law and sister-in-law were awake and 'Are you hungry and don't you want something to eat first?' 'And listen, it's Erika's birthday today and . . .' "

Frau Fest was back in the nearly overwhelming embrace of almost all her family. But it was her mother, who had been living some nine miles away, she was especially concerned about.

Telephoning and transportation being all but impossible, the next morning she began the walk, with Otto, to see her.

"And then I started off to my mother. . . ."

Frau Fest stopped speaking. After an unusually long time, obviously spent trying to collect herself, she continued. "Ja. Then came the bad awakening. My husband told me, my mother no longer lived."

Frau Fest began to cry. I scrambled in my belongings and found a tissue, for which she paused to thank me before wiping her eyes and nose. She finished her story through tears. "She was operated on, and anesthetized, and never regained consciousness. Essentially, she had an easy death. But you know, with us, it was as if we weren't finished."

Frau Fest collected herself. "Ja. That was in the main what happened. And eventually we built something up and today our children don't really understand why we'd rather not be active in politics, but would rather just appreciate a little bit of what we've accomplished, and have some quiet. One simply experienced too much."

As part of the terms of her 1947 release, Frau Fest was told to take her numerous legal papers to city authorities and reregister. She did. Years later, she received an unexpected judicial communiqué in which "they quasi-excused themselves that I'd been imprisoned for two years for nothing and said I was due some compensation." Furthermore, she learned, her experiences had placed her in the category of prisoner of war. The next thing she knew, she was called to the Sonnenfeld city hall, where she was issued three hundred Deutsch Marks as "POW compensation."

The Fests spent it on a new cupboard for their front hall.

At the conclusion of our final meeting, my mind too sapped to ask anything specific, I asked Frau Fest if she had anything she wanted to add. She did.

"You know," she said, "when I think about it in hindsight, during that whole time, one really had a pretty thick 'board in front of one's face.' There was so much one simply did not see. Even today, when our daughter asks, 'Mutti, what was it really like then? Did you both have any relations with Jewish people?' That we did have, but it never occurred to us as such. For example, I had a colleague at work, at Behringwerke, who was half Jewish, and at the time she was kind of set upon. There were many who avoided her. And I always said, 'What's that all about? Why are they doing that?' I picked her up in the morning and we always went to work together, we sat together at lunch, and generally talked among ourselves.

"When I was away afterward, she came to our house and told my husband, 'Herr Fest, I would like to give testimony on behalf of your wife, how she behaved toward me back then.' I really didn't see what there was to it. My husband also had Jewish acquaintances, and, well, you didn't think anything about it.

"We absolutely could not understand what difference there was supposed to be," she had said earlier. "For instance, at home we loved to eat goat meat and lamb, and one got it only from the Jews. There was a Jewish store in our village and two Jewish stores in the nearby village, and the Jews came and brought us meat and we got matzohs from them, and we found it all completely in Ordnung. And we were supposed to think later somehow those were our enemies or something? The picture that was drawn of the Jews was inaccurate coming and going. That certainly caused one to think."

As for anti-Semitic actions, "We simply couldn't understand it. Those were stores where we'd shopped and people we knew. What was the reason? I could just as well have said okay, all of you who wear a different native costume are different from us and we'll play the devil with you."

Asked if she had ever heard the comment about Jews having been at fault themselves, Frau Fest said never, but added, "It was said some Jewish business people cheated others. But we have a saying. The worst is the 'white Jew.'"

The "white Jew" is a Christian.

Frau Karma Rauhut

A Child Not of the Times

"In the German ideal of upbringing, whatever was creative was killed. If it danced out of line and did something that did not reflect the authoritarian father or mother, it got thrashed." Furthermore, "in Germany, when a child of nine months still wets its pants, it is a catastrophe. And mothers among themselves were proud [if they could say] 'Ja, my child is already clean.' That was such a tradition. One should not undervalue these small things. These little mosaic stones, I find, were already there and really paved the way for something like Hitler. I must honestly tell you, I was not raised that way."

That is putting it mildly. Frau Karma Rauhut, almost the youngest woman in these pages, was born in 1925 in the village of Glienicke-Nordbahn, just outside the northern rim of Berlin, to very young and, as she described them, rather Peter Pan–like parents. She pictured her mother as someone who mostly enjoyed herself by reading or partaking in Berlin's spirited cultural life. Karma's father was a banker (his "rank" was bank director) who "played at the bank" and speculated at the stock exchange. Neither parent was interested in child-rearing, so for that they hired teenage farm girls, who were not interested either. Karma and her one-year-older sister grew up "drilled in freedom." It was not good training for the Third Reich.

The friction within a free spirit within the Third Reich was intriguing (as was a German who had been named Karma), but I must admit to being reluctant to hear her memories. Her youth, to my mind, removed her from the weight of the moral choices the Third Reich both offered and demanded. On the other hand, Frau Karma Rauhut had a stellar recommendation. Asta von Moltke Henssel, the sister-in-law of Freya von

Moltke, described her younger friend from painting class as "urehrlich [honest to the core]." Still, it was with hesitation that I rang Frau Rauhut's doorbell in the pleasant Charlottenburg section of Berlin one afternoon. By the time the afternoon was over, I had recognized that moral choices are the provenance of children, too.

An unquestionably youthful-looking Third Reich witness opened the door. She had a smooth and casually sophisticated appearance—silver-gray pageboy, black stretch pants, espadrilles. Her home was atypically modern for Germans, or Germans in their sixties, with abstract paintings (not by her), black leather furniture, a glass coffee table, an art deco teapot. She looked and lived smooth, one might say, but she did not talk or act smooth. She had an aura of frankness about her, both in her vocabulary and the way she seemed to think and rethink out loud, her words rushing through cigarette smoke and coffee, and around family members and an affectionate Afghan dog. She was partly consumed by the Third Reich, it was evident, and why not? It had stolen her childhood, and, in a way, her parents.

Karma's early years had not lacked shadows. In 1929, after the stock market crash, her father lost his job and all his money. Unlike his colleagues, however, he had no debts. He happened to have been hospitalized for an internal problem for months before the crash, and had not been speculating.

After having flown, Peter Pan–like, over much of the financial disaster, he did try to work for a while as a carpenter, a phase his daughter recalled with wonder bordering on bemusement. "He was a completely, I would say, *un*craftsmanlike human being."

Her own family's economic circumstances at the time affected her less than did those of other Berliners. "I can remember as a child, that while traveling on the streetcar, people on the platform fell over from hunger." She saw "people everywhere on the streets offering themselves for *any* work. Like experienced salesmen stood on the Kurfürstendamm or Unter den Linden, carrying cardboard signs saying who they were and that they desperately needed work."

Also, a friend of her father's took it upon himself to show her and her sister more, "because we were such protected city girls." He owned a small factory in a "workers'" section of eastern Berlin and took them to see the workers' wretched homes. She recalled being aghast at the sight of tiny buildings in rows one behind the other, each darker than the one in front, "without any comforts, only toilets in the yards or maybe in the stairwell." Worse were the interiors. "One room with a kitchen, and dark and dirty." And crowded. To earn some money, women with "an insane number of children" rented out one of their own beds for a number of hours a day to "sleep guys"—men who could not afford to rent a whole room. While the "sleep guys" slept, the children lay in their parents' bed or on the floor. The tour met its purpose. "We were so shaken."

Frauen

Just before the Nazi takeover of Germany, Karma's own family had a break. Her father got another bank director job, at a private bank.

Just after the takeover, his many Jewish colleagues and friends began trying to leave Germany. She said he often helped them sell their possessions quickly to get money to leave, and probably did not realize how illegal his actions were. In one of her many descriptions of him, she said, "He was a very soft human being and also very cautious."

By the following year, Karma's life had changed completely. The memory of a nine-year-old: "I can recall as a child someone coming to us asking for help and money. It's a little vague. I was young. It must have been 1934. It was a completely harmless man. He had a daughter who was a chambermaid in one of the big hotels. And the SS believed she had enabled this writer, Erich Maria Remarque, who wrote *All Quiet on the Western Front*, to get certain papers so that he could flee the country. And the daughter somehow had also disappeared. I don't know if she went with this man. In any event, they [took] the poor father into the SS barracks, there was a big Gestapo headquarters, and then they interrogated the man and smashed his glasses, smashed out all his teeth, and [beat him] 'blue' and. . . . And this man, they didn't get anything out of him. Then they let him go. And he came, because he heard about us, 'There you'll get help,' to my father. And wanted money because he had none at all." The man especially needed to buy new glasses. "I saw this man. And we as children somehow figured it out. It was whispered, of course. And children, as much as possible, should know nothing at all, because that was too dangerous." I asked if her father gave the man money. "Ja, of course. Certainly."

It is perhaps not surprising that as the years passed and the Third Reich intensified its presence, Karma followed her parents' earlier example and sprouted her own wings. "I must tell you completely honestly, I went through this time as in a dream. The way of living did not suit me, and I knew my parents were also completely opposed to it and friends, too, our whole circle of friends. And during the whole time I fled into a dream world. For me, America was simply *the* land of freedom. Up until America entered the war, we still could see American films, ja, Hollywood drivel. We went to *every* American film there was anywhere. We didn't go to school and went to any matinee to watch every American film, no matter how bad. And collected pictures of the American actors there were then and they hung in our rooms." Robert Taylor and Clark Gable thus decorated at least one bedroom wall in Glienicke-Nordbahn. Also, "there were stores here where, if they knew you, you could get jazz records in the back room. And those of course were *the* things to have. That was just what you did."

What you did not do, she said with impatient scorn, was emulate the Nazis' version of beauty, sex, or culture. "Women under Hitler, that was something completely dreadful. A German woman does not wear makeup, she may not smoke, she should have a thousand children and. . . . Ach, that

344

still brings a chill to my spine. A little like the Greens, but in many ways more oppressing." She called the Nazis' output "pseudo-culture." And everything having "a tone of physical desire," she said with increasing anger, was called "Jewish piggishness. It had nothing at all to do with Jews. It was just passed off as that in the ideology. It was dreadful." She said German romance films showed no more than a kiss. "Later, during the war, things got a little looser, so that people would think about something other than just always listening to bombs. Perhaps from far away a bed could be seen, but there were no naked women and naked men. . . . It was so prudish, hypocritical. What the Nazi bosses did in bed, I don't know." She added, "Sex was only to give the Führer children. And when you consider these insane punishments, having to do with abortion or birth control and so on. They migrated into a KZ for that. It was *impossible*." She paused. "Those are all such things that seize your life. One cannot convey it to [younger people] today. They say, you are insane."

To escape the Nazi life, Karma also flew to her attic with a girlfriend, and read the forbidden books her parents had dutifully "cleansed" from their collection, if not, as ordered, from their home. The books would have been too boring for her and her friend otherwise, she said, but "it was clear, if they were forbidden, they were very interesting."

Back on German ground, Karma continued her flight. She evaded the Bund deutscher Mädel, a notable feat.

"One really *had* to be in the BdM. The trick was that I went to school [a private girls' school her mother had attended] in the city of Berlin, but lived so to speak in another district, so they never figured it out, because they had no communication with each other. In my village I always said more or less, 'I'm in it in Berlin.' And at school I always said, 'I'm in the BdM at home.' One could always create certain freedoms, nicht? But naturally the thing was, I didn't have a uniform. And when there were big marches or school festivals, the teacher always said, 'Put on a black skirt and a white blouse, so it's not so noticeable.'" Karma complied, relieved not to have to wear the BdM outfit.

"This odd jacket and the scarf and this leather scarf holder and the shoes, I would have died rather than put it on." She said her teachers "silently overlooked" her avoidance of the BdM because the school, although taken over by the Nazis, still retained the tone of its old director, a Social Democrat and "very emancipated woman." She had hired teachers "who were no one hundred percent Nazis. They did all afterward have to be in the Party or leave. I had an 'aunt' [a family friend] who was a grade school teacher, who did not join the Party." The "aunt's" husband, also a teacher, refused as well. Both were fired. "He later worked in a factory and she became a salesclerk."

Karma's school luck ran out when she had to transfer to a school which was "quite Nazi-infested." One day the director called her to his office and said, "Well, my dear child, I cannot give you your diploma. And I must tell you, you will never amount to anything. You are not in the BdM, you don't join the Party." He told her she might "become a worker, but you'll never be anything." To that, "I said, out of stupidity, 'Well, the world is round. It revolves.' And of course he then reported me." She said she saw in her school file that he had done so, and had knocked her down a grade in every subject.

During her school days, she also did something she now considers beyond stupid. She said she had forgotten about it until she attended a forty-year class reunion in 1984. Some former classmates had met sporadically before, but this was "the first time a lot of the women talked about their views about the Nazis, whereas in previous years no one risked either defending her previous views or talking about them." She said she noticed "that many still actually had the impression it really had not been so terrible. That shook me up *so* much. Several in the class had parents who were convinced Nazis and who themselves enthusiastically had participated in the BdM as 'Obergruppenführerinnen [senior group leaders]' or whatever. For example, one in athletics. She was a year older than I, born in '24, was in my class. Her father was unemployed when Hitler came to power. This she now told me, I didn't know it at all, and was some kind of tailor in a factory. And before Hitler came to power, [he] was in the Party and through Hitler attained a position of junior director in a uniform-making company or something like that. And the daughter went to the Lyzeum [girls' secondary school] with us, which earlier was not necessarily the case, that workers' children or children from poorer homes and so on could go to higher girls' schools. Because there was tuition, which later was slowly done away with. Anyway, the father was naturally very ambitious for his daughter and she was also convinced [pro-Nazi] and through athletics she tried to be somebody. And this woman, she is now a high school lecturer in Hanover, she said to me, 'You do know that you were always an outsider, that we could *never* stand you.' I say, 'Why could you all not really stand me?' 'Because you were not athletic.' That is, I was not at all *un*athletic, but did not like to take part in these massive sports things.

" 'And because you were politically unreliable,' she said to me. Then another said, 'Well, you still are today.' Outsider, nicht? Well, it was somehow so unnerving to me and then she said a very strange thing that I had already repressed." The year was about 1942. "She said to me, 'Did you really know that I wanted to report you?' Say I, 'Why? I can imagine that you wanted to report me a couple of times. Others reported me, too.' She said, 'Once you came to school and brought sort of a suitcase record player and brought *The Threepenny Opera* by Brecht [with the score by Kurt Weill] and during recess played [the records] and wanted to show us that this Jewish music is really very nice.' " (Brecht was not Jewish, but Weill was, and the songs were verboten.)

"I somehow had completely repressed it. For days after this conversation, I could not sleep and thought to myself, what did you do to your parents? You did something that could have . . . in an impossible and simply *un*political . . . Ja, it had nothing to do at all with resistance. That was not in it. We did such things from an inner opposition against this feeling about life."

Frau Rauhut asked the classmate why she had not reported her. "Then something very strange came out, that really probably rescued me a little throughout my whole life. She said, 'I talked about it with my parents and [they] said not to do it. You don't know what her parents are and what kinds of connections they have.'" Frau Rauhut paused. "*That* was the reason. And that was really how one came through the Nazi time quite well, ja? One had connections. If one had no connections, one was done for."

Outside school, Karma also noticed how the Nazis had affected some family friends. In her Weimar Republic childhood, theater and painting were "strongly Jewish," she said, adding, "That was *the* cultural life." People took part in it "with enthusiasm. . . . And then when Hitler came, one said, 'It's time they all get out, they have only stood in the path of us Aryans.' And all at once!"

She especially noted the change in one older woman, the woman who, in fact, had given her the records of *The Threepenny Opera* as a present. Frau Rauhut said she liked her personally, but was struck by how she was both "so enthusiastic" about Hitler and "so enthusiastic" about the Jewish artists whose paintings hung on her walls. These were artists she "even also *helped*, whom she must have liked from a purely personal angle. And [she] did not even recognize she made only anti-Semitic remarks." Frau Rauhut said once she took the woman on, knowing, she added, the woman would not denounce her. When questioned, the woman told her that an artist whose works she kept up had been "a friend of hers and she had not known he was a Jew. So, completely schizophrenic, ja?"

Although the family friend did not denounce Karma for her frankness, denunciation became more likely the closer Germany got to war. That war was coming may have been evident to many Germans, but saying so was another matter, especially on the twentieth of April, 1939 . . . Adolf Hitler's fiftieth birthday.

That day "there was an insanely huge parade with the military," as Frau Rauhut described it. The parade went right by the bank at the Brandenburg Gate, where her father worked. Bank employees, from directors to secretaries, stood on the balconies to watch. "Then my father, who was also kind of a dreamy type said, 'Well, this guy will bring us to war yet. Look at that, what else is it there for?' And naturally someone immediately reported him.

"But because my father had a lot of connections and . . . also was very friendly with 'appearance Nazis [Scheinnazis],' that is, who were very brown on the outside and had a completely different color inside, he always could get off. That is, he had to go to the police and was imprisoned for two days. Then he was allowed to spend five thousand marks for something or other, for some kind of organization. He could get off with money. But only through his connections. Suddenly, the [telephone] lines hummed. 'Could you not help?' and so. He could always bring it back 'to order,' nicht? I know my father did it deliberately. He cultivated these connections. He tried to get to know people who could help him in need, but he also helped many."

She said he also met often with a group of men friends in a kind of inner resistance. "One could create a certain free space for oneself. I don't know if you understand what I mean. In one's mind and in one's style of living, one could create a free space if one had enough connections, and maybe also a little bit of money." Her father's "neutrality" affected his career, in that he could not have been part of a government bank. He did not want such a job anyway, she said, at least during the Third Reich. "You did not want to stand out. You only wanted to try to carry on with your style of life without selling yourself."

Frau Rauhut related a furious attempt by a young soldier named Karl, one of three sons of the pro-Nazi Jewish-art–collecting woman, to show he was not selling himself. One of his brothers was a "one hundred percent Nazi" and a "guard officer" in Hitler's headquarters. Karl and his other brother were, in Frau Rauhut's description, "absolute anti-Nazis. And I was part of a scene. . . ."

It took place in the woman's home on the occasion of a festive gathering and meal to welcome home Karl from the eastern front. Frau Rauhut had known Karl "very well, since school days." In an attempt to stay out of the way militarily and politically, he had joined the navy, partly because of his interest in sailing and partly because of its reputation, she said, of not being "so political." Later, he was transferred to the army.

Like most young men, in high school he had been in the Hitler Youth. "People who had been in [it] up to the war were automatically made Party members, upon application. And these parents, these politically Nazi parents, simply applied on their own for their son to be received into the Party. This day, he returned from the front, the battlefront in Russia. And the mother, the father was not so bad, the mother had laid next to his place this recognition, 'Accepted into the Party,' and said, 'Son, I have a nice surprise for you.'"

Karl's initial reaction was silence. Nobody spoke about the Party acceptance.

"Then he took the piece of paper and [briefly] left. We sat there and chatted, several people were there, and then the mother went to the toilet and came back, and from behind, hit her son. And he still said nothing. Afterward, I said to him, 'Karl, what did you do?'" The answer was that he had torn the Party acceptance up into toilet-paper size and put it on the toilet paper hook. "And whoever wanted to wipe his bottom," she laughed, "would do so with the Party insignia."

Frau Rauhut had said earlier that two of the woman's sons were killed in the war. I asked if he were one of them.

"Ja, he died in the Caucasus, in Russia." Frau Rauhut then fell silent herself.

Karma Rauhut spent almost all the war in Berlin, trying to evade both bombs and Nazis. She maintained that anyone who was not there cannot understand that she could have done no more.

"Jewish friends now reproach me, saying we could have gone into the resistance, we could have switched our identities after each bombing attack. They say it would not have been so dangerous, [that] one could have changed identification by saying one lost everything, papers, house, et cetera. Ja, oddly, that did not work, because there were always survivors and they would be asked immediately, 'Do you know him?' One had to bring a guarantor who stated that one was someone entirely different. And that would not have been possible at all. I told them, 'You are picturing it as too easy.' In spite of these huge, heavy, bombing attacks, there was never such chaos that one could have done that. One could have gone under, disappeared, somewhere completely different, but in Berlin, one could not have changed his identity and continued to work somehow as a resister. Because everything was organized. It might have happened once or twice, but not organized somehow."

She said no matter how much she tries to explain how life was, that "the organizations were *everywhere* and the human beings reported each other and one watched the other," including who entered and left every apartment, the Jewish friends do not believe her.

She remained firm in her sense of the past. "It was like you were in a spiderweb and the spider always noticed if something vibrated somewhere and did not ring true. And that simply cannot be conveyed to them. They said, 'Ja, one could flee.' *Where* should one flee to? You could only do resistance if you took death into consideration. Or horrible torture and also torture for your whole family, and death and KZ. And we were not all heroes. We shat in our pants from fear. Not everyone is born to heroism, nicht? And you cannot convey that to them. Where should we go? Switzerland was so tight, no one could get through. The worst things happened when people tried it. And France was occupied, Denmark was occupied, Italy was fascist, the whole Balkan lands were occupied. Poland. One had no more free room to flee to."

Her father did get out once. It was a business trip to Switzerland. In Zurich, he went to a movie theater to see a film that happened to be preceded by an English newsreel. The spiderweb vibrated. His action was reported to Berlin. Once back, he was ordered to explain his action. "To that he said he had gone to the theater because he wanted to see a film and did not know an [English] newsreel would be played, that they could not demand of him he should have known." He was let go.

In July of 1944, just after the failed assassination attempt against Hitler, Frau Rauhut learned that her father's own web of connections extended to some of the plotters. "My father simply did not come home for several days." He went to the home of a woman he knew, the widow of an SS officer, who was hiding a half-Jewish friend of his. Frau Rauhut believed that her father sought shelter mostly as a precaution. "He did not know [about the plot], but he was in that circle. He knew them all through his career." She said some of the plotters were his supervisors at the bank, and that his direct supervisor was a baron who jumped out of a window after the Gestapo summoned him for interrogation. Her father returned home "only after all the arrests had run their course and he was not being searched for."

While he was in hiding, the family heard from the "aunt" who had to give up her teaching job because she would not join the Nazi Party. She was working in the Luftwaffe ministry building, in the section where uniforms were distributed. "The day after the assassination attempt she called us from her workplace, over the military telephone lines, and said to my mother, 'Have you heard? Even the devil won't take this terrible criminal.' Because he wasn't dead. And my mother, who thought our telephone was being tapped, [dropped] it like a hot coal. She said, 'How *can* this woman!' But nothing happened." They knew they had been lucky. The "aunt"'s comment was "essentially a death sentence."

Did Frau Rauhut really think her father was unaware what was being planned for the twentieth of July? "I believe [he did] not [know]. He did nothing," she said, half laughing, "that was dangerous." She called her father at another point, "kind of a clown who came out of everything. He was completely unpolitical. He was weak. He was no hero. And somehow he always came in contact with things that were risky." Being a clown made sense, she implied. "In these serious, terrible times, there was so much in life that was comedic, anecdotal, crazy, this maneuvering back and forth."

She learned that same year that she had not maneuvered enough herself. Under the National Socialists' mandatory "work duty" system, she was assigned to a work duty camp south of Berlin. "Not officially, but unofficially, [there was] a very severe gradation. There were, so to speak, noble camps, where the 'higher daughters' of Party members were, or people who had devoted themselves to the Party. They went to some estate or a large camp. And then there was a gradation downward to a regular punishment camp. And I was sent to such a wonderful camp as that."

It sounded, from her description, much like a concentration camp. "Around the camp were barbed wire and guard teams with dogs, and we had three or four [female] leaders in uniform. And in each room was a guard. We always said *Kapo*, because it was the analogous expression for a KZ leader."

The camp's centerpiece was a sandy windswept Platz in the middle of which was a flagpole with a swastika flag. "Every morning we had to get up at six o'clock and then do 'flag roll call,' the flag was raised up high, a Nazi song had to be sung, and then we had to work within the camp and always keep up the Flag Platz, that is, pour sand on it, make it flat again, and then the wind blew twice and it was all blown away and we had to do it again." The girls also had to "walk briskly past the Platz, not just saunter past it. And the toilets were such, the seats were not comfortable, forward at an angle, and ten in a row, not so that you could shit privately, or have a cigarette."

The food was awful ("I could not eat the fodder") and the nightly Nazi political lectures worse. Yet, she said, she had "insane luck" in the camp. "With me were all girls from reform schools in the Rhineland. And among them were a lot of prostitutes." She whispered, "They were fantastic. You cannot imagine. They could organize *everything*. They had so much courage." New arrivals had to give up "bra, panties, everything one had" and were issued "horrible underwear" that was thick, raw, scratchy, and brown. "Then this uniform. And one constantly had to make the skirt longer. They came again, 'The skirt is too long.' One had to shorten it. And another came and said, 'Do you want to be a streetwalker? The skirt is much too short.'" The real streetwalkers, for the price of cigarettes or even "fodder," used their forged key to the room where the personal items were locked up, chatted up the male guards and . . . "One day later I had my underwear from my suitcase."

The prostitutes helped her spirits, but Frau Rauhut (among others) soon became so sick that she was placed in the sick bay, although without proper medical care. Her illness included "a good case of jaundice, an angina," she said. "And I must honestly say, relatively often I was not even conscious."

To her rescue came a young Luftwaffe officer, who was also a medical student. His name was Rainer Rauhut. One of his friends was engaged to Karma's sister. Officer Rauhut had met Karma, but he did not know her well. During a visit with the betrothed couple, Karma's parents begged him to find out why they had not heard from her. And so, in his Luftwaffe uniform, he made his way to the camp.

The heavy fortification surprised him. So did the welcome of a guard, who said, "Ach, there you are! Come in, we've been expecting you." Rauhut said nothing and kept walking, past barracks of decidedly atypical 'work duty' girls hanging out the windows. Frau Rauhut recalled from his tale, "They were fresh and said, 'Man, do you have anything to eat?' 'Such a terrific guy!' and 'Have you brought us some food?' He thought, 'What *is* going on here, that they have nothing to eat?' And he had chocolate or something and gave it to them." They told him Karma had been sick a long time, and pointed to where he could find her. "He then marched over and came in and saw me lying there. And someone was lying in the next bed with unbelievable appendicitis cramps and another had tuberculosis. And he as a prospective doctor said, 'What is the matter with you all?' I was completely yellow. And suddenly the door opens and in comes the leader of this camp [a woman]. 'What are you doing here?'

"And he was already an officer, nicht? and he said, 'What's going on here? Shall I report you? So and so many people are lying here, it's impossible, the people need to go to a doctor, you can't just let them lie here.' 'Ja, that's none of your business and how did you get in here?' He said, 'The guard said you were expecting me.' It turned out that she had a boyfriend who was a Luftwaffe officer and had told the guards to let him in. They didn't know him, and now came an officer with a Luftwaffe uniform. Such *chances* just happen in life."

Officer Rauhut said if a doctor were not called, he was going to his general. The Führerin got scared, an ambulance was called, and the patients were all taken to a hospital in Berlin. But before she was to return to the camp, Officer Rauhut and Karma worked out another plan.

"And then I disappeared. And then I married him."

Frau Rauhut, still married to the friendly-looking man, with whom she had two daughters, did not speak a word about attraction or romance. She spoke in practical terms. Because the Nazis would be looking for her under her real name, she obviously needed a new one—like his. But the couple could not marry because she had never bothered to get her "Aryan" ID. "I am 'Aryan,' I have no Jewish relatives, but I simply hadn't collected the identification and the papers. How could I get them now? I couldn't go to some administration office and say here I am. They would have arrested me immediately, nicht?"

To the couple's rescue came Officer Rauhut's general, who, she said, was also in the resistance. He somehow furnished the necessary papers and told the couple to marry and disappear.

The wedding took place in the evening at a mayoral office in Berlin. Just as it began, so did a bombing raid. "The mayor didn't look to see at all who was getting married. There were so many dead and he had to arrange a place for them. He was always on the telephone, and our whole wedding lasted two and a half minutes. Because he had no *time*. He just signed the papers."

The newlyweds took off for Austria, to a field hospital where Officer Rauhut had been reassigned. Along the way, they stopped in Bavaria, near Obersalzberg, where one of Karma's uncles temporarily hid them. From the hiding place, she said, "I could see Hitler's house. And then to Austria and I was gone."

While Officer Rauhut reported to his new assignment, his leave having ended differently than he might ever have imagined, his new wife stayed "in a hotel room on the edge of legality." The marriage had not begun in a traditional manner, but was evolving along traditional lines. He went off to work in the morning and came home in the afternoon. She spent most of the day at home. She also became pregnant.

She knew the search for her had begun. "Of course, they went to my parents, and they said they knew nothing. But they did know." The police also sent letters, to Karma's christening name of Johanna. Her mother sent back the letters, "telling the postman she has no daughter called Johanna, which he knew she didn't." The bride-in-hiding risked sending letters, too. "The organization was not as tight as it had been. One noticed that immediately." She is certain her freedom was linked to her nonimportance. "If one really were *important* enough, the whole apparatus was put in motion to find you. That I was not." She was "just a badly raised child, nicht? But if they wanted to find someone, they *would* have found him. [A person] could have held out illegally only so long."

One day toward the end of the war, her husband returned to the hotel room as usual, but "spoke not a word. I said, 'What happened?' And he said, 'I have now seen for the first time something I will never forget in my life.' They had liberated Mauthausen KZ. And herded along these emaciated KZ people with dogs, and when they could not go any farther, the dogs bit them, and then they were shot in the back of the neck, and they died. We all knew there were KZs and so on, but my husband, after he saw it with his *own* eyes, only then did he really know it."

Frau Rauhut all but said that she already had known more. "The reports about these insane cruelties did seep through. But you know, with all things that are so completely horrible, one does not comprehend it right. One does hear that Jews are being gassed."

It was, among the German women I met, a rare statement.

"There were even jokes made about it. The political joke was indeed an enormous release valve when things were almost unbearable. For example, it was said . . . During the war we got really terrible soap. It swam on the water, that was somehow . . . And it was said it was made out of Jews. Such was *said*, such was circulated with a joking *laugh*. Ja. But the people, they did not realize what they said."

She said, as intensely as before, with such a report, "You cannot correctly realize what it really is. And that's how it was with KZs. We knew that Jews somehow were being gassed, but we repressed it. We did not picture it to ourselves." She added, "One did know, but did not *realize* it fully. One could not, because we would have gone insane."

She had heard another example of massacre. "A friend of my father's came to our house and told us he had seen, in Poland, an entire airplane hangar full of corpses." A long pause followed.

Such information just does not "fit in your head," she later said. "Can you picture a whole airplane hangar full of corpses if you haven't seen them? It surpasses one's power of imagination. This inhuman criminality surpassed every power of imagination."

I asked her at some point how and when had she learned about the gassing of Jews. She answered, "I knew it as a child. I heard it from my parents." She said she did not know how they knew. She believes the source may have been a Dutch man who was in the resistance and lived in part of their house with his family.

Within the story of her own life during the Nazi regime, Frau Rauhut spoke repeatedly and always adamantly about the difficulty of active, as opposed to passive, resistance. She said some people have suggested there could have been more resistance from within concentration camps. But she said that even in her own small quasi-camp, she saw the effect of the Nazi machine on the individual. "Everything was done to destroy a personality. And it happened very fast. Astonishingly fast. It happened under these conditions: withholding of food, withholding of sleep, away from everything, and always living under a threat. One becomes kaputt very fast." People who can survive such things better than others are those who are simply dulled [stumpfsinnig], she said. "But the more intelligent and sensitive a human being is, the faster he goes kaputt. Takes only days."

I asked Frau Rauhut about her opposites, not in action, but in knowledge, people who said they did not know what was happening to the Jews. "I cannot pass judgment about others," she replied. "Maybe they did not know. Maybe they really were in a circle in which they experienced nothing." She added that if people were strong Nazi supporters, no one would have said anything to them out of fear of being reported. "I would not have gone up to someone I knew was a one hundred percent Nazi and said, 'You all are gassing the Jews.'" She also thought that Nazi supporters "in subservient posts" could well have "shut their ears." But the fact of anyone not knowing "is a puzzle to me." She acknowledged that the raids and roundups, none of which she said she saw, mostly took place at night. The Nazis "tried hard to do it so the population did not necessarily see it. Whether a very small moment of *shame* was still in them, I don't know, or [if it was] simply for security reasons." But "when such a big machine is running, there are always holes, and one talked about it."

Toward the end of the war, a time of so much gruesome tragedy, Frau Rauhut's father inadvertently took part in a comedy of sorts. It was somewhat like the clown having a laugh on the circus. Because of his age and uneven health, he had not been a soldier, but "was only drafted toward the end, maybe five weeks before Berlin fell into Russian hands, into the Volkssturm." She began laughing. "That is actually very funny. One often has to laugh about some things, sad as it was. He was so untalented with his hands. And all these footsore old men and the whole Hitler Youth had to go to a field together" and learn how to fire a bazooka, a weapon she described as cumbersome and heavy. Every Volkssturm man and boy was to hoist it on his shoulder and shoot. But the village only had two bazookas to practice on, for the thirty or so Volkssturm Hitler Youths and old men "who were supposed to defend our village against Russian tanks. And stupidly, my father was supposed to be the first to shoot this thing. And he did it so stupidly, and shot down the electric transformer."

Frau Rauhut began laughing so hard, she could hardly speak. "With the result that the whole . . . All of these villages now had no electricity."

The instructor told his recruits to go home.

Frau Rauhut said she has found letters her father wrote during the very last days of the war. They showed her parents "fleeing as far into a dream world as we children had. They were going to every concert, they saw every movie, they read, nicht? They got together with each other and they also tried to shut their eyes. And they did shut them. They took part in no resistance at all. But I cannot criticize them for it, because it would have meant [that] the whole family was done away with, nicht? One *knew* that. And I was so afraid. [She once spoke of always turning on the water before talking.] In my circle of acquaintances, one or the other got caught and then disappeared. And we knew what happened." They had known since the man with smashed-out teeth came to their door in 1934.

When I mentioned that Freya von Moltke (whose sister-in-law introduced us) says that anyone who survived made compromises and therefore bears some of the guilt, Frau Rauhut replied, "Well, I must say that, too. The life of my parents consisted of *only* lazy compromises. And I believe, too, [the Third Reich] also deformed people psychologically. That is, people who could make these compromises constantly." She said she grew up watching individuals "repress everything. In a certain sense, we all are neurotic from it. We are fearful, in part dishonest, yes, and never have a good conscience. One always tried to repress it. *I* do it, too. I certainly repress a lot of things, because one always has fear and feelings of guilt.

"And my parents, too, for all practical purposes, did not get on with their lives after the war. My father committed suicide."

The year was "'52 or '51." He had a good job "as a bank director again and so on." But he could not "gain a firm footing, spiritually" after the war. Her mother could not either. She "fled into alcohol, basically died from it." Her father's course was more direct. "He simply drove into the forest and poisoned himself. He was supposed to visit me here, in Berlin. My children had some kind of celebration, I don't know, Communion or something." The poison, she said, was sleeping pills. The police found him four days later.

Had he felt responsible?

"I don't know if it was *conscious*. He somehow no longer came to terms with his life." She stumbled around in attempted explanations and unfinished sentences, then said, "It *was* indeed his life. And this life, according to my comprehension, somehow was made neurotic. It is terribly hard to get through it and then come to terms with it. Of course, maybe other reasons, acute reasons, could have been there, but he simply could not get on with his life any longer. My mother either." She paused. "And if you think about it, our entire youths also were, so to speak, stolen from us, nicht? We only lived in shock, in fear."

And in shame and in guilt, she said. "I must be ashamed about it. We *are* the Germans and I cannot imagine that others are not ashamed. Maybe they don't admit it or maybe don't say it to you as a foreigner. Because the older people do have a kind of feeling of nationality and say, we cannot tell an American that we're ashamed, better we bite our tongues than admit it."

She said the only kind of older German without it is "a crazy Nazi, who's still a Nazi and thinks it's all good. But all the others, who did not do anything, let's say it completely straightforwardly. We all were cowardly and all were afraid and arranged ourselves, maneuvered ourselves through this life. We all *have* feelings of guilt and we all *had* feelings of guilt. But at the same time, I know exactly," the question was, "what *should* we do?"

There may be no other German town more famously photogenic, more popular with besmitten
camera-toting tourists, than thousand-year-old
Rothenburg ob der Tauber. Its picture-perfect façade extends from cobbled streets up to graceful,
gilded iron signs signifying Gasthof or Bierstube,
then up to columned fountains and cascading window boxes, and upward still farther to the red clay
roofs above half-timbered houses.

Unifying the snappable splendor is a series
of handsome gated towers connected by the old
city wall. Its top is now a promenade, beckoning
admirers to walk and to focus outward and downward on other picturesque views, the forest and
fields of the Tauber River Valley.

The wall seems not so much to surround
Rothenburg as to embrace it. But its purpose, of
course, was to protect it. Over the centuries, the
fortification system did keep out small affronts. In
the face of larger offenses, however, Rothenburg
was plundered with impunity, sapped of blood,
and ransomed dry. Tourists who bask in the visual
harmony that is Rothenburg today cannot see much
evidence of the ravages of the Thirty Years' War.
But if they look closely, they can see clues of more
recent discord. Roofs whose red tiles look much
fresher than others. Painted walls and cobbled
streets that seem merely decades old. They are.

At about 9:30 on the morning of Saturday,
March 31, 1945, almost half of Rothenburg ob der
Tauber was bombed to the ground. The gated
towers and great thick wall meant to keep out centuries of invaders (and to let in centurions of
friendly visitors, including Adolf Hitler) were no
use at all against the 9th Air Force of the United States.

Frau Anne Hepp

"A Very Unpolitical Woman"

Frauen

Frau Anne Hepp heard the warning on the radio. "We always had the radio on. Then suddenly came this signal, first a forewarning, then the signal an attack was coming, then the voice. 'Sudden approach of American bombers.' The route was described. I don't remember it all, but I still hear in my ears, 'to Rothenburg.' It was already roaring. I took the children and quickly went down to the cellar. It was no air raid shelter, only a simple cellar." Her daughter was five years old, her son seven. Frau Hepp was not only frightened but shocked. "One *never* thought Rothenburg, too, would be bombed."

Somehow, the Hepp family home escaped damage. Frau Hepp said she cannot remember how long she and her children stayed in the cellar, but she remembered what they encountered when the attack ended and they climbed out. "The first thing we saw was a running cow with horrified eyes. And already there were people saying, 'It's burning, it's burning, it's burning.' " She repeated the words as if speaking a liturgy.

"They were all wounded and I took them all in, and tried," she continued. "What can one do? When there is bleeding, to bind someone up, to get someone something to drink." And she was not seeing the worst. The wounded reported that farther on, in the center of town, the situation "was very, very, very bad."

Ironically, part of the reason for the human casualties was Rothenburg's picturesque defense system itself. "People could only get out of the city through these few gates. That's the problem in Rothenburg. There's no open access."

As to why Rothenburg was bombed, the answer is still debatable. The same fleet of 550 medium and light bombers of the 9th Air Force that hit Rothenburg also bombed other targets that same day, including a militarily strategic part of Würzburg. Rothenburg, which had no obvious military value, at least to its residents, may have been hit simply because the pilots had extra bombs, or because it was part of the Third Reich.

Frau Hepp referred at various times to the bombing as "horrible," "terrible," and "very tragic." She stopped well short, however, of assigning blame. I asked her at whom one "schimpfte" [the word ranges from "reviled" to "scolded"]. She said that came later. But later, at whom?

"Of course, one schimpfte at the Americans. But one didn't know at first if it was English, or . . ." She stopped. "What does it mean? You can't blame soldiers who are under orders. We also shot at England." Frau Hepp, it was clear from the beginning, tried to see things rationally.

She lives in a three-hundred-year-old home she and her late husband remodeled from an old carriage house and moved into in 1947. Among her possessions are photographs of Rothenburg that certainly do not appear in the town's multilanguage tourist brochures. Herr Hepp, a professional photographer, took them the day Rothenburg was bombed.

358

He had been exempted from military duty by a bad leg, but in the last-ditch months of the war had been drafted to be part of the Volkssturm. While on duty in a neighboring village, he saw the attack on Rothenburg, and rushed back with his camera. The resultant photographs of the ruins (ruins that were still smoldering when the first American troops arrived, said Frau Hepp) are astounding. It is hard to believe that anything was salvagable from such rubble, much less a tourist mecca of homey splendor. I realized that all afternoon long, while strolling around Rothenburg, I had been unknowingly admiring a visual lie.

Literally true to its image, Rothenburg has lived more comfortably in past centuries than in the twentieth. The sharp-eyed proprietess of a local inn said that when she was going to school just after the Second World War, Rothenburg's teachers had no idea how to teach students about the Third Reich. In history classes, she said, whenever the Nazis shimmered in the future, teachers kept starting over with the Ice Age. "Ice Age, Ice Age, Ice Age," she said. "All I ever learned about was the Ice Age."

Frau Hepp herself looked like a representative from an earlier age. Ensconced in centuries-old surroundings whose burnished beauty was at once sensual and austere, she wore native dress of a dirndl-type skirt and a close-fitting blue sweater with silver buttons, a white collar peeking over its neckline. In aesthetic harmony with her adopted town, she seemed considerably more at ease talking about the years before, rather than after, 1933.

The eldest of three children of a self-made Rhineland building contractor and his Hausfrau wife, Anne grew up in a home that emphasized hard work and perseverance. Her father's company, which he "started completely alone," sometimes had two hundred employees, she said. They built private homes as well as city halls and "worked on dams, laying water pipes, great big ones between Wuppertal and the Ruhr. It was very interesting."

In her eyes, her father was a "very, very social human being" who "did a lot of good for his workers" beyond what the government required. "We visited the poor, the workers who didn't get a lot of pay." She did not suggest that her father could have, or should have, paid them more. "We had to bring them food; clothes for the children. And when they were older, things were also done, that they have homes that were"—she paused for the word—"habitable."

The business fluctuated, taking an especially sharp downspin in the inflation of the early 1930s. "It was very difficult. There was no work. Hardly any. Only repairs. No contracts."

Anne worked for her father for several years, until 1930, and then decided to pursue her own career. She reasoned no one in the office would be out of work if she left, "and I was off." She went to a small town in the Black Forest to work as an apprentice on a poultry farm. "I really wanted to work with my hands and be in nature and work with animals. We'd had a big garden at home, many fruit trees, and also animals. I was used to it and liked it." At the poultry farm, she faced a situation typical of the period. "I had to work very, very hard. When one wanted to be an apprentice, one had to pay the owner fifty marks a month, to guarantee the job. We only got our food and could sleep there."

When I commented it sounded exploitative, she said, "Ja. Of course. But they couldn't exist if they didn't do it that way. We were six or seven young girls there." She said the parents of the others paid for their daughters to learn the poultry business, but she had money she had earned and saved from working for her father. The farm work proved too hard for her. "I got a heart problem and the doctor said, no more work like that or you can get very sick. Then I worked in the farm office. I said if I do that, I'm not paying the fifty marks anymore."

In the meantime, she had been in touch with a young man, Herr Hepp, whom she had met in Rothenburg while attending a home economics school. Her parents had suggested the school after touring the old town themselves. "They saw the girls all wore the same clothes, white collars, and aprons, and thought, that's something for our daughter. Those were still good times, then. My parents had money and could pay. The school was expensive."

While she was at the school, an interest in photography led her into a photo store owned by her future husband's father. After her year at the school was up, she and Herr Hepp Junior "wrote each other a letter now and then and he once visited me at my parents' home. And I was in Rothenburg sometimes. It was a casual connection. Without obligations," she laughed.

He then wrote her he was opening a his own specialty photo store on the Marktplatz, the center of Rothenburg. "He asked if I would want to help. It came at the time the doctor told me I couldn't do hard physical labor and therefore couldn't finish my education at the poultry farm. And I wrote, ja, I'm coming. My parents were *mad.* They said, when I make up my mind to do something, I don't stay with it. Earlier that was stricter. Today, with the youth, it's accepted more. It's something we learned from America, to be more flexible."

She moved to Rothenburg in 1932. "I found it wonderful here. I felt very well here. But, naturally, we had a profession in which we met many people from different cities and from other countries. Americans came. I could freshen up my school English." She said her move to Rothenburg had little to do with romance. "That came somewhat later. Congeniality [Sympathie] naturally was there. But at the beginning, there was no thought of a common future." Not in her mind, maybe. "Two years later, we married. Everything was good with my parents, naturally."

By the time she married, the Nazis were in power. Her parents' early response to National Socialism, she said, was to be "very depressed. My father was a Free Democrat and had a lot of worries about how it would turn out." Her husband, she said, was not for the new regime, either. He was "skeptical." Why? "He was a little skeptical anyway. He was not for enthusiastic things."

She said he was the oldest of nine children, three of whom had died. "And"—she paused—"he was sick. As of sixteen years old. He had a leg injury which was very bad, involving the bones. It made an impact on his life. He was"—she paused again—"a somewhat quiet man. Ach, you can't say that either. His siblings were more *lively*, more *spirited*. One brother was a sculptor and a younger brother was also a photographer, a very good photographer." She sighed.

Her closest relatives may not have been on the Nazi bandwagon, but she was. She sighed again. "You've probably already heard it many times and perhaps cannot believe it. Because one could not initially recognize these terrible developments that became apparent later on. But at the beginning, each human being was spoken to [and asked] to give the best and to work for a Germany that promised social well-being.

"After '33, it simply was better. The times of depression were over. There was work again. How it hung together, I can't tell you. Unfortunately, I'm a very unpolitical woman. I only know that not just in the construction company, but in general, there was work. And human beings were appealed to, to do good work. That's a very important point. And everyone worked with joy, I'd say, because one thought a better future was coming."

Her father reaped two years of National Socialist prosperity, then died in 1935. His company was dissolved. In the meantime, Herr Hepp, who like her father started with "nothing at all," was working hard at his own business, his new wife at his side. "In general, we all believed this idea that each person has to work not only with his hands, but with his mind, and must be ready to help. And through the youth movements, the younger people were pulled idealistically. Each should be honest. That was talked of a lot. Honest, comradely. And ready to work.

"It was 'the silver stripe on the horizon.' I don't know myself how it all happened. All of a sudden, there was something one could build up again. People also made things with their *hands!* And when one does something and sees one has done something, that's a reason to believe things will be better."

Frau Hepp's enthusiasm, I later thought, in part may have been connected to what she described as a "relatively isolated" life. Her husband was a lone wolf—"ein Einzelgänger," she called him. For one thing, he did not join the Nazi Party. For another thing, because of his bad leg, he did not join anything athletic, other than a rifle club.

Frauen

As for her, other than being a housewife and eventually a mother, she spent much of her time working with her husband in the store. And, she said, most of their customers (including "Mr. Hearst the newspaper king, with his whole entourage") were out-of-towners. Her husband started a second business, an art publishing company specializing in photographs of church art, and she was busy helping him with that, too. Furthermore, she was not a native Rothenburger, but an outsider, and felt it. "We built up friendships much later," she said. All in all, "we stood apart a little."

That is why, maybe, she noticed as little as she said she noticed.

There must have been Nazi hoopla in Rothenburg, I said. She replied, well, Rothenburg is such an historical city anyway and has its own traditions which "always were highly maintained."

What about Nazi parades?

Ja, she acknowledged, flags were hung out. And Hitler did come to the Marktplatz. But it was a private visit. She had not known about it and had not seen him, although "there certainly were many people who saw and cheered him."

And? And? Frau Hepp had been to the dentist the afternoon before our evening meeting, but it was I who felt I was pulling teeth. "You really should have talked with a native Rothenburger," she said.

Then a clue emerged that Adolf Hitler had made more of an impression on Anne Hepp than she had indicated.

The clue was thanks to the Ice Age expert at the inn, who had asked me if I knew what day it was. With embarrassment, I realized I had not noticed it was the 20th of July—the day, in 1944, when Claus von Stauffenberg tried to assassinate Hitler.

Frau Hepp, I said, the proprietess at the inn was asking me if I knew what day this is. Do you know?

She searched awhile. "The 20th of July. Ach so, ja!" She paused. "Führer's birthday, I think. Or, what was it? Nein. Nein. Stauffenberg. I told you, I'm unpolitical."

Her attempt to cover her own embarrassment was almost touching. But she not only had mixed up Hitler's celebrated birthday, the twentieth of April, with the day of his attempted assassination. She also had called Hitler's birthday the "Führer's birthday." That was the phrase of a follower.

And indeed, close to midnight, hours after talking of her parents, her husband, and the bombing of Rothenburg, and after a modicum of good Franconian wine, Frau Hepp volunteered that she had been a member of the Nazi Party.

"I had the feeling, who knows what one thought? I should be there." She said she was influenced by a woman friend who had gone through hard times and was particularly hopeful about a new future. Frau Hepp also said she herself was afraid her husband would suffer the consequences of *his* not joining the Nazi Party. "It unfortunately was the case that people who didn't join the Party were attacked or had business difficulties." His obduracy had no ill effects, whether thanks to her Party membership or not. (And it helped him with the Allies after the war. He went from photographing German soldiers in uniform to photographing American soldiers in uniform.)

What was his response to her decision?

He told her, she said, "If that's the way you feel, then do it." She added, "I wasn't active."

If not, what had she seen through the lens of her own eyes? Anyone in a small town like Rothenburg (the population then was about 9,000) must have noticed what was going on with the town's Jewish population. That Rothenburg had had a Jewish population long ago was evident. On my own casual walking tour, I had paused at the Judentanzhaus [Jewish dance hall]. It was built in 1613, burned in 1945, and restored in 1953, said the sign. I had also walked along a street named Judengasse [Jew Lane]. The name, which exists in other German towns and does not seem to startle Europeans, obviously is from an era well before the Third Reich. I read in a guidebook that the Jews were first expelled from Rothenburg in 1350. (The book's first mention of their existence was their expulsion, with no reason given.) Then, said the book, they came back in greater numbers, and in 1520 the Rothenburgers destroyed the synogogues and again chased the Jews out of town.[1] Then the Jews came back again and built a dance hall? The history was almost as bewildering as it was sad.

The book did not mention Rothenburg's Jewish population during the Third Reich. But I read between the lines and saw it. And she must have seen it for real. For whatever reason, I decided to wait and see if she would bring it up herself, or if her recollections would end with no mention of the words *Jew* or *Jewish*.

She talked, and talked, carefully, guardedly. Late that evening, weary of mostly futile attempts to draw her out, I asked if there were anything she wanted to add, anything she especially thought about when she thought about that time.

There was.

The words did not come easily. "It . . . It . . . has been imprinted on my life, that this belief that one had, that things would be good, was false. I cannot yet free myself from it, from this shattering. What one had to experience, what happened. Of which we really had no idea. Of this persecution

---

1. Willi Sauer and Wolfgang Kootz, *Rothenburg ob der Tauber* (Heidelberg: Edm. von König-Verlag, 1985), 11.

of the Jews. And of the extent of the war." She paused. "I'm speaking just of myself, personally." She paused again. "It was so incomprehensible. We did not learn it gradually. It came quite at the end, when everything became public."

For instance?

"Like I said. Persecution of the Jews. Concentration camp things. Also these terrible reports from the front, the Russian campaign. Everything came, one after the other. And you said to yourself, how can this be, when you were idealistic and it went such frightful ways?" She paused a good long while. "Into the inhuman. Incomprehensible."

Was there a Jewish population at the time in Rothenburg . . .

She interrupted. "Yes! But, well, there was already something, that the Jews . . . But they could leave."

Did she have Jewish customers?

"Nein, I believe not. Nein. That I don't know. That is, of the families that were here, I don't believe . . . *Ja.* Ah, I cannot tell you. Certainly someone came inside to my husband and they spoke and, I don't know. They did have opportunities to sell their houses. Germans bought the houses. And mostly then they went to America."

What did she think about it then? The sense of it?

She sighed, remained silent for fifteen seconds, and sighed again. "First, I have to say that in my parents' home I never had anything to do with Jewish questions. It was never spoken of that there were problems, then." She sighed once more. "One thought, ach, it's better they leave, if they're going to be set upon."

Were they "set upon" in Rothenburg?

"Well, you just heard, they had to sell their homes, *could* sell their homes. I personally knew no Jewish human beings here." (The Jewish population of Rothenburg was comparable to what it was in Germany as a whole before Hitler—less than one percent.)[2]

I would have thought they had stores, I started.

"There were *good* stores here. But by the same token, they were very clever and grasped very quickly what was coming."

Was she never a customer in these stores?

She said she was not. "You see, we lived very, very simply. We had to. As I said, we started with nothing. What did we buy? Food? Sometimes a bit of clothing. I don't know anymore where we bought it."

She then remembered something else.

---

2. For example, the 1933 edition of *Der Grosse Brockhaus* (16:132) encyclopedia says that in 1925 there were 80 registered "Israelites" among 8,830 Rothenburgers. Thanks to Linda Wheeler.

One day, while visiting the city of Würzburg, she saw a woman wearing a Star of David walking in the street. She asked someone why the woman was not walking on the sidewalk. Frau Hepp was told that Jews had to walk in the street.

That was, she said, the beginning of her despair. Seeming most uncomfortable, she said, "The deeper you feel something, the harder it is to talk about it."

Frau Doktor Margret Blersch

"I Was Alone. And I Had the Whole City Against Me."

The country-browned woman in a big straw hat, white blouse, long skirt, and sandals stood on the train platform of the out-of-the-way village of Riedlingen in rural southern Germany and waved with vigor. Even from fifty yards away, standing alone, something about her dress and her verve indicated she would have stood alone in a crowd. And she had. My visit was motivated solely by a tale about one such time.

Up close, seventy-nine-year-old Frau Dr. Margret Blersch had a finely weathered face, a great arch of a nose, and wide and sparkling eyes. Her blouse was starched linen, a ladylike touch, and more evidence that her world extended beyond a country village. But there was no time for much reflection. Within a minute, she was driving us swiftly over hills, around corners, then up a driveway to a stop. Within another minute, her large dog, Dior, was happily barking and leaping on us both, and Frau Dr. Blersch was striding across the lawn to a wire-enclosed pen of exotic Kenyan fowl. As she entered it, they shrieked and flew about, Dior continued to bark, a large wet tongue slapped the back of my neck, I added a yelp to the cacophony, jumped a foot, and turned to see a most affectionate horse. Frau Dr. Blersch emerged from the pen, two speckled eggs in hand. "For breakfast," she said, smiling.

In the midst of the congenial pandemonium, the thought emerged that not only did Frau Dr. Blersch stand alone, she celebrated doing so.

That afternoon she gave a brief tour of her pleasant, modern, memento-packed house, which stands high in splendid seclusion among grain fields. She had it built after the war for herself, her family, and her medical practice. Although she transferred most of her practice to a son who lives nearby, she said, she still treats some old patients. Her specialty is homeopathy. It was only one of the disciplines she practiced during the Third Reich.

To talk of it, we sat on her terrace much of that day and the next. Away from the menagerie, the setting was peaceful, the interruptions few; a distressed friend telephoned for comfort, and two smartly dressed soldiers appeared to assess the damage their military maneuvers had done to her fields. She went off with them, and returned, smiling. She had asked what division they were from, because their uniforms were so elegant and well cut. They had replied, "We are French."

Although I was anxious to hear Frau Dr. Blersch talk about the time she stood alone, I was at least as curious about her personally. I had been learning that standing alone—for a noble reason—rarely happened without a background in compassion, and that compassion rarely appeared without experience in questioning the status quo.

Frau Dr. Blersch fit the mold. Her first questioning began early, she said, with her own Catholicism. "As a child, I opposed the conventional religion. And at the age of fourteen, I left religious instruction. It was all too pious." Not only was one of her uncles the Catholic deacon, but she had an especially pious aunt. "I always resisted her. She was too Catholic for me. She was my godmother, the youngest of my mother's sisters, and always took me with her on vacation. I found that *horrible*. The first years of study, she gave me thirty marks each month, sometimes sixty. But of course that wasn't much. I still had to work a lot."

She did? From almost the minute we sat down to talk, Frau Dr. Blersch had been dropping the most respected names of Germany (while, in a populist counterpoint, swatting a number of flies). I therefore assumed her own name was droppable, too, and bespoke some wealth. She had mentioned her godson marrying into the von Weiszäcker family, former patients being Stauffenbergs, her French daughter-in-law's distinguished ancestors. Then there was a row of judges and doctors whose names meant nothing to me, but whom she touted as friends from student days and esteemed today.

Lofting above them all was mention of her neighbor, Ernst Jünger, the famous and controversial writer then in his early nineties, a man she had known for decades, a man who had written about her fictionally,[1] a man married to someone she did not dismiss. Pictures of him and inscribed by

---

1. She says she is Ulma in *Besuch auf Godenholm* (Visit to Godenholm), written in 1952. It is a tightly woven allegorical novella about the postwar spiritual journey of two men trying to harmonize the contradictions of life. Ulma is a minor but critical character whose unself-conscious physical way of being is so pure that she raises physicality to a spiritual level, in the tradition of German heroines. *Werke*, Vol. 9, "Erzählende Schriften I" (Stuttgart: Ernst Klett Verlag, n.d.), 311–369. Thanks to classically educated Rita Kuhn for helping enlighten me.

him were everywhere. She acted somewhere between shocked and disappointed that I knew little more of him than that he first made his prose reputation by praising noble battle. (In fact, by the eloquent glorification of his First World War experiences, which prompted other writers to follow his lead, he arguably fostered a yearning for war in the next generation of German youth.)[2]

The reason her apparent bedazzlement with famous people mattered at all was that especially during the Third Reich, heroes and heroines mattered. And the heroines included the curious amalgam that is Margret Blersch.

The "years of study" she mentioned referred to the study of medicine. They started in 1932, in Freiburg. It was there the then-twenty-four-year-old Margret Links met her future husband, Konrad Blersch, a former linguist and scholar who specialized in ancient languages. He was from Riedlingen, which was and remains, in Frau Dr. Blersch's opinion, "the deepest province." He taught at the local high school, she said, but gave up trying to interest uninterested children and decided to become a doctor. Her decision to become one, too, necessitated taking a number of part-time jobs. They included teaching anatomy to younger students, by dissecting corpses.

"Freiburg had a number of Jewish professors," she added. "As long as they were there, we didn't get any assistantships. My girlfriend and I together had *one* assistantship after our state exams. Because the Jewish professors mostly took Jewish assistants, nicht?" Asked if they did so to help them, she answered, "No, not to help them, but because they credited them with more intellect."

She later indicated that she agreed with the professors. "The Jews in general are cleverer than we are," she said. Why did she think so? "I believe through these thousands of years of tradition and also the Bible they see relationships much better." She said "it's the same" with the training of Moslems, who learn parts of the Koran by heart. When pressed, she said, eventually, she thought Jews have "another mentality" because of having had to fight for centuries to survive, but she did not know if that necessarily was a result of genes. "Out of this mentality, out of this *life* of having to protect oneself, certain strengths became more forceful than they were among people who could live in peace and quiet." Whether such strengths were learned or inherent was "difficult to say." She thought "upbringing plays a great role." But a "natural gift also comes into play." We finally left it at that.

When Hitler came to power, Margret and Konrad and their friends

---

2. Gordon A. Craig, *Germany 1866–1945* (New York: Oxford University Press, 1980), 492–493.

already were part of what she called a resistance group. They were "Anthroposophen," followers of the progressive educator Rudolf Steiner. She and Konrad were the only students, the other members having already started their careers, mostly as teachers and lawyers. As she described the group, it was spiritual rather than physical. That hardly mattered to the Nazis.

"In '33, we were all arrested." The group had been holding a conference in a local castle. "As a conclusion to the conference [about German and Roman justice] we had a party with . . ." She paused. "These were all such idealists, with minuet dancing and a little pathos, nicht?" She laughed. "Suddenly we heard, no one may leave, the castle is surrounded by the SS. [She corrected herself to say the SA.] All the papers were seized. *Everything* was seized, what we'd written for eight days. Then all the names were written down. Anyway, it was bad."

She said the conference was purely academic, "*but* those were all people the Nazis were suspicious of earlier. None was in the Party. Later, I worked as an assistant at the Freiburg nerve clinic and my professor said over and over, 'Please, *go* at least to the . . .' where one had to go on Sunday to some kind of a club of theirs. He said he was constantly getting complaints that one of his assistants was in none of these Nazi clubs at all, nicht?"

Nicht? The word, which literally means "Not?" (short for *Nicht wahr?* [Not true?]), proved to be a frequent interrogative for Frau Dr. Blersch. The expression implies concurrence, as did hers. With each *Nicht?* her voice hopped higher and her eyes were especially direct. One could scarcely refrain from at least nodding in agreement.

After the SA surrounded the castle, she continued, "The word was, that it had been, so to speak, a whorehouse. Ja! Nicht? Nicht? But it was bad, nicht? One could not defend oneself at all." She said of the SA men, "They all came inside and we had to show our identification and we were locked up in a room. All other rooms were searched and they took everything they wanted. Then the word was, they had captured a nest of conspirators."

Of the SA men's demeanor, she said, "I believe it was most embarrassing to them, because everyone was from the region. The son of the high school principal was there, too. And the daughter. I think it was highly embarrassing. But it was the same with the synagogues. They couldn't do otherwise, nicht? They were ordered there." She went on, "And a Jewish woman was there, too. A lawyer. Who later took her own life. Much later, when she was threatened with deportation. Many took their lives."

Frau Dr. Blersch insisted she had not been frightened by the SA action. "To the contrary. I'd gone there only on a test basis. My [future] husband was a member." But sometime in the middle of the action, when members asked if she wanted to join the group formally or remain on a "test" basis, "I said, 'I want to be a member *now*.' And I did so. Nothing happened to [Konrad] and me except for our names being written down, but we were not in public office. We were still just students. But all the others were fired. All. All. All. All."

Did the group stay active?

"And how! And how!"

How active?

"It was not a resistance group in the sense they conspired against Hitler, but it was a group that tried in a spiritual and Christian way to push through its goals and thereby to be a fortress against the Nazis."

As we talked, the summer sun lowered, the number of flies thickened, and Frau Dr. Blersch soon regularly punctuated her recollections with the blap! of her fly swatter. Later in 1933, she said, she and Konrad moved to Vienna and then to Munich, to continue their studies. (It was common for students to move from one university to another.) She passed her medical exams, becoming a member of a professional organization she said was obligatory for her and had been for Jewish doctors, too.

"In 1933, they were all thrown out. There were very famous Jewish doctors in it." She said she thought it shameful that physician groups lent themselves to the order, which, she said, did not come from her medical organization. "It came from above. And then instead of the caduceus being the mark of distinction, there was the swastika. Then everything was taken over. Many doctors also went along with it willingly. Many doctors were, after all, for euthanasia, nicht? They said it themselves. 'There is unworthy life.' "

She said she understood how Hitler got the early support he did. "Unemployment was much worse than today. Then, there was great hunger. Then, the youth were in the streets. Then, many artists had no bread, and went along the roads as vagabonds, nicht? Then, was a very bad time. And *then* someone came and said I'll help you. Everyone come! You'll get work, you'll get bread, you'll get, nicht? It was believed only *too* happily."

In 1938, two years after they married, the Blersches moved to Riedlingen to set up a joint medical practice. She said that because they shunned the Nazis, they lost out on financial backing that other doctors got, like state insurance reimbursements. Nonetheless, they managed to do all right. Then came the war.

Herr Dr. Blersch was drafted almost immediately as an army doctor. Frau Dr. Blersch continued to work and soon directed "a gigantic practice. We began in the mornings about eight and stopped in the evenings at eleven or twelve or one." There were 150 to 160 patients a day, she said. "It was bad."

Among her staff were five nuns, all members of an order that had been thrown out of its cloister by a local Nazi. The nuns not only worked for her but lived with her in the ever-growing Blersch household. She and Herr Blersch had their first child in 1937, and one almost yearly after that, the fifth being born in 1942. She also took in a bombed-out friend and her three children. Also, a bombing raid killed one of Frau Dr. Blersch's brothers (a Luftwaffe pilot), their sister whom he was visiting, and two of the sister's three young children, so she took in the surviving child. Toward war's end, the Blersch household numbered eighteen people, including eight children under the age of seven. One nun worked solely as a "Kindergärtnerin," another in the household, the other three in the laboratory.

The medical practice, contained within two examining rooms, a large laboratory, an X-ray room, and the waiting room, took up one floor of a large three-storied house. The household took up the rest: a general living area on one floor, bedrooms for the children and the nuns in the attic. There also was a cellar, which in the last days of the war hid several German officers and soldiers who had refused orders to blow up the local bridges. "The SS was looking everywhere for them, but not in our cellar. Then all the people who were considered deserters were hanged. Bad!"

A disadvantage of the house, for Frau Dr. Blersch's purposes, was its location. Not only was it near the center of town ("Riedlingen was very transparent, like a glass window," she said), it was next door to the post office. And the postmaster was the Nazi Ortsgruppenleiter. She still was not cowed.

"I did really bad things. You see, if one were brave, one could do resistance. In our waiting room we had to hang up a plaque, a new one each week. On it was a Party saying, like a saying from the Bible. The Ortsgruppenleiter came and brought the saying and said I had to hang it up in the waiting room. And I said, 'Is that *law?*'" One could hear the might in her voice. "He said, 'It is not law, but one expects it of you.' I said, 'I won't do it. I don't hang up Bible sayings and I won't hang up Nazi sayings, either. Furthermore, I'm no Nazi.' Then he came again and said I had to give a reason. My nuns were terribly afraid something would happen to all of us. But nothing did. It really wasn't the law, so they couldn't do anything. If it had been the law, I couldn't have done anything about it. So in a *certain* sense, one could go a *little* against the grain. Because, nothing happened. One was looked upon as not quite belonging."

Another act of legal resistance cut closer to Nazi sensibilities. "When one had five children, one got an Honorable Mother's Cross, nicht? From the Nazis. Sort of a mark of distinction. And I sent it back to them." She laughed again. "I said I won't allow myself to be rewarded. I didn't bear my children for Hitler. But that was bad to say."

She also annoyed the Nazis by her treatment of a Russian woman doctor who had been hauled to Germany as a factory worker. The annoyance was not in providing her shelter and giving her work (in the household), but in treating her humanely. "She ate with us. That was bad, nicht? One was not allowed to let Russians eat at your table."

But her worst-known infraction, to the antireligion Third Reich, was providing work and shelter for the five nuns. When I asked if she had been afraid to oppose the Nazis in the ways she had described thus far, she said, "My nuns much more than I. Because they were suspect anyway. Just because they wore their habits. They were in much more danger."

Proof the Nazis did not like Frau Dr. Blersch's attitude soon became evident. "They informed on me for faith healing," she said, seeming more bemused than angry. In addition to the patients who came to her, "at night we also went to pay house calls, the nuns and I. If someone were at the point of death, we called for the pastor. That was forbidden too, or not well liked. And they said we were engaging in faith healing! Nicht? Ha ha ha." Somehow, she was cleared.

On the surface, the Blersch medical practice covered a range of disciplines, with specialties in homeopathy and neurology. But Margret Blersch also had another specialty. In a regime obsessed with cleansing "unworthy life" from a "master race," she helped save people the Nazis would have murdered.

Her acts were doubly defiant. She treated patients other doctors might have shunned, people who were mentally or physically handicapped or who had a range of contagious diseases. And she did not report them, as Nazi law required. Although it obviously was a great risk for her (and her family) to flout Nazi law, she had learned it was deadly for the patients if she did not.

The person she had learned it from was one of her medical professors, "a wonderful man" who himself suffered from clinical depression. He was the beleaguered director of the Freiburg nerve clinic. "When he noticed what was happening to the people, he sent a lot back home." What was happening, as is well documented, is that "unworthy life" was killed.

What Frau Dr. Blersch heard about in Freiburg, she observed in Riedlingen. "The buses went past our house. They were gigantic buses with curtains over the windows. They went from here to the Alps where the institute [was], where one said they'd shower. And then came . . . gas inside." She said the gas was Zyklon-B, the type used for the massive killings in concentration camps. But in the time and circumstances she described, the Nazis probably murdered with a more "primitive" gas—carbon monoxide.[3]

"If there were a mentally ill person in a family and someone took him to a psychiatric clinic, they were held there perhaps a couple months, and then they were loaded into a big bus and sent to an institute to be gassed. It was near here, forty kilometers away. We knew that. We knew that from our professor. We knew they did not want the mentally ill to live." The gassing

---

3. Thanks to Agnes Peterson. Further information may be found in Ernst Klee's *Euthanasie im N-S Staat* (Frankfurt: S. Fischer, 1983).

started in her area about 1940, she thought, and she believes many local people learned about it. "After all, they did see the cars [or buses] that drove by with curtained windows. And when the people came out of the facilities, they screamed. They knew something was going to happen to them, nicht? They didn't want, they . . ." She got lost in stumbles, and restarted. "It was like this. Here we had homes run by religious orders, of nuns, for debilitated children. Retarded children. They were all taken, too."

She said the truth made its way to the victims' families. "They knew it. That got talked around. Somehow, these Swabian families always had a mentally ill relative somewhere. And when the cases of death piled up and it was said he died of typhus, he died of tuberculosis, or whatever, one already had suspicions." By 1943, she said, after the murders were quite well known to the local public, "it was done more secretly. The mentally ill were killed in the clinics themselves. Simply injected, nicht? Or left to die, nicht?"

Had she attempted to spread the news about what she knew?

"Nein. Neiiiiinn. That was *strictly* . . . Nobody could talk about it. That was kept the strictest secret. But ten kilometers from here was, still is, a psychiatric facility. A woman ran it, a crazy Nazi. She injected the people by her own hand. There were many, many, many sisters [nuns] who were my patients. That's how I knew something. But that was exactly why it is absolutely possible that these people who say they knew nothing of the gas chambers and ovens in Auschwitz are telling the truth. It was kept *so* secret, one was arrested for only speaking about it, nicht?"

She returned later to a variation on her point. "*Everything*, everything that had to do with the SS and all these death camps, also in regard to the mentally ill, was handled as the uppermost secret. Certainly some people knew about it, who had something to do with it. But I ask myself if, eh"— she paused—"you see, I ask myself whether even the wives of these people who ran the annihilation camps, how much they knew about it. Mengele, who was sought throughout the world, must have been such a lovable human being. Soft and, nicht? Nicht? That he had friends all over and . . . That *is* the story. That the outer [and inner] beings . . ."—she paused again— "often do not seem at all to intermesh."

She had no doubts about keeping quiet herself, she said. "It was fully enough that I stood by the people who had congenital diseases. And said, 'You may not go to another doctor. You must stay here. That is, I won't report you.' But one could not say, 'If you are reported, you will be gassed.'"

Frau Dr. Blersch had spoken of one Nazi she trusted, a man who joined the Party early and thereby had amassed considerable influence. Could she have talked to him about the killings?

"I'd *nevvvver* do that. One never could do that. One could not tell the other what one knew, because that made him know it, too. One beleaguered the other with it, nicht? All the things one knew, that my husband told me, one kept *completely* secret, only in the family or with the most trusted people.

You cannot imagine it at all. It was . . . One thought there are microphones everywhere and people listening. It was a terrible time."

She recalled a story about two sisters, one of whom had been her patient. The patient was upset that her sister and not she was in line to inherit the family farm, and "reported that the one who was to have inherited the farm did poorly in school because she was feebleminded, nicht? She was sterilized, because of the report. And the farm was taken away from her, because of the report. Then the sister who reported her got the farm. And then hanged herself. After the war."

Frau Dr. Blersch also maintained that farmers in and around Riedlingen would have done "nothing at all" about the killing of their mentally and physically handicapped relatives. A major reason was poverty. "Many farmers were happy if they were free of the people to whom they had to give half their farm. If they had a mentally ill child and had to put it in an institution, they had to pay for it. And if it died, they didn't have to pay anything more. And it hadn't helped them anyway, nicht? In that way, the farmers think very practically. Many farmers, many people, were happy when they were rid of someone who was dangerous. For [the mentally ill] often were dangerous. They could begin to rave or, nicht?"

I asked at one point if she knew before the end of the war about full-scale annihilation. "*Ja*, we knew," she said. "That we knew exactly. We saw it here. There was a Jewish settlement. We saw the Jews in rows, sent away, to a house in the Alps, and then sent farther." She insisted it happened in 1940 or 1941, early in terms of the "final solution." That made me question further, asking if she knew the people would be killed. "Nein. That one did not know at the time."

When I said that is what I meant, she insisted she did not think the people were to be killed, but were going to Theresienstadt, the so-called new Jewish city. Then when did she know of the whole Holocaust? "Not until after the war, I believe. It was kept very secret." When I commented that many Americans do not believe that, she broke in, "We couldn't have known. It was kept so secret. We did know of concentration camps. We knew of terrible circumstances, but if anyone got out, he was not allowed to say a word, nicht? And from Auschwitz, no one who could say anything got out."

Incidentally, Frau Dr. Blersch said she saw no films or documentaries whatever relating to the Holocaust until 1985. That year, after a sister moved to Hanover, the two toured the exhibits and site of the nearby Bergen-Belsen concentration camp.

Meanwhile, during the Third Reich, more and more intended victims of Auschwitz or its lethal way stations found their way to the medical practice of Frau Dr. Blersch. The word had spread that she would treat them and not report them. Also, because of her training as a neurologist and her use of shock therapy, among the people who came a great distance to her were an increasing number of schizophrenics. "I injected them with insulin. Then they were unconscious. And afterward injected sugar and they came to again and had lost their crazy ideas, nicht?[4] If these patients had gone to a clinic, they'd have been removed immediately and been gassed. One did not allow them to live. Also all crippled children and tuberculosis patients and all incurable sicknesses."

The surest way to protect the schizophrenics was to go to them, rather than have them come to her. "I treated them at their homes. I had a couple. That was, of course, very dangerous, nicht? Here in the village, I injected them. They came through. That's why so many people came, because they knew here were nuns, we're not handing people over to the health ministry. We don't notify the state about them."

Was there an order that she had to?

"'Had to,' yes, but no one could prove it of me. I could say, I didn't notice it at all. That I'd thought it was a passing illness, that I didn't consider it a mental sickness. That was not so bad. The bad thing was when one was convinced the people had to go and then helped it take place. Nicht?"

While Frau Dr. Blersch was tending her array of German civilians on the home front, Herr Dr. Blersch was tending German soldiers on the battle fronts. In Russia, he, too, learned of the deaths of innocents. "My husband said on his first leave from Russia, he had seen terrible things and that we do not want to remain in Germany, if he returns from the war."

What he had seen were "shootings. He saw that Russians were shot in their graves. Russians and Jews. That one lined them up and . . . that the Wehrmacht then had to march next to them." She said the SS had done the shooting.

Had that not made him want to leave his post?

"Nein. I believe he would not have, out of comradeship to the others. He was a troop doctor and responsible for many. Although he loved the Russians very much. He always said how educated the Russians are."

The war against them claimed their admirer's life. Herr Dr. Blersch died of typhus. "Because he did not have enough vaccine for everyone. And he did not vaccinate himself." She paused. "He was . . ."—she paused again, ever so briefly—"wonderful." She speeded up. "My son's the same."

---

4. The insulin-shock form of treatment was relatively new then, but common for the era. It was replaced by electroshock, which is considered less detrimental to the body and allows a doctor more control. (In eastern Europe, however, insulin shock was used much longer, because the electricity often could not be controlled.) Thanks to Nurse Robert Holtz, Marin General Hospital, Greenbrae, California.

I asked how she learned what had happened.

"The pastor wrote me. And one of his friends who returned wrote me from the field hospital, he died like a saint. When the vaccine came, he was already infected but didn't know it, because it incubates for fourteen days. Then he inoculated himself and was already infected. That was a double infection. Ja. And . . ." Frau Dr. Blersch hurried away, saying she had to wash her hands.

Konrad Blersch died in April 1942. His widow was thirty-three. That October, she gave birth to their fifth child, a boy.

Speaking later of her children, she said only three of them, two boys and a girl, reached adulthood. "One child died of diphtheria when he was three years old. The *only* child in the whole practice, of all my patients and children, who died of diphtheria was my small child. The son who was born after the death of my husband."

She never remarried. "One doesn't know what would have been better. But I had many nice people who helped me and the children."

Perhaps, too, her husband was not an easy man to replace?

"That, too. Nein nein, nein nein. And I had my work here, that I liked very much. And, nicht?"

Frau Dr. Blersch continued that work and continued thwarting the Nazis. (It was the fatherless fifth child who earned her the Mother's Cross she sent back.) She was not alone in her battles, however. She had several "guardian angels," as she called them. The two most active ones were Nazis.

One, a Dr. Reinhart Gmelin, was the earlier-mentioned man to whom she would not talk of the gassings. He was "the head doctor here in the whole area, a *won*derful human being [who] had the Golden Party Badge of Honor." The insignia, usually given by Hitler personally, signified a very early member of the Nazi Party. Dr. Gmelin joined in 1923, she said.

"He was a good human being. He was an *idealist*. After all, there were also many idealists in the Party." She said he joined because he believed the Nazis would solve unemployment. He became, she said, "the foremost doctor in the Party."

If he was so wonderful, why did he not quit once unemployment was "solved"?

"He could help *many* more people by being in the Party, nicht?" In fact, he "protected my life during the war." He knew "that the lower-ranking doctors were very much out to get me. They took away my car. Throughout the whole war, I traveled for my practice by horse."

Her main medical nemesis, she said, happened to be one of her husband's former classmates. "He was with the SS, a Count von Ziegel. [At her later request, a pseudonym.] He had a castle near here. It was even said he

376

pushed his brother out a window so he'd get the whole estate. Ja. And he was a doctor. And was an SS doctor. And was an SS doctor in Auschwitz. I believe he was killed after the war, before he was brought to Nuremberg. And he controlled this region here and especially tried to waylay me. He paid very close attention to what my nuns were doing, what I was doing, nicht? And he was extremely malicious. Therefore, my husband was afraid for me and wrote to Dr. Gmelin, he with the Golden Party Badge, that Dr. von Ziegel made so many difficulties for me, that he'd taken away my car and not allowed me gasoline. And he was the same one who had thrown my nuns out of their cloister and requisitioned it for a field hospital or something. Then this Dr. Gmelin wrote a very nice letter to my husband, 'Dear Herr Blersch, you may set your mind completely at ease.' He knows me, he knows how hard I work, and he's so happy I have the nuns, for otherwise I couldn't do so much work. And my husband could be completely reassured he would protect me against the impediments of the Party and the SS. He wrote it, the top Party doctor!

"He wrote this letter in March or the beginning of April, '42, and on the fourth of April my husband died. Then the letter came back with all his possessions. After the war, I sent the letter to Stuttgart to exonerate Dr. Gmelin, to show what Dr. Gmelin also did *against* the Party, nicht? It helped him a lot."

Frau Dr. Blersch's other Nazi guardian? Riedlingen's own Ortsgruppenleiter, who had asked her to display Nazi sayings in her waiting room. It happened that his family knew that sloganless waiting room well. "He had three or four children and they were patients. That was a plus.

"He always told me when the Gestapo had been back again and asked him about me. He always told me. Near the end of the war, he said now I had to keep quiet, there was nothing more he could do for me, that they were all so loaded against me. Now I was to be very, very small."

But did he really help her?

"I do believe so. I believe he was an honorable negotiator. Also, there were far too few doctors. They needed me, too."

Why did he say that the Gestapo . . .

"Because of different things," she broke in. "First, because I refused the Mother's Cross. Second, because I didn't have these sayings up. Third, because I had the nuns. Fourth, because I was denounced for faith healing. And, what else did I have to answer for?"

What else, indeed. Discounting her still-unknown subterfuge in regard to the mentally ill, she had been friendly with members of the family of Claus von Stauffenberg, who tried to assassinate Hitler. His father's cousin, Franz Schenk von Stauffenberg, was a regular twice-a-month patient. A daughter-in-law was her friend. (She added that the woman, Camilla, was a granddaughter of Pierpoint Morgan. Actually, she was a great-granddaughter.)⁵ "When the assassination attempt happened, she called and said, 'Margret, I believe we will all be picked up. May I leave my bicycle with you?' She then said, 'Be careful, it clicked on the telephone.' That means we were being listened to, nicht?" Frau Dr. Blersch said she was not disturbed "a lot" about being overheard. "They couldn't do anything. We were not conspirators."

After the failure of the assassination, her friends were "very low." All had hoped "we'd be free because of our *own* strength, not because the Russians or English conquered. But we had done something our*selves.*"

As dusk approached, and the name Stauffenberg still hung in the air, I asked Frau Dr. Blersch about her own background. She said her family was "very simple." Her father was a shoemaker, the eldest of fourteen children of linen weavers. He had a store in Celle in northern Germany and also made orthopedic shoes and riding boots, was the head of the regional shoemaker guild, and the "Shooting King" of the local rifle club. He was red-bearded and witty, and she spoke of him fondly. Her mother was one of eight children of farmers. (Konrad Blersch came from a background similar to hers, she said, his family having been farmers and brewers.) "We came from the people." The Links had six children. Margret, the eldest, was born in 1908.

She was the first person in her family to go to college. For a daughter from such a background to attend not only college but also medical school was extraordinary. Wondering about her parents' influence, I asked what sort of politics they had.

"Ha ha!" she said. "My father was a Nazi." Before a second passed, she amended. "Or, not a Nazi, but was with the SA." The SA brownshirts were, however, Nazis. She said she never saw him in uniform except in a photograph and does not know when he joined or what he did. The "SA was more like a community club, nicht? Sort of like a rifle club, nicht? At home in Celle." She also said she never heard her father say anything anti-Semitic, and that he helped the children of Jewish shoemakers.

She also said that during the Third Reich she and her father did not talk about each other's political opinions, that he would have been upset about hers. She said politics per se "*never*" were talked about at home (and she left home in 1928), so she did not know her mother's opinions. "She was Catholic and very conventional. Always somewhat beyond her position in society, in terms of bringing up her children."

She did credit her mother for her own interest in medicine, which "requires [the] supernatural sensitivity and intuition" that she felt her mother had. (She added that natural healers from the East have it, too, and that her

5. Gerd Wunder, *Die Schenken von Stauffenberg* (Stuttgart: Müller-Gräff, 1972), 486. Thanks again to Linda Wheeler.

mother must have had "some eastern blood," because she herself has a grand-son who looks Chinese.)

As for her upbringing, "I was always very individualistic. All my broth-ers and sisters are. Each is a person unto himself." Did she and her siblings have more or less the same opinion of the Third Reich? "I don't believe so," she said, with a sound of finality.

She said she herself never liked anything about it. "From the begin-ning, I was so infuriated about Hitler personally. About this primitivity. And I am certain I foresaw all that was coming, nicht? Ja. Absolutely certain. Known from within." She continued, "I never agreed with anything. I never made a concession. That certainly is remarkable. I never made the smallest concession."

From the beginning, she and Konrad Blersch were "absolutely" of the same anti-Nazi political opinion. "Whenever there was a procession, my husband and I went into the mountains. That got on our nerves so much."

Did she sense that on the street, in whatever city, she was a minority?

"Ja. Ja. Absolutely. One had to be *very* careful. When my husband and I didn't raise our arms during processions, or greet correctly [by saying "Heil Hitler!"]." She said she replied to someone else's "Heil Hitler!" with the Ba-varian greeting "Grüss Gott!" She laughed at the memory.

The Nazis' girls' organizations attracted many admirers, but not her. "It was grotesque for me. *Ach*, these dames with the wreaths in their hair." What about the Frauenschaft? "Oh nein, horrible."

Her overriding interest, outside of her family, had been and remained medicine. To become a doctor, she "absolutely boxed" her way through. If her mother was otherworldly about medicine, her father was extraworldly about it. He opposed her study because he could not pay for it. By 1930, he had "lost almost everything in the depression." And because she had not done well in her high school final exam, she had no scholarship. So, while she was preparing to take the government's medical entrance exam, she went to work, giving English lessons, working in a library, earning money wher-ever she could. She then not only passed the exam, she was the only person who got a "one"—the highest grade. Her feat was considered so exemplary that she immediately got a scholarship. Her parents' reaction? She said they were unimpressed. It was a matter of course that she do well, because she had to.

In six years of study at various universities, she received tuition waivers wherever she went, and the small stipend from her "too pious" Catholic aunt. Much later, the aunt also gave her a memorable lesson in defiance. In 1942, a Nazi Gauleiter [district leader] made an address to a gathering of some three thousand Catholic teachers, among them the aunt, who taught lan-guages. "He spoke against the sacraments and against the priests and so on. She stood up and she said, 'I will not put up with that.' Nicht? As the *only one* among three thousand teachers! Brave, yes.

Frauen

"She was *immediately* fired from her school. Immediately. Then she had to go to Berlin, to the Culture Minister Lammers." (Hans Lammers was not the cultural minister, but chief of the Reich chancery and a close legal advisor to Hitler.)[6] "She said what the Gauleiter said, and [Lammers] said that was not right. And she should try to be reinstated. She said, 'That I will not do.' Because if she stands up the next time, something much worse will happen to her."

The aunt retired early, with only half her pension.

During the Third Reich, the risks Frau Dr. Blersch took also included speaking her mind, mostly privately. Some conversations were with patients, especially old farmers who came to her for relief from their rheumatism. She said many farmers supported Hitler because he flattered them, but "there also were those who weren't for him. For whom Hitler came right after the devil." All the farmers she confided in proved trustworthy, she said.

A fellow doctor did not. He was a surgeon to whom she sent patients and with whom she sometimes did X-rays. He was the "chief doctor in the hospital [and] a head military doctor. Was also a Nazi." She said "everyone" knew it. "But still I trusted him. I had human trust, nicht? I thought, we have always worked together. There were very few of us doctors.

"In the beginning of 1945, we left the hospital together and I said, 'Things are so bad, if I could just kill Hitler. The war *must* come to an end. We're losing it.' Then he said to me along the way, 'I could have you put in a concentration camp now for what you've said.' That was bad. Coming from someone I thought would stand by me. From then on, I hated him. I despised him. I thought, you are a pig, nicht?"

But what did she say?

"I think I said, 'You *could* do that, but you will not.' Something like that. I couldn't . . . I *did* say it, nicht? *Many* human beings met their deaths because of such accusations. Much lesser ones."

One week in the spring of 1943, some tests of caution and bravery were behind her, others were years in front of her, and one, the one that had brought me to Riedlingen, was only days away. Frau Dr. Blersch, then a widow with five young children, took what she called a "leave," her first vacation in a long time. She went alone to a mountainous retreat in a southern tip of Germany. "It was a lodge belonging to the German Alp Club, where the Alp Club guides ate and where people who hiked the mountains spent the night. A very pretty house. The Kölner House. It was over two thousand meters high and bordered directly on Switzerland."

---

6. Lammers was considered "an unimaginative bureaucrat." Dr. Louis L. Snyder, *Encyclopedia of the Third Reich* (New York: Paragon House, 1989), 204.

Among the guests was a young woman who also had been attracted to the lodge by its location, but for a reason other than the view. She hoped to escape to Switzerland.

Her name was Hildegard Dannenbaum, she came from Berlin, and she was Jewish. Her papers did not give her real name, nor were they stamped with a J for *Jude*. She was identified as Eva Puppel, a nurse, the German-born daughter of an Argentinian mother and a German father, and by default, "Aryan." It must have been a painful pretense; her family had been Jewish Germans for centuries.

Frau Dr. Blersch summarized. "The parents and both brothers were gassed, killed, by the Nazis. Is that not horrible? A family which had settled in Westphalia for three hundred years and, you know, who felt more German than most Germans."

She said Hildegard's only sister had managed to get to England, but the Dannenbaum parents had not tried to emigrate until 1939. Then they tried to go to Canada, where they had relatives who were citizens, but the Canadian government, she said, did not want any more Jews. "In any case, they did not get immigration visas."

Not only had Margret Blersch and Hildegard Dannenbaum both gone to Kölner House the same week, both ended up sharing the same room. Each had booked a private room, each having her own good reason to treasure privacy. Upon arrival, however, each learned she would have a roommate. "But I didn't know who Hilde was. [One] evening around eleven or twelve, a young girl came in [the room] to sleep in the second bed. I thought, odd, a young girl arriving so late at night. What's she doing?"

Frau Dr. Blersch estimated that her roommate was fifteen or sixteen years old.

No, said Hildegard Dannenbaum Lawrence, she was about twenty.

In New York, in the spring of 1986, she talked with me about the encounter. I knew little about her or her story, having not yet been to Riedlingen. I did know, however, that our lunch appointment was scheduled to precede her chemotherapy treatment in Manhattan. Her husband was driving her in from their home near the New Jersey shore.

Watching for the Lawrences outside a Greenwich Village restaurant, I overlooked her. Then a very pretty woman, much younger looking than I expected, smiled a greeting and introduced herself. Although mammothly cursed twice in her life, she was enchanting, with lovely eyes and lovely skin. She wore simple clothing, including a knitted cap she never took off. She seemed weak, but still she charmed.

After we ate, Mr. Lawrence discreetly left for a walk, and Hildegard Dannenbaum Lawrence recounted her version of what happened in and around the Kölner House. We had agreed that our talk would be informal, and unrecorded. Later, in a letter and an extensive phone conversation, she corrected the sometimes false recollections both Frau Dr. Blersch and I had.

Hildegard Dannenbaum had been living underground in the fashionable Grunewald section of Berlin, in a "very lovely home" belonging to a mixed-marriage couple who had separated. A Dannenbaum family friend, Hildegard's Tante Puppie [literally, Aunt Dolly], had made the arrangements. She could not hide her where she lived. Tante Puppie had been a girlhood tennis-playing friend of the Christian wife of the couple. The Jewish husband, a doctor, lived in his office in downtown Berlin but came to the house every day for the noon meal, to help show the Nazis he was still married to an "Aryan." It was all that kept him from deportation. He did not know that Hildegard was Jewish, and in hiding. He thought she was Christian, and a housekeeper.

"I did clean her house and I received a lot of verbal abuse," she wrote. "I was at her mercy. I was made to understand that she came from an aristocratic but impoverished family."[7] To support herself, the woman rented out rooms, and Tante Puppie paid her "handsomely" in cash and ration cards to shield Hildegard. Tante Puppie also was behind the effort to get Hildegard into Switzerland.

"I had false IDs that were given to me from a friend of Tante Puppie, a woman by the name of Isabella Puppel," she wrote. The woman was born in Argentina, but her daughter Eva was born in Germany. "She gave me her daughter's driver's license, which stated that she was a nurse and German. German drivers' licenses required a photo, and somebody put my picture with an official stamp on it. Eva Puppel's mother allowed me to use her daughter's papers as soon as she was 'über die Grenze [over the border]' with her two daughters. Isabella Puppel had been married to a German Nazi, who supposedly was wealthy. She had been very unhappy over his political thinking and divorced him. Somehow she managed to leave Germany via Switzerland, then Spain, to South America in the beginning of 1943."

Once the Puppels were over the border, Hildegard moved to get out, too. She was to take a train to the conveniently located Kölner House, where as a cover she had reserved a week's stay. In reality, she planned to stay only briefly. On a certain evening, she was to hook up with a certain cowherd who was to guide her over the border to Switzerland.

The plan, in Frau Dr. Blersch's telling of it, got off to a frightening start on the train itself. "She told me that on the trip from Berlin to the Kölner House, SS people constantly propositioned her. She . . . she was absolutely beautiful. She's still beautiful, but as a young girl she was remarkably beautiful, nicht? Remarkably beautiful and remarkably lovable. Sort of from an inner, beaming lovableness." No doubt, it hid terror. "The people gave her

---

7. Letter, April 1992.

compliments and also very crude offers. Bad. And this fear to be noticed, that was much worse than with me."

The fear must have been intensified after knowing, or rather not knowing, where her parents were. "She knew they had been picked up. And, and I find that so ludicrous. So many people say today that they didn't know anything. That is really not believable."

The supposed Argentinian-German background was fitting, said Frau Dr. Blersch. Hildegard "looked very much as if she came from a southern country." But most evident was "her large amiability [Liebenswürdigkeit]. She had a special charm, even as a young girl, nicht? She still does."[8]

Hildegard Dannenbaum got to the Kölner House, her identity undiscovered. Learning she had to share a room was a prospect less annoying than frightening, for she had reason to be scared of strangers. Still, she did not plan to stay long. The border was just a walk away. But crossing it was not easy. One problem, she said, was knowing *when* you had crossed it, and which one it was. The area, called Drei-eck [Three Corners], bordered not only Germany and Switzerland but also Austria. Another problem was evading the Swiss border guards, who often sent the desperate refugees back to Germany.

On the day arranged, Hildegard Dannenbaum left the Kölner House in search of the man who was to guide her across. After a long walk, she found him. He told her he could not help her, after all. He could not leave his cows that long.

Shaken, and knowing she could not find her way across the border on her own, she started the long walk back to the lodge. When she finally reached it, late that night, it was all lighted up—because of her disappearance. She made whatever excuse she could and went to her room.

Her new roommate and she had talked earlier, but only a little. That night, said Hildegard Lawrence, Margret Blersch asked her what she did. She answered she was a nurse. Frau Dr. Blersch responded, "Then we have much to talk about," she being a doctor. Hildegard, who knew nothing about medicine, said she told her she was exhausted and really could not talk, but that Frau Dr. Blersch responded, "Nonsense! One is never too tired to talk about medicine."

Hildegard Lawrence said she panicked, but managed just to be evasive. She said the conversation so upset her she wanted to go back to Berlin before her cover was blown. But because she was supposed to stay a week, she thought she should stay rather than arouse suspicion by leaving early.

---

8. The Lawrences visited Frau Dr. Blersch in the 1980s. They loved seeing her, they said, but were appalled at the backwardness of the area and amazed that she had stayed.

Frau Dr. Blersch said she has no recollection of the conversation, but that it sounds plausible. "Could be, could be," she said.

The next day, something happened that both women remember clearly, if a little differently. Frau Dr. Blersch's version: "We sat together in the dining room, this young girl, too. And these mountain guides were talking horribly, about the Jews, that one should hang them, and so forth, nicht? And I became so infuriated, and, eh, stood up and said I will not stand for that at this table, that's unheard of, that they're speaking that way and . . . Ja, then they said no more, the mountain guides. They had only said bad things about the Jews, that Hitler was right, to exterminate them and so on. . . ."

They really said exterminate?

"Ja, that was already '43, or to send them away, nicht? And that really upset me a lot."

In Hildegard Lawrence's written recollection, the people at the table were older women, not mountain guides. "They talked about the 'Kristall Nacht' [*sic*] and about Jews being dragged thru the streets and beaten and that it served them right." She said as they talked, she felt herself become paler and paler. And she recalled Dr. Blersch saying that although she did not have any Jewish friends herself—something Hildegard Lawrence thought was said for protection—she had known many wonderful Jewish doctors, and that Jews were indeed human beings.

She remembered especially that Frau Dr. Blersch was the only person who spoke up. "There was no humanity in the hearts of these people except for Frau Dr. Blersch," she wrote.

By that evening, Hildegard Dannenbaum had spent a decade regarded as a subhuman in Nazi Germany, knew that her parents and her brothers had been picked up by the Nazis, had learned that she was trapped in Germany, and had just endured the anti-Semitism of her tablemates. She wanted to die.

As soon as the meal was over, she went back to her room and threw herself on her bed. Frau Dr. Blersch, upon returning to the room, asked if she were suffering from "Liebeskummer [love sickness]."

Hildegard Dannenbaum said no, she was not suffering from lovesickness. But because Frau Blersch was a doctor, could she please give her something to end her life? She said Frau Dr. Blersch answered no, she would not give her something to end her life, but she would try to help her live. What about it? I asked Frau Dr. Blersch. "Could be, could be."

She remembered the encounter in the room this way. "On *that* evening, this young girl talked with me. She said she heard what I'd said and that she trusted me. That she's a Jew. And was trying to cross the border. And therefore she came back so late at night. And that she could not tell a single person. At the time, border soldiers were patrolling with their big dogs, with German shepherds. It was completely impossible. English and French officers had just escaped from a camp and gone over the border and that's why it was so strongly guarded. That it didn't work. So Hildegard could not get over the border. And then I told her, 'Ach, I'll go to the pastor.'

"I went to the Catholic pastor. But at the time it was all so difficult, because the pastor didn't know either whether or not I was testing him, nicht? In any case, I told him I had the five nuns in my household and in the practice, so he would trust me. But. That was *very* difficult, nicht?"

Did she think he himself agreed with Hitler at all?

"*No* one could rule that out. There were some who agreed with Hitler, who against the Jews because of religion. But that I couldn't know."

In short, the pastor refused to help. But he did give her a suggestion. "He sent me to two mountain guides, having said a mountain guide *maybe* would do it, if we'd give him enough money. And I went there. But *him*, I really had luck I got out. He told me immediately, 'If you say anything more, I could report you. And you'd be put in a concentration camp.' That I'd wanted to try to ask him to take someone over the border." The guide, she said, was an Austrian, for the route in question belonged to Austria. "He was to take Hildegard from Austria into Switzerland. It was one *step*. One step." She said she "pleaded with them to take someone over the border. But I didn't name Hildegard, nor did I say it's a Jew. All I said was that it's someone in need, nicht?"

Where, then, could Hildegard Dannenbaum go? To Riedlingen?

"Hildegard? To us? That would have been completely impossible! That wasn't even a question. I would have *gladly* hidden her, but . . ." Frau Dr. Blersch paused. "At the time in 1943, in such a small nest, that probably would have been insanely difficult. My husband had been killed. I had five children. I was alone. And I had the whole city against me. People came constantly to interrogate me." She added, "Hildegard would have been a lot less protected here than in Berlin, nicht?"

Hildegard Dannenbaum Lawrence said she felt she had no other choice. She must return to Berlin and continue to live underground, but now with an emphasis on living, as Frau Dr. Blersch insisted. She recalled her saying, "If you give up, that's just what they want. So you can't give up."

Hildegard Lawrence, ending her story as her husband returned to the table, said Margret Blersch gave her an enormous amount of courage to survive.

With that courage, she returned to Berlin. At some point, the Grunewald house was bombed. Then, for a number of months she "lived alone in the basement with some of the walls being exposed to the outside." Later, "a well-known physician" and his girlfriend hid her in their home in the Lichterfelde area of Berlin. "After we were bombed out there, he and his girlfriend moved into a one-room summer bungalow. I slept on a folded rug under their roof." She said it was a crawl space she reached by climbing a ladder. In a phone conversation, she softly summed up her years of hiding, "I went through hell."

Frau Dr. Blersch continued, "We never heard anything else from one another afterward. Hildegard went back. I always sent her bread and so on, but everything without return address. I mean, what we could spare I sent to Berlin and I didn't know at all if anything even reached her. After all, one couldn't ask. She couldn't thank me and I couldn't write her. She was, she really did not exist, nicht?"

Frau Dr. Blersch said she sent the packages to an intermediary in Berlin, whose address Hildegard had given her. When I mentioned this to Hildegard Lawrence, she said she never received any packages, something I mentioned, hesitantly, in a letter to Frau Dr. Blersch, who wrote back she was very sorry the packages did not arrive, that she regularly sent such items as bread, which also was expensive, and worn but good shoes. This I imparted to Mrs. Lawrence. It turned out she never met the intermediary, who had left the country, and she was never at the address. Tante Puppie had given her the address only in case the Gestapo arrested her and demanded to know where she lived, so that she not endanger anyone else. (She gave Frau Dr. Blersch the address because it was the only one she had.) Because Frau Dr. Blersch did not know until 1992 that Hildegard Lawrence never received the packages, Hildegard Lawrence did not know until then that Frau Dr. Blersch sent them. But, using the formal form of address, she wrote to thank her, "even though I was not the recipient."

Frau Dr. Blersch had given Hildegard the name of a doctor family. "I looked them up," she wrote. "They gave me some food to take home, but they were so scared of my being there that I never returned." She said many people behaved the same way.

The courage bequeathed her at the Kölner House had to be stretched for two more years of Nazi rule. Throughout that time, Frau Dr. Margret Blersch had no idea if the woman she had urged to live even had been able to, packages or no. "But the first package *after* the war that *we* as a family got ["a package with coffee and the most wonderful things" she added—and which seemed a thank you for the packages she had sent to Berlin] was from Hildegard, from New York. And then I knew that she had made it through."

In letter and on the telephone, she emitted organization and no nonsense. In person, she emitted both, and more. A tall, thin, bright-eyed, animated woman, with a girlish, turned-up nose and every-which-way teeth, she seemed eager to talk, and even more eager to instruct. She also was an avid hostess. In her neat, compact Stuttgart apartment, she produced daunting arrays of drink and food, and food and drink, that lasted nonstop from one rainy afternoon to late that night, and continued unabated the next day.

She also obviously enjoyed embellishing her assumed roles as teacher and hostess with the more theatrical aspects of the German language. Although her voice was at times crackly, she spoke with great enunciation, often drawing out words for emphasis. Her grammar was proper, her vocabulary picturesque. She spoke, too, with her eyes and hands, especially when exasperated. Then she might lean forward, increase her volume, bore her eyes into mine, and crook a long forefinger inches from my face. One might pull back a bit from Frau Frankenfeld, but no one nods off on her. Throughout the hours, however late they became, her views did not waver, nor did her stamina noticeably wane. Even toward midnight, when I finally pleaded exhaustion (both my mental and physical states were flagging rapidly) and suggested we resume in the morning, her response was as animated as anything she had said.

"Frühschoppen!" she exclaimed.

Good Lord. That meant morning *drinks*.

Frau Regina Frankenfeld

"I Am Never Dishonest."

Frauen

The next day, fortified by as much hotel breakfast as I could down, I knocked on her door. Opening it, she looked distractingly exuberant. Had the echoes of the horrors we had been talking of not followed her to bed? She positively beamed, readying glasses for Frühschoppen. As we sat down, it dawned on me. For better and for worse, the Third Reich had been Frau Regina Frankenfeld's golden age.

Within minutes of the first interview session, another part of the persona of Frau Frankenfeld became apparent. She wore honesty like a cloak and truthfulness like a badge. "I always said the truth," she stated at one point. "Even in school as a child, I never lied, because in my upbringing at home I was 'inoculated' that one doesn't lie, one always says the truth. To lie is not proper."

Her first reference to honesty and/or truth stemmed from 1916. Regina, then a little girl, was living on her parents' farm near a village which is part of Prussia. "In the First World War, we had a so-called war mass every Wednesday in the church. We pupils from the village school were to go, too. Ja, I went. As my mother later told the story—I myself can't remember so exactly, but it must be true because it made an impression on my mother— the pastor included in the prayer, 'God, grant victory to our soldiers, our troops, our people.' Then I am to have said when I came home, 'You know, Mutti, the others, the English and the French, pray exactly the same thing. What should the dear Lord do?' " Frau Frankenfeld smiled.

That war's impression on her was gentle. She recalled her school class going to the train station and proudly helping Red Cross nurses distribute coffee to "lightly wounded" soldiers in the halted troop transports. Her father, being relatively old and having been classified as "indispensable to the rural economy," was never drafted.

War's end made a greater impression. "Plunderers went through the village." They were "Communist rebels, released soldiers, everyone possible. They came into the houses, into the smoke cellars, cleared them out. As a child, one registered that as simply unfair. One may not take something of someone else's."

Regina was the eldest of three children, and the only girl. "All three of us were brought up, I won't say strict, but very goal-oriented. But not to slavish obedience," she added. She had wanted to become a doctor, influenced in part by an uncle and great-grandfather who had been veterinarians. "But a woman doctor was not as matter of course as today. I liked having to do with such things. I would come across a chicken that had just died and absolutely had to cut it open to find out what was going on inside. And later in my professional studies, I determined that chicken had a liver illness and the liver was full of small white growths. As a child, I recognized it." Frau Frankenfeld chuckled as she often would when speaking of her childhood.

388

A woman who never married or had children, she somehow seemed to regard her younger self as her own delightful offspring.

The studies were part of six years of training she undertook to become a "Landwirtschaftslehrerin" [an agricultural home economics teacher]. She mentioned that her home ec studies were in Frankfurt an der Oder, which lies on the eastern edge of what until recently was East Germany. In chatty conceit, having visited the city, not a common destination for Americans, I alluded to its being on the Polish border.

"Well, not Poland, but," she chuckled in a not very chuckly way, "what is now occupied by Poland. Frankfurt an der Oder, on the left or the right side of the Oder, actually is as German as it ever has been." The chuckle became a laugh. "Ja, there you already see a generational difference. For your generation, it's already Poland. For us, it's an annexed piece of Germany under Polish administration." That was the first clue to Frau Frankenfeld's political sentiments.

The second clue came after I told her, for some reason, about the cab driver who had brought me to my hotel barely an hour earlier. Within one minute of my getting in the cab (time in which he noticed my accent, asked me why anyone would come to Stuttgart, and heard my brief answer), he began an emotional outburst about how his anti-Nazi father had secretly and illegally slaughtered his chickens and rabbits for Jewish neighbors (the meat from which the cab driver, as a boy, delivered to them at night), and how his father was so smart and good and how he himself was "such an idiot," in 1943 lied about his age to join the war, and to this day is ashamed. The Allies did not kill him, but his father would have, he said. To Frau Frankenfeld, I said mistakenly that the cab driver volunteered not for the army, but for "Arbeitsdienst" [work duty]. She met the story with a long pause before speaking.

"Work duty was definitely not the worst thing in National Socialism's inventory," she said. "When I see what kind of youth is hanging around here today, sometimes something similar would not be the worst thing at all. They did useful things in the work, that naturally went on under N-S [National Socialist] flags and songs and so on."

In regard to the Third Reich, she added, "To my way of thinking, it is a great mistake to throw everything in one pot." Clue number three was the "everything in one pot" phrase, about which she willingly elaborated. "Everything that came within the time period of the Third Reich. Let us say, from 1933 to '45. Whether music, whether literature, whether handicrafts, whatever, today it's *manure*. It will not be seen as art, will not be seen as literature. I'd like to give you a very typical example. Hitler was an admirer of Wagner, ja? One can be of *very* different opinions about Wagner and his music." She went on to say that people who attend the Wagner festival in Bayreuth are considered not to have conquered their past. "I say that is throwing things in one pot. The comprehension of participants for this somewhat bombastic music won't be seen. And another example I remember *very* well. The New Year's reception of Adolf Hitler. That would have been in '34. Ja, they all came with *waving* flags," she said enthusiastically. "Today that's considered to have been a crime." She resumed, "Do not misunderstand me. It is no defense of whatever measures . . . not at all, in no way. But only that the contemporary view tends toward nonobjectivity, because one throws into one pot things not at all measurable with the same ruler. Everything's discredited because of the accursed war. That was the root of all evil."

Asked to describe the root's beginnings, she paused again, then spoke slowly and not about the war at all. "What was repugnant to me personally, I must say, was how they began with acts of violence. The Jew had to leave, the stores should be boycotted and, well, these first violent measures. I found them repulsive. And I did not understand them, either."

Had she herself known any Jews?

"Certainly. At home, in the country, Jews played a large role, as grain dealers, as cattle dealers. One was not in business with them, but they were well regarded. They were esteemed. And when Uncle Philipp hung his coat in the hallway, I still remember as a child [her chuckle returned], I sniffed, my mother told me this later, '*Ach*, Uncle Philipp is here.' 'Ja, how do you know?' 'Those are his cigars.' And then I knew, I was not interested in the smell of his cigars, that Uncle Philipp always brought us chocolate. I know that as if it's *today*. And chocolate was our *favorite* thing to eat." Another chuckle.

He was a grain dealer?

"Ja, he was the Grain Jew, nicht? Had a large grain store, in Frankfurt or Berlin or wherever, nicht?"

The Grain Jew. Did she as a child know he was Jewish?

"Ach, not at all, for God's sake," she chuckled again. "That first became a concept in the Third Reich, nicht? Where they spread it all and played it up. And naturally too with ill-meant [ungut] measures."

So that now she uses the expression Grain Jew. . . .

"Ja, ja, that was the expression. That was not an insult. He was for the grain, among other things, and the other was for the cattle."

Yes, but she said she did not know he was a Jew.

"Ach, that was the *expression*. That was not discriminatory. Jew was really no insult. Not at all. Those were later reflections."

But as a child she did know the expression?

"That was an expression one used *at that time*. Like a cobbler or a tailor or a miller or whatever. As profession."

How would one use it with them, as an example?

"The cobbler, one is going to the cobbler."

One would not say, one is going to the Cobbler Jew?

"Ach, not at *all*. He was no Jew."

Well, she *had* said Grain Jew.

Frau Frankenfeld became impatient. "Ja, ja. That was the common *expression.*"

Two more attempts to rephrase what seemed a basic question nearly had her out of her chair. "We connected only pleasant memories with the *concerned.* And when the smell of cigars wafted out of his coat, I was glad it was hanging there, for we'd get chocolate. That's childhood logic. As a child I wasn't interested in what a Jew is, or whatever is. That was the usual designation." She paused yet again. "Nein, nein, these things got their edge much later."

Grain Jew, in sum, had nothing to do with being Jewish and had no edge then, or now.

Fräulein Frankenfeld started her studies while barely in her teens. She learned "everything that belonged to farming and home economics. Gardening. Raising animals. And home economics, to which belonged cooking, nutrition, needlework." She also studied pedagogy and psychology. "If you want to be a teacher, you can't do it without psychology."

In 1926, when the six years of study were over, she took and passed her state exams. She got her first regular teaching job at a school in the eastern German province of Pomerania. She was twenty. Her pupils, girls sixteen and up, were mostly future farm wives from relatively well-off families like hers, who could afford the tuition.

Did she like her work?

She glowed. She liked it "unbelievably much."

Teaching was not the only avenue that appealed to Regina Frankenfeld in the early 1930s. National Socialism, she said, had a "resonance" that was "simply undeniable." It "made young people enthusiastic. There's no question at all."

There was no question, either, that on some level she was defensive about her enthusiasm. Similar to other Nazi supporters who made peace with their pasts, she compared certain features of Nazism to their benign equivalents. Asked if the torchlight parades at the takeover were impressive, she said, "Dear God, today they demonstrate. And then they celebrated their election victory with torchlight parades. That was nothing unusual."

Did she vote?

"As long as I was able to vote, of course I voted."

She waited until asked, in tiptoed politesse, for whom.

"Naturally I voted for the NSDAP. Obviously. Which young person would not have, who was open-minded and enthusiastic? Was also no reason at all *not* to." She added, "That did not have such a terrible importance. You see it today as much more important than how it was for human beings then. Maybe, I would like to add, it might have been better if we had regarded it as more important. For we could not sense what came of it afterward. No human being could have." Her voice had become less enthusiastic.

What about early resisters who did not support it?

There were "just a few who had some kind of personal reasons." Then, "maybe they were more clever than the majority, I don't know." She also said of other resisters, "In my eyes, they were heroes, who brought forth the courage to resist and even paid for it with their lives, later, where things came to a head. But they didn't change anything."

Nothing-I-might-have-done-would-have-helped has become another psychological mainstay in postwar Germany. Frau Frankenfeld used it again after I mentioned a woman who had defiantly shopped in a Jewish-owned store during the boycott. "This form of protest in an authoritarian state does not mean a thing, anyway. As sad as that is."

She spoke again of "acts of violence" upsetting her and again mentioned the boycott, but distanced herself the while, not mentioning it happened only months after the Nazis took over (when her enthusiasm was ever-growing) and implying it did not take place near her. "It certainly happened more in the cities than in the small towns. There they certainly had slogans like 'Don't buy from Jews,' for example, nicht? My God, the Jewish stores later were closed, so the situation for all practical purposes was settled. I mean, it was not so that it was an obvious and visible number. They were such individual cases it wasn't apparent. And therefore one perhaps thought about it too little."

But she was closer to the boycott than she had indicated. During the Weimar Republic, she joined the local branch of a nationwide rural women's organization, the Landfrauenverein. The branch's treasurer, who also owned and ran a candy store, whose wares Frau Frankenfeld happily recalled, was Jewish. "Suddenly one day the small store was closed. One could not buy there anymore. I cannot tell you whether Frau Rosenthal disappeared on her own accord or if the store was closed and she was banished. I don't know. One did not think about it terribly much or make problems. We just regretted that Frau Rosenthal no longer did the bookkeeping at the Frauenverein. That was the only thing we were confronted with, you understand?"

What happened to Frau Rosenthal?

"I don't know."

There was silence.

Late that night, after filling many glasses of champagne and wine, Frau Frankenfeld filled other moments of silence with bombshells. She had been talking of attending an international home economics congress in Toronto in 1949. One evening she went to a pub with a group of young Canadians who wanted to know all about the Third Reich. "Naturally, they also asked if I had been in the Party. Ja, I said. I was. Went in young and enthusiastically. Then I tried to explain how it could have happened from our economic . . . I told them the naked truth. Nothing prettied up, nothing swallowed. And nothing"—she paused—"repressed."

She joined the Nazi Party, she said, "because I was idealistically convinced that was the single correct way to lead us out of the whole mess [Schlamassel]. As a *young* person, convinced and idealistic to kingdom come. That is the privilege of youth, nicht?" The chuckle was back. "In later years, one is not so idealistic."

Her conviction and idealism came years before Nazi rule. "But the decision to strengthen the Party through my membership was realized in the beginning of 1932. I would *never* have joined the Party during the war. Or when one saw, for God's sake, where the way was leading. Until [1932], *nothing* unjust had happened."

Frau Frankenfeld must be credited with making the disclosure of Party membership on her own. But precisely because she recognized its significance, statements she made shortly thereafter were all the more explosive because of her apparent ignorance that they were even remarkable. The fruits of German vineyards should be credited with moving her toward these "truths" and in some cases moving me from the role of interviewer toward that of challenger. Frau Frankenfeld did not seem to mind. It was apparent she liked a fight.

The conversation first veered toward confrontation after she asserted that during World War II, Norway might just have well have been occupied by England as by Germany. "What's the difference?" she demanded.

She was upset, she said, that "so many" people outside Germany took part [mitmachten] with the Nazis. "In my eyes, those are even worse traitors than the criminals here. ["Traitors" usually means anti-Nazi Germans, but she could have meant war criminals.] When they took part in their own country. Against their own people."

What? Worse than the Germans?

"That's not how I mean it. But those who, so to speak, worked against their own country. The others believed they were working *for* their country. That's quite a difference.

"You know," she said, not long thereafter, "when one must atone for, should atone for, what one did, or more correctly said in this case did not do, that is, 'used one's elbows at the right time,' then we really are the ones, in that we lost a lot. I consider it a piece of atonement for *not* having paid attention at the right time. What we experienced in the last part of the war, that was something, nicht? And afterward at home, with the Russians. That was something too, carefully expressed."

Her reference to "the Russians" prompted me to fulminate about a book a former East Prussian (Frau Burchert) had given me. In grisly descriptions and photographs, it documented how ghastly Russian soldiers were to German civilians at war's end, but it gave no mention whatever to what Germans had done to Russian civilians. It was as if, I groused, Russian men woke up one morning and said, Let's murder German babies and rape German women and commit atrocities. When Frau Frankenfeld responded, her voice was oddly mild.

"You know, to that I would say this, from my own completely personal experience with the Russians. Naturally, everywhere there are these sorts and those sorts. But one thing is constant. In disposition [von Natur], the Asiatic cruelty of the Russian is *far,* far greater than any European or German or whichever."

Worse than *Auschwitz?*

Frau Frankenfeld seemed not to have expected the reference, nor its fury, but she did not waver. "Auschwitz is, I would like to say, a thing unto itself. . . . Not to excuse, for *God's* sake. Auschwitz is as bad as there is."

Did not come from the East, I managed.

"Nein, of course not. But Auschwitz is not the single horror that happened as a consequence of this war. And that is something that again today, well, I would like to call it a tendency to picture [events] very one-sidedly. There's still only Auschwitz, there is still only Holocaust. But everything else, what *ghastly* crimes took place in this regard, is hardly talked about or not talked about. And from a psychological viewpoint, that is the reason such people, the author of this East Prussian book, feel themselves provoked and motivated *now* also to present that which no one speaks of today."

The conversation veered, but soon returned, for Frau Frankenfeld had bitten on something she would not surrender easily. "I am *far* from making speeches defending terrible things that happened. I comprehend those as a"—she paused—"disgrace for the twentieth century and a disgrace for the Germans. That is completely clear. *But* I turn away from the one-sidedness of *only* this injustice existing in publications. And we're on that path. That does not lead to anything good. That leads to such dumb things as you told about in this book." She paused again as she refilled her mouth and continued through the food. "One thing is completely clear. I mean the atrocities [Greueltaten] of the German army, which was absolutely disciplined, should never have occurred, of course not. That is completely clear and also should not be meant as some kind of glossing over. But its extent is not at all comparable with what happened on the other side." Russians committed more horrors in Germany, reasserted Frau Frankenfeld, than German troops did in Russia. "*That* you may believe."

The statement, upon later somber, sober reflection, could conceivably be less monstrously wrong than it first seemed if Frau Frankenfeld were referring solely to the behavior of regular German army troops and not the SS. At that moment, however, her remark elicited a sputtered challenge to comment about thousands of Jews in the Soviet Union being lined up and shot.

She paused, chewing. "Is a criminal act. Absolutely. *If* it happened."

It's been *proven*. Some German soldiers themselves . . .

She interrupted softly, as if being helpful. "Furthermore, you also may not forget that in war, it was a military order."

Russians also lined up women and children and shot them to fall backward into a mass grave?

She was silent for exactly thirty seconds. She then said, at first boldly, then softly in repetition, "Difficult to say. Difficult to say."

She soon recovered, her tune unchanged. "One thing is certain. In the day-to-day, let's just say propaganda and it is political propaganda, the 'Kontra' [counterargument] in regard to the cruelties of the Germans, which was bad enough, bad enough, but everything, everything *without* end. . . . I sometimes ask myself how many more generations will it go on, be talked about, be judged. But of the other things, which were *exactly* as bad, *exactly* as terrible, you hear nothing." She continued, "What stirs me up is the sense of justice."

I asked her if it is difficult to be a German.

Frau Frankenfeld started and stopped, started and stopped, then said, "I would like to say it this way. If one feels collectively guilty, I would say to your question, it is very difficult. If, however, I would apply that which I *did* and also that which I did not do, unfortunately, and stand them side to side before my own conscience and strict criteria, then I must say, collective guilt, no. The other, yes."

From the beginning of the Third Reich and—she said—through the first war years, her regard for Adolf Hitler and National Socialism remained high. I asked if she had seen Hitler in person.

"Ja, of course. On the street. At the rallies. He never invited me to tea. This honor I never had. But I definitely would have gone, because it would have excited my curiosity."

What was it like being within a crowd at a rally?

"One only saw the *millionfold* agreement of the others. And as a young person one said, now look, here are these millions who are praising him and saying 'Jawohl' and saying 'We thank our Führer' and what do I know of stupid slogans. They are not all crazy. There must be something *to* it." She felt "a *confirmation*" that she was "on the right path."

In the earlier years, she almost revered him?

"'Revered' is too much. His thorough measures, for all things in the economic realm, in terms of unemployment, were exemplary."

But when asked how one actually became a Nazi Party member, she became impatient. "Ach, you got a form to fill out like in any organization. *Exactly* the same."

What did it cost?

"Not much at *all*. What did I pay? Maybe three or four marks a year. Laughable, nicht? Even for lower-income people, it was a laughable amount for dues. And contributions and so on were left to each person, on a voluntary basis. I never was very active in that."

Did she get an identification card?

"Of course. Membership card, like in any organization. If I'm a member of the Federal Union of Health Education in Bonn, I get a membership card. It's the same everywhere."

Does she still have it?

Frau Frankenfeld exploded. "*What?* Now listen, I'd sure be stupid if I did. I ripped it all up when it was time and threw it in the water." She simulated quickly ripping up the card, her long pale fingers tearing apart the air inches from my nose. I may have pulled back some. When?

"*When?* During the war, at the end. Would have been an idiot if I'd saved such a document. I reported everything afterward at de-Nazification anyway. They didn't ask for any membership cards. *Really.*"

Frau Frankenfeld was in much better humor when the subject returned to the beginning of the Reich. In 1934, after eight years of what she called "school duty," she was promoted to an administrative position in the Pomeranian branch of the family and home economics division of the Agricultural Board, by then the Reich Food Production Department. In German, she was a "Referentin" in the "Volkswirtschaft-Hauswirtschaft" division of the "Reichsnährstand." (She never abbreviated any of the above.)

She said my generation would not experience the work of the Reichsnährstand as she did. And how did she experience it? "Positively! The work went along, the work was orderly, we could accomplish something." As she described it, the work involved coordinating home economics advice centers throughout Germany. (As far as the Nazi leadership was concerned, of course, it was part of a larger effort meant to keep "Aryan" Hausfrauen happy and breeding.) She asserted that Agricultural Board employees faced no pressure to join the Nazi Party when it took over, nor did they lose their jobs or advancement opportunities for not joining.

"At the time, almost no one was let go when it was taken over by the Reichsnährstand." Although some people said, in her words, "I'm not taking part anymore," most continued as if nothing had changed. "They were the same people. They all did their work *exactly* as before. That is something distorted today. As if everything were disarranged and turned on its head. It's not the case at all. They stayed, kept doing their work. *Continuity* held."

And to hear her tell it, the Nuremberg laws of 1935—the "Reich Citizenship Law" and the "Law to Protect German Blood and Honor"—were in part just annoying impediments to that continuity. One law ordered Germans to trace their family tree back generations to show whether they were "Aryan," Jew, or, as many Germans knew or found out, both. Frau Frankenfeld talked about colleagues learning of Jewish relatives as if the matter were light office gossip. "He can't come up with his Aryan identification. Well, well, then there were difficulties, nicht?"

396

Did she know anyone who could not prove to be "Aryan"?

"Nein. Also many at the time," she paused, "went away, emigrated. Who said we're not going along with this 'Quatsch [nonsense].' And for them, at first not a hair of their heads got bent. They could take money and possessions with them and in no way, in that sense, were they persecuted at all. They went of their own accord because they saw it's a precarious thing that was going on. 'The clever man builds in advance.'"

The euphemistic interpretation hardly requires comment. As for hair getting "bent," she doubtless was referring to the familiar exculpation, "I did not bend a hair on a single Jewish head."

Did she herself feel protected after getting her "Aryan" ID?

"What do you mean, protected? The Aryan identity card," she said, chuckling, "was derived from birth and ancestors. It was a legal decree one had to assume. I never had the idea, for God's sake, a Jewish forebear or whatever would show up in my case. I just was annoyed I had to spend so much time writing to civil offices to haul up my documents. Especially since I had the bad luck that a great-grandfather, or great-grandmother—the key date was January 1, 1800, one had to have proof up to then—was born in 1804, which meant I had to show one more generation." She chuckled again. "So, that was an effort, that annoyed one."

Did she ever think about "Uncle Philipp"?

"No, no, no, that lay too far back. I am certain my father often thought about him. And maybe also sometimes said, I'd like to know what became of Herr Philipp or Herr Whatever. That for the *most* part they took off in time and also," she sighed, "did not have any great losses."

If Frau Frankenfeld considered the identification provision of the Nuremberg race laws mostly annoying, she considered another provision completely pragmatic. It involved, in her description, "inheritance laws not specifically against Jews, but inherited diseases. For instance, I now sometimes think when I see it here, if only we still had the law for the *protection* of a congenitally ill new generation."

The phrase she used, "Verhütung erbkranken Nachwuchses," was another Nazi euphemism. The law was not designed for the protection *of* anyone congenitally ill, of any generation. It was meant for the then-congenitally ill to be sterilized, disenfranchised, and murdered, so as not to give birth to a new generation. (The phrase may be translated as protection *from* a congenitally ill new generation.) To what extent Frau Frankenfeld knew that then or recognized it later is debatable. But her sentiments are not. "Today, things completely without sense are coddled to the nth degree and kept alive artificially, nicht? That which one did forever and ever in animal husbandry, what these laws addressed, is suddenly considered criminal, nicht? Have you ever been in a home where completely idiotic children, youth, and adults are kept?"

Ja, I said, stretching the truth.

"When, now or then? In your country anyway, there were after all other preconditions. Well, when I as a young teacher saw [such beings] for the first time during a day trip near Stettin, I thought, for God's sake, that was only comparable to animals who don't know who they are and in every function [are] physically *and* mentally out of control. For what? For what should one 'keep them on the bottle'? And they themselves have no joy in life either. And for the parents, when they visited, *horrible.* I didn't want such children. For God's sake! I mean, this law had its justification. As for the race laws, one thought, what's this rubbish really about? But then, no one knew or thought, let us say, which consequences could result. Those are two completely different things."

What does she think one should do when a mentally impaired child is born?

"That's something for the parents to decide and think about. I find it sad that it exists, but I'd never say it belongs in the gas oven. I'd only say, would that it *were* prevented, when it's an inherited disease. Schizophrenia and so on, that we also have in great measure today. And they did not get permission to marry. A schizophrenic woman or a schizophrenic man got no marriage permit, as a way to stop that disease from being passed on. That was the sense of the laws for the 'protection of the congenitally ill new generation' and a rational human being cannot find that criminal."

Were not some congenitally ill killed by injection?

"That could have happened in difficult cases. I don't know. That was, however, not spelled out in the law."

She would have been against it?

"Death by violence is a crime. One must impede something like it from ever seeming to appear necessary. And that was the intention and the purpose of this law. There was no word in it they are to be killed and they must get an injection and all that stuff. Not a word. But *impede* it from being formed."

She continued, "And therefore the obligation to establish proof, like with the Aryan identification, which you bit on a little strongly. It all hangs together. That you must declare among other things, *when* your parents, your grandparents, died and from *what*, which disease. You understand? One already had in mind not to allow unnecessary congenitally ill human beings to increase. And that is something to which today I say *ja.*"

Did not one of the Nuremberg laws forbid intercourse between Jews and Christians?

"Ja, ja, that naturally was all part of it, of course. The 'heirlooms' should not increase. For instance, because you always like experiences from one's own surroundings so much, a cousin of my mother's was the 'Hausdame' [literally, house lady] for *very* many years in a Jewish household."

Frau Frankenfeld then carefully set a scene about a Jewish widower who wanted to hire a woman not just to take care of his house but also to be a mother-substitute for his two daughters. Frau Frankenfeld's unmarried aunt fulfilled both jobs. And to her death near the age of ninety, she had a connection to both daughters "who were not killed in the concentration camps nor the father, either." But that was only partially the point. The family "stayed in Germany a long time and then moved. Probably Herr Klein, who was a very smart man, said, 'All right, we'd prefer not to go along with this or expose ourselves to whatever difficulties.' Completely legally and normally with all their money, with everything they had, they left. They did have that possibility the first years. And if more *had* made use of it, it wouldn't have become as evil as it did afterward."

Interrupting herself, she said she "wanted to say something completely different." It was about "these two young Jewish women" staying in touch with her aunt, who in her older years had such poor vision Frau Frankenfeld wrote dictated letters for her, "to her Greti in Israel and her Alice in Australia." After the aunt died, Frau Frankenfeld found among her "modest legacy" a silver pin. On the back was engraved "from Greti," who had visited the aunt twice from Israel. Frau Frankenfeld sent it back to Greti with a letter informing her of the beloved aunt's death, and also invited Greti to come for a visit. In return, Greti wrote "a *very* nice thank-you letter," saying how sorry she had not seen the aunt again and thanking Frau Frankenfeld for her invitation to visit. (The visit did not take place.)

"So, I want to say with all this, not everything was terrible, hostilities in every case. Contacts with Jewish 'fellow inhabitants' and friends were not all ripped apart by means of pressures or whatever." That was Frau Frankenfeld's illustration of the Nuremberg race law about intercourse.

Eventually she also addressed what must have sparked the memory in the first place: the part of the law forbidding Jews from employing "Aryan" women under forty-five years old, such as the aunt. "She wasn't old enough. She was too young. Plainly spoken, she was still reproductive. At least biologically, nicht? There was never a, a relationship, from which some kind of half-Jewish additional children, eh, could have resulted. Herr Klein would not have wanted that and my aunt neither. But with reference to the law, it was recommended she give notice. That was enough of a reason for Herr Klein to say, 'The girls indeed have grown up, but I cannot get used to having other people in this house. We are moving anyway out of this Germany which makes such assaults into personal matters.'" The aunt, she said, "was a little ashamed she had to leave."

Frau Frankenfeld's tone became defensively defiant, and a forefinger began tapping out each spoken syllable. "The law commanded, up to the age of whatever, employees could not be active in Jewish households. She could not do anything against a *law*." Frau Frankenfeld got caught up in a paroxysm of phrases, then said angrily, "I can't even talk with someone who did not experience what could be in store, more or less slowly, earlier or later, from the transgression of a law of this kind."

But did people think the law was just?

"God, what was one to do with this law? It did not have to do with me and who bothers with such trash [Kram] when one has one's profession and one's work and . . ." She said with spitfire delivery, "We *laughed* about it and said they must be *crazy*. No one took it *seriously*." Her voice slowed. "It only made us sorry, because the aunt had been in the house over ten years and had such a nice familiar relationship with the old gentleman and his daughters." After false starts of other sentences, she repeated her earlier theme. "There weren't only horrible drawbacks, which is all one talks about. No one talks about the other."

In roughly the same period of time that the Kleins fled the Third Reich, Frau Frankenfeld advanced within it. The Reich Agricultural Board promoted her to management, and transferred her to headquarters in Berlin. "When one was older and had accomplished something" was how she put it. The work continued "in bester Ordnung."

"My responsibility was to keep two thousand [home economics] advice centers in the Great German Reich running orderly and rationally. That involved making sure there were rational advice center leaders, not only little mother Müller who meant well."

Frau Frankenfeld emphasized that in the prewar years many foreign visitors, especially American women, came "of their own accord" to observe the advice system. Being "relatively capable with language," she was assigned such visitors. "They were always full of, well, 'praise' sounds so dumb. Always taking notes." She said she and the visitors often went to dinner or the theater after work and talked into the night, although her secretary had to go home "punctually after eight hours of work." Frau Frankenfeld said, vis-à-vis her own unpaid socializing, she has sought international cooperation in the home economics field her entire life, adding with what seemed an aggrieved smirk, "and the interest for all of that stemmed from the years, the first beginnings of the unloved, terrible, horrible Third Reich."

In addition to evenings spent squiring around home economics enthusiasts, Frau Frankenfeld sometimes took work home, like lectures she was to give, "to think things really through." However late the night before, she arrived at work at eight in the morning, Saturdays, too, and began again. "Mein Gott, the desk was covered." She had so much mail she did not have to think about what to do, but just keep to it. Asked what might be in a typical letter, she said a group wanting to hold a conference for advice center leaders would ask for program suggestions. "And you can imagine, the Great German Reich was not so shriveled up, so chopped up, like today [1987]."

Each center purportedly was responsible for making the lot of "Aryan" German women easier. When asked for an example, she said, "Women came by the hundreds and said, we cannot make it with these ration cards." So the women were advised how to make the most of what they could get. Like, said Frau Frankenfeld, " 'Don't peel the potatoes, but rather cook them with the skins on.' Just a very common example, nicht?" Another example was advising a woman to spend her clothing rations on a warm winter coat rather than on a bathrobe.

The person putatively in charge of such helpful hints and related endeavors was one Gertrud Scholtz-Klink, literally "die Führerin" of Third Reich women's organizations. Even though hers was truly a kitchen cabinet post, it too came under male jurisdiction. I had read scathing accounts of Scholtz-Klink as a toadying anti-Semitic opportunist[1] and, keeping them to myself, asked Frau Frankenfeld her opinion of her former "Führerin." She took a deep breath, as if readying consideration of a Personage.

"She was a great idealist. Perhaps not realistic enough. She often had a lot of difficulty with the men of the Party. Especially later on, in terms of the war, when she had no more direct access to Hitler at all. There was always only the representative there, [Martin] Bormann. Bormann was an ass in the form of a human."

Had Frau Frankenfeld read any of Scholtz-Klink's books?

"The one she wrote a few years ago. Well, for us those are known things, nicht? I guarantee she was beside herself when for the first time, I don't know when that was, she learned, for example, of Jewish concentration camps and afterward Auschwitz or whatever else. That was not at all in the line of women's work."

I beg your pardon?

"Ja, not the object she had in view. She had completely different goals and completely different tasks and not the annihilation of the Jews. And those are things which the younger generation doesn't even see, because it's hardly talked about." She went on to discuss the "social realm" of Volkswirtschaft-Hauswirtschaft and politics.

Did she mean Frau Scholtz-Klink was not political?

Frau Frankenfeld again chuckled. "Well, 'not political' one cannot say. When one is in such a leadership position, politics cannot be avoided. But I mean politics did not consist only of annihilation of the Jews. As it is pictured today. And that is what I guard against, out of a sense of justice. Everything else is suppressed, won't be talked about, either because one does not know it or because of other reasons, for all I know. There *is* only the one thing, the horrible terrible things the Germans did. There's nothing else."

---

1. See especially Claudia Koonz, *Mothers in the Fatherland* (New York: St. Martin's Press, 1987). Koonz not only looked into Scholtz-Klink's Third Reich career, she interviewed her.

Perhaps it has to do with what people believe is more important?

"Well, these things that were worked on were very important."

To Frau Frankenfeld, so is her own brand of honesty, which apparently has merged almost completely with her own conscience. "For me, the only truth is that what I myself experienced and saw. No one can sway me. And I see it *sober*, with all pluses and minuses."

Has she ever changed her opinion over the years?

"I? No. Why? What opinion should I change? The injustice that happened we did not know about at all. No person knew that the Jews were being transported away. Work camps it was called. Ja, we also had work camps that were built here." (For "people who didn't work," she said, echoing the propaganda line.) "That is why it did not attract attention at all. It really became *public* to the last citizen after the collapse. An authoritarian state has *very* good means for making sure one does not find out what's going on."

That certainly was true, up to a point. But what of Frau Frankenfeld's other "truths"? They came after a dip into her private life. It was curious that she, having spent so much time, energy, and certainly belief on behalf of German housewives, never became one herself. When I finally broached the subject of a man in her life, she said, "The one I would have liked I didn't get and the others I didn't want." She laughed. "To put it very clearly. But not because of politics or any such nonsense, but from purely human personal considerations."

At one emboldened point, I brought up a related delicate matter. Even with a perhaps dumb question, I began, one hoped for an honest answer. Through a full mouth she said, "I am never dishonest." I went on, it is said in regard to Hitler that many young women found him sexy. (I used the English word.)

Frau Frankenfeld, using the word too, but pronouncing it in a German way, said, "I never found him zexy."

Never?

"Never."

Someone told me that single women in particular . . .

"Quatsch."

Why was he not sexy to her?

She began to yell. "I did not *find* him zexy. Why shall I now give a reason? It is my view." She calmed down momentarily. "And with single women also not necessarily."

Then what was *not* sexy about him?

"Zexy," she scoffed, impatiently. "You'll have to ask other people. I do not know if the man was zexy or not. He had something fascinating in speech and appearance, in his ability to convince. He was himself *so* interested in his things, one just had to believe him. That was what was fascinating. And also why he found such approval. It's completely clear. But zexy, I can only laugh. I don't know if he was zexy."

Did other women she knew find Hitler sexy?

"Nein. We talked and palavered about everything possible in regard to Adolf Hitler, but whether he was zexy or not we did not talk about." She went on to say she and her friends almost died of joy when a jealous husband of a movie actress punched out Joseph Goebbels for having an affair with her. She said after Goebbels spoke on the radio, she and her friends would say the next day, "Did you hear clubfoot's fairy tale hour?"

The comment sounded totally plausible and likely would have been made in the mid-forties, when German women in particular knew ever more graphically Germany was losing the war.

And when, in 1944, the well-publicized assassination attempt against Hitler failed, Frau Regina Frankenfeld was, she said, among those who regretted the failure. "My reaction was this. Shame that it went off next to where it was supposed to, nicht? Shame that the assassination was unlucky."

Did she want Hitler killed to end the war?

"That was primary, that was primary."

Or because she thought "he misled us"?

"Nein, nein, not as punishment, but for God's sake to bring an end to this insane war."

So not because he "mishandled" Jews?

She interrupted before I got my sentence out. "Nein. For everyone 'the shirt is closer than the skirt.' What we went through, we wanted finally to be done with it, that was primarily it, nicht? Not the other things. Each person is closest to himself." She elaborated about situations she then labeled "the natural self-preservation urge of human beings. And it's all the same, if he's American or French or German. It's my experience from the war. It's hard. Very hard. But when it has to do with survival, this smarmy pity [Mitleidsgedusel] ends at once."

Frau Frankenfeld spoke with conviction, but her true view, or views, of the war required deciphering. Although in her first mention of war, she expressed herself strongly as having been against it, when it was brought up later, sideways, at intervals, a more intricate "war-anschauung" emerged. The following, in chronological order, is what she also said.

1. Asked if she did not think the war was one of defense, as the Nazis always proclaimed it was, she said, "Of that I am not convinced. That's how it was presented." She added, "At the beginning, yes," then said a few moments later, "The war was a criminal act. With everything that was part of it."

2. Asked if she ever considered quitting the Nazi Party during the war, she said no. "But as long as one hoped the war was not yet lost, nor not necessarily would be lost, I did not withdraw my Party dues contract from a certain sense of *fairness.*" She used the English word.

3. Her reaction when she heard about the war with Poland? "Well, I didn't find the war with Poland so upsetting because the differences between

the two sides had become very hard. I mean, today it's said we attacked Poland, nicht?"

4. Her reaction when France was conquered? "What do you mean, conquered? It was only occupied. We did not conquer France. That's not the same. And one thought, how will it all end? One asked oneself that as a rational, realistic, thinking person. But I could not write a long letter to Adolf Hitler, 'Finally stop this crazy war.' Apart from the fact that it would have had no effect. It would have landed in the wastepaper basket. Adolf Hitler would never have got to see the letter."

5. Asked when her first hesitation came (I had not said about what), she said "the beginning of the war." So, with Poland? "Nein, nein. Poland was just a first skirmish. From a military point of view, that was no regular war. But when America entered the war, my father said that is the beginning of the end. For in the First World War, it was exactly the same." He meant, she said, the masses of materiel the Allies had.

6. What did she think when Germany "entered" the Netherlands? "Well, in *war* that was a necessary evil. It was just like with Norway. If we hadn't got a foothold in the Netherlands, the others would have and would have been closer to us." So she was for the war against the Netherlands? "I was for the victory of the Germans. Would you have been for the victory of the Germans if you were an American? Nein. You would say, 'We Americans must be victorious.' It's clear. One must really sometimes *try* to put oneself in the other's place."

7. Asked what she might have been thinking in January of 1945, she replied, "I was a realist. In January '45, there was no more thought about a German victory. Until '43 one perhaps hoped it *could* be. After the havoc and the total defeat in the east, it *could* perhaps still go well. Some believed in the Wonder Weapon, the V-2 and all of that. But afterward, one only said, bring it to an end. Oh God, bring it to an end."

Frau Frankenfeld turned out to have two personal reasons for decrying the war. When asked what the worst thing about the war was for her personally, she had only replied in a general way, citing the "*senseless* sacrifice of human beings on all sides, whether Germans or Americans or French or English."

Then I asked if she had been bombed out in Berlin. "Of course, totally." She laughed. "Totally. As long as I wasn't, I kept taking people in, because at my place the balcony doors and the windows and everything had blown out only twice and I had to keep schlepping [the door] to the glazier and then pick it up again weeks later. You schlep such a balcony door to the glazier and you'll know what you've done." The third time the bombs made it "ka-putt again," she decided to leave it as is. Summer was coming on, anyway. "You become stoic. Really. Not only I, the others just as much."

The second reason resonated in her earlier comment that what "we experienced" at home with the Russians was "something too, carefully expressed."

Toward the end of the war, Frau Frankenfeld left Berlin on weekends and took a train to visit her mother and grandmother. Their village lay in what had become a war zone—the last main battle line in Brandenburg. She had to get special military permission to make the trip; regular tickets no longer were being issued. "I said to myself, 'You can't leave the old 'Weiberchen [little women]' alone.'" One weekend, she got to the village as usual, planning to return to Berlin as usual on a 5 A.M. Monday train. But "in the night the tracks were totally bombed and no more trains moved. So I was stranded at home and heartily welcomed the Russians, nicht?" She took a deep breath. "Ah ja, let's not talk about it. Those are not good memories."

The remark came well after a rather idle question: whether her parents survived the war.

"Not my father, thank God. He died during the war."

Why "thank God"?

"Why? What do you think they would have done with him?"

I said I did not know what he had done.

"He didn't do anything at all. He wasn't even in the Party. But as the Russians came, they just raped the women. They lined them up against the wall, they dragged my mother and my grandmother out. What do you think, my father would have watched it? He would not have watched it. He would have tried to stop them and then they would have put him against the wall and shot him."

Thinking I had misunderstood, I asked what the Russians did to her grandmother.

"They raped her, too." Frau Frankenfeld began yelling, "Just like they did me, dear God. What, what do you think happened, what we *experienced* from the Russians? Who wants to speak about it? It's over. It happened. Done. But I can't *stand* it, when one shoves only the atrocities of Germans 'into the shoe.' That I can't stand. Nicht? And if my father had experienced it, he would have intervened. He would not just have watched, that they threw his wife on the potatoes and tore the clothes off her body. No. Come on. Ne ne."

The three women had gone to the cellar to seek shelter from shelling, then heard tanks rolling by. They knew the tanks were Russian; the German soldiers had long gone. It was not really a battle zone any more, said Frau Frankenfeld, for only one side was left.

All three generations of women were raped where they had sought shelter. Frau Frankenfeld paused. "And as we were then all hauled out of the cellar and as they stood there with their machine guns, my mother said, 'Well, now we'll probably be shot.' And I said, 'It's all the same to me.' It *really* was all the same to me. I mean, we had nothing more to lose. And this whole massacre. Well, no one had any interest in going on with life, not at all. But then we weren't shot. A Russian officer came and thundered terribly to his guys. In Russian, I didn't understand it, but one saw the results. They all left with very long faces and didn't bother themselves more with what they'd already dished up. So anything additional was left undone. At least for this day. In the weeks to come, others arrived and then the *same thing* happened again, nicht?"

She continued, "Do you think it happened just once? We always kept getting other troops. Then the Kalmucks [part of the Mongols] arrived. They were the best, these Asians." She laughed, bitterly. "You can imagine, Asian cruelty." She said the Russian commander ordered the local populace to stay off the streets because the current soldiers, the Kalmucks, had freedom to plunder. "And freedom to plunder, of course, was connected to everything else. So he tried, at least on the outside, to prevent further trouble. They [German women] were grabbed on the street, the way it happened to me by some kind of sheik, as I returned from work." (The "sheik" is no doubt meant sarcastically. The work was forced farm labor she was doing by then for the Russians, in exchange for food.) "So, 'Frau, come,' that was the slogan. 'Frau, come.' And I was *so* furious, because I'd had it up to here, that with my elbow, with my elbow," she repeated, slapping it, "he had me in such a clinch I couldn't free myself, with my elbow I hit him in the pit of his stomach. That definitely hurt him, and he yelled, 'You, I shoot.' And he was brandishing this kind of machine gun around my nose and then I said, '*Then shoot.*' Yelled it, yelled it just like he did. '*Then shoot.*' I didn't make another move. Then he looked at me and let me go. Ja. You see, that happened, not once, a thousand times. The past is not *so* simple as one makes it out to be today, believe me."

She said her only lingering physical consequence from the Russians was that one of her fingers got badly infected after a fragment of a shell hit it. "I said, na, at least you're lucky that, I mean, I wouldn't have carried a Russian baby to term, that you can believe."

Her mother was philosophical, too, about being raped. "My mother said, '*Good*, Father did not experience it.'"

Frau Frankenfeld also spoke, at some length, about "proper and lovable" young Russians, "Stalin pupils," who arrived in town and spoke some German and were nice to children and even slipped her some bread crusts so that she could give her rationed slices of bread to her mother and grandmother. "I mean, of course that happened, but that doesn't annul the other, nicht? I only say always, one may not generalize. In my eyes there are not *the* Russians, there aren't *the* Americans and there also aren't *the* Germans. . . . Meanness is *not* the mark of a nation, it is human and happens everywhere. And the same with decency. My view, from which nobody can dissuade me and also my life experience, nicht?"

After describing one young Russian, Sasha (with "a face like a baby's bottom") who helped her carry a bag of potatoes home (not knowing she had stolen them) and who kissed her on the cheek, she repeated, "I mean, that happened too, you know, and in my sense of righteousness I am not for seeing *only* the negative, nicht? I'm against that. One must see both sides, both atrocities and both friendliness and decencies of the human way. Human beings are everywhere, this kind and that."

Where did Jewish human beings, apart from those already mentioned, fit in her philosophy? Again, the evidence was scattered, and often turned up after an elliptical journey into other subjects. For example, wondering how clearly someone who spoke of writing an antiwar letter to Adolf Hitler had seen another aspect of the war, I said I guessed she did not say on the street Germany would lose. "Not in public. 'Doubt about victory' would land you in a KZ. That was the official designation for such a degree of punishment. 'Doubt about victory [Zweifel am Sieg].' Ja. The People's Court then decided. What was the name of this horrible guy? Freisler. Who then delivered his verdict."

Regarding the infamously merciless Judge Freisler, who had condemned so many resisters to death, after screeching at them, humiliating them any way he could, I mentioned I had just read about his widow getting a government pension. (The news was causing an uproar in Germany, but bureaucracy held; Frau Freisler *was* a civil servant's widow.) Frau Frankenfeld said she did not know about it, then added, "Listen, you may not believe everything you read in the newspaper. What kind of a newspaper was it?" When I named a large respectable one, she brought up another large respectable one. "Well, in the *Frankfurter* [*Allgemeine*] which is decidedly, not in a negative sense, but factually a *Jewish* informed and financed paper, there was *nothing* about Frau Freisler getting a pension. I didn't read it."

It did not matter, of course, that she had not read it. What did matter was how she described the newspaper. The question was due: Would she describe the source of anti-Semitism?

"Ja! That I can tell you," she replied, chewing loudly. First she listed from her childhood a number of situations one might have thought were laudable. Jewish businessmen paying in cash for grain or cattle. Jewish department stores having goods of more variety and lower costs. Jewish businesspeople working hard. Then she came to a familiar verse. Jews "also got money in part through very cunning methods" and engaging in usury.

When I commented that Jews were said to be the only people in those years in rural Germany who took financial risks, she responded they were not the only ones, but "were overwhelmingly predestined for it." And, in brief, "The German has not been as good a Händler in business matters."

Why then did postwar Germany become an "economic wonder"? There having been precious few Jews involved, I had to add.

"Because of *insane* diligence, renunciation, and perseverance. Through nothing else."

Another elliptical journey had a different kind of ending. It began when Frau Frankenfeld, speaking of a bombing raid, pointed out a large glass and wooden bookcase (filled with German classics) which she said had been damaged in one attack. She added that she had it repaired after finally managing to have it and a few other pieces of her furniture shipped to western Germany after the war. She did so, she said, "with ruses and tricks and the help of my cousin, who was married to a half-Jew." This was the first mention of the woman's existence.

Frau Frankenfeld said that when she tried to get her furniture moved, the occupation authorities looked her up in the records and decided, "She was in the Party for God's sake, old Nazi pig, she won't get her furniture. To the contrary, we will requisition the desk." She added, scoffing, "Very democratic. As if I were a war criminal, nicht?" Her cousin then wrote a letter to the authorities. She recited as if from memory. "My cousin, Regina Frankenfeld, in spite of her career beliefs, and moreover in respect to her character, never broke off the connections to my family, including to my half-Jewish wife.' That was true. We got together just like before. They lived in Berlin Lichterfelde [part of southern Berlin] and so did I. Why should we suddenly not visit each other anymore and not get together? There was no reason at all."

The furniture was shipped. Frau Frankenfeld laughed, saying she recalls the episode as a small "amusement" (she used the English word). She added that the half-Jewish wife still laughs about it too, and once told her, "You *were* a good girl and never harmed anyone." Frau Frankenfeld added, "If I speak the truth, nobody can put me in danger."

The truth, she often said, included acknowledging her past. "I was never requested to report to the de-Nazification [office]. I reported myself, filled out the questionnaire, and sent it [to Allied headquarters]. Because I said, now please, I have nothing to hide and I have done nothing that is in *any* way criminal. So, *everything* written out as it *was*." She was designated a "Mitläufer" [one who goes along with]. "The name says it all. The most harmless, the most foolish, but not in any way," she said, drawing out the word loudly and slowly, "*h a r m f u l*."

She also mentioned having a hearing. "They said, 'Mitläufer' like many others. Two hundred and fifty marks atonement. That was a monthly salary for me then."

Did she pay it?

"Of course. I wanted finally to be rid of the Quatsch." She said that when she wanted to attend the earlier mentioned conference in Toronto, a trip that would take her through New York, she had to go to an American consulate in Germany and show both the outcome of her hearing and a receipt that she had paid her "atonement." She said she did so, smilingly.

(Her Party membership did not harm her later career. Almost to the contrary, she claimed that the postwar chairwoman of the federal "Association of Farm Women," who was half Jewish, hired her because of her experience, most of which took place during the Third Reich. Eventually, Frau Frankenfeld became the manager of the organization, a post she held for twenty years.)

Frau Frankenfeld said she never considered lying about her past. "I told myself, why should I be silent or imply something false? That is against my sense of honor. And also against my conviction. I personally took no Jew to a concentration camp. I did not mistreat any. I did not call the whistle on any or denounce any. 'That is a Jew, you have to go pick him up or take him away' or whatever. Never in my life."

The compartmentalization of Frau Frankenfeld's conscience was a model of its kind. And it must have been the core of her good opinion of herself, along with her knowledge that her entire career in the Third Reich was based on helping others. But how was that conscience formed during the Third Reich? Three steps backward are instructive.

The first involved her response to being asked if she had seen transports in Berlin. With notable roughness, she asked back, "What kinds of transports?" That people were pushed together and had to get into trucks and were taken away, I said. She replied, "They did not do that during the day so that all could see, for otherwise the population would have known a lot more about these things than it did. That happened at night, if then, in the quiet."

When she added she had never seen one herself, I mentioned a Berliner told me she saw one during the day. Again, roughly, angrily, "Ja, what kinds of people were they? Did they pick up Jews or what?" Her voice got louder, intimidating. "What did they pick up, *whom* did they pick up?"

In this case, it was Jews.

Inexplicably, her attitude changed. "Well. That certainly can be. That certainly can be. As sad as it is. I myself, thank God, never had to see anything of the kind with my own eyes and am glad about that. For it certainly would have distressed me very much. Because I abhor all force."

The second step back involved the yellow Stars of David. Frau Frankenfeld said she was "shocked during the early time [stars were first worn in 1941] when one saw someone with a yellow star, who had to stand in line for food or so." Asked about children wearing them (as was mandatory at the age of six), she said she never personally saw any. "I believe there was such a thing. But if you ask me if I saw it, I must say no, for otherwise I would be lying." She added that she had seen the sight on television, when "old things *eternally* are brought up and served up *again* and again." This time, after going on almost word for word as before, she said, "That does not produce understanding and is a *completely wrong* tactic."

Perhaps the broadcasts were meant for younger people?

"Ja, but unfortunately all they get is a completely wrong picture from the one-sidedness of what's shown. When I sometimes discuss it with my niece. . . . 'It was on television,' she said. I just say, 'Everything political does not only consist of the Jewish question. We don't want to go to the ends of our lives occupied only with that.' "

That certainly was the truth. But the last step back was something else. Whatever it was, it resulted from another inadvertent question. And it led to her placing what seemed like one last card on a house of them.

The subject was "Kristallnacht." Most women interviewed had vivid memories of it. If all Frau Frankenfeld knew was what she herself had witnessed, I wondered what she had witnessed of "Kristallnacht." I asked if she had had a particular reaction. She said no, because "Kristallnacht" was in Berlin. "That was, let us say, a highly distasteful occurrence, which every person who abhorred force rejected, of course. I experienced no 'crystal night' in Pomerania. Certainly the boycott of Jewish stores, but you know," she again chuckled, "where there were no synagogues, they also had no inducement to destroy them."

Although distracted by a seeming anachronism in her response, I moved on, asking if she read a lot about the Third Reich. She first said she did not need to because she experienced it, then said she does read about it because it is "interesting. I hear pro and con in the most remarkable forms and sometimes say to myself, that is not right at all, for I lived through it, or regarding others, you all are crazy, you must have forgotten to bury your crazy perverse idea. We always say, 'That's a leftover old Nazi they forgot to bury,' nicht?"

Even the distasteful lure of finding out what she considered "a leftover old Nazi" to be was pushed from my mind by the anachronism. One date just did not make sense. At the nearest possible juncture, I asked if she had been in Pomerania when the war broke out.

"No," she said briskly. "I was already in Berlin."

She went to Berlin in '39?

She figured a second. "I took the Reichsstelle [Reich job] in Berlin in '37."

She *really* meant 1937?

She said, still briskly, "From '37 to '45, I was in Berlin." It was as if she were placing her last card herself.

So, she was in Berlin in '38?

"Ja."

As the tip of the card touched down, I said that was when "Kristallnacht" took place.

She responded immediately. "Nein, little child ["Kindchen"! she said]. 'Kristallnacht' was indeed '34. In the first years after the seizure of power. There was no more 'Kristallnacht' [in 1938]. That had long been taken care of. I did not experience it in Berlin, as it happened in Berlin in '34, when I was in Pomerania."

410

The word *Kindchen* and her impatient tone were like slaps in the face. She really meant "Kristallnacht" was in '34?

"Ja, ja, ja."

And that is why she did not see it in Berlin?

"No, I did not. It was in the newspapers. One said, 'It's crazy. What is force for? Let them be, nicht? Please.'"

Just when it seemed that all the cards of the house of honesty began to fall, she interceded. "Wait a minute, what do you really mean by 'crystal night'? So that we don't talk past each other."

That in many German cities, synagogues . . .

"Ja, that happened in '34 . . . "

Store windows were broken . . .

"They did that too, ja, ja."

And many owners were hauled away.

"Well, hauled away is an exaggeration. In part, were picked up and got an arrest warrant and such things."

There was no point debating what happened on "Kristallnacht," or where it happened. She may have been somehow thinking of the Roehm Putsch of 1934. But no adult living and working in Berlin, a center of Jewish German life, could have missed the enormous conflagrations, the destruction, the widespread "crystalline" aftermath, or at the very least the talk about it. Frau Frankenfeld's repeated assertion that she saw nothing, for it all happened years before she was there, said more. Her carefully constructed house of cards seemed to lie at her feet. It was an oddly pitiable sight. Much truth and honesty may well have been in the debris, but precisely where was not certain.

Frau Christine (Tini) Weihs

Life as a Cabaret

Frau Tini Weihs may have told all. She certainly seemed to have that intention. Even on the phone, she said come over as soon as possible, for she thinks about the Third Reich more and more and there is so much to say. A whirling sprite of a woman opened the apartment door, all but pulled me inside, almost immediately said let's call each other *du* (she is an old friend of a friend, but this is not done), took my hand, led me on a tour of every intricately cared for little room of her apartment, including a kitchen on whose wall hung two red ceramic breasts, sat me down to coffee, lit a cigarette, imparted appalling and intimate details of the behavior of her knave of a late ex-husband, whom she still mourns, and went on about the personal lives of others, including a man who during the Third Reich accepted his adulterous wife's child as his own, while knowing the father was a Jew who had fled Germany.

Along the way, Tini (she accepted being called Frau Weihs for about a minute) spoke specifically about her own experiences during the Third Reich. That is, sort of specifically. She paid no heed to dates, such as 1933 to 1945. The triumphant implication was that her life had not been part of the Third Reich as much as the Third Reich had been part of her life. She paid little apparent heed, either, to names and places. Jumbles of references, all in different voices (no "he said, she said"s, for Tini) arched in streams of consciousness back and forth over decades and dialectical boundaries. Although she lives in Stuttgart, she is a native of Cologne (the mutual friend said he considers Tini the epitome of the "Rhineland temperament") and relishes her mother dialect, as well as other dialects she mocked with gusto. She also had an evident fondness for colorful and arcane phraseology, and spoke faster than one imagined a tongue could move. And, adding to certain acoustical concerns of mine, she did not precisely speak, not to mention speak precisely. Rather, she put on a one-woman two-day performance of frenzied, buzzing, anachronistic narrative flights studded with non sequiturs and mime. Tini rarely sat still, or sat at all. She paced, marched, acted out, with song, shout, outrage, gesture, and, most of all, with whisper.

From all she said, or seemed to say, Tini Weihs's Third Reich was not clear-voiced and public, but mostly hushed and private . . . and remained so. I strained my ears, amped the mike, tried to track her, tried, too, to rely on her movements to get a gist, yet some of what she said simply vanished.[1] Occasionally, when the alternative was to go mad with confusion, I interrupted. But at center stage in her living room theater, Tini Weihs, like any actress within her role, did not accommodate distractions well. Among the few times every word rang out was when she imitated a Nazi. (Admittedly, I became grateful she knew some.) But although the majority of her testimony often approximated a murky, tangled skein of sounds, there was no question that the effort to retrieve them and put them in some order had to be done. Tini Weihs's examples of the soul-battering affronts and uncommon goodness within the Third Reich then speak for themselves.

Botching my wish to begin at the beginning, the one thing Tini Weihs never mentioned was her birth. (The mutual friend said, though, that Tini was born in 1915.) She did say that three weeks after she was born, her father died.

He was killed in France, at the front. His survivors included his wife, his three-year-old daughter, and baby Tini. An independent businessman, he left his widow very little money and one large wish. It was that his children should be "masters, not serfs." The widow took the wish to heart. Knowing she could barely support her children on the pittance she received as a war widow, she decided to start a dry goods store. Her late husband's brothers, also proudly independent business people, cosigned for the collateral.

Tini's mother worked all day at the small store and also learned to tailor. In the evenings she made clothes, which she sold for extra income. After five or so years, the business did well enough that she no longer spent evenings sewing, but employed three seamstresses. She also was able to afford the luxury of sending her daughters to a private Catholic day school.

In the 1920s, the family of three rented the third floor of a house owned by an older Jewish couple, the Menckels. The Menckels themselves

---

1. Special thanks are due Petra Gampper, for doggedly extracting every speck of transcribable syllable from the tapes.

lived on the second floor and operated their business—a butcher store with connecting back office—on the ground floor. They had one child, a married daughter who lived elsewhere. Tini never said her family and the Menckels were close. Her stories did.

One evening, her mother mentioned, while eating dinner with the Menckels, how she missed going to concerts and the theater as she used to with her husband. Tini, who would have been about six, either was there too and has wonderful recall, was told everything by her mother, or used her imagination. In re-creating the dialogue between her mother and the Menckels, Tini used the formal pronoun. "Then Herr Menckel said 'Ach no, you don't need to [stay home].' 'Ja,' she said, 'what can I do, Herr Menckel? I really cannot leave the children alone.' 'No problem. If you want to go to the theater or to a concert, bring the children to us. They will sleep with us and when you come back, we'll carry them to you.' And then I can remember that my sister and I woke up in the morning and my sister lay in Jewish arms [Judenarmen] to the right and I in Jewish arms to the left. When she [their mother] then came home after the performance and softly knocked on the door, she [Frau Menckel] got up and said [Tini whispered], 'Do let the children sleep.'"

Tini raised her voice. "These people we should hate because they were Jews? I ask myself, has humanity never had such experiences? And when Christmas came—they celebrated a completely different Christmas than we—and the housekeeper decorated everything. Mother was at the store until the last minute and distributed all the presents [to her employees]. And then they [the Menckels] said, now we should go to Christmas matins and when we came back, presents would be given out. Mother with both her children to the ice-cold Christmas matins in the church. And when we came back, there in the alcove the Christmas tree was lighted. . . ." She later circled back to the same scene, describing the tree as having "lights in it, that my father forged himself. The Jew there, the Jewess there."

Although she never said in whose home the Christmas scenes took place, in both recollections Frau Menckel intervened before the presents were opened and made the girls follow the German Christian tradition of reciting a poem before receiving a present. "Then the Jüdin said, '*First* a recital of the Christmas poems.' They were pretty long. And we said the Christmas poems. You, it was. . . . I sometimes ask myself. How am I supposed to hate the Jews and say kill them? Was a sport club. It was a nephew of the Menckels. Bruno was my first great love. I was his first great love. And as the number one in gymnastics he got a victory crown. Above were the bedrooms. The little dress I wore was [so small]. My doll wore it afterward. *I* proud of Bruno. He had the victory crown. How old were we? Let us have been twelve. And he came home. He had a house key. I had none. He had to go in the door, I in the door. And then he said, 'Are you really proud of me?' And he gave me a kiss. *I* into our girls' room, stumbled over my sister, did not sleep at all that night, had to write a French paper, missed it. I had my first kiss. And *he* already left in 1927, to America. And on New Year's at home we [made crafts]. I just made roses and little boats. And then he said, 'It has a meaning.' I said 'What then, what kind of a meaning?' He said, 'I am emigrating. A time is coming when one will kill the Jews.' I say, 'Bruno, what is coming?' In Jewish circles it was already talked about a lot more than in ours."

Tini's disjointed reminiscences returned again and again to the Menckel family. "This Jew there in the house where we lived, he also went through the First World War. And today I still can see the scars on him and where he got shot. Ja, when we were children, it was always talked about. That we lost the war. And then my mother finally realized she can indeed go to the concert again and go to the theater again as she was accustomed to with father, because her children were taken care of. I cannot say anything. Capable business people they were. They were capable."

Around 1926, after ten years of widowhood, Tini's mother remarried. In 1928, she gave birth to a boy, who was named Hubert. Tini referred to her stepfather as "Vater," but spoke little of him. Her attention then, and a half-century later, focused on her baby brother—"mein Brüderchen." When he was three months old, he developed what she called "brain convulsions." At the age of six, he went to school, but "it didn't work, he didn't understand." He then went to a school for retarded children.

The dates add up to Hubert being in the public record as having a learning disability one year after the Nazis came to power. Tini did not point that out, yet in her spinning monologue referred to what it meant. "First the Jewish children who were not capable of life, then ours, too, went to an institution." It was Catholic-run (or had been) and was located in Essen, not far from Cologne. She said her family visited Hubert frequently. She did not say whether they tried to bring him home.

One day Tini (then about nineteen) realized Hubert was in an isolation room. "And I [said] to my mother, *ask* the doctor why he's in isolation. She didn't want to . . ." (Her whispers involved her mother's fear about the boy's being handicapped.) "Then I asked and the doctor said 'Ja, the lungs are not completely in order.' " She said she did not quite believe him.

"He [Hubert] was indeed in the isolation room a fairly long time. And then Father was killed in an accident." (She said no more about it, but answered the year was 1935.) "And I brought him the news that Father is dead. 'Bigoted' pious we were not, but religious. And he wanted to know who made the coffin, who carried the cross, where they buried him. He understood everything. And the Nazis were at the steering wheel. One already experienced it with the Jewish children, also that they were taken to Theresienstadt." She shouted, "NO ONE CAN TELL ME HE DIDN'T KNOW ANYTHING ABOUT IT. I asked my closest neighbor who was a Jew, 'Where *are* they then?'

"'The people played ostrich politics.' To the contrary, the hate campaign against the Jews was such that one said, they came from Poland and had nothing and one day they had a chain of stores here. I was in a sport club and then we had a monthly meeting and our chairwoman said at the end, 'Ja, I have something to announce. We are closing. The entire women's squad is being transferred to the BdM.' And I said, 'But without me.' 'So, without you? You're a born BdM leader.' '*Nein*,' said I. 'Nein.' Really, I did have a certain leadership ability. I don't deny it. And then I was publicly scorned and my mother trembled and 'Did you and would you'? Nein! And then they sent for me. *Why* I wasn't in the BdM. *Nein*. I say, no, I know the way of thinking. I am Catholic, I remain Catholic, I am not going along with it. I do not disavow God because of the BdM. And one demands that of us. That I won't do. Ja, and then I was 'outlawed [a civil version of excommunication].'"

Tini may have been describing her situation accurately, but National Socialism's basic antichurch stance manifested itself differently according to location and leaders, and there was no national "demand" that BdM girls disavow their faith—at least none that any other woman mentioned.

Tini's impassioned and increasingly whispered remembrances included the following. "Many Jewish girlfriends. 'Man, Tini, can you help us? Tini, can you give us a hand?' I said 'I'll try.' But it kept going further. And then came the question of 'duty obligation [another Nazi youth mandate].' My mother said, 'I need her in the store and I went through enough in the First World War.' Therefore I was allowed to stay home. And therefore I could help a lot of people. I got them cloth, clothes ration cards. I really always stood with one foot somewhere in jail. I was lucky. And then I went to Essen. . . ." At this point, knowing Essen meant a trip to see Hubert, I asked when, for she might have meant any time. After calculating the year was 1939 or 1940, she resumed precisely where she had left off.

". . . and I wanted to go to the ward, to the little one, and the ward nurse was called to the telephone and I was alone in the room with my little brother. Suddenly from the room next to us I heard *cries*. A child's cries. Cries of pain. The little one looked up, looked at me, 'I will stay very still.' And then I pushed down the door handle and there lay a child, perhaps ten years old, a boy, in the bed. And his scalp had been opened and the brain was gushing out. Of a living body.

"I pulled the door shut again. Sat down on the bed. In that moment, the nurse came in and said to me, 'Why are you so pale? What have you done?' I said, 'I went to find out about the screaming. What is that? That is only a child. And my little brother, my Hubert, is said to have something wrong with his lung.' 'Well,' she said. 'Come outside with me. I must tell you something. Ja, we have had inspections here, by the SS. It was determined that your little brother is incurably sick.'

"'No,' I said, 'he is not incurably sick. He is some years backward with his understanding.' I said, 'You can have a conversation with him. He *just* said to me, he is very good, [but that] he is continually being put in a straitjacket. I should take him home.' 'I can't take you home.' 'Am also very good, don't want ever to be naughty again.' I say, 'Hubert, you can't come home with me. You *must* stay here a little while longer.' And then she told me he would have been taken care of. I say, 'Taken care of, what does that mean?' That these incurably ill children are put into 'gassed' cars and one drives them through the city and the relatives get a notice, 'suddenly died of an infection.'"

Tini's account raised many questions, but all seemed superfluous, because what she described was believable. She later referred to the other child as Jewish. She may have assumed this, or have been told so by the nurse.

She said she became close to the nurse, presumably a nun. (She referred to her as "Schwester," which means "nurse" or "nun" or, literally, "sister.") "We *often* talked about our upbringing in the cloister school. And she understood me and I understood her. And then suddenly [Hubert's] condition worsened so badly. Was it physical? Was it mental? I don't know. But then one Sunday morning I was in a hail of bombs between Cologne and Essen. I would not get out of the train alive. I got out. And I went there and he lay in his little bed and he had stuck his foot out. And then I said, 'Nurse, the foot is completely black. What is happening to the child?' 'Ja, must die.' I say, 'Has the child been given something?' 'Nein, Frau Weihs, I swear it to you.' He really did have something wrong with his lungs. In the end he was very feeble. Then he looked at me and said, 'You are wearing such a pretty dress, is that new?' It was a blue-gray, a color Mother wore. 'Ne, I've had it quite a long time.' And I said to the nurse, 'I am not going home. I'll call my mother. I am staying here.' Then around two or three o'clock, he stretched, and I turned on the little lamp and he said, 'Now I must die. And heaven is opening up and Father is standing there. Auf Wiedersehen.' With clear understanding. Turned over and was dead."

Tini was silent several seconds. "At the end, the nurse only said, 'Thank *God* on your knees, you saw him die. How many mothers, how many brothers and sisters do not see their next of kin die.' But I say, with my own hands I would have killed whoever killed that child. I say, you cannot *do* that." She began shouting. "You CANNOT square that with your conscience. Why were the Jews of Cologne on the east side of the Rhine transported away in *cattle* cars and one *never* hears from them again, *never* again hears a word? The populace cannot say *today* we did not *know* about it. One did *see* it. Where then did the human beings stay? And then today one still wants to revise the penalty of 'lifelong.' He's become so old, he won't live much longer anyway. He cannot say he was only the executioner's executioner. If you [said] to me, I was upset about someone, so kill him, I would say you are not normal. That is not *done* with me. For what could the child do about it? He was born *healthy*," she continued shouting, "and at the age of three months got convulsions in the bathtub. He strained for a very long time, but then was himself again. But I could talk with him. I could remind him of things. He *was* not incurably ill. They wanted to do away with them, they were too much for them. I was *also* once young, I wasn't old. And as I saw that Jewish child in the next room, she was furious I figured it out. What do you think, if a supervising doctor had seen how shaken she was."

I asked Tini if she had told anyone about the child in the next room. She barely registered the question. "God, in the narrowest circles. Told my mother once. [Inaudible whisper.] 'Come, don't get so upset, it happened, it's over.' I know, from Jews, of one family there were three children, with feet that were sort of pigeon-toed from birth. When I think about it, not a single one of them is alive because, because . . . those were physical crimes. That was no reason to *kill* somebody. That was *only* to do away with the Jews. They wanted to foist a pure race on us." She had resumed shouting. "What was that? They were at the time highly bred, the men. A man was blond, blue-eyed, he has to breed such children. Listen, that was *Quatsch* what they talked. And the wide masses believed it. One should look this way. One should be this way. A nation should be embodied this way. What can one do about it if he has dark skin? He can't do anything about it. But I am so happy I saw him die, really. Really, I am so happy. I could still hold him. Can really say he died a natural death. So, I watched it. Why suddenly so fast that I don't know. But better than if they had killed him."

About the same time Hubert was sent to the institution, Tini was involved in another human drama. At its center was someone else close to her and whom the Nazis wished gone. Herr Menckel.

The infamous anti-Semitic newspaper *Der Stürmer* began to "set upon him," as Tini put it. (Why *Der Stürmer* singled out Herr Menckel for vilification is not clear.) She went on, the paper claimed "he is a filthy Jew lout [Judenlümmel] who would molest all women and girls. That is not true. That he did not do. It was written in the newspaper. That he's a whore-monger, that no woman is safe from him. The Jew whose arms we lay in. It was in the *Stürmer*." Tini may unwittingly both have explained and been part of Herr Menckel's "crime." A Nazi neighbor could have remembered that the little "Aryan" sisters sometimes stayed overnight in the Menckels' home, and then reported him.

One can scarcely picture how upset he must have been by the *Stürmer* diatribes, not only because of their mendacity, but their danger. "He did not comprehend it. And *all the people* they were good to, whom they helped financially, it wasn't a few, assailed them. *Der Stürmer* made him look outrageous. He molested 'Aryan' women. And that he did not have the strength to overcome." The story, which she brought up twice, continued. "I was in the apartment above with Mother. At the time I wasn't married. And then under us, I heard this *thump* in the apartment. I run down below. I say to my mother, 'Mother, come quickly, something must have happened at the Menckels'.' There he was, between the electric stove and the cupboard and he had collapsed. Then we quickly called a doctor. All he could do was confirm the death."

She later indicated the cause of death was a heart attack. "He got a clogged heart artery and he was dead. He just fell over. I have thought about it so *often*. One woke up. 'Mother? No, oh yes, ja, we're lying in bed at the Menckels'.' And he kept us until it was time to get up." She paused. "Ja, *ask* someone. Why did one kill the Jews?"

When Herr Menckel's death was confirmed, "Somehow I could not bear their crying, their screaming, that they didn't know what do we do now. I returned home that evening. They had a very large hallway and I came through the gate. I know when a Jew dies that all the mirrors are covered. Then all the Jews come together. There were still a lot of Jews. Then I thought, it's going to end sooner, it won't be long, it's already ending. There the mirrors were hung, everything that glistened was hung. That I know, she told me that once. *Hate* is with us Christians. It's true. I had a girlfriend, they had a furniture-making store. I went there bawling, I say Herr [?], what is that for a box standing there? The Jew is not buried in a pompous coffin like we are, but in a glued-together box. Not nailed, glued. And there is a small pillow he had for under his head.

"And I saw it through a crack in the door, how they alternated with praying and crying, and then when the Jew has died, when you go to God, you have salt and a little bag of money under your pillow. But when you see the Christ, stone him and maybe you can buy your way free with the money. That was the sense of the thing, but can be off. It's a lot different than what we do." Tini's understanding of Jewish funeral practices was questionable, but her tone of empathy was not.

"And my mother's sister," she continued, "loved him. Earlier, when there were these church festivals, she went dancing with them. And when they visited us, but it was kosher. That means they ate no pork. And he liked to eat pork so much." As if she were back in the Menckels' kitchen, she spoke of separate dishes, washed separately. "And each Friday there were matzoh dumplings and then candles were lighted. They observed the Sabbath. We lived like little rascals. In any case, they knew, Moritz was his first name, Moritz is dead. And then *they* said *we* will go to his burial. That was all the same to them. All went along."

The funeral procession, which she acted out, but did not say she attended, went from the Menckel house to the Jewish cemetery. "And then the Nazis crossed the path. Then they filmed. The whole burial." Tini's mother did not attend, out of fear. "Then my mother said, 'Do you all think they filmed it to leave you in peace? I mean, what do you think will happen next?' *That* was all the same to them, that had been worthwhile to them. And they should think once about the time we spent the night there."

What happened afterward?

"Nothing happened afterward. It was in *Der Stürmer* that the whore-monger is dead, et cetera, and the 'Aryans' should be *ashamed* of themselves, to help bury a Jew. Was all the same to them." She added, "What was important was that they were not arrested."

Asked what happened to Frau Menckel, Tini's answer was typically elliptical. "She had a son-in-law and she had a daughter. . . . The relatives, as I told you, all were born with such pigeon-toed feet, were all very nice, very hard-working. And then they all had the curved nose, well, one could see they are Jews. And they [Nazis] had them on the spot. Incurable sick ones, cripples, and like that. That was the *worst*, when those with inherited diseases. . . . For them, everything was incurably ill. Hitler wanted a pure race." She continued, "He was only interested in the Siegfried masses. You couldn't be short. Tall. Could not look Romanian [Gypsylike]. Then Herr Feuerstein, the son-in-law of this Jewish woman [Frau Menckel], he was a Jew, too. And he came from Leipzig. A very nice man. And the daughter, a typical Jewish woman. Black hair, black eyes, curved nose, legs a little bent, had . . ."

Bent legs?

"The Jews [had] bent legs." Tini stood and demonstrated an oval-shaped walk. "They walked this way. The Jews always walk this way. Bent. Preferring to point the feet inward. Not all Jews. The oldest was quite straight. He was completely straight. He and my sister [got along] well. But the others . . ."

Where had she got the notion about Jews having bent legs?

"Through observation," she said. "Look sometime. They all walk sort of . . ."

I rather insisted that I knew no Jews with bent legs.

"Well, they have certain characteristics a little bit. Always that their ears stick out somewhat. And Herr Feuerstein said you should get your finances in order. . . ."

The upshot seemed to be that Frau Menckel got her finances in order and emigrated to England. But because of some "clause," she continued to own the house she had lived in, as well as another house, and was entitled to the rent from both. "Almost all had some property. Hardworking business people they were. And then Frau Menckel, the [wife] of the Jew who died, wanted to come once a year, to get the rent. She could, in part, take or invest the money. Then she came one day. Things were getting so far, it was dangerous to receive her. And we had found sort of an emergency exit at our place, to climb through a window. She arrived and said, 'Deutschland, Deutschland, über Alles.'

"My mother said, 'Frau Menckel, you're saying *Deutschland, Deutschland, über alles*?' 'Well,' she said, 'perhaps you all picture when we emigrate, we come into ordered circumstances? We get assigned a room, and so on. Here everything really is still more orderly than anywhere else.' "

The yearly visits back to orderly Deutschland ended at one point, and the Menckel family stayed in England. Tini implied that Frau Menckel died there of natural causes before the war was over. (After the war, at her mother's request, one of Tini's uncles bought from the Menckel heirs the Cologne house they lived in.)

For all the interaction between the two families, the closest relationship seems to have been between Tini's mother and Frau Menckel. In Tini's recollection, they continued to address each other formally, as would have been proper deference from her mother toward the elder Frau Menckel. The latter influenced Tini's mother, at times in unusual ways.

Tini said her mother "naturally was pressured" to join the Frauenschaft. Joining would have been wise for business reasons, she said, for the shop was going through rough times, but her mother resisted. Then "our Jewish Frau Menckel herself said, 'Do join the Frauenschaft.' She [Tini's mother] said, '*You* say I should [join] the Frauenschaft?' For the business. She would get more contracts. 'You're still young,' she said."

Tini's mother joined. No doubt as a result of her membership, she and Frau Menckel were characters in a remarkable incident. Tini did not recall the date, but the year probably was 1935 or 1936, after Herr Menckel and Tini's stepfather both had died. By then, the two women had in common their address, their widowhood, a common partaking of Christmases and kosher meals, and what might be called a certain ecumenical pragmatism.

"Then came the first of May, the national holiday," said Tini. "And they [the Nazis] approached her [mother] with a contract for eighty red flags. She was to sew them, and with swastikas on them. Now listen closely. Was a gigantic contract. Did us good. Business not doing well. No money. What we bought on credit, I had to collect. Sometimes . . . Ja, she got the material. The swastikas were on white felt. Now they had to be sewn. Frau Menckel said [to Tini and her sister], 'So, you now get in bed. Go to sleep.' It was evening. The day after that, the flags had to be hung up. All the streets would be hung with flags. She stayed up until my mother had finished the flags. Through the night. Frau Menckel made coffee, talked with my mother, got out bread. My mother sewed and sewed and hemmed. And the morning broke. Both the women dead tired. We got out of our beds. 'Didn't you both sleep?' 'No, sleep we did not. But the flags are ready.' Someone came from the Party and hung up the flags."

On her way to church that next Sunday, Tini took a close look at the waving swastikas. In church, she whispered to her sister, "'For God's sake, our mother sewed the swastikas on upside down.'

"Neither of them noticed," she continued, "that it was the other way around. But it was windy and the flags waved, she got her money, and the person who was happiest about it all was Frau Menckel, the Jüdin. Please. I ask you. If that is not a life, I don't know."

After the war started, said Tini, young men from Upper Silesia were drafted and sent to the Rhineland to protect it from an expected attack from England. Three soldiers were bivouacked with Tini and her mother. Tini spoke at length of that relationship, too, and of her mother's care and concern for the soldiers, who were not accustomed to the damp cold of the region. I asked if the soldiers were eager and enthusiastic about the war. "They did not believe in victory," she said, adding that they hated the drill. "It disgusted them."

One morning they were gone, having left a note saying they had been sent to the western front. Two of them died there. Tini's mother was grief-stricken.

About the same time, shortly after the war started, Tini met her future husband, one Konrad Weihs. As earlier indicated and as she continued to describe him, he seemed a man whose charm was so great he felt it overrode any necessity for decency. He and Tini had spotted each other one evening at a dance in Cologne. Waltzes were being played. He was Austrian, she was enraptured, and they waltzed to dawn. Tini, humming and swooping in her living room as she spoke, said he could lead wonderfully. He told her he never knew a German girl could waltz so well. He already had a girlfriend.

When Tini's romance began, she was working in her mother's store. It may be assumed that she did her work with alacrity, but there was one thing she did not like. "The endless greeting of 'Heil Hitler.' You could not say a normal 'Guten Tag' anymore. The moment you did not say the [Hitler] greeting, 'What's going on?' Nicht? When they bought things at our store. 'Heil Hitler.' I think, man, what does it have to do with Hitler when they're buying something?"

She did have an idea of the consequences of not saying the greeting. One of her male friends was cleaning his car when an Ortsgruppenleiter greeted him loudly with "Heil Hitler!" The young man "could not bring the words 'Heil Hitler!' over his lips," but instead muttered "Good morning." The Nazis requisitioned his car the next day.

Konrad had different problems with the Nazis. Working in downtown Cologne as a technical draftsman when he met Tini, he was ill-treated (she said) because he was considered a foreigner. "His boss was a Nazi dog [ein Nazihund] and he had a dame, blonde. If she wasn't, she bleached it. She was a customer of ours. She had ration cards and then she got patching thread and sewing thread and so on. Got it stamped. In any case, Konrad came by during his lunch break on his bicycle." Tini said he leaned on his handlebars and exchanged a few words with her. "And this beast saw us. He [the Nazi dog] came in the office and screamed at him. 'You filthy Austrian,' and so on."

Being an Austrian was bad enough, presumably. Worse was not being a soldier. He was called up, said Tini, but was deemed unfit to serve because of an earlier kidney operation. After she and he became lovers, they rented rooms across the hall from each other. (She said, confirming the social mores of the time, which were quite separate from Nazi mores, that living together would have been out of the question.) They then decided to marry and went to Austria for Tini to meet his family. She said that everyone from his parents to siblings were lined up at the station to greet her. All were wearing swastikas.

"What is *that?*" she said she asked herself. Later, she asked them. Imitating an Austrian accent, she said they replied that because she came from the "Old Reich," they thought maybe she was in the Party or in BdM and they therefore would "match ourselves to you."

"'Schwachsinn [imbecility]!' I said. That's the way it was."

The couple married in 1940. Among their wedding presents was the standard one from the state, a copy of *Mein Kampf*.

Did she read it?

"And *did* I. There was even a dedication in it, To the wedding couple on November 1940. It was all in it, how he went to Vienna and told himself he knows the Jews and they have to be annihilated. Ja, child, I don't know anymore. Why did the English . . . And *that* is the other way I see it. The others aren't so completely guiltless either."

She returned to the theme of international responsibility more than once. "*Then* I always say to myself, *why* did foreign countries [das Ausland] not do away with Hitler? If you read a book about Rome, [about] a Roman commanding general who was fit for nothing, one served him a poisoned goblet of wine and he was out of the picture. Unemployment was going on in England, it was in America, it was in Austria and everywhere. But why didn't they do away with him? We tried it a few times. 'Divine providence' as he [Hitler] said, 'protected him from it.' Did they *need* him? Did the Ausland need him, knowing he'd start a war? That I do not comprehend. It had been possible for all of you to block the whole thing. Whoever read *Mein Kampf* . . ." She mentioned the book several times and insisted she had read it all. "It fascinated me so much."

Asked if her husband also had read *Mein Kampf*, she answered, "Certainly he read it. I mean, he even had, to some extent, ja, you could assume, yes, yes. I would indeed say he was very much for the National Soc . . ." Her words dropped off to nothing.

What? Had he been a Party member?

"That he was not. No, no." Her next words dropped again into the inaudible, then back up. He wanted to be a German citizen, she said. "I did not want him to. I said, 'We'll lose the war, what then?'" She paused. "You know, I always had a bit of an impression that he 'turned his flag to the wind.' He was also known in my circle of friends. . . . We had overwhelmingly good people as friends. . . . Many friends said, 'Well, you are heartily invited, but please do not bring your husband.' He politicized. We can't sleep at night because . . . they had a different opinion than he, couldn't stand him. He always tried to convince people it was right, what the National Socialists . . . it wasn't worth it. He didn't kill anyone, but . . ." she said, fading off.

She was so loyal to his memory, she continued trying to picture him as best she could. "He could not think objectively enough," she said. She asserted he was not anti-Semitic. Asked why, then, did he like National Socialism, she said she did not know, but he may have been influenced by a "Machtrausch [delirium of power]" from the movies.

Late one evening, "around 1941," she and Konrad were bombed out of their home. For whatever reason, they were not living with her mother, nor did they seek shelter with her. Tini spoke so disjointedly of the aftermath of the bombing that it set more a mood than a foundation. A store customer who was "a leader of the Frauenschaft" had offered shelter. "She had said if we had no more place to live, we should ask there. If we could have a room or a room and a half. I was pregnant at the time. And I had to . . . one had to stay somewhere. Then we went there that evening, around half past eleven. The Frauenschaft leader had a relationship with a Gestapo man, who was married, and one word led to the next, about the war, and winning and losing, and she was one hundred percent convinced about it, was also a one hundred percent Nazi, that we'd win. And suddenly the Frauenschaft leader stood up and said to my husband, 'I will tell you something. You should be *ashamed* of yourself as a foreigner, as an Austrian, that you're not on the front. You are a *shirker* if ever I have seen one.'

"Just picture it. Newly married. In love over my ears. And someone attacks your husband. Then a woman calls him a shirker. The others were all on the west front, that I admit. And then I said, 'WHY then? Why then, Fräulein Brost? Why should he voluntarily enlist? First, he had a kidney operation and was declared unfit for service. For what?" Whether or not Tini was yelling then, she was now. "'For *Hitler*? Should he perhaps just let himself be shot out of hand? *No.*' So we got terribly excited and then my husband said, 'Now you be very, very quiet, think about, with your miscarriages, every time, either a big bombing attack or you get excited.'" Tini, who never had children, told me she was pregnant three times during the Third Reich, and miscarried each time. And each time she had to contend not only with her own grief, as when once a fetus emptied out of her into a toilet, but having to prove to the Nazis, if they should demand an explanation, that she had really miscarried and had not had an abortion.

Continuing the story about the consequences of her outburst, she said she and Konrad left the apartment of the Frauenschaft woman, and "went to other friends and lived there. The next morning, I was in my mother's store. Suddenly the door opens. I was at the back, in the office. 'Heil Hitler! You do have a daughter, a Frau Weihs, is that so?' 'Ja, I do.' 'So, where is she?' In the meantime, I heard what was going on. Came out. I say, 'Here she is.' Gets out the handcuffs and says, 'You have to come with me to the commandant's office. You're under arrest.' What? Me? My mother [Tini whispered in imitation], 'Will it never come to an end?' 'Mother, calm yourself. Come, be still, it will be all right.' So, to the regional commandant, of the Gestapo. Gauleiter. 'Enter.' " She added, barely audibly, "My cousin was secretary to the mayor. And she said, 'Man, what have you done?' What did I really do? 'Tini, you'll never get out of here. You will not get out of here at all.' "

"'COME IN,'" Tini spat out the order. "There sat ten or twelve at a long table. In full uniform. SA and SS. 'Sit down.'"

Her imitation became a whispered spray. "'*What* did you say last night?' One who knew our family well, he kept looking at me so timidly. He was already older. What had I said?

"'Last night, at the home of the *Brost* family, at the home of the Frauenschaft leader, *what* did you say? About Hitler, that your husband would . . .' I say, 'It's true. Why should he get shot? Why? For *what*?' For God's sake, the family friend, he looked at me, and . . . 'Would you say that today?' I say, 'Of course I'd say that again today and it is true. And one must finally stop. About a foreigner. Austria did return *home*. He is no foreigner. I ask you again, why should he register voluntarily? He was called up, he is unfit. They should finally leave us in peace.'

"They were eighty percent against me, except for the one [who knew] our family and our fate. One, mother a widow. Two, father killed in an accident. And then about the child. That was finally enough. *Ja.* Then they conferred with each other. Where should they put me now, nicht? Until the befriended Gestapo said, 'Gentlemen, listen to me. What did she really do? She married young, she defended her husband. She really did not do anything bad. And we cannot demand that of her mother, too. The family has gone through *enough* sorrow.' Then, conference. The handcuffs taken off. Went back to my mother's. Store closed. No one knows where my mother is. 'Yes,' says one. 'I saw her. She went to the church.'"

Tini dramatically enacted the next scene, more with gestures than words. Of finding her mother in the church, praying. Of her mother's despair turning to joy. The church whispers between them are lost but for fragments, having to do with her mother begging please do not do anything like that again and Tini responding she cannot promise. Then, somewhere or other, Konrad enters the picture. He says to Tini, "Well, this thing was really your own fault. You shouldn't have said anything."

In the years before and during her marriage, years in which the Reich made life ever more precarious for Jews remaining in Germany, Tini, as she cursorily described her activities, spent a good amount of time and effort scurrying about Cologne trying to keep such lives intact. "Scurrying" is perhaps not the correct word, but reflects both her acted-out and spoken language.

One ongoing effort involved a Frau Kaufmann, who lived in what Tini called a "Judenhaus" ["Jewish house" or "Jew house," depending on who is talking]. Presumably it was an apartment building where Jewish families had moved after being evicted from their other homes, by decree or financial necessity, or was a building the Nazis had not yet requisitioned for "Aryans." It can be assumed that Frau Kaufmann, like almost all other Jewish Germans, was more and more restricted in terms not only of housing, but of food, clothing, and anything else. And unlike other Germans, especially city women, Jews could not easily go off to the countryside to trade what they had for what they needed. Fear, curfews, and the dual indignities of having to wear yellow stars and being prohibited from using most public transportation kept them home. Tini, as she described her actions, basically stepped in as a go-between, engaging in a complicated and very illegal exchange of goods (involving the use of her own clothing ration card), to help Frau Kaufmann and her family and friends.

The subject of these activities came up by way of a small explosion of information. "My brother-in-law himself was in the SS." Willi, by name, had married Tini's sister, who herself, Tini revealed, had once referred derogatorily to "these Jews." Had she attended the funeral of Moritz Menckel? "Please, I beg you," scoffed Tini. Why were the sisters so different? "You have different genes in your body," said Tini.

Tini's activities put Willi on the spot. "My brother-in-law called up my mother and he . . . 'Your daughter, she goes into a particular house. She still [takes] coffee beans there and that is a Judenhaus and things are always exchanged there and if it does not stop, she'll end up where she belongs.' My *own* brother-in-law. My *own* brother-in-law. And that was the one thing she [Frau Kaufmann] pleaded for every weekend." Tini said, dropping her voice, "'Can you get me a little coffee? I have no more beans left.' So, I was already . . . I had to be careful. There were four flights, only Jews."

She sketched the intrigue in barely audible breaths of phrases. "Had to give Frau Kaufmann my clothing ration card. She needed a few points, I don't know. She must have [hidden it] in her girdle. And the clothing card. Signatures. Otherwise wasn't legitimate. Write down points, so and so many. You still could buy some dry goods. Wasn't much food. 'Ja, Frau Kaufmann, I'll bring some.' 'You be careful.' 'Ja, sure.' 'Will you come Saturday morning?' A little coffee. You can get some from Holland, a little at the border. Oh God, oh God. I say to my mother, 'If I am to get some coffee, I have to leave now.' Phone rings. My brother-in-law on the phone. Aie, aie, aie."

Willi, a Nazi, is most audible. "Just tell your daughter she should not go into that house today, for *we* are going to be holding a police raid in the house across the street and whoever comes out will be arrested immediately."

Tini got on her bicycle and took off for Frau Kaufmann's. Reading between the lines, or phrases, it becomes clear her recollections involved separate incidents and that she had managed to get to the Dutch border and procure more coffee—probably for trading as well as drinking—for she was hiding it in her sweater as she raced to the house. A more dangerous component in the barter system, and the reason Tini took off so fast, was to recover the clothing ration card she had lent Frau Kaufmann. If the SS found it on her, both she and Tini would be in trouble. In her telling of the tale, the closer she got to the apartment house, the more she whispered.

"Left my bicycle there. Looked around. Up the steps. And, door opened. I say, 'Frau Kaufmann.' Knock immediately. 'I have to come in now.' I say, 'Frau Kaufmann, very, very quickly, before I tell you anything else, I have to have my clothing card.' 'I'll give it to you right away. What is it?' 'I say, all of you be careful, hide from the SS. Police raid going to happen in house across street. We have learned that Aryans still get things here from the Jews that aren't available anywhere else.' Told it plain. Then, me out the front door. Now they can come. Nothing can happen to me. I have the card. Slipped it into my panties. My clothing card. It was like a pass. No one came after me. Ach, I can tell you how my heart beat."

It was the only time she mentioned being nervous.

Adding to the danger of Tini's actions was that social relations between "Aryans" and Jews had been verboten for years. And in 1942, when Tini thought the incidents took place, she and Frau Kaufmann were endangering each other and themselves simply by meeting, let alone doing illegal business.

Tini also spoke about engaging in some subterfuge involving the kinds of ration cards people got after being bombed out. Her aim was either to get her mother more customers or wares. "I stood with one foot in jail. But I had given myself the assignment. [She] brought us through the First World War and I would bring my mother through the Second. No matter at what cost." Asked if her mother always had been against National Socialism, Tini answered "always" and added later that her mother "did not understand on religious grounds" the campaign against the Jews. "She always said, 'One can talk about everything.'"

As the war raged above and around her, Tini seems to have dashed through the days and nights of Cologne in states of passion, outrage, and clarity. "And the troops kept coming closer and closer. And the Jews became fewer and fewer.

"I also experienced that they were deported. That was on the right side of the Rhine. And one could look over from the left side and see it. There were the train cars. They traveled down below, along the Rhine. And I, fast over the bridge and saw how they loaded them all on. And not a single human being came back. Not one of them came back. *Nothing*, nothing heard from them again. Like swallowed into the earth." Her voice went from hard to soft. "And they didn't do anything to anybody. I do not understand that. Even *today*, I do not understand it."

The sight doubtlessly contributed to her involvement in a much more dangerous scheme. In the latter months of 1944, when deportations were relentless, Tini helped hide and nourish "four or five" Jewish acquaintances. They had worked for Ford Motors in Cologne, she said. (Incidentally, Tini told me at one point that she was often put down for not joining what she called the "underground movement," since she had read *Mein Kampf.* "'No,' I say, 'I was still too young to join the underground movement.' 'Ja, as a spy. You should have done something.'" She seemed to feel she had not.)

She spoke in such a disjointed manner about the hiding of the Jewish acquaintances that once again the impression came through, she was seeing so much in her mind's eye that words were superfluous. "Then we had, at a friend's, she was well over eighty, they had parquet floors. We kept and hid the Jews under them. Then we opened the parquet to reach the food down to them." Prodded and prodded, Tini elaborated, a little. Because the house was in the heart of Cologne, her friends had constructed the hiding place with extreme care and quiet. "The breakthrough was done using sacks as a sound wall, so no one could hear the work and no one could be discovered taking food directly to the cellar. Nobody was allowed to see that someone . . . Until someone somewhere noticed that something moved, and then naturally we jumped out of our skins." The someone was "in the neighborhood." What did that someone do? "Told us, 'Children, be careful. You'll land in the devil's kitchen.'"

But their goal was the angel's cellar. After prying loose a number of parquet floorboards in the ground floor of the house, the friends cut through the subfloor and constructed a trap door, under which was the cellar, or a portion of it separated from the regular cellar. When the trap door was not being used, the parquet was put back in place and the octogenarian's living room looked perfectly normal.

"We did the whole thing at night. Friends organized the cellar, also with eating. All the friends organized the food. A lot of it was got by trading with farmers. Naturally, too, with personal cutbacks, or sales." She said not many people were involved in the project, because those in hiding were concerned about being discovered.

What about Konrad? Did he know about the Jews in the cellar?

"No, he didn't know that."

The people lived in the cellar, day and night, for nine months, she said. "They were so afraid," not only of being discovered, but of being bombed. "They couldn't go to a bomb shelter." The cellar offered little more protection than luck. And in heavily bombed Cologne—ninety percent of the center of the city was destroyed—luck did not stretch far. Tini described the raids over Cologne and the fighting in it as if both were happening that minute. After she was bombed out, "we had an emergency home directly on the Rhine and had just had our pitiful Christmas Eve meal. And then came a big alarm and then came a squadron of Americans above us and [attacked the bridges]. One still stood. And then when they threw the bombs on them, the houses lifted up so each moment you thought it was going to collapse. And the worse it got, the farther it went into the earth.

"Children, the last bridge gone. So the escape route was totally cut off. No one could get out. Then Mother. The responsibility for our mother. We stay here, we *cannot* run away from the front. Mother, *where* can we go?

"And then another day. They noticed that the Americans kept coming closer and then we all had to get out. All out. [As Goebbels ordered.] Many Cologne residents are there. Not a step do I take away from the front. If we die here, then we're home. We know where we belong. And then Goebbels said, 'As for the *Cologne* population, we will deal with them after the war.' And I said, 'Mother, here's hoping he even experiences the end of the war alive.' You can*not* picture how it was. Then the Americans pressed forward up to Cologne. The German army stood on the other side. *Very* many [soldiers] fled. And the Americans shot at the Germans and the Germans at the Americans, where there were Germans again. So many Germans were killed because they did not want to leave Cologne, because they did not know where to go. You simply cannot picture it. You cannot picture it. It was so horrible."

She said that after one "awful" bombing attack on Cologne, an aunt (the one who liked to go dancing with the Menckels) went to search for her son, Fritz, Tini's cousin, who had been home on leave from the eastern front. The aunt took a young grandson, Fritz's nephew, with her and headed to a newly bombed section of the city. The dead were piled all over each other. The grandson looked around. "And then he said when he saw a hand stretched out, 'Grandma. That is Uncle Fritz. That is his wedding ring.'"

When the war finally ended, no bombs had fallen through the parquet floors of the Cologne town house. "The Jews all survived, whom we hid."

Tini said that as soon as the American troops arrived, a girlfriend's husband who "spoke *excellent* English" was taken immediately to the American commandant to be a translator. (The man's military status is unclear.) "And he told them that so and so many Jews were hidden there and that we had kept them alive and he asked where the people should go now. They were physically and mentally at the end of their ropes."

Tini, however, continued as before. Shortly after the capitulation, she saw a woman on the street "looking so depressed and thin. I said, I have to speak to the woman, maybe I can do something, I have good connections. Then I brought her to me and cooked her something, she already trembled so, and her eyes, the tears poured out, so weakened, until we could talk to each other." The woman brought her son with her. "That first evening they met in my home and talked through the entire night. And how they got through the Nazis' net, that was really remarkable." The woman was Jewish.

Her son was half Jewish. He was devoted to her and embittered toward his father, who had bowed under pressure to get a divorce rather than lose his coveted job as a fine arts teacher. But as was often the case in Nazi Germany, things were not that simple. The son had confronted his father as a coward, but apparently was not unsympathetic to his father's explanation and attempts to help his family. "But, but," said Tini, "'Angst im Nacken, Angst im Nacken.'" [The untranslatable phrase involves a kind of overwhelming fear at the back of one's neck about something that has not yet arrived.] "Man, your existence. You could be deported, too." Tini rambled about pressure, betrayal, and about the woman's brother who had emigrated to the United States, and had such a difficult time finding work and help. Tini added, "That is always my fury against the others. You did not take them in, either."

Tini eventually befriended American soldiers, too. "[They] came to where we lived. The one thing they never did, they *never* put down their weapons." She added, "One always said the Americans are cowardly. No, how? They don't know what we'd do to them." How did she (and Konrad, who was jealous of her attempts to help anyone, she said) and the soldiers communicate? Via the other new friends, the mother and son. "The Jews spoke excellent English."

I asked Tini directly if she had known that people in the camps were being gassed.

"Eh, ja. One knew that. That had seeped through. And exactly . . ." She diverted into something about clothing ration cards, then redirected. "I heard they were being deported, and it was named Theresienstadt and it was called gassing." How did one know that . . . "I don't know," she interrupted. "Someone or other. And there were always messengers, who said now *that* quarter is next, or *that* quarter, nicht? Only this specific Auschwitz and Theresienstadt, the details we did not know. But when we knew they're standing there or now have to get in these wagons, these cattle cars, ja, *where* then? Ja, on a vacation trip they are not going, ne? And they never reappeared. And I tell you, it was those who physically and psychologically had something wrong and it was those who had reached a certain age."

After another diversion, she sarcastically imitated her contemporaries. "Ja, what should we have done? What then?" She continued, after another diversion, "The wide masses are dumb. You can look back in history. There's always a Pied Piper of Hamlin. Ooooh," she piped. "And they came from all the holes. Ooooooh." The note was higher. "And if it continues with unemployment in the Ruhr. . . . It began like that. We were all unemployed. And that was the stirrup for Hitler." After another diversion she said, "I don't know, were the others all *dreaming* or was I alone completely awake? I don't know. No Jew tormented me. They were so fantastic."

Frau Erna Dubnack

A Natural Matter of Friendship

A block off Berlin's famously frantic shopping street, the Kurfürstendamm, stands what must once have been an elegant apartment house. Through its tall, nicked, art nouveau entrance, past the stairwell and out a back door, is a large courtyard—a common, quiet, and hidden garden. In its midst and unseen from the street stands another apartment building, known in Berlin as a "garden house." Through its own old, nicked entrance, past bicycles parked in a dark vestibule and up four winding flights of stairs, a door opens to a modestly appointed apartment. For five decades, it has been the home of Erna Dubnack.

Born in Berlin in 1909, Frau Dubnack never has left, as her accent and pride testified. "Bin eine Berlinerin," she said more than once. She also fits the German concept of "worker," as evidenced by a lifetime—from childhood to her sixties—of low-paying, physically demanding jobs. It has not been easy, she said matter-of-factly. Now that she is "pensioned" by the government, she is slightly better off. She could afford to "travel someplace once."

She does not spend much money on appearance. When we first met, her hair was straight and plain, with bangs, her housedress loose and plain. But her blue eyes lit up like an imp's and her smile was quick. She was a little self-conscious about gaps from recently pulled teeth her dentist had not yet replaced. Sometimes she covered her mouth in mid-smile.

Besides being a Berliner and a worker, Frau Dubnack belongs to a rarer category. In the vocabulary of post-Holocaust consciousness, she is a "righteous Gentile," a non-Jew who during the Third Reich saved a Jewish life. Implicit in such righteousness is not having acted for any material gain. Also implicit is having acted at the risk of one's own life. Righteous Gentiles typically provided food or shelter for varying amounts of time, depending on circumstances. Erna Dubnack provided a woman named Hildegard Naumann with both food and shelter for over two years.

Offering such help obviously was dangerous in itself. But in the years Frau Dubnack provided it, 1943 to 1945, a time marked by the extensive roundups and slaughter of Jews, it was almost suicidal. One writer put the situation this way: "Nothing could be more miraculous than the survival of a Jew in Berlin during the last years of World War II."[1] In this case, the danger was compounded. Frau Dubnack's neighbors were Nazis.

The years of her righteousness also coincided with the increasing miseries felt by almost all Berliners. There were shortages of food, water, heating fuel, clothing, and housing. But there was no shortage of Nazis, watching who went where, listening to who said what, and there was no shortage of bombing raids. As photographs and documentary film footage show, Berlin was increasingly uninhabitable. Yet to hear Frau Dubnack speak of what she did, dangers seemed beside the point and personal deprivations irrelevant. Frau Naumann was her dear friend.

The friendship did not evolve because the two women had anything obvious in common, for they certainly did not. Indeed, if Hitler had not come to power, Erna Dubnack (then Erna Krzemieniewski) and Hildegard Naumann might never even have crossed paths. Theirs was a friendship the Nazis brought about.

They met in the summer of 1935 on the shore of a Berlin lake. Both were twenty-six years old. Frau Dubnack, her high-pitched voice delivering fast, clear Berlinerisch, described the scene as if it had happened five minutes, not five decades, earlier.

"We'd all gone swimming. We were a clique, my husband and others, although I wasn't married then. We were a lot of young men and only two or three women. And she sat there looking so lonesome. I saw she was a Jew, a 'full Jew.' She really looked very Jewish. I thought, God, she's sitting there so alone. She can play with us and we can swim together and so on. And then a friendship developed. She visited me and soon after that we made a bike trip. That was '36. We even went to Italy and Switzerland. We didn't take the bikes to Italy, because that would have cost one thousand marks and we didn't have that kind of money. She did somehow have . . . Well, her

---

1. Leonard Gross, *The Last Jews of Berlin* (New York: Simon and Schuster, 1982), author's note.

father was a judge, but he was dead. She still had a mother and sister, but she didn't live with them."

Frau Dubnack's speaking style not only was artless, but so divergent, with a sentence or thought finished often only after several parenthetical asides, that I feared I had missed a subtlety. Did she mean, I asked, she had gone over to the woman at the lake simply because she looked Jewish?

"Ja, *natürlich*. She just made me feel sorry for her. And we weren't against Jews or such anyway. We had no hate. We hadn't been that way at home. Of my brothers, one was unemployed seven years and the other four years and they didn't join any Party. A lot did join and that's why it got so big, because they just didn't have any work. And many because of enthusiasm, no? And afterward some were, well, silent. That's how it was then. But we had little to do with such people. I didn't have a job either, for a whole year. Earlier I'd worked in a sewing factory. In any event, I wanted to tell you about my friend. So, I just went and got her because she sat there so alone and probably saw that maybe we . . . Maybe that's why she was in the vicinity, too."

Asked if she herself already knew, that . . . Frau Dubnack broke in before I said what "that" was. "Ja, of course. It had already started. Not that they were persecuted so directly, but '35, yes, it had started. We already knew . . ."—she paused, dropping her voice to a whisper—"that many people were against the Jews. And one had another religious belief. But she was not pious." Frau Dubnack suddenly laughed a friendly and brisk, seemingly nervous laugh with which she would punctuate many sentences. "She wasn't pious at all. But she was intellectual."

Frau Dubnack later said that "my friend [meine Freundin]" knew English, French, and Latin, having had "a good education." She added, "The parents were rich." The connection was appropriate. In the early decades of the twentieth century, a German high school education was mostly for the well-to-do. It cost not only money, but time. Children going to school could not work full-time to help the family. Such an education was beyond the expectations of poor Germans like the Krzemieniewski sisters and brothers.

Hilde Naumann had used her education to become a librarian. But one of the first acts of the Nazi regime cut her career short. Civil service jobs were for "Aryans."

"Afterward, she couldn't get a job. Then she worked at a furniture store, then here, then there. And later she had to work in the factory, for the war."

In Frau Dubnack's recollection, as soon as Hitler came to power, there was work, but all connected to an arms buildup. One company looking for workers was Siemens, the huge electric corporation. Despite its obvious ties to the military, the allure of employment made her apply. She was hired to train for a job adjusting electrical components. (She qualified for the training, she said, becuase she had "very good eyes.") She still seems uncomfortable about even approaching Siemens. "I told myself, apply so at least you have a job. We were poor. We were *very* poor, in fact. As children we carried newspapers, putting them in front of the doors at five in the morning. And I was in the country, too, working for farmers." She laughed again. "Ja, ja, we went through a lot. As poor people . . ."—she corrected herself—"as poor human beings, you go through a lot anyway."

The Krzemieniewski family—grandmother, parents, four children, and eventual in-laws—was and is close. One obvious state of accord is that between Frau Dubnack and her younger widowed sister, Elsa Blisse, with whom she lives and who, seemingly as a matter of course, joined us for the interview. Frau Blisse had her own wartime traumas, including the Nazis' torture of her husband and her own rape by at least one Russian soldier. She is a heavy-set woman with a soft way and sad eyes, and has some trouble with her legs. The long flights of stairs must be agony for her. Although the sisters revealed different personalities, both naturally completed or echoed each other's sentences as if they really were of one mind.

Apparently their parents were, too. That meant not being for Hitler at all, said Frau Dubnack. Their father always voted for the SPD, the Social Democratic Party. She referred to it as the "workers' party." He also opposed the aristocracy, she said, grinning bashfully as if she had said something naughty.

But he did not oppose the Jews. "Not at all. To the contrary. He bought from them, did business with them, bartered with them. No, our father wasn't that way at all." It was clear from her tone that Frau Dubnack adored her father. Herr Krzemieniewski worked for a time for the Berlin gas utility, for little money, she said. "But my father did a lot of things. He was a musician, too. He played in the winter, before he had a job with the city and wasn't married or anything. And summers, he went everywhere. Then he wanted to emigrate to America, because he didn't want to be in the army. He served just a year, because his mother was old. By then, he couldn't go to America. Our father worked in an office, too. He could do *everything.*"

The embracing circle of the Krzemieniewskis and friends immediately widened to include Hilde Naumann. "She always came to see me and my acquaintances. My [future] husband and all, she knew them all, because we were very interested in sports. My husband played punchball. We all were sort of tossed together. It was a group, no? We were *youth.* Anyway, a friendship developed. She visited my sister and I took her once to visit my mother-in-law." In turn, Hilde Naumann brought her new friend Erna to meet her relatives.

The friendship began only a month or so before the Nazis decreed the Nuremberg race laws, which banned, among other things, such friendships. Frau Dubnack said she knew that "one should not come together with the Jews anymore."

434

What was her reaction?

"We both wanted to emigrate later, to Canada." That she knew so little about Canada "it was not even a concept to me" did not matter. "Ach, I thought, maybe my husband will follow us there, or whatever, because the Nazi time. . . . I thought, *away*. I was not for it at all. Many did leave, and she always wanted to. But we didn't manage it, because by then she couldn't get out."

Asked if Frau Naumann was aware of the danger in which she was putting her just by being with her, Frau Dubnack said, "That she knew, that she knew. We both were on our guard, that's clear." Being on guard extended to the 1936 bicycle trip, which cemented the burgeoning friendship. "I had already known her a whole year. And I too," she laughed, "was ready for adventure. We both said, good, we'll plan a trip together."

At the time, she said, Germans were not allowed to take more than ten marks out of the country. But Hilde Naumann was able to get ninety-five marks apiece for them. "She probably had connections, or what do I know. Ninety-five marks was not a lot of money, but still."

A shortage of money was not the only obstacle the women faced. Travelers who wanted to spend the night in a German town had to register with the police. "When it came time to find a place to stay, I always went in to the police. She didn't trust. . . . There were police already who were, well, if they weren't *all* for Hitler, nonetheless they made a lot of police quit and put their people in their places. I knew a policeman who was supposed to join the Party and didn't and he was fired."

Even when entering the police station, Frau Dubnack said she never once said "Heil Hitler!" as was ordained. Nor, by her account, was she assiduous in following other Nazi orders. "When I was supposed to hang out a swastika flag, I pulled the blinds down. I said, 'What do you want with me? I'm working, I don't look left, I don't look right.' They came to me, why I'm not hanging out a flag, why I'm not 'waving,' nicht?" And during Nazi parades, "we got out of the way a little, on the other side or something, nicht? Because . . . I mean, she looked genuinely Jewish."

Asked what looking genuinely Jewish meant, Frau Dubnack said, "Well, the eyes. Many used to look that way, nicht? But not all. Many were blond. There was that, too."

Frau Blisse said she thought Jews were another race. She added, "When they left Galicia and wanted to come here to Berlin, somehow they had to pay for something or another. One didn't allow them to learn occupations and that's why they all became bankers and studied. They weren't allowed to learn trades."

Frau Dubnack, who had been out of the room during the brief discussion of race, said only at one point, "Well, if you'd seen her on the street, you would have said, Jewish heritage."

Getting back to the bicycle trip, she said that once she registered with the police, "I always went and got us a place to stay. And she [Hilde] knew Latin and so on and always explained the churches and ornaments and everything and the Latin inscriptions, what it meant and all. So," she laughed happily, "we balanced each other."

What kind of a woman was Hilde Naumann?

"What kind of a woman?" Seemingly unaccustomed to such a question, Frau Dubnack repeated it, paused, and finally responded with an accolade. "A simple one. She was not for riches. She was more, well, for the poorer population." The old friend paused again as if making sure she got it right. "Ja."

"She didn't like it at her family's house, the opulence and everything," she continued. "That's why she moved out, at twenty-one. There had always been social gatherings and whatever. She didn't like that at all. Even before Hitler, she left home. That's why she felt well when she was with us."

The women's friendship was captured in a few snapshots. Frau Dubnack, having dashed away for a minute (and so missing her sister's comments on race), dashed back with a fistful of photos. One showed the new "clique" at the beach. On the far left of a large smiling group of young people in bathing suits is Hilde Naumann. She is looking down. Frau Dubnack frowned. "She's lowered her head. Maybe on purpose, you know? On purpose." She looked closer. "Here she doesn't look so good," she said, and laughed apologetically.

"Here. She's smiling!" Frau Dubnack had found another snapshot. Fourteen people at a home wedding—Frau Blisse's. It is unquestionably a happy and by no means elegant group. Girth in the grandma, buck teeth in the teenage boy, and both looking as happy as can be. Standing behind the seated bridal couple (Frau Blisse, a solidly built bride in a flowered dress, smiling next to a happily smiling man) is a row of family and guests. On the far left is Hilde Naumann. She is attractive, dark-haired, and is smiling into the camera. Next to her is her also-smiling friend, Erna Dubnack. "There, you see her quite clearly," she said. On Frau Dubnack's other side, one person away from her, is Herr Dubnack, looking at the ceiling.

Frau Blisse then looked for some time at the picture of her own wedding day. Would she comment about the ceremony? Her husband? Their plans? "She had beautifully thick hair," she said.

Film or memory could preserve some moments, but the private and public world in which the moments took place, as well as the vast arenas where they intersected, was changing fast. In 1937, Frau Dubnack, by then married, gave birth to her one child, Peter. (He is an engineer, and her pride.) After his birth, she repeatedly tried to quit her job at Siemens, an action her husband also favored. But, she said, the Nazis ordered women to keep working unless they had two young children. So she kept working.

Her son stayed in a Siemens kindergarten, where "he had it relatively good."

When the war started, Herr Dubnack was drafted almost immediately. "He didn't think that way. No one. Unfortunately, so many [from the young athletic "clique"] were killed in the war. So many of them. Good friends. Ja." Frau Dubnack looked inexpressibly sad.

About to affect her personal life as acutely as the war were the Nazis' deportations of Jews. Both she and Hilde Naumann knew about them. "In 1942, she told me that so many were picked up, even earlier. She'd already had a cap made for herself and had a rucksack ready for when she was picked up, so she'd have her luggage together, she told me. And I said, 'You know what, Hilde? If it gets to that point, you come to me. And then we'll see how it goes, nicht?' She didn't ask me."

The test of the friendship came the next year.

"Her mother lived on Nürnberg Street, and her nanny, too. Anyway, they had staff at their house. A nanny, household help, and a governess, I think. In the meantime, the nanny had grown old and was blind. She still stayed with the mother. She was from East Prussia. They'd had a nursemaid, too. They were *rich*."

After Hilde Naumann's father died (in the pre-Hitler era), her mother moved to a smaller house. "She [Hilde] took me with her a few times and to her cousin. I knew her sister, too. And what happened was, one day before she came to me, she told me her sister was hauled off. She never came back. And I said again, 'Then come. If it gets to that, you come to me.'"

Hilde Naumann moved in with Frau Dubnack and her son, Peter, in January 1943.

Oddly, hiding brought freedom. Hilde Naumann took off her star. And like many people who chose the risks of living underground to other risks, she felt she could walk outside, in almost-safe anonymity. Whatever emotional respite she had attained, however, did not last long. She soon learned that her mother had found a different escape from the Nazis.

Frau Dubnack's recounting was wrenchingly sparse. "Her mother took her life. She had poison. When it gets to that, when they want to haul her off, she would take the poison capsule. And did just that and was dead. [Hilde] went there to visit her and she was still warm."

Almost immediately upon seeing her mother, Hildegard Naumann saw her old nanny. It is not known who told whom what had happened. We do know that the blind "Aryan" nanny, either knowing or learning that her longtime employer was dead, gave the woman she had once taken care of a fast and final bit of care. It was a warning that the Gestapo was looking for her.

The kaleidoscope of Hilde Naumann's thoughts is not known, but her actions are. With time neither to grieve for her mother nor to bury her, nor to grab a memento of her childhood before the Nazis confiscated it, Hilde

Naumann fled back to her hiding place. Erna Dubnack's apartment must
have been the only place in her world she felt safe at all.

What meant safety for Hilde Naumann meant danger not only for Erna
Dubnack but for her son, by then six years old. She acknowledged, "I knew
it was dangerous. We already saw, after all, how the Jews were hauled off.
We knew them. We always said the 'Egg Jew' where we bought eggs. We
saw how they hauled the Jews away." She said it happened during the day.
"They had to climb up [into the trucks] and if they weren't fast enough, well,
they helped."

Had the people screamed as they were being hauled away?

"Nein, not at all," she said. "They were very quiet."

She knew full well that what the Nazis did to her Jewish neighbors
they could do to her. "If they'd come here, if I'd been hauled away to the
camp, I wouldn't have come out again either. Natürlich. I knew it was verboten." Frau Dubnack pulled her index finger across her neck. "Death
penalty."

Yet when I asked how often she had thought about the danger, she
said, "Ach Gott, well, I, I," and stumbled until finding her place. "You know,
one worked. I don't know. I didn't concern myself with it at all. But I have to
say, I am a human being who's not so very scared. . . . "

"Above all," interrupted Frau Blisse, "we were young."

Frau Dubnack echoed, "We were young. And we were opposed."

Despite knowing that Hilde Naumann and Erna Dubnack faced death,
the sisters seemed not to have known about gas chambers. Asked outright if
they knew then what fate awaited the people who had been taken away,
both sisters said they did not. To the question of whether Hilde Naumann
knew that she herself could be exterminated in a camp, Frau Blisse replied,
"Certainly. She knew that, at the end." ("At the end," could mean, however,
at the end of the war, when the liberation of the camps and the existence of
the gas chambers and ovens were widely publicized.)

Frau Dubnack interjected. "If she had been grabbed [geschnappt]
here, they might have killed her, nicht? I don't know." But when I asked her
if Frau Naumann knew that Jews were being transported to annihilation
camps, she said, "No, I don't think so. I don't think she knew that at all."

To that Frau Blisse said, "Where I lived, Frau Koch once told me, 'We
are not returning. We will all be killed.'"

"Ja, ja," interrupted Frau Dubnack. "That she was not coming back.
That, yes."

"Some of them already knew it, what was in store for them," said Frau
Blisse.

"Maybe she knew it too," conceded Frau Dubnack. "I don't know at all."

Frau Blisse added, "It's obvious. When they were taken away, they were taken to work, terrible nutrition . . ." And so, it seemed what she had meant all along was death by deprivation, not by gassing.

Frau Dubnack had interrupted again. "The only one was Theresienstadt. There they had older people. There different people remained alive. There they did not ga . . ." she stumbled, "gas them as much. They also hauled away people of other religions. They came to the concentration camps exactly the same, not only Jews. My brother . . ." She embarked upon a rambling if ultimately related story about his work as an electrician, a profession that helped keep him from the front line. After he worked at Siemens, she said, he was sent to the Peenemünde complex with Wernher von Braun and then to the concentration-work camp, the Lager Dora. Put in charge of installing and maintaining the camp's electricity, he had groups of eight prisoners a shift assigned to him. Because he felt sorry for them for being so exhausted (they were generally allowed only an hour's sleep at a time because of air raid alarms every two hours, and even that sleep was overseen by "the SS jumping around"), he set up a bed in a small room where the controls were. On the door he put up a sign: Life Threatening Danger. Entrance Strictly Forbidden. There he had the people assigned to him ("It was all the same to him if it was Jews or whomever") take turns getting a couple of hours of sleep, undisturbed by the SS. "He had so many invitations after the war," Frau Dubnack mused, adding, "and he didn't want anything."

She continued her earlier topic as if having taken time out for only a comma. "And many died, too. Then they shoved many in the ovens. Who could not work, and so on. They had huge ovens there. He saw that too, ja. They were just shoved inside. Jawohl. He told me everything because he knew I wouldn't talk about it. I didn't tell anybody."

Frau Dubnack guessed it was in late 1944 when her brother confided in her. And she confided in him about hiding Hilde. "Both my brothers knew. My mother-in-law knew, too. My husband also knew. Naturally, they all knew."

Were they for it?

"Well, they were indeed for it. Naturally, they weren't against it. But they were afraid, too. That is clear. If my husband had been here, he wouldn't have said anything. No one would have. Your husband either," she said, turning to her sister.

"My husband, they all knew it," replied Frau Blisse.

"They took him away once," said Frau Dubnack. "Tell about it."

"Ach," said Frau Blisse, looking uneasy. "That was a long time ago."

"A long time ago, ja," repeated Frau Dubnack. "The Nazis, they made him stand in water a couple of nights. Then he was sent to the hospital. They actually . . ."

"They simply took him with them, picked him up on the street," said Frau Blisse. Quietly, she began to cry. "Then they arrived somewhere and then, I don't know. They did everything possible to them." She looked tormented by the memory.[2]

Seeing her sister's distress, Frau Dubnack briskly took over, telling me that her own husband was caught by some Nazis before Hitler was in power, but freed himself. Another time, she said, they got him and thrashed him to the point he became "krumm" [bent]. She began telling of an acquaintance who was taken to a cellar, when Frau Blisse broke in to remind her to get back to Hilde.

"Ach! Of course, that is more important," responded Frau Dubnack, adding apologetically, "You could just drop all the other."

It was difficult not to break down.

"One doesn't remember everything," she continued. "But it was the time when one had one's eyes open. And we had them open. Not everyone did. Many said, and still say today, they saw nothing and knew nothing." Her reaction to such people is, "I tell them what's what. And sometimes we have a real entanglement [ein Techtelmechtel]. Jawohl. Some are still for it today, have not even swerved. There are some such. Let us say, not exactly for it, but they found the time not at all bad, because they had high positions and had it good and so on. Ja, many were after the money." She summed up. "It is astounding."

By the time Hilde Naumann became completely a part of the Dubnack household, there was little adjustment to make.

"She always came to my place before. Then she came and simply was just there. Also my acquaintances who came, all of us felt differently, nicht? They could see and knew, too, that it's a Jüdin. But when she was living with me, I had to work and because I had the boy, the child, eight hours of work and then with shopping and everything, it was twelve hours until I got home." She also said, "I didn't have so much time to reflect."

The sentence shimmered with memory. Other women had said the same thing, almost word for word. But Frau Dubnack spoke it in the context of dismissing her bravery. Other women spoke the sentence essentially as a defense.

A major element of the risk Frau Dubnack took on involved her son, Peter. It was self-evident that he, too, could be killed (or at the very least be

---

2. According to a book that came to light after the interview and included brief remarks from the sisters, Frau Blisse said her husband was standing in a city square when an SS dragnet surrounded it and took all the men away. Her husband was thrown in a cellar, interrogated, and beaten. He then had to stand against a wall for eight days, before finally being sent to the hospital. Hans Wienicke, in *Schon damals fingen viele an zu schweigen* (Even then many began to keep quiet) (Berlin: Bezirksverordnetenversammlung von Charlottenburg [literally the "district delegation assembly" of Charlottenburg]), 1986.

taken from her) if the Nazis learned Frau Naumann was hiding in their home. To help them not learn, Frau Dubnack managed to hide the truth from him. "In the morning, she always lay in the other room, in the living room. It was very cold in the winter. That room was heated a little. We heated with coal. We didn't get much during the war, and we had hard times to get through." Frau Dubnack, having slept in the cold bedroom with Peter, brought him into the warmer living room in the early morning. "I always dressed my boy by the warm stove, he was tired too, and distracted him so he didn't see that someone was sleeping in the bed, or was lying there. He wasn't supposed to know, because you know how children are. He was six years old. That's just a child. Afterward he was eight, at the end of the war, and somehow he could have given something away. I mean, completely harmless. But when she was there in the evenings or when we came home, or was there Sunday, well, that was Tante [Aunt] Hilde who just was there. That didn't matter. The thing was, we didn't want him to see she lived there or slept there. And she couldn't let herself be seen as much. When there were bombing raids, they always got worse, she went to a public air raid shelter." To protect Frau Naumann further, the Dubnacks and their friends developed a playful code name for her of "Otto Otto," in case anyone, including Peter, was overheard speaking about her.

The situation for Berlin, and the Dubnack-Naumann household worsened. Frau Dubnack spoke a volume in one sentence. "Then I was bombed out and brought her here with me."

The bombing raid killed a lot of people, she said, including three people in her own apartment house. Had she not followed her instinct, she and Peter might have died, too. "I didn't always go down [to the shelter] when there was an alarm. When the alarm sounded that day, I told myself, today I just have a feeling I have to go down. I already had my papers in a pouch. We were below less than five minutes when it happened. My house was kaputt. Not completely gone, but kaputt." Also, she sat way back in the shelter, rather than near the entrance where she usually sat, "or we would have been killed."

The new apartment the Nazi government assigned Frau Dubnack provided another irony for the Third Reich archives. The apartment had been Jewish-occupied. So it would be again.

The government also told Frau Dubnack she had to take in a paying tenant. (The government was not aware of various friends and relatives she was sheltering already—at one time seven in one room.) She managed to find a tenant she trusted, a young woman. "She was not for it. She knew it, ja, but she would not have betrayed me." Frau Dubnack's "it"s are clear. The first referred to the Nazi regime, the second to the hiding of Hilde Naumann. "She was already more for the workers anyway," added Frau Dubnack. "I believe even a Communist. The Communists also helped and hid people.

Ja, the workers. I would say the intelligentsia sometimes refused. Refused as a matter of course. I mean, Hitler would not have made it. And then they say the workers are at fault." She laughed in an unlaughing way.

In her new "garden house" apartment, Frau Naumann either slept in Frau Dubnack's room with her, or "in the maid's room, because of my son. It was good for sleeping. Sometimes I've had guests of my son here, in fact, one from a 'good house.' He was satisfied. It was not that small, the room. There was nothing in it, just an old bureau. Ach, she was satisfied she had the room."

The door of the room faces the entry door of the apartment. Frau Dubnack pointed out that the location was practical; Hilde could get out fast during bombing raids. At my request, Frau Dubnack (with an unusual hint of hesitation) opened the door to let me see the room. It was about ten feet by seven, with built-in cupboards, a large window at the far end, and a nice high ceiling like the rest of the apartment. Now the room obviously was being used for storage, among other purposes. Laundry on clotheslines crisscrossed above us. Frau Dubnack apologized for the appearance. That, it seemed, was why she had hesitated to show what was, of course, a sanctuary.

Back in the small living room (which I later learned was Frau Blisse's bedroom) Frau Dubnack continued speaking of Peter, who never knew until after the war that Tante Hilde slept over every night. But hiding her status from him was a relatively minor concern. Hiding her presence from neighbors was a major one.

"I had to be on my guard about them. Below me was a doctor who was in the Party. I don't know whether he was for it. My son was very beloved here in the apartment house. And [the doctor] sometimes gave him something or another as a present, like a little piece of chocolate. He probably liked children very much. He had none of his own. But of course he was not allowed to know, nicht? That is clear. One trusted nobody. I mean, there probably were some who were not that way. . . ." At the words "that way," Frau Dubnack, as if distracted, patted her upper left arm. It is where the swastika armband was worn.

She added that because she had little time for neighbors, she had little contact with them. Nonetheless, she and Hilde were well aware they included Nazis. The memory must have reminded her that the dangers posed by such neighbors were real. She immediately told of being in her local dairy store where "the milk woman [die Milchfrau] told me that a grandfather, a Jew, a Jewish religion let us say, I don't want exactly to say Jew, nicht?" Frau Dubnack interrupted herself with her short fast laugh. "He told her, 'They just hauled away my little grandchildren.' Imagine that. Five and six years old. Ja, without parents, without anything. She [the Milchfrau] was so beside herself. She was bombed, too. She lost her life. That apartment house nearby, where so many were killed." The bombing raid was the one that destroyed Frau Dubnack's first apartment.

The night raids caused particular dangers for the household. Frau Nau-mann could not risk being seen by Peter or by curious neighbors. So, at the first tone of the warning alarm that preceded the regular alarm, she raced outside and to a public bomb shelter. "No one did a thing to her there." Meanwhile, in a more leisurely race, Frau Dubnack got Peter ready to go down to the apartment building's own shelter. She and Frau Naumann had worked out the return, too. Peter was to be back in bed first, his eyes closed to the latecomer.

For Hilde Naumann, days provided different dilemmas, like what to do with the time, and where. Sometimes, when Frau Dubnack had a day off, the two friends went out together. "We went to Werder, to pick some fruit. But she looked very Jewish. One had to be very careful.

"She had a cousin, Ilse, who lived at number 24 something in Schöne-berg. I was there, too. She was a doctor. I also felt sorry for her, but I could not take two. It was so dangerous and also I didn't have much money. And she had none, my friend. And one did not know at all how everything was going to go and we didn't know at all that it had to do with losing one's life, in these camps. We didn't know that at all. Perhaps my friend didn't know that either. I don't know." In other words, Frau Dubnack seemed to have been saying, she still feels bad she could not hide the cousin.

Most days, Frau Naumann either stayed at the Dubnack apartment, often reading, or "she cleaned up a bit," or ventured out. Frau Dubnack had left her a key to come and go as she pleased, or risked. "She had a girlfriend in East Berlin, where she went. She had acquaintances, where she went dur-ing the day. And here, we made dinner. We always prepared things ahead of time. Sometimes she got it ready, then ate, her noon meal and so on. When I arrived, she had already cooked it and then we just ate."

Just ate what? Frau Dubnack did not say so in regard to herself, but it was common for mothers to hunger in order to feed their children. She did say she once had nothing for two days but spinach. "I felt so sick to my stomach. We had no bread, nothing, until my next ration card. I always traded things [for food]. We went through bad times. Well, it's over with. In exchange, we're doing better." She seemed embarrassed to have complained, and laughed her quick laugh. But Frau Blisse broke in to emphasize what her sister did for Hilde Naumann. "She had to have twice as much food for the both of them."

The point cannot be overstated. In fact, it was seconded by a Jewish survivor[3] who lived in Berlin during the same time Frau Naumann lived with Frau Dubnack. She said she was impressed that Frau Dubnack hid her friend, but was staggered that she *fed* her. Ration cards, which had to be stretched

---

3. The survivor is Rita Kuhn, whose interview follows.

thin even for the person they were meant to nourish, provided essentially the only way, other than the black market, or trading teapots for flour, to buy food. Hilde Naumann, whose money was used up and who clearly was out of the ration card system, thus was unable to provide even a morsel of her own meals.

Immediately after the evening meal, Peter was put to bed. Often, members of Frau Dubnack's large circle of acquaintances then came over to visit. What was discussed? Politics. "Of course. We were opponents. We were opponents of the Nazis."

One subject that must have crossed the evening table in July of 1944 was the assassination attempt on Hitler. Frau Dubnack said she had been walking along the street when the news came over the Nazis' ever-present loudspeaker system. "I heard it. People came by and said, 'Too bad that he's not dead. Too bad it went off next to him.' I mean a lot. In public." She dropped her voice. "It astounded me." She added, in her usual way of trying to be accurate, "Perhaps it happened to be those who were not for it so much."

In the last months of the war, Frau Dubnack's food situation changed from dire to almost princely. Her husband, who by then had been a soldier for more than five years and who was sent to Denmark at the end of 1944, arranged the food channel. "He got me eggs, so we could live. He sent ham and everything, or I picked it up from Denmark, where he bought it. But I had to send him money. I had to borrow. I sent him two thousand marks. That was a lot of money for me. I borrowed it from everywhere. I believe I borrowed from you, too," she said, turning to her sister. "I paid it back, step by step, nicht?"

Once food was relegated to the second-most concern in the Dubnack-Naumann household, danger stood alone in first place. Hilde Naumann must have felt it keenly. Frau Dubnack said, "Her nerves were pretty much shot. She had gone through all kinds of things. Her mother dead, her sister taken away. And the whole thing, anyway. She was pretty much at the bottom with her nerves. But one was still young. You can bear a lot then."

Frau Naumann did. She even continued to risk day trips outside the apartment. As for the possibility of being caught, inside or outside her sanctuary, she had a plan. It was to follow her mother's example. "If she were grabbed, for that she had a poison pill, nicht?" said Frau Dubnack. "She would have taken it."

An increasing element of Hilde Naumann's fear, and perhaps a reason for her excursions, was very close to home. The apartment house that sheltered her also sheltered not only a number of Nazis, but an SS man a stairwell away. "He paid such attention, looking at everything," recalled Frau Dubnack. "And my friend got scared. I thought, what do you do? What do you do?"

The options were few. If Frau Naumann continued as before, the SS man, or someone else, might spot her running to a public shelter during a bombing attack and wonder, among other things, why she was not going to the building's own shelter. Frau Naumann could, of course, have stayed in the apartment and been killed not by Nazis but by Allies. "The bombing attacks were bigger and bigger and she couldn't stay in the little room when there were attacks. She could have been hit or something. That is bad."

And the nearby public shelters were not completely safe. Adding to the dangers of being seen or recognized was the nondiscriminatory danger of the direct hit. "The attacks were terrible. The attacks were really terrible," said Frau Dubnack. "Here on the Kurfürstendamm there was a public shelter, where she happened not to be, and two hundred people died. The whole house was destroyed. I went there afterward that night, with my son, to look at it. We could not sleep anymore."

Erna Dubnack finally decided to extend the net of safety, with a trick. She went to the home of a woman, "a good colleague and friend," who lived outside Berlin's heavily bombed center. She told her a friend needed a place to stay. "I said, 'You know, she's bombed out and has no one.' I didn't say at all it's a Jew. I knew she wasn't for it. I said, 'Can't you let her stay for just a few weeks, until she has her own place or somewhere else to stay? She's a friend of mine,' and so on. Later, she saw what was going on. But she didn't say no then, either." Frau Dubnack laughed a good long laugh. "But she said, 'Erna, if I'd known her earlier and seen her, I've have been afraid.' Fear! Many were afraid. Many would have helped too, but were afraid. Very much afraid.

"We had to tell her [the colleague] the naked truth," she added. (The German expression translates literally as "We had to pour her the pure wine.") "Because she was there longer than I said, 'two, three weeks at the most.'"

Soon, Hilde Naumann slept again in relative safety. And, "I brought her food, so she would have something to eat. She came back here during the day. It was just so she would have shelter at night." The arrangement lasted "five, six weeks, before the end of the war."

Hilde Naumann survived the Third Reich and the war.

Frau Dubnack did not volunteer a word about the moment she and Hilde Naumann first met again, in postwar peacetime. After my leading questions went nowhere (I was longing for an image of tearful embraces), I finally asked directly. What happened when you two saw each other again?

Frau Dubnack replied, "We were all pleased they were gone."

Frustrated, I kept going. Did Hilde embrace her? Or . . .

"Ach, well," interrupted Frau Dubnack. "Back then we didn't hug each other so much, like today. They copied that from the Russians. I saw it the first time with Khrushchev, how they all kissed cheeks. Now they do it here, too. That didn't used to happen. Except with diplomats or wherever they did that."

It was time to give up, and acknowledge again that Hilde Naumann's life was saved not by gushing sentimentality but by plainspoken decency. Frau Dubnack finally did confirm "my friend" felt easier.

"The torment had ended," added Frau Blisse.

Like her friends, Hilde Naumann soon had other perils to face. Some she may have seen coming; another she did not.

In many German towns, the war ended in a burst of silence. But in Berlin, the surrender could not be heard above the fighting. Last-ditch defenders of the Reich shot at the conquering Russians, who shot back. Civilians dived into cellars to escape ricocheting sniper shots. For women, the danger of being found by a bullet was compounded by the danger of being found by marauding soldiers and raped. No wonder Frau Dubnack did not recall an onslaught of peace. She did recall the confluence of American, English, Russian, and German shells and psyches that shot from day through night and again to day.

She also remembered an earlier overwhelming presence in Berlin—the wounded German soldiers. From a Berlin beach in '35 to a Berlin street in '45, her reactions to suffering had not changed.

"One of them had no leg, everything bloody here, and the other had a wounded arm and the other somehow was wounded in the leg but could sort of hop or was taken care of better. The one who, where it was so bloody, he had a fever and was so thirsty, I said to put his arm over me and let me take him to the streetcar to Westkreuz where we wanted to go. Anyway, I had eggs. [She did not mention that at the time they were worth gold.] The eggs were raw, in a glass, and he had such thirst and nothing to drink and I stirred up a couple eggs for him, several eggs, and he was so thankful to have something liquid. He had such a high fever, nicht? And I went with him to Westkreuz and then there were nurses who took the wounded to Spandau. The Russians weren't there yet. And you know, we always prayed, prayed we did not, but always wished the 'Amis' came to Berlin first. The Americans. We wanted the Americans here. In spite of the fact that we were workers and more for workers. We had heard a lot about the Russians. Seen and heard, ja? And I believed a lot, too. I also experienced a lot. Well,"—she paused—"they didn't have anything to eat either."

In a sense, she judged miscreant German soldiers the same way—speaking of their wrongs, then explaining them briefly in context. "The soldiers took away many bicycles. Our soldiers, nicht? I had nothing. It doesn't matter. They also wanted to save their own lives." One German officer tried to take her bicycle (by war's end it was an invaluable means of transportation), and ordered her to lean it against a wall. "I moved as if I wanted to put it to the side. And I went a little bit, and get up, and away I go. They didn't come after me."

One of her worries at the close of the war was her father—her mother had since died—who lived on the edge of Berlin in a small house near a forest. She and Hilde Naumann used to take the streetcar to go visit him, until the risk of Hilde's being spotted as Jewish was too great. During a pause in the postwar shelling, Frau Dubnack and Frau Blisse, with Peter, managed to get to Herr Krzemieniewski. They found him unscathed, but they unwittingly risked being raped. On a walk in the nearby woods they came across several Russian tanks. They raced back to their father. "He said, 'You both, get in the house right away. Hide. But Peter can stay outside.' They didn't do anything to children. In fact, they were very good to children. One cannot say otherwise. To be sure, they did sometimes rape a child, a girl who was a little older. But they really were good to children." The Russians, as expected, soon came by. "My father and Peter went to the door. He simply went outside with the boy." Somehow Herr Krzemieniewski managed to keep the Russians out. "The whole night long, they crept around the house, but did not come in. I was awake all night. My sister slept, my father too. My Peter too. I couldn't. I was *so* upset and had such a fine sense of hearing, now I don't hear as well, and all night long they crept around. They saw no women and went somewhere else and there raped all the women."

In the following weeks and months, true to her expectations about human behavior, Frau Dubnack encountered Russian men, for better and for worse, as individuals. She and her sister happened upon a younger soldier by himself, who "wanted to talk, and was from the Ukraine." They communicated by kneeling down together and drawing pictures and letters on the earth. She decided he was very good [ganz gut], and got her sister to agree to draw where their father lived, so he would come and protect them. And he did. He also spoke enough German to tell them his politics. He said, "Stalin Schwein. Hitler Schwein." He also warned the sisters about a Soviet officer who was a Schwein too. The officer lured women to his house with the promise of butter. Postwar food shortages being even worse than war shortages, Frau Dubnack went, in a group of four. "He treated us to butter. Well, it wasn't everywhere. And we had nothing to eat. We had no more food at all. Then I wrapped up some here, and here in my bra, for my boy and for Father." She laughed, "There were four of us. He didn't do anything. If we had been alone. . . . Ach, then I wanted to get out of there."

After their young protector left, the situation at Herr Krzemieniewski's worsened. "Then another Russian came, a higher one. And we all had to get out of the house. We were plundered. What I still got later, they took too. My suitcase, for air raids. The most necessary things. Afterward I had nothing at all. What I had on my body. Today one laughs about it a lot. But then, it was not so funny."

Another episode at her father's house must have been, in fact, terrifying. Frau Dubnack spoke of it with her usual understatement. "The Russians came too, my sister was also raped, and I made myself look old and held my Peter to me and they probably overlooked me. They had enough women in the vicinity. That was the worst for us. Ja, that was the worst."

Hilde Naumann, like other Jewish women who survived the Nazis, also faced being raped by the liberators, but apparently was not. (One Jewish survivor, who had been living underground with her mother, said her mother frantically tried to forestall rape by showing their Jewish identity cards to a Red Army soldier, but to no avail; he could not read German.)[4]

Meanwhile, the friendship that was forged in difficulty and tested in trauma stayed strong. Instead of evading Nazis, the two women evaded Soviets. Frau Dubnack happily recalled another joint excursion to gather fruit, during which the women accidentally walked into a Soviet army camp. "I said, 'We have to be very, very quiet, as if nothing's the matter.' We did it very casually, but inside we trembled. Perhaps they would have done nothing to us other than rape us. But that was enough. Anyway, we walked through real fresh, and they didn't do a thing."

The two also accidentally wandered into the American zone too late to get back home before a 9 P.M. curfew. After nobody would open a door and let them in to sleep over, they finally found a shed to sleep in. It was in view of American soldiers. This time, Hilde intervened with the authorities. "My friend knew English, nicht? *Perfectly.* She talked with them and they watched over us. The next day, we went on."

The friends' common adventures and dangers continued, as the two did what they could to get food (Frau Dubnack happily stole it from Russian occupation troops, for whom she had less sympathy than for the fighting troops). Housing was less of a problem. Frau Dubnack's apartment was intact, if full. Hilde Naumann found her own place to stay, and "came to see me all the time." She survived for little less than a year of peacetime.

One April night in 1946, when she was walking alone down a Berlin street, an Allied patrol car ran over her.

Frau Dubnack spoke of the events with a sadness that permeated every word. "She wore glasses and she was so . . . It was probably late. Everything was still dark. There weren't any lights yet. She had gone along the street, for things lay everywhere." She added, "She probably didn't see the car at

---

4. Inge Deutschkron in Helke Sander's 1992 documentary film *Befreier und Befreite* (translated as "Liberators take liberties"). For a superb and personal look into the reactions of a Jewish family as the Third Reich gathered power, see Deutschkron's autobiographical book, *Ich trug den gelben Stern* (I wore the yellow star) (Cologne: Verlag Wissenschaft und Politik, 1978; Munich: Deutscher Taschenbuch Verlag, 1985).

all. An Allied car." Because the police did not tell her otherwise, she deduced the Allies in the car were Americans. She also believed that Hilde had been visiting her longtime boyfriend, a German soldier back from the war. They had met in Frau Dubnack's old athletic "clique." Frau Dubnack believed they were planning to marry.

German medics took Hilde Naumann to a hospital. There she died.

"Gone through the whole war," said Frau Blisse.

"Ja, ja," said Frau Dubnack. "Afterward, both of us were . . ." She cut herself off. "A week before her death she was here. We were here Saturday or was it Sunday and at the time everything was going every which way and she told me, 'I was almost run over.' 'Well,' I said, 'I'll have to collect money for a wreath for you, I can already see it.' Nicht? I was just joking. I didn't mean it earnestly at all. And in a week she was run over." Frau Dubnack paused as if trying to think of what she could say. "Because she was so . . . careless."

Frau Dubnack got the news from one of the medics, who happened to be the husband of a classmate. He said they put her on a stretcher and brought her to the Westend hospital. "Then he, I was still, he told me every-thing, exactly. After one and a half hours . . ." Frau Dubnack stopped and restarted. "She had a concussion. In one and a half hours she was dead."

Hilde Naumann was buried in Berlin's Jewish cemetery in Weissensee. Frau Dubnack said there were "four or six" mourners, among them the boy-friend and herself.

"For a long time, I could not cope with it [Ich hab' das lange nicht verkraftet]." She said nothing more for many seconds. Finally, she said one word. "Ja." She repeated it over and over.

Frau Dubnack filled the decades to come with hard work. She named many jobs, and how long she had them. Five years cutting out patterns for men's coats, two and a half years as a hospital orderly. "Once I worked in a women's clothing company, which I liked a lot. But we had to work fast, everything to the minute and second. It has not been a nice life." Sometimes, she worked two jobs. In her sixties, she cleaned houses. "That was not so simple at all, to earn something."

Her life was not made easier by her marriage. "I was with my husband for twenty-seven years, but not married that long. But . . ." Frau Dubnack stopped, as if getting up her nerve. "The way it was, the men did not return, three million of them didn't come back. And the women were there. My husband also was good-looking." She paused again. "And I didn't pay atten-tion. But he didn't stay with her. Now he's somewhere else. Since '57."

Her son was twenty years old when her husband left her. She did not remarry. "My son had not finished his education, you see. We paid for ev-erything ourselves. There weren't any scholarships and so on, or whatever they get today. We had to pay for it ourselves, school and so on. Then he became an engineer. I wanted that he—he was intelligent, nicht?—that he become something. And then you don't know to whom you 'hold to' afterward. Your son or your husband, your second husband. It's always such a thing when you have children." She said she considered, when she was fifty-five, marrying a fifty-seven-year-old teacher who proposed to her, but she decided not to. "I always thought, ach, now you've become so old, nicht?"

What about when she was so young, I wondered. Did she ever regret hiding her friend?

"Nein. Otherwise I wouldn't have done it. I didn't think about it at all," she added. "What I did, I was responsible for, nicht?" She laughed. "I didn't worry about it. I could laugh. Stupidity must be punished. It is so, nicht?"

You were very brave, I said.

"Do you think so? Ach, well." She muddled about for an explanation. "We went through thick and thin. As children we already had to, nicht? We certainly were not spoiled. And we worked. And when one worked like I worked, you don't have that much time for reflection."

The reason anyone other than the rest of an aging "clique" knows what she did is that years ago (she has no idea how many years) the German government asked anyone who had hidden anyone Jewish to register by a certain date. "I didn't put such a value on it. I reported myself in the last weeks, before it was closed up. I thought, ach Gott, I registered for the sake of Berlin. Really for Berlin. 'Bin eine Berlinerin.' That Berliners were not all so bad. Because it wasn't the case that it all came from Berlin. We weren't at all so very much for Hitler.

"And an acquaintance of [Hilde's] aunt, who was married to a Jewish doctor," said Frau Dubnack, "strongly urged me to go and report you hid a Jewish woman. I thought, well, so that all Germans weren't bad. There were many who also helped, nicht?"

"I am a medievalist," she says in an almost ironic manner. "My dissertation is on the Grail." After getting her bachelor's and master's degrees in Greek and Latin classics at Cornell, she jumped forward a few centuries and got her Ph.D. in comparative literature at the University of California at Berkeley. In her dissertation, she compared Wolfram von Eschenbach's Parzival with the Perceval of Chrétien de Troyes, then brought in last-chapter classics of Virgil and Ovid. She "really had fun working on it." Since then, she has been torn between the academic pleasure of writing more about past millennia and the emotional anguish of doing "something with my story." She has read so much good literature on the Holocaust, she said, and so much bad. "It's so easy to trivialize it."

Rita Kuhn is like all the other women of this book in that she spent the Third Reich within Germany. Unlike them, however, she grew up considering herself Jewish. So did the Nazis, up to a point. The point was her "Aryan" mother.

In the autumn of 1933, when Rita was five and a half years old and just starting first grade in Berlin (she is also the youngest woman in these pages), she was not sure what religion she was, but knew that her world was not what it had been. "My father said, 'Be careful about the men in the brown uniforms.' He said, 'Be quiet, don't attract attention to yourself, don't look at them, and just walk straight.' Possibly with your eyes cast down. That was the first intimation I had that something was amiss. I'm not sure I even knew why I had to be careful of the men in the brown uniforms. I think my father said they don't like Jews. I don't remember. . . ." She recalled, "And from that day on, it was just, I had to be invisible, practically."

Ms. Rita Kuhn

Talking about Silence

"In school, after a few weeks or so, the teacher had to ask the whole class who's Jewish. I looked around the classroom and nobody raised [a] hand. And I remember I wasn't really *sure* whether I was Jewish. It wasn't ever a conscious thing for me. I mean, I went to synagogue, but I didn't know really clearly, Jewish or non-Jewish. And I raised my hand, because," she laughed, "I knew I had *something* to do with being Jewish. And I went home and asked my father, 'What happened, Papa? Am I Jewish?' And he said, 'Yes, you are.'" She said she asked him if she should have raised her hand. "And my father said yes."

She does not recall any anti-Semitism directed at her or her two-years-younger brother, Hans, before the Nazis came to power, but she knows that children in the Charlottenburg area where they lived must have picked some up from their parents quickly. "I remember kids would tease us on the street where we lived. They would call us names. And my brother even remembers some of the rhymes that they said. One day they would call him a 'Dirty Jew' and the next day they would play with him [and call him by an affectionate nickname]. And I remember an incident when . . . I can't have been more than six or so, when the kids on the street, especially boys . . . I played with the children in the street, too, but one day the kids forced me to, to say something in Hebrew. All I knew in Hebrew was what we call the Sh'ma, which we say in extreme situations. And a few prayers that I heard my father say for High Holy Days. I knew a few of them. And I didn't want to use those. They were not to be taken in vain. And they threatened to beat me up if I didn't and they pushed me into a corner. So I said the Sh'ma. And I said maybe half of a prayer. And they left me in peace. I knew right away," she said, that her life had changed.

In January of 1933, her father's life already had changed. "He lost everything. The minute Hitler came to power. Any Jews that had anything to do with money, they were the first to go.

"He lost his job, and I think they confiscated everything he had. Probably whatever savings he had, assets he had. I have no idea. All I remember is that he was just desperate. For four years he didn't have any work. He literally went begging." She remembered him coming home day after day "discouraged and despairing. Couldn't get a job and also couldn't get anyone to help him financially."

Herr Fritz Kuhn had been a kind of combined banker and stockbroker, said his daughter. "I was too little to know" exactly what he did, except that he worked in a bank with connections to a "Börse [stock exchange]." She also knew that at one time in the 1920s, "he was a very rich man. He had two cars, and a chauffeur. He had an American Pierce Arrow and a French little sports car. He courted my mother in it." Her mother, a Lutheran, came from a family that was "all working class. And that was one of the reasons that my father's family didn't want him to marry her." She laughed. "He waited for her for *four* years, he fought it, overcame the opposition of all his family." What about her mother's family? "Oh it was all right with them, I think. I don't think that family had an ounce of prejudice, the ones I remember." Was his family's objection based on religion or snobbery? The latter, mostly, she thinks. "They wanted him to marry a rich Jewish girl." But he married Frieda Krüger, the daughter of shopkeepers, in 1926. The shop was a "soap store," in which laundry products were sold and bed linens were pressed. In the Kuhns' wedding picture, the only members of his family who attended were his parents. "Then, after they got to know my mother, it was 'Friedl' and 'Friedlchen.'"

The extravagant style of the bridegroom did not last long. He was not a very good businessman, his daughter thinks. He lost most of his money in the stock market crash of 1929. He was, however, able to keep his job at the bank.

The family's life was modest; they lived with Herr Kuhn's mother in her apartment. In 1929, the same year as the stock market crash, Hans was born. Sometime after that, possibly before the Nazi takeover (Ms. Kuhn is not certain), the family of four moved to their own place, a small apartment in a dank cellar. "In fact, my mother contracted TB there." She was hospitalized and given an emergency tracheotomy. For a while, she was thought to be near death.

Although Rita Kuhn never said so, once the Nazis took over power in Germany, her mother's health became important to the family for reasons other than affection. Her status as an "Aryan" marriage partner would keep her husband from certain deportation and her children from possible deportation. She also insured, if inadvertently, that her daughter would know two worlds, and become both a "German" witness and a Jewish survivor.

The Nazis classified Rita and Hans Kuhn as "Geltungsjuden," a word that means they "counted" as Jews. The reason they did is that Frau Kuhn, who "wasn't much of a practicing Christian," converted to Judaism when she married, and her children were raised as Jews. Also, in Ms. Kuhn's opinion, the Nazis were so male-oriented that they considered children of Jewish fathers more Jewish than children of Jewish mothers, the opposite of traditional Jewish law. If the Kuhn children had not been raised as Jews, they may have faced fewer strictures. In general terms, all half-Jews, including the Kuhn children, were classified as "Mischlinge [mixtures]."

Rita Kuhn is a mixture in many ways. She is a medievalist who lives in Berkeley, California, and tutors reading and writing at Berkeley High School. She looks young for a survivor. She is simply pretty, with fine gray hair, minimal makeup, delicate features, and a silver-dangle-earrings Berkeley kind of look. Although she is a serious person, she has an impish sense of humor. She mentioned that shortly after the Third Reich ended, someone in Berlin started a school for students like her, half-Jews who had not been permitted to complete high school. The name of the school, she said, breaking into laughter at her English translation, was "High School for Hybrids." Her apartment is a hybrid, too—cats, plants, mementos from the arts-and-crafts days of her four children (she is divorced from their father), a menorah, and a lot of hardbound German classics. It looks like the home of a graduate student. She has been speaking English for so long, with a mixture of British accent ("cahn't") and American slang ("you know"), that we opted to talk in English. It seemed an appropriate choice for someone who has had very ambivalent feelings about the German language.

For her and her family, the trauma of the Third Reich was so great that until a few years ago she "didn't want to have anything to do with Germans at all." She "didn't trust them, didn't want to hear their language spoken," she said. "I have denied my Germanness, my cultural Germanness. I am [now] very proud to be a German, culturally, intellectually. I feel very much an affinity." She half laughs, as she often does, usually at something too ridiculous to be true. "A lot of good has come out of Germany."

Her views are at odds with those of some other survivors, and of some American Jews who have never lived in Germany. "I come to the defense of Germans. When people say, the . . . I say, let's make a distinction between Germans and Nazis. I really insist on that." She said she lost all her friends in the Holocaust and most of her father's family, and has "no reason" to defend Germans, but "I want to be fair." (In one attempt to be fair, in 1988, on the fiftieth anniversary of "Kristallnacht," she returned to Berlin—in defiance of some male leaders of the Bay Area Jewish community—with the express purpose of addressing Berlin high school students about her life during the Third Reich. Their attentive reception was "incredible," she said.)

Back in the early days of the Third Reich, Rita continued going to a regular German public school. "I don't remember any particular anti-Semitism in school, no teasing." But one day her teacher, one Fräulein Opitz, made an announcement. "She told us that any of us interested in joining the BdM . . ." Ms. Kuhn laughed, "I raised my hand. I mean, who doesn't want to be part of a group? And she says, 'Well, Rita, you come up to me after class,' and she talked to me and told me I can't join. So."

What had Fräulein Opitz's attitude been when telling her?

"She was very kind. She was very sympathetic. I think that's why I remember her name. She tried to explain as gently as possible why I couldn't."

And Rita's reaction?

"Disappointed, I suppose," she said, laughing a little. "I couldn't understand what was the matter with me."

Not long thereafter, she recalled, the school's principal asked her father please to take his children out of school because he did not want Jewish children there. Rita and Hans then went to a Jewish school, well before the official order to do so.

Why the Kuhns, so typical of other families who emigrated early, did not emigrate is a question their daughter cannot answer. "I think my father saw the writing on the wall." The only reason she knew of that her father did not try to get the family out was that his mother was alive. (She died in Berlin in 1936.) And in the first years of the Third Reich, the Kuhns basically got by. Rita had enough to eat, thanks to family help and a Jewish welfare organization. And someone sewed clothes for her. But the overall situation, especially her father coming home discouraged every day, was one of increasing emotional strain.

"I remember one incident. It's indelibly etched. My father adored my mother, like a saint, really revered her. At least that's my memory. He always spoke about her in endearing terms. 'Die gute Mama.' 'Our Mama.' The only incident I remember, and it must have been very, very early after Hitler came to power, because I *remember* it. I see in front of me the room where it took place." It was the dank apartment where Frau Kuhn got sick. "I can't have been more than five at the time, when I witnessed a fight between them. An argument, a very bitter argument . . . It was about a racist argument, my father accusing my mother's family of being anti-Semitic and trying to influence her or something, to get her, I don't know, to leave him. My mother defending her family, saying 'They have nothing against you because you're Jewish.' And then it focused maybe on her sister, or something, not all members of the family. 'Your sister doesn't like me because I'm Jewish,' or the son. And I remember that argument. I think there was a time after Hitler came into power, when the Gentile partners were encouraged to leave their Jewish partner." Then "I remember that my father pushed her physically, and that she fell, against a cupboard. I remember that." The family "only had one room. Father already lost his job. It was just crazy, going crazy, you know. What's happening?"

At Frau Kuhn's doctor's orders, the family moved out of the dank apartment and into an above-ground apartment a few houses away. Not long thereafter, the Nazis passed the Nuremberg laws regarding race and citizenship; people registering as Jews, which the Kuhns did, had different citizenship from "Aryans." They were now "Reichsbürger [citizens of the Reich]," whereas Jews became "Staatsangehörige [basically subjects of the state]."[1] From Rita's point of view, the laws meant that Jewish Germans like herself simply were no longer protected by law, and "anyone who wanted to do us harm could."

In 1937, Staatsangehöriger Herr Kuhn got a job. It was with the Jewish Community Organization, the Jüdische Gemeinde. "He helped a lot of Jews leave Germany," she said. "But you know, things were happening all over."

---

1. The *Wegweiser durch das jüdische Berlin* cites the laws, including the stipulation that the Reichsbürger has "German blood" and is the "sole carrier" of "full political rights" under the laws (363).

Frauen

A main thing the next year was "Kristallnacht." Rita was ten years old. She remembered walking as usual to school, about fourteen blocks away, and passing broken shop windows. Suddenly she encountered classmates who told her their synagogue was on fire. Rita turned to passersby, telling them, "Our synagogue is burning!" She remembered them looking away from her, as if they were "ashamed and embarrassed." They said nothing. (One theme she wants to explore in her memoirs is silence. Not to be silent was another reason she returned to Berlin.)

Sometime after "Kristallnacht," she thinks, her cousin—her mother's nephew—joined the Hitler Youth. "We grew up together. We were very close when we were children. He was almost like a brother to me. And when he joined, I was very disappointed." Furthermore, "we had arguments about it. I don't remember what I said, but I remember arguing with him about Hitler. I said, 'How *can* you fall for this? Don't you know what he's doing?' He says, 'Well, but he's good for the country. He's good for the German people. He's got the economy' and blah blah blah." Ms. Kuhn said he "didn't believe anything really bad would happen to us. I remember arguing with him, and my mother . . . turning to me afterward. 'Never do that again. Never talk to him again.' Like that. I said 'Why not?' 'Because you can't trust him.'" Her mother also told her not to talk with her aunt (her mother's sister), because even though she was not for Hitler, she would defend her son. Ms. Kuhn moved her shoulders in a gesture of distaste and said, "Uccccchh."

Another tale about family "race" and rifts was evolving on her father's side. It involved Rita's Tante Ilse, her father's cousin. She married a count, said Ms. Kuhn, with some amusement. "She was Countess von Rohde." She was so striking that she was featured in magazines as one of "the four most beautiful women of Europe. She represented Germany," she said, smiling. "You know, blonde, blue-eyed, kind of like Greta Garbo. So, she married this count without telling him that she was Jewish. And they went to one of those affairs, a ball. One of the gentlemen told the count, 'Your wife, she's so beautiful. . . . It's really hard to believe she's Jewish.'" Ms. Kuhn started laughing. "And the count says, '*What?*' And he went home and confronted her with it. They had a two-year-old son by then. And the next day, [her husband] divorced her."[2]

In 1939, Herr Kuhn, whom his daughter "vividly" recalled as getting many Jews out of Germany, decided to try to insure his children's safety through Christianity. "The only thing that my father did, I was twelve, my brother was ten, he wanted us to be baptized. I refused. I just really fought it. . . . I said 'No, I'm Jewish and I want to die Jewish.' Anyway. His will

---

2. The former countess was deported to Theresienstadt concentration camp and survived. Shortly after liberation, she developed an infection, was given an injection with a dirty needle, and died of blood poisoning.

prevailed. Sunday school. I was baptized." She said the move was too late to help them at all.

Also in 1939, Ms. Kuhn remembered, she and her father listened with increasing fear to the sound of heavy boots coming up the staircase. The fear escalated with each step. Then, a knock on their door. It was a policeman, coming to take away their radio. As of that year, Jews could no longer own them. Cameras either, she said.

The war began. The possibility of leaving Germany was even more unlikely.

The next year, the noose around existence got tighter. The goods allowed on the Kuhn family's ration cards were halved. And the Kuhns were ordered to leave their home. Jews now were prohibited from living in a dwelling owned by a "German." The Kuhns moved into part of a spacious, if subdivided, apartment in a building owned by an American Jew. The building was just doors away from Frau Kuhn's relatives' home and store. It also was across the street from a Gestapo branch office.

The main tenant of the apartment was a Jewish woman, about eighty-five years old. She seemed like a witch to Rita. "Very strange person, never talked to anyone, except the birds." The woman had crammed the contents of her house into the one room she now had, and fed the birds on her balcony. In one sublet section of the apartment lived an anti-Nazi "Aryan" named Frau Schmidt, whom Ms. Kuhn referred to as a "gem of a person" and one of dozens of German women who helped her and her family. Frau Schmidt was not particularly attractive, but "such a loving person," she said, laughing. While Herr Schmidt was off fighting at the front, Frau Schmidt extended her affection to any number of boyfriends. The Kuhns moved into three rooms in another section of the apartment. Rita and her brother and father slept in one room, and her mother alone in another, because of her tuberculosis. (Years later, the Nazis ordered the family to give up one room, which they did. The Jewish widow of an "Aryan" moved in.) Despite a certain closeness, and shared kitchen, the Kuhns realized they now had more space, for a time, than in their former home.

In the meantime, the bombing of Berlin had begun. During air raids, the residents of the four-story building, all "Aryans" except for the Kuhns, ran downstairs and took shelter together in the reinforced cellar. Herr Kuhn missed the daytime bombings; in 1941 he was drafted as a forced laborer and assigned to a railroad station in Berlin. Also that year, he and his children were ordered to wear the star. "By the way, I kept this." Rita Kuhn handed me a yellow piece of cloth with the word *Jude* on it.[3] Actually, it was two pieces of cloth. Her mother had sewn on a lining. That made it more

---

3. The stars were not printed with the female *Jüdin*, so Jewish girls and women lost their sexual as well as individual identity.

durable when being washed, said Ms. Kuhn. Also, it could be pinned on by the lining, and more easily (and illegally) removed.

She said she remembered wearing her star while walking with her mother, who, because of being "Aryan," did not wear one. She remembered her mother being cursed and called a whore. She also said, in one of several conversations we had, that when she was alone and wearing the star she was never harassed. "People looked pained and embarrassed and looked away." More silence.

About the time they got their stars, the Kuhns got new across-the-hall neighbors: a Gestapo woman named Frau Boger and her daughter. Frau Boger was, in fact, "very, very" high up in the Gestapo. Shortly after the Bogers moved in, there was an air raid. Everyone again ran to the cellar. "But when the Gestapo woman . . . saw the star, three stars, [she] said she didn't want to be in the same room with Jews. And so she threw us out. During an air raid. *Bombs* are falling around us. And she wanted us *out*. And I panicked. I just freaked out. I started crying. I don't know what I said, 'I don't want to go out, I'm afraid to go out.' And this woman, a doctor's wife, took me, she put her arms around my shoulders and led me [to an adjoining room] and comforted me. And it was okay in the small room. I felt safe there. I never expected to die in the air raids. Never." She said for the doctor's wife to "declare her loyalty [to a Jewish child] in front of a Gestapo woman, that was not safe to do."

Eventually, Frau Boger, a "mysterious woman, full of contradictions," got to know "our circumstances and realized my mother was an 'Aryan,'" and "she befriended us. She liked us. She thought we were"—Ms. Kuhn paused, laughing slightly hysterically—"'good Jews.'" Frau Boger also told Herr Kuhn that "if all Jews were like you, we would have nothing to hate, or persecute."

The Kuhns apparently were the only Jews Frau Boger had met. "Otherwise, Jews were an abstraction" to her. The families got so close, in fact, that "I had an argument with her, too." Ms. Kuhn laughed. "We were sitting in [Frau Schmidt's] living room, in the apartment. My mother, she, and I and over tea or something. [Frau Boger, like everyone else, was fond of Frau Schmidt and often came to visit.] I said 'How can you believe in the Führer, and what he is doing?' My mother was just . . . out of her mind, you know. She just sat there quietly." And, Rita Kuhn said later, laughing again, "looking paler and paler."

In 1943, Rita also was drafted as a forced laborer. She first worked in an ammunition factory, from 7 A.M. to 6 P.M. There, too, she said, people seemed embarrassed by her star. She recalled that with the hours, and several bombing raids a night, she was tired, as well as numb. "People were anesthetized. I believe that. *I* was. When I think of what we went through . . . There's something that happens to you. I know when we were arrested . . . Panic."

She was arrested twice. The first time was on February 27, 1943. Joseph Goebbels wanted to give Adolf Hitler a birthday present of making Berlin "Judenrein" ["clean" of Jews]. To do so, he instituted the infamous Fabrikaktion [factory action]. Seven thousand Jews still working in Berlin factories were seized, including Rita Kuhn.

She remembered that it was ten minutes after seven. "All of a sudden the whole place was full with SS men, rounding up the Jewish workers. [They were shouting "Juden raus! (Jews out!)" she later recalled.] I was alone then. So. When they loaded us on the trucks, and closed the curtains, and drove off, after a while I know I panicked. I said to the lady next to me, 'They're going to blow up the truck.' She said," Ms. Kuhn whispered in imitation, "'No, they won't do that. In the middle of the city?' " She laughed a little. "So I calm down and a moment later I remember being unloaded. I still see it, a row of SS men on both sides of us. And we go to this building and [are supposed to] go through it. And I did not think I would get through this line, get where I was supposed to go. I was calm, you know? I walked through. And once inside I saw other people. . . . It was better then. And from that moment on, I didn't care what happened to me. I really didn't care. I was numb. I knew that if I have to die, I am going to have to die. . . . You needed that internal defense, or armor, to put on. I think that was true for a lot of people." She added, "The only thing that troubled me was my parents. Also not knowing what happened to them. Being separated. And my mother particularly. I worried about them, and if I would find them again, if I ever get out. What if I don't ever see them again, you know. I worried more about how they would feel."

She said the women in the building, who had been separated from the men, "felt a real solidarity" and began talking to each other and getting rid of any jewelry and money they had on them, flushing it all down the toilets. "They didn't want to give anything to the Nazis, the SS." Ms. Kuhn said she had little more than her subway fare, and for some reason, kept it. She and the other women were held at the center all day and into the night. At about ten o'clock they were told to line up. What she called a "selection process" began. "All the people were going left, or right. Most of the people went left." She paused. "That meant to the camp."

"There were rows of SS, at tables, and looking through their papers. And most of the people went left. . . . And when it came my turn, there was a girl before me, and when she went through her papers and [an SS man] asked questions and told her to go right. She was released. When it came my turn, I didn't think it would happen twice." She laughed, a little. "So I gave my name, and whatever questions they asked me and I think they asked me about my mother. 'Ist sie arisch? [Is she Aryan?]' they asked." Her identification stated that both parents were Jewish. But her mother's name did not include the middle name Sara that the Nazis insisted be on the identification cards of all Jewish women. The SS man continued his questions.

459

"'Wohnst du mit ihr? [Do you live with her?]' 'Ja, ich wohne mit ihr.' And, hm, go right, you can go home.' And I didn't believe him. I stood there. 'GEHEN SIE NACH HAUS! SCHNELL! [Go home! Fast!]'" She laughed again. "And I went out, and I wasn't very joyous. I wasn't very joyous. I remember that. I was really saddened."

Outside, she saw the girl who had been ahead of her in line. She was just standing there. "I said, 'Where are we?' And we had no idea. In those days, Berlin was black. There was no light anywhere. Everything blacked out. And we walked around and found a U-Bahn [subway] station and I went there. . . . We hadn't eaten anything all day. We were not supposed to take our lunch with us, anything. I wasn't even hungry. I just couldn't think of food. But I had money to get home. And so I went home. She had to go another way, I went my way. And I'll never forget, it was late at night, it was almost eleven at night. People on the subway. And I looked at them. They were all sleeping, [or] sitting there. I felt like I was in another world. From that moment on, I felt such, I don't know what it was. . . . A feeling of, if only you knew what is happening. I looked at them and I said [silently], 'How can you be so indifferent? How can you go about your own way? When there are thousands and thousands of people being sent to their death?' And there were thousands of people in that hall. Really, thousands."

Did she know they were going to certain death?

"Oh yes. Yes." She added, if not to immediate death, then to eventual death. When questioned more closely, she said, "We really didn't know what was happening. [We] knew Jews were dying of disease and starvation." But she "did not know of crematoria and shootings . . . until after the war."

When I later called her to double-check some of her testimony, I asked about that, and if she had not known of the gassings. "Not at *all*," she said. In a speech she delivered in August 1992 at a rally opposing Serbian human rights abuses, she said, "It was not until 1945, after I had seen the liberation of the concentration camp at Buchenwald on a movie screen and learned of other death camps that I knew that many members of my family and all those friends who had disappeared after 1942 would never return."

As for her own fate the day of her arrest: "I knew if I was sent away that I wasn't going to come back," she whispered, "and wasn't going to see my parents again. I really was just prepared for death. I just remember that feeling. I almost felt a kind of superiority." On the subway ride, she said, she thought she covered her star, as she often did. "I was afraid," she laughed, "they would come and get me again. Just my luck.

"Then I finally found my way home. And . . . it was eleven o'clock at night. And I rang the bell. My father didn't answer the door. Neither did my mother." She paused. "Or my brother." That day, she later learned, the Nazis had come and taken away the old woman who talked to the birds. So, when Rita rang the bell, her family was inside, terrified, and sure the bell meant the Nazis now had come to get them, too.

Finally, Frau Schmidt opened the door and saw not Nazis but Rita. When her father, overcome by a mixture of relief and joy, came up to her, he collapsed in her arms.

A week later, as the Fabrikaktion continued, the Nazis arrested Herr Kuhn and both his children. "We were home. It was a Saturday. And my mother went to get the ration card[s]. . . . She went to the school where she usually got them. . . . And she came back and said we have to get them ourselves. So my father knew then that they had made a mistake when they released me. And they got wise, or examined the records again. [He] said, 'This is it.' He said, 'Put on a double layer of clothes.' My father was a very strange man, a very difficult man. But there was one moment when he was strong. He broke down very easily, anger and all that, complained about this and that. But boy, whew, he was so calm then." He made sure his children were extra-warmly dressed and then took them to where the ration cards were handed out. "We were the first ones to arrive in the school and they closed us off in a room, and locked the door behind us.

"And then my father knew, for sure, he had been right. Then we waited and waited, and eventually more people from the street came." One was "a good friend of ours," their subtenant of sorts, the widow of an "Aryan," with whom she had two daughters who (unlike Rita and Hans Kuhn) had never been registered as Jewish. "And pretty soon the whole room filled up." One person showed up voluntarily. It was a "German" friend of her father's. "Here's another example of a German . . . declaring his loyalty to a Jew. He pushed his way through the SS and forced his way through the opening in the door, and peeked in and said, 'Hello.' And brought us something, or wanted to bring us something." She said the man could have been punished for his act, but was not. "In '43, I really feel the Germans were not as secure anymore. . . . They yelled it over the radio that they are going to be victors. But I don't think deep down they really felt it. So they had to be a little more careful about what they were doing, because they knew they might be held to account." At another point, Rita heard "a woman crying outside, wanting her children and not just wanting to see them, but 'I want to *be* with them, I want to *go* with them.' And I would hear that. . . . I didn't even recognize the voice. But my father said, 'That is Mutti, our Mutti.'" She was not let in.

When enough people for a transport had gathered, they were led outside. "Then we were loaded on the truck." While being loaded, Rita saw her mother. She "just stood there. And we were on the truck. And there she was, waiting. The daughters of this friend of ours were there too, looking. I'll never forget my mother's face. Just white. And stony. By that time, everything had gone out of her. I mean, she couldn't even *say* anything to us. She could hardly wave. Anything." One daughter of the Jewish mother fainted. Her mother on the truck cried out to her and tried to move forward. "We were right at the edge of the opening, and I saw on both sides there were

SS men. I saw this very young SS man, with his gun over his shoulder. I watched his face. [He was] moved, somehow. He looked embarrassed. He looked *pained*. There were a lot of tears as we were leaving. Our family was left behind. You know," she said, half laughing, "he was really moved. And," she laughed again, in a choked way, "I felt like putting my hand on his shoulder. It's the craziest thing. It was crazy. I mean, he was so young. He was obviously uncomfortable. And here the mother was crying out because her daughter had fainted, and here this young man, I think he had tears in his eyes, actually."

The trucks drove off. They were the army type, she said, with canvas "curtains" in the back, drawn closed so people on the streets could not see inside. "They really tried to conceal as much as they could." The trucks arrived at a holding center on Rosenstrasse. The females and males were separated. "I came into a room with just women, maybe four or five women in there, lying on straw mattresses, and they had been there the whole week. I remember three of them didn't even talk. To me, or anyone. They were already like . . . I don't what happened to them." One woman did finally talk to her. She told her about what had been going on outside, as of Sunday, February 28, the day after the first mass arrests.

As is well documented, the arrests, mostly of Jewish husbands of "Aryan" wives, prompted those wives to stage a mass protest outside the Rosenstrasse center. The women's numbers and courage grew hour by hour and day by day, through the nights, as they shouted, "We want our husbands." They were ordered to disperse. They refused. Other Germans joined them. The Nazis aimed machine guns at them. They still refused to move. The Nazis did not fire. The crowd grew. The demonstration, unique within the Third Reich, lasted for several days. The woman on the straw mattress had heard the chants and so had SS men inside the center. The woman told Rita that one SS man entered the room where she was and said of the women yelling outside, "These are *our* Germans. We are proud of them." He admired their sense of "deutsche Treue" [German loyalty]. (Hans Kuhn corraborated the story. An SS man had said the same thing in his room.)

The woman on the mattress also witnessed another scene. One prisoner was the Jewish wife of an "Aryan." He and their son, who was raised as a Gentile, came to the center to inquire about her. The SS checked into the case and told them that she would be free to go if they would take her home with them. They declined to do so. The SS men became so infuriated, they yelled at the "Aryan" husband and son that they were "Schweine" [pigs] and told them, "Get out of here. You don't deserve to be German."

Rita spent the night at Rosenstrasse. The night included a bombing attack. The prisoners were not allowed to seek shelter.

She spent most of the next morning standing in lines and showing her papers. As in the previous collection center, the Nazis "were always very civil to me. Not hostile at all. Just very official. Courteous, almost. It was very strange."

What happened next is "all a haze." She knows that on March 6 she and her brother were released. But even now she is not certain if her father was freed that day or later. She does recall that when she went outside, a civilian man across the street gestured in a kind of victory sign. And she is certain that without the protests by the "Aryan" women (which her own mother apparently had not known about), she and her brother and father would have been deported.

Home life continued, in its way. An "Aryan" moved into the bird woman's apartment. She, too, befriended the family and was "awfully nice." And she was a prostitute. She brought her customers, German soldiers and SS men, home with her.

After Rosenstrasse, Rita and her father continued to wear their stars, but Hans refused. He was blond and blue-eyed ("we did not look Jewish," said his sister) and was not stopped, even by the guards at the Gestapo branch office who must have recognized him. (She theorizes they let him have his way because they knew that his Hitler Youth cousin was by now a soldier on the eastern front.) But Frau Boger of the Gestapo certainly knew Hans was Jewish, and starless. What did she do about it?

She took him to the movies. Frau Schmidt went, too. Rita Kuhn had forgotten the incident, but Hans had not.

Once "free," Rita and her father resumed work as forced laborers, both in railroad stations. She did "different things, mostly outside work." She especially remembered a cold-weather job of cleaning the outsides of "very, very dirty windows" of army troop transports back from the eastern front, and carrying a ladder down the length of the trains. Sometimes she worked underneath the cars, oiling them. Her coworkers were "regular" Germans, as well as French, Spanish, and Ukrainian forced laborers, mostly women. She said only the Ukrainians expressed anti-Semitism toward her.

Herr Kuhn, meanwhile, loaded and unloaded freight trains. He was the only Jewish man among older "Aryan" coworkers, and his experiences with them, she said, were "all positive." All the men stole butter and cheese from the trains. "One time somebody noticed that my father had stolen some cheese. You could smell it, for one thing. And one of his coworkers defended him and got him out of the situation." Another time, Herr Kuhn was going home on a hot, packed streetcar after work, with cheese strapped inside his clothing, his star on the outside. Soon, people backed so far away from him that he even was able to sit down, something Jews were not usually allowed to do. He thought they were repelled by the "stinky Jew," she said, but then he realized that what they were smelling was not him but melting cheese. This is considered a very funny story in the Kuhn family.

In comparison to what was coming, it was.

Toward the end of the war, the Russians surrounded Berlin. "There was constant artillery. We lived in the basement for ten whole days." She said that after a while, there were intervals, then regular intervals, during which "we would go shopping. At least we had a bakery [nearby]." During one interval, Frau Boger went to get bread, and Rita and her father went upstairs to get something from their apartment. "While we were up there, we heard this tremendous sound, whistling. It was a bomb. We were in the living room and my father said, 'Come on, let's get in the hall, away from the window.' And it hit very, very close by. It was what they called the 'Stalinorgel.' It was very highly explosive and made a huge noise. . . . The whole house shook. And we went downstairs and then there was quiet again. And my father said to me, 'Puppchen [Dolly],' he always called me Puppchen, 'Why don't you go get us some bread.' I said, 'Okay.' So I went outside, and as soon as I got to the corner, I [would turn] left, and left again, and there was the bakery. And I came to the corner and everything changed. I couldn't recognize . . . I thought I was in another city. Everything looked very, very unfamiliar. The trees had lost all their leaves. And buildings on both sides were . . . little holes, big holes, and just the whole area is devastated. I thought this is strange, what happened?" She laughed. "But, my dad told me to get bread, I have to get bread. And I walked on, and I looked at the trees, and I saw pieces of clothing on the trees. Pretty soon, as I got closer to the bakery, there were pieces of human flesh. They were all over, everywhere. On the trees, on the balconies, pieces of clothing, pieces of human flesh. . . . I almost fell over a woman, lying there in the street, dead, with her legs blown off. And I couldn't find the bakery. I walked on and I passed a house, and I could see a lot of people, moaning, crying. And I came to where I thought the bakery was, and there was just a big hole. Sure enough, that's where it had hit, and people hadn't had time to take cover.

"So I came home, no bread. And the daughter of this Gestapo woman, we were friends, we actually were friends. Especially during those ten days, we got really close. And she said her mother hadn't come back from getting bread. Then we figured she must have been there. And nobody wanted to go see. Among either the wounded or the dead. . . . So my grandfather, who was a World War One veteran, he volunteered to go and look for her. He asked the daughter what she had worn." He did not find her.

"Now, we think she died there. The only other reason for her disappearance could be that she got out with the SS, and lived in hiding. If she did, she never contacted her daughter."

The reason for the speculation was an unnerving postwar experience. The four Kuhns all survived, but learned that the Nazis thought they had not.

"After the war, my father was walking down the street to work and he heard his name called. He recognized the man he had worked with in the Jüdische Gemeinde. He was in an American uniform, of a major. And the man couldn't believe that was my father he saw. He said, 'You're *alive?*' He said, 'Yes, I'm here, it's me.' And he said, 'What about your family?' And he said, 'My immediate family, my wife and children survived. But I lost all my other relatives. Twelve,' he counted. He had a very small family, fortunately. . . . I remember aunts, uncles, never came back. 'But,' [the man in uniform] said, 'I still cannot believe it.' He said, 'I just came from Gestapo headquarters,' which was just around from Rosenstrasse. 'It's my job to look at the files of Berlin Jews and what happened to them. And I looked through all files and came across your name. Kuhn, Fritz. Rita. Hans. And right across the file was [the word] *Erledigt.'* " The word basically means "done," and implied the family was dead.

"So when he saw my father, naturally . . . My father mentioned that incident, and we never thought about it. It came to me one sunny day in California as I was walking, grocery shopping. I felt, you know, what a beautiful day, how wonderful life is. And all of a sudden," she sort of laughed, "I remember how close I came, not to be here. And I remember this and I thought, who could have put it on? I mean, I think it was an inside job. I don't think it was a mistake. . . . My theory is, either it was done on Rosenstrasse, while we were there, to prevent any such thing again, for our protection. Or it was done, and this might be the most bizarre thing, and there's no way I could ever prove that, it was done by [Frau Boger].

"She was very high up in the Gestapo. And she liked my mother particularly. She also liked my father. And when we were arrested, maybe that's what she did. She went and put that stamp on it."

Back in May of 1945, just after Frau Boger's presumed death, Russian troops took over the neighborhood. They ordered the residents of the Kuhns' apartment building to gather in a room on the first floor. They did so. The group, including from one apartment the four members of the Kuhn family, the very affectionate "Aryan" (Frau Schmidt), the prostitute, and, from across the hall, the daughter of the presumed dead Gestapo woman, may not have been the most diverse assembly of Germans that day, but it may have come close.

At the time the group assembled, the raping of German women, whether "Aryans" or Jews, was rampant. Rita was then seventeen. "We all sat there, and were hiding our faces, with kerchiefs on. You've heard stories like that. And we waited there. And three Russian officers came into the room. I think they were officers. And they looked around at everybody, and they looked at me. And they came toward me," she said, half laughing. "And she [the prostitute] saw that. Lydia was her name. She saw them come toward me, and she came to them and she says"—Ms. Kuhn gestured with her forefinger—"'Come.' And she took all three of them. They all followed her. So, that was another German woman."

One of Rita Kuhn's themes, in recounting her experiences in the Third Reich, is that over and over, "Aryan" German women helped her live. They included the doctor's wife in the bomb shelter, the strangers in the protest outside Rosenstrasse, maybe Frau Boger, and certainly Lydia the prostitute. And most of all, they included Frau Frieda Kuhn.

Much later, Hans, wrote his sister a letter about their mother's role. (The Kuhns all planned to emigrate to the United States, but after Rita got permission first and left in 1948, expecting her family to follow, Frau Kuhn came down with Parkinson's disease and could not be moved. Her husband stayed with her. And Hans decided to stay, too. He became a Berlin police-man.) This is part of Rita Kuhn's translation of his letter: "It is true beyond question that we owe our survival to Mama. That should diminish neither her memory nor her dignity. But I take it for granted and don't consider it a special merit, if you do not part from people you love in times of crisis." He continued, "It was not a question of sacrifice or courage for Mama to remain at our side. We gave her life meaning and purpose, and that is not something one parts with easily. It's as simple as that."

One time Ms. Kuhn and I met just after I had attended a colloquium about revisionists' views of the Holocaust.[4] The revisionism in question did not have to do with disputing the facts of the Holocaust but with suggesting it is only one of many massive slaughters in history. Ms. Kuhn said she thinks there *is* indeed a danger in maintaining the uniqueness of the Holo-caust. "If it is a one-time freak event in history, then you don't have to worry." She added, "The uniqueness about the Jewish murders is it was geno-cide, it was planned genocide. And if the Allies hadn't won over Hitler, he really would have made it worldwide. He really was out after the extinction of the Jewish people. I mean, that is unique."

What is also frightening, she said, is "that Hitler tapped on something that wasn't only German. He had collaborators." She spoke of pogroms and massacres in Russia and Poland "long before Hitler." And as for the Third Reich, she said, survivors from Auschwitz have told her that "sometimes the Ukrainians were more cruel and more vicious than the SS." One example she heard of was of Ukrainians loading prisoners into coal cars steeply slanted like a long *V,* to go (she thinks) to Dachau. The shape of the cars insured that people literally slid down on top of others. During the long ride, those below slowly suffocated, while those on top fought desperately to stay on top. When the transport arrived at its destination, accompanied

4. The colloquium, called "Rewriting German Fascism," took place at the University of California—Berkeley in March 1988.

466

throughout by Ukrainians, the SS people who unloaded it "were horrified." She cited Ukrainians supposedly being particularly ruthless at Treblinka, and Poles massacring Jews who came back from the death camps. "And there were French collaborators," she added.

She said what is frightening to her is that "it could happen in America. If we didn't have the government we have."

If one could say that German women were confronted by a great test and for the most part failed it, what can be said about American women, if they were to face it?

She said that she rejects the assertion by some survivors that "there is a Hitler in all of us," because he was a "systematic killer." But if one were to say there is "evil in all of us, yes." She said she believes that "Hitler tapped on something that's not particularly German. I mean, there is prejudice all over the world. There's fanaticism, intolerance for other . . . I mean, that is basically human nature."

Conclusion

Long before the interviews ended, I feel compelled to say, I was almost immobile from sadness. I wish so much that a *handful* of hateful men had been taken seriously and had been dissuaded, or had been locked up, or had found good jobs and loving women, or men, or that at some early point, Germans and non-Germans butted into, meddled, intruded into things that arguably were none of their business, and that consequently nearly *forty million* people either born in the European (and west Asian and north African) continent, or sent to fight what the handful of men unleashed, had died naturally. I wish so much that this book did not have cause to be written.

Because there was cause, however, it is appropriate to take a backward look at what we have just seen, whether in printed words or in our minds' eyes, and try to examine it unblinkingly. We know that none of us will understand all of why what happened happened, why the handful of men (brought from infancy to childhood to adulthood mostly by women) became so hateful, and why their hate was so contagious. Short of such understanding, we look for answers in the evidence accumulated here before us. At first glance, it may seem that all we have are female-related pieces of the Third Reich puzzle spinning by, taunting attempts to be placed within a greater picture, much less to be accorded any significance.

Perhaps because I have been with the women so long, a kind of group portrait has emerged in my own mind's eye. To me, it is enormously revealing. I see women from highly diverse backgrounds, women mostly in the prime of youth, health, and high-mindedness, being met head-on by the aggregate force of National Socialism, itself buttressed by the aggregate forces of German traditions. I see some women embrace National Socialism, others waver in its shadow, then fall, and others never even stumble. I see the women cheer, doubt, fight, and tremble. I see them inhale idealism and exhale enmity, and vice versa. I see them make up their own minds and I see them let their minds be made up for them. I see them look to the outside world for reaction and watch the outside world pay homage to Adolf Hitler by sending their diplomats to meet him and their athletes to compete under his swastika flag. I see a surprising number of the women's families divide and unite, and unite and divide. I see the women's own lives expand and contract. I see the women coping, or not, with logistics, with doses of still-potent propaganda, with babies, with orders and more orders, with bombs and more bombs, with ill will and good intentions, with atoms of decency and crates of cowardice—both theirs and others'—with fear that explodes from tension to terror, with death and more death, with reticence, with opportunism, and with courage as pure as light. I see privilege and formal education taking a back seat to lessons in decency and fairness learned at home. I see the women face day-to-day consequences of the Third Reich with varying morsels of impudence or despair, with hesitation or hope, or humor, with prejudice, with contradictions, with shame, with first refusals and second thoughts, and with blinders.

Later, I see many of the women gradually, or suddenly, learning they had been had, and by whom, and about what, and I see them either take a step toward or a step away from learning more. I notice those who had opposed and risked their lives taking no pleasure in having been prescient, and being the most self-critical later. And I notice something of the opposite phenomenon taking place, too.

Some pieces of the puzzle form what looks like a kind of tortured ballet of exoneration danced over the women's and their country's past. Not all the pirouettes are false, if we take the women at their word. Some women really had meant well. Some really did sense a call to idealism. After the Nazi takeover, there really was more work and more food and less political gang warfare in the streets. And life really did seem normal again, at picnics and hikes and birthday parties and romantic encounters. Whatever women meant by "politics" really did not welcome them, never had. (What sphere of nation-directing influence ever had?)

As for anti-Semitism, some women really did not know any individual Jews well. Some women really did feel helpless before the cynically masterful anti-Semitic propaganda machine. Anti-Semitism really had been around before the Nazis. (Where did Erna Dubnack's "Egg Jew," the "Eierjude," come from? Or was that just a figure of speech, like Gretl Sasowski's "the Jew Boehm"?) Some of the ballerinas' most desperate leaps fill the stage. There really was a high percentage of Jews in glamorous careers. Some Jewish businessmen presumably did swindle some customers—just as other German businessmen did, said those who did not need to leap. The Nazis' anti-Semitic actions really could be seen as a passing phase. (Some German Jews certainly believed that.) And they did not want them killed—just curtailed.

One thing the women did not mention directly was that by the time large groups of Jews disappeared, they were all but out of sight already (if not as far out of sight as the Gypsies long had been). Jews were out of "German" classrooms. Out of "German" homes, offices, and hospitals. Out of "German" apartment buildings. Out of the stores at certain times. Out of the movies. Off the streetcars. Off the streets.

And when they began disappearing from the streets, there really was no way to find out where they—or anyone else—had gone, that is, without endangering oneself. There really was reason to be afraid. As the actions and years of the Third Reich accumulated, as eyes were opened and borders were closed, there were many, many reasons to be afraid.

The hard-core Nazis, as we all have seen, spent most of the performance backstage, fogging up their dressing room mirrors with exhalations of alibis. They look, and see nothing. The hard core know they are not as supple as the others, that if they do not stick with what they used to believe, they would crack.

One element of the ballet of exoneration that is especially striking was how many women, even the old Nazis, grasped at the one dance partner who could perhaps grant them salvation: the Hausjude [the "house Jew"]. The well-known, and disparaged, phenomenon refers to a Jewish person whom a non-Jew can point to as having known and liked, and thus prove an absence of anti-Semitism. I was unaware how many Hausjude ghosts exist—in the face of a shopkeeper, in a teacher's visit to a child's sickbed, in memories of neighbors. The leap to salvation is not just in knowing one had a Hausjude, but in knowing that the Hausjude left in time. Even Mathilda Mundt spoke of delivering food to a Jewish family which, she claimed, later lived in splendid wealth in New York. She, too, can sleep. The Hausjude who escaped and prospered in America became the first patron saint of post-war Germany.

The ballet occasionally takes shameful pratfalls. Some women need to point out that they did not *personally* murder, or to put it even more coarsely, did not *personally* push their Hausjude into an oven. So many Germans must have made similar comments that an expression has evolved. "I did not bend a hair of a Jew's head." (I heard it and its equivalents more than once.) Ellen Frey's friends did not personally know anyone who was gassed. Regina Frankenfeld explained that the persecution of the Jews was not in the women's division.

A couple of women also needed to point out that "the Jews" are back and doing well in Germany again. They are on television again, own department stores again. A reemerging Jewish community in Germany, as well as tales of success of Jews anywhere in the world, may act as more psychological salvation. It shows they did not kill them all, after all.

I saw too, as a finale to the ballet, that many women did reproach themselves. Many rued that by the time their eyes opened to the Nazi agenda it was too late to act. An East German (whose interview is not included) specifically criticized herself just for being "dumm." Many women recalled a particular Jewish person whose murder they guessed, or knew about. Unless I was conned over and over, the women still seemed affected.

They also rejected, even as a topic of conjecture, the possibility of intervention, especially late intervention. More women than I anticipated spoke of cowardice. The cynic in me sometimes saw cowardice as an alibi nearly as airtight as two others that spin by in the puzzle, ignorance and

fear. What could presumably terrified, uninformed, unorganized, women civilians in the spiderweb of the Third Reich do to stop Hitler and his war?

Yet, almost every woman wanted Hitler and his war to stop, at least by
the last years. What about wanting, or trying, to stop earlier acts against
one's neighbors or colleagues? (Actually, the Nazis sometimes announced
anti-Jewish strictures only in Jewish newspapers, to keep the news from the
German public.) Or were such acts, and responses to them, repressed?

Repression. The word warrants its own picture. It is a delicate, intricate
matter in Germany. Indeed, the word *repression* [Verdrängung] has become
so well known among the generation to which it most frequently is applied
that several women spoke of it rather like a psychological companion, as in
"Maybe I 'verdrängt' what happened." Perhaps the best explanation may be
found within the widely cited thesis by a German sociologist team, Alexander and Margarete Mitscherlich, in their book *The Inability to Mourn*. To
put part of the thesis in lay terms, immediately after the stress and terror of
the war, Germans faced a number of emotionally stressful circumstances.
Their country had been bombed into rubble. Many people had lost their
homes and all or much of what was in them. Their government had presided
over the second unconditional surrender of the century. Many men they had
known and loved were dead, for a cause that in its "idealistic" swaddling
many people (especially impressionable young people) had believed in
blindly. By the time the cause was lost, it proved to have been reprehensible.
A predictable response would have been mass exorcism, sought individually
in psychiatrists' offices, alcoholism, acts of penance, or just weeping and
talking it through. In the Mitscherlichs' word, mourning. Instead, as Margarete Mitscherlich said in a later edition of the book, there ensued a "psychological immobilization of the German postwar society."[1] Germans
imploded into repression.

They were aided in doing so, it seems almost too obvious to say, by
the all-encompassing physical challenge, that is, the postwar turmoil of
hand-to-mouth survival many Germans say was starker than the war. The
often-repeated slogan, "If you think war is bad, wait until you have to go
through peace," proved especially true in urban areas. (In 1946, an estimated
75 percent of Berlin children were undernourished.) I believe that Germans,
including many in these pages, were aided in repression by another obvious
fact. The victims were gone. Many Germans, especially women, still on the
home front, had to see the victims on the Allies' documentary film footage,
but not in person. Accusatory eyes of the Hausjude did not follow a woman
home. And gone from sight were not only the victims but places associated

---

1. *Die Unfähigkeit zu Trauern* (Munich: R. Piper & Co. Verlag, 1967). Citation, my
   translation, from 1985 edition, 368.

with them. Much of urban Germany, where many of the victims had lived, worked, and worshipped, was unrecognizable.

The passage of time helped develop repression, too. To take an extreme example, if a woman saw Jewish neighbors being dragged away by the Gestapo, she might later have comforted herself by saying she could not have stopped it, then, she wished she had not seen it, then, she did not see it that well, then, it is hard to remember, and finally, she does not remember. It is possible, in my opinion, that her conviction is honed to the point a lie detector would register that she is telling the truth. The phenomenon, as psychologists around the world might agree, is hardly German.

Verdrängung (in addition to Allied money) must also have speeded Germany's famously fast postwar rebuilding—got the streets cleared faster, the mortar mixed faster, the curtains hung faster. New buildings hold few reminders of the past.

As our mental picture shows end and the range of repressions has been noted the related issue of truth remains. I may as well say point-blank, I believed most of the women most of the time. That includes believing what I did not want or plan to believe, including that Anna Fest, the concentration camp guard, was not anti-Semitic. I also believe that fear was a factor in almost all lives. I do not believe that all the women confided their most anguished memory, or had not repressed it, or had not forgotten other things (including "good" things), or that the women did not at times try, as most people probably would, to put the best light on their actions and inactions. But I believe that most of the women thought what they did say was true.

Perhaps I believed them because they could have said no to an interview, or because of their body language, or because so much of what they said simply rang true, or in general terms was corroborated by books as well as by accounts of survivors I read or heard or watched in films or on television.[2] Perhaps I believed the women because they often fretted about accuracy, about what happened when, about what they knew when. And perhaps they were wrong or I was fooled. I learned that my own memory about at least three interviews was wanting. The tapes corrected me, while confirming my trust in tape recorders over people with pencils. In part because of my own lapses, I think more in terms of the women's "truth" and truth, than Truth.

Where is "truth"/truth/Truth in regard to the answer to the question many non-Germans (not including myself) think the most important one—what did the German women know of genocide?

Apart from my view that this one question must be answered indi-

---

2. A major source was the illuminating once-a-week cable series by the Holocaust Oral History Project of San Francisco.

vidually because of the vast differences in the women's lives, there are reasons to believe women who said they did not know what was happening in the camps. One is that they did say they knew the camps existed. Another is that the Nazis made great efforts to keep information about what was happening in all the camps from the German public. The efforts began with threats against inmates released in the early years of the regime, and ended with locating specifically intended death camps out of Germany and murdering the wretched prisoners who were forced to "staff" the gas chambers and the ovens.

Another reason to believe the women is the testimony of people we have reason to trust, like American GIs. Many have been quoted as saying they did not know what had been going on in the camps until shortly before their macabre hour of liberation. One veteran who helped liberate Dachau recalled, "The people came walking out of these buildings in all stages of emaciation and they wanted to hug us, embrace us, and we kept saying no." The soldiers saw the striped camp uniforms and assumed that the prisoners were criminals.[3] Other people we have reason to trust include Jewish survivors. Why have so many survivors and families of survivors spoken of Jewish Germans fearfully, but in heartbreaking innocence, following orders to pack their clothes for a move to some "work camp" in the "east"? Many did believe. Why was the Nazis' ghastly ruse about taking a "shower" in a gas chamber so successful? It was not only intimidation; many still believed. And in Auschwitz itself, a few (whose testimonies I am aware of) believed. One woman testified, "Even though I had been in Auschwitz, I did not know about the gas chambers. Can you imagine that?"[4] Another survivor of Auschwitz told me that when he was in a labor camp in 1942, a Jewish man came into his barracks and said that elsewhere Jews were being gassed, and that he did not believe him.[5] The exchange is not unique in the annals of Holocaust testimony. And Rita Kuhn said she did not know. And Freya von Moltke spoke of the difficulty her husband had—he, a member of the German high command—in finding out what was going on. But he did find out.

There also are reasons *not* to believe women who said they did not know. The killing apparatus was so big, holes developed. That is what Karma Rauhut said, and she said she knew. Tini Weihs said she knew, too, in part because the Jews were not coming back. Margret Blersch knew about murders of "Aryan" innocents. So did Wilhelmine Haferkamp. If news of individual murders (although committed close to home) of hapless mental

---

3. Paul Parks, former soldier of the Army Corps of Engineers, quoted in the *New York Times*, June 3, 1988.
4. Marika Frank Abrams is quoted in Sylvia Rothchild, ed., *Voices from the Holocaust* (New York: New American Library, 1981), p. 190.
5. Conversation with Hans Hirschfeld in San Francisco, 1988.

patients got through, would news of mass murders not get through? It did, in a way. But apparently not by way of the strictly forbidden radio reports; as far as I know, the BBC and other broadcasters were not well informed, either. Instead, sometimes reports of genocide got through via witnesses, whether survivors or soldiers, whom people either believed or not. Or they got through via rumors (a staple of information and misinformation within the severely censored Third Reich), which people either believed or not. One rumor was that the Nazis could listen to everything in your home through your telephone, even if it was not in use. (Just to be safe, some people covered their phones with a tea cozy.) One rumor was that after the war all couples without children would be forced to divorce. Another rumor was that somewhere the Nazis were gassing the Jews.

I do not know who heard that rumor, or report, or who believed it, much less risked the danger of repeating it. I do believe that some Jews could not or would not believe it, and that some Gentiles could not or would not believe it. Both groups certainly had their reasons.

As indicated earlier, however, what the German women knew or did not know about the "final solution" is not, to me, the most important gleaning from their testimony. To me, the most important parts are what happened much earlier, at the personal stages mere mortals can comprehend. Surely that is why it is so much easier to condemn what others did at Auschwitz in the 1940s than to condemn what one oneself did at home in the 1930s. Surely that is why it is easy to decry the soul-searching atrocities being perpetuated (as I write) in Bosnia, like that of a young mother being gang raped by four Serbians, enduring it silently, then asking to nurse her baby crying by her side, and in response one Serb cutting off the baby's head and handing it to her.[6] Who could not cry at and decry such abominations? But who is trying to stop them? Who is willing to die to stop them? On the home front of my own country, it is easier to decry abominations in Serbia than to give more than a dollar and a glance and a mumbled word or two to any of the countless homeless people I pass when venturing not far at all from my home. There are levels of abominations, including the responses to them.

So, what of the German women's response to the coming of, middle of, ending of, aftermath of, the abominable Third Reich? On a basic level, one can say of the fraction who have been asked to speak for the record and the majority who have not, that they faced an enormous test of morality and courage and intelligence, and for the most part failed it. To pass it would have required at the very least for them to have had less trust, prejudice, bigotry, and nationalism, and more bravery, insight, and rebelliousness, as well as, perhaps, power.

---

6. *The New York Times*, December 13, 1992.

But they are indeed individuals—at least, I hope they emerged as such—and one cannot come close to an individual for long without making comparisons with one's own character. Maybe because I was literally close to them, the German women made me wonder how American women, or women in other countries, would have done if they had taken the same test. It was, incidentally, a question no German woman raised.

Being in Germany made the test feel closer. Sometimes scenes, or sounds, the look of an old street, made me feel I am *there*, and I sensed a terrible might. Then came the moment in East Berlin alluded to in the Preface. In 1985, while in the office of a friendly American consular official, to whom I was chatting about maybe coming back and interviewing other women on the sly without government approval, he began writing something on a slip of paper. How rude, I thought. He then passed me the paper. It read, "Everything you are saying is being overheard." He then took the slip of paper *back* from me. That and two other incidents the same day within East Berlin did not ignite valor in my soul. They made me nearly nauseated with fear that I would be arrested, and trapped.

Speaking only for American women, I still like to think that they, that we, as a group would have done much better on the test than the German women of the Third Reich. I cannot believe that would be because of a more felicitous genetic bequest. Unlike many of the German women, I do not believe a citizenry's behavior is determined by "blood," whether "German blood" or "Gypsy blood," "black blood" or "white blood," "Mongol blood" or "Jewish blood." I think that American women would have done better because their fate was to have been born into a democracy (however flawed) of legislated liberal will, free education, a free press, and at least a grudging acceptance of the heterogeneous nature of its people, and not to have been born in Germany in the first decades of this century. The basic thought is not my invention, but should be credited to the late Reinhard Bendix, the man who said he hoped this book would not make Americans smug.

Why should it? As all of the women in these pages demonstrate, the Third Reich was both simpler and more complex than it might seem because it was made up of individual human beings. Furthermore, doesn't every human being have capabilities and shortcomings that can lie fallow or be inspired or exploited? That is why I find it difficult, finally, to judge the German women, collectively or individually. I cannot claim I do not want to. Who does not want to judge Germans from the Third Reich? But I was not there.

In everything the women said, I hope they helped demonstrate that it is worthwhile to consider women's testimony. I talked with only about fifty women, and sometimes think of those whose testimony is still available and whose is not. Perhaps I should also state again that I recognize I merely looked eye to eye at mostly unknown members of an underrated sex for information, and paid little attention to the massive effects of the international economic depression, or the financial and military consequences stemming from the Treaty of Versailles, among other significant forces that helped moved the Nazis into power. But, again, I figured that had been done.

Finally, the words of the German women imply, to my rather pummeled mind, a multifaceted warning. It may be simplistic, but is a warning nonetheless. It is that we are all well advised to take seriously and keep honed and in good repair our peace-minded instructive freedoms—especially public education and a free press. It is that anyone of good will cannot happily go about a private life, but must be alert enough and brave enough to butt in and be assertive the minute that injustice or intolerance, not to mention despotism, is spotted. It is that ignorance, avoidance, and stereotypes of any kind certainly are time-savers, but in the long run break down, and reveal plain old human beings, who have a lot more in common as human beings—such as not having chosen where, when, or to whom we were born—than as members of any group. It is that we must cross superficial boundaries and get to know each other as individual human beings. It is to remember that as individual human beings, we are all connected.

The following words and terms come up more than once within the interviews, and in most cases are explained here only.

Abitur / Final high school examination. Because it was a precursor for university study, students who took the test came mostly from relatively well-educated and/or well-off backgrounds.

Arbeitsdienst / Work duty. The once voluntary, then compulsory program the Nazis instituted for German youth, the voluntary part actually started in the Weimar Republic.

Aryan / Nazi term for a supposedly Nordic type of non-Jewish descent. It has no validity as an ethnological category.

Bund deutscher Mädel (or BdM) / League of German Girls, the girls' division of the Hitler Jugend (HJ). (*See* Hitler Youth.) Both the BdM and HJ were essentially mandatory for "Aryan" German youth. On the surface, BdM and HJ activities were somewhat like those of Girl Scouts and Boy Scouts. Unlike scouting, however, the BdM and HJ were very pro-Nazi and political, whether or not the members and lower-level leaders realized it. Girls' League handbooks (and historians) substantiate that the League was political in its songs, slogans, and attempts to encourage German girls to think a certain way, to become a certain kind of German mother, and to be loyal to the Nazi government that started the groups. The guise mainly worked; some older women might be alarmed to rediscover what they once innocently sang and read.

Concordat / Treaty between Hitler and the Vatican. Signed on July 20, 1933, within half a year of the beginning of Nazi rule, the Concordat was an enormous coup for Hitler, in terms of international stature and domestic politics. The supposed aim of the Concordat was to protect Catholics and Catholism in the Third Reich, but it is doubtful that Hitler meant to abide by it, and he did not (at least not all of it).

Frau, Fräulein / *Frau* means "woman," "wife," or "Mrs." *Fräulein* literally means "little woman," "maiden," or "Miss." In German, any woman is formally addressed, or referred to, as Frau, whether she is married or not. Fräulein is used for any girl up to the highly subjective and variable point at which she no longer passes muster as a "Fräulein" and does pass muster as a "Frau."

Frauenschaft / Women's Auxiliary of the Nazi Party. Membership was encouraged, especially for wives of Nazi Party members, but was not mandatory. It, too, had a façade of innocence, that of a social civic organization.

Gel? / Right? Pronounced with a hard *g*, the South German expression is used only as a question, one implying agreement. It is like the "nicht?" or "ne?" that mostly North Germans use.

Gestapo / Secret police. The word was short for Geheime Staatspolizei. The group was independent, ruthless, and loyal to Hitler.

Hitler Youth (Hitler Jugend, HJ in German) / The Nazis' all-but-mandatory youth organization for boys. The term is sometimes used to include the girls' division, which was indeed part of it, rather than autonomous.

"Kristallnacht" ("Crystal night") / The Nazi-organized night of terror against Jewish Germans took place on November 9, 1938. (In English it also is called "the night of broken glass.") Nazi packs smashed, burned, and/or looted Jewish stores, homes, and synagogues, and mistreated or arrested many Jews themselves. If "crystal night" sounds cynically festive, it is; the term is a Nazi invention.[1] The Nazis even called it *"Reichs*kristallnacht," as if it had a government imprimatur (which indeed it did), while maintaining it resulted from a spontaneous eruption by the angry Volk. Among some survivors and Jewish groups, the night has come to be called the "November pogrom." (Not knowing that at the time, and trying to use terms the women knew, I always said "Kristallnacht.")

KZ / Concentration camp. The letters come from Konzentrationslager, a general term that takes in a spectrum of different kinds of concentration camps. They range from the deadliest, a Vernichtungslager [annihilation camp] to the euphemistically named Arbeitslager [work camp].

Na / "Well" or "so." An amorphous word that can start or finish a sentence, or stand alone.

Ne? Nicht? / *See* "Gel?"

NSDAP / Nazi Party. The initials stand for Nationalsozialistische Deutsche Arbeiter Partei.

Ortsgruppenleiter / Local Nazi boss (or "local group leader.") To my knowledge, the position—often of considerable power—always was held by a man.

---

1. Thanks to Rita Kuhn for alerting me.

Polish Corridor / The part of Poland that connected (or separated) the bulk of Germany to (or from) East Prussia. It came about as a provision of the Versailles Treaty. Poland's reputation for closing the Corridor in response to political conditions, thereby isolating East Prussians and their exportable produce, was a major reason for anti-Polish feeling among East Prussians, among other eastern Germans.

Roehm Putsch / "Night of the Long Knives" or "Blood Purge." Fearing the SA (see below) was becoming too independent and powerful, Hitler organized a murderous rampage against his earlier supporters, and set it loose on June 30, 1934. Some two hundred men, including Hitler's old friend SA Chief Ernst Roehm (spelled Röhm in German), were killed.

SA / Storm troopers, or brownshirts. The initials stand for Sturmabteilung. The members were the Nazi Party's early thugs, used as guards at Nazi meetings.

SS / Known in English, too, as SS. They were the blackshirts. The initials stand for Schutzstaffel, translatable as "defense echelon" or "defense detachment." The word *elite* often is used in describing the SS, whose members had been first Hitler's personal guard, then became a kind of precision army of killers. The SS ran the concentration camps.

Terezín, Theresienstadt / The so-called model Jewish concentration camp near Prague, which later proved as deadly as others.

Volk / People. Often used as "das deutsche Volk" [the German people], it implies a unified "Aryan" mass.

Volkssturm / "People's Army." More accurately, it was Germany's sacrificial last-ditch defense force made up of drafted older men, young boys, and invalids.

Acknowledgments

Ach, *how* I have looked forward to writing these lines. And what a contradiction they represent. How could I have felt so alone during most of the work on this book, when such a wealth of people—friends, acquaintances, colleagues, and strangers—proffered help? I could not have managed without them. But before naming them, I must reach back and pay respect to my first German teacher, Marie Wolfe of Conestoga High School in Berwyn, Pennsylvania, who energetically taught first-year German *in* German.

Leapfrogging to the project at hand, I come to another teacher, whose generosity to me is the more astounding for having no formal teacher-student basis whatever. He is Gordon A. Craig of Stanford University. It was Professor Craig I first contacted about the notion of doing this book, he whose immediate and enthusiastic response launched me, he who provided the first suggested reading list and ideas of how to bring up certain questions, he who volunteered the first list of German friends to contact ("a bit heavy on professors," he wrote, in his lovely calligraphy), he who helped me figure how to manage my avalanche of material, and he who became my academic anchor and best pep talker. My friends know who I mean when I refer to "my sainted mentor."

Then there is the astonishing Agnes Peterson, curator of the Central and Western European Collections of the Hoover Institution Library at Stanford. Besides imparting years of helpful musings, Agnes made sure I knew about new books or manuscripts relating to my subject. And, being a native German speaker who knew the epoch of the Third Reich well and has studied it since, she has a knowledge of German language, life, and history that, I realized, made her the perfect prepublication reader. Accepting the role with alacrity (but with stubborn refusal of compensation), she read almost every word of the manuscript, and lifted an enormous burden of anxiety from my heart. I can never thank her adequately.

Enormous thanks also are due Linda Wheeler of the Hoover Library for her research help. Perhaps twenty times or more, when frustrated at not being able to find in my own modest collection some nub of information (the origin of a phrase, the detail of a bombing), I availed myself of Linda's lavish offer to look up anything. She did so with academic gusto and good humor.

Acknowledgments

One strand of Professor Craig's network led to a treasure of an advisor, the late Reinhard Bendix, of the University of California at Berkeley. At first distressingly unenthusiastic about my plans, he kept pressing me until his criteria were satisfied. He also helped me in my search for interviewees and gave valuable and personal insights into what life in the Third Reich was like for a young man who hadn't known he was Jewish. This is a better work because of him.

To Renate Bridenthal of Brooklyn College (and to Nancy Lane for suggesting her), I give many thanks. Renate's own work not only helped mine, but her impulses to a nonacademic newcomer were munificent. She offered friendly scrutiny, sisterly suggestions, and, not least of all, contacts. Thanks, too, to Claudia Koonz, whose work became one of my touchstones, and who gave me not only reading suggestions and wisdom but encouragement. And thanks to another member of that fine circle of women historians, Marion Kaplan. An historian who extended an early helpful hand by mail is Jill Stephenson, of the University of Edinburgh.

The myriad paths that led to the Frauen involved many people, including Americans in Germany and Germans in America.

First of all, special thanks to Herbert Paas.

In addition to others previously named, I wish to thank Suzanne Lipsett, Annegret Ogden, the late Milton Mayer, Frances Goldin, Walter Thabit, Brigitte Petty, Jackie Baker Plötz and Jürgen Plötz, Hedwig Dost Sasowski, Sylvia Erdmann, the Thurauf family, and the fireline of Berliners from Ilse Beck, to Gerhard Schönberger, to Frau Ehmann, to Martine Voigt, that led up the stairs to beloved Frau Dubnack.

In a related category, I am especially indebted to wildly generous friends who *volunteered* to transcribe some audio tapes. Tausendmal Dank to Hedi Göpfert of Bad Tölz for transcribing otherwise impenetrable Bavarian and to Hildegard Ibing of Hamburg. Both helped in many other ways as well, Hedi providing essentially a clipping service from German newspapers about the Third Reich, Hildegard providing bed, board, and Gemütlichkeit during my Hamburg stays.

The search for other transcribers led me to an organization I would not have approached had I not been enjoined to do so, and which I thank for its unexpected help and encouragement: the Holocaust Center of Northern California, in San Francisco. Thanks to Joel Neuberg and most especially to Lani Silver and also Karen Amital of the Holocaust Oral History Project. It is a source of enormous pride that they consider my project valuable.

Through the Holocaust Center, I reaped a great cache of volunteer transcribers, to whom separate thanks are due. They are Rita Kuhn, herself a survivor (and the final interviewee), Stephan Nobbe of the Goethe Institute, and Britta Reinert of the German Consulate of San Francisco. Supplementing the volunteers were people who doubtlessly worked more for their interest and kindliness than my pay. Vielen Dank to Hannelore Stein, Petra Gampper, Sigrid Novikoff, Diedre Kennedy, John Salomon, and capping the list, the inestimable Nina Tatjana Helgren.

Another component of a project this extensive was funding it. To that end, I am grateful to the individuals who offered ideas or wrote fellowship recommendations, especially Gordon Craig, Lucy Komisar, Hans Wiessman, Bill Raftery, Lee Townsend, Hartmut Lehmann, the Reverent Douglas Huneke, Mike Kesselman, Fred Rosenbaum, and Susan Brownmiller.

Susan also deserves separate thanks for years of helping me in a myriad of ways one woman writer can, and did, help another.

Three funding efforts bore fruit. So, further thanks to the German Consulate of San Francisco, in particular Friedrich Conrad, to the former German Democratic Republic for travel accommodations (albeit restricted), and to the American Council on Germany, which granted me a John J. McCloy Fellowship. Special appreciation is due to Don Shanor of Columbia University and the endlessly enterprising Karen Furey of the ACG.

As I began to assemble the Frauen and write drafts of introductions and interviews (not knowing they were drafts, of course), I sometimes reached out for reactions from trusted colleagues and writerly friends. Years of thanks are due to Mary Brown for reading so many versions of the preface, and for her unflagging interest from the get go. I also am pleased to thank readers not previously mentioned for their time, wisdom, and/or welcome jolts of enthusiasm. They include Kathy Dickson, Suzanne Simpson, Rainer Baum, Eli Evans, Ellen Hoffman, Charles Kuralt, John Weitz, Ella Leffland, and Richard Hunt.

A battalion of other people in the United States and in Germany offered diverse assistance. In Germany, in addition to those already thanked and whose contributions span almost all categories, I wish to thank the helpful Hamburgers: Marian Dönhoff, Marianne Popist, Sybil Schönfeldt, Herta Schöning, Marianne Grothe, and Peter von Zahn. In then West Berlin, thanks to Ursula Goldschmidt, Karin Hausen, Asta and Karl-Heinz Henssel, Marie Herzfeld, Elizabeth and Gunther Langer (via Friederike Brause in Salobreña, Spain), Marianne Wagner, Myra Warhaftig, Marion Yorck von Wartenburg, and Gerda Szepansky. Former East Berliners I wish to thank include Edith Anderson (in whose apartment I inhaled welcome intakes of "frische Luft") and my appointed guide/companion, Wolfgang Thormeyer, who stoically put up with my tweaking. (Wo sind Sie jetzt, Herr Thormeyer?) Thanks in Bochum go to Annegret Hilsinger-Reinhardt and Horst Hilsinger, and to Lotte Elschner. In Göttingen, where I passed one of the most enlightening evenings of my life, thanks to Professor Rudolf and Wiebke von Thadden. Thanks to Elke Fröhlich, Ingrid Kinzel-Amuzer, and Mary Sue Packer in Munich, and Hermann and Dorothea Katzenstein in Freiburg.

In this country, many thanks belong here in the Bay Area: to the late

Acknowledgments

Dieta Muench, to Leah Garchik, Jerry Feldman, Willa Baum, Nadine Joseph, and Matthias Stein. For clippings and books, thanks to Jerry Garchik and Milt Moskowitz. For patient computer aid, thanks to Jack Curley. Thanks to Bob Hirschfeld, and many more to his parents, Inge and Hans Hermann Hirschfeld of San Francisco, for allowing me into a portion of their own anguishing memories, so that I might better hold in my mind a sense of whom the Third Reich affected the most cruelly.

Many people proffered various valuable forms of help from other parts of the country and the world and I thank them: Fritz Stern, Thomas Behrendt, Ann Jones, Sibylla Zinsser, Claudine Pachnicke, Eileen Max, Jeff Masson, Elizabeth Midgley, Wolf von Eckhardt, and the late and very much missed Hughes Rudd. He, too, never forgot the Third Reich, having done all he could to end it.

Thanks to master interviewer Studs Turkel for his exuberant interest, and for a delightful lunch during which I learned we used a same secret interviewing technique.

Although my gratitude to the interviewees may be inferred, I wish to thank them here for giving me, for whatever reasons, some of themselves. I regret that not all of them are included. But their words will be available to those who wish to hear them: at the Hoover Library archives at Stanford University.

My agents, Sydelle Kramer and Frances Goldin, know well the thanks I give them both. It helps to like and trust your agency.

And it helps to like and trust your publisher. Rutgers University Press and its compact, superb team of professionals have been a joy to work with. Above all, I want to thank my extraordinary editor, Leslie Mitchner. She made this a better book and, difficult though it may be to believe, a shorter one. She is the editor every writer dreams of and I got.

I also am very grateful to the managing editor of the Press, Marilyn Campbell, the copy editor, Willa Speiser, and the proofreader, Adaya Henis.

Finally, never before did I realize how valid are the thanks that go to family members. To my brother and sister, Warren and Michele, I give thanks for their sweet ways of being. To my much missed parents, who somehow encouraged both writing and laughing, both of which were useful these years, I have dedicated this book. To the Reverend William Perdue, and the late Ann Perdue, for their spirited affection, I give more thanks.

Above all, I thank the person who lived the closest with the separations and anguish and very long time this work entailed, who helped me think and rethink, acting both as a sounding board and angelic devil's advocate, who never suggested I not continue and who in many ways helped me to continue. That person is my man, Jonathan Perdue.

484

Index

East Prussia, 125, 280; deportations from, 147–148, 147n3; gathering of former residents of, 83, 266, 268; and Poland, 92, 94, 137, 139; and the Soviet Union, 83, 84, 273, 278; women fleeing from, 83

Enabling Act, xxxi, 249

England, *see* Britain

Fabrikaktion (factory action), 459–460, 461–462

farmers (*see also* women: on farms): and Nazi Party membership, 231, 235, 380; propaganda about, 231; and World War II, 231–232

Fatherland Women's Club, 216

FDP, *see* Free Democratic Party

feminism, xxx, xxxiv, 10

France and the French: occupation of Germany by, post–World War I, 87; perceptions of, 216, 222; POW camps in, 132; and World War II, 51, 63, 65, 89, 93, 94, 96, 253, 287, 292, 295, 349, 404

Frauenschaft, xxxii, 146, 222, 313, 316, 424; Allied treatment of, after the war, 334, 336; perceptions of, 10, 379; pressure to join, 221, 234, 421

Free Democratic Party (FDP), 25, 25n1, 361

Freemasons, 175, 175n1

genocide, *see* Holocaust

Germany: Allied bombing of, 241–242; ambivalence of natives toward, 70, 100–101, 454; contemporary, xvi, 114–115, 135, 137, 470, 475; divisions among peoples of, xxxv-xxxvi, 68; emigration of "Aryans" from, xvi, 9, 65, 435; envy of, 279; ideological dowry of, xxv-xxviii; militarization of, 284–285, 287; and Poland, 389; racial violence in, xvi,

68, 100, 115, 136, 199; religion in, xxxv; repression in, 355, 410–411, 471–472; reunification of, xiv, 81–82, 136, 199; and World War I, 1, 56, 60, 63, 137, 153, 157, 175; and World War II, 4, 28, 38, 63, 66, 70, 108, 122, 142, 148, 153–154, 241, 253, 268, 269, 271–272, 287, 309–310, 327–328, 357–358, 393, 403–404, 422

Gestapo, 43, 110, 161–162, 190, 263, 344, 377, 437, 465; arrests made by, 48, 119, 259, 472; fear of, 44, 49, 458; and informers, 41, 42, 45, 48; interrogations by, 122–124, 350, 425

Goebbels, Joseph, 58, 65, 255, 313, 429, 459; perceptions of, 47, 120, 133; propaganda spread by, xxxii-xxxiii, xxxv, 188, 201, 274, 403

Goering, Hermann, 255, 275

Greens' movement, 199, 345

guilt, 67, 69, 101, 101n2, 195, 258, 276, 291, 356, 395; in the United States about Vietnam, 101

Gypsies, 113, 135, 155, 168, 169, 469

Hamstern (bartering), 231–232, 231n3, 240–241

Harnack, Arvid, 39, 39n1

Hausjude (house Jew), 151, 470

Heine, Heinrich, 304, 306

Hess, Rudolf, 27

Heydrich, Reinhard, 111n6

Himmler, Heinrich, 5, 96, 251, 255, 256, 263

Hindenburg, Paul von, xxxi, 88, 141, 160, 188, 301

Hitler, Adolf, xxvii, 167, 168, 401, 459; assassination attempt on, 12, 39n1, 79, 66, 124, 177–178, 227, 255–256, 257, 260–262, 350, 362, 377–378, 403, 444; attractiveness of, 159, 402–403; deification of, 66, 71, 304;

Index

Hitler, Adolf (*continued*)
early successes of, 36, 47, 58, 59, 88, 177, 284, 370, 395 (*see also* Nazi Party: early successes of); election to power, xxiii, xxxi, xxxv, 313; encounters with, 15–16, 159–160, 201, 220, 268, 395; and the Freemasons, 175, 175n1; and the idealism of young Germans, 183 (*see also* Nazi Party: and the idealism of young Germans); and the Jews, 6, 87, 96, 104, 183–184, 248, 384, 385, 423, 459, 466; and nationalism, xxxvi; opposition to, xvii, 165, 174–175, 176 (*see also* Nazi Party: opposition to); as perceived outside Germany, 6, 275; perceptions of, xxiv, 5, 16, 19, 47, 48, 55, 59–60, 71, 74, 86, 87–88, 116, 120, 121, 139, 143, 153, 160, 173, 176, 177, 181–182, 183, 190, 194, 195, 200–201, 219, 221, 222n1, 226, 236, 243–244, 248, 268, 287, 295–296, 297–298, 301, 347, 362, 379, 380, 395, 402–403, 456, 471; responsibility of other countries for, 275, 423; suicide of, 149, 229, 270; views on women, xxiv, xxxiv, 2, 10, 73, 73n1, 269, 344–345; and World War II, 9, 63, 65, 67, 93, 95, 122, 143, 177, 194, 224–225, 227, 243, 250, 268–269, 295, 347, 403, 404
Hitler Jugend, *see* Hitler Youth
Hitler Youth, xxxii, 15, 19, 88, 196, 219, 234, 243, 303, 456; for girls (*see* Bund deutscher Mädel); Jews banned from, 174; members of, made Nazi Party members, 348; as preparation for war, 236; pressure to join, 3, 162; in the Volkssturm, 354–355
Holocaust, xxiv, xxvi, 132, 136, 142, 176, 298; awareness of, 210, 211, 374 (*see also* concentration camps: knowledge of); compared to Soviet treatment of German civilians, 149; films on, 374, 409–410 (*see also* concentration camps, films on); ignorance of, 29, 472–474 (*see also* concentration camps: ignorance of); number of victims of questioned, 97–98, 102, 113, 183, 275–276, 290; uniqueness of questioned, 101–102, 152–153, 394, 466
"Holocaust" TV series, 133, 133n1, 182
Hungarians, 129, 319, 320–321

IG Farben, 74, 316
Inability to Mourn, The (Mitscherlichs), 471
Iran/contra scandal, 100, 112–113

Jehovah's Witnesses, 256
Jews: aid to, 30, 73, 77, 96, 198, 249–250, 283, 300, 306, 308, 309, 344, 381–386, 389, 416, 425–428, 429, 432, 437–438, 439, 440–441, 442–445, 447, 448, 450, 466; boycott of stores owned by, xxxi, 22, 37, 71, 73, 139, 176, 177, 189, 199–200, 237, 267, 283, 303, 307, 390, 392, 410; in contemporary Germany, 87, 470; and culture, 346, 347; deportations of, 7, 76, 78, 101n1, 111n6, 131, 134, 212, 224, 251–252, 277, 409, 417, 427–428, 430, 437; disappearance of, 469, 471; early immigration to Germany of, xxxv; emigration of, 7, 65, 76, 77, 78, 90, 119, 122, 179, 224, 249, 289, 293, 306, 344, 364, 381, 397, 399, 415, 420, 430, 454–455, 456; and the Freemasons, 175n1; and the German ideological dowry, xxvi, xxvii; insular life of, xxviii; married to Aryans, 105, 296–297, 297n4, 453, 462; Nazi policies against (*see* Nazi Party: policies against Jews of); perceptions of, 6–7, 8, 13–14, 25–26, 48, 52, 55,